HOMILIES FOR THE CHRISTIAN PEOPLE

CYCLES A,B,C

HOMILIES
FOR THE CHRISTIAN PEOPLE,

CYCLES A,B,C

Edited by Gail Ramshaw

PUEBLO PUBLISHING COMPANY

New York

Design: Frank Kacmarcik

Printed in the United States of America

ISBN: 0-916134-92-X

TABLE OF CONTENTS

INTRODUCTION

"Then the records of the apostles or the writings of the prophets are read for as long as there is time. When the reader has concluded, the presider in a discourse admonishes and invites us into the pattern of these good things."

Justin, 150 CE

With this volume Pueblo Publishing Company presents a collection of liturgical homilies. Currently there is considerable conversation about how the discourse described above by the layman Justin ought to be carried out today. Responding to these conversations, we have commissioned seventy-five people, guardians of their traditions, to offer liturgical homilies for each set of lessons in the three-year Roman Catholic, Episcopal, and Lutheran lectionaries.

The editors believe that the sermon is to serve the eucharistic liturgy of the assembly. It both proclaims in contemporary speech the gospel as received in the readings, and it leads the assembly to Christ in the bread and wine. The homily usually springs from the language and imagery of the gospel reading. As well, in the Roman-Episcopal-Lutheran lectionary, the interplay between the gospel and the first reading inspires the preacher to seek ever deeper dimensions of meaning, and often the second lesson provides an angle from which to hear the gospel. Eucharistic preaching leads the people to their life outside the liturgy by leading them first to communion with God and with one another. The liturgical homily is mystagogy, baptismal cathechesis for the eucharistic community. The homily leads us from the font to the table and from the table to the world, walking together, one in Christ. It is only one part, but an extremely significant part, of the assembly's praise of God.

While the lectionaries of these three churches are nearly identical, our preaching styles are quite varied. This collection includes homilies by Roman Catholics, Episcopalians, Lutherans, Presbyterians, and Methodists. Some of these preachers deal with all the appointed readings, some concentrate on the gospel, some explicate the biblical images, some relate biblical stories, some share personal experience. Differing theological emphases are evident, and a wide tonal range is heard. These liturgical homilies allow us to hear the proclamation of the gospel across denominational lines, in outlines and phrases other than the familiar. The diversity is a concert that all can enjoy.

It must be said that a published homily is something of a contradiction, for a homily is an oral proclamation to a specific community. But there is good tradition of such a collection of homilies: the church of the middle ages and of the Reformation circulated postils (from the Latin *post illa verba*), books of model homilies as an aid for the clergy and as liturgical devotions for all the people. In our time such collections can continue their work among both clergy and laity. In this book the sermons are printed not as texts to be read in the assembly, but as inspiration for any Christian who desires yet another view of the Sunday's readings, another door into the Sunday's assembly. May these eucharistic homilies accompany us with a new ecumenical vision "into the pattern of these good things."

Gail Ramshaw, editor

R   *Is 2:1–5; Rom 13:11–14a; Mt 24:34–44*
E   *Is 2:1–5; Rom 13:8–14; Mt 24:34–44*
L   *Is 2:1–5; Rom 13:11–14a; Mt 24:34–44*

When St. Augustine was forty-three, not long after he had been made a bishop, he tried to recapture the youthful struggle out of which he was delivered, drawn ultimately to God. This he did in a religious autobiography entitled *Confessions*, thirteen "books" of praise characterized by an anxious turning to the past. He had all but broken with his incontinent life when, living in a rented house with two men friends and his mother, he found himself dipping into the epistles of St. Paul. He tells of hearing the sing-song chant of a child from a nearby house, boy or girl he could not tell, intoning repeatedly, "Pick it up and read it." Going back to Paul's letters he opened randomly to what we now designate as Romans 13:13 and read from the middle of the verse: "Let us conduct ourselves . . . not in reveling and drunkenness, not in debauchery and licentiousness, not in quarreling and jealousy. But put on the Lord Jesus Christ, and make no provision for the flesh, to gratify its desires." He stuck a marker in the place and brought it to his housemate Alypius, who had been thinking similar thoughts about a change of lifestyle. Alypius took the book from him and read on a little further to: "As for the one who is weak in faith, be welcoming." That, said Alypius, describes me. The two young men shortly thereafter made a radical change and, together with Augustine's teen-aged son, asked for baptism.

The Romans passage is designated as our second Bible reading on this Advent Sunday for at least two reasons. The days grow shorter all over the globe, the nativity feast following the winter solstice which marks the beginning of the sun's slow climb; and secondly, not every kind of revelry at the holiday season is in the spirit of the gospel. Thus:

"The night is far gone, the day is at hand . . . . Let us conduct ourselves becomingly as in the day. Put on the Lord Jesus

Christ, and make no provision for the flesh, to gratify its desires."

"The flesh" does not mean sexual sin in Paul's writings, although it may. Neither is flesh a blanket term for bodily needs. It is all of the human that escapes God's control, what St. John calls "the world" as opposed to the "life" that Jesus said he would give. So, as the days continue to darken earlier in this season, we are summoned to the light at the end of the Advent tunnel. That light is Christ: chiefly as he is to come in glory at the end but also, prefigured as that coming is by his earthly coming, the Christ of Christmas. The coming of our God in final consummation of the mystery we call life is primary. We have no better symbol of this future event, however, than the familiar one we know of from Luke and Matthew's gospels, the birth of the Savior.

Do not be surprised if the next three weeks in the Sunday liturgies prove not to be devoted to preparation for Christmas. That begins only one week before the feast itself. It comes with the prayer that brackets Mary's song at vespers: an antiphon begins to address Jesus as, "O Wisdom, holy Word of God," then, successively: "O Lord, O Shoot of David, O Key of David, O King of all the nations," and "O Emmanuel." From the seventeenth of December onward you will know that Christmas is coming. But for now, look for the coming one at an hour you do not expect him.

Advent is our time of making ready. It is a brief season, to be lived as if each day will be our last. Our faith is not lugubrious, a daily dose of *Angst*. It is, however, a matter of deep seriousness. We know the possibility of living in darkness. Some of us have lived there. We wish now to live in Christ. Ancient Israel longed for life on the heights of Zion. It ached to walk in the light of the Lord. The Christian hope is the same. Worshiping in spirit and in truth is its dream, not on this mountain nor in Jerusalem but "what we know" in "an hour that is coming."

It should not be indelicate to speak of the "works of darkness" that surround us. They are not terribly different from those of St. Paul's day. We speak freely nowadays of alcoholism. We seldom speak of the frequent drunkenness of Christians who are not alcoholics. "Chambering" was a word in the epistle to the Romans in older Bible translations. It has become "debauchery," which sounds like frequenting the red-light district or descending to skid row. Paul was talking about something very close to today's "safe-sex" for the young, marital "lapses" as we so gently describe our nasty infidelities, motels near the airport for the married and harried executive. These are not the works of darkness of people who never go to church. They are the self-destructive behavior Christians turn to in every age. There are very few new sins.

The light in our lives is the light of Christ. Slouch or stumble toward Bethlehem as we may, let us in genuine repentance proceed toward the one true Light which is Christ.

Gerard S. Sloyan

R E L SECOND SUNDAY OF ADVENT

R   *Is 11:1–10; Rom 15:4–9; Mt 3:1–12*
E   *Is 11:1–10; Rom 15:4–13; Mt 3:1–12*
L   *Is 11:1–10; Rom 15:4–13; Mt 3:1–12*

> There shall come forth a shoot from the stump of Jesse, and
>   a branch shall grow out of its roots. . . .
> His delight shall be in the fear of the Lord. . . .
> With righteousness he shall judge the poor. . . .
> The wolf shall dwell with the lamb. . . .
> The suckling child shall play over the hole of the asp. . . .
> In that day there will stand as an ensign to the peoples the
>   root of Jesse, whom the nations shall seek, and whose
>   dwellings shall be glorious.

"The voice of one crying in the wilderness: Prepare the way of the Lord,"

Today's reading reminded me of Jesse Jackson. No matter the criticisms of this contemporary black preacher—his ego, his moth-like attraction to the spotlight—is there not something of Isaiah in his bones and of John the Baptist in his marrow?

Every generation needs its own shoot springing up from the stump of its own tradition. Every generation needs those who are not co-opted by the good times and monetary prosperity of the moment, usually at the expense of the powerless, who recall for their time the original vision: that there once was an Eden in which there was enough for everyone's need, though insuffucient for everyone's greed. These folk will raise up and facilitate the imagination of a people to the possibilities for justice, freedom, righteousness and peace in their time and place. Jesse Jackson did this repeatedly in Campaign '88 and at the Democratic Convention in Atlanta. Pointing out injustice after injustice, he admonished, "America, we are better than that!"

Isn't this what Isaiah is doing here? He comes on as a new breath (a *ruach*) of fresh air, even as a wind blowing a new Spirit across the land. Once again Isaiah recalls the shalom vision that has been defined from the biblical perspective as central to world history: "All creation is one, every creature in community with every other, living in harmony and security toward the joy and well-being of every other creature."[1] In this vision, none shall hurt or destroy, all will be in balance, all creatures and creation so interrelated and harmonized as to result in healthfulness and wholeness.

The prophet's task is both to imagine and to generate a people's imagination. Way back in Egypt-land when a seemingly God-forsaken, pitiful pack of Hebrews were stuck in Pharaoh's mud pits making bricks for pyramids, and their plight seemed hopeless, and all they could do was moan and groan from their common misery, someone heard their cries. From somewhere there came a voice: from "Jehovah's" household no less, from one who also had sojourned in a foreign land, one to whom the Lord spoke with a new vision. "I have seen the affliction of my people who are in Egypt, and have heard their cry. . . . I know their sufferings, and I have come down . . . to bring them up out of that land to a good and broad land, a land flowing with milk and honey."

And so it goes biblically. Jeremiah, Amos, Ezekiel, John the Baptist, all were looking for one who would enable the blind to see and the lame to walk. Martin Luther imagined a church where the faithful would be free from the terror of the hereafter, and once again grace would flow freely, gushing from the inexhaustible wellspring of one who forgave even from the cross. Martin Luther King, Jr., climbed to the mountaintop and saw for his own people, for all people, a promised land of equality and freedom for his and Coretta's children, for all children. So even Bishop Medardo Gomez envisions for El Salvador, and Tutu for South Africa, and Sakharov for Russia, and Walesa for Poland.

The prophet's vision comes even to you. Perhaps you live in a marriage that is more captivity and abuse than ecstasy and delight in one another. Perhaps you are experiencing a teenage emergence into a world of falseness and contradictions instead of encouragement and promise. Some of us whose lives have been bent on "having it all" find at the last we have nothing! Whatever our situation, these texts teach, as did St. Paul in Romans, that we are embraced and inextricably held by a God of steadfastness and hope.

This gospel truth Martin Luther King, Jr., drives home in the opening words of his sermon, "At the center of the Christian faith is the conviction that in the universe there is a God of power who is able to do exceedingly abundant things in nature and in history."[2] Even to achieving peace on earth! At this prophetic word, this Advent we rejoice in hope.

John Steinbruck

[1]Walter Brueggmann, *Living Toward a Vision* (Philadelphia: United Church Press, 1976), p. 15.
[2]Martin Luther King, Jr., *Strength to Love* (Philadelphia: Fortress, 1963), p. 106.

R   *Is 35:1–6a,10; Jam 5:7–10; Mt 11:2–11*
E   *Is 35:1–10; Jam 5:7–10; Mt 11:2–11*
L   *Is 35:1–10; Jam 5:7–10; Mt 11:2–11*

At beginnings and ends of years, we try to discern the signs of the times. Newspapers run retrospective articles seeking key events that unlock the year. Television networks gather pundits who, like seers of old, read these key events, thought to be the signs of the times which explain the past and predict the future. Is Black Monday a sign of the times? Will the stock market signal a new depression? Who will succeed to the presidency? What are the signs of the times, and what do they tell us of the future?

Discerning the signs of the times is a central concern of our gospel lesson. From his prison cell John heard of the deeds of Jesus and sent his disciples to ask, "Are you the one who is to come, or shall we look for another?" By asking for the one who is to come, John the Baptist, the political and religious prisoner of the king of Judea, was asking whether Jesus was the expected Messiah. Jesus replies by pointing to what he considers the signs of the times: "The blind receive their sight and the lame walk, lepers are cleansed and the deaf hear, and the dead are raised up, and the poor have good news preached to them."

Let us contrast what we list as the signs of the times and what Jesus lists. We check the stock market and the White House. We list the opinions of pundits, we seek the wisdom of economists who read the leading economic indicators with the same gravity that ancient Roman priests read the entrails of a goat. We look to the high and mighty to check out the signs of the times. Jesus, in stark contrast, attends to how the blind, deaf, lame, dead and poor are doing. When they see, hear, walk, rise, and have good news, the dominion of God is at hand. And the one at whose hand these marvels take place, this one is the Messiah.

When he offered this set of signs, Jesus was only citing the prophet Isaiah. He knew John would understand, for John knew the prophesies and was himself a prophet. In Matthew a prophet who is a political and religious prisoner asks Jesus about his messianic pretensions. On the other hand, in Mark it is Caiaphas, a powerful political and religious official. In Matthew John questions because he is desperate for a messiah, not because he fears for his position of power and comfort, like Caiaphas in Mark. John is open to the advent of the Messiah, while Caiaphas is not.

What of us? Are we satisfied to gauge the times by the stock market and the White House, or do we too look to the blind, deaf, lame, dead, and poor? Can we point to the Messiah's work among the likes of those of whom Jesus spoke? Are we willing to find among them the dominion of God? Are we like Caiaphas, worried about our position and power, or are we open to the advent of this Savior among the likes of these?

Most of us are blessed with modest security. Looking upon those who do not have all that we do is frightening. When we see a blind person cross the street or a funeral procession pass us, we may feel sympathetic or courteous. But do we look for the Messiah among the blind or dead? Rather than being signs of the realm of God, are the needy more often than not awful reminders of how tentative and arbitrary life is? Do they not simply reveal how vulnerable we all are? We seek signs because we fear the morrow. Because we fear the open and uncontrolled future, we look for signs to predict it and relieve our anxiety. Our worst fears are embodied in the blind, the deaf, the lame, the poor and the dead. We anticipate hard times, and we have no hope.

However, most of us are neither John, the religious and political prisoner, nor Caiaphas, the religious and political power. Most of us are like the crowd who watched from a distance as John's disciples asked Jesus their question. We, like them, keep our safe distance from these events. We are curious but do not want to become involved. But Jesus will not allow us this safe distance. He turns to the crowd and asks leading questions, "Why are you curious? Why do you come out to see John? I have pointed to the sighted blind, the walking lame, the cleansed lepers, and the poor who have heard the good news. So where are you?"

Will you get caught up into the dominion of heaven? Will you preach good news among the poor, cleanse lepers, make the lame to walk, the deaf to hear, and the blind to see? Will you seek your signs for a hopeful future among such as these, or will you seek soft raiments among the rich and powerful as your signs of hope?

We, already caught up into the kingdom of heaven, cannot remain cool, curious, and distant. The sign of our time is marked upon our foreheads and breasts. The cross of this Messiah which has already claimed us is the sign of our hope. When it stands before our eyes and is traced upon our bodies, we are reminded that our future has been secured for us in this Messiah's death and resurrection which we share through baptism. Our fear of death, though powerful, is tempered with the promise of eternal life. Our anxiety for the morrow is broken, and we can give ourselves to a future that begins with preaching good news to the poor and healing the sick.

Through our baptism we entered a community which takes such as signs of hope. We gather regularly on the Lord's day to be his guest at his table. Through this bread and wine, this body and blood, we are renewed in our baptismal hope. In our worship, we are confirmed in our commitment to preach the good news and to love our neighbor. We seek to include all those who are open to the advent of the Savior. The blind find in our parish the necessary tools for participations. The deaf find signers who share with them our worship. Those who are the lepers of our society, the homeless and those ill with AIDS, find here hospitality. For at this table, in this company, we all are blessed and redeemed.

Patrick Keifert

R   *Is 7:10–14; Rom 1:1–7; Mt 1:18–24*
E   *Is 7:10–17; Rom 1:1–7; Mt 1:18–25*
L   *Is 7:10–14; Rom 1:1–7; Mt 1:18–25*

In a small English parish church, behind the pulpit, is a sign which reads, "We would see Jesus." This sign reminded me of my love affair with the film *Ben-Hur*. There was hardly a line that I, as a teenager, did not know or a scene that I could not anticipate. Much of it has faded from memory, but one scene remains fresh. Esther, the former slave, stands at the opening of a leper colony preparing to take Miriam and her daughter out to freedom. Having suffered under Roman tyranny they are now lepers. As Esther helps them to leave, they stop, paralyzed in fear. Esther sees their fear and says, "Do not be afraid. The world is more than we know. I have seen a man whose name is Jesus."[3]

I will never forget the tenderness in her voice. She knew and understood their fear. She, however, had been moved beyond fear into an incredible calm and a sense of certitude and peace.

Fear is a fact of life. Is anyone completely unafraid? The angel tells Mary not to fear, and Joseph also is told not to be afraid. Fear is no respecter of persons. Many psychiatrists tell us that the most common and subtle of all human disease is fear. Where humanity can find no answer, we will find fear: we fear the future, danger, nuclear war, disease, poverty, and death. We are unnerved by crippling disturbances that refuse to let us know lasting peace.

Fear can grip us and twist our behavior. It is an emotional force that has an insidious power to make us do what we ought not to do and to leave undone what we ought to do.

Isaiah wrestled with the meaning of faith in the midst of threat. For Isaiah faith meant to be at rest in times of threat. It is not to be stoic, but to know God is engaged for us. Faith is a religious posture in the midst of the holy war: not a crusade, but God fighting for us, God with us, Emmanuel, in the battle. Faith is the bet that God will turn out to be the conqueror in the conflict. For Isaiah the bottom-line question was, "Who governs history?" The kings always thought they did. Isaiah says, "No! You've got it all wrong. God is a free agent who will work God's way in the world."

Our ultimate question is, "Who or what shall we trust?" A wise old Jewish psychiatrist once said, "Fear must be replaced. The only known cure for fear and anxiety is faith." During the Dunkirk disaster England was threatened by a possible German invasion. Yet, written over the entrance of the Hinds Head Hotel near Dover was a sign that read, "Fear knocked. Faith answered: 'No one is here'."

The central mystery of Christianity is that God would take on our flesh, our mortality. This is not what we would have expected. Jesus explodes the term Messiah for he was far more than a king, rabbi, or an expected savior.

A mother tells of her daughter complaining that she was afraid alone in the dark. Her mother said, "Remember that Jesus is with you." The child replied, "I know, but I want someone with some skin on them."

In Emmanuel God has taken on our skin. God becomes skin of our skin and flesh of our flesh. God shares with us our trials, pains, temptations, disappointments, and fears. That skin is finally pierced by nails, and the God of creation would share even the taste of death with us. Ponder the passage in Genesis where God looks for Adam asking, "Where are you?" The incarnation is the finalization and fulfillment of that question. God has sought us and has, in Jesus, shown us God's own face. In doing so God assures us that God's word will be the final word, God's love the conquering of all fear.

The mystery of Emmanuel is the incarnation of the invisible immortal God. God has been in love with us from the beginning of time, and that is the real mystery of the Word that was enfleshed in Jesus.

God comes to us still. It was no accident that the Scripture states that the child's name shall be Immanuel, God-with-us. This is not only a statement, but a promise, a fact for now and for eternity. God comes to us still. In each moment of eucharist we touch the precious hem of Christ's garment; we touch the kingdom.

Do not be afraid. Come. Emmanuel is here. God is with us. Believing that we can also say, "Do not be afraid. The world is more than we know. I have seen a man whose name is Jesus."

Virginia L. Bennett

[3]*Ben-Hur* (Metro-Goldwyn-Mayer, 1959).

R   CHRISTMAS MASS AT MIDNIGHT
E   CHRISTMAS DAY I
L   THE NATIVITY OF OUR LORD, 1

R   *Is 9:2–7; Tit 2:11–14; Lk 2:1–14*
E   *Is 9:2–4,6–7; Tit 2:11–14; Lk 2:1–14*
L   *Is 9:2–7; Tit 2:11–14; Lk 2:1–20*

The woman working in the gift-wrap department neatly made the final fold in the red paper, fastened it with a piece of tape, and passed the package back over the counter to the customer. As she did, she glanced at the long line of people waiting with Christmas gifts to be wrapped, each person burdened with items hastily purchased and wearing that strained and impatient I'm-tired-and-in-a-hurry look. To no one in particular, and to everyone in general, she sighed, "Isn't it terrible what's happened to Christmas?"

We know, of course, what she meant. The birth of Jesus Christ, the coming into our world of the Word made flesh, what the writer of Titus calls "the appearing of the glory of our great God and Savior," all of this has been nearly lost beneath the mad rush of buying and wrapping, fighting traffic, standing in line, and beating the deadline at the post office. We no longer count the days of Advent, but rather the "shopping days until Christmas." The angels' song, "Glory to God in the highest, and on earth peace," is now merchandising background music heard through a tinny department store speaker, surrounded by the ringing of cash registers. "Isn't it terrible," she sighed, "what's happened to Christmas?" "Yes," we say. "It's terrible. If only we could get back to the *real* meaning of Christmas."

When we talk about getting back to the "real" meaning of Christmas, what we mean, of course, is the "religious" meaning. After all, Christmas is the celebration of the birth of our Lord. Christmas is about what God in Christ is doing in and for the world, the joy, the grace, and the hope for peace which the birth of Jesus brings into our lives. These are religious convictions, spiritual truths, and Christmas is a holy day. It seems to us to be a sad failure that Christmas must now take place in a materialistic environment which obscures its genuine splendor. Small wonder that we yearn to go back to the real, and religious, meaning of Christmas.

As strange as it may sound, though, whenever we think this way, whenever we long to have a Christmas as pure and as holy and as innocent as the scenes on our Christmas cards, we run the danger of missing the whole point of Christmas. The writer of Luke is careful to remind us that the very first Christmas, the day of Jesus' birth, was not a holy day, but a working day. Jesus was not born during a worship service, but during a tax census. The day when Jesus was born was a time, so to speak, of the ringing of cash registers, the filing of 1040 forms, people standing in long lines to beat the deadline, snarled traffic, and crowds so thick there was not a hotel room to be found. When the angels announced Jesus' birth, it was not to priests lighting candles in the temple; it was to shepherds earning their livelihood in the fields.

This does not mean, of course, that the true meaning of Christmas cannot be trampled and turned into one more commercial for buying and selling. What it does mean, is that the true meaning of Christmas is that God entered the real world of flesh and blood in Jesus Christ. God did not choose to enter the safe world of silent sanctuaries and hallowed spaces, but the rough and tumble, workaday world of people with jobs to do, fields to tend, more anxiety than they know how to deal with, and the government breathing down their backs at tax time.

If this were not so, the news of Christmas would not be the good news that it is. If the news of Christmas is only fit for the religion page of the newspaper, then its power is limited, its impact restricted to a small compartment of life. But Luke wants us to know that the birth of this child takes place in the middle of life's swirl, and it is therefore news to be heralded in every section of the paper, the politics page, the business page, the front page. The promise of Christmas, as Isaiah put it, is that the oppressor's rod will be broken, the government will be upon his shoulder, and his rule will be a time of peace and justice without end. In every arena of human life the Christ child is born to save and to restore.

So, the next time we hear the angels' song being sung above our heads as we push our shopping carts down the discount store aisle, we can know this was the way the world first heard that music, as it went about its weary and worldly business. And as we look around us at the long lines and the people whose eyes betray their many burdens, glimpsing the tired clerk as she pushes back her perspiration-soaked hair, we can know that the news of Christmas is truly for them, and for us, too. "To you is born this day a Savior."

Thomas G. Long

It was the most precious of the gifts of Christmas. Every year it was given in the same way. After the tree was decorated, the trimmings hung, the stockings pinned to the mantel, the last tiny box would be opened. Inside was a tiny nativity set. A simple manger scene. The family had a big expensive creche, but this was for the children. It was the most precious of gifts.

The tiny nativity scene was for the children their Christmas toy. Often you would see them arranging the characters in all sorts of ways. Sometimes they would play together, each taking a part of the story. Other times one of them would play in a sort of contemplative solitude, re-imagining that sacred event.

So it was this year. For the days before Christmas they played their nativity game and enacted the drama over and over again. In their imaginations the simple clay characters were full of life.

In fact the gift of the nativity scene was so special that on Christmas morn when they prepared to go to worship, the children would fight over which character would accompany them in their pocket or purse.

The youngest child always carried Jesus. It was a tradition, and traditions are so very special at holidays. Gloria sat in worship watching the familiar drama unfold, hearing the words, some of which she even understood, spoken. And, as always, Gloria watched the candles. Oh, how she loved the candles. The precarious flicker of light was always an adventure to watch. But she saw differently this Christmas. She was carrying Jesus with her. What is more, Gloria knew what that meant. She was aware, as she had never been before, of how central this baby was to the story, to life.

As the service moved on, Gloria sat in wonder fondling the simple clay character in hand. Caressing the baby Jesus, she watched, listened, and in a special way felt a part of this holy drama.

Then it happened. Gloria knew what was going on. She had seen it many times before. The pastor was setting the table. A cup. A loaf. Special words and prayers. All the while she tightly clutched the baby Jesus.

Then the procession began. Again, it was not new. She had seen it and had come to the table many times. But this day it was different. For as Gloria held the baby Jesus in her hand, she saw them differently. Those who knelt with hands uplifted, they were the shepherds. Those who came carrying their children in their arms, they were those common people who gathered in the stable many years ago. Old and young, men and women, they were enacting the same drama that she had played. What she saw, and it was so clear to her, was a living nativity scene.

It was months later. Christmas was now a distant mystery to most. The tiny nativity set was again packed away. Now her parents stood in the doorway to her room and watched Gloria play. Her dolls were all placed around a low simple table. Those that could be coaxed into a posture of reverence were. On the table was a cup and plate with candles on each side. Gloria was telling the Christmas story.

Gloria's parents' eyes glistened as with the brightest of all stars. Nothing more need be said. The truth was clear. This was the nativity scene. Christ was born again.

A simple cup. A common loaf. The gathered who long for the promised life. A nativity that happens again and again.

Mark A. Olson

R   CHRISTMAS MASS DURING THE DAY
E   CHRISTMAS DAY III
L   THE NATIVITY OF OUR LORD, 2

R   *Is 52:7–10; Heb 1:1–6; Jn 1:1–18*
E   *Is 52:7–10; Heb 1:1–12; Jn 1:1–14*
L   *Is 52:7–10; Heb 1:1–9; Jn 1:1–14*

Among us, in our congregation, this celebration of the holy communion on Christmas Day always seems to be very much a family celebration. By this I do not mean so much that our assembly includes our parents and our children; I mean instead that the eucharistic assembly on Christmas Day is "just us." Last night at midnight we opened our doors and our arms and our hearts to all kinds and conditions of people. Some of them were complete strangers, some looked a bit familiar, perhaps from last year on Christmas Eve, and some were people whom we recognized from the neighborhood but seldom see in church. But this morning it's "just us" once again.

Maybe that is as it should be. Centuries ago, when the great St. Augustine preached on this gospel for Christmas Day, he pointed out that the exalted words that St. John uses to proclaim the good news of Christmas are not for everybody. Those who are only casually attracted to the Christian faith will not be able to follow John to the mountaintop, to gaze with him into the deepest mysteries of creation, or to soar with him in the Spirit beyond the reaches of time and space to hear that Word beyond all words, that Word through whom the universe came to be, the Word that became flesh on that holy night in Bethlehem, the Word that continues to bring light into the darkness of this world for those of us who see the world through the eyes of faith. These words are not for everybody. St. John speaks only to those of us who strive day after day to live out our new birth in baptism, to those of us who struggle day after day to be people born not of merely human desire, but of God, and who Sunday after Sunday reach out to hold in our hands the grace and truth shown to us by God in the person of the Word made flesh, Jesus Christ our Lord.

For most of the society around us, the celebration of Christmas is already over. For many weeks now this city has glutted itself on Christmas carols and Christmas decorations, often concealing with hollow and brittle revelry lives bereft of any joy beyond getting, any hope beyond the gratification of the present moment, and any love beyond the narrow boundaries of the self. We, on the other hand, have spent the weeks of Advent in prayer, waiting and hoping for the coming proclamation of good news from God, news good enough to transform the desert places of our souls and make them lush and green, news good enough to call us out of loneliness and alienation into a new community of faith, news good enough to bring some hope into our lives, not only for ourselves but for this suffering world around us. Perhaps this morning you noticed the Christmas trees already abandoned on the empty sidewalks of the neighborhood. Our parish Christmas tree is always gotten at a good price, since we don't go out to get it until just before solemn vespers on Christmas Eve. Our tree will remain to grace our worship of the newborn king throughout these twelve days of Christmas, as we proclaim together and sing together the good news that our God at last reigns among us in the child of Mary, Jesus Christ our Lord.

Those of you who have been part of our parish family for a while know that this lovely tree will play a part in our worship life even after the twelve days of Christmas have come to an end. It is our custom here that after the Christmas season, our tree is not thrown out but set aside until Easter Day approaches. On Good Friday, this tree that now proclaims our Savior's birth will be transformed into the cross that we venerate as a symbol of our crucified Lord.

Last year our tree was somewhat smaller than usual, and when the time came, we discovered that we didn't have enough Christmas tree to make a cross for Good Friday. During Holy Week I was standing in front of the church with our sexton Jim, wondering how to get enough Christmas tree for a cross. And this is what happened: Along the street on that April afternoon came a little old man, dressed in rags, talking loudly in some foreign tongue to his imaginary companions. He was dragging a Christmas tree, little bits of tattered tinsel still clinging obstinately to its dried-out branches. When he reached the church, the man let go of the tree, wiped his hands triumphantly, apparently congratulating himself in his native tongue, and then walked off down the street.

Jim and I ran down the street after the old man. "Are you finished with that tree? Don't you want it anymore? Can we have it?" It was not clear to any of us who was mad and who was sane. The old man was the first to gain his composure. "Finished with it!" he screamed in his thick accent. "I don't even know what it is! It was not mine in the first place even. I cannot carry it anymore. You take it, please." And take it we did. Into the church, and on Good Friday into the sanctuary came that symbol of Christmas joy, used for a time as a symbol of madness, loneliness and isolation, transformed now into a symbol of the Word who became flesh to share our human frailty and weakness, transformed into a promise of the resurrection.

Our task as baptized people is to look at this world around us through the eyes of faith, to see this world through the eyes of the Savior who loved it enough to become part of it. Our calling as baptized people is to look for ways of bringing the joy of Christmas into the lives of those who know no Christmas joy. Our privilege as baptized people is to be God's messengers of good news to the people who shuffle aimlessly through the streets of this neighborhood and this city: the poor, the hungry, the elderly, the infirm, the lonely, the sick, the insane and the dying.

These people have something to teach us, too, about the meaning of Christmas. In them and in their lives the eye of faith can discern the child of Mary already making his way to Golgotha, begging us to help him carry the cross. These are the people who will make sure that our Christmas celebration leads all the way to Good Friday and into the light of Easter Day, because it is for them as well as for us and for all the people of this city and this world that the eternal Word of God became flesh in the child of Mary, in Jesus Christ our Lord.

Martin Hauser

R HOLY FAMILY
E SECOND SUNDAY AFTER CHRISTMAS
L FIRST SUNDAY AFTER CHRISTMAS

R *Sir 3:2–6,12–14; Col 3:12–21; Mt 2:13–15,19–23*
E *Jer 31:7–14; Eph 1:3–6,15–19a; Mt 2:13–15,19–23*
L *Is 63:7–9; Gal 4:4–7; Mt 2:13–15,19–23*

Over and over again we are reminded by the prophets of Israel that God is the great deliverer. Jeremiah is wonderfully graphic in one of the texts for this day. It is the Lord who preserves a remnant of Israel. It is the Lord who gathers the scattered and then escorts them home. It is the Lord who comforts their sorrow and watches them on the way. It is the Lord who makes the path straight and safe. It is the Lord who makes the land fat and the garden fruitful and fills the people with plenty.

And the Lord does all of that without any help. So Isaiah declares it. It was no envoy, no angel, but the Lord who delivered them. It is the Lord who acts for us through all the years gone by. That is what we believe. That is what we have to declare, says Isaiah. That is what we have to announce to the nations. That is the promise by which we live. God acts for us. Directly. God is pictured as the active one, who intervenes on our behalf.

The verbs that point to God's acting are equally strong in the Pauline letters. In Christ, Paul says to the Ephesians, God chose us before the world began. God has purchased our freedom, Paul writes to the Galatians, so that we might be heirs. Even while we were held captive by the spirits of the world, God determined that we would be the recipients of more graciousness than we know how to receive. And God continues to forgive lavishly. The intent of God's actions is that the whole universe is united in Christ.

The story of the birth of Jesus gives a similar picture. God is the actor. God announces to Mary and to the shepherds a birth for which God is responsible. God guides the three astrologers and warns Joseph to flee to Egypt with Mary and the Child. Never mind that an angel is the envoy. The message is the same. God is acting for the sake of the world. God is the deliverer.

It is very important to the writer of Matthew that we understand how the birth of Jesus is part of God's great plan of deliverance. And God continues to watch over the Holy Family in the midst of forces that threaten the life of the Child Jesus. In response to those warnings from the Great Deliverer, Joseph leads his little family to safety in Egypt and from Egypt to Nazareth. From the beginning of the birth story to the end, the picture is the same: God acts to save God's people.

There are really two actions in the story however. God delivers, but Joseph decides. That is the story of faith and our lives. Like the fragile Holy Family, our lives are held in the providential care of God. It is God's watchfulness that keeps us from harm. The God who delivered Israel out of Egypt and led the Holy Family to safety is the same God who rescues us from threatening peril. Deliverance is God's responsibility and not ours. And yet, like Joseph, we must decide and we must act. We must decide how to respond to what we perceive to be the plan of God.

The story of Christmas is not just about God's deliverance. It is also about our response. The innkeeper and the shepherds and the astrologers and Joseph all had to make decisions about God's interventions. We must decide too. And yet we believe that no decision we make is final. Everything is provisional in the light of God's providence. That is the liberating word that the story of Christmas reaffirms. It is the Lord who acts for us. Always has. And always will. Even so, we must act too. But that is seldom easy.

Even if our decisions are not final, they are serious. We still have to sort out a responsible course of action from among competing options. We still have to decide between two equally valid choices. We still have to ask the hard questions about long-term consequences of our actions. We still have to know the difference between what we need and what we want. We still have to be alert to the values that influence our choices. We still need to decide and then act on that decision even though it will probably be a flawed decision.

All our achievements are provisional and finite, but so are our failures. Our lives are finally judged by limited possibilities. There is a kind of graciousness in finitude. But it is not enough. We will make wrong choices. It is impossible to avoid deciding in ways that are contrary to God's plan. Our vision is limited, our hearing is impaired and our courage is faulty. And so we need to experience again and again in the eucharist the promise of God from the beginning: we decide but God delivers. That's how it was for Joseph and how it will always be for us.

Herbert Anderson

R L SECOND SUNDAY AFTER CHRISTMAS
E FIRST SUNDAY AFTER CHRISTMAS

R *Sir 24:1–2,8–12; Eph 1:3–6,15–18; Jn 1:1–18*
E *Is 61:10–62:3; Gal 3:23–25,4:4–7; Jn 1:1–18*
L *Is 61:10–62:3; Eph 1:3–6,15–18; Jn 1:1–18*

On this Sunday of the Christmas season, does it seem out of place to you to hear proclaimed again the prologue of St. John's gospel? It shouldn't. It is read today that we may understand even more deeply the mystery of the incarnation.

I recently was intrigued by the title of the book which read *Too Much Holly, Not Enough Holy?* It was one woman's approach to recapture the true meaning of the Christmas season. In the form of a diary beginning on January 6, the author searches for Christmas, and shares her struggles throughout the year with us of how hard it is to find the holiness needed to counteract all the window-dressing, like holly that our world offers us. This writer shares with her readers how she sidestepped the obstacles which stand in the way of our receiving the full enjoyment of the season. She discovered that she had to live each day of the year with this Christmas spirit.

So the church, in directing us forward, tells us with the prologue of John's gospel what our focus should be. The prologue becomes our companion on our journey of spreading the good news of the kingdom. May this homily then be a meditation for all of us as we make this journey.

Verses 1 and 2 of John's gospel: "In the beginning was the Word, and the Word was God. The Word was in the beginning with God; all things were made through the Word, without whom nothing that was made was made." The incarnation brings this limitless power and majesty of the word of God into our world in the form of the little babe of Bethlehem. Verses 7 and 8 of Luke's gospel: "She wrapped him in swaddling cloths and laid him in a manger because there was not place for them in the inn. And in that region there were shepherds out in the field."

Verses 4 and 5 of John's gospel: "In the Word was life, and the life was the light of all. The light shines in the darkness, and the darkness has not overcome it." Have we understood the meaning of this life? Has it challenged us in the search for its meaning? Verse 9 of Luke's gospel: "An angel of the Lord appeared to them, and the glory of the Lord shone around them."

Verses 9 and 10 of John's gospel: "The true light that enlightens every one was coming into the world. The light was in the world, and the world was made through the light, yet the world knew him not." Have our lives been so filled that we have not recognized him? Are we like Herod before the Magi? Verses 8 and 12 of Matthew's gospel: "Go and search diligently for the child, and when you have found him bring me word, that I too may come and worship him. And being warned in a dream not to return to Herod they departed to their own country by another way."

Verses 11 and 12 of the prologue: "He came to his own home, and his own people received him not. But to all who received him he gave power to become children of God." This rejection of the Lord is still present today, even from among us who were once baptized in his name. Why have we rejected him? Didn't we know the cross would be a real part of our acceptance of him? Recall the words of Simeon to Mary. Verse 34 of Luke's gospel: "Behold, this child is set for the fall and rising of many in Israel, and for a sign that is spoken against (and a sword will pierce through your own soul also) that the thoughts out of many hearts may be revealed." Finally, the prologue brings us to the ministry of John the Baptist who heralds God's presence among us. Verse 16 and 17 of the prologue: "From the Son's fullness we have all received, grace upon grace. For the law was given through Moses; grace and truth came through Jesus Christ." The baptism of John leads us to the ministry of Christ.

I hope this meditation has offered us a sense of rededication to the Lord. May we know the power that is ours in becoming God's daughters and sons. May the days ahead with all the festivities gone find us striving to increase our faith and hope and love. May we become better instruments in doing God's will so that the Lord's dominion will be real to one and all. Perhaps today we could begin to write a diary that shares our search to live out the true meaning of Christmas and to make the prologue of John's gospel our words of encouragement when the days seem dark and the challenge too great.

Timothy O'Connor

R E L THE EPIPHANY OF OUR LORD

R *Is 60:1–6 Eph 3:2–3a,5–6 Mt 2:1–12*
E *Is 60:1–6,9; Eph 3:1–12; Mt 2:1–12*
L *Is 60:1–6; Eph 3:1–12; Mt 2:1–12*

The star of Bethlehem, the symbol of our festival of Epiphany, is an unequivocal sign of God's blessing. Its light is the revelation of Christ to the magi, as Christmas was Christ's revelation to the shepherds. The unity of creation and God's plan for our redemption dwell in its light. On the twelfth day of Christmas, Augustine said, East and West are joined together. The lowly and the well-born, the Jews and Gentiles, today these two walls are made one in the cornerstone that is Christ Jesus.[4]

Augustine honed this metaphor in sermon after sermon on the Epiphany, and we who are now the church must take it seriously. Those of us who want our holidays to be sweet with nostalgia and self-congratulation must beware lest we hear only the cliché in this manifestation; we do not want to admit Epiphany's challenge to the way things are, or admit that revelation is a vision given to outsiders, to those who come late to work in the vineyards, to those who have not earned their salvation.

Consider our position: we are not outsiders like the magi, but members of a faithful people like Herod and the people of Jerusalem. Our turn has come to be keepers of holy writ and the prophets; we know where the Christ is to be found, but we have long ago stopped looking for God. "Herod," the Bible says, "was troubled, and all Jerusalem with him."

As children we identified with the magi. We joined their caravan to adventure and despised the people of Jerusalem who hid in the darkness. Today we are wiser women and men; if the star is still our hope for the future, it also reveals us as we are. We have done nicely; we have made a living for ourselves in the world as it is; we have shared in Herod's presumptions of rank.

Perhaps we do not want the light. Assuredly we do not want to be governed. We do not want to see ourselves as we really are, dependent on one another in our maturity as we were in our youth. We are never quite certain if revelation will be a blessing or a curse; we suspect that it may be both.

What has gone wrong that we are suddenly the ones threatened by darkness? We are good people surely? Indeed; and God has not only make known to us the mystery of Christ but has also made us stewards of this mystery for the world's good. The sign of the star is eternal; it says that God's light is stronger than a lifetime of exile and estrangement. Revelation comes to those who have been in a great darkness. And prophecy is a vision that we hope our grandmothers-and-fathers will inherit before they die, when in the return of their sons and daughters the abundance of the sea shall come to them. Isaiah's message is not an empty promise; it is a light from the end of life, a vision of how things will be when we stop depending on ourselves alone. When we recognize the end of the distance between ourselves and others, then will God be in our midst to save us. Until then, the glory of God's light shining through our exile, the star of Bethlehem, upholds us in our struggle against the darkness.

It was this self-reflection that we forgot when we puffed ourselves up against Herod's perfidy and spoke evil against the Jews, our sisters and brothers in God's covenant with the world. We forgot that the light upholds us equally—not as Jew or Christian, not as Catholic or Lutheran or Episcopalian or other, but as co-inheritors and members of one body. The star speaks hope for the poor ones of God, the afflicted who have no one to help them. May it be so, today, in our community.

For today, the patient, expectant waiting that we began in Advent is fulfilled. The plan that God had prepared for the world's salvation, the revelation foreshadowed in so many ways in the long course of Israel's history, moves forward again. Rejoicing, therefore, we come again to the ancient sources of our story to drink deeply of God's love and to seek the light of revelation.

That God's vision should be for all of us without distinction, that none of us can shape it according to a private tradition—this is the revelation, the blessing and the curse. It is so hard because it is so simple. The unsearchable richness of God's plan is a great mystery, not as something secret, but as unsurpassable glory. We have caught its splendor enshrined even in such ancient systems as the code of Hammurabi and in the wise sayings of Confucius in China. In this way at Epiphany our humanity is married to the divine. The great exchange has been made. From now on, to be truly godlike, we need only be ourselves—truly human. Everywhere under heaven, among all the peoples of the earth, the question is the same, "How shall we live?" and the answer comes back from as far away as China: a good monarch is one who cares for the oppressed, who rules by heaven's will, who causes the people to give thanks. And a good people is one that has become like their king.[5]

So is it for us. The vision of life for humankind is the revelation of God appearing in our midst. It is the nativity of the child-king, the birth of the holy one, the coming of the Lord who makes us holy. Not the code, not the law, not our own deeds, but the Christ into whose death we are baptized and at whose table we eat as one family—only this one gives us bold access to God. This is the word of God and the vision we shall live by. This one is Jesus, and today this one lives in our midst.

Rachel Reeder

[4]St. *Augustine Sermons for Christmas and Epiphany*, tr. Thomas Comerford Lawler, Ancient Christian Writers 15 (New York: Newman, 1952), p. 164.
[5]*The Sayings of Confucius*, tr. James R. Ware (New York: New American Library, 1955).

R L THE BAPTISM OF OUR LORD
E   FIRST SUNDAY AFTER EPIPHANY

R *Is 42:1–4,6–7; Acts 10:34–38; Mt 3:13–17*
E *Is 42:1–9; Acts 10;34–38; Mt 3:13–17*
L *Is 42:1–7; Acts 10:34–38; Mt 3:13–17*

The serigraph is simple but aflash with color. The artist calls it "The River." The art world labels its style "naive." The perspective is askew: upriver at the horizon, a farmer as large as any figure tends a garden of vegetables; at the mouth of the river in the foreground, the figures of John and Jesus at his baptism are no larger.

What river is it? It must be an important one since there are so many people on its banks. One is reaping grain, another tending sheep; several are swimming or drawing water while others are washing clothes or bathing. And all of this activity is alive in festival colors.

What river is it? Is it perhaps one of those mighty rivers which Abraham's family crossed before the patriarch received God's call? Or was it the great Egyptian river which was the lifeblood of that ancient land? Or was it the Jordan, the one the gospel reports?

The people of God have forded many rivers.

The artist has captured the moment that Jesus emerges from the river's baptismal water. Soon the Spirit which had moved over the waters in the beginning will come to hover as a dove over this baptized man. Soon the cloud which led the Hebrew nation from slavery in Egypt will come to cover the scene. This is the moment before the voice speaks the hope of the prophet Isaiah: "Behold my servant, my chosen, upon whom I have put my Spirit."

It is a glorious moment. The colors in the picture say as much. It is a time when all righteousness is fulfilled and the heavens are opened.

But when the heavens are shut again and the glorious moment is gone, the Spirit leads Jesus into the wilderness.

The Hebrew nation had known the same experience. They too knew the glory of God opened before them as God parted the sea. But the cloud led them after the miracle into a desert. In this desert was temptation to idolatry and mistrust of God. And to these temptations they succumbed.

Therefore the cloud led them in that desert until all who had come through the sea had died. Only their descendants would inhabit the promised land. The cloud led them from glory to the desert and accompanied them to death.

So too the Spirit led Jesus into the wilderness to be tempted by the devil. But there Jesus overcame the devil's temptations. In the wilderness world, throughout all Judea, he preached good news of peace, and went about doing good and healing all that were oppressed by the devil, for God was with him. God had anointed this Jesus with the Holy Spirit and with power. God's Spirit led him to the wilderness, and accompanied him through his life.

But the devil found an opportune time and placed temptation to jealousy and fear before the descendants of those who had been led by the cloud. This time the devil succeeded: Jesus was taken and ridiculed, beaten and given to soldiers. Soldiers, not the cloud or the Spirit, led Jesus to a cross and hanged him there. The cloud then turned the sky to darkness and the Spirit left Jesus crying out, "My God, my God, why have you forsaken me?"

There Jesus was hanged to die. And just to make very sure, Jesus was pierced by a sword and from his side came a river of water.

It is, of course, another river, just as it is for us another wilderness in which we live. But the river of his death invites us back to the river of his baptism—the river of our baptism. There sheep are tended by the Good Shepherd, water is drawn from the wells of salvation, and our robes are washed for the marriage feast of the Lamb. There we shall be born again and again and again each time we return.

Isaiah writes of the Lord who has called us in righteousness, taken us by the hand, and kept us. In our baptism we are called still in righteousness. In our wilderness lives, God takes us still by the hand. God grant that we be kept close to Jesus and his cross. Standing there under his riven side, may we ever be called back to our baptism, to a river and a life of joyful color.

Let Jesus' death become our life. Let his crucified body, which calls us ever back to the river of our baptism, become visible through bread in my hands and yours and wine shared among us.

Mikkel Thompson

R   SECOND SUNDAY IN ORDINARY TIME
E L SECOND SUNDAY AFTER EPIPHANY

R   *Is 49:3,5–6; 1 Cor 1:1–3; Jn 1:29–34*
E   *Is 49:1–7; 1 Cor 1:1–9; Jn 1:29–41*
L   *Is 49:1–6; 1 Cor 1:1–9; Jn 1:29–41*

The ancient Hebrews knew that God was more visible than any creature, that God had a face and a heart the way no creature ever could. God had given them eyes to see. When a prophet confronted them, filled with passion to save the poor, the widow, and the orphan, people knew the prophet was not God, though he said "I" when he condemned them or gave them hope. Idols had faces but no hearts. The powers of nature were heartless, drought and plague, though people called such powers gods. Human beings on the loose for booty were worse than idols and nature, faceless and heartless humans behind helmet and shield. But the Suffering Servant of Isaiah was different, he was God-With-Us, a beautiful human formed by a woman, one who did not do evil in return for evil, but good instead. He became thereby a salvation for everyone. Or the Suffering Servant was a beautiful people who were to absorb evil and make the goodness of God manifest. In its better moments, Israel knew the lineaments of the divine face. In its better moments, it longed to be like God.

The ancient Christians saw the face and heart of God in Jesus Christ, the one who stood before them suffused with the passion of God for the world. Such intensity of love, such intensity of truth was more than human, yet so at home in flesh and blood that the followers of Christ knew they were touched by God and could touch God in return. In their better moments, they longed to be like him.

When Jesus Christ was destroyed by crucifixion, his disciples were destroyed also. Both the human and the divine vanished for them. In the gospel descriptions they are empty, empty of him. They have the love, but it is a love with no one there. When he is restored to them, they know him from what he looks like and from what he feels for them and for the world. From then on he is always there to love, in everyone they see, in everything they touch. They become him, the way Isaiah's Suffering Servant became God visible, the way Israel became God's light to the world. The ancient Christians do no evil in return for evil, but good instead, wherever they go.

Those who see them are like the Baptist at the Jordan when Jesus comes to be baptized. John senses the coming of God, so the gospel says. John also senses that he himself is precious to the one who comes, that Jesus brings out in him everything that he, John, has ever wished, and John has wished that the world be holy with the holiness of God.

When Christianity was at its best, when it is at its best now, it has the face and heart of Jesus Christ. It brings out the best in everyone and everything. When it is at its worst, it is faceless and heartless, like idols, or forces of nature, or warriors. The world watches the faces of things, to see if things have a heart. And we do too, but for a different reason. Once we have seen Jesus, we have seen what everything else can become. His whole being is so inviting! He tells us we can invite in his name: not to a submission, but to family with God, and family with this world.

We are like the man who was walking by a department store one day. Belief or unbelief made little difference to him. The peaceful life did. A bomb blew up in a litter barrel and hurled him forward into a woman walking in front of him and took both some yards down the street where they fell to the sidewalk. He had shielded her from the blast, and she had cushioned his fall. It had just happened that way. He rolled off her and while still on the concrete felt himself for damage. None that he could tell, some blood on his fingers, but not from a gusher. She was not harmed either as he looked. But she was pregnant, very pregnant, and she knew the blast and fright had begun the process of birth. The man saw her contractions and he looked around for help, but the pandemonium was so great he could not catch anyone's attention. It took twenty minutes before a medic arrived, and he and the medic had to deliver that baby in the middle of a scene from the end of the world. The man was on his knees helping the medic, holding the woman's hands; so he saw the birth and the woman giving it so vividly that the scene of carnage around him seemed to disappear until both woman and child were gone in an ambulance and he realized he was slightly wounded himself and asked the medic to help him. He saw the face of God that day. In the woman, the baby, the medic, in his own hands. And he saw the face of evil in the carnage. But it was the beauty of birth that stayed with him, not the horror of death. And he saw Scripture as he had never seen it before.

God is visible to us today in ways we do not expect. But God has given us eyes to see as well.

Francis P. Sullivan, S.J.

R   THIRD SUNDAY IN ORDINARY TIME
E   L   THIRD SUNDAY AFTER EPIPHANY

R   *Is 8:23b-9:3; 1 Cor 1:10–13,17; Mt 4:12–23*
E   *Am 3:1–8; 1 Cor 1:10–17; Mt 4:12–23*
L   *Is 9:1b-4; 1 Cor 1:10–17; Mt 4:12–23*

Nothing changes as fast as the ad campaigns for beverages. The slogans are redone, new jingles suddenly appear, all trying to give a fresh appearance to the same old product. The half-life of the average commercial for a softdrink or a beer seems to get shorter every year.

Yet one ad has seemed to hang around forever, the Bud ad geared to particular types of work. No matter what you do, unless you are a criminal or a member of the clergy, "this Bud's for you." Odd, isn't it? One of the most enduring commercials is successful because it celebrates work, day in, day out work.

We know about this kind of dailiness. Day in, day out most of us do pretty much the same thing. This workday routine is familiar, and most of the time it fits. Oh, we may gripe about the routine, but usually there is more good than bad about all we do. It locates us, defines our place in things, provides a sense of security, shapes our identity. Our role comes with its own lore, its own language, and its own rhythm. We are identified by what we do; we even promote that identity. See the bumper sticker telling you that "If you can read this, thank a teacher." When you hear that Simon and company were fishermen, it tells you something. We know their daily routine, and we know how that served to identify them.

It is interesting how power weaves its way through daily routine. We find security through work and play, but we bump into some authority or other defining our lives. We find that instead of shaping our own identity, we are being shaped by some power outside ourselves. Here all along we were buying slogans like "Have it your way," yet in the process we were pledging allegiance to some principality or power out there. This is reflected in our dress codes, in the uniforms we wear. Walk down the main drag of a university town to see all the enforced dress codes. Adolescents self-consciously titter along, all looking like fashionably dressed college students, brand names blaring from every piece of clothes. The college students themselves walk more at ease in their wardrobes of jeans and sweats. In rebellion against such conformity, sullen punkers and rockers are outfitted solely in black and white, the only color being the dyed hair. All of these statements are made in the name of freedom of choice. There are authorities in the world with real power over us, and most of them function without our even knowing it. We are caught in our own nets.

Into this world Jesus walks. "Follow me," he announces, calling us by name. Jesus summons us to follow him and leave all our nets behind. There is a call here that demands a response, and a mystery in the invitation, for it comes with the authority of our creator God. For those fishermen, the word goes out and does not return empty. Look at the nets lying draped over the rocks, the boats tilted at odd angles where they were dragged up on the beach. Call and response. "Follow me," Jesus says, and they drop everything and go. "Follow me," Jesus says, and you see it happen again. A woman who had finally achieved job security is called and she packs up her car, says goodbye to her friends and heads off to seminary. "Follow me," Jesus says, and after three or four tough years she is crammed with term papers, finals, and internships, kneeling before an altar in a church packed with people; a stole is placed on her shoulders and she rises to assist at the holy meal. Call and response. "Follow me," Jesus invites, and the disciples drop everything and go. All of us got the same invitation as we went through the waters of baptism. Jesus walks into our world and calls us out of it. With the authority of the everlasting God, Jesus calls us by name and invites us to be disciples. "Follow me," Jesus says to his church. "Leave your nets and follow me."

This way of Christ we follow is different from all those worldly authorities. The invitation is to share in the work of Christ, to show forth God's dominion. Interesting: such fishers can't find a home in the world in the same way. The old identities don't stick with conviction any more. And yet, following Jesus leads you right back into the world, right into the thick of things, principalities and powers and all. But those authorities no longer enslave. Look at some fisherfolk who heard the call and are involved in a prison ministry in what was their spare time. Instead of outdoors, they are behind bars this weekend, leading a group of inmates through a guided tour of the life of faith. "Follow me," they say, in the name of Christ, through prayer, Scripture and personal testimony. And through them, Jesus speaks to some prisoners. "Follow me," he says. Redeem the time. In the midst of this world, join me in the Way. And in the grace of God, some drop their nets and follow.

So here we are again. Maybe we are minding our own business and tending our nets as hard as we can. Yet we are not surprised when we hear somebody call our name, or even when we follow. Fisherfolk indeed.

Richard Eslinger

R   *Zeph 2:3,3:12–13; 1 Cor 1:26–31; Mt 5:1–12a*
E   *Mic 6:1–8; 1 Cor 1:26–31; Mt 5:1–12*
L   *Mic 6:1–8; 1 Cor 1:26–31; Mt 5:1–12*

Each of us who gathers here today was once given a name at the time of birth. Yet that may not be the name we have been known by among family, friends and co-workers. It is not unusual that an adult might be given a lifelong tag. Have you ever met men still called "Sonny" and women still called "Sissy!"

What is true on the personal level is also true in a larger context. We tag certain mundane realities and give them meaning beyond what they are. Advertisers are good at this. Pepsi is the drink of a new generation. Coke is the real thing. You go for gusto, you only go around once, and it never gets better than this: these tags relate to beer!

Both examples indicate that we are more influenced by our namings than we realize. We are deeply touched by images and metaphors. For us who are Christian we can ask: what images enliven our lives? What ways, tags, and metaphors do we use to describe what we are about in the Christian life?

Until recently the image of heaven enlivened Christian living. We engaged in human heroism because our reward would come in heaven. We knew that the heavenly city was to be matched by the earthly city of God. We fasted with the knowledge that someday, after this journey, we would feast at the table of an abundantly generous God. We gave up many things because eventually we would know the bliss of paradise. For many of our family members these images gave meaning to their lives. They helped them endure enormous hardships for the sake of something yet to come.

There is one image, a neglected one, that expressed heaven. It came from those of Jewish-Christian heritage. The image was that of Christ the heavenly Rabbi. Christ the Teacher was sitting on a throne of wisdom. Gathered round him were other blessed followers. Each of them was attentive to the wisdom of Christ. Heavenly fulfillment meant a sacred learning that satisfied those who had spent a lifetime yearning for divine wisdom.

I have always found this image appealing. I don't know what one does with this if one hated school and if one equated learning with the ennui of classes. Nonetheless I have always loved and cherished this image. Jesus is the heavenly Rabbi who invites us to wisdom and knowledge. We shall be satisfied in our yearnings to know the great mysteries that we know so incompletely and after which we strive through such hard work.

The gospel story we have just heard is one of the best examples of Jesus the Teacher. Matthew depicts Jesus as the Moses-like figure who went up the mountain. He sat down, as if in the chair of Moses, and the blest ones, the disciples, came to his feet. He opened his mouth and wisdom came forth. He taught them. Both Jewish-Christians and Gentile-Christians, both living in an age of conflict and choice, could learn how to follow Christ wisely.

What is it that Jesus the Rabbi offers? The Beatitudes are not easy, clear answers. The learning is not neatly packaged like a television commercial. He offers a new set of attitudes, a style and stance of paradox. The disciple is given no other-worldly reward system which will make the practical living-out bearable. The Jesus of Matthew's Beatitudes offers criteria that place the Christian in the midst of the world and at the heart of its conflicts in an age where various religious allegiances vie with one another.

Poverty in spirit will bring the dominion of heaven. Mourning will issue in comfort. Meekness will overturn the isolation of greed. Righteousness will be satisfied. Merciful action will result in mercy given as gift. Purity of heart, seeking God single-mindedly, will allow one to see God. Peacemakers will be children of God. The persecuted will be victors. The rub is there: we rejoice in the midst of persecution. These criteria put us into the midst of the this-worldly. The wise, teaching Rabbi is Emmanuel. He is always with us as we are baptized, immersed in the concerns of this world. Doing justice and peacemaking and giving the cup of refreshing water will be a costly discipleship. We count not the cost because we have no right to. Discipleship, paradoxical as it is, brings a heroism in the here-and-now. How surprisingly God works. God uses us in our weakness to shame the strong; God chooses our limited knowledge and giftedness so that all humans might boast in the presence of God. The source of our boasting is not our achievement, is not our knowledge, is not our taming of the universe. It is our knowledge of God learned in discipleship and service. God is the source of our life in Christ Jesus, whom God makes our wisdom.

We come to the table today, a table that is foretaste of the heavenly banquet. But we come to the table to eat the scroll of wisdom. This wisdom is from Christ the Teacher, Christ the Rabbi. Its eating brings learning for Christian life and wise action in our world. Such wisdom can enable us to help fashion God's reign in the human city where Emmanuel dwells.

John J. O'Brien, C.P.

R   FIFTH SUNDAY IN ORDINARY TIME
E L   FIFTH SUNDAY AFTER EPIPHANY

R   *Is 58:7–10; 1 Cor 2:1–5; Mt 5:13–16*
E   *Hab 3:1–6,17–19; 1 Cor 2:1–11; Mt 5:13–20*
L   *Is 58:5–9a; 1 Cor 2:1–5; Mt 5:13–20*

When I was a little girl, I sometimes sat staring at the Morton Salt box while my mother was cooking. The box was blue with a picture of a girl carrying a yellow umbrella; she also carried a little Morton Salt box. Over the picture read the caption, "When it rains, it pours!" I could sit for a very long time, imagining that if I had a strong magnifying glass, I could see another little salt box on the one she was carrying, and another on that salt box, and on and on forever. Millions of microscopic salt boxes . . . finally, it made my eyes hurt.

I didn't know it then, but such an enterprise could be called speculation. It was something like the ancient conundrum, "If angels are spiritual beings without height or weight, how many of them could dance on the head of a pin?" Religion can be filled with speculation because so many truths cannot be proved. How many people will really go to heaven? What does heaven look like? If you lived on an isolated island and had never heard of Jesus, would you be saved? You can speculate about such questions for a very long time, until your head hurts.

So we might speculate about what Jesus meant when he said, "You are the salt of the earth, you are the light of the world." Such metaphors are perfect territory for speculation because Jesus doesn't say exactly what he means, only that we are to *be* salt and light. We can begin with what we know about salt and light, for Jesus often used common images to help us understand a deeper truth. Salt, before the days of high blood pressure, was thought to be essential to life. It was salt that preserved food and kept it from spoiling. Salt was traded by caravans just as people traded gems or gold. Nothing could take the place of salt; if it lost its saltiness, it was worthless.

We also know something about light: a dark room can be changed by lighting one candle. A frightened child can be soothed with a light on in the hallway. We know what Jesus meant when he said that no one lights a lamp, then puts it under a bushel basket. For we don't turn on the light switch to look at the light bulb. We turn on the light to see around the room. The light Jesus is talking about is not for its own sake: rather it helps us see something beyond the light.

Salt is something essential to life; light is something which points beyond itself. Now this is where serious speculation can begin. What's essential for life? Well, some might say prayer in the schools, another might say women staying at home to care for children, still another might say being a Lutheran or a Roman Catholic or a born-again believer. And light? Light must point toward the truth: then we would argue about what the truth really is, quoting Bible verses, preachers, and probably a bit of our own opinions. We could speculate on and on without boundaries; or could we?

For Jesus, salt and light had particular meaning. They weren't simply two common experiences among many others. For Jesus salt and light came out of a long tradition of biblical teaching: salt and light were images for the law of God. Just in case we missed that point, Jesus says it clearly, "Think not that I have come to abolish the law and the prophets; I have come not to abolish them but to fulfill them." Thus, salt and light cannot take us into any direction. Salt and light must take us back to the fulness of the law and the prophets, and the fulness of Jesus' radical teaching in this Sermon on the Mount. So it is that on this day we also hear a reading from the prophet who sees light breaking forth. But it is not just any light, pointing anywhere; this light shines from the fulness of God's law. The prophets plead for fulness of life: freedom from oppression, bread for the hungry, homes for those who have none, clothing for the naked. Is this not what it means to be the salt of the earth, to keep this prophetic word alive in the midst of our world? If we lose this vision, if we give in to other values, if we forget God's longing for justice, our salt has lost its taste.

We are not left alone to speculate forever. Jesus Christ, God's own word, has come to earth. Jesus comes, not replacing the law and the prophets, but fulfilling them. So it is that when we gather at the table and hear the words, "Do this in remembrance of me," it is not a speculative ritual. Nor is it disconnected from the rest of life. Whenever we receive the broken bread, we remember the prophet's vision to share our bread with the hungry. This holy meal invites us to break our isolated fasting and be part of God's community of grace, a community which continues to be shaped by the calling to the salt and the light in the world.

If you think salt and light can be whatever you might speculate, read the prophet again. If you think Jesus' call is impossible, remember that the One who is our bread is with us and within us, empowering us to be salt and light in this world.

Barbara Lundblad

R SIXTH SUNDAY IN ORDINARY TIME
E SIXTH SUNDAY AFTER EPIPHANY, PROPER 1
L SIXTH SUNDAY AFTER EPIPHANY

R *Sir 15:15–20; 1 Cor 2:6–10; Mt 5:17–37*
E *Sir 15:11–20; 1 Cor 3:1–9; Mt 5:21–24,27–30,33–37*
L *Deut 30:15–20; 1 Cor 2:6–13; Mt 5:20–37*

"Think not that I have come to abolish the law and the prophets; I have come not to abolish them but to fulfill them." With these words the writer of Matthew introduces a section of the Sermon on the Mount which contrasts the teaching of the law with the teaching of Jesus. These words were addressed to folks who have lived their whole lives under the influence of the law. What a startling claim it must have been for them to hear that Jesus had come to fulfill that law! And what could that mean? It meant that the law was no longer the final word on the relationship between God and God's people. It meant that the coming of Jesus moved people beyond mere observance of the law. It meant a new covenant, a new relationship. It meant the dominion which Jesus preached. It was not a new law, as one commentator points out, but a whole new frame of reference. Jesus reinterprets the law. Jesus takes the place of the law. And in place of the righteousness of the Pharisees and doctors of the law, the righteousness demanded by the dominion of heaven is relationship, allegiance to, following Jesus.

Jesus' fulfillment of the law does not lighten the expectations. Rather, it asks for a deeper connection between the inner attitude and the outward actions. Allegiance to Jesus is more complicated than simply observing a list of rules. It requires following where he leads, to a new understanding of the covenant with God and to a new standard of judgment. Following the will of God as revealed by Jesus is not easily reduced to a written code. Rather, obedience finds Jesus' new, radical claim of love. This new claim of love recognizes that the consuming preoccupation with details and correctness of the law could pull the people of God away from being concerned with what really mattered.

It is this transforming new attitude which Jesus is beginning to teach here to the people gathered to listen to the Sermon on the Mount. He is urging his hearers to look at the choices they make and the motivations for their actions in a new way. That change of perspective starts with an inner transformation. It is almost like the transition from child to adult. The questions change from "How much can I get away with?" or "What is the absolute minimum I am required to do?" to an emphasis on caring and responsibility arising not from external limits, but from an inner sense of what is right. For those Jews who heard this message, it represented an important change and was an essential ingredient in understanding Jesus' teaching and ministry.

But we are mostly not a people who experience ourselves as being bound by law. Even in a year like this marked by the impact of changes in tax laws and no-smoking ordinances, civil laws are not a major factor in our lives. Our religious lives also are lived under the new covenant. What then do we hear as we gather to listen to these words from Matthew's gospel?

We are no strangers to preoccupation with the external. In many ways, our culture encourages us to skim the surface and to ignore what is underneath. We have failed to grasp the secret which the fox shares with the Little Prince in Saint-Exupery's story. The fox tells the prince, "It is only with the heart that one can see rightly; what is essential is invisible to the eye."[6] We still need to hear the emphasis in this gospel on what is internal. We need to hear the invitation in Jesus' teaching to go beyond the surface of things to discover what is essential. We need to hear the call of the radical new claim of love in our lives, so that we are delivered from doing things merely because they are expected or correct or because they look good. We need to face our inner motivations, desires, and priorities and to hold them up to the new standard of honesty and love which Jesus gave to his followers. We need to examine and respond to the demands of relationship to Jesus.

Of course, this response comes from individual self-understanding and action. But it does not stop there. Jesus' preaching of the kingdom was not addressed to individuals, but to a community. Matthew wrote the words of this gospel lesson for a community of believers. We gather together as a community to hear and respond to those words, to that preaching and teaching. We may come to church seeking inner transformation, but we also come to a place where that deep spiritual experience is spoken about and shared. Not long ago, a friend and I were discussing his recent spiritual searchings. "What would a spiritual experience be like?" I asked. "To be deeply known and understood," he said, "and to feel that I was among people who shared that experience." I don't know where his spiritual journey will lead, but he has grasped the essence of what is internal and identifies its important impact on the external response we make.

The love, the new covenant, is not just an abstract philosophical concept or a moral precept each individual Christian seeks. It is a reality here among us. We are brought in touch with the reality of the love of Christ each time we celebrate the eucharist. This reality of God's presence is available, not just for personal renewal, but for strengthening the community for living the radical new claim of love. One of the eucharistic prayers in the Episcopalian liturgy asks that we be delivered "from the presumption coming to this table for solace only and not for strength, for pardon only and not for renewal."[7] Even when we are encouraged to pay attention to our internal motivation and transformation, we are not encouraged to get stuck there. We are called to go beyond mere observance of conventions and commandments, to go deeper into a relationship which calls us to respond. And then our response will be action to show ourselves far different from the Pharisees and doctors of the law. In that way we will begin to understand and to participate in the fulfillment Jesus offers.

Leslie G. Reimer

[6]Antoine de Saint-Exupery, *The Little Prince* (New York: Harcourt, Brace and World, 1943), p. 70.
[7]*The Book of Common Prayer* (New York: Church Hymnal Corporation, 1977), p. 372.

R   SEVENTH SUNDAY IN ORDINARY TIME
E   SEVENTH SUNDAY AFTER EPIPHANY, PROPER 2
L   SEVENTH SUNDAY AFTER EPIPHANY

R   *Lev 19:1–2,17–18; 1 Cor 3:16–23; Mt 5:38–48*
E   *Lev 19:1–2,9–18; 1 Cor 3:10–11,16–23; Mt 5:38–48*
L   *Lev 19:1–2,17–18; 1 Cor 3:10–11,16–23; Mt 5:38–48*

Our Lord has great expectations of redeemed disciples. Today they seem to focus on the words, "You, therefore, must be perfect, as your heavenly Father is perfect." But the "therefore" alerts us to a previous climax of our Lord's words. In effect he says, "I say to you that you should be perfect in all these ways so that you may be children of God." He does not say "so that you may *become* children of God," but because you already are. We are to be perfect in order to be what the loving Father has made us, God's children.

It can be apt, if somewhat labored, to paraphrase Lincoln's Gettysburg Address as a way to confront these texts.

Four score and eight years ago, plus thousands of years—(two thousand, if we think of Jesus here sitting on the Mount giving this sermon, plus even more thousands, if we think of Moses reporting God's words to Israel, "You shall be holy; for I the LORD your God am holy")— Four score and those thousands of years ago our heavenly Father brought forth on this planet a new nation, a holy nation, a chosen race. That royal priesthood, God's own people, was conceived in liberty by God's gracious love, through the Son of God made free indeed, and in baptism dedicated to the proposition that all people should be re-created *perfect*.

Now we are engaged in great civil war, against flesh and blood, against principalities and powers and the rulers of the darkness of this world, testing whether we in this parish or those in any other parish, so conceived and so dedicated can long endure, can turn the other cheek, can give up the extra cloak, can walk the extra mile, can give to the borrower and the beggar, can love their enemies and pray for those who persecute them, can, in sum, be the children of the Father who is in heaven, who makes the sun rise on the evil and the good, and sends rain on the just and the unjust.

We are met on a great battlefield of that war, *as* a great battle-field of that war. We have come to dedicate anew, to dedicate another area of our life's field to God, not for a resting place, but for increased effort, remembering the martyrs who have given their lives that God's church might live. It is altogether fitting and proper—it is altogether meet, right, and salutary—that we should do this.

But in a larger sense, we cannot dedicate, we cannot consecrate, we cannot hallow this ground of our living. The brave man, Lord Sabaoth, Lord of Hosts, who struggled here, by his living and in his dying has consecrated us far beyond our poor power to add or to detract.

[That is the fact, is it not? We have been made perfect in God's sight by God-in-Christ. He was in the form of God, our Lord Jesus was, but did not count equality with God something to be grasped. Instead he emptied himself, taking the form of a ser-vant, being born in our likeness. And being found in human form, he humbled himself and became obedient unto death, even death on a cross. Because of all that, God highly exalted him giving him the name above all names, and—remember—has highly exalted us as well, giving us the name children of God! St. Paul says, "have this mind among yourselves, which is yours in Christ Jesus." The perfection which God has given by grace includes such a will to love God and to love our neighbors as ourselves.]

We can never forget what Jesus Christ did here. It is for us, the living, to be dedicated to the unfinished tasks which he who fought here has thus far so nobly advanced.

["Dedicated": that is the description given of us in the second reading. We are God's temple. Jesus Christ is its foundation. He who was laid in the grave is risen. His life and power permeates the temple building's stones, rising up through the joints defin-ing each one of us, making us living stones, able to house God's

Spirit. God's temple is holy, and that temple you are! We are able to live as fools in this world and so be wise, to love and endure and strive, to *be* the children of God we have been made, to *be* perfect as the heavenly Father is perfect. We are made more than "able to": we *want to*! Our wills have been "highly exalted" to follow God just as these disciples were called up to the Mount by Jesus. They had heard Jesus say, "Follow me!" And in the following they were transformed into disciples. And so have we too been changed. We are those who are glad to hear the Lord's "therefore": "You must be perfect as your heavenly Father is perfect."]

It is for us, then, the living, to be dedicated to the unfinished work which our Lord who fought here has thus far so nobly advanced. It is for us to be here dedicated to the great tasks remaining before us, to take increased devotion to this cause of God from him who for us gave the last full measure of devotion.

We here highly resolve that our Lord shall not have died in vain, that this parish, under God, shall have a new birth of freedom-in-Christ, and that this church, of the Father, through the Son, in the Holy Spirit, shall become ever more perfect in the earth.

Come then to the thanksgiving feast of our Lord. Receive his body and his blood for the perfecting of your life. Pray, "Lord, I believe; help thou my imperfection."

George W. Hoyer

R   EIGHTH SUNDAY IN ORDINARY TIME
E   EIGHTH SUNDAY AFTER EPIPHANY, PROPER 3
L   EIGHTH SUNDAY AFTER EPIPHANY

R   *Is 49:14–15; 1 Cor 4:1–5; Mt 6:24–34*
E   *Is 49:8–18; 1 Cor 4:1–5,8–13; Mt 6:24–34*
L   *Is 49:13–18; 1 Cor 4:1–13; Mt 6:24–34*

Once in a while we read or hear a news item about a child accidentally left behind at a rest stop. When children are numerous, and outings involve more than one vehicle, such a temporary loss may well occur. Usually the omission is quickly discovered and corrected. Similarly, even good parents may become separated from their child in a store or at a crowded event. The poor parents feel terrible, but these things do happen, despite their deep love and concern.

It's much harder to mislay an infant; babies do not wander off in search of a drink of water, or stop to look at the toys. And the child yet-to-be-born cannot be lost at all. He or she is part of the mother's physical being. That close and wonderful relationship between parent and child is the basis of the image God uses in today's scripture from Isaiah. Even if a mother or father could wipe out the memory of a child, even if a woman could forget the developing infant in her womb, God promises that we will never be forgotten. We are held in God's hand, the beloved ones, embraced and held safely forever.

We find it hard to imagine the nature of God's unconditional, unlimited love. In the first letter of John, we marvel at the revelation, "This is love, not that we loved God but that God loved us and sent the Son to be the expiation for our sins." God loves us not because of our goodness; instead, anything of good in us is there precisely because God loved us first. From the first instant of existence, God loves every individual in the only way God can love: perfectly, completely, with no possibility of change. This love is personal and even more intimate than that between mother and child. It is faithful, despite our sins and our betrayals. It always fulfills what love promises, offering us salvation through the redeeming actions of Jesus.

Sometimes we find this powerful truth frightening. To be loved in such a fashion demands a total commitment from us who are loved. Often the sacred Scriptures remind us of this whole-hearted response. In today's gospel, we again hear how the reign of God is to be first in our lives. The gospel underlines the radical nature of our response: not even those things which we consider necessities are to get in the way of loyalty. And, aware of our fearfulness, God again promises that we will not be lost, we will not be abandoned, we will not cease to share in providence. Everything we need will be ours, if we allow God first place.

The great tragedy of human history is that humanity has deviated from God's plan. We have not put God at the center of the world, and we have denied divine sovereignty. Everything is out of order, not in harmony. We easily recognize the disorder and confusion within ourselves, in our social relationships, and in our world, yet we do not admit the basic cause. We keep on trying to find solutions based only on human ability. We keep on trying to serve two or more masters, with power or wealth or security receiving a great deal of our time and energy. Although we claim that our allegiance is to God, we want a few more dollars in the savings account or a few more weapons in the national stockpile—just in case.

Our many concerns and our many fears rob us of happiness. Above all else, the gospel message is meant to be good news. We are meant to be happy beings, as a secure, well-loved infant is happy. We live our routine day after day, aware that we are not fully committed to the coming of God's reign, but unable to change, for we believe such a life must go on.

By ourselves and our own power, we will not change. Only by giving ourselves over to the power of God's love will we become able to return a part of that love. Appliances do not work unless they are plugged into the source of power; we do not become God's co-workers until we are united with God's power—through worshiping together, through sharing with one another, through taking risks in the name of love. God tells us, "Look up!

Lift up your hearts! Rejoice! Do not fear." Something wonderful has entered our world: God has entered our history, and God's love has lifted us up forever.

Katherine A. Lewis, O.P.

E LAST SUNDAY AFTER EPIPHANY
L THE TRANSFIGURATION OF OUR LORD

E *Ex 24:12,15–18; Phil 3:7–14; Mt 17:1–9*
L *Ex 24:12,15–18; 2 Pet 1:16–19; Mt 17:1–9*

I recognize you. You are a pilgrim. You are on a spiritual journey, and you have taken the snaking route up from the commerce of the valley, past the planted fields, through the patchy forest, to this pass.

And now you hold out your papers and ask to be permitted to cross the border, but I must tell you to put the papers away. "To enter this country," I continue, "you need to be glorified." As you puzzle on this, I explain, "You need to go from darkness to light." You pause, and shift nervously. In the silence, I say, "There is a place you must go to, and a time you must use to get there. The place is the Mountain of God, and the time is forty days. There you will behold God face to face, and you will be glorified."

Left to your own devices, as often the pilgrim is, you may ponder those words. You may remember from Sunday School that forty is a holy number, that pilgrim Israel is in the wilderness forty years between Egypt and the Promised Land, and that their leader Moses goes up the mountain of Sinai for forty days before he receives the Ten Commandments. Do you recall that when Moses came down off the mountain, his face shone, so that he had to put a veil on his face to be able to talk to the people? Perhaps you also recollect that Elijah is commanded by God to trek into the wilderness forty days, until he comes to the mountain Sinai, where he perceives God, the "still small voice."

Today Jesus goes up the mountain with Peter, James and John, and is transfigured, that is, glorified. With him are the other two forty-day visionaries, Moses and Elijah. You remember an intense light that emanates from Jesus, his glorification. And God says: "This is my Son, the beloved one; listen to him."

You may have been trying to listen to Jesus for a long time already. That's why you are on the pilgrim's route to the spiritual border. And you are in the right place.

This church this morning is on the mountainous border. And today there is a place you must go, and a time you must use to get there. The place is the Mountain of God, and the time is forty days. There you will behold God face to face, and you will be glorified.

The borderland is this day of transfiguration. It is the border in your life in this community between the birth of Jesus and his death. The transfiguration of our Lord happens on this last Sunday on the upward climb we take from Jesus' Epiphany, when the magi visit the baby, and he is revealed to the nations. This epiphany is paralleled in Jesus' baptism when coming up out of the water Jesus hears the voice of God: "You are my Son, the beloved one, with whom I am well pleased." At the transfiguration we hear that voice again, but it is the last time that God speaks in words in the gospel.

For we pass border control this day, and we descend toward Jesus' death. And it is a road for forty days that we are going to travel, forty days of preparation for those momentous events through which we struggle in Holy Week. The church has set these forty days aside, so that you can travel the hard journey of self-examination and prayer which must precede glorification.

In the history of Christian worship, the observance of Lent grew from one day of fasting between Good Friday and Easter to a period of observance, forty days before Good Friday. These forty days have always been a time of reflection and renewal for the church. Adult converts who are being instructed in the mysteries of the Christian faith wait for the Vigil of the Resurrection to be baptized, so that their entering into and rising out of the baptismal waters would be seen alongside the descent into the tomb and rising out of death of Jesus himself. This border crossing from death into life has always been the center of the Christian experience, when all the baptized are marked with the cross of Christ forever.

But the words that accompany the ashen cross this coming Wednesday are different: "Remember, O man, O woman, that you are dust and to dust you shall return." The ash formed on your forehead into that fateful cross is your passport to glorification. And you pass the border into the forty days of Lent. The next time you will find yourself on the mountain, it is not an unfamiliar setting. Again you are with Peter, James, John and Jesus. Again there is an eerie light. But this time Jesus is asking whether this cup might pass from him.

Were he not willing to suffer, we would not be able to cross the border. In his suffering we see the suffering God face to face. As Christ is transformed into death, we are brought, through our baptism, to life, being changed from one degree of glory to another into the likeness of the Lord.

This church is the border land. This altar is the place of transformation. Your baptism into Christ's death is the passport. Come now to the mountain of God, and be glorified.

Jeffrey A. Merkel

R E L   ASH WEDNESDAY

R   *Joel 2:12–18; 2 Cor 5:20–6:2; Mt 6:1–6,16–18*
E   *Joel 2:1–2,12–17; 2 Cor 5:20b-6:10; Mt 6:1–6,16–21*
L   *Joel 2:12–19; 2 Cor 5:20b-6:2; Mt 6:1–6,16–21*

On this day, Ash Wednesday, we begin Lent, which was originally a period of preparation for Easter baptisms. During this time of instruction the catechumens fasted and prayed. The climax came in the all-night vigil Easter Eve with baptisms and the celebration of Christ's resurrection. At a later time, all church members joined in making Lent a penitential season of mourning for sin. As time went on, more interest was shown in the trials and sufferings of Jesus than in anticipating his victorious resurrection.

Let us remember that Ash Wednesday begins the forty day season of preparation for Easter, our great celebration of the resurrection of our Lord and the celebration of our resurrected life in him. Lent is not a period of preparation for Good Friday, but for Easter. Easter precedes Good Friday in the church's memory of the Christ. Any Lenten discipline, any Lenten practice of piety is to shape us to live the resurrected life in Christ. And this is what the gospel lesson is all about.

In the gospel lesson for today Jesus talks with the disciples about the practice of piety. He urges the disciples not to practice this piety so that they will be praised by others, but to practice their piety in such a way that others will be helped and God's name will be glorified. Throughout the lesson Jesus is concerned with the motives for the piety they practice.

First he speaks to them about almsgiving. All Christians are to give so that others might have, but this giving is not to be done for the esteem of others. Do not sound a trumpet as the hypocrites do. There is evidence that in the synagogue the amount donated and the donor's name was announced, and sometimes a trumpet called attention to a large donation. The hypocrites, the "play-actors," make a big scene of their giving, but the disciples are to do their giving in secret. In fact, it should be so secret that the left hand should not know what the right hand is doing, an anatomical impossibility, but an image of giving that eliminates any system of measuring what one does.

Jesus urges the same thing with regard to prayer. Don't pray in public places so that others can see you, but pray in private. We pray not so that others can see how prayerful we are, but we pray so that God's will can be done.

And the same is true of fasting. Do not make it a public occasion, but do it in secret and God will reward you. Do not disfigure your face, but anoint your head and wash your face; that is, act as if you are preparing for a feast, because real repentance is not just sorrow for sin but joy in a new way of life.

These illustrations which Jesus used to describe the practice of piety are not nearly as important as the deeper point he is trying to make with his disciples. That point, which is more profound than almsgiving, than how one prays and how one fasts, has to do with renunciation and self-denial. Jesus is inviting the disciples to renounce one's self for the sake of the kingdom of God. Because we are in Christ Jesus we can renounce the self; we can say "No" to the ego that is always looking for public affirmation. And this is not just a Lenten discipline, but it is living the baptismal life: crucifying the old and bringing the new to life. It is living the Easter vision by refocusing our habits, our priorities, and our direction.

Renunciation of the self during this Lenten season is much more than the renunciation of some of our petty practices. It is more than the giving up of certain things, such as cigarettes, no matter how valuable that may be. Too often we Christians tend to think of renunciation in terms of material things. We think that we should renounce the body, put down our sexual impulses, deny ourselves a certain food, give away an extra dollar or two.

Renunciation has to do with more serious things. When we renounce the self, when we forget about the public praise of who we are, we are renouncing a whole way of life, of attitudes, values, and perspectives. We are saying "No" to the attitude that we are better than others; we are saying "No" to the value that God answers only some people's prayers; we are saying "No" to the perspective that our position is the only possible correct position.

In the baptismal liturgy of the Episcopal Church the candidate renounces Satan and all the spiritual forces of wickedness that rebel against God, the evil powers of this world which corrupt and destroy the creatures of God, the sinful desires that draw one from the love of God. This is renunciation with a purpose beyond itself. This is renunciation that fosters living the Easter vision. This is renunciation which extends the lordship of Jesus

Christ and promotes and fosters love. This is renouncing all that which impedes my being a servant to my neighbor.

May you have a holy Lent. With these words the church calls us to begin our preparation for Easter. Nothing that we do in Lent will make us more acceptable to God. God has already accepted us in the saving work of Christ. Our practice of piety is to glorify God not so much by giving up something but by taking up something—the cross of the risen Christ—and following him.

Donald S. Armentrout

R E L   FIRST SUNDAY IN LENT

R   *Gen 2:7–9,3:1–7; Rom 5:12–19; Mt 4:1–11*
E   *Gen 2:4b-9,15–17,25–3:7; Rom 5:12–19; Mt 4:1–11*
L   *Gen 2:7–9,15–17,3:1–7; Rom 5:12,17–19; Mt 4:1–11*

I want to suggest a project for Lent: humility. Yes, humility. What a quaint word that sounds like, how old-fashioned and even a bit demeaning. Many of us have probably had it with humility. We hear the old tapes played again by parents, friends, the ministers of the church: "Don't get too big for your britches . . . don't be uppity . . . pride cometh before the fall . . . well, mister (or miss), just who do you think you are? You really think you're somebody, don't you?" Everyone of us has heard phrases like that sometime in our lives, and we don't like it one bit. After all, we should be somebody. We want to achieve, to make our mark on the world. We don't want to be put down: in fact, we avoid it at all costs. We want to be looked up to, to be respected, and to be liked. What's the use of humility then?

I don't care very much for the old-fashioned meaning of the word humility. But there's a trick to the word. Humility shouldn't mean a put-down. It means being close to the *humus*, the Latin word for the earth. Humility is being down to earth. Real humility isn't being less than yourself; it means being both no greater than yourself and no less than yourself. Real humility means being honest, being real.

This is the secret of the readings proclaimed from the Scriptures today. They are an important kick-off for Lent, the church's annual retreat and effort at self-examination, the church's traditional time for preparing itself to receive new members at the Easter vigil.

The point of listening to both the first reading about the sin of Adam and Eve from Genesis and the gospel reading about Jesus' temptations is to recognize in them the great reversal. Adam and Eve got taken in. The tempter says to them: "Listen, if you eat of the fruit of this tree in the middle of the garden, you're going to be like gods. You're going to have it all. Go for it, grab it, do it your way." In other words, "do as I say, and you're not going to have to worry about God at all. You can do anything you want. In fact, you'll be little gods yourselves." And it's a lie. They get tricked into trying to become gods by pulling themselves up by their own bootstraps. And this is what the author of Genesis sees as disaster for humanity, not just for the first pair of human beings but for all of humanity. There's something perverse about our human condition. We all try much of the time to make ourselves into God. And it's a lie, and it spells disaster.

Now consider the gospel, Matthew's account of the temptations of Jesus. The tempter is saying basically the same thing to Jesus as to Adam and Eve: "Go for it. Be the Messiah your own way. Perform impressive feats of magic and wonder. That's what's going to make people listen to you and follow you. Then you'll really be the kind of Messiah the world wants." In other words, do it my way, bow down before me and worship me; do it the way the world would expect you to.

And how does Jesus respond? He responds to the temptations by refusing to be somebody he isn't. He responds by being humble. There's a profound lesson here for us all. The true way to being like God is not to grab at it, not to try to make ourselves into little gods, but to accept the human condition. This is the root of sin: that we're unwilling to accept our human condition for what it is, unwilling to recognize that life is full of challenges, pain and struggle, as well as of joys. I'm not suggesting that we should stand by in the face of unnecessary suffering, either in ourselves or in others, and do nothing. That would be crazy. I am suggesting that we can't avoid hurt in life. Avoidance leads to further pain, misuse of others, unhappiness and sin. When we as mature adults recognize that God loves us as human beings, we come to accept our human condition and are willing to live lives of self-sacrifice, generosity, care and concern. Only when we are willing to follow in the steps of Jesus do we really become like God.

My suggestion is the following: work this Lent at being yourself by being humble. Know that God has made you to participate in that wonderful and sometimes scary project of being human. But take courage. God doesn't ask us to do it alone. It's through the obedience of the one person, Jesus, that we've all participated in reconciliation with God. So as we turn to the table where the love of that same Lord Jesus is poured out for us to be shared with one another, let us rejoice in the invitation to Lent, an invitation to be ourselves, to be down to earth, to be humble.

John F. Baldovin, S.J.

R   SECOND SUNDAY IN LENT

R   *Gen 12:1–4a; 2 Tim 1:8b-10; Mt 17:1–9*

We have only recently begun our journey toward the paschal feast. This Lenten season, as we well know, is a time for deeper reflection, for taking stock, for getting up and getting on. It is traditionally a time in which the community joined in fasting and prayer with the candidates for baptism and with the public penitents. As is true of any beginning, the road seems to stretch out far ahead of us, and we are perhaps tempted to speed down it without much thought, to loiter and meander on the way, or just to stay put where we are, not going anywhere.

Today's readings are intended as a reminder to us as a community that the journey is worth all the inconvenience and trouble. Our Lenten journey is a symbol of our lives as we experience them: lives marked by hardship, by monotony, sometimes by pain and suffering, by changes, and by the need to move on, to move out, to grow. From all our readings today come three main points:

1) God takes the initiative
—in calling Abram,
—in making known who Jesus is,
—in calling us as followers of Christ in baptism.

2) A promise, a vision, an incentive, comes to strengthen us in facing difficulties:
—the promise that Abram's seed would prosper,
—the vision of Jesus' role as Messiah called to glory,
—the manifestation of Jesus which makes possible the faith of Christians.

3) We hear the fact that our lives involve hardship:
—for Abram an uprooting from his native land,
—for Jesus, his passion and death,
—for Christians, hardship and troubles.

First of all, it is God who takes the initiative. We are not assembled here today primarily because of anything we have done, but because God has called us, sustains us in our calling, and gives us strength to be here. Abram was not out looking for a suitable place to move to; the disciples were not wandering around looking for the Messiah; and Paul reminds Timothy that his call was from God, and not because of any good works on Timothy's part.

Abram is promised that he will become "a great nation"; the disciples hear in a vision that Jesus is God's beloved Son; and Timothy is reminded that Jesus Christ has destroyed death and restored life. But the vision of the goal, the destination, must be held onto because there are difficult days ahead. Abram must fold up his tent and set out toward a place as yet unknown to him. Timothy must "share in suffering for the gospel," not in a spirit of cowardice, but rather in power, love and self-control. And Jesus, descending from the mountain, must go forth to face the hostility of the religious leaders, the bored indifference of the colonizers, the fickleness of the crowds, and finally his death.

This is what we are celebrating today: our conviction that God has called us, not as individuals, left to face our lives alone, but as a great nation, as the community of Jesus' disciples, those willing to learn from him. The gospel reminds us that Jesus is the embodiment of all the promises to Abram. The symbols of divine presence so familiar to his disciples, like the high mountain are, like Jesus himself, transfigured, alive with a new meaning. Jesus was transformed, as was Moses on Sinai. His clothes became white as light, and there appeared with him Moses, symbolizing the law, and Elijah, symbolizing the prophets. They conversed with Jesus, the embodiment of the law and the prophets. Then a bright cloud cast a shadow over them and a voice came from the cloud, the bright cloud a familiar sign in the Hebrew Bible of the presence of the Lord.

Clearly the gospel is saying to us that the promises made to Abram, the law given to the people through Moses on Sinai, the prophets like Elijah who from the mountain of Horeb called the people to renewal, all are enfleshed in this man Jesus. He has been transfigured: the disciples have an inkling of who he is, and they are afraid. Jesus, human as always, came to them touched them, saying, "Rise, and have no fear."

We celebrate today our calling as those who have been touched and reassured by Jesus in the gospel, his living word, that we need not fear his glory and his brightness. We need not fear whatever lies ahead. Most of us live very ordinary lives, so ordinary that we find narratives such as this one far-fetched and removed from our rushed and demanding lives. But is it so far removed? The call to "Go from your land and your kindred to be led up a high mountain" is a call to us today. Take time, make time for visions and dreams; take time, make time to see once more, hear once more our call. We often scoff at dreamers and visionaries because as Americans we are justly proud of our know how and practical gifts. But without visions and dreams there can be nothing new, there can be no straight line of meaning in the intersections and criss-crossings of our lives. Every Sunday we come together to hear again, together, our common dreams, our common visions, provided we come as attentive, active listeners and not merely as passive members of a vague church group.

And we hear today a special Christian call: "Go from your land and your kindred." Go forth from your fixed mental boundaries and your restricted sense of family, sisterhood and brotherhood. Go forth to an open-bordered land God will show us. Go forth, grow. But for that we need a vision and we need courage. Paul writes to Timothy that God gave us not a spirit of cowardice but of power love and self-control. And soon, in our sharing of the bread of thanksgiving, united more surely one to another, confirmed in our will to faithful discipleship, we will be touched by Jesus who says, "Rise, and have no fear." Do not be afraid to dream, to go forth from the limits of conventional ways, to "share in suffering for the gospel in the power of God."

Marian Bohen, O.S.U.

E   SECOND SUNDAY IN LENT

E   *Gen 12:1–18; Rom 4:1–5,13–17; Jn 3:1–17*

Nicodemus is in a painful spot: caught between two worlds. On the one hand, and not to be lost sight of, he has done something outrageously daring and open. A Pharisee, a member of the Jewish council, he has come to Jesus in secret, by night, risking his position and putting himself painfully on the line, for the sake of a vague something that tugs at his heart. But having made that enormous first step, he now balks at the second. "How can a person be born when that person is old?" The mind boggles, snaps shut. And as a result, what he receives is not an answer for his search, a balm for his soul, but scorn heaped upon his head. Unable to throw himself across the abyss, he winds up nowhere.

I often think that Nicodemus has received unfair treatment, from that first encounter with Jesus right down to our own day. His faith is often contrasted with that of Abraham, who receives a message, promptly dissolves his worldly affairs, packs up his household, and heads out into the unknown. For most of us, faith is more like Nicodemus's: one step forward and two steps back, two steps forward and one step back, pushed and pulled by a vague tug in our heart that can be neither satisfied nor denied. The Abrahams of the world, by contrast, while numbering among their ranks some paragons of sainthood, also contain their fair share of crazies—those of demonic compulsion or at least monomaniacally swelled egos, who willingly throw the stable tissue of life—their own and others—into the void, to march toward what may be only the vastly amplified voice of their own imagination. Most of us pull back, weighing the urgency of our own inner stirrings against rationality, considering the needs of others—"reality testing," they call it. And properly so, one might add: for if the will of God, the love of God, is destined to manifest itself ultimately in the human condition, it is important to meet God with our humanity intact. Sometimes the only way to meet God is to resist, and to wait between worlds, for a long time.

I have often wondered how Jesus might have answered Nicodemus's question later, after Gethsemane. For in a sense, Jesus has not flung himself over the abyss yet either. God-bred, spirit-born, he still lives lightly in the human condition; the unbearable solidity of this beautiful, fragile, broken sphere has not yet caught him. Only later—weeping before the tomb of his friend Lazarus, or wracked and broken on the cross, in that final wrenching cry, "My God, my God, why have you forsaken me?"—does Nicodemus's question finally pierce to the heart, and there find its extraordinary answer.

"That which is born of the flesh is flesh, and that which is born of the Spirit is spirit." It is a jagged dualism, but wait; for it is not forever, and it is not the root. Beyond the cross, where two

dissolves to one, we will see spirit, in love, give birth to flesh;
and flesh, borne of spirit, move lightly as the wind.

Cynthia Bourgeault

R E THIRD SUNDAY IN LENT
L SECOND SUNDAY IN LENT

R *Ex 17:3–7; Rom 5:1–2, 5–8; Jn 4:5–42*
E *Ex 17:1–7; Rom 5:1–11; Jn 4:5–26,39–42*
L *Gen 12:1–8; Rom 4:1–5,13–17; Jn 4:5–26*

A painting in the Metropolitan Museum of Art has captured me,
snared me, pulled me into its frame and searched me. It is a
landscape, a boundless autumn wilderness panorama with a distant shimmering ribbon of falls. Painted by Sanford Gifford, it
was titled "Kaaterskill Falls." Every visit to the museum includes
a vigil before this icon, which has a mysterious power over me.

I was startled to read that there is a Kaaterskill Falls, the highest
waterfall in New York, which has powerfully affected a whole
generation of Hudson School painters. The author of the article,
who lived for several summers less than three miles from the
cataract, never managed to locate it. Moreover, she couldn't find
anybody who could tell her where the water was.

The gospel this morning is like that painting. It points to the
central role water plays in our longing for life's fullness. It draws
us as do icons of the saints into the Christian life. In the lessons,
we easily identify with the Lenten struggle and longing for rebirth, for a future.

Jesus encounters a woman at the well. Now as this woman we
do not make a social event out of going to the well in the morning to get water when the rest of the village is there, exchanging
stories and gossip. No doubt, we are more than likely to be the
object of the gossip, living an unorthodox, many-spoused life,

and now living with someone but not legally married. So, we are startled when Jesus, thirsty from his journey, breaks the silence there by the well-wall, since it was most rare for a Jew like Jesus to give even the time of day to a Samaritan. Undaunted, Jesus gently but firmly brings us to a deeper perception of life through a conversation about water.

He asks us to give him a drink, but only as a lead-in to the central difficulty confronting us, which is for us to come to perceive Jesus as the Messiah, from whom we could drink living water. First we concern ourselves with ordinary water, observing that Jesus has no bucket. Jesus parries us with a test: he talks about our marital status, and touches the heart of our sorrow. We respond, going deeper into our wilderness. We ask about the crux of the antagonism between our people and his, which is the nature of worshipping God.

Jesus' direct response indicates that we are finally on the right track, as he tells us that true worship is not tied to nationality or place, but to spirit and truth. Here we have come to the rock. We suddenly perceive our deep and overpowering thirst. We reveal to Jesus our deep longing for the salvation a messiah would bring. And Jesus finally can give to us the water of rebirth he has come to bring as he reveals that he is the one our hearts have been longing for.

As Christian people we are called to be people of water, people of tears, people longing for justice to flow down, people called through the water to a new life of reliance on the God who saves. From very early the people who follow Christ have set aside the season of Lent as a journey toward authenticity. We live close to redemption in our daily lives, but fail to be washed fully in it. Can we experience the grace of water shimmering in the distance along our journey, rushing down, splashing, beading on our bodies? Can we take the frame off the painting of baptism and plunge deeply into the experience of it?

The treasure of the real Kaaterskill Falls was indeed a hidden one. Possessed during the height of the autumn colors to find this cataract, I drove to the Catskills to look for water gushing from the rock. A lower cascade, visible from the road, could not have been the nineteenth-century wonder. Trail markers led up beside the stream, but without any indication of a destination. A half-hour's hike brought me to the sound of immense crashing water, but the trail veered away, straight up. Another hour's bush-whacking revealed the source.

Without any doubt, this giddy torrent of water leaping from the dark rock into empty space, to be swallowed in a fathomless pool, was the Kaaterskill Falls of the pioneer painters. Thirst assuaged, I sat for many hours on a rock splashed by the spray.

Baptism is the cascade we live, not several miles from, but beside and within. It is water from the rock of Christ, which is ours not because we knew where to find it, not because we knew how to ask for it, but because God is God. It is the water which cleansed all the saints, gave them hope and a future. Knowing now its many joys, as well as its source, we should paint ourselves a world in which no one is thirsty.

Jeffrey A. Merkel

R E FOURTH SUNDAY IN LENT
L THIRD SUNDAY IN LENT

R   *1 Sam 16:1b,6–7,10–13a; Eph 5:8–14; Jn 9:1–41*
E   *1 Sam 16:1–13; Eph 5:8–14; Jn 9:1–13,28–38*
L   *Is 42:14–21; Eph 5:8–14; Jn 9:1–41*

The healing of blindness has been preached in Lent for almost as long as the church has lived. As the days are Lenten ones, that is, as they lengthen towards more and more sunlight in our days, so we are urged to let more and more light into our lives. The Easter baptisms were once called *photismos*—enlightenment, letting in the light. We keep this symbol before us still—the blessing of new fire, the paschal candle, the candles handed to the newly baptized and to all the faithful at the Easter Vigil. In the light of Jesus Christ we have a new and different look at things.

We begin to look not at mere images and outward appearances, but at realities, at the heart of things. This radically different vision is the one the Lord urged upon Samuel the day he went to Bethlehem to offer sacrifice and find a new leader for the nation. Never mind about appearances, never mind about the cleverly designed public relations image. God does not see in this human way; it is human to look at appearances, but God looks at the heart.

Even the disciples don't see things right at first: "Rabbi, who sinned," they ask, "this man, or his parents, that he was born blind?" Blindness was as much associated with sinfulness then as AIDS is by some people nowadays. Jesus asks us not to look at blame, but at opportunity, at occasions for epiphanies of light and vision, at human beings needing the pool of Siloam, the bath of forgiveness and healing and acceptance that is "sent" from the ocean of God's love. Neither inherited blame or individual blame is the issue, but that the work of God might be seen in new vision, new life.

Jesus moistens clay with his own saliva—an old-fashioned remedy—applies it to the eyes of the man born blind and sends him off to a sacred pool to wash. He comes back, seeing. Somewhat. It's not complete. For although he knows he's able to see, he doesn't know where to look, or where Jesus is in all this.

"Where is he?" the neighbors ask him. "I don't know," he answers. The act of baptism doesn't complete our own illumination, either. Nor does confirmation, nor indeed does ordination! The Pauline writer reminds us that children of light must walk in the light, for the fruit of light is in the walking. It's not enough to blink at the brightness. We are to walk in what is good and right and true, and to continue to learn. A personal commitment needs to be made; the gifts need to be appropriated and tested. The testing is all around us, as it was all around the man who came back seeing.

For neighbors have a vision problem, too. "Isn't this the guy who used to beg?" they ask. "Yes, he appears to be!" "No," said others, "but he looks like him!" Once we begin to look at things in a different way, once our consciousness is raised to see the world the way it is, to see its contradictions, to be led into the light, then some of our own friends and neighbors who have been comfortable with our beggary and our blindness may find that they have difficulty recognizing us! Those whose lives have been profoundly changed are often seen as strangers by those who shared the former narrow viewpoints, the limited vision, the common blindness.

Even his parents distance themselves. "We know our son, and we know he was born blind." The old son they are familiar with, comfortable with. But they can't deal with his new vision, nor with who gave it to him. It is risky for them to be involved with this radical change in him. They feared the punishment of authorities who threaten excommunication to anyone with a new vision of society. "Go talk to him about it!"

The Pharisees are short-sighted. They can't see the value of a ministry of healing performed in violation of perfectly honorable and traditional ways. Their view—a dominant, establishment view—was that anyone who would violate Sabbath rules could hardly be a prophet, no matter how much good came from his work. And they could not learn from someone "born in sin." Congenital blindness was evidence of an outcast, disgraceful status. For such, they have nothing to offer but anathemas.

The forms of blindness diagnosed in the gospel are varied: the blindness of faithful disciples, who speak in trite religious slogans, and phrase their theology of illness in terms of blame and shame; the blindness of neighbors, and of family, who will not be involved in the new vision, out of discomfort or out of fear; the blindness of a religious establishment, which could not see that anything good might happen outside its own system.

It is in the midst of this night time of blindness that the man born blind—he is all of us—has his healing made complete. Though he did not know where Jesus was, and in their blindness, those around him cannot help, it is Jesus who finds him and confronts him with the need to make a personal commitment of faith in the one who gives him vision.

"Who is he, sir, that I may believe?" And Jesus says: "You have seen him: the one speaking to you is the one." The gift of enlightenment, the baptismal light, comes to us from the word, who calls us to faith, for faith comes by hearing, a way of seeing, and hearing by the Word of God.

Grant M. Gallup

L FOURTH SUNDAY IN LENT

L *Hos 5:15–6:2; Rom 8:1–10; Mt 20:17–28*

We live in a time of excellence. The word is indispensable to what we believe to be the forward march of humanity. That is not to say that the present age is characterized by ever higher levels of achievement among people, ideas and things. It's just that excellence appears more sought after than ever before, and peppers so much of our communication.

It should be a good thing, that more and more, all of us are consciously set upon reaching higher and nobler expressions of endeavor, honing and refining skills, talent, intellect and will, coming closer to the top. Excellence becomes the way one finally arrives.

But is it all that simple, all that right and proper?

How much of the intense flaunting of "excellence" is just so much rhetoric, a flag waving to capture some unannounced battle? Does a college president incessantly thundering "excellence" have an eye in and for the students, or on the checkbooks of would-be donors? Is there necessarily any correlation between the two?

What do we mean by excellence? How does one achieve or accomplish it? Standing out above, excelling all others, has been done by many throughout history. Some heroes have reached the top by less than noble means. Hard work, determination, persistence may have marked the climb for some, but others have seized the short cuts, sneaked in the back doors opened for them. The cynic counters that it isn't what you know, but who you know.

That *yiddische mama* in today's gospel knew that. Somewhere in the words she kept hearing from and about this *rebbe*, was a promise, a reward. She may not have grasped the import of all he said, somber words about personal sufferings, a cup to drink, but one thing was certain: there would one day be a banquet, a kingdom, and she wanted her two boys in the front row, close to the host, influential enough to get her a seat too, small reward indeed for all she had suffered because of their prolonged absences following the *rebbe* from Nazareth. "Promise they'll sit on your right and on your left!" Most mothers will do almost anything to move their kids ahead.

That's not the way it works, she was told. Someone else is in charge of the seating arrangements; another passes on the list of promotions. It isn't that there are no places of preferment, no pinnacles of excellence in the coming dominion. There are. Not everyone is equal. Excellence still has a place in the family of the redeemed.

Had the voice stopped there, the rebuke would have been sufficient to deal with an overly ambitious mother and, perhaps, two eager sons. But others had heard the scolding, others were annoyed at the impertinence of some of their own company. The quest for excellence had infected them. Jealousy and anger sneaked in; so the voice had to continue.

There is nothing wrong with seeking out preferment. If you would be great, you must be the servant of the others. Your words and deeds must be caring, considerate, loving. So much must you live for others that the goal to reach the top is forgotten and dies. The life of such a one will be the greatest among you. Serving, slaving to do for your brothers and sisters, perhaps even dying for them: the Father sets priority on such a life.

The message is a hard one. Who measures excellence among the lowly of the world? Do we look for leadership within the company of those who have little? The voice pointed to the back rows, the lower stools. He didn't just talk about it, but walked himself this strange and unusual road to excellence. In that wondrous supper, bringing with its food and drink mixtures of ancient memories and new annoying signs of the future—soon and at the end—in that meal we have one more reminder.

The voice that talked about excellence and how it came from being a servant, a slave, gave life to those words, making them real, vivid, forceful. As host he was presiding, breaking the bread, blessing the cup and passing it round. Suddenly he is the servant, crawling around on hands and knees to wash the feet of those at the table. Dirty, stinking, sweaty feet. He takes each one and despite a protest bathes it and dries it with a towel.

What I have done, he says, you should do.

The supper goes on. It has never stopped; it never will.

Edgar S. Brown, Jr.

R E L   FIFTH SUNDAY IN LENT

R   *Ez 37:12–14; Rm 8:8–11; Jn 11:1–45*
E   *Ez 37:1–3,11–14; Rm 6:16–23; Jn 11:18–44*
L   *Ez 37:1–3,11–14; Rm 8:11–19; Jn 11:1–53*

Imagine yourself alone in Death Valley. It is summer. The sun keeps pressing its heat relentlessly through your skin to the muscles, organs, and bones of your body; and the dry winds keep taking your breath away. All about you, you notice bones, bones parched by the sun and wind, the bones of those who have succumbed to the dryness and death of the desert. You are bewildered, almost delirious, as you grow faint. You are alone, weary and hot, hungry and thirsty. Finally, exhausted, you begin to dream of restful shade and cool breezes across your hot forehead. And you know, know surely, that your very life depends upon the soft winds of companionship and the cool refreshment of food and drink. You know that you need help.

Moses knew it. When the people of Israel were captives in Egypt, Moses went to Pharaoh. His message was simple: "Let my people go," And the story goes on to tell of the wonderful help of God as the people leave Egypt and enter the promised land.

The prophet Ezekiel knew it, knew it long before the coming of Jesus. After the destruction of Jerusalem in 587 B.C.E., he imagined Israel in its captivity and exile as dry bones strewn in a desert. And he dreamt of a time when a cool breeze, the refreshing breath of God, the Spirit of God, would breathe life into the bones. Even graves would be opened; and the people would be restored. Israel would live again, at peace, in their own land. After all, God had promised help, and God's promises are sure.

The apostle Paul knew that we need help. He knew it because of Israel. And he knew it because of Jesus. For Paul, the choice is between the dry desert of the flesh and the refreshing oasis of the Spirit. Life in the Spirit is life with others, life where we are helped, life where we gladly share food and drink. The ultimate choice, the choice between life and death, is the choice between the death of apartness and the life of fellowship.

And Lazarus knew it. His name Lazarus, from the Hebrew Eleazar, speaks its reality. Lazarus means "God helps," or "God has helped," or "one whom God helps." The story of Lazarus, as the gospel of John tells it, is detailed and vivid. It is a story of illness and death, of burial and resurrection. Told as a sign of Jesus' power, it includes the shortest verse in the Bible, "Jesus wept." And in it we know the compassion of Jesus. Yet at its heart is the message that Jesus, like Moses, is engaged in God's work of helping. And the goal, if you move on to the rest of the story, is the meal which Jesus shares with Mary and Martha and Lazarus. For Jesus, as for Moses, life finds its possibility and its meaning in a feast. We are helped by, and towards, a table.

But as you heard the story, did you notice something else? Lazarus responds to Jesus' words, "Lazarus, come out." And Lazarus hops (or hobbles) out of the tomb. His hands and feet are "bound with bandages, and his face wrapped with a cloth." Like the slaves under Pharaoh, he is still a captive. He is all tied up. And his eyes are covered. He can scarcely move. He cannot even see where he is going. Clearly, he is not yet ready for the feast. He cannot even see the table. He still needs help.

So, Jesus turns to his followers. They too are a part of the story. And Jesus' words ring out, "Unbind him, and let him go." And in that moment, the name Lazarus, "God helps," has a new meaning. God helps, yes. And we help too! Our efforts are a part of God's plan. They always are. Mercifully, history is filled with the stories of those whose efforts have helped. Moses, Ezekiel, Jesus, Mary and Martha, and countless generations of the faithful, both men and women. And, now, God wants our help.

Now, especially, just now, during this season of Lent, when many, old and young, are coming from death of the desert to the new life in Christ, God welcomes our help. Those among us who are soon to be baptized need our help. And for many, whose lives we may touch, what we do may be a matter of life and death, death and life. Life together in Christ.

John E. Burkhart

R L SUNDAY OF THE PASSION
E PALM SUNDAY

R *Is 50:4–7; Phil 2:6–11; Mt 26:14–27:66*
E *Is 45:21–25; Phil 2:5–11; Mt 27:1–54*
L *Is 50:4–9a; Phil 2:5–11; Mt 26:1–27:66*

On this Sunday of the Passion a common thread that runs through the readings is the dual theme of servanthood and glory. One might wonder what the one has to do with the other!

Yet if the dual themes of glory and servanthood are separated or pitted against one another, the entire mystery of the Passion, and in turn the mystery of our life in Christ, will be thrown hopelessly off kilter.

The passion of Jesus carries within it this dual reality, which is often split apart by various segments of the church. We hear ourselves speak of a theology of the cross versus a theology of glory, as if one is forced to proclaim either Christ's cross or God's glory. Either side of the mystery of Christ's passion, if separated from the other, will result in misinterpretation or abuse.

One side proclaims that Christ's passion, and therefore life in Christ, is about humble servanthood. The cross of Christ is a servant's burden. We are Christ's servants as Christ is the servant of God. All this is true; however, our servanthood needs to be balanced by a healthy dose of glory, a joyous realization that Christ has won the ultimate victory over sin, death and the devil, thus freeing us for service in his name. Without this, servanthood can degenerate into self-flagellation and false modesty. A skewed notion of servanthood will lead us to believe that God loves us because we suffer or grovel.

The other side of passion is that of glory. The cross of Christ is the throne of victory; therefore, life in Christ is to know that we are the heirs of salvation and heralds of that salvation to the world. All this is true; however, when we focus solely on the the glory of Christ's passion and the victory of the cross without a healthy dose of servanthood, we will degenerate into self-congratulation and false pride.

The two sides of the passion, and therefore the two sides of life in Christ, are to be held in balance. When we have a balanced understanding of the meaning of the passion, there will be no need to choose between servanthood and glory, between social ministry and evangelism, between action and adoration. Holding to the dual mystery of the passion is our key to maintaining a balanced and faithful life in Christ.

The dual mystery of the passion is proclaimed boldly in the second reading. In this text Jesus, being in the form of God, took on the form of a servant. Let us view this hymn not only as a description of the dual reality of Christ's passion, but as a description of the dual reality of our calling as Christians and the mystery of our faith. This dual reality is one of humanity and yet divinity, it is of servanthood and yet glory, it is of a loaf which is body broken and yet is the bread of heaven, it is of blood that is spilled that is yet the cup of salvation.

On this Passion Sunday, let us have this mind among ourselves, that though we are in the image of God, we will not count equality with God a thing that we should grasp. Instead let us empty ourselves and take the form of Christ's servants. Let us humble ourselves and be obedient bearers of the cross. We can do these things, because God has highly exalted us in our baptism and has bestowed upon each of us the name which is above all names, the name of Christ, that calls all our knees to bow, and all our tongues to confess always and forever that Jesus is Lord, to the glory of God our Father.

Karen M. Ward

R HOLY THURSDAY
E L MAUNDY THURSDAY

R *Ex 12:1–8,11–14; 1 Cor 11:23–26; Jn 13:1–15*
E *Ex 12:1–14a; 1 Cor 11:23–26; Jn 13:1–15*
L *Ex 12:1–14; 1 Cor 11:17–32; Jn 13:1–17,34*

It must have been a night somewhat like tonight. Friends of Jesus gathered with him around a table. A sense of stillness, of expectancy, maybe of sadness, certainly a sense of the sacred hung in the air. The twelve didn't realize (except perhaps Judas), but Jesus knew: His hour had come! You and I know: and so the impact of what was said and what was done takes on all the more significance, for one treasures every word and every gesture of the last hours of a loved one's presence.

Come, sit at the table; truly you were present to Jesus that night. As his loving glance passes over each face, let his eyes meet your own. What must have been his thoughts? "Is there anything I've left unsaid for you? What word can I yet speak that you will always remember? A word that would call to mind all that I've said, all that I've done, a word that will help you grasp the meaning of my life. Even more so, a word that will strengthen you and help you grasp what I perceive as the meaning of my death. I have said it in so many words, in so many stories and parables. Tonight, perhaps, a parable in action you will always remember."

"He began to wash the disciples' feet, and to wipe them with the towel with which he was girded . . . I have given you an example, that you should do as I have done to you." The Master at your feet, serving! Like Peter, are you uneasy? All that society tells us of what a Master should be and should do are violated. Yet Jesus held his own: he would be Lord and Master who serves.

There is no question about it: Jesus was clear about his identity. "You call me Teacher and Lord, and you are right, for so I am." Jesus knew, through prayer, through reflection on the Hebrew Scripture, and through his own experience of life and of God, that he had come from God, the source of all love; that he was going to God, the fullness of all love; and that his mission here was to mediate that God of love and compassion both in his words and in his deeds. Nothing, and no one, not even Peter, could sway him from that.

Jesus knew the compassionate, liberating God of the Exodus who had seen the miserable state of the people and heard their cries to be free, a God who knew their sufferings and lured the servant Moses to lead the people out of bondage and oppression. Jesus knew that God was faithful to the promise to be with the prophets and leaders: "Say this to the people of Israel: 'I AM has sent me to you.' " Jesus knew that I AM had sent him, the new Moses, to lead God's people, to lead you and me, out of the bondage of sin, of suffering, and of all that impedes full life. Jesus claimed his identity as Lord and Master, but not as the world has known lords and masters, not as those around him would have him Lord and Master, but as Abba would have him Lord and Master, that is, as servant, full of compassion, mercy, and love.

One of the twelve could not live with his Master as Servant, could not believe in such gratuitous love and mercy. He went out into the night. Others, washed and fed, and moved by such powerful memories of love, went through the night of Friday to the light of Sunday.

And now, at the table, Jesus turns to you anew and says: "This is my body which is for you. Do this in remembrance of me. This cup is the new convenant in my blood. Do this, as often as you drink it, in remembrance of me." We are washed by him, served by him, now fed by him. His is a love that so longs for union, a love that longs to be forever!

We know that we, too, have come from God, the source of all love. Because of this Jesus, we, too, are going to God, the fullness of all love. We have been washed, baptized into his mission to mediate in this little part of God's world, in this week, with these people, the God of love and compassion in our words and our deeds.

Our competitive, ladder-climbing, be-No.1 society does not highly prize the servant role: our God does. We are fed and strengthened at this table to go through the darkness, anticipating the dawn. Our lives of love and service will evidence our deep memory: "I have given you an example, that you should do as I have done to you." Remember, and do this!

Joan Delaplane, O.P.

R *Is 52:13–53:12; Heb 4:14–16,5:7–9; Jn 18:1–19:42*
E *Is 52:13–53:12; Heb 10:1–25; Jn 19:1–37*
L *Is 52:13–53:12; Heb 4:14–16,5:7–9; Jn 18:1–19:42*

If only the powerful people of this world could stay tight-lipped before Christ, behold and say nothing, they might see what they had never been told; they might learn something they have never heard of before. It is the simple invitation of the liturgy of Good Friday to all of us to be silent before him. There is much to be known, on the condition of our silence.

If Jesus was a king, then Pilate had reason to worry. Pilate had to know where all the other kings were so that he could be on the lookout. Like Herod the Great, who some years before had heard that people from the Orient were in search of an infant whose new life was revealed in the heavens, Pilate now had to keep track of other important stars in his own constellation. He could not turn his back on any promising, exciting person who would necessarily threaten his own position. Pilate had to keep his diplomacy and his troops, and his wits, at the ready. It is the business of all powerful and important people to be nervously alert in a volatile world. The Praetorium is an anxious place, and the one who is reputedly in command must shuttle back and forth, between the accusers who have taken their stand outside, and the accused man who now, in the space of a few hours, stands in his fourth place of judgment, exhausting and frustrating his fourth panel of inquisitors.

If Jesus was a crank, just some pitiful fellow suffering from delusions of power, then Pilate could freely toss him back to the crowd. Jesus could be handed over to the Jewish authorities to keep them busy and out of any real mischief, at least through this keyed-up time of holy days. Let this Nazarene absorb the attention and anger of these nagging, irritating people. It could be done without jeopardizing the major power points.

But what if Jesus had a real following, if significant numbers of serious people took him seriously, if he *could* sway the gathering crowd? What if he did have armed followers mingling in that crowd, or waiting in the groves of Olivet, or over the hill in Bethany and in the caves of Jericho? Then Pilate had reason to be nervous. Perhaps this man's substantial power is in hiding. Bound and guarded as he is, maybe he holds some advantage or threat. People with power can sometimes size up a mystery in no time; sometimes the situation may call for time and a measure of caution. Pilate must think out the possibilities and contingencies. He doesn't have the freedom just now to speculate about loftier truths.

So I think Pilate was sincerely puzzled when he said, "What is truth?" But when the evangelist put the question in Pilate's mouth, the evangelist was certainly being sarcastic. He obviously had no sympathy for Pilate's predicament. Religious people think that truth is everything, and they have no appreciation for the dangers of being caught in a powerful position. They have a naive trust in mysteries that pragmatic rulers and dealers cannot afford to indulge.

Jesus replied to Pilate's question: "You say that I am a king." You are the one who's worried about the state of the Empire, where the lines are holding, where chaos might break out. But "for this I was born, for this I have come into the world, to bear witness to the truth."

Jesus witnessed to the truth in private and public places, before many gatherings and in the face of variously persuaded factions of the people: as when he washed the feet of his disciples, and identified himself with the bread and the cup they shared at the Passover meal; and when he called Lazarus back from the tomb, and restored the sight of the man born blind; and when he fed the multitude of people with the few loaves and fish they had at hand in that remote gathering of anxious, questing folk; and when he paid attention to the woman at Jacob's well, drew out of her the pathos of her life and the abuse she had suffered, and then enlisted her help in stirring up the interest and attention of her townspeople; even when he upset the temple commerce and insulted the pride of the tradition by calling for worship in spirit and "in truth." And he had witnessed to the truth when he worked his first sign, among his own kinsfolk and neighbors, when he kept the party going at Cana in Galilee.

There was a sort of power in such showings of truth, a power to set some people free. But what effect did these revelations have on the nervousness of Pilate and the rantings of the priests? What impact did his "truth" have in the face of an excited, rabid crowd? Did his witness to a mysterious truth stir any memories or strengthen any of the bonds of discipleship in those he had just called friends?

Truth seems so vulnerable, so forgettable and dispensable, in the turbulence of power. Like freedom it must struggle to survive the anxiety of powerful people. Or it may be free enough to let them play out their own anxious struggles.

John Gerlach, O.P.

R   E   L   EASTER VIGIL

R   *Rom 6:3–11; Mt 28:1–10*
E   *Rom 6:3–11; Mt 28:1–10*
L   *Col 3:1–4; Mt 28:1–10*

One foot after another.

"Now after the sabbath, toward the dawn of the first day of the week, Mary Magdalene and the other Mary went to see the sepulcher." There was doubtless no hurry. The Marys were on their way to meet an exceedingly sorrowful obligation. The Marys proceeded slowly to see what they dreaded seeing, "Jesus who was crucified." One foot after another.

What was waiting for them was hardly expected. An angel of the Lord, dressed in raiment white as snow, had rolled back the stone and was sitting on it! There, before their very eyes, a messenger of the Lord, lounging on the tomb's stone, feet dangling, just waiting for the first witnesses of the resurrection.

It was a sight to be sure, a sight to behold. The Marys edging forward in wonder and fear, carefully stepping over the bodies of the soldiers, who by the angel's appearance had been knocked off their feet. "Come, see the place where he lay." The dazed and amazed women, on tiptoe, peering around the corner, hoping now not to see what they had come to see, yet hardly believing it possible.

The testimony of the angel, "He has risen!", is followed by angelic instruction, "Go quickly." And the Marys are off. Feet flying! For fear. For great joy. Running for their Life.

"And behold, Jesus met them." "And they came up and took hold of his feet and worshiped him." They took hold of his scarred, calloused, spikenard-anointed, crucified, having-trampled-death-beneath-them-sure-as-he's-standing-there, risen-from-the-dead feet, and worshiped him!

And this is the picture we have walked rather a long, circuitous, homiletical way to see: Jesus Christ. Risen from the dead. Standing on his own two feet. And the faithful, hanging on for dear life.

This is what we have been waiting for this whole Lent long. It is for this that we have rehearsed his passion and his dying. It is this for which we were baptized. "For if we have been united with him in a death like his, we shall certainly be united with him in a resurrection like his."

This holy eucharist provides us another occasion to hold the Risen One. This is another resurrection reunion with the First-born from the Dead. We gather at the foot of the cross, at the feet of the victorious Christ, to worship him. Here we celebrate his life after his death and ours. Here we find the strength to hang on.

"Then Jesus said to them, 'Do not be afraid.' " Bending at the waist, offering to each Mary a hand, in the midst of the tears and the laughter and the relief one can almost hear him say, "On your feet, my friends." "Go and tell . . . ."

"We were buried therefore with him by baptism into death, so that as Christ was raised from the dead by the glory of the Father, we too might walk in newness of life." The Risen One not only gets us back on our feet again but does so with purpose: that we might walk in newness of life.

As the Day of Resurrection dawns let us be on our way, one foot confidently in front of another. We have seen what we have longed to see. We have held him whom we longed to hold. And he has redirected our steps. We have died to sin. The new life we have in him we live to God.

The Lord is risen!

He is risen indeed!

Alleluia!

Christopher Hoyer

R E EASTER DAY
L THE RESURRECTION OF OUR LORD

R   *Acts 10:34a,37–43; Col 3:1–4; Jn 20:1–9*
E   *Acts 10:34–43; Col 3:1–4; Jn 20:1–10*
L   *Acts 10:34–43; Col 3:1–4; Jn 20:1–9*

"They have taken the Lord out of the tomb, and we do not know where they have laid him." Thus Peter and the other disciples were greeted on the first Easter Day. Mary Magdalene's announcement opens the question to you and me as well. Do I know where they have laid Jesus? How do I find him on this Easter Day?

Peter and John ran to the tomb, but all they found was an empty space and empty wrappings. Later that evening they were to find where he was: not laid in another tomb, but alive in their midst. Moments after they left the tomb, Mary found where Jesus was; he was alive, and she fell at his feet in worship. That afternoon two disciples on their way to the village of Emmaus found where he was: not dead, but walking along the road, explaining the Scriptures to them, and present to them in the breaking of the bread. A week later Thomas finds him again in the midst of the disciples, alive and still bearing the scars of his passionate love for the human race.

But can you and I tell today where he is to be found?

A preacher I heard a few years ago noted that in the encounter Mary Magdalene had with Jesus, she did not recognize him. The disciples on the road to Emmaus did not recognize him, and other resurrection accounts indicate a similar problem. This preacher suggested that this was necessary because Jesus' friends had to become detached from his flesh in order that they might become attached to his body. If they were to carry on in relationship to Jesus, they must learn to look for him in forms other than the human flesh in which they had known him.

It is that process of discovering Jesus in their midst in new ways which occupied the disciples for the remainder of their lives. Their discoveries are the substance of the New Testament writings. Jesus did not depart but remained present. The body of Christ was found in new and different forms.

Today's reading from the Acts of the Apostles is a case in point, in fact one of the most important of those discoveries. It takes place a few years after the resurrection. The church, once a group composed of Jewish believers, has grown, has been persecuted, and has spread to areas beyond Jerusalem. It has found that the bread and wine of its common meal provide a place of encounter with the risen Christ. It has discovered that its gathering as a community is a manifestation of Jesus' presence. But something new happens to Peter.

He was asked to visit a Gentile named Cornelius. Peter, a devout Jew, was resistant to this request, still assuming that Jesus was to be found in Israel alone. In a dream God revealed to Peter that all people are acceptable to God. Now Peter discovers, in his own words, "that God shows no partiality, but in every nation any one who is God-fearing and does what is right is acceptable to God." The body of Christ is to be found in all of humanity, not merely some part of the human family.

Often Christians have seemed to proclaim a Christ who has vanished and left no traces behind. We appear to be proclaiming nothing more than a historical event which happened once upon a time. If we communicate a faith about something that happened long ago, a man who lived in times past, such a faith is no more than belief in a historical record.

The original Christians experienced Jesus in their midst. As Peter told Cornelius, Jesus appeared to them, who ate and drank with him after he rose from the dead. But you and I are often left with the impression that for us today there is not a direct encounter with the risen Lord. We sing "Jesus Christ is risen today," but mean "Jesus Christ was risen once upon a time." We call upon people to place their faith in Jesus, by which we mean that the Bible's story is true. Where has Jesus gone? How can you and I have our own meeting with Jesus and come to know him directly?

You may be saying to yourself, "But we do meet Jesus in the breaking of the bread, in his body and blood in the eucharist." "We do meet Jesus in his word as we read and share the holy Scriptures." Perhaps you are even saying, "We do meet Jesus in his body the church."

Last night in the Easter Vigil we saw brothers and sisters plunged beneath the waters of the font and raised into new life. We saw the resurrection with our own eyes. Those new members of the body greeted us with the very words Jesus used to greet his friends on Easter, "Peace be with you." What happened to them and to us in baptism reveals the mystery of where Jesus is to be found.

Yes, they have taken the Lord's body from the tomb. Where have they laid it? They have laid it in the midst of the world, in the midst of this city, in the midst of this gathering. We sing that Jesus Christ is risen today because we see the risen Christ all around us, in the eyes and faces of those sitting beside us, in the newly baptized, in the bread and wine of the altar, and in the people we encounter in each moment of our lives.

Christ is risen indeed. His body walks the earth today, healing, teaching, feeding, suffering, dying, and rising. You and I and all the human race are the living answer to the question Mary Magdalene posed that first Easter. The Lord is taken from his tomb and placed in the center of his world. He is risen indeed! Alleluia!

Michael W. Merriman

R E L SECOND SUNDAY OF EASTER

R   *Acts 2:42–47; 1 Pet 1:3–9; Jn 20:19–31*
E   *Acts 2:14a,22–32; 1 Pet 1:3–9; Jn 20:19–31*
L   *Acts 2:14a,22–32; 1 Pet 1:3–9; Jn 20:19–31*

Although it may not, in fact, be one of our cultural charisms, I think we Americans at least imagine ourselves to be a bold, self-possessed people. We condition our children to have a "winning attitude," promote the power of positive thinking, and proclaim as part of our national heritage the conviction that any position can be attained and any goal achieved as long as we possess in sufficient quantities that indispensable American virtue, confidence. For those afflicted by self-doubt or even quiet caution, we readily prescribe counseling or assertiveness training, and hope that after these experiences such individuals can attain at least those minimum levels of tenacity and self-assurance which our society demands.

Given this cultural context, it is possible that the gospel just proclaimed could be construed as subversive and quite un-American: for it unabashedly features a doubter at center stage, surrounds him with a timorous group of disciples (who hide behind locked doors even after they have experienced the risen Christ), and presents a Jesus unphazed by the skepticism and anxiety which run rampant among his followers. Such a gospel certainly does not serve to strengthen the national will or motivate the faint-hearted, and instead appears to be an unsettling proof text for fear and doubt. Quite frankly one wonders how such a skittish band of disciples ever gave birth to that idyllic, faith-filled community which we heard about in today's first reading.

What this gospel offers us in Thomas, however, is probably not an apostolic coward or even a first-rate skeptic, but rather a flesh-and-blood representative of the fledgling church in its pre-Easter faith. Stunned by the arrest of Jesus, and scattered by his trial and death, the early disciples were unquestionably a bewildered, floundering group following that Friday we have come to know as "Good." It is clear, however, that at least initially this eventful day was not good for them, and it appeared to be the definite end to an impressive, but short-lived, success story named Jesus.

Yet it was from the ashes of this apostolic doubt that faith arose. Moreover, the early community's experience of disbelief was probably an important preparatory step for its future life in faith: for doubting, like believing, presumed abandoning human surety in the search for other truths. Consequently, the first disciples needed to surrender much of what they believed about the earthly Jesus so that, like Jesus himself, these first truths could be transformed through resurrection. It is exactly such a transformation which is symbolized in today's gospel story, where brash skepticism yields to unrestrained belief. Ironically, it is Thomas dubbed "the doubter" who eventually makes the most explicit profession of faith recorded in the gospels.

This reading of the gospel story, however, could precipitate an unanticipated dilemma for those of us who imagine ourselves to be members of such a "transformed" community. Because we live after the resurrection, it is easy for us to presume that we should therefore possess a post-Easter faith as well. This presumption may be especially acute in these days after the great Vigil, when fresh images of fire and water dramatize anew the conversion which baptism says is ours.

Yet today's gospel reminds us that, like Christians of every age, we need to make the pilgrimage from Friday to Sunday, from a pre-Easter to a post-Easter faith. This is precisely what the author of I Peter proposes in that great baptismal hymn which formed our second reading: celebrating the passage from distress to new birth, and from trial to rejoicing in Jesus Christ.

Happily this is not a journey we need or even can make alone. Just as Jesus and the early community are remembered as having invited Thomas to publicly probe his doubts, so are we invited to face our own faith struggles within the community. Those fresh from the font are contemporary reminders that faith is not an isolated process, but is adequately explored and confirmed only in the context of a community.

Today's word does not, therefore, offer us a biblical precedent for fear and doubt, but a foundational story of journey in the midst of community to a post-Easter faith. May this day's celebration be for us a significant moment in that journey, so that we too may learn to be faithful to the apostolic instruction and the communal life, to the prayers and the breaking of the bread.

Edward Foley, Capuchin

R E L THIRD SUNDAY OF EASTER

R   *Acts 2:14a,22–33; 1 Pet 1:17–21; Lk 24:13–35*
E   *Acts 2:14a,36–47; 1 Pet 1:17–23; Lk 24:13–35*
L   *Acts 2:14a,36–47; 1 Pet 1:17–21; Lk 24:13–35*

Friends often invite one another for a walk. Especially in time of trouble, one might receive such an invitation. Perhaps along a wooded path, two friends discuss the hurts and the disappointments found in family or at work. Unfortunately, there is the chance that the two friends might address one another in such a way that the conversation never really plunges into the depths of the difficulty. The two may mirror one another's pain, rage and hurt. All told, the end of their walk finds them arriving only at more bitterness than they had at the beginning of their trek. However, there is the possibility that they will truly listen to one another. The end of their journey might find them not at the point of resolution, but at an understanding of the significance of life's hurts within the larger picture of life. This latter conversation only happens when the two friends are open to the presence of a third partner in the conversation: reflectiveness.

We hear today of Cleopas and his companion, early disciples, on the familiar road to Emmaus. They have witnessed the death of Jesus. This Jesus was the hope of all Israel. This Jesus had seemed to be the one that would lead the people to freedom and peace. And yet he was executed as a political but innocent victim by the Roman authorities. Certainly the dreams of these two disciples had been dashed. The one in whom they had placed their trust was seemingly gone, and with him, the hope of liberty. But suddenly, someone was in their midst who enticed them to see beyond their limited memory. This sudden partner in their conversation broke open to them the meaning of that death and once again their dreams were kindled. But this stranger was completely unknown to them. This seen and invited guest was revealed to them in the intimacy of their evening meal. Broken Bread and Blessing. The one who was dead lives. "And did not our hearts burn."

If we take seriously this familiar story from Luke, we are given today a blueprint for celebrating the Christian life as an Easter people. Cleopas and his companion went for a walk. The journey they took was far more than the merely physical. They engaged in the journey of faith. And it began for them in the throes of hurt, disappointment and, perhaps, bitterness. Their conversation had no movement save for a circular bantering. It was not until the Risen One interpreted for them, in the larger picture, the meaning of death, that they could see the realities of human living within the context of saving faith. But though they came to understand with their minds, they still needed to see the author of their understanding. In the breaking of the bread, they came to faith in the crucified and risen Christ.

All Christians, like the two companions, must enter into the three rhythms of faith's story as we find it today in this narrative. First, the pilgrimage of the Christian life is not a guarantee that our daily existence will be exempt from the rocks and dust that are part and parcel of simply being human. We encounter the harsh realities of our personal and societal lives, and we know that there is no escape for believers from the problems of loneliness, despair, violence and poverty. It is imperative that we walk the road if the word is truly to set the world on fire.

Second, in walking the road, we must take the risk and allow the Lord to walk with us and help us to understand. As one of my colleagues is often heard to say, "Jesus was a walker." Jesus walks with us in our lack of understanding, our hurting, our bitterness. Christians will encounter the evils of life. But there is the invitation from God that we surrender our lack of understanding into the hands of Christ who is always there to console and heal.

Finally, we must remember who it is that walks with us in our daily labors. This Christ is no mere supplier of answers to human questions. This Christ embraced the very deepest questions of what it means to be human. Jesus embraced our fear of death, the abandonment of the cross, the frail wood of human nature. But where do we find the presence of the Risen One?

Like Cleopas and his companion, we gather for our meal and we remember. We remember that God and all women and men discover one another in bread and its shaping. There it is that we meet and discover life itself, a life that goes beyond death. We discover it again and again in the crumbs that fall upon our table of thanksgiving. We discover it in the crumbs that fall from the tables of our daily living. And when we, a pilgrim people, have taken our walk with a God who, in Christ, walks with us in this life, we then are sat down at table and there we break bread to satisfy our hungers. And when we do this, do not also our hearts burn?

Edward Francis Gabriele, O.Praem.

R   *Acts 2:14a,36–41; 1 Pet 2:20–25; Jn 10:1–10*
E   *Acts 6:1–9;7:2a,51–60; 1 Pet 2:19–25; Jn 10:1–10*
L   *Acts 6:1–9;7:2a,51–60; 1 Pet 2:19–25; Jn 10:1–10*

In our society of electric and automatic doors we do not think of doors as symbols of recognition. We seldom have a door slammed in our face, so we do not think of doors as thresholds of rejection. Rather we think about doors as territorial barriers against our fears of being robbed or otherwise violated.

But what are doors that our Lord should say,"I am the door"? Doors stand between life and death. Doors stand between public and private. Doors stand between mine and yours. Doors offer protection and privacy. Doors establish a boundary between the self and the other. Doors allow entry and offer escape. Doors signal hospitable greeting or blatant rejection.

Doors are the last barriers across which guards throw themselves, for the invading enemy will enter only through their death! The final value of a door lies in the flesh of those who defend its threshold. The final value of a door hinges on the will to defend and protect to the death the life within.

Imagine: You are a cosmonaut out in space, umbilically attached to the craft. Out before you, the earth spins in beauty. Your space mission is completed, and the air reserve for the "walk" is almost gone. You reach for the hatch lever. There is nothing there. The door you came out is gone. You scour and claw the bolted surfaces of the craft. The way in is gone and you are lost. Suddenly, from within, a new and unseen door is thrown open, and you are pulled through it to escape into life. The one who threw open the unseen entry becomes for you the gate of life.

You are a miner, a mile or so under the earth. The shaft collapses. The dust of the earth becomes poison inbreathed. Time passes, and there is no escape. Air diminishes, your flesh is parched. Far off a voice cries out your name saying, "A door will be carved out of the rock." Time passes and you cling to the echo of the voice. Suddenly making the night of your death as bright as day, there is a door. A way out splits open above you, hands are laid upon you, and you are carried home.

You are a full-term baby, trapped inside a mother whose labors are unable to birth you. What was your life water becomes slowly a flooding threat. Your heart beats harder under the stress, then weakly. Into your hiding place pierces a cutting blade. A blaze of light, and a leaping up out of the darkness, and you are lifted out of death through the door in the flesh. You gaze upon the company who delivered you.

You are a secretary descending in an elevator from the 106th floor, long after hours. The car jolts and jerks and bounces to a stop. The phone fails. There is a blackout. The guard does not know you are there. The building is deserted for a three-day weekend. Hours pass. Panic envelops you as the walls of the elevator seem to shrink. Your thirst and craving for light overtake you. Then unimaginably, the ceiling of the compartment is thrown back. Hands grasp you and deliver you from your prison. You are free and embraced in welcome.

You are a Jewish adolescent girl. With 700 others you have trudged from a cattle train into showers for what the soldiers have called disinfection. From the shower heads the sickly gas clouds the locked chamber. In trampling panic the naked hordes beat upon the barricaded doors. There is no way out. In the midst of this fear-filled company, despite the barred doors, there appears another Jew. This Holy One of the people of the promise shows you and your dying company the wound in his side. With pierced hands, the Jew points to the wound in his side and invites you all through it. You are shepherded through, a flock fleeing to life.

As our door into the dominion of God, Jesus is our shepherd. Through Christ we find our way home to God. By Christ we are gathered in despite our tendency to stray, despite our stupidities and despite false trapdoors. Christ died before the enemies of God to protect the dominion of God. The pattern of God's will in Christ is cruciform. On the axis of the cross the stranger is called sibling, the threat is overcome forever, and life spreads out before us abundantly. Christ is guardian of the threshold of God's mercy for us. Christ is the one who bore the burden of us across that gate, carrying us inside the borders of the Trinity.

Christ as our door is the wide-flung hospitality of God, calling us home to the feast. Stand in the threshold in this assembly. Pray, standing at the altar with open hands and look up to see the heavens opened. Gaze upon the baptismal waters to see the river that washes us through Christ and beaches us at the throne of God. Be mindful of God's approval and of the power God gives. These promises this day are for you, for your children and for all who are far off, for everyone whom Christ invites. So dear people, heed the voice and be shepherded through.

Jann Esther Boyd Fullenwieder

R   E   L   FIFTH SUNDAY OF EASTER

R   *Acts 6:1–7; 1 Pet 2:4–9; Jn 14:1–12*
E   *Acts 17:1–15; 1 Pet 2:1–10; Jn 14:1–14*
L   *Acts 17:1–15; 1 Pet 2:4–10; Jn 14:1–12*

Over half a century ago Romano Guardini wrote that the church was awakening in the hearts of humanity. Others have pointed out that the third section of the creed, belief in the one, holy, catholic and apostolic church, has become a subject of intense theological speculation only in this century. Reflecting this interest two major documents of Vatican II deal with the church, *Lumen Gentium*, the Dogmatic Constitution on the Church, and *Gaudium et Spes*, the Constitution on the Church in the Modern World.

Today's readings can shed light in the ongoing discussion about the church through the image of "paradoxical house." In Acts 6 we see church as household. We are presented with an everyday occurrence: disagreement, discord in the community. The Hellenists, those Christians who spoke Greek, are not receiving their share of the communal goods. A resolution is required. The text does not tell us what the solution is, but rather continues to speak of another problem: Some of the members are overworked in the service of the community. Their many duties lead them to neglect those they think are the most important. A solution is found. A new office is created, new people are selected to become leaders in the community. This all bespeaks flexibility and growth, optimism and imagination. In the remark "a great many of the priests were obedient to the faith" we sense the excitement in the community of new converts, the newness of the message, the pride in the community in the spread of the belief in the proclamation of Jesus as the one sent by the Spirit. Here we see the church as "organization," as institution with the need for means of settling disputes, for expanding governance, for allowing equal sharing for all, a household in which solutions are sought in an atmosphere of love, consideration and enthusiasm.

Acts 17 presents us with the picture of church as the house of Scripture. We see Paul following his usual custom in the synagogue, discussing Scripture with the people as a means of convincing them of his message. We also see the community using the written word as a standard for the accuracy of the message proclaimed, "examining the Scriptures daily to see if these things were so."

In 1 Peter the faithful are exhorted to become living stones in the structure which is the house of God. The metaphor draws on two qualities of stone as an image. Stone as material used for construction of a building is used in a positive sense. We are the building blocks through which the house of God comes into being. Stone as dead, as opposed to living matter, is used to emphasize the contrast between a physical house of stone and the house of God which is build of living units replete with life, not only physical, but spiritual. In a further step this reading speaks of the stones which church members are, as more than living, as precious, as jewels calling to mind the holy city of the Apocalypse gleaming with "radiance like a most rare jewel." As a continuation of the image of house, this reference ties the household of spiritual stone of the church today to its promised glorification in the heavenly city.

The gospel reading speaks of the inside of the house that is the church. Its setting is the most intimate form of community, the meal. In this context we hear Jesus speaking of the house of the Father, where he will prepare dwelling places for those who believe. In Jesus' farewell address, dwelling becomes the metaphor for living united with God. Jesus stresses that not only will he prepare a dwelling for the faithful with the Father, but that he *is* the dwelling place of the faithful with the Father. The Father also dwells in the Son. Just as faith is needed to grasp the value of the living stones which make up the community of the people of God in 1 Peter, so too in John 14, faith in Jesus is essential. Jesus is the way to the dwelling place with the Father.

Thus the readings for today present many levels of the life of the church: (1) the practical institutional "household," (2) the place in which the living dialectic between the written word and the interpreting community is conducted, (3) the structure composed of living inspired beings united in faith to form the body of Christ, and (4) the Father's house of many dwellings which Jesus has prepared for us.

Pamela Kirk

R L   SIXTH SUNDAY OF EASTER

R   *Acts 8:5–8,14–17; 1 Pet 3:15–18; Jn 14:15–21*
L   *Acts 17:22–31; 1 Pet 3:15–22; Jn 14:15–21*

Throughout the gospel of John there is a pattern in which a lengthy discussion unfolds the meaning of a sign which Jesus has performed. The loaves are multiplied to feed a multitude, and in the following verses Jesus speaks about the bread of life. The blind man is healed, and Jesus speaks of the light of the world.

At the end of the gospel there is also a sign and a discourse. Only now it is the greatest of the signs, the sign toward which all the other actions of Jesus have pointed. That sign is the death and resurrection of Christ. And it is the lengthiest discourse, the so-called Farewell Discourse, together with the High Priestly Prayer. Here, too, the words mean to gather us into the meaning of the sign.

We read from these words during the great fifty days of Easter. Do not be confused with the ostensible original setting of the words, which are delivered before the death of Jesus. These words are set in the gospel before the account of the passion and resurrection, but they are intended as discourse for that great sign, the death and resurrection of Christ. How can we possibly say what the resurrection means? Here are words for the fifty-day feast. Here are words intended to draw us into the great sign itself, to make the meaning of Easter entirely available to us.

Then we understand: Jesus' "going away" is his death. His not being seen is what happens in the world because of his bitter execution. His coming again to us is the resurrection. And this all is for us, that we may live in trust, that we may be in the risen Christ, that we may know ourselves in God. As the letter of Peter says, "Christ also died . . . that he might bring us to God."

But how is this so, in this fifty days or at any other time? It seems we are left desolate. It is a desolate time. What we see is indeed the death of Christ—at least in this sense: he is gone. And we keep seeing the little ones of the earth, the wretched ones, the hungry ones, die. We ourselves die. God is silent, un-seen, unknown.

Yes. But listen again! These words of Jesus are kept alive in this assembly. This assembly does not mean to hide itself from the desolate times in the world, nor from the silence of God in our own lives. On the contrary, in our prayers we beg God for all the hopeless needs we can remember. Indeed, remembering Jesus' death we remember one slain among the most wretched of the earth. And the meaning of Jesus' death, in the midst of the desolation, is borne to us now in these words. By this discourse Jesus' death is shown to be a great sign among our desolations.

If we have nothing else of God, we have these words. We keep these words, present in the Christian assembly, living them out in love turned toward the needs of the others around us. So we find ourselves in what Jesus calls the Spirit of truth. The words themselves come alive for us, giving us the meaning of Easter. So do the baptism and the cup we share, enacting the words as a sign. These words say: God is with the wretched. Jesus' death brings God to the most silent places, the places we think God cannot be, and so brings us to God.

Listen to the words. They are the meaning of the assembly, the Spirit of God alive in this assembly, coming to comfort humanity. By these words the risen one comes to you, promises you that God's intention is that you live. Listen: "God will give you another Counselor. I will come to you. You will see me. You will live also." And listen further in this assembly as these words are put next to the words and signs of the eucharist: "My body for you, my blood for you." By the Spirit in this meal he does come, we do see him as he promised.

It is as if with these words and this meal among us, the risen Christ, the living Spirit of Jesus, visits the prisoners of desolation again, and pulls us and all humanity up and out of hell, to be in God and to live in love. This fifty-day feast and this assembly, whenever it meets, mean joy for this human city, news from the unknown God, the proclamation that God has shared our desolation and pulled us up to joy.

My brothers and sisters: Christ calls us to see the wretchedness of the world more and more clearly. But do not give yourselves over to despair. Give yourselves to love for the wretched out of faith in these words. Live!

Gordon W. Lathrop

E SIXTH SUNDAY OF EASTER

E *Acts 17:22–31; 1 Pet 3:8–18; Jn 15:1–8*

The gospel offers us two images for reflection. The first is Christ as the vine and we as the branches. Christ's power flows through us like juicy sap through the vine into the farthest branch, like blood into the tiniest artery. The second image, suggested by the idea that we live "in Christ," is that we are afloat in Christ, like fish in the sea or cells in the bloodstream. That second picture reverberates with echoes of Paul's sermon in Athens, with its message that "in God we live and move and have our being." Both images suggest things about our relationship to God in Christ considerably more radical than we might be comfortable with.

Christ flows through us as life flows through the vine into the branches. The language is familiar: Christ is in us and acts through us; we are the body of Christ. Though the image is familiar, we rarely take it seriously. We would be much happier, under most circumstances, to have someone else be Christ's body—Terry Waite or Mother Teresa of Calcutta, for instance.

The early church had a richer understanding of this image. They believed that as the body of Christ God entered them; they were "divinized" at baptism. They became, quite literally, God— incompletely and in a sacramental way, to be sure, but the identity was established, to be completed in heaven. But this language was too much for later generations, who spoke of being made "like" God instead of being made God. Yet the stronger language remains in the Scriptures, still challenging us to move away from our fears, to think what it means to have God flow in us and our actions, to have God depend on us and our actions.

This is a vision of God that is not familiar to us or that we seem not to like very much. It makes God too close, too fallible, changeable and dependent. But this is part of the vision that formed the early church.

Another part of the vision is Paul's picture of all creation, especially all humanity, aswim in God. He borrowed the image from Stoic philosophers, but Christians were quick to make it their own. Paul used it to describe God's grace flowing over us, sweeping us up into Christ. Tertullian later adapted it to baptism, describing the water bath as the sea of God's love in which we swim. "We, little fishes," he said, "after the manner of our *ichthus* Jesus Christ, are born in water; nor have we safety in any other way than by permanently abiding in water."[8]

Christians have used this image to try to convince others of the truth of the faith. Down the years, from Paul at Athens to Karl Rahner's notion of "anonymous Christianity," Christians have been collaring non-Christians on streetcorners, in markets and even in slave ships, urging them that they really are Christians in their heart of hearts, and all they need to complete their identity is baptism and a quick study of the catechism. Not surprisingly, most people so confronted have resented such suggestions.

Rather than continuing to force this metaphor down unwilling throats, we might do better to let people be comfortable with their own self-definitions. What we might do, meanwhile, is try to live that image ourselves. If we believe that everyone lives and moves in God, why don't we treat them that way? Why don't we acknowledge the presence of God in them and around them? How would people react if we treated them as if we were saying to them, "You are the presence of God to me?"

We probably won't find out, because we have more problems with this image than we have with the first image of the vine. If we have trouble picturing ourselves as God's body, we have even more trouble imagining other people as God. Sneak a glance at the person next to you: does God really look like that? Christian faith says, yes, God does look just like that. In fact, if you really want to know what God looks like, picture the face of your worst enemy. In God, that person lives and moves and exists.

The God revealed in Jesus is that confident of us. God is in our hands and our hearts; God wears our face and the face of our enemy. In such weakness is God strong; in such immediacy is God's universality. With such a God, the only way to show faith in God is to show it in one another; the only way to love God is to love one another; the only way to touch the face of God is to kiss the face of our enemy.

Gordon E. Truitt

[8]Tertullian, "Treatise on Baptism," tr. S. Thelwall, in A. Hamman, *Baptism: Ancient Liturgies and Patristic Texts* (Staten Island, NY: Alba House, 1967), p. 30.

R E L   ASCENSION DAY

R   *Acts 1:1–11; Eph 1:17–23; Mt 28:16–20*
E   *Acts 1:1–11; Eph 1:15–23 Lk 24:49–53*
L   *Acts 1:1–11; Eph 1:16–23; Lk 24:44–53*

Nikita Khruschev once ridiculed Christianity by remarking humorously that his cosmonauts, on their journeys around the earth, had never reported seeing Jesus passing by. His remark may well cause some unease in the most thoughtful modern Christians. What is left of our proclamation of the ascension of Christ if we refuse to take literally the archaic cosmological picture against which Jesus is described as moving from an earth down here to a heaven up there?

In fact, popular cosmological pictures, archaic or modern, have less to do with displaying scientific data about the universe than with bringing out assumptions about the nature of life within it. The popularity of such works as H. G. Wells' *Wars of the Worlds* or the recent *Star Wars* series lies in their ability to express our common fear of the universe as forbidding and alien, careless of human life if not positively hostile to it. They reflect our sense that we are alone and afraid in this world, a world we never made.

The accounts of the ascension of Christ we hear from the gospel of Luke and the Acts of the Apostles—as well as in the proclamation of Christ's assumption of heavenly power in the epistle to the Ephesians—employ bits and pieces of a cosmological picture which views these matters in a very different way. This picture was already archaic when these accounts were written, and we should not assume that their authors were necessarily unaware that the earth was round or that heaven and earth were not so simply up there and down here as they seem to suggest. Nonetheless, it was a picture which would have been familiar to any reader of Jewish apocalyptic writing, the Book of Daniel for instance, or the passage from the prophet Ezekiel just read.

In this picture, the universe is certainly awesome. But we are far from aliens in it. It is the work of God, God's glorious throne room. It is run according to God's mysterious purposes, which must finally control the destiny of all of us. If we are "alone and afraid" within it, that is because his purposes are different from ours. We want to live for ourselves, to promote our own concerns even when they clash with those of God or our neighbors. We want to run as much as we can of the universe on our own terms, however impossible that may be.

It is against the background provided by this picture that our readings set the suffering and death of Jesus at our hands, and his being raised again to life with God. The picture is in the background, and actually only the useful bits and pieces of it remain. Jesus, dead and risen, is in the foreground for all to see. What the disciples have been witnessing these last weeks is the actual, visible event of God's reaching out to reconcile the whole creation, to save it from the confusion it has brought on itself, to bring it back together in the new life of Jesus Christ. There is no question any more about the mysterious purposes of the one who sits on the heavenly throne. They are clear now. If the death we tried to use to stop them will not work, no power can do so.

This feast, then, has to do not with speculations about the universe we do not know but with God's involvement with the human life we know only too well—with the conflict of human wills, personal, social, national, seemingly even cosmic, which threaten to overwhelm it. It has to do with that—and with our confidence in the ultimate triumph of the new human life which God is bringing into existence in the death and resurrection of Jesus Christ.

We cannot end, however, without noticing how the disciples are portrayed in the accounts of the ascension we have heard. As is often the case in the gospels, they are unaware of the real purposes of God unfolding before them. Despite all they have witnessed these last weeks, they still ask the risen Christ: "Will you at this time restore dominion to Israel?" Now that you have been restored miraculously to the human scene, will you not finally get down to doing what a Messiah is expected to do, for instance redressing the balances between Israel and the nations? The disciples have little notion of the scope of God's plans for human reconciliation, or of the role of Christ in their being brought to fulfillment. They have to be prodded back to Jerusalem to await the gift of the Spirit which will make them bearers of a message they do not as yet understand.

We Christians are, unfortunately, more likely to see ourselves mirrored in the disciples as portrayed here than in the disciples as we will encounter them again in the accounts of Pentecost next Sunday. Despite the gift of the Spirit at our baptism, we secretly tend to think that the death and resurrection of Christ has something to do with the success of "our side" in the conflict of human wills which still dominates our lives, personal, social, national, most of the time.

We must, on the Ascension Day as well as on any other day, pray for the renewal of the Spirit to enable us to see more, far more, absolutely more than that in the work of reconciliation to which we have been called as members of the body of the risen Christ in the world.

Lloyd G. Patterson

R   *Acts 1:12–14; 1 Pet 4:13–16; Jn 17:1–11a*
E   *Acts 1:8–14; 1 Pet 4:12–19; Jn 17:1–11*
L   *Acts 1:8–14; 1 Pet 4:12–17;5:6–11; Jn 17:1–11*

One of the great joys of reading St. John's gospel is its glorious poetry, the majestic webs of words it spins to draw us into the depths of Jesus' message. From the very first phrases which show us the Word made flesh, we are swept along, wrapped in language of incomparable beauty. As the story approaches its end in the seventeenth chapter, Jesus prays, and his prayer is the poetry we have come to expect in this gospel.

Precisely because this passage is so poetic, our attention is caught by a phrase that doesn't quite seem to fit, a verse that breaks the flow. In the middle of lofty words about God's glory is a clarification, an explanation: "And this is eternal life, that they know you the only true God, and Jesus Christ whom you have sent." What is so important about these words that John allowed them to intrude on the rhythm of this prayer? Clearly John wanted to emphasize the importance of knowing God; but what does it mean to know God?

In an age of information processing and endless educational opportunities, most of us recognize the value of knowledge. Books, newspapers, television, radio—all offer us facts, ideas, research, information on every subject imaginable. Hardly any decision is made without first learning something. At times we bring that same sort of intellectual concern to our faith. We want to know God, and so we attend classes, we read theology, we think and talk and argue. We support educational ministry in our churches, so that our children, too, may know God. And all of this is no doubt a part of what John had in mind. Intellectual grasp of Christian teachings does play a role in faith, but it is not all there is. Alone, it does not lead to eternal life.

There are other ways of knowing, of course. When I was a child, I went through a stage, common to many little girls, when I was fascinated by horses. I read everything I could find, from classic novels like *Black Beauty* and *National Velvet* to histories of horsebreeding and manuals on training and grooming. I dreamed of owning a filly and was sure that I would know just how to care for her. The reality, of course, was that I wouldn't have known where to begin, because I had never been within six feet of a real horse, and diagrams are no substitute for horseflesh.

So, too, with knowledge of God. Even though John writes so movingly of the Word, it is a Word whom we know not just on paper but in the person of Jesus Christ. "To know" as Hebrew uses the verb involves direct experience and intimacy, and there is an element of this meaning in John's thinking. It is not enough simply to be in agreement with the teachings of the Christian faith. Eternal life also entails an encounter with the living Lord, and experience of what God has done and is doing, not just in history, but in our own lives. To know Jesus is to live in relationship with God.

But it seems to me that there is yet another level of knowing involved here. For John, even experiencing the Word made flesh was not sufficient. Knowing God also meant living a life of obedience to God's commands. Just as importantly, it meant being a part of the community of believers. To know is to share in the life of God's people. And that is precisely what we see happening in our lesson from the first chapter of Acts. Those who had been closest to Jesus during his ministry, the eleven and the women who had followed him, as well as his mother and brothers, had seen him and had heard his message. They knew God, and that knowledge continued even after the Ascension. They returned to the upper room, we read, and there "all these with one accord devoted themselves to prayer." This is the fullness of the knowledge of God: to have met the living Lord, to have heard the word of life and then to join together in worship and in service.

In that spirit we meet today. We hear the word and learn from it, but there is more. We encounter the One who is the Word, but there is more. In joy and humble obedience, we gather around the table, in communion with one another because, as we read in 1 John, our communion is with the Father, and with Jesus Christ, the Son. Here we know God, and here is eternal life.

Catherine A. Ziel

R PENTECOST SUNDAY
E L DAY OF PENTECOST

R   *Acts 2:1–11; 1 Cor 12:3b-7,12–13; Jn 20:19–23*
E   *Acts 2:1–11; 1 Cor 12:4–13; Jn 20:19–23*
L   *Joel 2:28–29; Acts 2:1–21; Jn 20:19–23*

A fantasy conversation: "Our congregation surely has a good spirit."

"Yes, but is it the Holy Spirit?"

What comes to mind? Pentecost has come: is it fully realized?

Our Scriptures tell it like it is, and like it could be or should be. We are candidates for an infusing of God's Spirit, Christ's mind. In Christian practice Pentecost occurs as the fiftieth day of Easter: the time in between Easter and Pentecost are times of festivity and joy. Originally, fasts were not to be observed, and people prayed standing, symbolizing the resurrection. And now, following Pentecost, the mood is festive: a new age has broken in, the church is reconstituted. Christ's work begun at Easter comes to fruition. We're empowered; the church gets new action. The early church has a visible display of signs and wonders attesting God's presence. People are asking what must they do as they are confronted by God's word. Gathered together, people hear a great sermon by Peter. There's spectacular vision, and they experience a shattering noise.

We too could have the "old" shattered. We too may have a spectacular vision. We too may have the four wonderful experiences of Pentecost:

1. *We have dreams fulfilled*. How we all long for dream fulfillment: "That's something I always wanted . . . it's a dream come true . . . I really looked forward to this day." Old Testament Joel longed for the day when exiles could come back home, when things would work out for good, when the people of God could realize new visions.

We all wonder whether it is possible for our dreams to be fulfilled. When, Joel asks, will our wastelands of desolation be redeemed? When will our catastrophes turn out to be blessings? Peter preaches: and we paraphrase, "I have a dream that some day this world will be cleansed of war and of the idols of status and class. I have a dream that young people will work for justice. I have a dream when old people will know that they are not has-beens. I have a dream."

2. *We have conflicts processed*. Interpersonal communication "how-to's" abound. In genuine communications, our uniqueness is respected and affirmed. And so are our individual differences. Bland and insipid uniformity does not obliterate individuality. We create corporate understandings and harmony. We share a common language: now another's speech is our own. We share a common planet and a common life. There is peace. We are hopeful!

Pentecost is the tower of Babel reversed. No longer are our languages confusing or our relationships conflicting. There's a given: we have a Spirit given to us. We are provided with tools of understanding which lead us into a fellowship of reconciliation. In President Reagan's hometown, in his own "home church" in Dixon, Illinois, was a talk-back session. A senior citizen and a teenager were both speaking. One said, "I want to see you after the service." And this is what the Pastor overheard: "Thank you for taking me seriously, for talking to me face to face rather than behind my back." Then a response, "And thank you for addressing me and granting me that dignity." They hugged: one clean shaven, with wrinkled skin and hunched back, the other bearded with ragged shorts. But both big and tall. That's the Spirit of God for you.

3. *We have gifts exercised*. Jesus still breathes upon us and says "Peace." What a gift. And in recognition that we are all equally inherited, ours is a common confession: Jesus is Lord. Before we know it, we've got the Spirit, one that recognizes our diversity, even our division of labor. But ours is a common source. And ours is a common mission and goal. We are different people and differently gifted, but we're unified. We are multi-membered with many parts and yet one body, says Paul in Corinthians.

That Spirit within is working throughout for common good. Our diversity is productive when and as we exercise our gifts in the interest of others. We have a good spirit, and it is the Holy Spirit. We are an energized people.

4. *We have joy and faith shared*. There's a dynamic deep joy among us. We've forgiven each other. People who come and who attend experience a new tone. One wrote about it this way, "It was the spirit that we saw in you and in that church that helped us hear for the first time those words, 'Follow me'."

Who's humming that tune? We are. And we also hear it from somewhere else. It seems to be coming from within and from without, from God, from the lips of Jesus. It is now obvious: it is channeled by the Spirit. What if some say we're drunk? We'll have to tell them, "It's only nine in the morning." Let's tell it now to all: "This is that which was promised of old; the Spirit of God is with us."

LeRoy E. Kennel

R *Ex 34:4b-6, 8–9; 2 Cor 13:11–13; Jn 3:16–18*
E *Gn 1:1–2:3; 2 Cor 13:11–14; Mt 28:16–20*
L *Gn 1:1–2:3; 2 Cor 13:11–14; Mt 28:16–20*

Let's begin with the third element in the "apostolic greeting," the fellowship of the Holy Spirit.

The word translated in our English Bible as "fellowship" or "communion" means the possession and enjoyment of something in common. For example, concert-goers have a fellowship in their common enjoyment of the music. Citizens of a country possess the advantages of their government together, and crowds on the beaches in the summer find a fellowship in the water. There are thousands of different kinds of fellowship, all the way from two people establishing a home to all people setting up a United Nations of the world. But of all these the highest, deepest, and broadest communion is that of the Christian church. It is broadest because it is the most catholic, including in it all sorts and conditions of people, from every part of the earth and from every period of history. It is deepest because the bond among all these people is not some temporary pleasure or ephemeral interest, but a thing that is infinitely lasting, a union that cannot be broken by time or circumstance. It is the highest communion because what is enjoyed and possessed in common is nothing less than the God of heaven. There is hardly anything to compare with the fellowship of the church.

It is usually said by commentators that the union of the faithful in Christ is a spiritual one, created and sustained by the Holy Spirit. That is certainly true; but that is not the whole story. What we have in common is not merely faith in a body of truth, though we do have that. Nor is it even a common spiritual experience, of the kind that we enjoy on the great festivals, like Easter. Let us be more precise and say that we enjoy God together; our communion consists in our mutual enjoyment of the third person of the Blessed Trinity. The Spirit dwells is each of us and among us as a community. St. Paul says that this community is so intimate that we are actually one body in Christ. What makes us one is more than a doctrine, more than a creed, more than a force or an ideal or a philosophy of life; it is God, in all of God's fullness, power, and love. God shall be with you and shall be in you, said our Lord, promising to send the Counselor. Last Sunday we observed the anniversary of the Spirit's coming. The Spirit came, as Jesus had said. The Spirit has since then not withdrawn from the church, but is still personally and powerfully present, not as a vague abstraction, existing in some no-man's land of infinite space, but definitely localized in our own souls and bodies, and in that other body which is the church. Individually and collectively we enjoy a person-to-person association with this Spirit who proceeds from the Father and the Son.

If what Christians have in common is the fellowship of the Holy Spirit, they certainly enjoy the association of the Lord Jesus Christ. For the whole work of the Spirit, in these New Testament times, is to bring to bear on human beings the full force of the work of the Savior. The Spirit is sent to bring all things to our remembrance, whatsoever Christ has said to us. Note the time-sequence: the Spirit was not poured out on the church until our Lord had ascended into heaven, for it was to be the Spirit's function to testify of the completed work of Christ, which obviously could not be done before that work was finished. So the Spirit brings about our fellowship with Christ by establishing the mystic union, as is adumbrated in that beautiful verse from Revelation: "Behold, I stand at the door and knock; if there are any who hear my voice and open the door, I will come in to them and eat with them, and they with me"— a verse which, incidentally, has marvelous overtones for our experience in holy communion.

And so we become members of the Christian family; by this means we come back to the Father of us all. Such fusion of human beings into community, the coming together of people in a holy communion, is God's own solution to the problem of world peace. That is why also everyone of us who continues in the communion is thereby making a contribution to the peace of the world, and everyone who brings a stranger into the communion makes an even greater contribution. For God knows, and so should we, that our common bond as human beings is not enough to overcome the hostilities which rise up among us. Human beings are born in sin, and to the evil they may perpetrate there is no limit. Some change must take place in them, some reversal of the hell-bent course to which they are naturally inclined. There must be a fellowship which is based on a deeper bond than our common humanity. And this happens, as we have said, in the communion of the Holy Spirit. To put it another way, the problem of world peace is not solved by making all people monotheistic and having them recognize one another as such; it is needful also that they become trinitarian. We hope and pray and work for the day when people all over the world will say, in the words of the ancient introit, "Blessed be the Holy Trinity and the undivided Unity: let us give glory to him because he has shown his mercy to us."

Herbert F. Lindemann

R BODY AND BLOOD OF CHRIST

R *Deut 8:2–3, 14–16; 1 Cor 10:16–17; Jn 6:51–58*

The mystery of today's feast is both subtle and rich. St. Augustine put his finger on it in the following section of a sermon:

"If you wish to understand the body of Christ, listen to the apostle address the faithful: 'You are the body of Christ and its members.' If, then, you are the body of Christ and its members, it is your own mystery which is placed on the Lord's table; it is your own mystery which you receive. It is to what you are that you answer Amen and in so responding subscribe to it. You hear, 'The Body of Christ,' and you answer, 'Amen.' Be a member of the body of Christ so that your Amen will be true."[9]

Perhaps the greatest grace given to the Roman Catholic Church in the years since the Second Vatican Council has been the gradual recovery of the experience of the church as the people of

God and the body of Christ. I would wager that only a short time ago many of us Catholics would not have understood what Augustine was talking about in this passage: "It is your own mystery which is placed on the Lord's table."

Augustine expresses the rich, many-leveled appreciation the church possessed for a thousand years of the sacramental presence of the risen Lord, both in the church assembled and in the sacrament of the communion in the body and blood of the Lord. This feast offers us an opportunity to reflect on Augustine's challenge: "It is to what you are that you reply 'Amen,' and by replying subscribe. For you are told 'the body of Christ,' and you reply, 'Amen.' Be a member of the body of Christ, and let your 'Amen' be true."

When the minister presents us with the eucharistic bread and says "The body of Christ," how do we understand this? When the eucharistic wine is offered with the statement "The blood of Christ," to what do we think this refers? Certainly, our "Amen" is a statement of belief in the presence of Christ, but how big is our picture? How wide is our lens for experiencing the presence of Christ in its fullness? This is by no means to downplay the presence of Christ in the bread and wine, but how do we resonate with Augustine's idea that we, too, are the body of Christ? Before distributing communion in the Orthodox liturgy, the priest holds up the bread and wine and proclaims, "Holy things for the holy!" How firm is our "Amen" to the statement that we are holy, that the holy presence of Christ is there to be experienced in my pewmates?

To help us appreciate the richness of Augustine's perception, let us note a few circumstances surrounding the origin of this feast.

It must be admitted that the Feast of the Body and Blood of Christ (a duplication of Holy Thursday) was instituted at a time in the church's history when eucharistic theology and piety were not at their traditional best. This was a time when the understanding of the church as a people of God who glory in their baptismal dignity was not widespread, when the traditional understanding of the eucharist as primarily food at a communal meal was obscured, when communion of the laity was infrequent and when theological speculation was preoccupied with questions such as how Christ was present in the consecrated species. Since the Middle Ages the church's eucharistic piety has not been characterized by an appreciation of the sacrament as an action of the believing community, but rather as a more or less static "presence" in the species brought about by sacerdotal power.

Gerard Sloyan wrote some years ago: "One can probably make the case . . . that there is a kind of disregard, though certainly not disrespect, for the character of the eucharist whenever it is dealt with on terms other than those of food at a meal."[10] We are challenged on this feast day to allow the mystery of eucharist to speak to us in all its fullness as we dwell on the words of the gospel.

Given our history, it is understandable how the important reading from John's gospel heard today, a section which scholars agree refers to the eucharist, often tended in the past to confirm the faithful in a belief in a quasi-physical rather than a properly sacramental presence of Christ in the eucharist. One must pay attention to the liturgical enactment of the eucharistic meal for a proper understanding of this gift of Christ. Jesus gave his body and blood, his life for us in his passion; he gives himself to us, truly present in this sacramental action. And he promises that if we feed on him, if he is the source of our life, we shall live forever.

No explanation can stand in the place of the liturgical enactment; no rational understanding of history offers the encounter with the Lord as does the sacrament. We must accept the invitation to the table of the Lord; come with our lives, hopefully bearing some scars received in selfless living. We must gather with one another, look at one another, hear the stories told, break the bread and share the cup in his memory. For it is in these actions that we encounter the body of Christ.

Lawrence J. Madden, S.J.

[9]Augustine, sermon 272, tr. Lawrence J. Madden, S.J.
[10]Gerard S. Sloyan, *It Is Your Own Mystery* (Washington, DC: The Liturgial Conference, 1977), p. 39.

R NINE SUNDAY IN ORDINARY TIME
E PROPER 4
L SECOND SUNDAY AFTER PENTECOST

R *Deut 11:18,26–28,32; Rom 3:21–25a,28; Mt 7:21–27*
E *Deut 11:18–21,26–28; Rom 3:21–25a,28; Mt 7:21–27*
L *Deut 11:18–21,26–28; Rom 3:21–25a,27–28; Mt 7:21–29*

Often, amid the complexities of contemporary life, we are confronted with the question, "How do I know what is the will of God for me?" In each of this Sunday's readings we can glean an insight into that abiding question.

Structurally, today's first reading from Deuteronomy forms the conclusion to the first part of the covenant formulary and serves as a transition to the Deuteronomic exposition of the law. The reading begins with an exhortation to Israel to keep God's word constantly on one's mind: "You shall lay up these words of mine in your heart and in your soul . . . teach them to your children . . . write them upon the doorposts of your house and upon your gates." As the Deuteronomic author continues the exhortation, he becomes more explicit about the meaning of keeping God's word. Within the context of his theology, keeping God's word or observing the law entails both loving the Lord, your God, and walking in God's ways. In other words, Israel is faithful to God's will when the people embody within their persons and existentially live out in their lives the attitudes and desires of the covenant God.

The beautiful words in this passage, especially the powerful metaphors used by the author to deepen Israel's awareness of its relationship with the covenant God—Bind these words of mine upon your hand—suggest a need on the part of the sacred author to bridge the gap in time between God's earlier revelation to Israel in the desert and the concrete circumstances of his post-Exilic audience. Not only does the author remind Israel of God's past saving deeds, but he confronts Israel and us with the need to ratify and deepen our own present relationship with God. It is today that we have within us the power to choose relationship with or alienation from God; today, each of us, in the concrete decisions we make relative to God and one another, truly chooses blessing or curse.

Today's gospel asks us to reflect even more deeply upon this same theme. The Matthean evangelist, writing during the 80's and 90's, is addressing a community in crisis, a community which did not always have a bedrock understanding of the ramifications of observing the new law. Whereas the early members of Matthew's community were predominantly Jewish converts to Christianity, and were raised in an environment which often reflected upon the meaning of the law, the community was increasingly Gentile in its membership. Those converts needed a fundamental Christian initiation and formation. In addition, Matthew's community was threatened by the presence of early Christian charismatics in its midst. These were people whose flashy words and showy deeds often cloaked a failure to understand and appropriate the meaning of doing God's will. Matthew warns them that various forms of ecstatic prayer are not a substitute for concretely living out God's will: "Not every one who says to me, 'Lord, Lord,' shall enter the dominion of heaven, but the one who does the will of my Father who is in heaven." Concurrently, the evangelist addresses those members of the community attracted to charismatic manifestations such as prophecy, exorcism, and miraculous deeds. Even those deeds, good in themselves, are not equivalent to assuming the attitudes and redemptive activity of the risen Lord, whom Matthew portrays as the fulfillment of the covenant law.

How can we contemporary Christians presume to take on such an awesome task? In his letter to the Romans Paul speaks encouraging words to those of us who recognize our shortcomings. Even though we have all sinned and fallen short of the glory of God, we have been "justified by God's grace as a gift, through the redemption which is in Christ Jesus."

Ultimately, we need not fear as we find ourselves overwhelmed by the complexities and ambiguities of contemporary existence. As we strive to discover "What is God's will for me?" we need, in the spirit of the risen Lord, to ask only one question of ourselves: "How can the redemptive love of the risen Lord be actualized in this situation?" If we act upon that, we will surely be akin to the wise person in today's gospel who built the house upon the rock. When the rain fell, and the floods came, and the winds blew and beat upon that house, it did not fall.

Margaret Page

R TENTH SUNDAY IN ORDINARY TIME
E PROPER 5
L THIRD SUNDAY AFTER PENTECOST

R *Hos 6:3–6; Rom 4:18–25; Mt 9:9–13*
E *Hos 5:15–6:6; Rom 4:13–18; Mt 9:9–13*
L *Hos 5:15–6:6; Rom 4:18–25; Mt 9:9–13*

One recollection that keeps me going in my life as a Christian is the marvelous quotation from Martin Luther: We are meant to be Christs to each other. I find this an exciting and challenging proposition for my life as a Christian. There is a similar challenge in the gospel for the day, in which there are two possibilities for faith.

The Pharisees and the scribes put a question to Jesus' disciples. Matthew writes, "Why does your teacher eat with tax collectors and sinners?" Mark writes, "Why does he eat with tax collectors and sinners?" And in Luke, the question to the disciples reads, "Why do *you* eat with tax collectors and sinners?" In Matthew and Mark, the Pharisees' criticism is directed against Jesus himself. In Luke, their criticism is directed against the disciples. There is, and there ought to be, connection and continuity between the work and witness of Jesus of Nazareth and the work and witness of Christian people. The congruence between Jesus and his people implies that Jesus and Jesus' people are up to the same business. It should be clearer to all who look at us that Jesus and Jesus' people are doing the same things, offering the same message.

Now, why isn't it? One conclusion we could draw is that we are not doing our job; we are not doing and saying the same things Jesus did and said. Remember Luther's marvelous phrase: You are meant to be Christ to your neighbor. Your life is the only Bible most people read. The unbeliever, the doubter, the wistful agnostic should be able to look at you and say: "That person is like Jesus." The resemblance ought to cut both ways: in praise and in criticism. If we are praised by the world for being like Jesus, then we should be criticized and condemned by the world for being like Jesus. If you are escaping criticism, condemnation, and questioning by the world for being like Jesus, then perhaps there is something wrong with your life and witness.

It would pay to ask yourself: What risk am I not taking that Jesus might have taken? Where would Jesus come in for criticism because of his compassion or his sense of justice? Am I burning with a similar compassion or justice? You've seen the legend on the poster: "If being a Christian were a capital offense, would the court find enough evidence to convict you?"

Let me cite one example. The Roman Catholic Archbishop of Seattle has urged the members of the churches under his jurisdiction to consider a tax boycott on military expenditures. Modern nuclear war is too horrible, says the bishop, for Christian people to condone its further development, and he has urged his people to consider doing something about it, in the form of a tax boycott on military expenditures. That's both illegal and unpopular, especially in Seattle where a cluster of industries are devoted to high-technology weaponry. It will not be simply non-Christians who find the Bishop's position distasteful, but many Christians as well, including some of his own flock. I hold this up, not for your praise or censure, but as a first challenge, an instance of one Christian's taking an unpopular stance and being willing to face the consequences.

Today's text offers us a second challenge. Jesus quotes from the prophets, "Go and learn what this means: I desire mercy, not sacrifice." Here Jesus repeats an old theme in the prophets of Israel: Israel was too concerned with ritual niceties, too absorbed in requirements of holiness, and thus ignored the demands of compassion. God is not pleased with a people who put morality above mercy. For Jesus here is not simply offending ritualist sensibilities; he is offending against popular morality of the day. It's not merely that Jesus refuses to wash his hands before he eats: he is eating with the wrong crowd, the moral and religious outcasts of his day. Jesus comes down on the side of mercy and compassion for the people involved, rather than moral judgments.

This narrative compels me to qualify what I know of morality, when the real needs of real people come into question. If I had to choose between keeping myself ritually clean, and helping the man lying along the roadside, stripped and beaten, there's not much question what Jesus would do and what Jesus' people should do. But the question is much more difficult when it appears as if the needs of people are conflicting with what I find a genuinely moral, ethical principle.

Since the third century, for example, some Christians have felt it necessary to break the fifth commandment. The fifth commandment is, "you shall not kill," and yet there are Christian people who serve in the military. Down through the ages, there have been men and women—remember Joan of Arc—who have seen it as their Christian responsibility to take arms and to kill, for what they perceive as the greater good, the protection of their society, homes, and families. That remains in my view a valid Christian position.

I can conceive that in his private prayers the Bishop of Seattle is praying quite a different set of petitions than is the Christian who opts to vote a larger military expenditure. But in our public prayers, for whose side shall we pray? For now we can pray for both. And we can ask for forgiveness for both. Someone has said that in our public prayers, the Christian church argues with itself. We often have no clear view of Christ's perfect will. We can pray for both sides, for forgiveness, and for our conversion that all our hearts may be turned to the will of God. We do have the Spirit of God. God will not allow Christian people to remain ultimately without a consensus.

Paul Bosch

R ELEVENTH SUNDAY IN ORDINARY TIME
E PROPER 6
L FOURTH SUNDAY AFTER PENTECOST

R *Ex 19:2–6a; Rom 5:6–11; Mt 9:36–10:8*
E *Ex 19:2–8a; Rom 5:6–11; Mt 9:35–10:8*
L *Ex 19:2–8a; Rom 5:6–11; Mt 9:35–10:8*

"You shall be my own possession . . . a holy nation." "While we were yet sinners Christ died for us." God's holiness, through Jesus Christ, continues to be shared. Jesus summoned the twelve and gave them power . . . to cure all kinds of diseases and sicknesses, telling them, "You received without paying, give without pay." God's love is a transforming power to the extent that it is shared in the manner of God's sharing. God's power is a transforming love when it is exercised in the manner of Jesus Christ's use of power.

Today, the readings point to the mystery of holiness as a mystery of life-giving and love-sharing power. Such power begins and ends with life and love shared. This mystery is revealed in Jesus Christ, who loved us even while we were sinners. This mystery is one the disciples of Christ are invited into, for he gives over his power to heal, to enlighten, and to love.

That ideal of Christian power, the power to care, to share, and to heal, has not been the power that humans have used through history. Power over others rather than power for others has been more typical, from personal relationships to those of more global proportions. The tension between Christian power and abusive power has at times been evident even in the people called to be a holy nation, the people for whom Christ died.

Camelot points to this tension of power with as many facets as people. In *Camelot*, Arthur and Guenevere discuss the idea of power that is about to be transformed. Though the context is the Middle Ages, the exercise of power sounds familiar to us. The reflection goes like this.

Arthur: Proposition: It is far better to be alive than dead.

Guenevere: Agreed.

Arthur: If that is so, then why do we have battles where people can get killed?

Guenevere: Because knights love them. They adore charging in and whacking away. It's splendid fun. You've said so yourself, often.

Arthur: It is splendid fun. But that doesn't seem reason enough. . . . Only knights are rich enough to bedeck themselves in armor. They can declare war when it suits them. . . . Wrong or right, they have the might. So wrong or right, they are always right. And that's wrong! Right? Suppose we create a new order?

Guenevere: Pardon?

Arthur: A new order, a new order. Where might is only used for right, to improve instead of destroy. . . . That's it, Jenny, might for right—Not might is right. Might for right! We'll build a whole new generation of chivalry!

Arthur questioned this dream that just might change the world. Could power be used for communion and not destruction? He asks, "Am I at a hill or is this only a mirage?" He soon must learn the tensions of power, power to love instead of power to destroy. The two people he loves most, Lancelot and Guenevere, betray him. His feelings are clear, and the actions those feelings suggest are also clear!

Arthur: I love them, and they answer me with pain and torment! They betray me in their hearts! I see it in their eyes! I shall not be wounded and not return in kind. . . . I demand a man's vengeance!

How quickly the battlefield has shifted from warring power of nations to the warring powers of the heart. How different the landscape becomes when it is one's own love that has been betrayed. Those who betray love should be punished, shouldn't they? Or is life not quite that black and white? Arthur muses.

Arthur: Could it possibly be civilized to destroy those one loves? Could it possibly be civilized to love myself above all? What of their pain and their torment? Did they ask for this? Can passion be selected?

Finally, pacing and wondering, Arthur comes to a decision.

Arthur: This is the time of King Arthur. Violence is NOT strength, and compassion is NOT weakness. This is the time of King Arthur and we reach for the stars! May God have mercy on us all![11]

You may know the story, and how such idealism ended. The Round Table, the dream that all could be one in communion of an ideal for the world, didn't take hold for long. "Might is right" became a larger part of the human story than "Might for right."

This day, we Christians gather in a different story, a story of might for right, of power for caring. Today we are called to receive again the power that is given to all disciples. This day we are called to be co-creators with Christ of a different story, co-creators of a world where Christ's power continues to heal, to affirm, to encourage, to empower others. In giving his gift of reconciliation, we receive more of that gift.

We gather around a table whose power is greater than that symbolized by the Round Table. Christ's table assures those who believe that they shall share his power to proclaim and manifest God's kingdom. For those who wish to receive this power as gift, the power must be shared as gift. In the giving is the receiving, and in the sharing is the reconciliation Christ promises. In the use of his power to empower all people, our lives proclaim again that the kingdom of God IS at hand.

Shawn Madigan, C.S.J.

[11]*Idylls of the King* and *Camelot,* ed. Allen Knee (New York: Dell, 1974), pp. 180–183, 215.

R TWELFTH SUNDAY IN ORDINARY TIME
E PROPER 7
L FIFTH SUNDAY AFTER PENTECOST

R *Jer 20:10–13; Rom 5:12–15; Mt 10:26–33*
E *Jer 20:7–13; Rom 5:15b-19; Mt 10:24–33*
L *Jer 20:7–13; Rom 5:12–15; Mt 10:24–33*

The word of God proclaimed for our instruction today has a deceptive power, and if we are not alert we may find ourselves seduced by it! Jeremiah had found that such a fate happened to him: "O LORD, you have deceived me, and I was deceived," he cried, when he found that God had attracted him to a ministry that would require more than he had bargained for. But by that time the prophet had reached his own personal point of no return: the only way out was to work his way through the trial by fire demanded by his prophetic mission.

This seductive power is typically accomplished by the dialectic of God's word. As living word, it is revealed to us in the dynamic tension of its message and in the dynamic circumstances of our own lives. Today's message seems to be released only when we have lived in the tension and with the truth of two very different revelations.

On the one hand, the prophet tells us in the first reading of his absolute conviction that God will support him in his trials. He goes so far as to anticipate the chagrin of his enemies when they see that God is on his side, not theirs. This message of consolation, of trust, and of fearless joy is proclaimed even more confidently in the gospel. For here, Matthew tells us that it is Jesus himself who assures us that we are priceless in God's sight, cherished beyond a calculus of sparrows in the sky and hairs on our head. Jesus himself will promote our cause before the Father. These words are profoundly consoling; they can even be soporific, giving warrant to those who accuse us of using our religion as a security blanket; and they are seductive.

In context, their truth cannot be heard without also responding to the challenge revealed for us this day by Jeremiah and Matthew. The great theologian, Paul Tillich, has shown how the dynamic of any faith that is truly one of ultimate concern occurs in the tension of a demand that requires an unconditional response but promises an absolute fulfillment. It is that very tension that is worked out in these readings that we have heard. The demand is the challenge to live and speak the truth of the Christian message, even in the face of opposition and rejection. The promise is the word of comfort: God's assurance that we will be protected from the only harm that really matters.

These messengers of God's word, Jeremiah and Matthew, remind us that our membership in this assembly requires more than that we be simply card-carrying Christians. We must acknowledge the truths that we believe; our lives must reflect the values and faith we profess. Anonymity is not an option. Jeremiah had found this out to his dismay: as he lived in fidelity to a prophetic mission, he was to be rejected and despised by those whose injustice he denounced. And Jesus, in the gospel text, instructs his first disciples on their responsibility to be fearless in the communication of his message. What he has shared with them in the intimacy of the apostolic community they must be willing to proclaim from the housetops.

We know what happened to Jesus in the service of truth. These words are his indication to those who accept his comfort that they must also accept his challenge.

So today's disclosure of God's will for us exists somewhere in the dialectical tension between comfort and challenge. We will have missed it if we settle for either one without the other. The challenge to be faithful to our identity as followers of Jesus is a daily one, encountered in the events and associates of our ordinary lives. Our presence here today attests to the fact that we have accepted God's invitation at some level of our being. (Jeremiah would call this God's seduction!) In choosing life over death, faith over disbelief, integrity over sin, we have long since given lip-service to these choices. But it is in the mysterious working of God's Spirit in our lives that the implications of these choices find expression in the dynamic circumstances of home and family, work and leisure.

It is not an easy thing always to stand firm; the defense of one's own convictions may lead us to the lonely isolation that Jeremiah experienced, and God's comfort may seem an empty thing when friends desert us. It will be some comfort to us, struggling to be faithful, to remember that the apostles who heard these words from Jesus were not immediately able to respond to his challenge. In the face of trial and opposition, they deserted him and denied their most firmly held beliefs. But God's promise sustained them, even in their weakness, and the Spirit would come to make them fearless.

The story of God's involvement with the chosen people is a story of how the divine plan continues to be accomplished, even through our weakness and infidelity. That is what makes it gospel, good news. Our developing maturity in a life of faith brings increasing realization of the challenges that follow upon the commitments we have made. But each challenge brings a deepened realization of the constant loving support of a God who needs us in the service of truth and who cherishes us beyond all sparrows, seeing us in the face of the beloved first-born son.

Ruth Caspar, O.P.

R THIRTEENTH SUNDAY IN ORDINARY TIME
E PROPER 8
L SIXTH SUNDAY AFTER PENTECOST

R *2 Kg 4:8–11,14–16a; Rom 6:3–4,8–11; Mt 10:37–42*
E *Is 2:10–17; Rom 6:3–11; Mt 10:34–42*
L *Jer 28:5–9; Rom 6:1b-11; Mt 10:34–42*

As you watch and listen to the performance of a great pianist, I'm sure you wonder, as I have frequently, what it takes to acquire that level of artistic quality and expertise. You think to yourself, "That seems so simple. How could I do the same in my own field of interest?"

Although not all of us play the piano, we can imagine the amount of work that goes into playing with great skill and artistic expression. Not only do many hours of immediate preparation for a particular concert need to be considered, but the years of practice beforehand as well: the tedious scales and finger exercises, the hours of ear-training to detect harmonies and dissonances in a piece, and the repetition of pieces of music to develop an appropriate style and sensitivity to them. But most essential to the development of high-quality performance through the long periods of practice is the ability to focus one's attention, to concentrate totally on the task at hand. The pianist who aspires to greatness needs to approach the task of playing the piano with such singleness of purpose that she or he is wholly centered on it. A disciple of Zen might describe this by saying that the pianist and the piano must become one in the playing. Experts have noted that the difference between the one who plays with the highest degree of excellence and the one who plays well is this ability to be single-minded. No small challenge to those of us who wish to excel in our own area!

Our following Jesus as described in today's readings is no less challenging. "They who love father or mother more than me are not worthy of me." The strength of this statement can be overpowering. Its meaning is clear. It can be neither questioned nor ignored. The disciple is called to a radical commitment to the following of Jesus. Nothing takes precedence over that commitment, not even family ties.

The radical nature of this commitment is emphasized by the author of Matthew with the use of the term "cross." Some commentators note that this is the first time in this gospel that "cross" appears, implying that no suffering or sacrifice is too great in the following of Jesus. Discipleship demands the total giving of oneself.

In the second reading from Romans today we are urged to recall the foundation of this radical commitment. Through our baptism we have been given new life in Christ. Our old self, enslaved to sin, has been put to death. Having died with Christ to sin in baptism, we are expected to live as those who believe that this transformation has been accomplished in Christ. We are challenged to appropriate and live out the reality expressed in our baptism: to carry our cross daily; to die to all that prevents us from giving ourselves over to God in our lives; to let go of all other priorities; in other words, to aspire to that singleness of purpose which is required of one who is serious about following the way of Jesus.

Whether one is a "prophet," a "righteous one" or one of the "little ones" of Matthew's church, the foundation of this radical call is the same. But in hearing today's gospel, one senses that the "little ones" hold a privileged place in the invitation to discipleship. We are invited to offer them hospitality with particular care. This attention to the unique call of the "little ones" is a needed corrective for those of us who would tend to rely on status or privileged position in the church for the effectiveness of our preaching. The author of Matthew would say to us today that those who dare to follow Jesus and proclaim the message of the cross need to assume the same humble posture as did Jesus!

This invitation to a total self-offering in Christ is given not merely to the individual disciple but also to the church as a whole, to that community of disciples who profess to live out the dying and rising of Jesus, the Christ, in a definitive way. Mandated to preach the meaning of the cross in each age, the church is a credible symbol insofar as it enfleshes the very message that it proclaims. It, too, needs to die to those things which are not of God, to adjust its priorities so that its mission is clearly focused, to let go of all that detracts it from its one purpose.

Today's eucharistic celebration can bring us to a new awareness of the meaning of our call to discipleship. We hear a word of challenge and judgment proclaimed in our midst and ask for a heart that is hospitable to the demands it makes on us. May the bread that we break and receive strengthen us to surrender ourselves entirely to the Christ "in whom we live and move and have our being."

Patricia A. Parachini, S.N.J.M.

R   FOURTEENTH SUNDAY IN ORDINARY TIME
E   PROPER 9
L   SEVENTH SUNDAY AFTER PENTECOST

R   *Zech 9:9–10; Rom 8:9,11–13; Mt 11:25–30*
E   *Zech 9:9–12; Rom 7:21–8:6; Mt 11:25–30*
L   *Zech 9:9–12; Rom 7:15–25a; Mt 11:25–30*

No problem! Two words: abrupt, dismissive, assuring, urgent; the contemporary panacea for all that riles human behavior; the universal antiphon shutting out the entreaties of all who cry in the wilderness. Two little words.

No problem!

In a moment, mouthed before the last words of lament pour out from hurting hearts; in a moment, two little words take charge. Promising to deal with whatever it is that troubles or assaults, the words assure victory and peace. Perils may ensnare; accidents, hurt, doubts wrack us. The road has become bumpy, apparently impassable; we cannot go back, and there seems no path open ahead. We cry out in a thousand different experiences born of the human condition, and out of the darkness we hear, "No problem!"

We have been heard; someone is answering our cry. What is more, whoever is speaking implies that help is forthcoming and that it will be given. We like that, for no one wants to walk a bumpy road throughout life. Life could be so much better, so much happier were there no annoyances! The slogan "No problem" proclaims the fervent desire of the human heart, a world free of distress, a life devoid of trouble. "No problem" laughs at our hurts, accusing us of a kind of self-pitying myopia. Put on your rose-colored glasses, this is really the best of all possible worlds. There are no problems. You're making them up.

But we know otherwise. We hurt; the hurt does not go away. A spoiled marriage, a floundering career, the little annoyances of other people, the noisy neighbors, surly kids, whining parents, demanding bosses; phony words by politicians, business leaders, advertisers and colleagues we want to trust; words that deceive and delude and mock: and I hear "No problem"?

Something inside me whispers with annoying persistence and frequency that I could be, should be doing better. My mind creates standards and guidelines to deal with my hurts: diet and exercise for my body; more and better reading and less TV for my mind; a lock on my lips and a cleaning out of ears and brain to be more willing to listen and not snap out. But the machines which promise to turn out a new person do not always work. And when I cry out, all I hear is "No problem."

Is there nothing else? Am I forever locked into a confinement from which my spirit demands escape? My spirit is me; I have created my spirit, built it over the years by careful (and some not so careful) scrutiny of options and well-balanced judgments. My spirit directs me, enforces my resolve, encourages my ambition, delights in my tastes. But my spirit must be doing something wrong; else why do I have problems? Often these problems arise because of disagreements, challenges, rejections by other people. What allowances does my spirit make for others? Is there no common ground, no mutual understanding from which we all can create new lives?

Such questions unsettle one. I feel myself being turned about, and I am not so sure I like it. Am I seeking a way to get rid of my problems? Or is there something outside of myself waiting to come in and take charge so that I can deal with the problems? Building within me is a more clear awareness that I am meant to be other than what I have allowed myself to become. My problems and the discomfort they cause me are real; they may not go away. The important thing now however is my attitude, which requires consideration of others beside myself. "We" has become more noticeable in my thinking than "I." Commonality must have something to do with it.

Against such honest scrutiny, the church holds up Jesus. Come to me. I will refresh you. My yoke is easy, my burden light.

Yoke is a nasty word; we need no other burdens, we say. But all of us are burdened and in one way or another live under the yoke. Some yokes of our own making are really the cause of our problems.

But the yoke Jesus offers steers us. Behavior learns to look after others, their needs, their persons. Trust, gentleness and concern rise within and take over. Simple human values become important, necessary, imperative. Gone are all the complicated devious mechanisms that we cranked out in our own interests. No more need we connive and pretend. The yoke is easy, the burden is light.

Reward no longer motivates our comings and goings. No more is happiness a product of our own production. Delight grows, knowing that the Lord is loving to everyone, with compassion for all.

And so we eat and drink, again and again. Hunger is fed by righteousness, thirst by the living God. The supper is our meal, the table the Lord spreads for us, and not for me alone.

Edgar S. Brown, Jr.

R FIFTEENTH SUNDAY IN ORDINARY TIME
E PROPER 10
L EIGHTH SUNDAY AFTER PENTECOST

R *Is 55:10–11; Rom 8:18–23; Mt 13:1–23*
E *Is 55:1–5,10–13; Rom 8:9–17; Mt 13:1–9,18–23*
L *Is 55:10–11; Rom 8:18–25; Mt 13:1–9*

The readings presented to us this morning speak loudly and clearly of hope. From the prophecy of Isaiah we hear:

"My word . . . shall not return to me empty, but it shall accomplish that which I purpose, and prosper in the thing for which I sent it."

Paul confidently writes, "I consider that the sufferings of this present time are not worth comparing with the glory that is to be revealed to us."

In our day, however, these passages, together with the famous parable of the sower, are proclaimed in a world that seems to be trapped in a cycle of hopelessness. This hopelessness, more virulent than the AIDS virus, threatens to destroy our capacity to imagine and wonder, and we must continue to protect ourselves from its destructiveness by listening attentively to the word of God.

I am often asked to give lectures on "Global Spirituality" to church or school groups, and I usually begin my presentation by asking people in the audience how many of them ever spend time imagining what it will be like when the world lives at peace. Out of at least two thousand people who have attended such lectures over the years, no one has yet admitted to such daydreams.

I follow this question, as you might suspect, by asking how many people have ever spent time imagining what nuclear war might do to the world. In answer to this question, by contrast, many hands are raised. This never ceases to frighten me. Civilization has dreamed its way into exploring the face of the earth and the mysteries of the universe. Might we not be dreaming ourselves into a nuclear holocaust? At the very least such speculations increase the threat of nuclear war.

"The problem is too immense!"

"I can't do anything about it, so why should I bother?"

"It's unrealistic to imagine that all the people of the world could live in peace. It will never happen."

Such remarks, common responses these days, are symptoms of the syndrome of learned hopelessness, and a further manifestation of this disease is seen in those who live as though hopelessness is all there is. Too many of us have become such pragmatists that we have lost the capacity to delight in possibility.

When I drive upstate to visit my nephews, I always bring them an interesting gift. I've been known to bring unusual branches or fruit, but on one such visit, I brought them a modular shoe rack that I was planning to discard. I opened the trunk of my car, and my nephew, then about five years old, cried out gleefully, "A radar station!" He thanked me profusely and headed off into the woods to set up his new radar station at headquarters. Only later in the day did he take me aside quietly to ask what my gift had been before it became a radar station, but he never for a minute doubted its new identity.

What has happened to that wonderful capacity God gave human beings to revel in possibility?

The word of God is love, and the Christian's mission is to continue to spread the message that peaceful relationships at all levels of society are possible. But how can we live in peace if we have given it all up as hopeless before we've even begun?

Yes, we should mark well the parable of the sower this day, and ask ourselves where we find ourselves in it:

Who will steal away from us that which has been sown in our minds? How deep are our roots? Are they sturdy enough to withstand drought and pestilence? Do we let worldly anxiety and the lure of money cut us off from living the gospel authentically?

Made in the image and likeness of God, we have been endowed with the capacity to create rather than simply to conform. The world will tell us again and again that creativity is not realistic and just won't work, for the world's stock in trade is conformity. It was true in Isaiah's day, and it is true in ours as well, but how we respond to such pressure will mark us as God's own.

Julia Upton, R.S.M.

R SIXTEENTH SUNDAY IN ORDINARY TIME
E PROPER 11
L NINTH SUNDAY AFTER PENTECOST

R   *Wis 12:13,16–19; Rom 8:26–27; Mt 13:24–43*
E   *Wis 12:13,16–19; Rom 8:18–25; Mt 13:24–30,36–43*
L   *Is 44:6–8; Rom 8:26–27; Mt 13:24–30*

> Time, like an ever-rolling stream,
>   Soon bears us all away;
> We fly forgotten, as a dream
>   Dies at the op'ning day.[12]

Whenever I sing these words from Isaac Watts' hymn "O God, Our Help in Ages Past," I see myself in my college chapel, hearing the organist play an improvisation on this verse. As we sang, we seemingly cried out the futility of time while the great rolling sounds of the organ came over our heads, then into us, around us and through us. The sounds immersed us into the shortness, even the hopelessness, of earthly existence. Time itself seemed to choke us in our words and the organ's sound. The opening lines of the last verse, "O God, our help in ages past," would then come like a cry for rescue from the suffocating reality of time.

Our age is very time-conscious. Our machines make it possible to do things with great speed, and so everyone expects things to be done even faster. We run from this place to that, from one project to another, and then go to seminars on stress and burnout, only to go out and start all over again. The church speaks of Sabbath, retreat and God's gift of rest, but its cry is drowned by advertisements for twenty-four hour supermarkets and all night department store sales. Time continues to choke and suffocate us.

The gospel text for this day speaks of the weeds that grow alongside the wheat. Even when the good seed is planted by the good sower, the realities of earthly existence allow the weeds also to be planted and to grow and thrive. The weeds can choke the wheat and stop its good growth. The wheat can also grow to its maturity within the weeds, waiting for the promised harvest.

We who are the children of God are the wheat. Our earthly existence, our limitations of time and mortality, are the weeds. As we live and grow in the grace of God, that growth promised to us by the gift of the Holy Spirit given to us in our baptism, we are constantly thwarted, held back, bent over and sometimes choked, by the weeds of time. Time's weediness closes around us and causes us to grow into ourselves, instead of into God. We want to grow to be healthy and strong, yet we constantly find ourselves in the suffocating reality of our limitations, in the reality of time.

But in our gospel text, Jesus assures us that the promises of God are sure. Jesus echoes the word from God to the prophets that we need not fear; God's care is for us all. We are the people of God, the first and the last, who calls us children to a life which reaches beyond the limits of time. The weeds cannot stop us. We are called to grow into the grace of eternity. We stretch always to the sunshine, lifting our heads to God's promised growth.

When we bring the gifts of bread and wine to the table for the feast, we Lutherans sing a song of God's harvest: "Let the vineyards be fruitful, Lord, and fill to the brim our cup of blessing. Gather a harvest from the seeds that were sown, that we may be fed with the bread of life. Gather the hopes and the dreams of all; unite them with the prayers we offer now. Grace our table with your presence, and give us a foretaste of the feast to come.[13] " And then, when we come to the table ourselves, we step for one moment out of the weeds of time and take our place in eternity. There, as we reach for the bread and our lips taste the wine, we know the limitless, freeing power of God's life. In that instant we know the God who stepped into the limits of our time, who shared our suffocating, choking existence. And in that same instant, we know the God who makes us the children of eternity, who draws us into whole and real life. And so with the joy that comes of the harvest of eternity, we can go back into the weed-choked world, confident in our growth in God's unchanging grace. Then will the righteous shine like the sun in the limit-less dominion of God.

Nancy L. Winder

[12]Isaac Watts, "O God Our Help in Ages Past," *Lutheran Book of Worship*, (Minneapolis: Augsburg Publishing House, 1978), #320.
[13]*Lutheran Book of Worship*, p. 66.

R SEVENTEENTH SUNDAY IN ORDINARY TIME
E PROPER 12
L TENTH SUNDAY AFTER PENTECOST

R *1 Kg 3:5,7–12; Rom 8:28–30; Mt 13:44–52*
E *1 Kg 3:5–12; Rom 8:26–34; Mt 13:31–33,44–49a*
L *1 Kg 3:5–12; Rom 8:28–30; Mt 13:44–52*

I've discovered some interesting ideas about treasure in our cul-ture. We live in a recyclable era, and we have names for what we throw away and recycle in a different way. On one level we call it junk and garbage, on another level we call it second-hand furniture, and on the highest level we call it antiques. At dif-ferent phases in the life of the same thing, as it is recycled, it may be perceived as garbage, as second-hand or as a priceless antique.

One person's junk is another person's treasure! Often treasures come to us, garbed in some other vesture that allows us to see them for what they really are.

All things have a value when they are prized; the game that elevates some things from junk to second-hand to antiques is a game that is played in a lot of fields. One week's hero in the art world is next year's wash-up. Lord knows you can get to feel that way about yourself. You can begin to think that you have no value because you are not popular or not as successful as the next person. Value seems to be so relative that you end up judging yourself in relation to others, and of course you always come up lacking.

The second lesson and the gospel speak as one to this point. The second lesson is Paul's testimony to the process whereby he was declared valuable in the eyes of God. He was chosen, predestined, called into this life together with God in Christ, in order to be glorified; he will know the weight of glory, because the presence of God will penetrate, sustain and support his life completely from past to future. Conformed to the image of Christ by baptism, we all pass through the process which God has in mind for us; we are transformed by the renewal of our minds in Christ. Our value is given us before we begin to search for it; we have been declared valuable and thus we need no longer compare ourselves to others in order to determine our value. The greatest point of comparison has been given to us, and that is our relationship to God, in the light of which nothing and no one is without value.

If we compare ourselves to others, some of us will need to be recycled. The rest of us will wind up either as junk, or as second-hand, or as antiques. But the determination of value will have been our own, and we will go on to market ourselves or to manipulate others into seeing our value or to write advertisements for ourselves. This is the path of delusion.

The gospel bids us to seek for that pearl of great price which is called the dominion of God, a mysterious reality which sounds alive and true and full of hope. We are bothered deep within by the prospect of a life in which we must always be on our toes, comparing ourselves to others in order to discover our value. Yet our only hope is to relinquish this comparison. The dominion of God exists, we know, wherever Christ has created the space for each of us to be most truly ourselves, where our value is underwritten by the love and the creative energy of God, and where we can find our sabbath rest.

The search for the dominion of God is valuable because in the search itself we may find our value. In seeking we find. The object of our search is found on the road. We are tempted to look constantly beyond ourselves, and so we never realize that the search, once undertaken, *is* the fulfillment and the joy which is promised to us. This is a hard saying but it is worthy of note: if we are to pray, then we begin by saying Our Father. If we are to enter the dominion of God, then we begin by entering the dominion of God.

The invitation to enter the dominion of God is perennial and eternal. Christ invites us from a place beyond place and a time beyond time. His invitation comes to us here and now. But the dominion of God comes garbed in some vesture that hides it from us so that we can see it. Come. Let us look.

In the dominion of God, we are all of value. We are all blessed by God to be citizens of this dominion; but since the dominion of God cannot be seen, we have to hear of it in ways that will make us see it even when we cannot see it. We must be invited into the deepest reality which cannot be seen. And so Jesus uses parable to invite us; the dominion of God comes garbed in a vesture that hides it from us so that we can see it.

Again: here is bread and wine. Shortly we shall pick up the bread and the wine, and we shall taste it and take it into ourselves. We shall do this after having been cautioned, if you will, that this bread and wine is something more than bread and wine: something is hidden in, with and under the bread and the wine. It is also body of Christ, it is also blood of Christ poured out for us. Christ comes to us garbed in a vesture that hides his presence from us so that we can see it.

The meaning of this event goes on and on as long as I engage in it. Its meaning is in the seeking. So it is with the whole of the dominion of God. Once you enter it—which you did at your baptism—you have only to live in it and to give thanks. The pearl of great price has been found and you have been called to glory; these truths come together at the eucharistic table. Christ offers himself to you in sacred story and in sacred food in order that you might know yourself valued, blessed and quickened.

It's a kind of a trick to keep you from falling into a place where you can only value yourself in comparison to other people. You have to stay focussed on the road and not on yourself and not on others who are in the road. The Christian community is an odd one, in that its focus is not upon itself, certainly not on self-improvement, but on the praise of God who has come to us in Christ to free us from the pain of creating our own value, who has surprised us with the presence of the One who valued us before we were born. God comes to us garbed in a vesture that hides God's presence from us so that we can see it.

Now look once more at that bread and wine and remember: here Christ and the dominion of God come to you garbed in a vesture which hides them so that you can see them. And, finally, if the truth were to be known, *we* come to this meal garbed in a vesture, the white robe of baptism, which hides us from ourselves in order that we might know who we truly are. And that may be the deepest mystery of them all.

Jay C. Rochelle

R EIGHTEENTH SUNDAY IN ORDINARY TIME
E PROPER 13
L ELEVENTH SUNDAY AFTER PENTECOST

R *Is 55:1–3; Rom 8:35,37–39; Mt 14:13–21*
E *Neh 9:16–20; Rom 8:35–39; Mt 14:13–21*
L *Is 55:1–5; Rom 8:35–39; Mt 14:13–21*

"They all ate and were satisfied," Matthew tells us today. This is a more remarkable statement than it may first appear. Of course, after a good meal one is no longer hungry; there is nothing miraculous about that. But the scriptural context of Matthew's statement suggests more than that common experience of physical satiation.

As Isaiah cried out, "Why do you spend your money for that which does not satisfy? Come, receive wine and milk." Deep, total human fulfillment is a gift received in the mutual presence and affirmation of a loving relationship. It is this which nurtures and deeply satisfies the human heart. The Bible affirms this when it says, "Not by bread alone shall one live." Food alone cannot satisfy, but a meal given in a context of love provides the deepest satisfaction. In such moments there may be an inflow of presence and love to one's deepest being, and one may be strengthened and filled with joy to the core.

It is something like this that Matthew means when he says, "They all ate and were satisfied." The people, longing for the presence and healing and wisdom of God, had followed Jesus out into the wilderness. Single-mindedly they continued to focus their attention on him, forgetting about their practical and physical needs. Seeing their longing and attentiveness, divine love overflowed in Jesus' heart. As Matthew says, "He had compassion on them"; he healed them, fed them, and most of all, rejoiced with them in mutually affirming presence. They were satisfied to the very core of their beings.

Jesus fed and satisfied the people in a communal meal. We now celebrate that same reality in our weekly community eucharist. These are the moments in which Jesus most concretely reaches out to fulfill our longing and to unite us with himself. Yet most of us experience other moments of deep satisfaction as well. Other moments—moments of shared love with spouse, family or friends, moments of contemplative prayer, moments of joy in nature or art—sometimes even seem to have more intensity and power than the experience of the eucharist.

It almost goes without saying that it is important not to be seduced by sheer experiential intensity. Life usually teaches us fairly quickly that intense highs can be illusory, and that following their lead may sometimes lead to disaster. Yet peak experiences of human pleasure and joy can also be one of the ways in which the ultimate and total kind of satisfaction—the satisfaction that can only come from God, and which is given fully in the eucharist—overflows into every corner of God's creation. Every authentic experience of goodness is a participation at some level in the goodness of God.

In fact, for most people human experiences of love and satisfaction are absolutely foundational to the ability to appreciate the love God has for us. A common image of total human satisfaction is the nursing infant in the arms of a tenderly loving mother. Psychologists now affirm that an adequate experience of being lovingly held and fed as an infant lays a foundation for all future love relationships, including the love relationship with God. Just as the infant's experience of love is a foundation for mature loving, so every human experience of fulfillment can point toward the reality of ultimate fulfillment in God.

Yet a mature Christian spirituality also maintains a clear awareness of the unique centrality of the eucharist. It is in the eucharist that Jesus brings diverse peoples into one worshipping community and feeds them with the concreteness of bread and wine, his own body and blood. It is in the eucharist that our own deepest satisfaction is united with the satisfaction of a community that stretches throughout the earth and throughout history. Other peak experiences—even when they are experientially more intense—lack this concrete depth and breadth. Only God can unite total intimacy and total materiality, radical diversity and radical oneness, into a single action. When we do not experience it with such depth, the lack is not in the eucharist, but in our capacity at that moment to experience it fully.

The danger, perhaps, of emphasizing the eucharistic model for our deepest relationship with God is that to some this suggests that the relationship with God is something available only in church and through the hands of the clergy. Indeed, the community eucharist is climactic and central for our love of God. Yet when Jesus said to the disciples, "You give them something to eat," his words echo far beyond the specifically eucharistic setting. To everyone who would be his disciple, in whatever time or place or situation, he speaks: "Let me be present to the people, let me feed their deepest hungers, through you."

Jesus warns all Christian disciples against two equally debilitating attitudes: thinking they can satisfy the world's needs by employment of their own human powers alone, and thinking they have nothing to contribute to anyone's satisfaction, since God alone can accomplish it. A common variation on the latter is the assumption that all that is necessary to fulfill one's discipleship duties is to attend the weekly eucharist where, through the clergy, God feeds and fulfills us.

This passive attitude is equivalent to thinking that all one has to do to maintain a good marital relationship is to be on time for dinner every night. In discipleship, as in marriage, one has to put care into every gesture and word and action, great and small, day in and day out. For Christians the astounding fact is that even though in and of themselves our gestures and words and actions are so often woefully small and inadequate, they can nevertheless be the vehicle for the overflowing compassion of God. Just as Jesus fed the crowds with the five loaves and two fish which the disciples regarded as impossibly little for so many, so God can feed many with our small and hesitantly offered gifts.

Mary Frohlich

R NINETEENTH SUNDAY IN ORDINARY TIME
E PROPER 14
L TWELFTH SUNDAY AFTER PENTECOST

R *1 Kg 19:9a,11–13a; Rom 9:1–5; Mt 14:22–23*
E *Jon 2:1–9; Rom 9:1–5; Mt 14:22–23*
L *1 Kg 19:9–18; Rom 9:1–5; Mt 14:22–23*

Sometimes in trying to understand the Bible, we settle for too little. Often, for example, today's gospel reading is taken to mean only that when the troubles of life assail us, we can prevail over these storms simply by having faith. After all, does not Jesus say as Simon Peter sinks in the sea, "O you of little faith?"

There is a grain of truth in such an understanding; yet to leave it there is to settle for too little. The point of today's gospel reading, as also of the Old Testament selection, is that God is ruler of creation and therefore is to be adored and served. The maker of heaven and earth still governs all that has been made; this is the basis for our worship and the foundation of our hope.

Often we do suffer from too little faith. But the matter is not remedied by sitting ourselves down and resolving to have more faith. Usually that is a futile enterprise designed only to make matters worse. We focus more and more upon ourselves and less and less upon God, as did Peter when he approached Jesus on the sea.

Attentiveness to divine strength and goodness is the remedy for lack of faith. The gospel calls us to look outward, not inward, and thus to behold the glory of God, who is our help.

Note the conclusion of today's story from Matthew. When the storm ceases at the behest of the Lord, the gospel writer reports that "those in the boat worshiped Jesus, saying, 'Truly you are the Son of God.' " The disciples recognize and acknowledge the power of God in the person of Jesus. The Holy One is in their midst; thus fear is transformed into hope.

To know the closeness of God in Jesus is a central insight of the Christian faith. But if we overemphasize that affinity of Jesus to us as human beings, we are in danger of losing something important: the crucial confidence that this one who is near to us is nevertheless vastly different from us. The One we address as the Christ is not merely a human companion with us on our journey of faith, but is the source and sustenance of our faith.

In today's epistle, Paul agonizes over the inability of some people to see in Jesus anything more than a good teacher and moral example. He wants all people to recognize Jesus as someone greater—as the One sent from God, as the Anointed One long expected by devout believers, as "Messiah." So important is this expanded understanding to Paul that the apostle says he would himself be willing to be cursed and cut off from Christ if that would help others see Jesus for who he truly is.

Is our understanding of the One we call Christ so rich, so important to us in our daily lives, that we are in agony because other people think too little of Jesus? Or are we like the disciples during the storm who need our faith in Christ expanded and intensified?

Perhaps that is an important question for each of us to ponder: with whom do I more closely identify in today's New Testament readings? Am I a disciple who cries out in fear for my own life because my understanding of Jesus is too small? Or am I an apostle who cries out in agony at the impoverished faith of others? Like the apostle, would I give up my own fellowship with God if only that could enable others to have the joy of that fellowship in their lives?

These are hard questions; and if we are not satisfied with our answers, that is good. For it is evidence that we see our need to grow in faith. But again let it be emphasized that growth comes not by looking inward and lamenting our lack of faith. Growth comes by concentrating on the goodness, mercy and power of God. Faith is a response to the faithfulness of God. We do not produce faith by deciding to have more of it. But as we witness and identify God's love again and again, faith springs forth within us and flourishes.

Is that not one reason we come regularly to the eucharist? Here the goodness of God is proclaimed, even in the midst of the greatest adversity. The more difficult and tortured our daily lives are, the greater the value of experiencing the grace of God at the holy table. The sacrament is not something we earn the right to receive by being people filled with faith. No! The sacrament announces to us the faithful power of God in the midst of our emptiness; and thus faith grows within us.

One of the ancient writers of the church called the eucharist "the medicine of immortality." So it is not a reward for our strength, but a remedy for our sickness: God's gift, given until we no longer are those of little faith; given freely until we are enabled to be those who see the glory of God and give thanks.

Therefore, let "God who is over all be blessed forever. Amen."

Laurence Hull Stookey

R   *Is 56:1,6–7; Rom 11:13–15,29–32; Mt 15:21–28*
E   *Is 56:1,6–7; Rom 11:13–15,29–32; Mt 15:21–28*
L   *Is 56:6–8; Rom 11:13–15,29–32; Mt 15:21–28*

Today's gospel is not easy to preach. In our minds, Jesus is the epitome of kindness, affirmation and compassion. Others may criticize us, judge us, misunderstand us, but Jesus loves and welcomes us. "Come unto me," Jesus says, "all who labor and are heavy laden," come to loving Jesus.

Except for you Canaanite women. In today's text, Jesus calls everyone to come be part of his dominion. A woman, a Gentile woman, comes to Jesus asking him to heal her mentally ill daughter. She is called a "Canaanite," a curiously anachronistic term which Matthew probably intends to underscore that this person who implores Jesus in not only a woman, but also a Gentile woman, an outsider. She has three strikes against her, as far as the insiders are concerned. Jesus' male disciple know that Israel's Messiah has not come for people like her. "Send her away," they say.

The disciples' rejection of this woman does not surprise us. We can explain their actions. After all, a teacher's disciples do not always hold or exhibit the same enlightened, exalted attitudes as those of the teacher. Many of Jesus' disciples in our day worship in churches where an outsider like this Canaanite woman is excluded or at least made uncomfortable because she is not one of "us."

But the thing which shocks in this text is that not only the disciples but also Jesus excludes. "It is not fair to take the children's bread and throw it to the dogs," he says.

Can it be that Jesus, the same one who said, "Come unto me," is also the one who rejects this pitiful woman as a dog?

I will not try to explain away the abrasiveness of this tough text. The harshness of this episode cannot be explained by saying that Jesus was testing her faith to see if she were really sincere in calling after him, or that Jesus was debating in his own mind whether nor not Gentiles were worthy recipients of the gospel, or that Jesus was using her as a good example of humility for others to follow. It is an embarrassing text.

Of course the stakes are high. And Jesus' actions can be partly explained by noting that this pleading woman was asking Jesus for a great deal. She was asking for the miraculous healing of her daughter. But more even than that, she was asking him to bestow upon her gifts that were not by right hers to claim. If he were the Son of David she addressed him as, the long-awaited Savior of Israel, then Jesus, and the benefits of his kingdom, belonged to those who suffered in Israel, not to Gentile outsiders. There were more than enough suffering people in occupied Judea, enough people in pain, enough trouble souls to be delivered without casting blessed bread toward this Gentile dog.

And it's perhaps right there, there, with this outsider who will not be sent away, that lies the *real* embarrassment of this story. Matthew writes for the insiders, for Israel, Jesus' own people, the children to whom the Bread of Heaven is meant to be sent. And yet, many of these on the inside, who take such smug delight in their inheritance (I tithe, my family helped found this congregation, I never miss a Sunday), fail to see in Jesus the one long-awaited whom this tenacious woman calls "Lord, Son of David." This outsider, this Gentile, this probably poor (because she was a woman) person refuses to be sent away from Jesus. First Jesus ignores her. Then the disciples rebuke her: "Send her away." Then Jesus says, "I wasn't sent for you—I was sent for Israel." But she threw herself before him crying, "Lord, help me." To Jesus' harsh rebuke she sagely replies, "Even dogs are allowed a few crumbs from the children's bread."

"O woman, great is your faith," says Jesus.

And isn't that the real scandal of the text? Great is this outsider's faith. And what about *our* faith? What about those of us on the inside, those of us who are the privileged first recipients of the blessed bread which Jesus brings?

In Korea, I watched people stand in line for three hours in the freezing cold for the privilege of attending one of the four morning services at a Presbyterian church. A friend of mine saw over a hundred persons baptized in a river in Africa, some of whom had walked over twenty miles through the bush for the privilege of baptism. The only food they received to enable them to make the twenty-mile walk back home after the service was the bread and wine of their first eucharist.

And for those of us whom this bread is our birthright, those of us privileged to be "insiders" in the family of faith, an early Sunday morning rain shower is enough to keep us away from church.

This pushy, tenacious, determined, Gentile woman saw in Jesus the nourishment her daughter so desperately needed. Her persistence is an embarrassment. Insiders take note. She hurt, she saw, she refused to be sent away empty-handed. "O woman, great is your faith!" said Jesus.

William H. Willimon

R TWENTY-FIRST SUNDAY IN ORDINARY TIME
E PROPER 16
L FOURTEENTH SUNDAY AFTER PENTECOST

R *Is 22:19–23; Rom 11:33–36; Mt 16:13–20*
E *Is 51:1–6; Rom 11:33–36; Mt 16:13–20*
L *Ex 6:2–8; Rom 11:33–36; Mt 16:13–20*

This word bears identity: God's and ours. Our identity is bound up with the God who addresses the ancient people of Israel, and with the one who questions his disciples at Caesarea Philippi. Yet God is revealed through the mystery of the mundane.

God is hidden within the mystery of a name: I AM. And God is hidden in the riddle of a question: Who do you say that I am? Even a hymn of praise leaves us gaping at the wonder of God: "O the depth of the riches and wisdom and knowledge of God! How unsearchable are God's judgments and how inscrutable God's ways!"

Yet identity is revealed in the mystery of the mundane. As on a day at Caesarea Philippi. Where is Caesarea? It might be anywhere; it is especially where people suffer and cry for a savior.

Come! This word beckons us to mundane Caesarea. Caesarea is a world of wheelchairs. The corridors are full of them. Wheelchairs move in slow motion to the beat of once radical Beatles' tunes, poured like syrup from the Living Strings. Gray-headed bodies slump in chronological disjunction against designer decor. Wilted bodies, enfeebled by a lifetime of two-legged exertion, roll themselves toward distant destinations. An appointment with the hairdresser is like a transcontinental trip. A visit to the physical therapist is like driving in Los Angeles, only more complicated. The traffic in the P.T. room makes the Ventura Freeway look like child's play.

But we are here to worship. We have come for the Lord's Supper: lessons read, prayers prayed, a bit of bread and wine consumed. It is a puny little feast, an almost microscopic meal. Still they come like flies to honey: 25 or 30 chair-bound Christians. Some sit fairly alert, others loll like heaps of boneless flesh: blinking eyes exhibit their only sign of life. A few sleep like babies.

One woman, Ella, flashes in and out of lucidity. Today is a bad day. Today Ella is more out than in. Her mind plays tricks, suddenly transporting her to unknown times and places. When she is lucid, she is right on the money. But when she isn't, she is frightened and paranoid, calling for her mother.

During the sermon, the room becomes hot and uncomfortable. Ella answers rhetorical questions and poses a few of her own. But at last the eucharistic prayer! Then we pray the Lord's Prayer. It is Ella's homing device, her liturgical North Star. The ancient words seem to clear her muddled mind. Even when she doesn't know who she is, she knows this prayer. When she prays it, her world is ordered.

If even for a moment, the prayer has cleared the air. We are all alert and leaning toward Christ, his body and blood. Gnarled hands reach like limbs extended from the grave. Hands reach from death to grasp the bread of life. They are like nestling birds straining for sustenance from their mother's beak, aged children of the kingdom craning to get a bit of bread, a sip of wine. Some eyes shed tears; others shine with the sparkling joy of a child's eyes on Christmas Eve. We are communing in the border country. We are in sight of the Promised Land, teetering somewhere between death and eternity. It is like celebrating the sacrament in some splendidly sacred place. It is like communing in Jerusalem amid glorious strains of the B Minor Mass. It is like heaven on earth.

Until Ella falls out of sacred time. Crying out for her mother, she drags us back to the rest home, back from the B Minor Mass to "Hey Jude" by the Living Strings. As the host is extended, Ella's eyes widen, her nostrils flare, her hands leap in self-defense. She grabs the pastor's arm. "Who are you?" she demands. "Tell me who you are! I'll call the police! Who are you? And what is this? You're trying to poison me!" She begins to weep.

Trying to get free from Ella's clutches, the pastor disturbs her rhythmic sobs. She lifts a contorted face and their eyes meet: "Who am I?" she cries, "Who am I?"

"Ella," the Pastor says, "Ella, you are Ella. And this is the body of Christ."

Ella takes the wafer. She takes it like a timid prisoner, afraid of being tricked. She studies it, tracing its edge with her finger, like a beggar considering the worth of a coin. Suddenly her finger stops, retreats, then probes again the surface. She feels something. It is the imprint of a crucifix stamped on as a sort of pious decoration. She caresses it. She gazes into the distance, and whispers, "Who am I? The body of Christ. Ella. The body of Christ." She eats.

It comes as a revelation from God. It comes as identity for the lost. The Christ of God, present as a gift from God, made known by the mysterious will of God alone. Christ and Ella. Christ and church. We cannot know one without knowing the other.

Jesus asks, "Who do you say that I am?" Peter answers, "You are the Christ, the Son of the Living God!" Then Jesus binds Peter's identity to God and church: "Blessed are you, Simon Bar-Jona: For flesh and blood has not revealed this to you, but my Father who is in heaven. And I tell you, you are Peter, and on this rock I will build my church, and the powers of death shall not prevail against it."

It is not that Peter is so smart, or even that he is so faithful. It is rather that God is so inscrutably gracious. God reveals the Christ even to fickle Peter who in the next paragraph will be Satan!

As with Peter, our identity is not a matter of our own will, but of God's. When it comes to identity, Peter is no different from Ella, and neither are we. When recognition comes, it is God's doing. When faith comes, it is God's gift. Against this identity, death has no power.

"For from him and through him and to him are all things. To him be glory forever. Amen."

Franklin A. Wilson

R TWENTY-SECOND SUNDAY IN ORDINARY TIME
E PROPER 17
L FIFTEENTH SUNDAY AFTER PENTECOST

R *Jer 20:7–9; Rom 12:1–2; Mt 16:21–27*
E *Jer 15:15–21; Rom 12:1–8; Mt 16:21–27*
L *Jer 15:15–21; Rom 12:1–8; Mt 16:21–26*

Most Christians in the United States have the impression that we live in a society that is reasonably favorable toward religion. In many senses they are right, of course. We experience no great persecution for holding our faith. We have an amazing range of freedom to express our religion and to commend it to others.

So it would be easy to conclude that our spiritual situation has very little danger, but this would be a mistake. For one thing, the very openness of our society toward any and all religions can give the impression that it doesn't make much difference what we believe or if we get around to considering the claim of God upon our lives.

But the more serious danger that confronts Christians in the United States is related to the great prosperity and affluence that most of us enjoy. Research has shown that very few Americans think of themselves as well off. There is too much sense of struggle and precariousness in most of our lives for that. But judged by how most of the people on this planet live, the vast majority of Americans, even those who do not have too much, are very well off indeed.

The Bible warns again and again that while God created the world full of good things and good opportunities, nevertheless all of this can become a temptation to spiritual blindness and indifference. We can be so busy with our things, or with our responsibilities, or with our families, that life rushes by and we give little thought to what is deepest or most important. Dare I suggest that such things can happen even to those who faithfully attend church and receive the sacraments? We mean well, but we have so much on our minds that we never quite settle down to thinking about our personal faith in God.

So you see, brothers and sisters, it is not just the crazy street preacher who warns people against the world and all the dangers that it contains. All Christians ought to understand the world's dangers and have a strategy for coping with the difficulty. The lessons for this morning remind us of this very basic point.

Paul, writing to the church in Rome, the capital of the world, a city of luxury and power and diversity, tells the Roman Christians that they must not be conformed to this world. Paul knew that this could happen to nice people, sincere people, well-meaning people, because they did not understand that at the deepest level there is real enmity between the powers of force and greed and lust that dominate every society and the gospel of the righteousness of God in Jesus Christ.

Likewise our Lord, in explaining to those who follow him in every generation that the way of discipleship is the way of the cross, has to warn us as well: Whoever holds on to life will surely lose it. What will it profit us to gain the whole world and lose our souls?

And here is the danger: such a path to destruction begins not with setting out to defy God and to identify with the world in its wickedness and sin. The path to conformity, to worldliness, to spiritual destruction begins with small, seemingly harmless steps. We are busy, we are tired, we are not ready for anything serious, we are just doing our duty. But eventually such small steps and such rationalizations can close our hearts and our minds to being able to hear the word of God at all.

There is a simple test that can help you diagnose your own situation. Ask yourself each day, at some regular time, whether you have remembered in all your doings and all your plans that you are a person who is certain to die. What will it profit any of us to get the raise, to pay off the debt, to take care of the family, to build the extra room, to settle our problems with our neighbors, to put our feet up to rest, if in the process we forget to come to terms with the God who has given us life?

That God comes to greet you in our worship this morning. God has come to the world in Emmanuel, God with us and for us in Jesus. God wants to interrupt us in the best sense of the word, not because God resents our lives and our projects, but because God intends to warn us from danger and keep us on the path to life. And God understands how strong is our temptation to be conformed to the world, to excuse ourselves with the thought that we are acting just like everyone else.

This morning you will receive the sacrament. And in that moment you will be bound into a different reality from the one that dominates our daily routine: the reality of Jesus who as he predicted walked the path of obedience and met his death on the cross. He did not deny that death was coming for him. And yet, in the night in which he was betrayed, he blessed bread and broke it and gave it to his followers, and to all who come after him. And when he rose from the dead he promised that he is with us always and everywhere, to the close of the age.

Do not blame Paul and Matthew for bringing you a warning that could save your life for eternity. Do not resent the interruption that this weekly gathering of the people of God constitutes. Rather, see that both in warning and in forgiving, in loving and in rebuking, in living and in dying, God comes to see that we do not lose our lives but find true life in the world that is restored to us through Jesus' death on the cross.

Timothy F. Lull

R   TWENTY-THIRD SUNDAY IN ORDINARY TIME
E   PROPER 18
L   SIXTEENTH SUNDAY AFTER PENTECOST

R   *Ez 33:7–9; Rom 13:8–10; Mt 18:15–20*
E   *Ez 33:7–11; Rom 12:9–21; Mt 18:15–20*
L   *Ez 33:7–9; Rom 13:1–10; Mt 18:15–20*

Confrontation is really a very difficult thing. Few of us do it well. There are so many escapes. Either we gunny-sack our feelings until we explode or we nag constantly. Sometimes we tell everyone we know about a problem except the one concerned. It is a rare person who can open a tender subject, discuss it reasonably, and then leave it alone.

The problems with confrontation seem to be twofold: too much fear, not enough hope. We are afraid of anger, rejection, another blow from the offender. We cannot arouse enough hope to believe that we can be reconciled.

A wise teacher once told me that to cease to expect anything from a person was the same as condemning that person to death. The person from whom I expect nothing might as well be a post on the side of the road.

Today's readings demand from us expectation when it is most difficult. They demand that we expect goodness from one who has wronged us. Ezekiel shows us a God who is willing to wait until the last minute, who is willing to value the present moment of righteousness more than any and all previous moments of wrongdoing. He shows us a God who demands perseverance from a prophet, who demands that a prophet never give up, never cease to warn a stubborn and rebellious people. Ezekiel show us a God of hope. It is the hope of God which makes possible the forgiveness of God.

The gospel makes the same demand of us. When we suffer wrong, first we must seek reconciliation without proclaiming to the world our own righteousness and the wickedness of the other. We must expect goodness from the other.

If that attempt at reconciliation fails, we still must take only two or three others in order to try again. Only on the third try may we involve the whole community of the church. But still we may not give up. Still we must expect goodness from the other. Only if the third attempt fails, may we write off the other. Only then may we treat the other as a Gentile (an outsider) or a tax collector (an outcast).

However even then we must not forget the passage that immediately follows in Matthew's gospel. Peter asks, "How many times must I forgive?" Jesus answers, "Seventy times seven."

The message today is to hope, to have the greatness of heart to hope even in the one who wrongs us. That is Paul's message about love, the ultimate debt we owe one another. Love supports our patience and creates true peace. It is, in the last analysis, love that never gives up on the other, love that expects goodness even from an enemy.

If to cease to expect anything from another is to condemn that person to death, then to continue to hope in another, even in the face of direct odds, is to gift that person with life. The meaning of our redemption is precisely that God, in the face of all odds, continued to hope in us. God's hope went to such lengths that Christ gave his life that we might be reconciled to God. Christ gave his life in the expectation that we would turn from our wicked ways and live. For God, Ezekiel proclaims, does not delight in the death of the wicked but rather that the wicked turn from their way and live. God's love is the love that overcomes evil, that overcomes death. This is the love that expects everything from us, that gifts us with life. This in turn is the love that we owe another.

Irene Nowell, O.S.B.

R   *Sir 27:30–28:7; Rom 14:7–9; Mt 18:21–35*
E   *Sir 27:30–28:7; Rom 14:5–12; Mt 18:21–35*
L   *Gen 50:15–21; Rom 14:5–9; Mt 18:21–35*

Jesus said that the kingdom is like a king who wanted to settle accounts with his servants. He then told the parable of the forgiving king and the unforgiving servant. It seems obvious that *receiving* forgiveness and *forgiving* are related. But how can we learn to forgive? How can we learn to forgive ourselves? How can we learn to forgive others?

In the parable, the king forgave the servant all of his debt even though it was enormous. That forgiveness meant that the slate was clean, that the servant owed absolutely nothing, that he was accepted as if the debt had never existed. What a gift, what mercy, what grace, what love! One would think that the servant would have felt so good that he could not have done anything but forgive his fellow servant a much smaller debt. But that is not what happened. Why not?

Perhaps what was operative in the life of this servant is something all of us struggle with daily. Even though his debt was forgiven by the king, he could not believe that he was really forgiven, so he could not forgive himself. He was angry with himself because he had failed to pay the debt he owed. His self-image was very low. One way to deal with such anger towards oneself is to project the anger onto someone else. So when another servant came along who owed the first servant some money, instead of being forgiving, he turned all of his angry self-recrimination onto the other person.

Haven't you sometimes had the experience of feeling anger toward yourself because of something you have done and then finding yourself almost inadvertently projecting that anger onto someone else, someone safe, someone who had absolutely nothing to do with the situation, perhaps your child? Here was a safe place for you to vent your anger, which was really anger towards yourself. Our human relationships are so complex, and we all so desperately wish to feel good about ourselves, that sometimes we do very foolish things to try to convince ourselves that we are okay, even if it means angrily putting someone else down in the process.

When we can't believe that we are really forgiven, when we can't forgive ourselves, it is easy to be like the unforgiving servant, isn't it? The unforgiving servant could not believe that he was really forgiven, that his slate was clean, and that he owed absolutely nothing. The unforgiving servant believed that his debt had been merely extended, not forgiven.

But the servant was in fact forgiven, and we are forgiven. We are forgiven: our slates are wiped clean; our debts are paid. No matter what we have done or not done, our God forgives us. And that means that God loves us and accepts us the same as if we were as perfect as Christ, because through Christ we are.

What if we really experienced that forgiveness? Recently my daughter shared with me an experience of being forgiven. When she was a teenager, her youth group spent a New Year's Eve gathered around a fireplace talking together about all that had transpired during the previous year. They concluded the evening by each writing a list of their failures from the previous year for which they wanted to be forgiven. Then each of them brought their lists of failures to the fire. Their adviser was a very wise woman who talked individually with each of them, conveying to them that God would forgive, would erase from their lives these things that they had written on their piece of paper. Just as surely as the fire burned up the piece of paper just so would God erase their failures, and they could start the new year, with a totally clean slate.

Can we believe that we are forgiven? Can we believe that God our King forgives us and gives us clean slates? Can you believe that God our Queen forgives us and wipes away our failures? Can you believe that through Christ we are okay? Can you believe that we are accepted, that we are loved, that we are forgiven?

In the assurance that we are accepted and loved and forgiven, can we not accept and love and forgive ourselves? Then, free from angry self-recrimination, can we not accept and love and forgive others?

Kathe Wilcox and Milton Crum

R   TWENTY-FIFTH SUNDAY IN ORDINARY TIME
E   PROPER 20
L   EIGHTEENTH SUNDAY AFTER PENTECOST

R   *Is 55:6–9; Phil 1:20c-24,27a; Mt 20:1–16*
E   *Jon 3:10–4:11; Phil 1:21–27; Mt 20:1–16*
L   *Is 55:6–9; Phil 1:1–5,19–27; Mt 20:1–16*

Sometimes we don't know what we want. A restlessness grips us, and we are not attentive enough to know that the Spirit of God often moves in us through a discontent with things as they are. So we cover up a seeking of the Spirit with food, noise or some other form of adult pacifier.

The word of God today plays no such games, and will not allow us to play them. It aims right for the target: life, the deepest yearning of the human heart. For Paul, any mention of real "life" is synonymous with his encounter with the real Christ. Somehow in Paul's experience this relationship became the core of what he lived for. This Christ Jesus was the risen one, the Word made flesh, the Word lived out in love.

But we are not Paul, we say. Life means other things for us. There are physical things, psychological things, even spiritual things I must tend to. In the face of our objections, Paul's words may seem like some obsession, granted a magnificent one.

The first reading for today has no mercy on our objections. Real life in its deepest sense comes from the Lord, and we have no alternative but to turn there for it. Life in its fullness is not found in some Thing. It is found in Someone. To hedge on entering that relationship is to settle for a life that is not worth living in its long-term significance.

But relationships are risky, and entering such with Christ Jesus leaves no doubt as to who is "in charge of the estate."

The gospel today speaks of the owner of a vineyard approaching people and making an agreement with them. These people are presented as standing around, waiting for they know not what. At the approach of the owner they are found and freely enter into a working agreement with him that satisfies them and satisfies him. This working agreement happens earlier for some and later for others. It turns out in the story that some are envious because the owner is generous to the latecomers, giving them as much as the early workers agreed to work for.

The parable remains a puzzle for us if we conclude that what is given the workers is some Thing. The parable takes on a new significance if the payment becomes Someone. What if all the workers are rewarded with that portion exceedingly great? It all begins with being found, called, needed. The parable is constructed on relational terms. Perhaps it uncovers for us what we all indeed really want: to belong to Someone. Any other payment pales in comparison. Are we still standing around, or do we already belong to Someone? Is Christ really in charge of our affairs?

We will leave this assembly and go on doing the things we must do for a living. Sometimes these occupations are filled with meaning; at other times we are sick unto death of them. What matters is the Someone in whom we live and move and have our being. What matters is that primary relationship which manifests itself in a life lived out in the truth of authenticity. What matters is life lived out in its deepest sense, human beings as human words for the Word made flesh. There is no room for rash judgment about fellow workers. We simply don't have all the facts about them. There is no room for idlers either, because the charity of Christ presses us in this estate of affairs. Still standing around? Choose life, to the hilt. He has agreed to pay in full.

Carla Mae Streeter, O.P.

R TWENTY-SIXTH SUNDAY IN ORDINARY TIME
E PROPER 21
L NINETEENTH SUNDAY AFTER PENTECOST

R *Ez 18:25–28; Phil 2:1–11; Mt 21:28–32*
E *Ez 18:1–4,25–32; Phil 2:1–13; Mt 21:28–32*
L *Ez 18:1–4,25–32; Phil 2:1–5; Mt 21:28–32*

Who is responsible? The question was frequently asked in racism-awareness workshops and black/white encounters in colleges and universities during the 1970's. At some point in the process, white students would address persons of color and say: "Why are you so angry at us? Are we responsible for what our ancestors did? We are not slave owners. We aren't the ones who kept the vote away. Why blame us?" Locked in their own defensiveness, the white students could not hear the message implicit in their questions: we are not responsible. We are not responsible for racism in society today. We are innocent victims of something our parents did. Look elsewhere, not at us. We are not racist.

The people of Israel were locked in a similar defensiveness in today's first lesson from Ezekiel. "We're not responsible," the people claim. "The fathers have eaten sour grapes, and the children's teeth are set on edge." Parents and grandparents are to blame for the current suffering and exile. The present generation is an innocent victim. Lashing out at God, the people ask, "Why are you so angry with us? You are unjust, O God!"

In response, the word of the Lord through the prophet Ezekiel comes back three-fold: as a welcome word, as a critiquing word, and as an imperative word.

The Lord speaks a welcome word: I am a God of compassion. I do not blame the sins of the ancestors on the children. Each generation is shaped by the heritage of good and bad it has received. But I take no joy or satisfaction in the painful results of human wickedness.

The welcome word becomes a critiquing word: I am a God of justice. I hold all persons accountable for their own actions. Blaming others for what they have done or failed to do is no excuse for personal irresponsibility. There is no evasion for each person's struggle to live faithfully. People are not as guiltless as they claim or imagine.

But finally the Lord speaks an imperative word: I want life and not death. Change is possible. A new heart and a new spirit can come because one is not bound by past generations or even by one's own past sins. Repent and live!

A welcome word, a critiquing word, an imperative word. It was a critiquing word that I heard one day as a woman described how a car owned by a member of her family had been stolen from in front of her house. The car had been stripped, but then found in a run-down neighborhood of Chicago. The man who found the car called a telephone number which he found inside to let the family know the car had been located. As the woman told me the story, she referred to this man, who was black, with a derogatory name. A white man finding a stolen car and taking the time to report it would have been called a hero, a good neighbor. A black man, doing the same thing, was called something demeaning. But the critiquing word came to me in that moment; I said nothing to the woman. Responsible for my own faithful response to the God who created all of humanity in the divine image, I remained silent.

Where could I find what I needed to confront the racism in my own heart and bring a change? What would enable me to repent of sin, that which separates me from brothers and sisters, separates me from myself, separates me from God? Who or what would help me respond to that imperative word of turn and live?

Only Jesus Christ is the source of that new heart and spirit. For sometimes I am the daughter who says, "I will obey," and does not. Other times I am the daughter who says "no" but even yet turns and obeys. Only Jesus Christ accepts the divine will with complete obedience, trust, and respect. It is Jesus Christ who "being in the form of God, did not count equality with God a thing to be grasped, but gave it up, taking the form of a servant. . . . And being found in human form he humbled himself and became obedient unto death, even death on a cross." In Christ alone do profession and practice meet and match.

And it is in baptism, and the reminder of that baptism, that I and you take on Christ. Clothed with Christ, we take on the possibility of a new heart and spirit. Dying and rising with Christ in those baptismal waters, we hear the imperative word become and continue to become a welcome word.

Who is responsible? We are. Who can repent and live? We can, through the victory won for us in Christ Jesus, our crucified and risen Lord.

Kendra Nolde

R   TWENTY-SEVENTH SUNDAY IN ORDINARY TIME
E   PROPER 22
L   TWENTIETH SUNDAY AFTER PENTECOST

R   *Is 5:1–7; Phil 4:6–9; Mt 21:33–43*
E   *Is 5:1–7; Phil 3:14–21; Mt 21:33–43*
L   *Is 5:1–7; Phil 3:12–21; Mt 21:33–43*

The parable in the gospel of Matthew is quite clear. The householder is God. The servants are the prophets. The son is Jesus. The story has to do with the hardheartedness or sinfulness of the people. Later in the gospel, Jesus exclaims, "O Jerusalem, Jerusalem, killing the prophets and stoning those who are sent to you!" Jesus, God's beloved son, receives the same treatment as the prophets who had preceded him. The prophets' messages fall on deaf ears. To the degree that the prophets are heard, they are rejected.

The Jesus story, however, has a different ending to it. The rejected one has become the cornerstone in the new foundation.

Matthew's insight clearly reflects that of a Christian community after the resurrection. The crucified one has been vindicated, and the gospel is now being preached to the Gentiles as well. Matthew understands the parable as referring to Jesus, to Jesus understood in the light of the resurrection. Yet the heart of the parable is about servants of the Lord and the servant par excellence all murdered by the people.

What is it that leads people to respond to God's messengers in this way? Would you and I respond any differently?

There is more similarity between the parable in Matthew and the story in Isaiah than the common image of a vineyard. Isaiah touchingly discloses God's love for the people. "What more could I do for my people than I have done?" asks the Lord. In spite of God's tender love, the vineyard does not produce a good harvest. Isaiah makes it very clear what God wanted: justice. And Isaiah also makes it clear what God received: violence. Injustice and violence are hardhearted responses to God's overtures of care and love.

Likewise in the New Testament parable: not much has changed. Injustice and violence mark the response of the tenants, most dramatically evident in the treatment they give God's own son.

Why are injustice and violence such characteristic responses? And has much really changed? Are we any different from the rotten grapes of Isaiah's vineyard or the tenants in Matthew's parable? We would like to think so. But why do we continue as a people to support or tolerate a nuclear arms build up? Why was Oscar Romero shot? Are we less violent? Would we not do the same as the tenants in the gospel to someone who challenged us forcefully to live justly? Why does the call to justice disturb and threaten us so?

Both Matthew and Isaiah are teaching us about hardness of heart and ingratitude to God. We may well prefer not to see ourselves in the texts. Yet we are there. So much of the Bible and the teaching of Jesus long to turn our hearts of stone into hearts of flesh. God, the compassionate one, longs for us to be compassionate as God is. Why should compassion be so difficult? Why are our immediate responses so often selfish or hostile? What is it in us that makes us proud of being tough?

Perhaps becoming compassionate is dangerous. It can change our lives. It will affect our relationships, in the family, among friends, at work. Some kinds of work may even become less tasteful, even impossible. Compassion will affect our politics. We will not look at some things in the same way any more. No longer will might or bigness or force imply what is right. We will see things through different eyes, as God sees things, and that may require a whole conversion of our hearts and our lives.

Compassion is not weak. It takes strength. Compassion is not foolish. It reflects wisdom. God longs for us to be compassionate because compassion will save us. Compassion keeps us human.

What good does it do if we gain the whole world, feel utterly secure, enjoy all kinds of power, become a success in our work, establish ourselves financially, but lose our soul in the process, find our hearts becoming like stone, and discard our humanity?

We need not be like the tenants in the parable, rejecting the word of the Lord. Today we can allow ourselves to hear that word and act accordingly. As the prophet Micah put it, "God has showed you what is good; to do justice, and to love kindness, and to walk humbly with your God."

Donald J. Goergen, O.P.

R TWENTY-EIGHTH SUNDAY IN ORDINARY TIME
E PROPER 23
L TWENTY-FIRST SUNDAY AFTER PENTECOST

R *Is 25:6–10a; Phil 4:12–14,19–20; Mt 22:1–14*
E *Is 25:1–9; Phil 4:4–13; Mt 22:1–14*
L *Is 25:6–9; Phil 4:4–13; Mt 22:1–10*

We are offered an exceptionally rich fare at the table of the word today. The mystery of the kingdom of God is disclosed as itself being a banquet. God's love excludes no one from the enjoyment prepared for all human beings.

As is the case with all parables, the story which is the gospel for today has but one point. It is that the king sees the banquet hall filled with guests. Doubtless, the story is not about an individual king nor about the kind of beef he served at his table. No, it is about human dynamics, such as preparing a wedding banquet, inviting guests to the feast, refusal by preferred guests, and finally inviting any and everyone so that the party may go on.

In all of this what does this parable tell us about God? God is like the great king who prepared a banquet for the wedding of his son. The wedding is, of course, the union of God with humankind in the person of Jesus of Nazareth. The banquet is an apt symbol of the fulfillment which comes to human beings by reason of their share in that ineffable union. The mystery expands when we see the invited guests refuse to come to the banquet. Somehow refusal on the part of preferred guests is related to the further call of any and everyone from the highways and byways to be guests of the king. This astounding turn of events illustrates just how wonderful God's deed can be.

To what does the parable call us who hear it? What will accepting the invitation cost us? To share a meal with anyone presumes a commitment to the person whose guest we are. It includes subscribing to the meaning of the occasion being celebrated. For us to say yes to God's invitation on this Sunday means being willing again to put on the mind of Christ and to follow his mode of behavior. This may entail having our usual set of values turned upside down in some area of our lives where we do not expect it. In some area it will involve a new dying in order to enjoy fuller life in the power of Christ.

The first reading from Isaiah 25 in its own way also opens up to us the deeper meaning of food and of celebration. This selection is part of a song sung at the celebration of a victory that Israel achieved. It speaks of juicy, rich food and pure, choice wines. It then leads into the deeper meaning of that food and drink when it reveals what God has done and will do for the people. On this mountain of worship, the Lord will destroy the covering and the veil which cover all nations. The covering hinders vision of what is right, and the veil entangles them so that they are unable to do even what they do see as right. The words: "This is the LORD, for whom we have waited," indicates that the people recognized God as being in their midst. Their faith helped them realize that their celebration was authentic. Salvation for them was experienced both as an accomplished fact and an on-going reality, since the "hand of the LORD will rest on this mountain."

Psalm 23, which was so much loved by the earliest Christians as well as their Jewish ancestors, is a most appropriate response to the first reading today. We realize anew that our Shepherd has been leading us safely. That God spreads a table for us in the sight of our foes is particularly apropos in the view of the victory sung about in the Isaiah text. Their striking appropriateness gives the words an added dynamism which can evoke profound gratitude and acceptance.

One aspect of our Judeo-Christian experience is the sense of continuity. This is part of keeping memorial. Within this experience connections are made spontaneously. On a day like today, it is quite natural for us to sense that Jesus is our food, the Living Bread come down from heaven. The cup of pure choice wine becomes the cup of the new and everlasting covenant in his blood. Once again the act of making such connections contains a hidden power to move hearts to be more fully open to the word of God.

It is certainly the Holy Spirit that directed the choice of the selection from Philippians. It would not have happened by pure chance. Placed between two banquet readings, this selection sheds a significant light on the table of the word of God today. Beyond any doubt, Paul knew both hunger and plenty during his missionary career. He had learned to cope with either one, and he knew that neither of them could separate him from his goal. He appreciated the help offered by his beloved friends. "My God will supply every need of yours according to the divine riches in glory in Christ Jesus." This line ties it all together, opening the view to a magnificent panorama. The food in both readings actually becomes Jesus Christ. And that leads us into the eucharistic liturgy per se, realizing that our own every-day life is being caught up into the glory of our God and Father for unending ages.

This reality of having our ordinary life become part of the glory of God calls us to the eschatological banquet. This term stands for the end time to which we look during these final weeks of the church year. We mention the final coming of Christ specifically in the eucharistic prayer, as we anticipate the end "when he comes again." We enter into the end of time when we make it part of the anamnesis in this way.

Finally, there is the great doxology which brings today's event to its high point and carries everything we do on this earth into the glory of God. We do share the joy and the fulfillment which is the kingdom of God.

Mary Pierre Ellebracht, C.Pp.S.

R *Is 45:1,4–6; 1 Th 1:1–5a; Mt 22:15–21*
E *Is 45:1–7; 1 Th 1:1–10; Mt 22:15–22*
L *Is 45:1–7; 1 Th 1:1–5a; Mt 22:15–21*

There is at least one word in the English language that has the power to elect politicians to high office, finance battleships, cause economic hardship, and get you to pull your hair out of your head. One word. Wars have been fought over this word, nations established, and people sent to jail for not taking heed when this word was spoken. The word is taxes!

Someone has said that there are only two things that we can be certain of in this life, and they are death and taxes. As Christians, we know that Jesus has conquered the first. But what of this second anathema that we face? The gospel seems to indicate that we are on our own and that Jesus expects us to pay them. "Render therefore to Caesar the things that are Caesar's," says our Lord, "and to God the things that are God's." Has Matthew, from the tax collector's office, been whispering in Jesus' ear?

A number of questions come to mind. First, who started these taxes anyway? My guess is that from when we first began to inhabit this earth, some sort of taxes were taken. But they were not part of God's order of things. Nowhere in the Genesis account do we read "and God levied taxes on Adam and Eve, and it was good." Nor was Moses given a tablet of stone with the inscription, "Thou shalt pay thy taxes." Taxes were levied and taxes were collected, but from the beginning they were a human invention for the necessity of earthly rulers, the building of temporal roads and aqueducts, and the financing of battles of the flesh and not of the spirit.

Yet, God has always required a rightful share for the work of God's dominion. The first fruits of every harvest were set aside by the early people of Israel for the Lord. Even a temple tax was established and gathered by the priests for the maintenance of the religion. Is this why Jesus seems to support the payment of taxes?

Perhaps it has something to do with his birth. As God would have it, not coincidentally, the Savior of the world was born where he was born because of a decree issued by Caesar Augustus "that all the world should be taxed (Luke 2:1 KJV)." If God wanted to be certain to enter this world clearly at its center, there could be no better time than at the taking of a census for purposes of taxation. Joseph went to be enrolled with Mary, and thus obedient subjects of Roman rule place the Christ child's birth where God has ordained and the prophets of old have promised: in Bethlehem.

Our gospel lesson picks up where that enrollment left off, with a conversation some thirty years later that all three synoptic gospels record, suggesting just how significant it was. On the surface, we have a simple story. A plan devised by the Pharisees and Herodians would trap the popular rabbi from Galilee. Should Jesus advise the paying of taxes, many Jews would consider him a collaborator to the Roman powers. But, non-payment would be dangerous, since followers of Herod would accuse him of sedition.

With a coin, Jesus appears to foil his enemies on both sides. Taxes are for Caesar, but those imprinted with God's image are for God. In one master stroke, Jesus is saved from both pious accusation and political self-incrimination.

But, for those who would hear it, the Man for Others is not interested in a crafty escape from the hands of his foes. He is mindful rather of their escape from the snares of this world. As our Lord reveals again and again in his life and words, his is not a preoccupation with self but with the life of his listener. He is forever waiting and watchful for the moments of grace when he can restore us to our rightful relationship with our Creator.

The master teacher does this skillfully wherever he finds us, revealing the eternal life that is ours in the simple things of each day's journey, be it birds of the air, wandering sheep, or kernels of grain. He lifts them up and reveals their secrets, for in them are hidden all of the answers we seek. He points to rocky soil, a city on a hill, or a fisherman's net and tells us who we are or what we can become. And today, he does it with the Roman forged coin of a day's wage.

"Show me the money for the tax," he says. "Whose likeness and inscription is this?" "Caesar's" they reply. "Render therefore Caesar the things that are Caesar's, and to God the things that are God's."

Our Lord is not telling us what we already know, namely that our taxes ought to be paid. He is also not telling us that payment to God is due. Rather, he is revealing to us who we are, what we are, and what we can be with a coin. This is what you work for and what you slave for. You have come to believe that this coin is the measure of your value, the symbol of your worth.

But the true measure of your value has to do with the likeness and inscription borne on your bodies and souls. As Caesar has cast the denarius in his image, God has cast each of you in God's own image. As Caesar sends out as wage and calls back in tax, God also sends out the bearers of God's likeness to be the golden coinage of a heavenly realm. But God also calls us back, demanding for God's own self the sum of our lives.

Jesus is the gatherer of this tax, God's collector of souls stamped with the divine image and inscribed with God's name. Come to me, he says. By your following, you will find your true self. In my words I will show you the way to the One who has made you. On my cross I will settle your debts. Lost coins are we all, and in Jesus has God invited us back to the eternal treasury.

Bruce J. Evenson

R THIRTIETH SUNDAY IN ORDINARY TIME
E PROPER 25
L TWENTY-THIRD SUNDAY AFTER PENTECOST

R *Ex 22:20–26; 1 Th 1:5b–10; Mt 22:34–40*
E *Ex 22:21–27; 1 Th 2:1–8; Mt 22:34–46*
L *Lev 19:1–2,15–18; 1 Th 1:5b–10; Mt 22:34–40*

The lawyer who asked Jesus which of the commandments of the law was the greatest received an answer that was a touch of both the familiar and the new. The Pharisee simply wanted to engage Jesus in a debate about which of the 614 commandments of the law were "great" and which were of lesser consequence. It was not an uncommon topic among the rabbis.

Jesus' response was, in part, no surprise. He identified two of the commandments—the love of God and the love of neighbor—as among the "great" ones. But he linked them to one another and to the whole of the law and the prophets in a completely unexpected way. Jesus claimed not only that these two commandments function as the principle of interpretation for the entire law in all its complexity, but also that the love of neighbor "is like" the love of God.

We have heard it so many times that the import of this paradigmatic expression of the good news may deafen us as much as it astounded the Pharisees and Sadducees. We tend to smile comfortably and nod our agreement when we hear the account of Jesus' reply to the lawyer. Yes, the most important thing in life is our love for God. We are to love God with our whole heart, our whole soul, our whole mind. God is the one who gets all of us. And we also must love our neighbors as ourselves. The second is implied, as we so often say, in the first. If we love God, we will love those whom God loves. The greatest commandment is, therefore, really two: love God and love one another. Everything else depends upon these two.

But if this is our understanding of Jesus' answer, we have only begun to plumb the depths of Jesus' comment that the second "is like" the first. Jesus did not simply mean that the command to love our neighbor as ourselves is the proof of our love of God. Nor did he say that the command to love one another "is similar to" the command to love God. He told us that the commands are inseparable. Jesus has told us that there is no love of God that is not at the same time the love of one's self and one's neighbor.

We do not merely illustrate or demonstrate our love of God in our love for one another; it is only in and through the love we bear for one another and for self that we actualize our love for God. The love of self and of neighbor is, we might say, the sacramental cause of the love of God. It is the expression and realization of our response to God's prior love for us. Our "Yes" to God is a "Yes" to self and others. The invitation to embrace the infinite is a call to unconditional surrender in the midst of the finite. We taste and touch eternity in our everyday human loves.

The love we bear for Jesus is, of course, paramount. In Jesus we love the human other who is in the depths of his person one with God. Our love for this infinite finite one, our love for the one who is in his person the unity of the divine and the human, is the prime instance and ultimate fulfillment of the great command of which he spoke.

The command to love God with one's entire self, the command to love one another as one's self, the command to love Jesus, is the one thing necessary. But it is the command to love with utter abandon at all times. It is the command to love without limit. It is the command to love as the Spirit of God loves. It is the command to let the Spirit love in us.

What would it mean if we actually believed that the Love that is the Spirit of the Father of Jesus lives in us as God's personal gift enabling us to love one another? What would it mean if we actually believed that our love for one another is one with our Spirit-empowered love for God?

What would it mean if we actually believed that the love we know from each other is one with the love that is God's Breath? What would it mean if we actually believed that the affection offered us in the ordinary little exchanges of life were one with

the affection that bonds Jesus and the Father? What would it
mean?

Barbara Finan

R   THIRTY-FIRST SUNDAY IN ORDINARY TIME
E   PROPER 26
L   TWENTY-SIXTH SUNDAY AFTER PENTECOST

R   *Mal 1:14b-2:2b,8–10; 1 Th 2:7b-9,13; Mt 23:1–12*
E   *Mic 3:5–12; 1 Th 2:7–13,17–20; Mt 23:1–12*
L   *Mal 2:1–2,4–10; 1 Th 2:8–13; Mt 23:1–12*

The San Damiano cross, that famous cross before which Francis
of Assisi prayed, is quite different in style from the familiar cruci-
fixes hanging in most or our homes and churches. It is actually a
Byzantine-style painting on a cross-shape which portrays Jesus
crucified, and surrounding him there on the cross are various
figures: John, the beloved disciple, Mary his mother, and the
other Marys, with angels looking on. Even in death, as in his
public life, Jesus is the center of a community, the focus of a
crowd, the hub of a circle of disciples. He drew people to him
with words and deeds of love, he bade them love one another,
and by his death and resurrection he became the bond between
them, forming them into a body by the power of the Spirit.

"Love one another," he said. It has been repeated down through
the ages, by Paul, by John, by Augustine, by every saint and
preacher and teacher the church has known. Love is the hall-
mark of the Christian, and the greatest in the reign of God is the
servant, the one who acts humbly, the one who centers on Jesus
and lives toward others as Jesus did.

"Why, then, do we break faith with one another?" The plaintive
question of the prophet Malachi echoes in our time as well as his
own. Why do the priests of Malachi's era cause people to lapse
by their teaching? Why do the prophets of Micah's time lead

people astray? Why do the scribes and Pharisees lay on heavy burdens, lord it over others, climb on the backs of others to raise themselves up?

"Why, then, do we break faith with one another?" Why do marriages fail and friendships grow old? Why do we belittle each other, betray each other, exploit each other, fear each other, torture each other, kill each other? Why do we, who were born for loving, for union with our God and one another, kill love?

Some would call the root ill of humanity, the wound that throbs within us, "alienation." Deep within us, we are at war with ourselves. As Thomas Merton writes, "The peculiar pain of alienation . . . is that nobody really has to look at us or judge us or despise us or hate us. Whether or not they do us this service, we are already ahead of them. We train ourselves obediently to hate ourselves so much that our enemies no longer have to."[14]

What we most want, love and union, we go after in disordered ways. Our lives become a constant reaching for ways to fill or to hide our neediness, ways that lead often enough away from God and our neighbor in a spiraling path downward and inward to the dark cell where we keep ourselves imprisoned. Like the little creature hidden in the conch shell, we hide away behind a carefully built and impressive exterior, presented as the "real" us. "See me! See how well I dress, how carefully I follow rules, how many important people I know, how often I am right, how willingly I help others, how much knowledge I have, how 'together' I am."

Why do we break faith with one another? Is it that we are wicked? Were the priests of Malachi's time, the prophets and rulers of Micah's day, the Pharisees of Jesus' time, and are we here and now bad people? No, not bad, but often not worthy of imitation, as Jesus pointed out. Not bad, but wounded and out of touch with the truth of God's love for us and our relatedness to one another.

Jesus, who was sent to us as a healer, calls all of us out of our glorious-looking shells, whatever they're constructed of, because with God's power and love we don't need them. Jesus shows us that we can, as the apostle Paul puts it, live unassumingly, unafraid to humble ourselves in love.

There's a story about a disciple who went to his master, a wise and holy man, to seek his wisdom. "Master," begged the disciple, "teach me how to love." The master answered, "You can no more make yourself love than you can make the sun rise." "Then why," responded the disciple, "do we spend so much time observing the commandments and doing good works?" "Ah," said the master, "That is to ensure that we will be awake when the sun rises."

When the sun rises, we will see ourselves in a crowd, with Jesus, who is the bringer of God's love, at the center. We will see ourselves bonded to one another, and we will have no need of shells, of honor, titles, recognition. We will not live at others' expense, but we will keep faith with one another, because of the one who remained faithful to us, even to death on a cross. The sun rises here at this eucharist, banquet of love. Do you see? Here we can recognize ourselves as one body, here we are taught about and taste of God's great gift of love in Jesus.

Fed and strengthened we are sent forth, awake, with a new capacity for receiving the gift and for giving it to one another.

Janet Schlichting, O.P.

[14]Thomas Merton, *The Literary Essays of Thomas Merton*, ed. Patrick Hart (New York: New Dimension, 1981), p. 382.

R THIRTY-SECOND SUNDAY IN ORDINARY TIME
E PROPER 27
L TWENTY-FOURTH SUNDAY AFTER PENTECOST

R   *Wis 6:12–16; 1 Th 4:13–18; Mt 25:1–13*
E   *Am 5:18–24; 1 Th 4:13–18; Mt 25:1–13*
L   *Am 5:18–24; 1 Th 4:13–14; Mt 25:1–13*

At midnight came the cry: "The Bridegroom is coming!" The cry fell on the ears of both foolish and wise. Everyone had to be awakened. Ten maidens sleeping. Not a one awake and watching. All were sleeping. What made the foolish to be foolish was their lack of oil. What made the wise to be wise was their flasks of extra oil.

The foolish were foolish because they expected everything to be on schedule. No delays. The foolish didn't anticipate a sudden change of plan. They didn't prepare for every possible contingency so as to insure their presence at the feast. They didn't realize that this feast was *everything,* that to be *there* called for investment of one's total being and every resource—surplus included. The foolish didn't know the importance of the meal.

What now are the expectations of your heart? How do you rank *this* feast? Are you here for a taste, or are you here to be dazzled by a foretaste? Foolish are you, or are you wise? And while we together suspect that the five and five somehow live within each of us, we are the wiser when we know too that the foolish ones today are still those who expect delay, who risk tentative investment in other interests. To be foolish like that is easy. Waiting for nineteen hundred years doesn't compel one to a tiptoe posture of expectation. We expect delay, and we have become experts at ordering interests, necessities, and the surpluses of life accordingly.

Are you here for a taste, or are you here to be dazzled by a foretaste? Taster's choice.

Who knows why the foolish didn't come better prepared? Obviously they had no idea the bridegroom would be delayed. In fairness it might be suggested that according to their best estimates the scenario would unfold with the speedy arrival of the bridegroom, a magnificent feast, and bride and bridegroom living happily ever after. For the ill-prepared five, the end of the feast probably meant: home, rest, and awakening to another day filled with a whole new schedule for tasting and feasting. Prudence would suggest keeping some resources in reserve—at home. So many feasts, so many opportunities, and oil needed for them all. And one maiden sang to another: bring the lamps, bring the flasks, let's drop in for a taste.

You don't have to be a party animal to be foolish. Are you here just for a taste? For a morsel the size of which in a convoluted way is a sign of your own diffuse gluttony of purpose and interest? Then hear the hard word: the delay of the bridegroom and the suddenness of his return is matched only by the abrupt shutting of the door. The day of the Lord cannot be wished away, especially by the foolish who habitually look for one feast more, one taste more to satisfy their nagging hunger.

Expecting a delay, we are all tempted to look here, there and everywhere for a taste of something, of something—how should we say—divine. Foolish ones come here seeking a morsel of god-stuff, a welcome change from the week's agenda. Foolish ones, we seek here a morsel which will supply relief from the complexities of schedule and vocation. A taste among many. A taste among so many more anticipated and sought. A taste for me while I retreat for a moment from dedication to the festival of life. Bridegroom delayed? Then let me enjoy the taste of the churchly community, or the taste of prestigious bureaucratic profile. Let me enjoy the mystery-filled ritual of it all; or let me taste the flickering lights, or the holy sounds of the ages. Are you here for a taste?

What makes us inclined to the detached, momentary sampling is the alluring ease of it all. But the delights of the foretaste are never savored. The bridegroom is never met. The wise were wise because they brought a flask of extra oil. Large quantities of oil in single flasks. It didn't matter that there might be other feasts, other seeming purposes to life. These had no value.

There was nothing else for which to save the oil. This feast was everything. This bridegroom was worth feasting with. And so they were wise. Even if he should be delayed.

From practiced lethargy today the liturgy calls us to be dazzled by foretaste. To be wise today is to receive the power of the signs. The wise among us see not a community dedicated to occasional charity or to routine pleasantry. The wise, blinded to all else, see starved sinners receiving satisfying signs of the presence of the bridegroom, nourished by his very body and blood. The wise hear the call of the future at this end of the church year, at this end of time, knowing that the design of it all is given. Here is the bread and wine. No need to snack at other meals, to explore the empty promises of other feasts. The wise hear the call of the liturgy: "until he comes as victorious Lord of all."[15] The wise grasp such promise as comfort; they know this meal as the most inclusive in town, embracing not only saints and angels but all those who have fallen asleep in the Lord.

Hear the claim of the liturgy, for it is power to be wise.

Are you here for a taste, or are you here to be dazzled by foretaste? Bedazzled ones are wise and—wonder of wonders—in their bedazzlement discover their flasks to be full of oil.

Mark P. Bangert

[15]*Lutheran Book of Worship*, p. 71.

R   *Prov 31:10–13,19–20,30–31; 1 Th 5:1–6; Mt 25:14–30*
E   *Zeph 1:7,12–18; 1 Th 5:1–10; Mt 25:14–15,19–29*
L   *Hos 11:1–4,8–9; 1 Th 5:1–11; Mt 25:14–30*

Several television commercials underscore one of the purposes of the parable of the talents. The caption for these commercials is "a mind is a terrible thing to waste." The viewer is transported into a series of scenes in which an obviously talented student is faced with the reality that his or her family is unable to pay for college education. In one of these commercials the request for financial support for black colleges is made by Leontyne Price, the renowned opera singer, whose artistic gifts were discovered and nurtured in racial-ethnic minority institutions, the black church and the black college. Would the artistic gifts of Ms. Price have been lost if these nurturing environments had not been available for her? How much God-given talent is being lost because of societal marginalization induced by poverty?

The mind, a gift of God, is indeed a terrible thing to waste. Any misuse or underuse of capabilities directly contradicts that which is required of us. The parable of the talents underscores the requirement that humanity should not bury any gift, any talent, no matter how small it may appear. The Lord will return unannounced, like a thief in the night, and will expect increased returns on our gifts. What, then, of the contemporary youth, gifted and willing, and yet faced with obstacles which are not of his or her own creation? How is God speaking through this?

We turn first to the gospel lesson, not to find answers to questions that we raise, but to listen for the word of the Lord. The parable must be understood in the light of the historical context of the story. The Jewish community, steeped in the law and its understanding of the truth and the demands of God, was under heavy burden of accountability. Strict accountability created a need for the religious leaders, the scribes and the Pharisees, to guard the law, to protect it intact, in preparation for the return of God. By their method of conserving and protecting the law, religious truth became paralyzed, partially understood by a few, unclear to most of the faithful. Like the single talent the truth was buried in the ground.

Too often talents are measured by the standards of one culture and then superimposed upon other cultures. Such measurement has discouraged many persons from discovering their own particular talents and usefulness in society. The gospel message is clear: each child of God is of worth and of value in God's holy purpose. Each person has something to offer for the good of the whole. These gifts are best identified when individuals feel comfortable, wanted loved and needed. People need assurance of their "somebodiness" in order to develop to their fullest.

The three men involved in the parable already had a sense of their somebodiness. They knew they were servants of a particular lord, bondservants entrusted with the property of their master, each according to his ability. Our gifts are gifts of grace. We are all bondservants entrusted with talents that are not ours. It matters not what talents one has. What matters is how one uses them. God never demands more from us than our abilities allow. What God demands is that one uses to the fullest what one possesses. As servants of God we are expected to return, with interest, the talents that have been entrusted to us.

The assumption is that we first accept what is given as a precious gift from God. We consecrate the talents to the glory of God and set diligently about using them. It is not our purpose to compare our gifts with others enviously and to limit ourselves to meager tasks. Our gift may be the ability to plant seeds of justice which can yield immeasurable harvest. One simple word spoken, one act of kindness, a life of love! Who can judge your particular talent in a world open to investments for peace? The contemporary environment is so constituted by the love of God that our one seed planted in fertile soil will germinate and flourish to the glory of the kingdom of God. When the master returns, unexpectedly, like a thief in the night, we might be lauded for breaking new ground. The Almighty requires of us the hazards of paths untrodden. God's "Well done" is our compensation for the tireless labor of using our gifts. Equally with artists, sculptors, or musicians using their talent to the glory of God, the ordinarily talented farmer and worker for justice and peace are also bondservants. To each faithful bondservant comes a place in the kingdom.

Finally, Jesus warns the hearer of the dangers in being the useless servant. The failure of the servant lay in his fear. The one who, even with one talent, did not risk using it for the common good is condemned for blaming God and others for this failure. It is better to venture forth with what one has and fail than to try nothing and live an empty life. To such a person can be traced much of the void and lackadaisical attitudes of society. The one-talented man in the story could not see that his talent was of value to God and humanity.

The good and faithful servants viewed God not as an officer of the law catching them in wrongdoing, but as one who freed them to invest their gifts. Life is much like a fertile field waiting to be tilled. They dared to venture into the openness of the field with open minds. They were faithful and persistent. They believed that hard labor in the use of their gifts was good for them. The ancient proverb of the Kikuyu of East Africa, "Kuguru ni irata thi," translates literally "the foot goes all over the world," or "it is perseverance that prevails." Devotion and faith require risks and daring if one is to persevere.

The good and faithful servants received surprising rewards. Rather than receiving license to sit back and relax, they were given greater tasks to do. Such is the reward of the new covenant in Jesus Christ. When we neglect opportunities to plant and nurture the Christian seed, opportunities will be cut off. If we trust in the protective love of God and remain open to possibilities, our own capabilities will yield increase. Any gift of grace provides an opportunity for divine investment. Enter into the joy of Christ and receive the glad greeting, "Well done, good and faithful servant." Anyone may receive this greeting, for each person is talented. Together, much can be accomplished to the glory of God!

Melva Wilson Costen, Ph.D.

L TWENTY-SEVENTH SUNDAY AFTER PENTECOST

L *Jer 26:1–6; 1 Th 3:7–13; Mt 24:1–14*

Her breath was labored; it came with rasping difficulty. I sat at her bedside watching, waiting and praying. Would this breath be her last? Would this sigh be her giving up of the spirit?

It was a strange and holy experience to sit at the deathbed of my mother. At one point, I went to the nursing station to talk with the head nurse. "What are the signs? What do you look for? How will you know that her death is imminent?" I asked. The nurse smiled, shrugged and responded, "Each time is different. Sometimes the breathing just gets increasingly shallow. Extremities get colder. The eyes get less responsive."

We stood together in silence for a few moments. "So what do you think?" I asked. "How long will it be for my mother?" Again she smiled, shrugged and responded, "I don't know."

I went back into my mother's room and sat beside her. Her left hand loosely gripped the bed's metal frame. I leaned over and lightly kissed her hand. Her hand was pale and cold.

Similar questions of discerning the end dominate today's gospel. The disciples asked Jesus for signs of his coming, omens of the end of the age. Jesus may have smiled and shrugged as he responded, for his answer was not very precise. He urged the disciples to take heed, observe the birth pangs of the end and be watchful. His response was full of dire warnings of false messiahs, war, famine and love grown cold.

This 27th Sunday of Pentecost is observed only occasionally. In those years wherein Easter is especially early, the season of Pentecost embraces fully half the year. This year we have thus moved through an especially long season of green. We have journeyed through Sunday after Sunday of lessons exploring discipleship, with its frequent motif of "how shall we live?" In this next to the last Sunday of the church year, as Christ the King Sunday looms, as we prepare to enter anew into Advent's themes of anticipation and second coming, we stand astride the turning of the cycles. Matthew's text points us already toward Christ's return. The question is not so much how shall we live, but how shall we wait?

How shall we wait? I asked questions of a nurse about the imminent death of my mother. The disciples asked questions of Jesus about the close of the age. Both sets of questions sought signs, clues and warnings. In a subtle way, such questions seek to resolve the tension by putting the questioner in control. We seek certainty and signs so that we may be sure. But that is not how we are called to wait.

How shall we wait? Jesus' approach to his own imminent death offers us clues as to how we wait for the closing of the age. Jesus' waiting centered upon community, prayer and the meal.

Jesus' discourse about the signs of the end was spoken in the context of the close community of the disciples. The same community surrounded Jesus as he waited and watched for his own coming death. Each of us comprise a part of the baptized community of God's people. In the presence of that community we find encouragement and support, mutual conversation and consolation. In the community of the church we are sustained amidst the birth pangs of the coming age. In the community of the church we are taught about the Christ in distinction from false messiahs. In the community of the church we are hospitably welcomed into the presence of Christ rather than being led astray.

Jesus' own anticipation and waiting for the end was marked by prayer. His prayer was for the community and for himself. As individuals and within that community we similarly pray. While that prayer might often take the shape of seeking to discern the signs of the end, at its deepest level that prayer is simply and profoundly a relationship with Christ. Within our prayer we live in relationship with God as we seek to be watchful, to take heed. By our prayer, in the midst of the birth pangs of the end, we intercede that we may be saved from the time of trial.

On the night before his death, surrounded by community and upheld in prayer, Jesus shared a meal with his disciples. In the community of the church, similarly gathered in prayer, we share the meal which proclaims Christ's death "until he comes." The eucharistic meal, this foretaste of the feast to come, is also among the signs of the close of the age. This meal of bread and wine points to the end of time to the dominion of God. It is a meal of hope and joy which stands in contrast to the horrors and devastations that Matthew's apocalypse describes.

Jesus described the signs of the end; and, of course, they define our age. All of us know events or circumstances which like earthquake, famine, war, or "love grown cold" threaten to shatter our lives, our selves. It may be the death of a parent or a spouse. It may be the deterioration of a relationship. It may be famine or war. It may be faith grown cold. Yet precisely in the midst of those events that threaten to overwhelm and shatter us we encounter the Shattered One who calls us forth to new life, new beginnings. And this one calls us forth from the cross, from the very place that would appear to be the ultimate site of devastation. We are called forth to new life and new beginnings by the one who in the midst of our turmoil and torment invites us to take and eat. The Crucified One recalls the image of the psalmist: in the presence of our enemies you prepare a table.

How shall we wait? We are called to wait as if beside a death bed. We are called to wait in confidence and trust that it is Christ who is in control, and not ourselves. We are called to wait in joy and hope, knowing that nothing—neither birth pangs of the coming age, nor tribulations, neither wars, famine, earthquakes, nor even death—can separate us from the love of God in Christ Jesus our Lord. We are called to wait amidst the community of the baptized, gathered in prayer, to be sustained and nurtured by Christ's own body and blood until he comes again at the end of the age.

Stephen M. Larson

R   LAST SUNDAY OF ORDINARY TIME, CHRIST
     THE KING
E   PROPER 29
L   CHRIST THE KING, LAST SUNDAY AFTER
     PENTECOST

The feast proclaims Christ as our king. But we must ask, how
can he be king for us in a land that knows no king, no queen, in
a nation founded in a revolutionary war against a distant and
unjust monarch? How can Christ be king for us when our only
experience of royalty is the folklore of Camelot and the weddings of Westminster?

Certainly in ages past, when monarchs ruled the West and
claimed the right to do so by divine will, the notion of Christ as
king could strike a responsive chord in the hearts of men and
women. But who among us today would entrust our lives, our
love, our trust, our very hope against death to a god clothed in
the heavy mantle of an ancient monarch?

How can he reign for us, be king for us? Indeed, how is it that
Christ truly reigns in the midst of a vast world in which so many
do not know nor even care to speak his name?

Some would suggest that we simply translate the meaning of
monarchy into the language of the modern world, and there we
will find the way to worship him as our king. But if we do so,
Christ only becomes the absolute power who demands our be-
grudging obedience, the judge before whom there is no appeal,
the political leader whose term of office limits the good to be
accomplished, the schemes to be hidden. It seems that neither
Camelot nor Congress will do.

The biblical word, however, offers us another vision of majesty
and power, a word and a vision so out of character with modern
notions of "leadership" and "charisma" that it begs a hearing.
"The lost I will seek out," says God our Shepherd, "the strayed I
will bring back, the injured I will bind up, the sick I will heal."
Against all our images of stern authority and capricious power,
we hear the Lord's voice, the voice of the shepherd who tends

the scattered sheep of the flock. We hear the voice of the one who judges us, not by our strength nor our cleverness nor our ability to keep the laws of the land, but by the depth of our need. And so the words of the psalm roll off our lips, "The Lord is my shepherd, I shall not want."

But in Jesus, even this image of shepherd-king is turned upside down in that mysterious wisdom of God. For as we know, the shepherd becomes the very lamb who is led to the slaughter, who is led to the cross, who, by entering into the death of Adam, embraces all our deaths before they have even claimed us, so that our sickness and our injury, our final enemy is at last put to death in his body on the cross. We see that this one, brothers and sisters, this Jesus whom the feast praises as king is, in fact, like no other king that has ever reigned. For the feast, the gospel, and the holy meal proclaim him king where we least expect it: in the depth of our yearning for life, our suffering, and our need. And in this he is no ordinary king.

If, then, we would look for his reign in this world, we need only hear his word: "I was hungry, and you gave me food, I was thirsty, a stranger in your midst, naked, ill, and in prison, and in my need you gave me water, clothing, comfort, and friendship." It is there in the suffering of the human family that we hear the voice of the shepherd-judge: there in the hungry and the naked, the stranger and the widow, in the world's fear and anxieties, in the private search for peace and the public quest for justice.

If we would look for him today, if we seek to worship this shepherd, we shall not discover him clothed in the garments of unbridled power which demand our attention and our respect. We shall discover him within and without where he robes himself in our frailty, in our flesh, in the rhythms of conflict and peace, of pain and pleasure which move through human life. "He is clothed," writes one poet, "with the robes of His mercy . . . not velvet or silk and affable to the touch, But fabric strong for a frantic hand to touch . . . Here in the dark I clutch the garments of God."[16]

Here in our struggle and desire to be witnesses to his life and his love for us, he reigns. And here in the world, hidden in the open hand begging for a taste of bread and a cup of water, in the struggle for justice and peace, in the lives of women and men who abandon the strategies of fear and intimidation for the politics of hope and mercy: here he reigns.

And yes, at last, he reigns among us in our meal of thanksgiving. The judge of the universe, coming in glory escorted by all the angels of heaven, sitting on his royal throne, has become for us the derelict upon the cross, the lamb of sacrifice, the wounded king. To those who thirst for his justice, he offers his royal body and blood, the cup and bread which are his judgment of love. The blood is poured out, the body of the king is broken that we might feast on his mercy, that we might taste it on our lips. God grant that, in a world which yearns for the kingdom of the just, we might become that very mercy which we eat and drink.

Samuel Torvend, O.P.

[16]Jessica Powers, "The Garments of God," *The Place of Splendor* (New York: Cosmopolitan Science and Art Service Co., 1946), p. 66.

FIRST SUNDAY OF ADVENT

R   *Is 63:16b-17,19b;64:2b-7; 1 Cor 1:3–9; Mk 13:33–37*
E   *Is 64:1–9a; 1 Cor 1:1–9; Mk 13:33–37*
L   *Is 63:16b-17;64:1–8; 1 Cor 1:3–9; Mk 13:33–37*

Of the many themes in Advent, I want to focus our attention on three: watching, waiting and hoping. These themes are, I believe, difficult for us Christians in this time and place.

Watching requires time to reflect upon the events in my life and in the world, time to reflect on the past, the present and the future. Reflection is a valuable part of watching. I cannot watch for a mishap unless I have time in the first place to imagine what mishap might occur. Likewise, I will miss opportunities unless I have thought about what opportunities might come my way.

I can remember spending long days as a college student working the summer fallow fields. There wasn't much to do except drive the tractor to one end of the field, turn around and drive to the other end. Unless the chiselplow hit a huge rock and broke a plowshare, all I did was drive up and down the field all day. Those long hours working out my relationship with God, I thought about how I wanted to live my life.

Today there is little time for such reflection. Life happens quickly. We react to what is happening, rather than reflecting upon certain actions and planning ahead to meet opportunities or prevent disasters. As a result of our frantic pace we no longer watch. We no longer anticipate God's action in our future because we do not take the time to reflect on God's actions in our past.

Advent calls us to watch, to take the time to reflect upon God's past, present and probable future action in our lives and in the life of the world. If we can anticipate it, we will watch for it, and we will be less likely to miss it when it comes.

We wait in a world which knows no waiting, a world that moves quickly and constantly. We have been trained by fast cars, rapid scenarios on TV and instant cash from bank machines. A post-World War II generation wanted its children to have what it did not have, and our economy was ever-expanding. We have been trained to get what we want when we want it.

Recently I acquired a new hard disk computer and a laser printer. As I was trying out all the fancy variations on my new toy, I constructed a complicated test: print a complex picture, turn it sideways and print it in high resolution text. Needless to say, my computer needed a little time to process such a complex task. As I waited, I went into the kitchen, filled a mug with water and set my microwave to heat it. Frustrated that I had to wait for the printer, now I had to wait for my water. And then I had a flashback. About twenty years ago in my parents' kitchen, where we had neither computers nor a typewriter, if I had wanted that cup of tea, I would have walked to the well, pumped the water, heated it on the wood stove, and about thirty minutes later I could have had my tea. Yet here I was, frustrated because I had to wait two minutes for my water to heat and a few minutes for my printer to produce a picture which in my youth would have taken several people hours of labor. How soon we forget! How quickly we want what we want, when we want it.

We live in a world of instant gratification. If we pray for something and don't get it promptly, we often conclude either that our faith is too weak or that God did not mean for us to have our prayer answered. It rarely occurs to us to wait. When we wait for something, we build anticipation, we watch for when it might be coming, and we prepare ourselves for its coming. When it comes we are ready and we value it.

Advent calls us to wait, to look for and await the coming of Christ into our lives and into the life of the world.

Hope: we watch and wait in hope. But hope for what? Many school children say that they don't hope for much because they expect the world will be destroyed by nuclear war before they grow up. If there is no hope, why take the time to watch and wait?

I suspect the children are only a bit more honest than adults are. We may expect to live out a natural life, but we live fast and hard and do not hope for too much. Some see the future Day of Judgment, whether by bomb or Bible, as a disastrous time. For them, that Day will be a time of weeping, wailing and gnashing of teeth. For most of us the Day of Judgment, the End of Time, the Second Coming of Christ, whatever you want to call it, is something without any real meaning. We don't look forward to it with dread, because we don't look forward to it at all. Our hope is what I would call "neutral hope" —not filled with fear and dread, but also not positive. We are too busy living in a fast-paced world to concern ourselves with the future.

Advent calls us to hope for the coming of Christ. This positive hope comes from watching and waiting expectantly. This hope comes from knowing that we already belong to Christ and already live in communion with him and each other. Without this knowledge, we would dread the revelation of Christ. For who among us can say with certainly that he or she is living a life which is ready to be judged and found without fault? If at Christ's coming, at the end of time or into our lives today, we would be accepted or rejected on the basis of our lives, none of us would be accepted.

The gift of Christ is that in him we have been graced, through him, and in communion with him, we will be without reproach at the day of his coming. Through grace we are made ready to meet Christ both in our daily lives and at the Day of Judgment.

So it is that in Advent, and throughout the rest of the year, we can watch and wait in hope. We can anticipate and prepare for the coming of Christ into our lives, knowing that no matter who we are or what we have done, we have already been accepted by him and we are already in relationship with him. Advent reminds us to take time to watch, to make space for that waiting which is so important to our spiritual journey, and to look to tomorrow in positive hope, living expectantly for the coming of the Christ. May your Advent be blessed by the God of our salvation.

Linda L. Grenz

R   *Is 40:1–5,9–11; 2 Pet 3:8–14; Mk 1:1–8*
E   *Is 40:1–11; 2 Pet 3:8–15a,18; Mk 1:1–8*
L   *Is 40:1–11; 2 Pet 3:8–14; Mk 1:1–8*

In the Middle Eastern desert, where once the Hebrew nation wandered forty years, is a highway. It is no superhighway, not wide, but it appears well-built with a good blacktopped surface. A strange phenomenon that travelers report is that the road seems to end suddenly just ahead but to resume a hundred feet later, only to disappear for some distance once again. The constant wind that blows sand over the surface hides and then reveals the black path ahead.

Joshua camped with the Hebrew nation like the bedouins who camp beside the road yet today. And as now the desert sands blow, so then and there they blew at the Hebrew camp near the banks of the Jordan River. Moses had seen the promised land beyond the Jordan before he died, but only Joshua with his camp prepared to conquer that land which the Lord would give them to possess.

When the spies whom Joshua had sent on reconnaissance returned, all departed the camp. As the priests who led the way with the ark of the covenant stepped into the Jordan River, it parted before them and there was a highway of dry ground for the nation to pass through.

Joshua came into the promised land with weapons of war. Jericho was burned; at Ai beside Bethel, Israel slaughtered all the inhabitants and made the city a heap of ruins. And from the camp at Gilgal the destruction went on until all the land was conquered

These cities were to be a confederation where the Lord ruled. But when the warriors took off their armor they took on other gods and forgot the faithful God who had given them the land. So God raised up Elijah to call the Hebrew nation back from pagan worship. Elijah performed wondrous miracles and demonstrated the Lord's strength over the idol Baal.

But this man, who wore a garment of haircloth with a girdle of leather about his loins, never eluded those who worshipped Baal and sought the life of this prophet. At the end of his life he went from the conquered promised land: from the camp at Gilgal to Bethel beside Ai, to Jericho, to the Jordan, where he took his mantle and struck the water, and it parted for a highway of dry ground for him to pass through. And he was taken up by a whirlwind in the place where Joshua's campaign had begun—in the desert where the winds blow the sand.

Centuries later another prophet speaks words of comfort. The warfare is over, and the iniquity of those who went after other gods is pardoned. In the wilderness desert there shall be a highway for God to come again, in strength, but not as a god of battles; and to come again with love as a shepherd for the flock, for righteousness and peace shall go before this God.

Remembering those words, one came from the desert to prepare a highway for God. It was a wilderness man named John, who, like Elijah come-again, wore camel's hair and had a leather girdle around his waist and ate locusts and wild honey. He came from the desert to the Jordan and in that river preached a baptism, a way for the forgiveness of sins.

Hearing that voice, one Jesus (whose name is Joshua in Hebrew) came to the Jordan. And when he stepped from the waters he began to proclaim that the dominion of God is at hand. Now God would indeed rule in this land given to the Hebrew people through the campaigns of Joshua.

But as Joshua came with armies into the land, Jesus comes and mercy and truth embrace, and righteousness and peace kiss each other. But the helmet of salvation he would wear becomes a crown of thorns and the breastplate of righteousness a thin purple robe and a mockery. And Jesus, his loins girded with truth, is hanged on a cross.

But the highway is still there, and God shall come again suddenly like a thief and with a loud noise and with fire and bring new heavens with a new earth. Then the promised land will become the place where righteousness dwells.

And this highway stretches out to us in our desert wilderness. Signs of water and a cross point us to this promised land, and along this road we are called to live lives of holiness and godliness until Jesus comes again. And we pray the Spirit will blow a clear path, to keep the sand and all that impedes us off this highway and to lead us to this altar which mediates between us and the new heavens and the new earth.

For we need a clear path as we bring to this altar the things of our wilderness. We bring no locusts nor wild honey, but bread and wine, gifts of the earth and products of our human ingenuity. These we taste as the gospel already, the promised land in which righteousness dwells.

Mikkel Thompson

R E L   THIRD SUNDAY OF ADVENT

R   *Is 61:1–2a,10–11; 1 Th 5:16–24; Jn 1:6–8,19–28*
E   *Is 65:17–25; 1 Th 5:16–28; Jn 1:6–8,19–28*
L   *Is 61:1–3,10–11; 1 Th 5:16–24; Jn 1:6–8,19–28*

Today's readings for the middle of Advent seek to bring us closer to an understanding of the coming Messiah by reflecting back upon us the problem of our own identity. In the gospel reading John the Baptist is asked, "Who are you?" This question, though unspoken, is continually asked of us by those around us, through their interaction with us, their perceptions of our behavior, and their understanding of our stance on the broader issues of national politics, foreign relations, and religion. What do today's readings tell us about the nature of this question and of the response to which we are called?

Looking first at the gospel, we see that John the Baptist is asked this question in the specific context of the messianic expectations of the Levites and priests, who represent the religious establishment of the society of which John the Baptist is a part. This establishment expects a messiah who fits into its preconceived notion of the extraordinary. John responds first by giving a negative definition of himself. He is not the Messiah. Nor is he the re-incarnation of figures like Elijah and Moses. We likewise need to be able to say who we are not. We need to have a healthy sense that we are not defined by the expectations of others, by our particular economic position, our job, or even our family.

The Baptist then moves to a positive definition of himself. "I am the voice of one crying in the wilderness, 'Make straight the way of the Lord'." Certainly not the answer the questioners were expecting, this answer startles, is unique, poetic and beautiful. We too are called to find such a positive definition of ourselves and to demonstrate it in our daily living through our words and actions. Our positive self-definition should, like John the Baptist's, give expression to our singularity, our creativity, our beauty.

A brief examination of the content of John's answer takes us a step further. By quoting Isaiah, the Baptist gives an answer that comes from the scriptural tradition of his questioners. He thereby establishes a connection with them as well as forcing them to re-think the tradition in which they seem so very much at home. Analogously there must be something in our self-definition which allows us to connect with others, while at the same time challenging them to re-think themselves.

As "the voice of one crying in the wilderness" the Baptist defines himself as deriving meaning through his relationship with another. He is the voice who prepares for the coming of the Lord. The reading presents John as knowing little more about the "one who is to come" than that he is unworthy of him. John lives in the element of risk, of venturing into the unknown. He lives in the desert, a place representing danger and hardship, the region through which the Israelites had to pass in order to gain their freedom.

In 1 Thessalonians Paul speaks from another vantage point. The one whom the Baptist is waiting for has come. No longer unnamed, the Lord for Paul is "Jesus Christ." The tradition out of which he speaks and the one in which his listeners stand is one that includes the experience of Jesus, the light of the world. Indeed in Thessalonians Paul refers to those listening to him as "children of the light and children of the day." Christians are those who live in the context of their relationship with the Lord Jesus. We are called to be open to doing the will of God in joy. In this passage the will of God is to give thanks, *eucharisteite*. Giving thanks will leave us open to the spirit, will not quench it, will help us to evaluate prophetic utterances, will give us the ability to discern good from evil. Giving thanks is the openness which will allow us to let God work within us and will make us whole for the coming of our Lord Jesus Christ. For we, like John the Baptist, live in imperfect knowledge of Christ. Yet we are looking forward to a fuller revelation of Christ, who is even now calling us, who is faithful to us, and who will accomplish what he has promised.

Pamela Kirk

R E L   FOURTH SUNDAY OF ADVENT

R   2 *Sam 7:1–5,8b-12,14a,16; Rom 16:25–27; Lk 1:26–38*
E   2 *Sam 7:4,8–16; Rom 16:25–27; Lk 1:26–38*
L   2 *Sam 7:1–11,16; Rom 16:25–27; Lk 1:26–38*

The church has almost made it. We are almost to the creche, almost peering into the human face of God's eternally self-giving love. We are almost stepping into all the splendor and mystery of the Christ Mass. But not quite: for on this day the church pauses.

In their wisdom the lessons of the church detain us. Halting our fast progress they bid us turn our greedy eyes from the folds of the swaddling clothes. Ponder, they urge us, blessed Mary's face. Mary, protector of frail flesh, protects us from falling flat in error before we kneel at last before her newborn son, the only begotten of God.

We are held back this day to see Mary and so to see the meaning of our bodily selves. Mary, mother of God, mother of faith, stands with us confronted by God. She witnesses that our flesh may serve as the vessel for God's life by the power of the Holy Spirit. Mary's body is the tent in which God chooses to dwell. Within her fleshly being, God as the developing child Jesus lived. From the sanctuary of Mary's hospitality, Jesus came forth.

Honoring God with her whole being, Mary displays our humanity when it is full of grace. She submits to the call of carrying and bearing another life within her life, and so keeps faith with God. Her will for God's gracious will is freedom. Mary's worship of the Lord is thus whole, an offering of her whole being.

The mother of our Lord stops us this day from the temptation to vivisect our being and disassociate from our bodily existence. The self and the body are one, as Mary's worship makes manifest. Jesus was not God veiled in flesh, but God enfleshed. Mary is a mirror in which we glimpse ourselves before we are caught up in the beauty of the flesh of Christ. In Mary's body, we behold the calling of our bodily selves as that which bears divine life into our world.

It is not insignificant that Mary is an unknown. Her untried and unknown capacity to bear life, her creatureliness, her frightened awareness of the unspeakable powers of God: all these things link her flesh to ours. She is, without God, finally no one, of no account. She is one of us, fully human being, fully undivine. Yet in her flesh, God calls forth a human one, the only begotten of the Most High. Mary's offspring Jesus becomes the womb from which all others and Mary herself are born into the dominion of God. So also Mary is the church from which spring forth the birthing waters of grace, where Christ's siblings are delivered into God's presence.

Mary says with her whole being that the substance of her createdness is a sign in service to God. Her word we freely echo as we daily remember our identity at the waters. In the annunciation of our baptism, God calls us to bear within our lives the very spirit of Christ. To truly echo Mary's word we must remember we are bodies created to live as the image of God.

Wholly to bear forth the life of God will cost us and will try our flesh. The scandals in our communities, the infidelity of those bound to us, the grind of the world snagging our days: these are only the beginning of the cost. There may be for us much to ponder, swords to pierce our hearts, snooping shepherds and foreign kings and most horrible pogroms. Perhaps we too will be exiles and refugees. We may face rebuke, even rebuke from Christ; and always there will be the strangeness of nurturing what is unnatural and finally still unfamiliar within us.

"Let it be," Mary said, and the future's unfolding was hidden from her. "Let it be," Mary said, and her future was embraced as God's. "Let it be," Mary said, and she sang the first phrase of the Easter song of praise.

We pause a breath away from seeing Christ face to face, and we gaze long upon Mary. Here in Advent with all creation in travail, we are Mary, bodies claimed for the life and purposes of God. Here at the waters, the Lord greets us: "Hail!" Here at the table, the Lord says: "Do not be afraid." Here in the assembly we are bodies joined by God's spirit to be more than we ever imagined, as in us the sovereignty of God is established in steadfast love forever.

Jann Esther Boyd Fullenwieder

R CHRISTMAS MASS AT MIDNIGHT
E CHRISTMAS DAY I
L THE NATIVITY OF OUR LORD, 1

R *Is 9:2–7; Tit 2:11–14; Lk 2:1–14*
E *Is 9:2–4,6–7; Tit 2:11–14; Lk 2:1–14*
L *Is 9:2–7; Tit 2:11–14; Lk 2:1–20*

It was Friday evening and I was caught in a bit of traffic on my way uptown. There was snow in the air, steam escaping from underground vents, and workers repairing a section of First Avenue up in the area of Harlem. At one point, I found myself sitting in my car for almost 45 minutes next to a row of abandoned buildings and burned-out tenements. I waited and watched. No one moved. Cars stood in a row.

Then some light coming from one of those soon-to-be-condemned walk-ups caught my eyes. Light came from a second-story window where I thought no one could possibly be living. There were no curtains, and from the ceiling a bare light bulb hung, wires exposed.

In the window were two young boys, maybe nine and ten years old. They had some sort of cardboard with letters cut out. With what seemed to be a bar of Ivory soap, they were stenciling something, some words, onto the window. The traffic was so snarled that I was able to watch these boys for many minutes as they inscribed across the glass, for all the world to see, two words, two magical words, so out of place and unexpected on this block. The words: MERRY CHRISTMAS.

Living in poverty, amid rats, roaches and drug peddlers, those two children unknowingly gave me one of the most wonderful Christmas cards I have ever received. MERRY CHRISTMAS. Soap caked on dirty glass from two youngsters with little to be merry about. Greetings and glad tidings from a hearth that old Saint Nick will probably overlook this night. I was filled with wonder and astonishment.

And how the angels must have been filled with the same wonder and astonishment when *they* saw, to their utter disbelief, the glorious Son of God when he left his magnificent throne in heaven, where unnumbered cherubim and seraphim worshiped him day by day, to be born in the filth and stench of stable. Not like those plaster-of-paris stables with little white donkeys, but a filthy stinking stable, where the Son of God was born. How the angels must have wondered at that!

The shepherds out that night must have been filled with as much wonder and amazement. The angelic announcement was, in itself, puzzling: "You will find a baby wrapped in swaddling clothes."

"Swaddling clothes? Are you certain that's what they said?" As if a stable wasn't humble enough a beginning. God's sign to the shepherds that they would know the Christ child, the Messiah of the chosen people, the Savior of the world, would be his diaper!

But there was no mistake made about it. The sign was part of God's deliberate plan. God's gift to the world, the Redeemer and Prince of Peace, was wrapped in the linens of humanity. No ordinary gift, this gift, from God, but a gift carefully labeled and marked by the very simplicity of life itself. The sign and presence of the Holy Child is given in ordinariness so that nothing might confuse us as to where the real gift lay.

Soap traced through a stencil. The words MERRY CHRISTMAS. Two children announcing for me, at least, the presence of Christ in this world. His presence from the beginning and to this very day is clearly directed to the places of pain and hurt, brokenness and sinfulness. "He is here, is he not?" I meditated, while other drivers blasted their horns and wiped foggy windshields, everyone now in a panic to get beyond this street and out of this part of the city.

But Bethlehem wasn't particularly appealing either, was it? It was away from the bustling and cosmopolitan Jerusalem. The crowds that may have lined its streets were also only passing through, for a census. Only passing through. And so, Mary and Joseph sought shelter in a stable.

Have you ever tried to camp overnight with a herd of cows or a flock of sheep? And to top it all off, God uses Jesus' swaddling clothes, yesteryear's Pampers, to identify the Christ child to the world. Jesus experienced all that swaddling clothes imply, including our human vulnerabilities, our needs for warmth, love and affection. Jesus knew our pain, the awkwardness of learning obedience, and the misery of being rejected, unloved and unwanted.

On the path from manger to cross, however, those swaddling clothes took on even greater meaning, with Christ not merely ensconced in our human condition, its messiness and stink, but also conquering our human condition and redeeming it. Swaddling clothes are traded in for the linens of death.

Who is this Christ Jesus? Who is this one whose birthday we celebrate this eve? It is none other than "God with us," Emmanuel, the living Creator of all the galaxies; that One from whose hand was flung the greatest of the stars; that One who created this earth; that One who owns all things, this planet and all its life and beauty. Christ Jesus is the One who is from everlasting to everlasting. He is the Alpha and Omega.

But in Christmas God tells us one thing more: God is not above and beyond our need and reach. God is revealed by a manger stall and swaddling clothes, by a bar of soap pressed across a cardboard stencil on a window pane. In Christ God loves us and is with us, wherever we are.

Emmanuel, God with us, Merry Christmas.

Bruce J. Evenson

R CHRISTMAS MASS AT DAWN
E CHRISTMAS DAY II
L THE NATIVITY OF OUR LORD, 3

R *Is 62:11–12; Tit 3:4–7; Lk 2:15–20*
E *Is 62:6–7, 10–12; Tit 3:4–7; Lk 2:15–20*
L *Is 62:10–12; Tit 3:4–7; Lk 2:1–20*

Does any homilist know what to say on a feast of the church like this one? Certainly not this homilist. The mystery is too deep, the expectations of the worshipers and their guests who have in the past been worshipers, too many. Christmas Day? The only person equal to the challenge is the one responsible for our presence here. That one is Jesus, the man of Nazareth, born to a set of briefly homeless young parents. They are victims of a political oppressor interested only in recording the number of those oppressed.

The one who speaks to us today is one of us, a person "born in other's pain who perished in [his] own." Francis Thompson wrote that line, an English poet known, in his weakness, for his addiction to drugs. But were it not for poor sinners like him—and you and me—what need would there be for the manger and the cross?

How does the child at Bethlehem speak to us in today's divine liturgy? He speaks as the Son of God enfleshed, dying as a criminal on a knob of Jerusalem earth. For the mysteries of incarnation and redemption are never separated in the church's public prayer. This child came to birth so that he could die. In our Christmas is our Good Friday and our Easter. The incarnation happened, quite simply, so that the redemption could take place.

Calvary thoughts at Bethlehem's stall? But of course. This event we memorialize is no idyll of infancy to be sentimentalized into a tale of the sugar-plum fairy. This is the story of the earthly beginnings of a man who died young, executed as an enemy of the state. Our capacity for self-deceit is such that we can sentimentalize even that. The birth of Jesus was cold and hard, relieved only by the love of parents and the breath of animals. His death was even harder. But privation and legal injustice were not what the young teacher's life was about. It was about a human obedience to God so great that the world has not known its like since, nor does it expect to.

The circumstances of his birth and death were such that many find them compelling. The evangelists have recorded them with simple artistry. But the person at the center of these stories was not a sentimental sort. He thought that life had a certain hard quality, that it made demands. One had to fulfill one's calling, he supposed. His it was to sum up in his person the vocation of his people Israel, God's own beloved son, the Jewish people.

> Behold, the LORD has proclaimed
> to the end of the earth:
> Say to the daughter Zion,
> 'Behold, your salvation comes;
> behold God comes bearing the reward,

preceded by the recompense.'
And they shall be called The holy people,
The redeemed of the LORD;
    and you shall be called Sought out, a city not forsaken.

All that old poetry! What can it mean, especially on a day when
Luke's nativity account rings so familiarly in our ears?

It can tell us what the gospel is about, for we might never know
if it were not for the Bible and poets like the one we call the
Third Isaiah.

The birth of Jesus is about a holy people, the redeemed of the
LORD. This LORD is to be given no rest by them until Jerusalem
is established as "a praise in the earth."

The people are no less than the people Israel become the
church—a reality now that is all European and Asian and African
and Australian and American, but meaningless religiously apart
from tiny Israel its mother which continues to flourish. We would
still be bowing down to wood and stone but for the Jews. We are
the peoples over whom an ensign is lifted up, the spiritual offspring of the people redeemed of the LORD. Without Abraham
and Sarah, Isaac and Rebecca, Jacob and Rachel, there would be
no Joseph, no Mary, no Jesus. Apart from the patriarchs and
matriarchs, no crib, no cross, no life beginning for us on this day.

It is all a gift from start to finish. The letter to Titus reminds us
what life might be like for us had God our Savior not stepped in.
We would have been "slaves to various passions and pleasures,
passing our days in malice and envy, hated by others and hating
one another." It sounds like life on South Fork, does it not, or its
California counterpart, Dallas with grapes? Your favorite morning "soap" that has as its profoundest problem which of these
three is the father of this child is what the birth of Jesus has
rescued us from. The events in Bethlehem mean an end to alcohol in the suburbs, crack in the ghetto, and an antiseptic abortion in a clinic "without the risk of backalley butchery with a
coat-hanger." From all this we have been saved "when the goodness and kindness of God our Savior appeared."

I do not speak in irony. I speak only the truth of God when I spell out what a life of fidelity to the newborn Jesus could mean. He teaches a way of human happiness, not human misery, of prosperity and peace, not wealth and anxiety. So, rest ye merry, gentle folk. Angels and shepherds bring you tidings of comfort and joy. A person who can change your life is born this day in Bethlehem of Judea.

Gerard S. Sloyan

R HOLY FAMILY
L FIRST SUNDAY AFTER CHRISTMAS

R   *Gen 15:1–6;21:1–3; Heb 11:8,11–12,17–19; Lk 2:22–40*
L   *Is 45:22–25; Col 3:12–17; Lk 2:25–40*

On this Sunday after Christmas, Luke tells a story about the family of God. But like all good stories, its meanings are interpreted anew by successive ages and peoples. Today's story about the family of God has its cast of characters who contribute to the unfolding meaning of Jesus Christ, the Word who dwells among us. You have just heard that story, and met the characters.

Simeon is an old man who has looked forward to the comforting of Israel. He senses a future story coming from the present. Imbued with the wisdom of the old, Simeon already senses the new. This child is the light of revelation for the Gentiles, the glory of God's people, Israel. This child is the one for whom the people hoped, and Simeon proclaims it.

Anna is a woman who is "of a great age" and who prays constantly. She too senses the future story which will unfold from the present. She also affirms that this child shall be a liberator of the people. Yes, this is the one for whom the people of God waited.

Mary and Joseph, as any new parents would, marvel at these happenings. The story of the child will unfold in its own time. The family goes to its home in Nazareth, where the child will be guided in the ways of life, of wisdom, and of grace. The future unfolding of this story will verify the hopes that were identified for this child. He would become light for the Gentiles, light of the world, and the glory of God's people.

That story of the family of God had its historical limits of time— a beginning, a middle, and an end. Joseph and Mary died. The child who grew in wisdom, age, and grace was crucified under Pontius Pilate, died, and was buried. That, for historians, may seem like the end of the story. But for us who gather here, the holy family of God was just beginning in the Spirit. Its story continues through history, created anew through the ages at the table of the Lord.

Today, in the shadow of Christmas and memories of family, we join together as the new family of God. Today, as in past ages, we continue to write the story that has no end. What is our part in the story? What do our lives write about the light of revelation, about liberation of the people, about the Word who was made flesh and continues to be present through his body, the church? Is our story one of sacrament or of sacrilege? Who are we individually and together?

Are we Anna and Simeon for the world? Are we the ones who sense and hope for a better tomorrow, something new to come out of the best of the past? Anna and Simeon prophesy that the one in their midst shall transform the old into the new. His presence calls forth the Spirit within them. Each proclaims that God's liberation is for all people. No one shall be excluded from God's love, a light for the revelation of the Gentiles and for the glory of Israel.

As the new family of God, the body of Christ, do our lives proclaim the same prophecy? Do we consciously work to shape the Christian story of loving liberation, dignity, and light for all people? Or does fear, prejudice, or antipathy for those of different races, social status, gender, sexual preference, faith preference make our light and liberation selective? Are there some within our own community of faith whom we marginalize for their stands for the poor, the oppressed, the burdened?

How does the story of light for the revelation of all continue today in the choices we make as the holy family of God? Has the story ever new, ever old, become so old in our hearts that the new has no chance of being? Has the meaning of the Christmas story ceased to be a source of active wonder about the marvelous mystery of God? Have centuries of strife between ethnic groups, nations, and even Christians changed the story of the family of God into sacrilege instead of sacrament?

Today, what do we do to renew and recreate the story in our lives, and so in the heart of this community? What do we do to become again like Simeon and Anna who see the presence of Christ in their midst, point to its meaning, and live in hope? Simply, we believe that Christ's story, which is ours to continue to manifest, unfolds and enlivens us who gather around this table of the Lord. Christ is in the midst of the new family of God and continues to create the story in every age. If the story has grown old in our hearts, let us at least desire the transformation of the old at this table of the new. In the light of Christmas, we reflect on communion in Easter faith.

Shawn Madigan, C.S.J.

R   SECOND SUNDAY AFTER CHRISTMAS
E   FIRST SUNDAY AFTER CHRISTMAS
L   SECOND SUNDAY AFTER CHRISTMAS

R   *Sir 24:1–2,8–12; Eph 1:3–6,15–18; Jn 1:1–18*
E   *Is 61:10–62:3; Gal 3:23–25;4:4–7; Jn 1:1–18*
L   *Is 61:10–62:3; Eph 1:3–6,15–18; Jn 1:1–18*

The late Anthony DeMello in his book *The Song of the Bird* wrote a particular meditation that gives us much to reflect upon in this Christmas season. DeMello tell us of a Christian who could not find the courage to look straight into the eyes of Jesus. Something inside this person made such an encounter almost an impossibility. Perhaps it was the memory of some failure. Perhaps it was the fear that comes with any act of believing. Perhaps it was a tragic lack of self-esteem. Whatever the reason, the Christian simply feared to have the Christ peer into the depths of his or her soul.

One day, this individual happened to meet the Lord Jesus on the street. At their meeting, Jesus invited the person to look into those deep and powerful eyes. At first, the Christian was more than timid. Buy slowly, and only slowly, their eyes met. The Lord looked long and warmly in return, seeing in this disciple exactly who and what was there. And then to the complete surprise of our fearful Christian, Jesus simply said, "I love you."

In this holy season of Christmas, we are too often misguided by the romance of the feast from tasting the awesome reality of its rhythm. Like the believer we just heard about, we also need to catch the stunning and brutal truth of the message of Christmas, that God has come among us and lives within us, loving us despite our own temerity and fear, despite our running from God's acceptance of our very selves. And it is this message, this truly good news that is at the heart of God's word to us this day.

Whoever it was that stitched this Christian hymn into the text of John provided Christians with a glimpse of the whole story of the remainder of the gospel. In this hymn the beauty of the whole of Christian faith is encapsulated. The Word, the self-disclosure of the God who is beyond our own words and thoughts, enters into the condition of being human. The Word becomes flesh and dwells among us. The God of the universe becomes the God of humanity by embracing that which God is not: human flesh. Heaven and earth are wed; the failure of Adam and Eve to trust is overturned; and sinful humanity is once again made whole. This very act should be the cause of our own joy and an invitation to a new way of living. But is it? Sadly, oftentimes it is not.

If we were to ask ourselves the question, "Has God really embraced my flesh?" we might have to answer that many times we refuse to believe this basic tenet of our faith. But why? Inasmuch as we are graced and saved persons, human beings can engage in a type of deadening self-concern over failures which can result in a lack of ownership of our salvation. We run far from the embrace that constantly seeks to make us whole despite our sinfulness. Even outside of ourselves, we look to our world and are tempted toward a dark despair when we view violence, hatred and war. It is too difficult for us to see the "beauty" of Christmas in the homeless, the abandoned and those who are most marginalized in our society. And yet the Word which we celebrate has indeed become flesh. God has pitched the tent of meeting not outside us, but within us. And it is pitched within all of us. If our reading from John's gospel this day means anything for us at all, then it must remind us that the presence of God is to be found deep within the human heart: in its joys as well as in its ugliness. The word this day compels us to examine the temerity of our own eyes to see the Christ precisely in the poor and the abandoned. It compels us to wonder if our rejection of God's special children is our escape from the gnawing fear that God will reject us. And we must again wonder if we have missed the point of this holy season: the Word has become flesh and made a dwelling among us.

We are the believers who are invited today to peer into the eyes of the Lord Jesus. Timid and fearful, we must gaze into the eyes of the Christ who bears us the gift of all reconciliation. And when Jesus tells us that we are loved to the depths of our being, then we will come to know the full meaning of reconciliation. A strange word, this reconciliation. It comes from the Latin meaning "eyelash." Today we stand eyelash to eyelash with God. God sees and loves us exactly as we are. We see in God all that we might dare to become.

Edward Francis Gabriele, O.Praem.

E   SECOND SUNDAY AFTER CHRISTMAS

E   *Jer 31:7–14; Eph 1:3–6,15–19a; Mt 2:13–15,19–23*

Even as the glitter of the secular holidays fades, our liturgical calendar insists that we still celebrate Christmas. We are still focused on the birth of the child, on the wonder of God with us, on the coming of Emmanuel. But even when we manage to keep the focus on the manger, we may not fully recognize the reality it represents. It is very easy to romanticize this baby who comes at Christmas. Although we understand that the birth was in the stable, we seem to make our creches either magnificent or cute. We may see either ornate, gilded, soaring angels and beautifully blue-robed madonnas, or a scene with a little Mary, Joseph, baby Jesus, and adorable, pet-like animals. Rather than the chill of night in a barn, we feel a warm, sentimental glow like candle-light.

This morning's gospel lesson comes along to jar us. We are torn away from our quiet contemplation of this lovely babe. We are pulled out of the starlit night and away from the peaceful angelic voices. This instead is a story of escape, of risk, of insecurity, of danger. It takes more than the strength of china creche figurines or soft-touch greeting card characters to undertake this journey by night, fleeing to Egypt.

Matthew includes this story in order to connect the birth of Jesus with the stories and prophecies of the Hebrew scriptures. He draws a parallel with the exile of ancient Israel in Egypt. As Joseph was taken down into Egypt in the old story, so in this story Jesus is taken there. The gospel also echoes the story of Moses, who was persecuted and in danger when he was a baby because of a wicked king. Moses also was put in hiding in order to save him. Even the words the gospel writer chooses show how closely he saw the comparison. The message to Joseph when it is time to return with Jesus and his mother is like the message that it was safe for Moses to return to his work in Egypt: "those who sought the child's life are dead."

These closely drawn parallels show the readers of Matthew's gospel that in all the details of the story, God's purpose of salvation is being worked out. These allusions remind those readers of the history of Israel, the exile and exodus in which God acted to save the people. The reminder here is of how God's promises were fulfilled, but it is impossible to retell the story, to remember Joseph and Moses, without also being clearly reminded that the history was not an easy one. The people of God did not start out in promised land flowing with milk and honey. It is the story of a long journey which Matthew's hearers will remember.

As we listen to the unsettling story of the flight into Egypt, we can also be connected to countless stories in our own time. Jesus was born into a world of oppression, injustice, and political upheaval. The people into which Jesus was born were not the powerful, comfortable, or secure of the time. From the beginning of his life, Jesus was vulnerable to risks and dangers, serious enough to require Mary and Joseph to be uprooted in order to protect him. The prayer for this day in the Episcopal prayer book prays that "we might share the divine life of him who humbled himself to share our humanity."[18] We see in this gospel story just what was involved for Jesus in sharing our humanity.

The baby Jesus, carried away to Egypt by night, shares the humanity of all of us: those whose lives are threatened by political unrest and upheaval; those who die in places where peace is replaced by conflict; those whose lives are affected by leaders and decisions over which they have no control; those who are forced to flee from home or country in search of safety; those who are imprisoned, silenced, or exiled because of their beliefs; those who are separated from home or family because of race or nationality; those children born into places or nations which will never know peace in their lifetimes; those women and children who run from abuse in their own homes; those runaway children and teenagers exiled in the frightening world of the streets; those whose families are uprooted by economic change and unemployment; those whose opportunities are limited because of prejudice or misunderstanding; and all of us in whatever ways we are unsettled by anxiety or lack of security.

This is the humanity, the risky, frightening, difficult life in which Jesus comes to share. These are the stories of our time which parallel the story of the flight into Egypt. The coming of the Christ child in our midst does not promise instant comfort and security. If we celebrate the birth of Jesus, we celebrate his coming into our human situation with all its pain and complexity. We may not like being reminded of Jesus' connection and ours to these intense, difficult human stories. We may find it difficult to, as the letter to the Ephesians urges, "Know what is the hope to which God has called" you. To look for hope, for promise, for salvation, is to look for the one who has come among us: not the romanticized baby of our creches, but the real Jesus living the risks and vulnerability of human life.

When we find hope, fulfillment, and light, we will find it even in the unsettling story of the flight into Egypt, in the story of a journey which reminds us that Jesus journeys with us in all our humanity.

We will remember the journey. We will find hope. We will celebrate. And we will understand, far beyond anything we ever imagined, the wonder of God with us this Christmas season and always.

Leslie G. Reimer

[18]*The Book of Common Prayer*, p. 214.

R   E   L   THE EPIPHANY OF OUR LORD

R   *Is 60:1–6; Eph 3:2–3a,5–6; Mt 2:1–12*
E   *Is 60:1–6,9; Eph 3:1–12; Mt 2:1–12*
L   *Is 60:1–6; Eph 3:2–12; Mt 2:1–12*

Today we are celebrating the Epiphany of our Lord Jesus Christ, what used to be subtitled the "Manifestation of Christ to the Gentiles." The Feast of the Epiphany, is one of the oldest of feast days and possibly one of the least understood.

This misunderstanding possibly goes back to its confused origins. Egyptian Christians dedicated January 6, a festival of the pagan god, Osiris, to the baptism of our Lord, claiming that it was at his baptism that the Lord's divine calling was first revealed. But as the celebration moved eastward to Jerusalem, more orthodox Christians insisted that Christ's vocation must be dated from his birth as the only begotten Son of God. So in the East, January 6 was kept as a celebration of both his nativity and baptism. Meanwhile in the West, another pagan festival, that of Saturn, December 25, was taken over as the feast of Christ's birth, and the Epiphany was used to celebrate the visit of the Magi.

Because the Magi were Gentiles, not Jews, western Epiphany celebrates the manifestation or the revelation of Christ to the whole world. It celebrates God's "showing up among us" in the person of Jesus Christ. Epiphany is a day of celebration of how we have not been left in darkness.

The Epiphany is a festival of light; it is a celebration of the manifestation of the light of Jesus Christ in the darkness of the world. Light is the theme of the entire epiphany season, because in Jesus Christ we see things in a wholly new way. Light is what Epiphany is all about. And light is what the story of the Magi is all about. Star-gazers from the East follow a star and find a baby in whom God will light up the world.

It is difficult for us in this age of electricity and artificial light to appreciate the symbolism of light, but for biblical people light was the fullest expression of God's work in the world. You remember some of those references to light in the Old Testament: "Arise, shine; for your light has come, and the glory of the Lord has risen upon you." "Your word is a lamp to my feet, and a light to my path." "I have given you as a covenant to the people, a light to the nations, to open the eyes of those who are blind." "The Lord is my light and my salvation; whom shall I fear?" "The people who walked in darkness, on them has light shined." Without light they were threatened with the chaos of darkness and confusion.

To say that God is light is to say that it is the nature of God to be manifest, just as it is the nature of light to shine. Light cannot help but shine, and God cannot help but reveal divine love, even if for a while like Moses all we can see is God's back. And if we cannot see the face of God, we can indeed see the very heart of God, that God is faithful and just.

Just as light, by its very nature, cannot be self-contained, but is ever seeking to impart itself, pouring through every crack and crevice, so by God's very nature God is revealed as being God. God is light, and as such is always seeking to shine on us who have been made in God's image. God is transparent; we can see right through God, and we can see that God loves the whole world. That is what God's "showing up among us" is all about.

But not only is God light, but that light which is life has been made manifest in Jesus of Nazareth, the one the astrologers came to adore. Those who saw the Christ had seen the love of God and knew that Christ came "through the tender mercy of our God, when the day shall dawn upon us from on high to give light to those who sit in darkness and in the shadow of death." This God who is light is now permanently present in Jesus Christ. The coming of Jesus Christ announced the dawning on a new age which will never be followed by night. With him, "Morning has broken like the first morning."

This Jesus is indeed the light of the world. But what does that precisely mean? It does not mean some of the things we may have heard in the past. Surely it does not mean that Jesus is the light at the end of the tunnel. Surely it does not mean what the little song claims: "If everyone would light just one little candle, what a bright world this would be." Surely it does not mean what the little couplet says: "How far that little candle throws its beam, so shines a good deed in a naughty world." Christ is not just a dim glow, or a signal, or a guide through the darkness, or a light on a question, or a ray of light in a dark world. He is the radiating, life-sustaining light who comes in power and glory like the sun bursting over the eastern horizon. He is the Sun of Righteousness with healing in its wings.

Old Simeon knew who the Christ child was: "A light to enlighten the Gentiles and the glory of your people Israel."

Jesus Christ is the light of the world because he reveals the very heart of God. He is the light of the world because in him we see the fullness of the love of God. He is the light of the world because when we see him we see the Father also. That is what we are proclaiming in the Nicene Creed when we confess Christ as "Light of Light, True God of True God." During this Epiphany season let that which was made manifest become our manifesto.

Donald S. Armentrout

R L THE BAPTISM OF THE LORD
E FIRST SUNDAY AFTER EPIPHANY

R *Is 42:1–4,6–7; Acts 10:34–38; Mk 1:7–11*
E *Is 42:1–9; Acts 10:34–38; Mk 1:7–11*
L *Is 42:1–7; Acts 10:34–38; Mk 1:4–11*

In the Eastern church the important truth at this time of year is not that our Lord was born, but that he was manifested to human beings as the incarnate God. Therefore the great festival among Orthodox Christians in not Christmas, but Epiphany. On that day, January 6, two manifestations are commemorated: Christ's baptism and his birth. The latter seems to have been included mainly because it was assumed that our Lord was baptized on his thirtieth birthday. The significant event was the baptism, when God the Father publicly acknowledged Jesus as the Son of God, and when Jesus was endowed with the Holy Spirit, who was made known by the visible sign of a dove. This, in the mind of the Eastern church, was the beginning of his manifestation as the Son of God and the world's Redeemer.

When later on the Western church began to observe the Feast of the Epiphany, Christmas had already become established, so that certain adaptations were made, notably that attention was directed to the visit of the Magi, and the story of our Lord's baptism unfortunately dropped out of the liturgical picture. Now, happily, with the revision of the lectionary. we have it back again, and the First Sunday after Epiphany is annually observed as the Baptism of our Lord.

So to today's gospel. If you read it carefully, you will see that St. Mark treats our Lord's baptism as a kind of inauguration ceremony. Prior to the event the Baptizer speaks of the coming ministry of Jesus, and the event itself is plainly the introduction to that ministry. This ministry, as well we know, was to reach its climax in our Savior's sacrificial death on Golgotha, which means that in a broad sense our Lord, when he was baptized, was beginning to tread the way of the cross. Certainly everything he did from this time on was in line with his redemptive purpose: his healing of the sick, his casting out evil spirits, his raising the dead, his preaching of the good news. He was committed to do these things; he had come into the world precisely to save, to liberate, to bring people into God's dominion. This was his task, and he undertook it on the day of his baptism.

Today's first and second lessons provide more details. Isaiah says that the Chosen One, who will have God's Spirit upon him, will bring forth justice to the nations, "to open the eyes that are blind, to bring out the prisoners from the dungeon, from the prison those who sit in darkness." One is reminded of the kind of work done by Amnesty International. The second lesson is more general; it speaks of how Jesus "went about doing good and healing all that were oppressed by the devil," and of the universality of this ministry, for "in every nation any one who is God-fearing and does what is right is acceptable to God."

With all this in mind, the tie between Christ's baptism and our own begins to come clear. For we too are committed by our baptism to the redemptive task, and we agree to do this by the same method, the method of the cross. Certainly this is not the most pleasant assignment in the world, or one that we would have chosen without God's suggestion. We recoil from sacrifice and suffering; we are interested in having a good time. It is sobering to reflect that we are committed by our baptism to a way of life that requires us to live no longer for ourselves but for him who for our sake died and was raised. We can of course refuse to follow through with this, just as our Lord soon after his baptism could conceivably have succumbed to the temptations in the wilderness. But to do this amounts to a repudiation of our baptism, and we must be perfectly clear about it. There are many baptized people who do not live like baptized people. The requirement however remains: to live before God in righteousness and purity forever. If we live as though we had not been baptized, we do so at our soul's peril.

The imagery behind this is the New Testament picture of drowning in holy baptism. St. Paul keeps talking about being baptized into the death of Christ, a death which, since it is associated with baptism, is to be thought of as a drowning. The threat is, that if you go all the way under the water, you may not come up again. And the apostle means this not only as a threat, but the actuality of death; there is to be a real killing of the old sinful self. This is to happen daily, so that, as Luther's Small Catechism has it, the person new in Christ can daily come forth and arise. Every day is Resurrection Day in the Christian experience!

Like the Israelites who passed through the Red Sea, we also have experienced a *transitus*, a passage through the baptismal water from death to life.

> From death to life eternal,
> From this world to the sky
> Our Christ has brought us over
> With hymns of victory.[19]

Herbert F. Lindemann

[19]John of Damascus, "The Day of Resurrection," *The Lutheran Hymnal* (St. Louis: Concordia Publishing House, 1941) #205.

R *1 Sam 3:3b-10,19 1 Cor 6:13c-15a,17–20 Jn 1:35–42*

Today's first reading is the winsome story of the call of Samuel. When we think of the great call narratives, we usually think of adults who are called from a dissolute or pagan life and respond with a radical conversion. We think of Moses or Paul, with their life turned completely around. But Samuel is no wicked adult struck by the vision of God and converted. No, Samuel is already in the holy place when he hears God's call.

The story of Samuel began back before his conception. His mother Hannah was barren, and thus disgraced in the eyes of her people. The story says that she prayed fervently for a child. In fact, the intensity of her prayer was mistaken by the old priest Eli as drunken incoherence. No, she protested, she is not drunk, only pleading that God will give her life. When her son Samuel was finally born, Hannah sang a song much like Mary's Magnificat, praising God for bringing life out of a barren world. In gratitude for her opened womb—she goes on to bear five more children—she gives the child Samuel to God. After he weaned, still only a toddler, Samuel is given to God as a kind of altar boy, a servant of the priest, a minister in the holy place, to attend the lamp of God.

It is as a young child that Samuel hears the voice of God. The story says he mistook God's voice for Eli's, so accustomed was he to respond to the old man's requests. Here I am, are the famous words of the eager youth. And so the child, born through the beseechings of Hannah, apprenticed to the priest, hears God's call to become a judge in Israel; and he responds, Here I am.

The text says that Samuel served Eli in the temple. This was of course not the famous Jerusalem temple, which was not yet built or even imagined. This temple was a local shrine, a holy place for the people's devotion. To this holy place the people brought their sacrifices and their prayers. Here was the lamp of God.

Here the people received the word of God, and here God was honored.

Our gospel reading finds the faithful at yet another holy place, the Jordan River. At this holy place, the ancient poems said, God would arrive. It was here that the first century Judeans expected to see the Messiah come. At this place the people had long ago crossed over into the promised land, and here at the coming of the age God would appear to give the people life. Today's story finds us here at this holy place, where John the Baptist is proclaiming the lamb of God to be the coming fire of judgment.

Suddenly John sees Jesus. Behold, the Lamb of God! Not in the Jerusalem temple is the lamb, slaughtered for the Passover meal, but here by the flowing waters of the Jordan is the lamb. By this lamb we will honor God and sign our salvation. The text calls Jesus "Rabbi," the one who teaches the word of God from the holy place. Jesus is called also the Messiah, the one who will make the whole land a holy place for the people of God.

Andrew and Peter are at this holy place, awaiting life from God. They hear the names of the coming one—Lamb, Rabbi, Messiah—and they, with Samuel, respond to the call. They follow the call and come to serve their Lord. They receive the life of God at the Jordan, though in a different way than they expected.

And us as well. We too come here to this holy place, ready to tend the lamp of God. We come to serve, to await the arrival of our Lord. In our place of assembly the light burns at the font, our lamp of God at our Jordan River. At these flowing waters we come to plead for life and to honor our God. At this holy place we hear the call of God, and from here we follow the voice of our Lord. We too like Hannah have borne life, and we too can sing her song of thanksgiving; for the water of baptism has signed to us entry into the promised land of God's grace.

But this building is not always recognizable as the holy place of God's coming. This time seems very ordinary to us, and like Samuel we cannot always distinguish God's call from all the noises about us. Yet Paul reminds us that the temple need be only our very own body. For God dwells within you, Paul tells the Corinthians. In their very bodies God is honored; in these very bodies God's word is heard. The holy place is this baptized body, all of us one holy place together. As baptized people our bodies are much greater than the sum of our single skeletons and individual skins. Our body, the holy place of God's call, is the whole community of faith.

And when we do not know which cries are the call of God, we can listen more closely to the cries of the rest of the body. The voice of God is calling to us from some part of this body. May we be ready, as the boy Samuel, to jump up ready to serve. May we be ready, as Andrew and Peter, to pay heed to John's call. May we, strengthened by this food before us, rise to follow the Spirit of Christ. God is born among us, we say to one another: come and see where God lies. Together let us go find God: together we shall tend the light of our baptism, hear the word of the Lord, and honor our God.

Gail Ramshaw

E L SECOND SUNDAY AFTER EPIPHANY

E   *1 Sam 3:1–10; 1 Cor 6:11b-20; Jn 1:43–51*
L   *1 Sam 3:1–10; 1 Cor 6:12–20; Jn 1:43–51*

The story in John's gospel about Nathaniel is a very odd story. This should not surprise us, though, because John's gospel is a very odd book. For one thing, John curiously does not inform his readers about the purpose of his book until the *end*. Most writers tip their hands on the very first page, saying things like, "This book is an exploration of the causes of the American Revolution," or "In the chapters that follow the reader will be introduced to the principles of basic physics." But John waits until the end, waits until we have read twenty chapters full of incidents like Jesus' conversation with the woman at the well, Jesus feeding five thousand people, Jesus on trial before Pilate, the crucifixion of Jesus, and the followers' encounters with the risen Jesus; then he tells us what this book has been all about: "These are written that you may believe that Jesus is the Christ, the Son of God, and believing you may have life in his name."

The reason for John's odd literary behavior, the reason why he makes us wait so long before showing his cards, is that John understands well what it takes for people to come to belief. John wrote his gospel so that people would be able to believe, but he knows that people do not come to belief in Christ in the same ways that they come to believe in other truths, like the fact that excessive taxation was a cause of the Revolutionary War or that Ohm's Law is a trustworthy measure of electrical resistance. People come to faith in Christ only by being drawn into the story and into the community of Jesus. Like Samuel in the temple, we do not instantly recognize the claim of God upon our lives. It takes time, and it demands the testing of our experience with others. Only when we have experienced the story of Jesus by listening to it lovingly told by the church, gradually learned to make it our own story, and slowly begun to see the world and ourselves in its light, can we truly say, "I believe." Full and authentic believing comes, in other words, at the end of the journey, and not at the beginning.

That is part of the message of this unusual story about Nathaniel. The story begins with Philip, a disciple of Jesus, telling Nathaniel about his own faith in Jesus. "We have found him," said Philip, "of whom Moses and the prophets wrote, Jesus of Nazareth." Today we might call what Philip did "witnessing," or even "evangelizing." It was as if Philip had turned to Nathaniel at the office and said, "Brother, let me tell you about Christ," or leaned over to Nathaniel on an airplane and handed him a religious tract. Some Christians think that this kind of witnessing is all that there is to it. You simply tell people about Christianity, they say, and then you hope they will accept it.

But John knows that there is more, much more, involved in coming to believe. Church history teaches us, as theologian George

Lindbeck has noted, that early converts to Christianity did not, for the most part, understand and believe the gospel and then decide to become a part of the church. They did, in fact, the reverse. They were first attracted to the Christian community, and only then, by living the lifestyle of that community, did they grow to believe. That is why, when Nathaniel scoffs at Philip's witness by saying, "What good can come out of Nazareth?" Philip does not turn away dejected. Rather he invites Nathaniel to come and see. Careful readers of John's gospel will recognize that this word to Nathaniel is more than an invitation to come and take a look. In John's vocabulary, "come and see" means "come and live," "come and experience," "come and be a part of the community of Jesus." Nathaniel does come, and it is then, and only then, there, and only there, that Nathaniel comes to believe.

There was once a downtown church that housed a soup kitchen providing a simple lunch each day for the homeless of the city. Volunteers from the church came daily to ladle the soup, to serve the sandwiches and coffee, and to provide hospitality for the people of the street. A woman who worked downtown and who was concerned about the number of homeless people in the city began to give her lunch hour once a week to work at the soup kitchen. She was not herself a believer, but she took her place in the serving line, standing beside the members of the church as they worked to feed the hungry. No one tried to convert her; no one read to her from the Bible. They just worked alongside her, serving others in the name of Christ. One Sunday, she appeared at worship. A few weeks later, she was there again, and then more regularly, until one day, she asked to be instructed for baptism.

How do people come to believe? John knows. By "coming and seeing." By responding to the open invitation which every true Christian community gives to all who will hear, an invitation to come and join us in worship and service. The invitation does not demand that people believe at the beginning of the journey. It rather beckons them to join us by rolling up their sleeves and pitching in as the Christian community serves others in Christ's name. For it is there, John knows, that they will encounter the living Christ and "find life in his name."

Thomas G. Long

	R	THIRD SUNDAY IN ORDINARY TIME
E	L	THIRD SUNDAY AFTER EPIPHANY

R   *Jon 3:1–5,10; 1 Cor 7:29–31; Mk 1:14–20*
E   *Jer 3:21–4:2; 1 Cor 7:17–23; Mk 1:14–20*
L   *Jon 3:1–5,10; 1 Cor 7:29–31; Mk 1:14–20*

A dog found near the Rose Bowl, California, wore a collar with the name of a city in British Columbia. When the owner was found, it became clear that the dog had followed some visiting friends who lived near the Rose Bowl. The dog's name was Rover, so named because of its tendency to stray. Animals stray, so do airplanes, and adolescents, and adults, let alone children and the elderly. The Old Testament lesson is a story of God's children straying and of God's straining to bring them back home, even through those who themselves have tendency to stray.

Those with conflict of wills tend to stray. If the covenant is broken, or about to be, then the condition is that of harlotry, Jeremiah insists. One of the partners is clearly faithless; a divorce is imminent. Duplicity and betrayal are obvious. Judah is following its treacherous sister Israel, who is now already in captivity. Yet Judah feigns a reform which is only pretense.

Jeremiah proclaims the covenant God. If there is any chastening, it is for the purpose of wooing the children away from false gods. God is the divine physician restoring those who are ill back to health. Inward cleansing, circumcision of the heart, breaking up the fallow ground are God's urgent pleas.

Grace pursues. Turn. Abandon the idols. Adopt a new orientation. Assert that "In God We Trust." The parable story of Jonah illustrates that God does not want us to get out of sync. We all stray, but we are also all sought, and in turn recruited to search for others.

God is not blind. Jeremiah's reference to Hosea and the claim of Micah 6:2 are always true: God has a controversy with people. God is at work in human hearts, human history, human affairs. Why? God sees us for what we are and where we are. God knows that we are all always straying people, selfishly preoccupied with ourselves, our wealth, our position, or future. God's controversy exists because we have too little recognition that our fate is bound up with others, that when one suffers we all suffer, and that our faith could enable others' faith. There's too little conviction of solidarity, too little corporate sense that if one part of our ship is sinking, the rest is up in the air. We are our brother's keeper. The stock market in one time zone affects the market in another.

God restores. To repent, to turn back to the apartment or house if one thinks one may have left the stove turned on, is prudent. God's first gift is to help us come to a new option that is possible for us. We see that we could have our prejudices and prides changed. We could have inner healing. Our inner turmoil could convert to outward peace, could be the war to end all wars. We could find what we've been missing. God gives grace. For the time being we sense we're no longer straying. We emerge, saying, "All right, we'll do it then." But is it full restoration? Is it but reluctant obedience, or is it a full change of heart? Are we still elitist, arrogant, first class nationalists, exalting our own kind and our own god?

God would restore Israel, Judeh, Nineveh, USSR, USA. The point is critical: Are they, are we, willing to change? Are they, are we willing to be found by the loving, gracious God? Are they, are we ready to turn from hatreds, prejudices and fears, and to accept openness, freedom and goodwill?

The basic thesis is a declaration of God's universal love, of God's willingness to receive and bless all who turn in humble repentance and obedience. All who stray may come into the kingdom.

And the next thesis is that it is the business of those who have strayed to seek and find those who are straying.

Yet other lessons of the day can be listed: that God doesn't discard people or stop divine blessing; that we are all strays, and we are all seekers; that God has unfolding purposes for the world; that mourning can turn to joy; that God has no class system; that we are invited to believe in the dominion of God, not as removed scholars but as involved students and faithful disciples; and that God puts pressure on us out of compassion for us. The kingdom of God is now here: it is the right time to enter.

LeRoy E. Kennel

R   FOURTH SUNDAY IN ORDINARY TIME
E L   FOURTH SUNDAY AFTER EPIPHANY

R   *Deut 18:15–20; 1 Cor 7:32–35; Mk 1:21–28*
E   *Deut 18:15–20; 1 Cor 8:1b-13; Mk 1:21–28*
L   *Deut 18:15–20; 1 Cor 8:1–13; Mk 1:21–28*

Recently, a number of theologians have focused their attention upon Jesus as the eschatological prophet of the end time. These writers see the ancient hopes for a prophet come to meet Jesus of Nazareth. Let us consider what this prophet image means for the New Testament and for us.

Today's first reading is part of a larger literary unit in which the Deuteronomists describe the governance of Israel once the people have established themselves in the promised land. In a manner which was unique in the ancient Near East, the Deuteronomic writers stress that for God's people life must be characterized by a just balance of judicial, liturgical, royal, and prophetic power.

The final and most important power outlined, that of prophecy, is described within the context of false human ways of encountering divine power: child sacrifice, sorcery, and necromancy. The Deuteronomists, by way of contrast, stress the absolute freedom of the covenant from human control and manipulation. According to those biblical theologians, the way in which the God of Israel reveals the future and interprets the present is not through human control but through the charismatic, divinely appointed prophet.

In this first reading, the Deuteronomists also allude to Israel's refusal to listen to God at Sinai. Their memory allows them to reinterpret that event and use it as the basis for the divine inauguration of the prophetic office. Since God cannot speak directly to Israel, God will raise up a prophet from among the people to function as an intermediary of the divine word. Israel's stance in relation to the divinely appointed prophet is to be that of listening.

In subsequent years of Israel's history, especially during the Maccabean and later periods when the prophetic voice in Israel seemed to have been extinguished, the Jewish community began to dream of a new prophet like Moses, a prophet who, in his call for inner renewal, would offer to Israel one final chance for conversion. If Israel could only respond to the eschatological prophet's call for conversion, then God would enter anew into Israel's history, freeing it from a whole history of oppression. Popular piety often identified the eschatological prophet not only with the description of Moses as a prophetic mediator, but also with the figure of Elijah come back to life.

In a real way, today's gospel picks up both of these themes. Our reading describes the first of many miracles performed by Jesus. In the account of Jesus' expulsion of the unclean spirit, the evangelist stresses that Jesus speaks with the same miraculous power by which he acts. Jesus has only to say, "Be silent, and come out of him!" and the unclean spirit departs from the man in the Capernaum synagogue. On another level, the Marcan evangelist is saying to us that the first miracle in Jesus' public ministry signifies that Satan's power over the world has come to an end, and that the dominion of God has broken into human history.

An additional Marcan theme present within today's gospel is that of the messianic secret. The unclean spirit avows in the presence of the synagogue assembly, "I know who you are, the Holy One of God," and Jesus rebukes him saying "Be silent." Of special interest is the title employed by the unclean spirit, "Holy One of God." Within the context of the story, one would expect a messianic title; here, somewhat surprisingly, the title has distinct prophetic overtones. Moreover, the title and the demon's previous questions, "What have you to do with us? Have you come to destroy us?" are evocative of the words of the widow of Zarephath's words to Elijah: "What have you against me, O man of God? You have come to bring my sin to remembrance, and to cause the death of my son!" Perhaps this literary borrowing intends to remind us that Jesus is a prophet analogous to Elijah. It is significant that the widow refers to Elijah as the man of God, a title which in the parallel text becomes the holy man of God. In today's gospel, the fact that the unclean spirit addresses Jesus as the Holy One of God suggest that the Markan evangelist connects Jesus with the prophet of the end time, the one who would like Elijah speak God's word to the world.

What significance do today's readings hold for us? Perhaps in them we can once again hear the call to conversion that Jesus as the prophet of the end time holds out to us. Perhaps, too, in these days of almost apocalyptic tensions, in this time of the terrible gulf which separates the rich from the poor, of humankind's pollution of the environment, of the possibility of nuclear disaster, we can reaffirm our faith in the final inbreaking of God's dominion on earth, an inbreaking which calls each of us to assume responsibility for the overcoming of demonic powers in this world.

Margaret Page

R   *Job 7:1–4,6–7; 1 Cor 9:16–19,22–23; Mk 1:29–39*
E   *2 Kg 4:18–21,32–37; 1 Cor 9:16–23; Mk 1:29–39*
L   *Job 7:1–7; 1 Cor 9:16–23; Mk 1:29–39*

Driving down the main street of almost any town today will reveal something about what sort of people we are. Burger King,
McDonalds, Roy Rogers, Wendy's—we know what we want, we
want it our way, and we want it now. This is an age and a
society of fast food, junk food. At home, microwaves promise
meals in minutes, and anything that is frozen, dried or packaged
is almost assured of success. We are people in a hurry. We don't
take time to cook, we can't slow down to eat, we no longer
spend time together at the table. We are a nation of Instant
Breakfast followed by fast relief.

Nor is it just meals we rush through: we rush through much of
life. We want not only instant soup but instant success and instant solutions to problems. Perhaps that accounts for the enduring popularity of Superman. His adventures never involve planning or wondering, uncertainty or waiting. There is just a hero
who swoops in, cape fluttering behind him, scoops up Lois Lane
and flies off to safety. That's how we like our heroes—fast and
flashy.

That's true of religion, too. Many of the churches we see growing today offer that sort of approach to faith: simple, unambigu-
ous answers, healing on the spot, perhaps even promises of immediate success in business. It's all very appealing. We'd like
Superman to save us, to solve our problems, to erase our sor-
rows.

The people of Jesus' day were not very different. They too were
impressed by miracle workers offering instant cures. They too
looked for a hero to save them. No wonder they were drawn to
Jesus. Here was someone special—a wonder-worker, a healer,
perhaps the solution to their problems. Here was one who could
say the word and make it all better.

But the evangelist Mark knew that Jesus was more than that, and for that reason he tells us something peculiar in verse 34 of chapter 1: Jesus "would not permit the demons to speak, because they knew him." Over and over in Mark's gospel, Jesus seems to want to keep his identity a secret. Why? Why doesn't he want anyone to know who he is?

The answer lies in how people saw him—miracle worker, healer, almost magician. At the beginning of his ministry, his acts revealed him as one with power, a superman doing mighty things, reaching out and curing instantly. But miracles were only part of the story. Jesus knew that those who saw him only as a wonder-worker would miss the real meaning of his life. Therefore he commanded silence until the rest of the story could be told, the story which leads to the cross. It was not that he wanted to hide his identity. Rather, it was that he wanted to reveal it fully, and that would be possible only after his death and resurrection. Only then could he be seen as more than a performer of miracles.

To us, Jesus' silencing of the demons serves as a reminder. We, too, may look for wonderful cures, miraculous answers, speedy solutions. The word responds by pointing us toward the rest of the story. To a world which wants a Superman, Christ comes not with a cape but with a cross, reminding us that there is more to it than that. God offers us not a hero but a savior, not magic tricks but victory over death. And when we look for fast food Christ offers real food, himself, body and blood given and shed for us. That's who this Jesus is—healer, wonder-worker, one with authority—all of those things, but only because he is also the one who has passed through death in order to bring us new life. That is the rescue that is offered. It does not involve easy answers of instant solutions. Instead, it comes through struggle and pain but leads ultimately to victory.

Come, then, and eat the meal that is offered. Come, not just to a miracle worker with instant cures and easy answers, but to the one who hangs on the cross. Come, and be fed, for here is real food, food to satisfy, food to give life.

Catherine A. Ziel

R   SIXTH SUNDAY IN ORDINARY TIME
E   SIXTH SUNDAY AFTER EPIPHANY, PROPER 1
L   SIXTH SUNDAY AFTER EPIPHANY

R   *Lev 13:1–2,44–46; 1 Cor 10:31–11:1; Mk 1:40–45*
E   *2 Kg 5:1–15b; 1 Cor 9:24–27; Mk 1:40–45*
L   *2 Kg 5:1–14; 1 Cor 9:24–27; Mk 1:40–45*

Naaman was a man of power. He came to Elisha with all his might, his armies and his gold and silver to see if the prophet could cure him of his leprosy. Naaman was a man of the world. He knew what the world, in its shadowy power, could do. He knew he could buy just about anything. Naaman knew what the world could do. He knew his body was rotting from a fearsome and fatal disease. Naaman came to the prophet Elisha knowing both sides of the world.

Elisha knew what the world could do, too. He knew the law in Leviticus prohibiting contact with a leper. But he also knew what God could do. Elisha did not meet Naaman's wealth and power. Elisha simply met Naaman with the word of God which over-comes the world. This word made Naaman angry. He couldn't understand something that didn't involve the world's power. Yet, through the common sense "it-can't-hurt" words of his ser-vants, Naaman heeded the word of God through Elisha. Naa-man washed seven times in the Jordan, and was made clean. God's word washed him beyond the healing of his disease. God made him all new, a fresh child, scrubbed and clean as though he had just come from a bath by his mother.

A leper also came to Jesus. Probably he wasn't rich and powerful like Naaman. Probably he knew only the life of the outcast and the desperation of disease. From his place in the world's weak-ness, he reached out for the word which Naaman couldn't hear: the word of God with the power to heal. Jesus touched him and said, "Be clean." Jesus' word was even more powerful than Eli-sha's. It asked no seven-fold dip in the waters of the Jordan. Jesus' word itself was washing enough. Jesus brought a new word from God, a word which washes over bodies, hearts and minds and makes them clean, clean like babies straight from their mothers' baths.

Whenever we celebrate a baptism in our congregations, we are all brought once again into the cleansing power of God's word. The water poured over the person baptized drowns us all anew in its healing flood. The Naamans of this world and the outcasts of this world all stand beneath the same great waterfall of grace and forgiveness. The powerful and the weak, the articulate and the dumb, the rich and the poor, we are all one in our need for cleansing and rebirth. We are together in our need to be scrubbed clean by the power of God's word at work within us.

Jesus is for us both the water and the word. He promises that we will be people of living water; we are made clean. In John's gospel, Jesus tells the disciples, "You are already made clean by the word which I have spoken to you." Already made clean! What a wonderful word! We are created in new flesh as God's children, forgiven, restored and renewed for life.

Jesus' power to speak the washing cleansing word finds its fulfillment in the cross. There, suffering in our humanity, Jesus accomplishes the work which brings health and wholeness to the whole world. Through a sordid, dirty, messy death, the whole world is brought to the place of healing and beauty with cleansed hearts and minds. We who were the outcasts are now brought into the household for the feast. We who saw the rotting side of the world are healed of our disease and ready to join the banquet. Jesus says, "You are already made clean by the word which I have spoken to you." Just as a mother reminds her children to wash their hands before supper, God reminds us that we are already washed in the death of Jesus and ready for the feast. Naaman's power is of no avail. The law's restrictions do not bind. The leper sits next to him at the table. We all join with them in the feast of those who have been made clean in the living water which is God's word in Jesus.

Nancy L. Winder

R SEVENTH SUNDAY IN ORDINARY TIME
E SEVENTH SUNDAY AFTER EPIPHANY, PROPER 2
L SEVENTH SUNDAY AFTER EPIPHANY

R *Is 43:18–19,21–22,24b-25; 2 Cor 1:18–22; Mk 2:1–12*
E *Is 43:18–25; 2 Cor 1:18–22; Mk 2:1–12*
L *Is 43:18–25; 2 Cor 1:18–22; Mk 2:1–12*

When Linus is asked how high the clouds are, he looks at Sally and answers, "Oh, they're at different heights. Some of them are far-away high and some of them are right-up-there high." Charlie Brown challenges him: "What sort of explanation is that?!" And Linus replies, "Sometimes it's best to keep these things in the language of the layman!"[33]

Linus is right. It's best to keep things in the language of common folk. Science has never been one of my fortes! Maybe Linus's explanation is too simplistic: there must be a way to calculate the heights of clouds. But I am convinced of the truism that if you keep things in simple terms, you greatly help the majority of folks. The lesson for this Sunday is an example in point.

In both the prophecy of Isaiah and the account that Mark gives us in today's readings, we are called to appreciate fully the reality of sin, in order that we may know why forgiveness is one of the most proper activities of God. Our theology teaches us that sin is the rejecting of God. Our biblical understanding of sin further teaches us that not only does sin separate us from God, but it leads us away from God. This is what we have come to call "the consequences of sin." While it is true that we must forgive the wrong done to us, we must remember that we cannot forgive the sin. Only God can forgive the rejection of God. Only God can reverse the direction that human beings have chosen. How right were the scribes in today's gospel when they said, "Who can forgive sins but God alone?"

Today's gospel, however, adds another dimension to your reflection upon sin and upon our needs for God's forgiveness. While God alone can forgive, the faith of others can help. This is shown in the gift of the four people who brought the paralyzed man to Jesus by opening the roof and lowering him down. They became instruments from God, and because of their faith not only was the man healed, but more importantly his sins were forgiven.

Today's gospel is not only a call to take up our own mat and walk, but also a call to help others to pick up their mats and walk. Have we ever been one of the four friends of the paralyzed man in today's gospel in somebody else's life? We all have heard stories of how the help of another has brought one back to God. One such story, a great source of comfort to many of us, is of St. Augustine and those who helped him on his way to conversion. Later in life St. Augustine wrote of that experience in these words:

> I probed the hidden depths of my soul and wrung its pitiful secrets from it, and when I mustered them all before the eyes of my heart, a great storm broke within me, bringing with it a great deluge of tears . . . . How long shall I go on saying "tomorrow, tomorrow?" Why not now? . . . I was asking myself these questions, weeping all the while with the most bitter sorrow in my heart, when all at once I heard the sing-song voice of a child in a nearby house. . . . "Take it and read, take it and read . . . ." I seized [the book containing Paul's epistles] and opened it, and in silence I read the first passage on which my eyes fell: "Not in reveling and drunkenness, not in lust and wantonness, not in quarrels and rivalries. Rather, arm yourselves with the Lord Jesus Christ. . . ." I closed the book. My looks now were quite calm as I told Alypius what had happened to me. . . . Then we went in and told my mother, who was overjoyed. And when we went on to describe how it had all happened, she was jubilant with triumph and glorified you.[34]

Soon our thoughts will be drawn to the season of Lent. Maybe this is the time for each of us in our own pilgrimage to realize both that only God can forgive sin and that we can assist one another in making the journey to God. Let us spend some time in reflection and preparation to make Lent what it's intended to be: a new spring, a return to forgiveness, and assistance offered to the stranger.

Timothy O'Connor

[33]Robert L. Short, *The Parables of Peanuts* (Greenwich,CT: Fawcett, 1968), p. 21.
[34]St. Augustine, *Confessions*, tr. R.S.Pine-Coffin (New York: Penguin, 1961), pp. 177–78.

R EIGHTH SUNDAY IN ORDINARY TIME
E EIGHTH SUNDAY AFTER EPIPHANY, PROPER 3
L EIGHTH SUNDAY AFTER EPIPHANY

R *Hos 2:16b,17b,21–22; 2 Cor 3:1b-6; Mk 2:18–22*
E *Hos 2:14–23; 2 Cor 3:17–4:2; Mk 2:18–22*
L *Hos 2:14–16,19–20; 2 Cor 3:1b-6; Mk 2:18–22*

The day begins, and we are at it again. Eyes open to familiar sights; the same sounds and smells assure us nothing has changed. The body stirs, a routine entered upon, often with consistent and identical repetition. Our path follows all too familiar landmarks, requiring if not demanding the same salute we gave yesterday and the day before that and all the other days we have been here. So is our life.

Even when we move to other places, look into the faces of strangers, take on tasks in foreign misty surroundings which require greater attention, more diligent consideration, we are not dismayed. We have made ourselves in our own image. Obstacles are but momentary, petty annoyances. These too will be fitted into roads we are making for ourselves and our families. The cocoon we have spun for ourselves is cozy, snug, secure. No one should disturb us. No one should try to.

Newness poses a threat. We are annoyed at those who dance outside the fences we have erected around our worlds. Life within the fence is smooth, orderly, productive, predictable. We know why we are here, or at least we say we do. We know what we are expected to do, and we continue even if at times we know that our actions aren't very productive, do not really make sense. If newness comes, if an alien spirit arises to question us, we meet it to defeat it. The force of the new is disarmed, its potency sapped: all is still secure. The easy speeches that comfort cruel men and women have won again. Complacency rules. Nothing has changed.

But when the new breaks through the rhetoric, the programs, the gold ribbon panels and all the other devices concocted to ensure that the pleasant status quo will not be violated, complacency must deny its very nature. It masks itself in indignation and rises to fight. Forced by the insistence of the new, it must, yet it cannot escape honesty. No matter how routine, how dull, deceptive, unproductive, even demonic we have become, we will not accept the new, the unknown. Better to be slaves and have meat to eat, than to starve out here in the desert because of some vague promise.

Jesus challenges our protest, taunts our cautiousness, mocks our cowardice. Newness promises freedom, freedom that breeds vitality. Life is meant to be abundant, bursting at the seams in all directions. Predictability, mechanical procedures, pious preachment full of traditional vocabulary doing nothing more than lulling to sleep: these are not the fruits of the spirit. Joy and love and peace are, and these erupt where the spirit dwells. Those who live in the spirit know that to keep these gifts alive, the old must be discarded.

How much like a wedding this sounds! The early years of a man or woman: building, planning formative years—all that has been done—must give way to newness, must willingly discard the past to embrace the future, to grow in it and to be glad for it.

From the beginning, humanity desired a love affair with the Eternal. There is Israel the bride of the Almighty, Christ the bridegroom of the church. A union in all its fullness, all its potential, could be, needed to be, must be achieved within creation. The garden once lost could be regained and once again enjoyed.

So he took bread and made it new, more than the product of work and sweat and desire. Bread, born of the soil and the seed, the rain, the sun, the seasons, the hands; bread that could be chewed and savored, broken into pieces and shared with others or put aside for another time, another place; bread, a constant necessity, the sign of all that men and women must do in order to survive and enhance life: he took the bread.

He made it new. He made new what I work for, what I pray for, what I need for life; my efforts to serve you and you and you and so many others. I eat with joy my little bit of bread, you eat it too. Together we share in my gift, my labors, my self. I in you, you in me, we all in the rest. He made it new: I am the Bread of Life.

He took wine too. He had it to give. Vines produce grapes, grow branches, for more and more grapes: grapes ripening in autumn sun to the rich, juicy bursting point; grapes dying to be born again in cool, bubbling, foaming wine. Rich, tasty drafts soothe parched tongues and throats, spill deep into empty places, make glad, and promise a foretaste of the feast to come.

He took the wine too and made it new: blood poured out, spilled to cover and wash the hurts of the world, demanding that all peoples ponder why only blood can shame human beings to be remorseful for their failures, to acknowledge their transgressions.

New wine, rich, potent, delicious, and hearty, demands vessels sturdy enough to absorb its vitality, guests zealous to drain happily its promise. For he has made us new as well. By this eating and drinking, words spoken, words heard, the drama is played out again and again. God's newness nourishes, delights, beckons, invites.

Edgar S. Brown, Jr.

E   LAST SUNDAY AFTER EPIPHANY
L   THE TRANSFIGURATION OF OUR LORD

E   *1 Kg 19:9–18; 2 Pet 1:16–19; Mk 9:2–9*
L   *2 Kg 2:1–12a; 2 Cor 3:12–4:2; Mk 9:2–9*

On this last Sunday of Epiphany, we stand on the cusp of
Lent. On the mount of transfiguration, Mt. Tabor, we are reminded of Golgotha and the empty tomb. This meeting of Golgotha and Tabor is our last epiphany of the season, our last
revelation of our Lord's true identity. This day joins together
two moments of Jesus' future: his death and resurrection with
his being the ultimate prophet and final judge of the people of
God.

This meeting of Golgotha and Tabor is especially clear in Mark's
gospel. The lesson does not leave us on Mt. Tabor but culmi-
nates as we stand with Peter, James and John at the foot of the
mountain and hear our Lord charging "them to tell no one what
they had seen, until the Man of Heaven should have risen from
the dead." Prior to our lesson Jesus taught the disciples that he
"must suffer many things, and be rejected by the elders and the
chief priests and the scribes, and be killed, and after three days
rise again." Jesus' epiphany as final judge on Mt. Tabor is joined
to his being judged by humanity on Golgotha and by God on
the third day.

It is as if the text is saying, if you want to know who this Jesus
is, you must see his future. It is not enough to see him
exorcizing evil spirits, healing the sick, preaching good news,
and teaching about the reign of God. One must see him suffer at
the hands of the religious establishment, die by the command of
the Roman governor, rise three days later through the power of
God, and finally rule as victorious Lord. Here, at what many
have called the "hinge" of the gospel according to St. Mark, Jesus' fate is joined to his ministry. The author invites us to see
and worship our Lord in the wholeness of his being. When Tabor and Golgotha meet, Jesus is profoundly revealed.

Our gathering around word and sacrament is gathering around such a wholeness of our Lord's being. We focus on the presence of this exorcizing, healing, preaching, teaching, crucified, risen, and reigning Lord. The lessons proclaim him, the liturgy prepares for and embodies his presence. The Sanctus greets the coming of this most blessed one, who comes in the name of the Lord, with cries of Holy and Hosanna! The Great Thanksgiving offers our sacrifice of praise and thanksgiving at the everlasting mercies and blessings of God. The words of institution proclaim that awesome presence for us, and we remember with joy all that our Lord has promised and done for us and our salvation. In memory of his promises and sacrifice we ask that by the power of the Holy Spirit we too might be joined to the life and purpose of our Lord in the unity of the triune God.

This prayer is generously answered. By the power of the Holy Spirit our lives are joined to our Lord's. His fate and ministry become ours even as our sin and bondage became his. In our baptism we were joined to his death and resurrection; in our death we are freed to rise into his everlasting life.

Our text, joined with the liturgy, not only reveals Jesus as final judge and prophet, but also reveals our unity with him. When we hear his word, take, eat and drink his body and blood, we are joined to his future. Being joined to our Lord's future has force for us, force with public and personal dimensions.

We have recently celebrated the birthday of Dr. Martin Luther King, Jr. His life responded to the meeting of Golgotha and Tabor. The force of the meeting of Jesus suffering with Jesus judging characterizes all of Dr. King's work. His "I have a dream" speech perhaps best illustrates the power of the meeting of Golgotha and Tabor. In that speech, he was mindful that some of those gathered before him "come . . . out of great trials and tribulation," "the veterans, of creative suffering."[20] Out of a creative suffering grounded both in his vision of the Savior and in the American dream, he dared to hope. Dr. King understood that when Tabor and Golgotha meet in our public lives, God is profoundly revealed.

This is equally true on a personal level. An incident three years ago during the last week of Epiphany comes to mind. Our oldest daughter had been particularly surly for a couple of days. I had surmised that it was related to the death of Trudi, a friend's younger sister, and the severe injury of Trudi's mother in a car accident two days before.

I was concerned about our daughter's response, but she did not volunteer and we did not push. Late in the evening, she came down from her room to kiss me good night. Her body was stiff and her touch cool, perfunctory. I asked, "What's wrong?" She replied tartly, "What do you mean?" "I mean, you seem uptight and a long ways away from me." She sat down and began to cry.

After a bit she said, "I am so ashamed and angry." "Why?" She hesitated, then spoke, "Because I don't feel bad enough about Trudi's death. I'm mostly angry. Just angry about almost everything. I feel ashamed because I should feel worse for my friend and her family, but I can only feel angry!" "Do you know why you feel angry?" I asked. She blurted out, "Because it could have been me! It's not fair that life can end just like that! It's not fair!"

Indeed, it is not. Together we wrestled with the arbitrary nature of death and suffering. I shared my fears of death and suffering; I also shared my faith and hope in the promise of life in Jesus Christ. Skeptical of my belief, she shared her doubts. In the midst of this conversation Tabor and Golgotha met. Our Lord's joining us in a world that is not fair was joined to his reigning as Lord of everlasting life.

The question this morning is not whether our Lord is revealed when Tabor and Golgotha meet but whether we slow down long enough to notice it. When I look at the chances I have missed to have such conversations with my children, my spouse, my friends, colleagues, and students, I can only pray that I seek out such opportunities. In this liturgy we are invited and enabled to do just that.

Patrick Keifert

[20]*The Words of Martin Luther King, Jr.*, ed. Coretta Scott King (New York: Newmarket Press, 1983), pp. 95–96.

R   E   L   ASH WEDNESDAY

R   *Joel 2:12–18; 2 Cor 5:20–6:2; Mt 6:1–6,16–18*
E   *Joel 2:1–2,12–17; 2 Cor 5:20b-6:10; Mt 6:1–6,16–21*
L   *Joel 2:12–19; 2 Cor 5:20b-6:2; Mt 6:1–6,16–21*

On this day, the first of Lent, the Wednesday of Ashes, I am remembering the stench of soaked and smoldering ash, remnants of a Twenty-Third Street dwelling. Friends searched the rubble (aftermath of all-consuming flame) for something that might be saved.

I am remembering today the finality of fine white ash, coating my hands, invading my throat, and tiny fragments of bone, resistant to the funeral pyre, as we buried my sister. She was a victim of violent death, and we returned to the earth in ashes all that remained of her laughter and her love.

I am remembering today the aftermath of Auschwitz and Bergen-Belsen, Nagasaki and Hiroshima. The suffering of strangers. International carnage. The thick smoke, remnant of the slaughter of our sisters and brothers, hangs as a pall over human history.

I am remembering and I am grieving the irony of Congressional receipt of billions in defense-dollar requests even on this holy day. I am horrified by the prospect of future footprints in blood and ash. The song of my youth has turned to ashes in my mouth.

Do not speak lightly then of "getting the ashes" today. The palms from which these ashes come are rooted in the remains of ten thousand ghetto fires: in the coagulation of sorrow that was Soweto, Jonestown, El Salvador and Vietnam, the Golan Heights, Gethsemane, and Golgotha.

Do not treat lightly this historical ritual of our faith. These ashes bear near to us the specter of death. The deaths of murdered millions. The deaths of those whom we have allowed to die. The death we cannot long escape—our own. The death of the Christ of God—for us.

Do not take lightly the step toward the imposition of ashes. Do not come casually seeking some symbol of personal piety. Do not come quickly to assuage a faithless conscience or to appease an angry god. Do not come prodded by some misbegotten sense of obligation. This is not an hour for the proud, but for the penitent.

There is no magic here, only memories. We are remembering today the Son of God, made flesh for us. The Son of God, who, joining one generation of his people on this earth, shared their suffering then and shares our sorrow now.

We are remembering today the Son of God, crucified for us. The Son of God, who resisting human hatred and violence, submitted to it, even to death. He laid down his life, a sacrifice and example, for those whom he loved.

We are remembering the Son of God, raised for us. The Son of God, who, having burst the bonds of death, calls us from our death-dealing existence to new lives of love and compassion.

Come then for confession, for shame and for sorrow, at our complicity in the cacophony of human destruction.

Come then in contrition, repentant and grieving, remembering the suffering of our Savior.

Come then for renewal, re-creation and reaffirmation of the vows of holiness made at your baptism.

Come now and be sealed with the cross of Christ as on that day when with this same sign you were called to be a child of God; when with this same sign you received the promised forgiveness of God, full, free, and forever; when with this same sign you received the Holy Spirit of God with her promise of strength and sustenance.

"Return to the LORD, your God; for the LORD is gracious and merciful, slow to anger, and abounding in steadfast love."

Christopher Hoyer

R E L FIRST SUNDAY IN LENT

R   *Gen 9:8–15; 1 Pet 3:18–22; Mk 1:12–15*
E   *Gen 9:8–17; 1 Pet 3:18–22; Mk 1:9–13*
L   *Gen 22:1–18; Rom 8:31–39; Mk 1:12–15*

If Ash Wednesday was the day of our humility, the first Sunday in Lent is the day of our joy. Today we witness God's covenant with Noah and through Noah with the living creatures of all flesh, and we are witnesses of the covenant foretold by the sacrifice of Isaac, the giving of the first-born for the world's salvation.

Today we are witnesses of Jesus' baptism and the beginning of his ministry, as today this anointed one emerges from the desert of time to announce a new day of salvation and belief in the gospel. And, as witnesses, we too are anointed and our participation in the sacrifice is assured. The Sundays in Lent call us to consider our lives as a journey with Christ away from the desert. Catechumens and holy ones—those who have been elected for the Easter sacraments and those whose progress in our communities is already well attested—are at the extreme way stations of the journey. They fill our imaginations so completely that we may not see ourselves beside them, though it is the whole church, ordinary seekers as well as neophytes and saints, who are called to make this journey.

The urgency that the evangelist communicates is our strength for the journey. Now is God's dominion at hand, today. By tomorrow, Monday, we may have forgotten this urgency. We have observed many Lenten seasons, after all, and the journey metaphor has worn thin in our time. "Tell me about your path," is already a cliché in some communities, about as meaningful as the roughly equivalent, "What is your sign?"

But still. Today we begin a new journey that will take us to Pentecost, and even then will not end. Today we take up life itself, under the signs and in the hope of God's covenant and everlasting love for the world. The Lord guides the humble to justice— that is what Lent is all about—with symbols: on Wednesday, ashes; throughout Lent, the waters of baptism. The bow in the clouds; the dust formed in God's likeness and alive with God's breath; the father who withholds nothing, not even an only child; the flood as a wall of water that destroys evil and brings us to life; ourselves, the church, as the sign of God's presence: the first step into God is to delight in these symbols, to play wholeheartedly with the clay of humankind.

Noah's ark-building efforts stand at the beginning of this journey because the earth, with its hills and valleys, its grasslands and rivers, its clouds and rainfall, is God's sacred place. Though we live in creation as in a place of exile, God bound it in covenant with Noah to God's self forever, with compassion for all living creatures. God's patience waited in the days of Noah, because the lives of eight people were at stake. Nor will God abandon us. Never again will the waters become a flood on all the earth.

Abraham thought God had called him to wield the knife against his only son. But it is not our sons, it is our very selves we must give. And Abraham knew that; he turned and saw the ram and called that place "the Lord provides." Ultimately, God's salvation is God's self, the death and resurrection of Jesus the Christ. Noah's flood is a symbol of our salvation, the apostle says, because it corresponds exactly to the bath that saves us; and it is the same with Abraham's willingness to sacrifice his only son. Life comes from death; the time to live this truth is now.

What then shall we say about today and about this holy season? Our Lenten observance is not like our celebration of New Year's Day. Some carefully prepared and heartfelt personal resolutions may be in order, but they will not cover our responsibility for this time. Today we are called "to understand the meaning of [Jesus'] death and resurrection"[21] and to walk, in the power of the one who knows our temptations, "through the wilderness of this world toward the glory of the world to come."[22]

Lent is our acknowledgement that all humankind is meant to be God's image and likeness in the world, to make accessible God's concern for all living creatures and to enjoy the unity of all creatures under God. This notion of humankind as a procession into the *imago dei* is God's revelation of the love that indwells the created world, seeking its peace.

Prayer, fasting, almsgiving—these have been the traditional means whereby we enter into the *imago dei*. But we risk an immature practice, a foreshortened journey, if we continue to do these things exactly as we learned in childhood. The child abstains from candy; the adult gives up alcohol. The child saves dimes for poor children; the adult makes a donation by check or money order. Each has made a beginning, but the church must do more than tend to private virtue. Rather, let grown-up hearts yield their complacency and toleration of poverty; let common sense refuse to sell any weapons, no matter how conventional, that maim and destroy any part of us; and let our sensibilities harden against the enjoyment of scandal, political, religious or personal, that keeps evil in the public eye. Then will our thinking, willing and judging be conformed to the likeness of Christ. Then will we give every burden and temptation to the crucified and risen Lord and receive victory from the Lord the sweet waters of baptism strengthening us.

Worshipers especially must know how hard the journey is. Love comes first, then prayer and fasting. Otherwise we may become a people zealous for justice but unable to inspire it in others. Indeed, we may be good people, benevolent and virtuous, but if we have not discovered in prayer the reason for our journey, it cannot succeed. It is difficult, yet so important, to let our Lenten fast and the Sundays of Lent overcome our less worthy notions: that our personal shopping habits are not contributing to poverty, for example, or that we are too busy working at jobs or rearing children to be implicated in the problems of the larger world.

As we approach the Lord's table of thanksgiving and prepare to eat the bread of life, can we resolve in all humility to undertake such prayer and fasting? May God do in us all that we cannot do to make this community a lifegiving symbol of the salvation appearing this day in our midst.

Rachel Reeder

[21]*The Sacramentary* (Collegeville: The Liturgical Press, 1974), p. 154.
[22]*Lutheran Book of Worship*, p. 17.

R   SECOND SUNDAY IN LENT

R   *Gen 22:1–2,9a,10–13,15–18; Rom 8:31b-34; Mk 9:2–10*

This Sunday the readings illuminate each other profoundly. The first and third readings seem like reverse sides of the same garment. In the first lesson, God calls Abraham. His answer is: "Ready." Abraham has had many experiences with God's calling; he has been led places and experienced realities he never dreamed of. Once again he doesn't know where he is going. God says, to "one of the mountains of which I shall tell you," but Abraham does know what he is to do: sacrifice his dear son. Of course, as we hear the reading, we breathe a sigh of relief. God was only testing Abraham. God didn't really mean it.

We'd like to have this happen all the time, but the angel doesn't always intervene. Someone dies in agony and darkness, the victim of anger, despair. In old age, someone loses the gift that was most cherished: the ability to sing, to see, to hear, to walk, to make decisions. Wars declared and undeclared take lives in a

seemingly purposeless way. On our TV we see victims of earthquake, flood, famine. And each of these people with and without faces is someone's beloved child. Like us, they are the body
of Christ, and often unaware of their identity.

The last reading shows us a transfiguration of the offering. The
beloved son is radiant and accepted, and in the acceptance, brilliant with love. This is the ending we are required to accept by
faith because we so rarely see it.

So everyday we prepare ourselves. We want to mean what we
say. We are yours, we tell God. But can we let go of anything,
let alone our dearest hopes, dreams and desires? Can we learn
how to take direction, and bear the feeling of being without direction if that is what is required of us?

The second reading spells out the strength: "If God is for us,
who is against us?" In Christ we live and move and have our
being. The call is all round us, everywhere and in ourselves. We
are like the acorn that holds the entire oak in itself. We are the
seed and the son. It is ourselves we are called to offer in places
and ways we cannot predict. It is ourselves that will be given
back to us one day, radiant and changed.

So how does all this relate to us today? We ourselves are God's
call. We must look into ourselves and read the word written in
our hearts to which we must respond: "Ready." All of us are
somewhere on the journey that began at our birth. Aware or
unaware we are responding to the insistent call. It is important
to take time to know ourselves, to love ourselves and to raise the
call that we are to our own awareness.

As we learn to know ourselves as the call we are, then we gradually grow in the understanding that all we are and everyone and
everything in our life is gift. All, all is to be held with open
hands and offered in praise at every moment. We need to live in
praise and readiness. This is quite different from living in fear
and trembling about what is ours today and gone tomorrow. We
can brood and anticipate with great anxiety what God will require of us next, but that is not the life we are intended to live.

Even the awareness of gift and the praise of every breath is gift. We must ask for this gift and practice praiseful giving even when we feel stupid and awkward and ungrateful. In the eucharist, it is all done once for all, everyday. In this moment we are all together the body of Christ, the gift that sums up all our lives and gifts. Here we are in community. Where I am weak, you are strong. If I cannot sing, you can sing for me. If I do not know how to praise, your praise becomes my joy.

In the eucharist we celebrate together our call, and we go together to that high place of which God has told us. There we offer together the beloved son who is us and each other. And there we celebrate what we cannot always see: the transfiguration of our gift and ourselves into radiance. We celebrate the journey and the arrival, the darkness and the light. We affirm that God is for us and will not abandon us. We get the strength from each other, today, to continue on the journey and to hold and offer our gifts with open hands, in readiness and praise.

Eileen Paul

E L SECOND SUNDAY IN LENT

E *Gen 22:1–14; Rom 8:31–39; Mk 8:31–38*
L *Gen 28:10–17; Rom 5:1–11; Mk 3:31–38*

We think we know what it means to say that someone has a cross to carry in life. But do we really understand that phrase based upon the injunction of Jesus: "Take up your cross and follow me?"

Often we think of the cross someone bears as a burden inflicted by nature or circumstance. Harriet was born without the gift of eyesight; that is her cross. John has lost his job because of a factory closing and is too close to retirement to find new employment; that is the cross he has to bear.

Such circumstances of physical disability or poverty are indeed very heavy human burdens which should elicit both our compassion and our assistance. But these are not the kinds of things the gospel for today is talking about.

The cross Jesus calls us to take up is modelled upon his own cross. And the cross of the Savior has two notable characteristics to be considered. First, it was taken up willfully. And second, it was taken up in sacrificial devotion to others. Let us look at how these two characteristics define our own vocation as cross-bearers.

To begin: The cross of which Jesus speaks is something we voluntarily decide to do. It is not something inflicted upon us without our consent, nor some unfortunate difficulty that befalls us because of our carelessness or neglect. Jesus does not tell us merely to bear the cross, but to take it up. Life is full of burdens we have to bear because we can't escape them. But the cross can be evaded. That is the meaning of Jesus' struggle in Gethsemane. Jesus has the power to avoid crucifixion; but he will accept it in order to fulfill God's intention: "If possible, let this pass from me. Nevertheless, not my will but yours be done." That is his prayer—and ours if we would take up the cross with him.

Moreover: The cross we are called to take up is there for the sake of others. It is not some suffering we accept so that people will pity us, or praise us for our endurance. It is not some act of penance we engage in, hoping for personal spiritual growth thereby. The cross is suffering we take up in order to help others, even as Jesus went to Calvary on behalf of the world.

Thus to be afflicted with cancer or AIDS is not the cross of which Jesus speaks, torturous as those diseases are. Rather the cross is carried by those who willingly minister to cancer victims, when they could avoid it. The cross is carried by those who show compassion to persons with AIDS whom they do not even know, by those who accept the scorn of others who think most adult AIDS patients deserve no sympathy, but only condemnation.

To be poverty-stricken due to circumstances of birth or loss of employment is not the cross of which Jesus speaks, unfortunate as such deprivation is. Instead, the cross is borne by those who do not need to work in soup kitchens or shelters for the homeless, but choose to do so. The cross is borne by those who call for higher taxes or a reduction of spending on armaments in favor of social services. Those who take such stands will be maligned by friends who want taxes lowered or military spending increased. The criticism such advocates accept is their cross. They assume it voluntarily, for the sake of others.

To have a son on drugs or an unwed daughter who is pregnant is not to take up the cross. Rather taking up the cross may mean loving our children when we might instead kick them out the door, telling them to suffer the consequences of their own action without any sympathy from us.

To take up the cross is no easy thing. Indeed it goes against the grain of anyone who is not masochistic. Thus when Jesus spoke to the disciples of his own impending crucifixion, Peter rebuked him, tried to argue him out of it. Jesus, in turn, spoke the most stinging word ever reported of him: "Get behind me, Satan! For you, Peter, are not on the side of God."

We are not inclined to take up the cross, nor even to watch someone else do it, without arguing or impugning motives. But this is the call of the Lord, pressed upon us especially during Lent. This is the true Lenten penance—not giving up of some pleasure for the sake of our own souls, but taking up of some difficult work for the sake of others.

What crosses are you capable of assuming this holy season? What can you do, without thought of personal reward or even satisfaction, but also without regard for the criticism or misunderstanding that may be generated among your family, friends, and even fellow church members? Therein may lie the cross you are called to carry.

But the power to carry it comes from the crucified one, who by his body and blood given us in the sacrament strengthens us. To him we may offer this prayer of Ignatius Loyola:

Teach us, good Lord,
to serve you as you deserve;
to give and not to count the cost;
to fight and not to heed the wounds;
to toil and not to seek for rest;
to labor and not to ask for any reward,
  except that of knowing we do your will.
Amen.[23]

Laurence Hull Stookey

[23]The United Methodist Church, *The United Methodist Hymnal* (Nashville: The United Methodist Publishing House, 1989), #570.

R E L THIRD SUNDAY IN LENT

R *Ex 20:1–3,7–8,12–17; 1 Cor 1:22–25; Jn 2:13–25*
E *Ex 20:1–17; Rom 7:13–25; Jn 2:13–22*
L *Ex 20:1–17; 1 Cor 1:22–25; Jn 2:13–22*

Some days ago, I learned something about two acquaintances of mine. They are a married couple with a child, a girl of eight years. Just recently they adopted a six year old boy from Peru. He is physically incapacitated to some extent in that he has been undernourished for years and is smaller in stature than he should be. But he is also emotionally underdeveloped and has the mental capacity of a three year old.

I recounted this story to a friend the other day. He rolled his eyes, swallowed slowly and said softly, "Wow!" That was my reaction too. This couple did not adopt a child who was going to be an unadulterated delight. Perhaps no child ever is, but people who do adopt someone into their family have the expectation that the child will be a delight to them at least most of the time. In this case, this couple bought problems from day one. It makes you stop.

I want to ask you a few questions to start our reflections on today's readings. Will you grant me that what this couple did was of God? Will you grant me that their gesture looks like a response to the word of God? Will you grant me that this is the kind of behavior that Jesus exemplified? Secondly, will you grant me that, if more people acted in this fashion in our world, the world would be a substantially better place? Will you grant me that our parish would be different, that our neighborhoods, our city, our country would be better?

Thirdly, will you grant me that, when you see what might be, it becomes obvious how prideful, how divisive, how riddled with self-interest we are? Our parish, our city, our nation, our world?

Will you grant also that this kind of behavior is life-giving for those who act this way? "Lord, you have the words of everlasting life," we sang in today's psalm. Do you find the action of this couple life-giving? In your experience and in your mind, is obedience to the inspiration of God's word life-giving? Or do you see such behavior more as an experience of death? A gesture like this couple's would mean dying to so many cherished things in my life. I know I would have to give up so much.

We have come into our artificially created desert of Lent to consider such things. We fast, so as to see what kind of slavery we are in, what alien gods we unconsciously worship. We pray, so that we might rid ourselves of the illusion that *we* are God. And we do works of charity and mercy to get us thinking more about the other and less about ourselves.

We also enter the desert to find out what God's will may be for us. This is difficult work, especially when we are subject to all sorts of strong attachments. God asks different things of each of us. Do you want to know what God's will is for you? There are all kinds of ways to avoid the knowledge that God's will for me may possibly be like the action of that couple. Do you *really* want to know what God's will is for you?

Here's the rub: we say we believe in the word of God, we say we believe that God's will for us means a true and full life. Can we trust enough to be open to what God really wants, as that couple probably was? They were buying into a real diminishment of their lives in some ways, a change in so many things they had. You might say they were open to downward mobility. They are both professional people, healthy, with a healthy, bright and well-developed little girl. They bought into a situation that will change their lives for years, perhaps for as long as they live.

How could this be a sign of life? It is an act of faith, isn't it? And we have our model for this sort of living: Jesus. The wisdom of God shown in Jesus was absolute folly to people. Jesus' life was a secular disaster; it looked and smelled like death. No worldly wisdom could justify the kind of life Jesus lived. He loved unpopular people, he took unpopular stands, being faithful to his Father's will as he saw it. Worldly wisdom makes no sense of that. Jesus' life, just like this couple's act, was what sociologist Peter Berger calls a signal of transcendence. By this Berger means an element of human experience that simply cannot be explained by the collective wisdom of the world. We do not want to live by the wisdom of the world. We want to live by the wisdom of God that is the source of true life.

And so we continue our Lenten, desert experience, but probably with some trepidation. God may ask something of us other than what we expect. I am tempted to say: "I'm basically a good person. I do try to obey God's law. Perhaps my behavior is good enough." Well, maybe being a good person is not good enough. Maybe I am compromising the true wisdom of God. The gospel story makes me wonder, "Am I behaving like the merchants in the temple?"

I suspect the merchants in the temple did not think they were bad people, yet Jesus kicked them out in a rage. They were providing a needed service for the worshipers. Roman coins, the coinage used in Jerusalem, could not be used to pay the temple tax: one had to use shekels. So the faithful had to deal with moneychangers when they went to the temple. People also needed animals to offer in sacrifice. Merchants provided a necessary service for the worshipers.

What caused such anger in Jesus, some scholars surmise, was the fact that the business of buying and selling had gradually moved from outside the temple into the very court of the Gentiles. He felt that the house and the worship of God were being compromised and insulted. Jesus' zeal for his Father's glory was uncompromising. Hence his justified anger.

To what extent have we behaved like the merchants in the temple? God's hard word faces us, challenges us, but also strengthens us. We believe what the psalmist says, that the law of the Lord is right and makes the heart rejoice. The commands of the Lord are sweeter than honey. We believe this. Lord, in the celebration of your holy supper reassure us that our dying with you shall be our rising with you to fuller life. Let us see in whatever apparent death we are invited to embrace the door to your kingdom of love and life.

Lawrence J. Madden, S.J.

R L FOURTH SUNDAY IN LENT

R   *2 Chr 36:14–16,19–23; Eph 2:4–10; Jn 3:14–21*
L   *Num 21:4–9; Eph 2:4–10; Jn 3:14–21*

In Chicago traffic I have repeatedly found myself up against a bumper sticker that says "Life's a bitch, and then you die." In bumper-to-bumper, rush-hour traffic, at a crawling pace or at a dead stop, as we try to keep alert through a windshield awash with rain, or as we breathe in the exhaust from semis and busses in summer heat, that cryptic comment says it right. No matter how much I abhor that attitude after I've thought about it, I know that I've been tempted to say, "You're damn right it is."

But because I want to think that I've been formed to some extent by the gospel, and because I'm temperamentally given to stringent self-examination, I can't let the frustrations of life go with a moment's cynicism and some spontaneous profanity. Something in me censors the cynicism, the language, bumper-sticker reductionism, the culture that plasters sentimentality, politics, and tiresome jokes on its bumpers and rear windows. All this tumbles about in my mind and combines with my dread of highway travel, my dependence on it, and my longings for fresh and quiet spaces in nature. I add some moralizing about this particular bumper sticker, never on Porsches or Cadillacs but on rusted-out wrecks that pass from owner to owner for a few hundred bucks, owners who have to think a lot about getting laid off and getting back on.

That guy ahead of me in this stop-and-start parade down the Northwest Tollway who pulled me into his life with that short sentence, thought nothing more about it than to slap it onto the rear end of his Mustang. At some point in this traffic jam and my own mental meanderings I will realize that my education and Christian formation, my habits of rumination and concern do not make much difference: We're all here bumper to bumper, we move ahead only as unmanageable circumstances permit, or we sit, suffer, and curse our common lot. An image of being free at last begins to loom in my mind: it's the last hundred feet of open driveway, which leads into the cool darkness of my own garage. I'm home at last, pulling in my own rear bumper that bears some message about peacemaking.

My mind went back to the tollway experience and the bumper-sticker commentary as I read "As Moses lifted up the serpent in the wilderness. . . ." When the Israelites were frustrated and disgusted and rebelling against the circumstances of their own forced march to freedom, Moses needed something to get them going again. It was a bronze serpent, raised up like a standard, an artificial symbol of whatever it was, a seraph, that had afflicted them. It became the effective agent of their healing and forgiveness, the sign that injected hope and a renewed will to keep going toward the promised land.

"As Moses lifted up the serpent in the wilderness, so must the Man of Heaven be lifted up, that whoever believes in him may have eternal life." *Must* it says, telling me, the preacher, the Christian leader, that I have to get Jesus up there before people's consciousness in a call for their faith; telling me and all of us who share the responsibility for moving the Christian community on in life that we must proclaim the Lord as the source of hope and energy in a world of confounding circumstances and in the face of the death that defeats all our hopes. This word "must" pressures the conscience of a church already touchy about the weakness of its proclamation and the ineffectiveness of its preaching in a world that prefers to sit in darkness. I see other bumper stickers going by with fleeting statements about Jesus being the answer, flashing assurances that Jesus loves me. "I believe it," I say, almost grudgingly, as I cringe once again at this competition of easy assertions and cynical rebuttals, opposing standards, mutually abusive interest groups. Here am I, the preacher, clearing my throat, searching for the proper qualifications, the intelligible language, to make a balanced and credible statement on behalf of the crucified and risen Lord.

The Man of Heaven *must* be lifted up. Is that obligation, that necessity—that pressure—something that is imposed upon us? Or is it something at the very heart of God? "The LORD persistently sent messengers to them, because the LORD had compassion on the chosen people." This world regularly ridicules the messengers and despises the word of God. But the messengers, the leaders, the liberating opportunities continue to come, not ending. But culminating in the One who "reflects the glory of God and bears the very stamp of God's nature." At the heart of our own faith is a conviction in God's unfailing love; for generations of recurring cynicism, indifference, and despair have never had the last word or given the definitive comment on our human situation. The love of God is persistent, and the Word of God always finds a new voice in the most hopeless circumstances.

We are hemmed in by circumstances, or crushed by them, discouraged or despairing; yet the One who has been raised up among us commands our notice and our hope so that we may believe that the life we have been given is beyond time and measure.

John Gerlach, O.P.

E FOURTH SUNDAY IN LENT

E   *2 Chr 36:14–23; Eph 2:4–10; Jn 6:4–15*

Our gospel today brings us into the very heart of Christianity, to struggle with its central image. This story of the feeding of the multitudes appears in all four gospels. Next to the crucifixion and resurrection themselves, this event has made the central impact on the New Testament. We are feeding and being fed; we are entering the mystery. Later at the end of the chapter, Jesus will have made the mystery explicit, the equation of inner and outer. "The bread which I shall give for the life of the world is my flesh."

Because this reading brings us so close to the heart of the Christian mystery, it is important not to talk about it too lightly. At worst, the lectionary has an annoying tendency to resolve itself into tidy lesson plans. Corinthians speaks of the "immeasurable riches of God's grace." The gospel gives us a stellar demonstration of this point. The message rings out loud and clear: God feeds the hungry. All we have to do is have faith, plunge in, open our hearts, not count the cost, it is self-evident, self-enclosed truth: the classic gospel good news. Q.E.D.

Only how do I tell it to Elise?

Elise lives in the women's room at Pennsylvania Station in New York City. I met her there in what is home to her and her three children. They were begging. Elise, two preschool kids, and a toddler. Sitting there with Dixie cups to hold the quarters.

I talked with her for a while. Begging was new to her, she said. Three months ago she had had a job and a house; it was all under control. But then they raised the rent in her rent-controlled house, and she and her kids were out. They found their way to Pennsylvania Station, to the ladies' room. But then, she said, she had to quit her job to watch the kids so they wouldn't play on the train tracks.

Every time I have started to write, presuming I have something to say about this central mystery of our faith, I see Elise. Sitting there in a pew, the three kids next to her, listening to what I have to say about this feeding business. It stops me cold. I can tell how it's supposed to work, how it works metaphorically. But she can't eat metaphors, and I can't multiply loaves. In the real world, it does not connect.

Or does it?

Later in that same New York trip, I attended Sunday services at the Cathedral of Saint John the Divine. I found myself a part of Volunteers Sunday, honoring the many people who work in the cathedral's lively social outreach program. Six volunteers gave the sermon that day; particularly one woman's story called me up short.

When she first moved to the city, she recounted, she had been lonely, emotionally fragile, completely preoccupied with self. Desperate for community, she had begun coming to church, secretively at first, covering her face with a veil so as not to be embarrassed if she should run into people on the street whom she knew. Gradually she settled in, got caught up in the spirit of the place, volunteered, and found herself working in the soup kitchen. Confronted with real poverty, she at first ran scared. But then something caught hold in her, started growing with a life of its own, which gradually became *her* life. For the first time, she said, she felt joy—real joy—and some coherence of purpose. Barely peering over the top of the huge, stone pulpit, she spoke in a quaking voice, yet rich with a presence and an authority which gave the ring of truth to her words:

"Believe me," she said. "Love is real. Community is real. It's not easy to find, but don't ever doubt that it's there: so simple, right under your nose. When we reach out to feed each other, we ourselves are fed. When we allow ourselves to be fed, we feed others. In the end, God is the bread."

Right under your nose.

So often our faith feels like mere words: comfortable, familiar— just words. To hold them up before the misery of the world feels like trying to bail the ocean with a thimble. But in truth these words are gates. When we enter them, we find ourselves in a

wide kingdom that lives beyond rhetoric, where evident para-
doxes resolve into larger life and God simply is bread. In the
end, the most profound mystery of this world is not that so
much misses, but that so much connects. Something bonds this
world right under our nose to God, and God, aching in our
hearts for form, to this world. That is the mystery of feeding,
ours to enter and share.

Cynthia Bourgeault

R E L   FIFTH SUNDAY IN LENT

R   *Jer 31:31–34; Heb 5:7–9; Jn 12:20–33*
E   *Jer 31:31–34; Heb 5:5–10; Jn 12:20–33*
L   *Jer 31:31–34; Heb 5:7–9; Jn 12:20–33*

In this season of Lent we are called through the threefold discipline of prayer, fasting and charity to examine ourselves in relation to the gospel of Christ. We move, in both thought and in
deed, as the expression puts it, from ashes to alleluia, and we
are now in the midst of reading the meaning of the ashes. This
season, more than any other in the church year, calls us to a
pensiveness which could be dangerous if we were to become
self-indulgent and self-centered. But the season offers us the
means by which our lives might be centered. In today's texts we
are offered the heart of Lent. We are called to hear that heartbeat
and to allow it to become the centering tempo for our lives.

Jeremiah looked to a time when the heartbeat would be written
within, by means of what he called a new covenant known by
all Israelites without reference to our benefit of priesthood. Each
person would know the law within and would be able to live in
resonance with it. No need for priests in such a time as this. The
people would be living in the time of fulfillment.

The time is fulfilled here and now, said Jesus, and the dominion
of God is at hand. In the coming of the Christ we see the fulfill-

ment of that hope of a new covenant for which Jeremiah lived. Christ is the one priest, according to Hebrews, in whose sacrifice we know the highest, deepest meaning of priesthood. Christ knew the pain of suffering and nevertheless was obedient until the end. Christ is given the crown of life through the resurrection. By his obedience he becomes the high priest for us all, and he now intercedes before the throne of God on our behalf.

This is the language of divine poetry and is not readily accessible to logical understanding. This does not mean we cannot understand it, only that we need to understand it in a different way from cooking recipe or a formula for making soap. The language draws a picture for us; Jesus offers God obedience as a gift, and at the same time his humanity shows forth in the loud cries and tears which he offers to God in a prayer of lament. God receives the obedience of Christ as a gift, and this obedience is the ground on which Christ is raised from the dead.

Here is a mystery of faith: what is the reason that obedience is the ground of resurrection? Here is one answer. In obedience, the self which we invent as our own is dismantled and discarded so that the true self which we are before God may come into being. But this true being is not ours to determine; it comes only from God, it is a gift and not a construction, it is a character and not a feeling. This self has the stamp of durability and substance given by God: this self is not a self grounded on the whim of feeling. In obedience, the self we invent is put aside so that a new self may be given us, a self truer than any truth we can speak to ourselves, a self spoken into being by God. As Thomas Merton once said, education in Christian faith is more than information, ideology, or even learning. It is radical discovery of the self before God. To this we are called in Lent.

Obedience takes us out of our own notion of who we are and puts us where we can hear another word which defines and says yes to our life. In obedience we hear the call of God to a life of service and caring, in which the old self that we constantly create is forever being discarded behind us, a new self arising as and when we forget ourselves in service.

We need to see ourselves as part of a larger body than we normally do to understand this Lenten way. The need for sacrifice arises because others need space and time and goods with which to live. Our culture has not yet recognized any limitations; we continue to think that we can use up the resources we have with impunity; that we will create more and more bounty to include the others. But the truth is that we are losing the battle against poverty; the so-called permanent underclass continues to broaden in our society; our natural resources are being depleted. The merry-go-round cannot continue to turn at such high speed. At the root of our inability to sacrifice is a belief that we own our existence and need not take others into consideration. We each consider ourselves to be, contrary to the poem by John Donne, an island, entire of itself. Or we would like to be.

Jesus directs attention away from himself to God, and he constantly empties himself on behalf of others. These two aspects of his life both baffle people and attract them to him. He is priest in the root sense of the word, namely that he serves as a bridge between you and another person, between you and God. His whole reason for being is to empty himself in order that in him we might find the meaning of our own lives. Alexander Schmemann wrote that "the vocation of the priest is to have no vocation so that others might find their vocation in God through him."[24] This is how Jesus serves us as priest. This is how we serve each other as priest.

The disciplines of Lent are one means for us to enter into obedience. When we relinquish the sin of excess, when we redistribute our funds to the poor and the outcast and the oppressed, when we redirect our whole lives to God through prayer, we are put in a place where we can learn the inner secret of Lent. That inner secret is that in dying we live.

To speak of offering in prayer and thanksgiving brings us to the baptismal font, where we were offered up in order that we might become servants of Christ, stewards of God's mysterious creation, and caretakers one of another. Prayer and thanksgiving bring us to this table set with bread and wine, signs of Christ's love poured out for us in order that we might be in turn poured out for others. At this table we are invited to offer up one another in prayer and thanksgiving in that offering of aunts and uncles, mothers and fathers, children and friends, which is the priesthood that redeems creation and celebrates life among us.[25]

Jay C. Rochelle

[24]Alexander Schmemann, *For the Life of the World* (New York: St. Vladimir's Seminary Press, 1973), p. 94.
[25]Robert Farrar Capon, *An Offering of Uncles* (New York: Sheed and Ward, 1967).

R L   SUNDAY OF THE PASSION
E   PALM SUNDAY

R   *Is 50:4–7; Phil 2:6–11; Mk 14:1–15:47*
E   *Is 45:21–25; Phil 2:5–11; Mk 15:1–39*
L   *Zech 9:9–10; Phil 2:5–11; Mk 14:1–15:47*

Today with the universal Christian community we enter upon the final week of preparation for our yearly celebration of the Lord's death and resurrection. Since Ash Wednesday we have tried to listen attentively to God's word of life and mercy in Jesus Christ calling us once more to a renewal of our baptismal commitment. The renewal of that life-giving stream within our hearts should flow anew into patterns of loving service in the midst of our sisters and brothers within the human family.

The readings of this day's liturgy seek to gather the weeks of our Lenten journey around the Marcan passion narrative and the story of Jesus' messianic entry into Jerusalem. These two foci represent two diverse traditions of celebrating the Sunday before Easter in the early church. The Roman tradition of the late fourth and early fifth centuries was to read the passion on this Sunday, hence its name, Sunday of the Passion. The Jerusalem tradition, more interested in re-enacting the day-by-day events of the last week of Christ's life, centered its liturgy in the Palm Sunday procession on Jesus' entry into Jerusalem. The medieval liturgical tradition, which we have inherited, sought to combine both traditions. Contemporary liturgical renewal has continued the celebration of both traditions but has placed renewed emphasis upon the reading of the passion as the central focus of today's liturgy of the word.

On this Sunday of the Passion we read one of the synoptics on a rotating basis, while every year we read the passion according to St. John on Good Friday. The horizon for interpreting the meaning of the passion within our Lenten journey is specified on this Sunday and on Good Friday by the first and second readings of the liturgy, and most especially today by the second reading from Paul's letter to the Philippians.

We read the passion according to St. Mark in the midst of the community on this day so that the story of Jesus' suffering and death will be a place where all our individual and communal stories of pain, loss, suffering, and death during the past year can find some meaning. For we are confronted each day with the tragedies of human suffering that seem to challenge the truth of God's love and providential care for us. The Christian response to human suffering is not finally a philosophically reasoned series of answers but an invitation to the *kenosis*, the self-emptying, of Jesus.

The Marcan passion narrative does not ask us to choose suffering as suffering, but it does bid us to enter into Jesus' struggle to accept in faith the reality of suffering in human life. Jesus' agony in the garden and his sense of abandonment by God on the cross reflect the truth of our own human experience.

Paul says in Philippians that our attitude must be that of Christ who empties himself by obediently accepting death on a cross. Jesus' obedient acceptance is not a passive surrender in the face of suffering but an active and faith-filled listening to his own role in God's plan of salvation. Such listening obedience does not remove the human agony or the feeling of abandonment that are part of our experience of suffering. But in Christ's self-emptying of obedience unto death we are opened as women and men to the mystery of God's strange ways of loving us through suffering and death unto newness of life.

God created us as human beings that we might have life and have it in abundance. In the self-emptying of Jesus' passion, death and sin are conquered because they are taken into the mystery of God and transformed into new life. As we gather on this Sunday of the Passion around the word of God's gift of new life in Christ crucified and risen, we bring the mystery of our own experience of the passion during the past year as individuals, as a Christian community, and as members of the entire human family. Most suffering and tragedy make no sense to us, and we have often wondered where the loving God is when we are surrounded by pain and loss.

Today's readings tell us that through self-emptying, the loving God, in, with, and through Christ, is present amidst all our suffering so that we will have life in abundance. God's self-emptying in Christ gathers all our experience of emptiness, nothingness, and meaninglessness in the face of suffering into the cup of Jesus' passion so that we may ever drink the cup of new life. This day let us allow our experience of suffering to flow into the mystery of the cup of Christ's passion. Let us eat of Christ's body and drink of the cup of Christ's blood, believing that the mystery of his self-emptying by obediently accepting death on a cross will sustain us amidst the darkness of our own self-emptying and our own struggle to be obedient to God's plan of life through death. Come to the table of the cross and share in the victory of Christ by drinking new life greater than all the forces of suffering and death. May the stream of Christ's gift of new life in our hearts flow into the compassionate service of our suffering sisters and brothers in this community and in the entire human family.

Thomas McGonigle, O.P.

R HOLY THURSDAY
E MAUNDY THURSDAY

R *Ex 12:1–8,11–14; 2 Cor 11:23–26; Jn 13:1–15*
E *Ex 12:1–14a; 2 Cor 11:23–26; Jn 13:1–15*

This is the night on which we begin once again the three days' observance of the Lord's death and resurrection. We begin it with a celebration of the eucharist which inevitably calls to our minds the final meal of Jesus with his disciples: the Last Supper. But before we proceed to the eucharist a ceremonial washing of feet will remind us of the account of Jesus' washing of the disciples' feet at that last meal, which we have just heard read from the gospel of John. And after the eucharist we will strip and wash the altar in preparation for the rites we will observe tomorrow.

Before we begin, however, the lesson from the book of Exodus requires us to ask what we are undertaking to do in these three days. That lesson is the ancient mandate for Israel's celebration of the Passover. It lays it down that Israel must every year recall the events by which it was brought out of Egypt and made people of God, and that this is to be done "as a memorial" set before God and the people. The Passover, the festival no less than the events it recalls, is constitute of Israel's identity. Israel lives its life in Passover time.

English is almost the only language in which the three days' observance we begin tonight is called something else than the Christian Passover. By a curious set of circumstances English speakers call it by the Saxon word Easter. But this must not obscure the fact that this observance is quite inexplicable apart from our belief that the God of Israel has brought us too into the plan of human redemption through the death and resurrection of Jesus Christ.

As the Jewish Passover and ours intersect with one another year by year, we cannot be unaware of the long history of misunderstanding, bitterness, and worse which has separated us. We must be particularly aware of that history in our time. But we must also relearn from Israel what our forebears knew to be the

Jewish roots of our observance. Like the Passover mandated by the book of Exodus, our Passover celebrates the events which give us our identity as Christians. Our recalling of those events, our setting them "as a memorial" before God and ourselves, is constitutive of our lives as people of God. The church too lives its life in Passover time.

To put matters this way is to say something very important about our eucharist tonight. This is no more a simple redoing of the last supper of Jesus with his disciples than is any eucharist. Even if such a redoing were possible, in the fashion of the Revolutionary War reenactments which Americans have undertaken these last few years, it would take us back behind the events of which that final meal was an anticipation. That is clear from the ancient "tradition" about that meal which Paul sets down in the first epistle to the Corinthians and which underlies the accounts of that meal given in the later gospel narratives. That tradition records that when Jesus recited the customary blessings over the ceremonial bread and wine, and broke the bread, and distributed the bread and wine, he did it as a foreshadowing of the breaking of his own body and the pouring out of his own blood. And when Paul says that Christians are directed to bless, break, and share the bread and wine of the eucharist "as a memorial," he means that they perform those actions before God to recall the death of the risen Christ, the means of our reconciliation to God and to one another. As he puts it elsewhere, "As often as you eat this bread and drink the cup, you proclaim the Lord's death until he comes."

It is in just this way that we celebrate the eucharist at the beginning of our three days' observance. It is not a reenactment of a past event, which was itself only an anticipation of something to come. When we receive the bread and wine tonight, it is, as clearly as at any other time, our partaking of the banquet of the Lamb that was slain for us in the Passover time which gives us our Christian identity.

Now when the gospel of John gives us its mysterious account of the events of that final meal, it omits direct reference to the tradition which Paul and the other gospels record. It may be true, as is often said, that the author wants to keep from sight the tradition about the eucharist as appropriate for Christians alone. As that may be, his account of Jesus' washing the disciples' feet is most certainly his way of interpreting that tradition. In his account, the disciples have been bathed already: the baptized Christians to whom he writes are mirrored there. But they still need Jesus to wash their feet if they are to have any part in him. There is John's reference to the self-giving of Christ in the broken bread and the poured-out wine which the baptized received in the eucharist.

But then the author adds this further point about what it means for Christians to receive that bread and wine. "I have given you an example," Jesus says, "that you should do as I have done to you." Our lives too are to be used up and given away for God and one another. They are to be taken up in God's plan of human reconciliation.

This is a good point to make and to make dramatically through the ceremonial washing of feet which we now do before we pass to the eucharist at this beginning of our three days' observance. It is a point which will recur again and again. The self-giving of Christ which brings us to this eucharist has an implication for the way in which our Christian identity is to be lived out. We enact that implication in the washing of feet in preparation for our receiving of the bread and wine of the eucharist on this night.

Lloyd G. Patterson

L   MAUNDY THURSDAY

L   *Ex 24:3–11; 1 Cor 10:16–17; Mk 14:12–26*

It was near the mountain Sinai that God made a covenant with Israel. We remember how God had declared the ordinances of the agreement in the form of the decalogue. And we remember how the people had declared their willingness to obey. And then we remember how the Lord promised to be their advocate. "If you harken attentively to (my) voice and do all that I say, then I will be an enemy to your enemies and an adversary to your adversaries." There is nothing tricky or complex about the covenant that God made with Moses and the people. I will be your God, says the Lord, if you will be my people.

What we may not remember is how the covenant was sealed with blood. Moses had thrown half of the blood from the sacrificed animals against the altar before reading the covenant agreement to the people. After they declared their agreement, Moses sprinkled the rest of the blood on the people as a seal and testinomy to the covenant the Lord had made with them.

I am glad I was not there. The prospect of being sprinkled with animal blood is vexing to me. It is not that I am squeemish about blood. I find the senseless slaughter of any of God's creatures to be a distortion of the sacredness of all life. But more than that, I would rather not be sprinkled with blood because of the power and primitive innocence of that symbolic gesture. There is something voluptuous about the very horror of blood because it is a signal of life and death. At the same time that blood is an encounter with death it is also a sign of life, something rich and stimulating and vibrating. Most of us would rather not see life and death so close together. If being sprinkled with the blood of innocent animals is too close, what can it mean for us to drink the blood of an innocent man?

Even though this covenant with God was clearly accepted and dramatically sealed, it did not last. The story of Israel is in fact the story of promises broken. And that is our story as well. Our best efforts fall short of our intentions. The human story is a chronicle of disobedience and unkept promises. We live with an aching awareness that how things are not how they ought to be. Our expectations are greater than our convictions.

No one has experienced this discrepency between is and ought more clearly than Jeremiah. He spent much of his life on the ashheap of unmet dreams and unkept promises. From out of the rubble of Israel's broken covenant with the Lord, Jeremiah summons the power to envisage a new covenant. This new covenant will not be like the old one. No more tablets of stone. No more periodic reforms. No more sacrificed animal blood sprinkled as a seal of the covenant. This time, Jeremiah pictures, God will write these laws on the hearts of the people. "But this is the covenant which I will make with the house of Israel after those days, says the LORD: I will put my law within them, and I will write it upon their hearts; and I will be their God, and they shall be my people." We will know God as we know ourselves, from the inside out. And God will do this.

On Maundy Thursday, we celebrate the establishing of this new covenant, written on hearts of people rather than on tablets of stone, and sealed with the death of Jesus rather than the blood of sacrificed animals. The new ordinance of the covenant is a new commandment: that we love one another as God has loved us. When Jesus washed the feet of the disciples, he gave an example of the kind of love to which he call both them and us.

To be washed with water and sprinkled with blood is still not enough. It is still outside us. But what Jeremiah hoped for was something much more intimate, something written on the heart, something that would make loving God and loving our neighbor like breathing. Even sprinking with blood is not enough. And so Jesus says, this is my blood of the covenant, which is poured out for many. Death and life, up close.

God's love for us transcends all boundaries. God's longing for covenant was so great that God entered our world, walked our streets, felt our pain, washed our feet, and finally died our death. The love that God commands is fulfilled. The blood of Jesus is shed for us. Even before his death, he invites us to have a part in him, to ingest what we could never emulate. It is not enough to be sprinkled with the blood of innocent animals. We are invited to take and eat his body and his blood and mix them with our own. Full of Jesus, fed on Jesus, we will love one another as God has loved us because God's covenant is written on our hearts.

Herbert Anderson

R   *Is 52:13–53:12; Heb 4:14–16;5:7–9; Jn 18:1–19:42*
E   *Is 52:13–52:12; Heb 10:1–25; Jn 19:1–37*
L   *Is 52:13–52:12; Heb 4:14–16;5:7–9; Jn 18:1–19:42*

It is now the center of the Triduum, the great three days of the Church. We gather with the taste of yesterday's feast still in our mouths: the feast of love, self-giving love, the feast served from a table decked in white, the meal shared in the midst of images of foot-washing and servanthood. We gather remembering the meal of the past day, yet hungry for more, always hungry for more. It is as if yesterday was but an appetizer. We long for the main course.

Hungry in our deepest parts we gather before a stripped and vacant table. Nothing adorns this place except emptiness. All that is present is absent. The white vestments of the last day have now been scattered, and darkness and nothingness now find their home in this place. It is to this foreboding place that we come hungry. We long to be fed. We have a passion to be filled. Our very beings growl for some nourishment.

The word is spoken, the word that describes the menu for this center day in the great liturgy of the church. We listen anxious to hear what will nourish us and give us strength for the coming days.

But the word is a hard word. It is the harshest of all realities. It is the deepest of all fears. It is the darkest of all nights. The word spoken is the word of death. That is our feast. That is our meal digested into our deepest hungers this day. Death is what is set upon the table.

The prophet Isaiah speaks well of the meal upon which we feast. He serves for us images to feed us this day, the image of one who "shall prosper, shall be exalted and lifted up, and shall be very high."

But this one is not beautiful to the world's eyes. "His appearance was so marred, beyond human semblance." We know of this for we have seen the ugliness of a creation once called good, now marred.

"He was despised and rejected by men." We come knowing of rejection and of being despised. In the painful parts of our lives there are scars that speak this truth. But more than that, we come sharing a world where people are despised and rejected because of the color of their skin, the language of their people, the status of their parents, or some other difference that is labeled as significant. We know of rejection and of being despised.

The prophet Isaiah tells of the meal upon which we feast this day. He was "stricken, smitten by God, and afflicted." It does not surprise us. It is a dark and painful question that occasionally sneaks out of mouths, but is so ever present in our souls. How can there be a God if . . . ? Where is God? How can God allow this or that to happen? Affliction is tragic. Affliction by God is horrifying.

And there is more to this feasting. "Yet it is the will of the LORD to bruise this servant; the LORD has put him to grief." We feast today on one who was bruised, broken, and himself died as an offering. We feast today on one who holds all of the bruised and broken, the smitten and afflicted, the oppressed and wounded, the marred and ugly, in his wounded and outstretched arms. We feast today on a feast of death, a feast of emptiness, a feast of nothingness.

So it is. The central day in our great liturgy of the church is a feast day, a feast of death, the death of Jesus. Come and share the feast. For it is an ironic truth, but a truth to be sure, that this day is Good Friday.

Mark A. Olson

R E L EASTER VIGIL

R   *Rom 6:3–11; Mk 16:1–7*
E   *Rom 6:3–11; Mt 28:1–10*
L   *1 Cor 15:19–28; Mk 16:1–8*

We have gathered in the darkness of this spring night around the wavering flame of the paschal candle. In the circle of its light we have marked in our ancient book the progress of salvation, of God's mighty acts in human history. Yes, we gather in the night with candle and story and song—but we are not alone. Standing in our midst, if we but have eyes to see, are Adam and Eve longing for paradise lost, Noah searching for dry land, the Hebrews crossing the Red Sea, Israel yearning for the return home, the prophets eagerly pointing to the dawning of a new age. With us they hold in their hands the flickering light of hope in the God who will not fail to act in our lives as God has acted in theirs. Those who stand among us from the past are, in fact, living signs of who we are today and that for which we yearn in the depths of our hearts: the world transformed into a peaceful garden, the nations of the earth cleansed of corruption and greed, a people liberated from every form of oppressive slavery, a church which holds forth and promotes, with utter clarity, God's endless mercy and justice.

With Adam and Eve and Noah, with Moses and Miriam, with the prophets and all of Israel, we too hold forth our vigil lights in the darkness of this night: signs of our deep longing that every human hunger might be satisfied, every cry heard, every need fulfilled. We hold our lights forth to God, we sing and recount our stories, themselves our prayer that the ancient wound which has marked our race since the mists of time would at last be healed. Yes, healed within us, our church and world; healed because with our first parents we too have felt shame and longing, with Noah we have shared the fear of destruction, we have experienced, in our own ways, the suffering perpetuated by the unjust rulers of mind, body, and spirit, and with the prophets we have longed—have we not? —for a land, a place, a home where we might live in faithfulness to God and each other.

On this night of nights, we mark within ourselves and the world in which we live this ancient wound, and yet we sing of it as our *felix culpa*, a happy fault! How strange, how ludicrous these words must sound in the ears of those who know so well the frailty of our condition. To sing with joy of human strife, of private fears and social conflicts must appear absurd. And yet it is the very cause for our gathering in the night: to name in our history and our lives the forces of darkness while holding in hand and heart our lights of faith toward that great light which signals for us the truth of God's final triumph over every power of evil. "O felix culpa," we sing, "that won for us so great a redeemer!"

We gather with our catechumens at the four rivers of paradise, on the waters of the flood, at the edge of the Red Sea, on the banks of the Jordan, and at *this font* in order to be immersed in the river, the flood, the sea of God's infinite life. We have gathered with them at the creation of our first parents, in the valley of dry bones coming to life, and now in *this new body* in order to be filled with the creative and prophetic spirit of God's own breath. And we have gathered with them on the ancient night of Passover, in the fields of the promised land, within the upper room, at the foot of the cross, and at *this table* in order to be fed on the paschal lamb, on milk and honey, on the body and blood of the redeemer; yes, on the bread of life and the cup of our salvation. For it is on *this night* that Christ, who shall never die again, yearns and longs to be revealed to the world through us, his wounded yet holy assembly. "O happy fault!" we shout, that God has chosen what is weak and powerless and frightened, that God has chosen us to bear in our minds, our spirits, our bodies that which our ancestors in the faith longed to see and that for which our world so desperately yearns: our human folly embraced and rendered powerless by God's near-unfathomable compassion.

On this night we mark the steps of that age-old dance between human suffering and divine mercy, between folly and compassion; we mark the progress of salvation from the creation of the world to this place and time in history. We do so, however, in the light of faith, that God-given capacity to see our lives and our world, not as random moments of birth, work, and death, but as the very sacrament through which the presence of grace is being revealed in the ordinary signs and rhythms of life, in our limitations and the fear, the doubt they produce; indeed in our suffering, in our passion, yes, in our deaths.

Brothers and sisters, the ancient wound which still marks our path through this world is, to be sure, not the sign of our abandonment to the power of darkness; rather, it is the meeting place between God and humanity, between heaven and earth, between our pain and God's healing balm. This has been revealed to us, neither through spectacular signs nor in sensible words of wisdom, but through one of us, a human being, in the wounded body of our Lord Jesus who now is with us, eager to wash us, renew his spirit within us, and feed us on his life in God.

We stand now beside the font, our watery grave, which has become in Christ the healing stream which flows from the very heart of God. "Come!" says the apostle, "Taste the water of life!" "Come!" says the seer, "Drink at the river flowing from the throne of God and from the Lamb." "Come!" he shouts, "Wash your robes clean and you will have the right to the tree of life."

And so we who are thirsty for mercy and peace, hungry for love and justice, come to the font and the table. "O happy fault," we murmur as the water of life gushes around our lips. "Christ is risen!" we whisper as wine and bread mingle in our mouths. And then as we glance to the left and to the right, we see Adam and Eve, Noah and Moses and Miriam, eating and drinking and—yes—weeping with tears of joy, for they, too, have come home: home to the cross, our tree of life; home to the grave, our doorway to the promised land; home to the banquet of the Lamb, our table groaning under the weight of God's infinite blessing on our step, our path, our dance toward the dominion of light.

Samuel Torvend, O.P.

R E EASTER DAY
L THE RESURRECTION OF OUR LORD

R *Acts 10:34a,37–43; Col 3:1–4; Jn 20:1–9*
E *Acts 10:34–43; Col 3:1–4; Mk 16:1–8*
L *Is 25:6–9; 1 Cor 15:19–28; Mk 16:1–8*

"The Lord is risen! He is risen indeed! Alleluia!" Such is our joyous proclamation this day, made with shouts and trumpets and chorus. The air is charged with our great rejoicing, and all creation seems to thrill with us and join our song. How different is the tone of our celebration than that of Mark's account of the empty tomb and the first response to the news that Jesus was risen. Mark says the women who heard this news "went out and fled from the tomb; for trembling and astonishment had come upon them, and they said nothing to any one, for they were afraid." Curiously, that is where Mark's gospel ends. We are left hanging on this ending, with many questions unanswered. Did the women ever tell their story? And if this Jesus is risen, where did he go? Did they ever find him? And what is he doing now?

Perhaps most curious of all is the "young man" at the tomb, dressed in a white robe, speaking to the women. Who was he? Whoever he was, this is not his first appearance in Mark's gospel. The "young man" was part of the story of Jesus' arrest in Gethsemane, dressed then only in a *sindon*, Mark says, a strip of linen cloth used for wrapping corpses in preparation for burial. When someone tried to seize him, he fled away naked, leaving the garment behind. Now he appears at the tomb, dressed, a witness to Jesus' resurrection. "He is not here. He is risen." How very strange!

Who was the young man? Whoever he was, Mark's earliest readers could scarcely have missed noticing how much he was like them, for most of them had been dressed in burial attire on a night before the day of Easter, and had appeared next morning dressed in a white garment, bearing witness to the resurrection of Jesus. In between they had been stripped of the old garment, baptized, crucified with Christ, born again, and raised to a new life.

Whoever this young man was, he was one of them, or they were now like him. . . . including the women, who fled when maybe there was more to do or say. But eventually they also returned and told the story which has us singing Alleluias still today. In between they had died a second death. It was bad enough that they had lost one they loved. Now they had lost him again. His body was gone and they could scarcely grieve a healing kind of grief. "What's that you say? He is not here? He is risen, gone on ahead of us somewhere?" It was too much. Death and grief, awful as they were, the women understood. But risen? What does that mean? The women, too, had died with Jesus. They had believed in him, given their hearts to him, and something in them had died as surely as he did on that Friday.

Now they had come to bury a corpse, and in a way they did, though not the one they intended. What got buried forever on that morning was themselves, their old selves which were handmaidens of death and grief. These were new women who left the tomb, and even as they fled in fear and astonishment, they were on their way to where they would be the body of Christ in the world. Their beloved Jesus would clothe himself in them, and say to those who came to dispose of the corpses, "She is not here, she is risen."

Finally, among the last to visit the tomb are you and I. We, too have been the handmaidens of death and grief, laying our loved ones carefully in graves and wrapping ourselves in the cloth of mourning. We have fled away naked, our dread and pain exposed. We have died a little each time, and we have buried so many pieces of ourselves by now. But we have also died with Jesus, drowned in the waters of baptism, so that even in our fear and astonishment, when our tongues are tied up in confusion, it is not we who live, but Christ. We are the body of Christ.

He comes to us again in this day of rejoicing, eating and drinking new in the reign of God, now with us, giving us in the bread and cup the life which was crucified but is also resurrected. In this meal he clothes himself in us, and says to all the world, "There are no corpses here. You came to see the baptized ones? those crucified? They are not here. They are risen. They are risen indeed." Alleluia!

Frederick A. Niedner, Jr.

R E L SECOND SUNDAY OF EASTER

R   *Acts 4:32–35; 1 Jn 5:1–6; Jn 20:19–31*
E   *Acts 3:12a,13–15,17–26; 1 Jn 5:1–6; Jn 20:19–31*
L   *Acts 3:13–15,17–26; 1 Jn 5:1–6; Jn 20:19–31*

Now Thomas, one of the twelve, said to them," Unless I see. . . ."

If we are going to be involved with Jesus, it is always helpful to be honest and frank. This why of all the disciples, Thomas rings most true for me. His exclamations says it for me: "Unless I see. . . ." Denigrate him if you will—as has history with the phrase "doubting Thomas." I too have always had difficulty believing a bowlful of impossible things before breakfast. I too have reached a point when I said, "Unless I see in his hands the print of the nails, I will not believe."

Frankly, should anyone? Should we believe because the church says so? That's not enough these days. Whoever observed that Sunday morning at 11 o'clock was the most segregated hour of the week was accurate. Where are our credentials for declaring "He is risen"? How can we say that we have "seen the Lord" and experienced the breath of Jesus' Spirit? Was it at Auschwitz? Or on the Selma March? On the freedom buses? Where were the baptized twenty years ago during war that was going nowhere and that terminated in a Southeast Asian graveyard consuming hundreds of thousands of lives? Where is God, at once refugee and host, as thousands of homeless sisters and brothers beat on church doors locked tighter than neighborhood banks? And where is the church, the body of Christ that is to bear the identifiable marks of all who suffer: the hungry, the imprisoned, the unemployed, the paranoid schizophrenics now legion on our streets, the terrorized victims of first world technologies of warfare waged on the third world's weak?

Back in 1939 Dietrich Bonhoeffer attended New York's Riverside Church and afterwards wrote in his diary:

> The whole thing was a respectable, self-indulgent, self-satisfied religious celebration. This sort of idolatrous religion stirs up the flesh which is accustomed to being kept in check by the Word of God. Such sermons make for libertinism, egotism, indifference. . . . I have no doubt at all that one day the storm will blow with full force on this religious hand-out, if God himself is still anywhere on the scene. . . . But only an American himself can shift all this rubbish, and up til now there do not seem to be any about.[26]

Bonhoeffer wrote almost fifty years ago. And today? Is God anywhere on the scene? What is the visible evidence? Do you see any imprints, any stigmata? Is there any apparent presence of the holy catholic and apostolic church walking the Via Dolorosa that winds its way on the downwind side of our cities? Are we doing the visible signs of Christ's committed, compassionate and empathetic love?

In a word, when a disoriented soul from the street knocks on the church door it should not require four years of seminary education to determine the appropriate biblical and theological response: just open the damn door! If they say they're thirsty, "Here's the water fountain." If they are visibly imprisoned in their mental illness, hold their hand and accompany them on their frightening journey. If they are strangers with no place to go, call them in, all of them, burdened down with plastic trash bags. "Bring your meager belongings; come in and I will give you rest."

Like Thomas, we would do well to look for Jesus, not in the religious, but among those who bear the telltale marks of human suffering, and amidst a scarred and polluted earth threatening to become a "greenhouse" tomb.

In his Holocaust remembrance, *Night*, Elie Wiesel recalls three executions, one of whom was a child, too light of weight to die instantly of a broken neck. As he was hanging between the adults for interminable minutes, gasping for life's breath, out of the assembled deathcamp victims a voice asked, "Where's God now?" The response came: "Here He is—He is hanging here on this gallows."[27]

You want to "see Jesus?" Again, like Thomas, pay little mind to homiletical hearsay. Rather, find Jesus there among those struggling to survive, among the sisters and brothers gasping at the end of their rope, and gently bring them down in order to lift him up.

John Steinbruck

[26]Dietrich, Bonhoeffer, *The Way of Freedom* (New York: Harper & Row, 1966), pp. 230–231.
[27]Elie Wiesel, *Night* (New York: Bantam, 1982), p. 62.

R E L   THIRD SUNDAY OF EASTER

R   *Acts 3:13–15,17–19; 1 Jn 2:1–5a; Lk 24:35–48*
E   *Acts 4:5–12; 1 Jn 1:1–2:2; Lk 24:36b-48*
L   *Acts 4:8–12; 1 Jn 1:1–2:2; Lk 24:36–49*

We should know God, Scripture says in today's liturgy. Then it makes an even bolder assertion: we should know God in Jesus Christ. Then it makes the boldest of its assertions: we should know God in one another. You should have known whom you were killing, Peter argues. You could not tell the difference between a murderer and an innocent man. The innocent man was the Holy One of God. You must not make the same mistake again, Peter argues further. Then St. John says, echoing Peter, that if we do forget and sin against innocence, we can yet return to God through Jesus Christ. For Christ pleads for us if we wish it. It is better, though, to know God through innocence of life.

That is what God is in Jesus Christ, innocence. Then St. Luke
says, "a spirit has not flesh and bones." He is arguing that everything about Jesus is recognizable, hands, feet, voice, appetite.
For Jesus made everything human speak of God. So they fed
him at his request. And then they made the test of their lives the
love they had for one another. For that is the test he gave them.
He was the visible result of such a love. He was alive again due
to his Father's love. He breathed God through every pore. He
seemed to contain what nothing could contain, but the contradiction made perfect sense to them. For they felt that he had given
himself to them, and that contradiction made perfect sense also.
They were more themselves than they had ever been before.
From that time on they treated others as he had treated them.
Or they tried.

We seem to move differently, from knowledge of one another, to
knowledge of Jesus Christ, to knowledge of God. We are like the
woman who loved tulips. Loved to photograph them and give
her best photos to her friends. Her own house had no more
room. She was driving to a flower nursery one day when she
spotted a small home surrounded by a magnificent lawn full of
tulips and daffodils. There was an old woman bent in among
them with a feather and a plastic envelope. She had on a broad
brimmed straw hat and wore a calico gown to her shoe tops.
The photographer stopped her car, took her camera, hailed the
old woman and asked her could she photograph some. The old
woman was more than happy to say yes and allowed the younger woman her choice for a good twenty minutes, then said,
"You've missed the best ones." She took the younger woman's
arm and led her to a red tulip with black edges, and the black
went down the petal to form what looked like a crucifix. "That's
my Jesus tulip," she said. "Took me years to do it. And this
one," she continued, "this is my Holocaust tulip." It was black,
but there were red streaks on each petal, and they were joined
at the bottom the way a menorah is. "This took me years also,"
she said. "You must be a religious person," the woman photographer said. "Thank you," said the old woman, "most people
think I'm dotty, that this is how I hide from the real thing."
"Well, why these two?" the photographer asked. "They are re-

membrances," the old woman said. "Are you Christian?" the photographer asked. "No," said the old woman, "but my husband was. This Jesus tulip is for him." "And the Holocaust tulip?" asked the photographer. "It's for me," she said. "I could give you some bulbs if you would like. When the bulbs are ready." "Yes," said the photographer. "Then let me write your name down," said the old woman. The photographer fished a pencil and paper from her equipment bag, then held the bag like a small desk between them so the old woman could write. She took off her plastic gloves and on her forearm was visible the tattoo of a number. "Oh!" said the photographer. The old woman looked up and saw her still face. "My husband was a U.S. soldier who found me half dead. He came back for me. And took me here and gave me life." "Why the flowers?" the photographer asked. "I am asking God," the old woman said. "For what?" asked the photographer. "To make them all beautiful again," the old woman answered. "For what they have been through."

Jesus was made all beautiful again for what he had been through. That is why his disciples "still disbelieved for joy, and wondered."

Francis P. Sullivan SJ

R E L FOURTH SUNDAY OF EASTER

R *Acts 4:8–12; 1 Jn 3:1–2; Jn 10:11–18*
E *Acts 4:32–37; 1 Jn 3:1–8; Jn 10:11–16*
L *Acts 4:23–33; 1 Jn 3:1–2; Jn 10:11–18*

This Fourth Sunday of Easter goes by the name of Good Shepherd Sunday. In our gospel for today, St. John portrays Jesus describing himself as the good shepherd or, perhaps more accurately, as the real shepherd of God's people. Throughout the pages of the Hebrew Scriptures, God is described as the shepherd of Israel and the chosen people are described as God's flock. We made that language our own today in the twenty-third psalm.

We Americans become far too sentimental when we think of Jesus as the good shepherd. Nowhere do sheep and shepherds figure as part of our daily economic life. Consequently, our thinking about Jesus the good shepherd is informed by stained-glass windows. There stands Jesus in long, flowing robes unstained by sweat or sheep manure. In one hand he carries a willowy shepherd's crook that would scarcely discourage even the most timid wolf or mountain lion. With the other hand he cradles a sleeping lamb with wool as pure and white as new-fallen snow. You would think sheep the most innocent and docile of all creatures and shepherding one of the cushiest jobs around.

I have been a student in Scotland, one of the few countries that still relies heavily on sheep for its economic well-being. You may have some Scottish woolens among your winter clothes. In my student days in Edinburgh, I occasionally went with friends on weekend trips into the highlands. One inevitable feature of those trips was stopping the car every ten miles or so while a seemingly endless procession of filthy, witless sheep crossed the road, each one marked on its soiled hindquarters by a mysterious blotch of red paint. Finally, the last straggler would be booted across the road by a ragged, weary shepherd, who would then signal with his heavy stick that we were free to continue our journey.

I got acquainted with one or two of these shepherds, and they taught me about the role of sheep in the Scottish economy. Until a couple of hundred years ago, the country was populated by tenant farmers who had worked the land for centuries. But then a new dynasty in Great Britain decided that it would be more profitable to replace the farms of the Scottish highlands with flocks of Cheviot sheep. And so thousands of poor families were forced to leave their ancestral homes forever and seek a new life in Canada, in Australia, or here in the States. Those farmers who were too old, too sick or too stubborn to leave were burned alive in their cottages. Thus the highlands were cleared of people to make way for more lucrative commodity, the Cheviot sheep.

In view of this history, every Scottish shepherd has an ambivalent feeling about his sheep. On the one hand, they are the most precious thing in the world, his only means of supporting himself and his family. On the other hand, each sheep is a symbol of a long history of economic injustice, of the oppression of the weak by the strong, of the triumph of profits over people. And in view of Scotland's staggering unemployment rate, every Scottish shepherd has the shame of knowing that the lives of the sheep are more valuable than the life of the shepherd.

But the question I most wanted answered was why every sheep had some kind of bright red mark across its backside. "Och," a shepherd replied, "that's tae tell ye which sheep belong tae ye, and which belong tae your neighbor. Wi'oot that mark, ye canne tell 'em apart." That mysterious red mark identified the sheep that decided to wander away from the flock.

So every time I see a Scottish sweater, beautifully crafted from pure, snow-white wool, I think of the horror of the highland clearances, of the human misery that was required for some sheep to graze and grow fat, of those filthy animals with thistle and Scottish mud clinging to their woolly bodies, of a shepherd wondering whether his life is worth more than his sheep, and of that bright red mark enabling the shepherd to recognize his own sheep. And every time I see the people of God gathered around this altar, I think about how deeply our lives are enmeshed in the violence and oppression of this world, how our standard of living is at the cost of monstrous poverty for the rest of the world, how every time we get dressed or drive our car or go to the store or eat or drink, we help some vast anonymous corporation pollute our atmosphere, our world and our bodies.

And I think about a man who loved this cruel and wretched human race of ours enough to give his life for us, not because he had to, but because he chose to. And I think of the night of the Easter Vigil four weeks ago, when several new brothers and sisters emerged from the water of baptism; perhaps with some of the grime and pollution of this sinful world still clinging to them; but nevertheless dressed in pure white robes as a promise of what we will one day be, a promise of the innocence that will one day be ours by virtue of our baptism into the death and resurrection of Jesus Christ. And I think about the thick, dark chrism poured cross-wise over their heads, marking them for a time with a streak of oil and myrrh, cinnamon and cassia, marking them forever with the sign of the cross. For us, that cross-shaped streak across our forehead is the sign of who we belong to, whose we are. But unlike Cheviot sheep, we wear our mark where our real shepherd, our risen Lord, can see it as he glances over his shoulder calling us to follow where he leads us.

The world around us may not be able to see that baptismal seal across our brow. But this world cannot ignore our risen savior when he raises his club to bring this world to a halt. This world cannot ignore a whole flock of people who follow their shepherd by saying No to oppression and violence, by taking the side of the victim, by defending the weak and helpless, by speaking for those with no voice in our society. This world cannot ignore a community of baptized people who are willing to put their time, talents, possessions and lives on the line to bring some mercy, compassion, and humanity into this society. This world cannot ignore us as our risen Lord leads us into the new creation promised by his resurrection. Sooner or later this world must hear the news that has changed our lives and made us new people. Sooner or later this world must know that Christ is risen.

Martin Hauser

R L FIFTH SUNDAY OF EASTER

R *Acts 9:26–31; 1 Jn 3:18–24; Jn 15:1–8*
L *Acts 8:26–40; 1 Jn 3:18–24; Jn 15:1–8*

Karl Rahner, one of the preeminent theologians of our time, once wrote about a conversation he had with another theologian whose attitude toward Jesus seemed to Rahner to be "rather rationalistic." At one point in the exchange Rahner attempted to bring the discussion to a less esoteric (but in fact more sublime) height by saying, "Yes, you see, you're actually only really dealing with Jesus when you throw your arms around him and realize right down to the bottom of your being that this is something you can still do today."[28] I thought of that when I read today's gospel.

Jesus says that he is the vine and that we are the branches. Insofar as we abide in him and he in us, we will bear much fruit; insofar as we do not, we will be absolutely ineffective. Furthermore, if we do abide in Jesus and bear fruit, we will be pruned so that we may accomplish even more.

Often, I suspect, we think too "rationalistically" about what that might mean. Often, I suspect, we analyze more readily than we visualize. Jesus' image is evocative, however, precisely because it is so concrete and vivid, so earthy. Jesus' allegory touched the hearts and minds of his disciples because it was so rooted in their experience, not only of vineyards, but also of the prophets of old.

The disciples knew how necessary it was for branches and vine to be one if there were to be fruit for the harvest; they knew how that relationship symbolized the interdependence of God and Israel. They knew. Israel could do nothing without God; God, remarkably, could do nothing without Israel. The work of salvation was to be accomplished through those people whom God had so gratuitously chosen; their identity as a people was to be inextricably bound with God's call.

Most of us are a bit removed from the vineyards, a bit removed from the values of pruning. We leave the vineyards to the wine conglomerates of California, France, or Germany; we leave the pruning to the electric company, the nurseries or the neighborhood children and their bikes! But we know about the importance of the vine to the branches and vice versa; we know about the value of trimming back oaks and elms, geraniums and roses. But mostly we know about love. We know about the importance of a caress, an embrace; we know about the value of encouraging and challenging our friends. We know the risks of complacency, the danger of taking one another for granted. Yes, mostly we know about love.

I wonder, however, how many of us consider frequently enough the love that Jesus bears for us, the love that Jesus invites from us, in the language of human affection. How often, for example, do we picture him glancing our way with delight? How often do we find ourselves grinning at the thought of his smile? How often do we imaginatively "feel" the strength and warmth of his embrace? Would such revelry in love's nearness be unfitting? Does such imagery detract from the sublime mystery of the divine encounter with humanity? I think not.

Perhaps we need to risk a touch of excessive piety now and again for the sake of the gospel. Perhaps we need to risk imagining our arms around Jesus, his arms around us. What else could it possibly mean to abide in the beloved? What else could it possibly mean to be filled with the Spirit—the personified love that bonds Jesus and the Father?

Barbara Finan

[28]Karl Rahner, *The Love of Jesus and the Love of Neighbor* (New York: Crossroad, 1983), p. 23.

E FIFTH SUNDAY OF EASTER

E   *Acts 8:26–40; 1 Jn 3:18–24; Jn 14:15–21*

The reasons behind this behavior may not be clear, but the behavior itself is undeniable. Though more apparent among urbanites and the middle-aged, it is nevertheless true that all Americans live a somewhat schizophrenic life. We have distinctive wardrobes, separate vocabularies and varying personalities for the different segments of our day. We wear old clothes at home, but they never accompany us to school; we shout in jubilation and frustration at play, but seldom vent such emotions at the office; we abandon every social convention when eating in front of the television, but reinstate them when dining with friends; and we reveal vulnerability and affection to our loved ones, but not to the lunch crowd we plow through each noon. It is a phenomenon so ingrained in our national personality that we actually applaud others for keeping their personal and professional lives separate, and think it complimentary to be told that we are "another person" away from work or outside of the home.

In his widely acclaimed study on American society, *Habits of the Heart*, Robert Bellah recognized this tendency to divide our day into isolated segments as typically American. According to Bellah, this activity may have originated as a defense against a culture where the demands of work, family and community are sharply divided and often contradictory. Whatever the explanation, however, this is a pervasive characteristic which manifests itself even in religion.

It sounds sacrilegious to suggest that Americans use religion like a wardrobe accessory, yet the urge is in all of us. We consistently relegate religion to specific times and places, controlled by well defined rules. We like our God the same way: well-defined and easily controlled. Thus we insist on a God who is not mother, brother or friend but Father, and is as predictable as "he" is well-defined: summoned from the heavens like a cosmic messenger boy when the need arises, and dispatched back into the cosmos when our request has been fulfilled.

One of the unsettling revelations about the God of Jesus Christ, however, is that his deity will not be accommodated to our categories. Instead of a grandfatherly figure on a throne of gold, we get glimpses of a divine insomniac who spends eternal nights pacing the heavens plotting our return. Instead of a God who follows our well-crafted rules of etiquette, we discover an unorthodox party crasher who brings the unwashed to our kingdom banquet, and expects us to toast them. And instead of a well-behaved demiurge who restricts religious commerce to Sunday morning at the local prayer station, we encounter a Holy One who neither keeps an appointment book nor spends much time in church.

This is something of the image of the divine intruder hinted at in today's word. It is true that, aside from the story of the converted eunuch, today's proclamation sounds like a relatively innocuous call to love. What lies at the heart of this word, however, is an unpredictable God who expects unpredictable responses.

We begin with the "eunuch meets Philip" story, which is not a commentary on apostolic rapid transit but a story about sharing the word with the wrong person. Our migrating court official, remember, was a pagan flirting with Judaism, and therefore an ideal symbol of the unexpected hearer. This Ethiopian banker was also an idealized symbol of the unexpected response: quickly translating word into deed, and explanation into baptism at the nearest roadside oasis. Fundamentally, this isn't a story about the eunuch at all, but about the divine word who intrudes in the most unexpected of lives and demands an unconditional response. As the gospel writer reminds us, the God of Jesus isn't a Sunday morning ecclesiastic who can be forgotten once we've hit the parking lot. This is a God who demands, in response to the divine commandment, a love which does not stay on the lips or in the church, but works its way into the body.

For all baptized this is the premiere season for action, when the God who could not be contained by death called forth in divine obedience the unexpected from Jesus and from us. Jesus' response, like that articulated in the second reading, was a response in deed and in truth, not just in words. To discover our response, we ask: Where is the secret from which we have barred the divine intruder? Who is the unexpected hearer who awaits our invitation to the gospel? What is our private death which awaits resurrection? Where is the place of prejudice or rejection which calls forth love in spirit and in truth? To ask ourselves the questions is to summon again the Paraclete, unrecognized by the world, but present in our response to a restless God.

Edward Foley, Capuchin

R *Acts 10:25–26,34–35,44–48; 1 Jn 4:7–10; Jn 15:9–17*
E *Acts 11:19–30; 1 Jn 4:7–21; Jn 15:9–17*
L *Acts 11:19–30; 1 Jn 4:1–11; Jn 15:9–17*

The alleluias rang out on the Easter night. They have multiplied and echoed over these days of Easter season. Somehow we who are church bounce with joy and with good reason. The once crucified one is raised up, victorious. We are not as we were. New members have enlivened us. Godparents and newborn bring a fresh outpouring of divine love. It is luxuriant and intoxicating.

It can also lure us into a banal euphoria, into a superficial enthusiasm! No one of us wants to diminish the strength of the alleluias. Let them ring out! And let us also learn what the risen one shapes in our inmost being during this wonderful season. The Spirit of the Christ, the one who inspires our alleluias, breathes life into these festive alleluias; this Spirit is shaping something precious that will endure long beyond Pentecost.

The Spirit is shaping an affective and apostolic heart in all of us singly and together. Let us listen to that Spirit-song well and learn its melody.

The melody is that of lovers. John's gospel places these words on Jesus' lips: "As the Father has loved me, so have I loved you; abide in my love." We learn a new melody. It is not the song that one sings to another in order to use the other for one's own purpose. Such a song makes another into an object. Such a tune manipulates the other into doing what I want. Such a song smothers love because it does not allow the other to become what he or she is called to become. This song is not a counterfeit song. It is instead a song of presence, of being with the other without calculation.

John's gospel goes on: "This is my commandment, that you love one another as I have loved you. Greater love has no one than this, that a man lay down his life for his friends. You are my friends; I have called you friends." There is cause for alleluia here. No one of us is present to the others among us in a second-class fashion. We sing a song shaped on sacrificial love and friendship. So strong has this been in Christian heritage that the medieval writers changed the Scripture to read: God is friendship and the one who abides in friendship, abides in God, and God in that one. We are not slaves; we are not members of Christ based on hierarchies of status or greater or lesser rank. We are, lettered and unlettered, male and female, newborn and long-born, friends.

The Spirit can shape affective and apostolic hearts when we see ourselves as church, as a society of friends. Such friendship in Christ makes us companions at the Lord's table. There is a scandal in this. It goes against the competition models we have learned. It brings us into a communion of people bonded together in affective ties because God chose us and loved us first.

The implications of this friendly society are powerful, as vibrant as the alleluias which ring out. First, our society of friends is open to all people, black and white, Indian and Asian, Anglo and Latino. It is expressed in our greeting of one another when we gather, when we exchange the gift of peace and when we come to the table. Second, it is not meant to be hoarded among ourselves. The Spirit who shapes affective ties also shapes an apostolic heart. We, a covenant people, a promised land flowing with milk and honey, covenant with others, with people of the first covenant, with other Christians, with people of sincere heart. The song we sing is a new song. It is a melody of friendship offered to our cosmos. We sing alleluia when we make commitments to our soil and seas, our air and our forests. We sing a new melody by being people whose mission is to newly arrived peoples, to those who are unemployed, to those who are downtrodden by unjust systems that deny just wages and deny access to resources that the able-bodied take for granted.

Peter lifted Cornelius up and said: "Stand up; I too am a human being." Some came to Antioch and spoke to the Greeks preaching the Lord Jesus. The one who is in us is greater than the one who is in the world.

Many false prophets have gone out into the world. We go out without fear, with love and with humility. The friendship we share here is one we can bring to others. Such a mission is a joy. Such action indicates a fresh initiative of the Spirit. Such a task brings delightful merriment and creative hope for our world.

John J. O'Brien, C.P.

R E L   ASCENSION DAY

R   *Acts 1:1–11; Eph 1:17–23; Mk 16:15–20*
E   *Acts 1:1–11; Eph 1:15–23; Lk 24:49–53*
L   *Acts 1:1–11; Eph 1:16–23; Lk 24:44–53*

Once a year the day of the ascension rolls around of the church calendar. The church calls it a feast, which means a celebration. We can have trouble celebrating the ascension when we get all tangled up in the mechanics of the event. The "how's" have a way of blinding us to God's truths.

The story of Jesus and Nicodemus is a case in point. Nicodemus came down with a severe case of the how's. How can I enter the womb again? How can I be born anew when I am a senior citizen? Being so concerned with mechanics can happen to us at the ascension. If "How" is our primary concern, the ascension is only a fantastic feat, a cosmic trick. To dwell on how the ascension happened will only turn it into a biblical sideshow, complete with wires and mirrors. We could speculate forever on what happened and never figure it out. Yet we are not supposed to figure it out. We are to be drawn into what the ascension meant for the disciples and what it means for us.

The ascension is about endings and beginnings. It is about joy and hope. The earthly ministry of Jesus had ended. He had taken up the cup prepared for him as he suffered under Pontius Pilate, was crucified, dead and buried. The time had now come for him to return to the Father and take his place at the right hand of God. We know this is true, but why the dramatic exit? Ultimately, God only knows; perhaps it has something to do with finality. This dramatic parting proclaims in a vivid way that Jesus' time with us in human form is over.

So what does this departure mean? Is "Out of sight, out of mind," what it meant? Obviously not. How about "Absence makes the heart grow fonder"? No, that won't work either. Neither cliche fits. Jesus is not "out of sight, out of mind," and it is not his absence but his profound presence that makes our hearts grow fonder.

The ascension signals the beginning of the reign of Christ. Jesus has left the boundaries of time and space and has taken his place with God. The ascension is not something to cry over, but rather something to cause joy. As Jesus told the disciples in John's gospel, "it is better for you that I go to the Father." He is now the great intercessor described in the book of Hebrews. He is above all and in all. All is now his: life, death, defeat, victory, sorrow and joy. Now nothing, as Paul tells us, can separate us from his love.

The ascension means he is with us in the most profound sense. He is with us when we gather, two or three in his name. He is with us in word proclaimed, he is with us in bread shared and wine poured. He is with us as Savior for he is able to save those who approach God through him. The ascension is no time for tears. In Luke's account, we are told the disciples went away to Jerusalem, not to hold a funeral, but to raise a few toasts!

This is why we too are gathered together. We are not here to hold a memorial service for someone who is absent, nor are we here to sit and reflect upon the vacuum created by his exit. No, we are here to celebrate. It's a party! The church calls it a feast, a feast in honor of the crucified, risen and ascended Christ who is with us till the end of the age.

We have every reason to be joyful and full of thanks, just as the disciples were on that very first Ascension Day. This Ascension Day is a feast, a time to make eucharist, a time to give thanks.

This day, as always, we have the joyful opportunity of approaching the throne of grace to receive mercy and favor. So come, let us feast.

Karen M. Ward

R E L SEVENTH SUNDAY OF EASTER

R   *Acts 1:15–17,20a,20c-26; 1 Jn 4:11–16; Jn 17:11b-19*
E   *Acts 1:15–26; 1 Jn 5:9–15; Jn 17:11b-19*
L   *Acts 1:15–26; 1 Jn 4:13–21; Jn 17:11b-19*

There is in today's gospel good news that invites us to celebrate the mystery at the heart of our salvation: that God longs for us; that God longs for us with passion and fire and spirit; that God longs for us in Christ. The readings from John especially and most graphically invite us to celebrate our thanksgiving for the good, ever joyous news that we are beloved. Our salvation could have been a divine gift from heaven, but our being beloved could only come from and be revealed to us within God's humanity, from God's heart—a heart that in the womb beat with the heart of the mother, a heart that was moved by the frailty of our human nature, a heart that humanly rejoiced and suffered and loved. Every time we celebrate God's love as revealed to us in the face of Jesus, we touch at the core of our faith: God never abandons us, never lets us go, never lets the world go, but seeks to reclaim it through the power of love. After the incarnation a part of our humanity is forever assumed by God; it is with God so that the love of the Father and the Spirit for us is made constantly available to us, God's beloved children. "Beloved, let us love one another; for love is of God." Love for us Christians is not so much a goal to be achieved as a gift to be welcomed and shared. We love because we are first beloved, because we share in the very source of love that is God.

Jesus has been sent to us so that our weakness may be strengthened and empowered, our indifference healed, our faults forgiven. We are not merely called to love. We are enabled to love in the measure of our faith and availability to God. Love consists of this: not that we have loved God but that God has loved us.

The first vocation of every Christian is to be loving towards others. Like Jesus who welcomed in his heart the poor and the sick, like Jesus who loved the enthusiasm of Peter as well as the doubt of Thomas, the humiliation of Mary Magdalene as well as the humility of his mother, the intimacy of John as well as the distance of Judas, like Jesus we welcome every brother and sister within the community of the church and the world. We forgive like Jesus, who died because of the most hateful things that human beings can do and yet refused to condemn humanity in himself or in others. Loving and forgiving others, Jesus came into conflict with every partial insight, ideology and system that would constrain God's love and forgiveness. But he could not live otherwise because he knew this was the way to implement God's loving compassion in a sinful world. Like Jesus we rejoice in the others' gifts, we listen and respect their diversity and uniqueness.

The love that God revealed to us in the face of Jesus is not possessive or exclusive but outreaching and universal. The more the Father loves the Son, the more the Father offers, hands him over to us, not in spite of but for our sins, for our forgiveness, especially in this mystery of the eucharist where Jesus becomes the humble, life-giving bread, the source of our witness and our love. Through this mystery and the love we bear to one another, God dwells in us and the gift of God's love is brought to perfection in us. Only when we are given of this love are we enabled to be sent to others, given to the world for its salvation.

Our thanksgiving for being beloved is also a commitment for us to share that love with the least of our brothers and sisters in the world. Our solidarity with those who suffer, our humble presence with those who are poor, our respectful proclamation of the gospel to those who are searching for the truth, bring to people the love we ourselves have first received and open for them the way to the only one who is truly gentle and humble of heart. Everyone who loves has knowledge of God, and everyone who loves makes known to others the gift of that God whom no one has ever seen. Jesus, loving us from his heart, made touchable for us the love of the invisible God. So we, loving from our hearts, make visible, authentic, and efficacious for others the proclamation of the good news. Just as Jesus was not shielded from pain and difficulty, our salvation does not mean that God rescues us from what is upsetting or frightening or painful, but that God is with us in anything that life can bring. God's power is never equated with force—even against those who would crucify Christ—but is the disarming appearance of love in this world.

But there is something else in the proclamation of Christ's love for us. Love tends naturally to conformity: two friends always attentive to meet the other's unexpressed desires; a child of simple faith, convinced to do something simply because Jesus would do it also. Christ in the humanity of his heart loved us so much as to become in everything like us. Yet in the divinity of his nature, so much more did he love us as to allow us to become like God. There is no limitation indeed in the humanness of his love for us. "Those who confess that Jesus is the Son of God, God abides in them, and they in God. So we know and believe the love God has for us."

Kathleen Cannon, O.P.

R PENTECOST SUNDAY
E DAY OF PENTECOST

R *Acts 2:1–11; 1 Cor 12:3b–7,12–13; Jn 20:19–23*
E *Acts 2:1–11; 1 Cor 12:4–13; Jn 20:19–23*

The Christian story of Pentecost is a story of wind and fire, a rushing, mighty wind, and tongues of fire on the heads of the disciples. Wind and fire are our images for talking about God as spirit, the Holy Spirit. They are good and valuable images, useful because they serve to remind us that when all is said and done, God remains a mystery, *the* mystery. We can measure the wind, almost predict it, but in the end it is invisible, restless, powerful, and mysterious. It blows where it wills. Fire we can usually contain and put into our service, but fire can be an over-zealous or unwelcome servant which consumes much more than we wish. The reminder that God is spirit, like wind and fire, is unsettling. Father and Son are so easily domesticated, but not Spirit, not wind and fire. To be sure, it is the breath of God blown into the earth creature which gives life to each of us. But the Spirit of God does not always blow gently, or fan a cozy, warm, safe fire. The Spirit has been known to blow down great institutions, or to incinerate whole crowds of people.

No wonder that one of the oldest names for God in the Hebrew Scriptures translates into English as Consuming Fire. The Hebrew expression for someone becoming angry is to say literally that someone's nose is hot or kindled. When it was God's nose that was kindled, the breath of God became the awful fire. It is said that the ancients had seen it happen. There were stories of the trip from Egypt to the promised land which told of fire coming forth from God to devour disobedient people.

Ultimately the kindled nose of God had blown on the whole people of Israel, and they became the valley of bleached, dry bones which the prophet Ezekiel saw in a vision in the days when the Babylonians came as agents of destruction. The people of Jerusalem didn't want to believe that it had been God's hot breath that withered them and laid them waste. But it was. There seemed no other explanation.

It was also the Spirit of God who drove Jesus out into the desert to be starved and tested after his baptism. The same Spirit urged him finally to Jerusalem, and to the cross. And the very same Spirit blew rushing and mightily upon the disciples and drove them out of Jerusalem, scattering them like seeds all over the earth, filling them with words which changed many lives but which eventually, if we can believe all the legends, got almost every last one of them killed.

It is a bit too early to say what the Spirit has done and is doing among us. Just as with the wind, one can oft-times tell where the Spirit has been but not where it is now, or where it is going. There are some great things aflame today, some strong currents, but it is hard to say yet whether that is the Spirit. There are amongst us, too, the blown down and the burnt out, those apparently consumed in a holy cause. There are some whose hearts have grown cold in the wind. They have not known the warmth of love for a long time, and the spirit has gone out of them.

When cold and dried up, we often pray in words like those of J.S. Bach's Pentecost cantata ("O Ewiges Feuer"): "O eternal fire, kindle, ignite our hearts. Let the heavenly flames flare up and penetrate them, for we wish to be thy temple." But the cantata later refers to God choosing "the tents of the godly to dwell in."

Do we dare pray that? Is it safe to invite fire and wind into a tent? Isn't that finally our problem, that we are not stone temples, fireproof and sturdy, impervious to the wind? We are flesh and blood, tents woven from the fragile stuff of earth. The wind and fire consume us, wither us in a day like the grass and the flowers, and we die. Do we who dwell in tents dare pray for wind and fire?

We do, for there is another side to the Spirit's story. The ancient Hebrew Scriptures tell of someone who came to speak as a prophet for God, but this time not with a kindled nose. "'Comfort, comfort my people,' says your God." Comfort. In the Hebrew that verb comes from a word which means to pant, rhythmically, as a woman does during childbirth. Thus, the biblical picture of comfort is a mother holding a child so that the child can feel the mother's warm breath and sense the rhythm of the very heart that beat only inches from where the child's life began.

When Jesus, following the custom of the Scriptures, called the Spirit of God the "Comforter," that would have been his picture of how comfort works. God as mother holds the wounded, frightened child and with her breath she makes a safe place, she inspires trust, she rekindles confidence. She gives life back again.

The same Spirit that pushed Jesus on toward Calvary found him then in the tomb, dead and broken. She held him close, and breathed him back to life. Jesus promised that the same Spirit would follow us, all the days of our lives. The Spirit will be with us in the times when we are blown down, too weak even to pray. The Spirit will hold us, and with sighs too deep for words she will breathe us back to life. That is promised to each of us in our baptism. And only with that promise do we, whose lives are housed in fragile tents, dare to pray for wind and fire.

And come the wind does into the tents, into each of us, to fan the fire, to accomplish what God wants done in the world. Sometimes frightening, most often surprising, the wind blows where it wills. Now it makes a blaze in our midst, now a steady, single candle in the night. But always the Spirit is ready, should we wither and fade, to gather us up for comforting, and always ready, too, to use our limbs, our heartbeat, our breath as the rhythm of God's own Spirit to work comfort in the earth. The Spirit is ready, too, one day, when the tents which we are become burnt and ashes, to hold us in peace forever.

Come, O eternal fire!

Frederick A. Niedner, Jr.

L   DAY OF PENTECOST

L   *Ez 37:1–14; Acts 2:1–21; Jn 7:37–39a*

"Can these bones live?" Hearing that question always makes me think of *My Friend Flicka,* and of the fateful day when Ken's father sees how sick Ken's filly, Flicka, has become. An infection from a seemingly healed wound has been spreading through her body, wasting away her flesh, until now she stands with her head hanging down, looking like a skeleton wrapped in dried-out skin. Ken's father gives the verdict Ken has been fearing:

these bones cannot live. The filly must be killed, for she is already as good as dead, and nothing can save her now.

That night, knowing that Flicka is to be shot in the morning, Ken goes down to the pasture in secret to stay with her. He finds her lying in the stream, the current dragging her down. With all his strength he hauls her head up on the bank, onto his lap, and cradles her that way all through the night. O'Hara writes: "The water rippled over Ken's legs, and over Flicka's body. And gradually the heat and the fever went out of her, and the cool running water washed and washed her wounds."[29]

Like Ezekiel's vision, this is a resurrection story. Into a scene of utter hopelessness, where death is a *fiat accompli*, there comes the miraculous renewal of life. Like the gospel of John, where the water of life flows with the blood from Jesus' wounds, this is a story of life renewed through sacrificial love: for Ken falls deathly ill from the night in the cold stream, even as Flicka is washed clean of the infection and set on the road to healing. And for me, this story has become a profound image of baptism. It is the water of the font that continually washes us clean and brings us to life.

"How can water do such great things?" Luther asks in his Small Catechism. "It is not the water indeed that does them, but the word of God which is in and with the water, and faith, which trusts such word of God in the water."[30] Water by itself is an ambiguous symbol, bringing to mind both rain and flood, drinking and drowning. This ambiguity is clear in the story of Flicka, for she would have drowned if Ken had not found her. It is Ken's holding her in the stream that transforms it for her into healing, cleansing, life-giving water. Even so, it is God's word of promise, God's holding us in the frightening, chancy water, that makes the water healing and life-giving. Without that holding, the water would drown us. But God comes looking for us and fights the currents that drag us down and the infection that rages within us, holding the life in us, holding us into life.

Faith, says Luther, is trusting the promise in the water. It is looking at a valley of dry bones and hearing the wind of the Spirit calling them to live. It is looking at our deathbound world, where the rain in New England kills the trees and the snow in Scotland is turned pitch-black, and hearing God tell us to prophesy to a despairing land. It is looking at conflict-ridden families and war-torn cities, and hearing the voice of one who can call not only individuals but whole communities out of death into life. It is looking at a world condemned to nuclear death, and deciding, even when hope seems lost, to wait through the night in love. It is looking into our own arid hearts and finding a river of living water, flowing from the heart of one who faces the night of death and despair with us and never lets us go.

That living water is the Spirit, who speaks the promise of God in your heart, and speaks it from your heart to all the world. You know it is the Spirit, for it enlivens this whole community, all of us who gather around this table to receive into our hands and mouths and hearts the promise of God. You know it is the Spirit, for it enables you to speak to other people in their own language, in the language of their own unique experience of struggle and hope and despair. In all those millions of languages, in the private language of each human heart, the Spirit over and over speaks the same word: "Live!"—till the Babel of our alienation finds healing in the babble of one great river of living water.

Elaine J. Ramshaw

[29]Mary O'Hara, *My Friend Flicka* (Philadelphia: J.P. Lippincott, 1973), p. 230.
[30]*Dr. Martin Luther's Small Catechism* (St. Louis: Concordia, 1943), p. 16.

R *Deut 4:32–34,39–40; Rom 8:14–17; Mt 28:16–20*
E *Ex 3:1–16; Rom 8:12–17; Jn 3:1–16*
L *Deut 6:4–9; Rom 8:14–17; Jn 3:1–17*

When we set out to explain the church year we point out that Trinity Sunday is the only feast day which celebrates a doctrine rather than an event. The other festivals celebrate such things as our Lord's birth, the crucifixion, the resurrection, the ascension, or the coming of the Holy Spirit. But on this particular Sunday, we celebrate a doctrine.

I believe this explanation is mistaken, particularly if we understand doctrine in the sense that the Bible understands it.

In the Old Testament reading today we heard about the God who says to the holy people, was there ever another God like me? I go forth and create, I challenge Pharaoh and take a nation for my own, I lead them through the wilderness, I speak to them, I speak my word to them through the fire and the smoke, I implant my knowledge and presence in the hearts of my people. Here is a picture not of a static doctrine and concept, but the God who acts in this world, a God who creates, a God who redeems, a God who inspires.

Part of our problem is that we have for hundreds of years relied on the language of dogmatic theology, the philosophical, logical, careful thinking which characterizes doctrinal statements of the church. These statements sound terribly static and absolute. We forget that such language is the language of imagery and analogy. The analogies provided by philosophy sound so impressive and so mystifying, and perhaps so obtuse, that we think they must be exact pictures of the truth itself.

The Bible uses less precise analogies. It uses analogies of creating, relating, and acting as we have heard in today's readings. It presents doctrine more often in events rather than in intellectual propositions. We see this in the iconography of the Eastern church. Its way of portraying the Trinity is either to show Abraham with his three mysterious angelic visitors who strangely, though they are in different postures, have identical faces, or to show the baptism of Jesus with a dove above his head and a hand above that, indicating the Father.

There are other analogies, of course. There's the analogy from our own ability to create. Created ourselves in the image of God, we bear the imprint of the Holy Trinity, and we ourselves engage in a three-fold process when we set out to create. An artist first *conceives* that which is to be done and then *acts* with the talent and the skill which give the *power* to make that clay or that stone or those sounds become that which was conceived.

These are analogies. The reason I like analogies that describe God the Holy Trinity in terms of action, creation, community, and shared love is because, if indeed we are created in the image of God, then our lives as individuals and as the community of God's people must have those same qualities: relatedness, sharing, love.

Think about what happens when you fall in love with someone, or even in "like" with someone. You see the person, and you suddenly realize in yourself that he or she is someone to be loved. You act and speak in the hope of producing a response of love back. And so you reach out, and what you give brings response, brings the other back to you.

Here is another image, one which doesn't fit quite so neatly into threes, but God doesn't mind, because even being Three is an analogy. It's what we do in the liturgy. Think about what happens. A group of clergy and laity of various orders come moving into the assembly. The people sing and then the choir sings and then the presider sings and then the people sing and then the celebrant prays and then we all pray. A lay person reads and then we sing and another lay person reads and then the cantor sings and then the deacon reads and the preacher preaches and we listen and respond. We all are relating and responding back and forth in the very image of the life of the Trinity.

In a few moments we will turn to each other and reach out and give Christ and receive back Christ as we say "Peace be with you." In our daily lives, in our families, in our relationships of love, in marriage, in parenting, in our work, in our play, again and again, the very nature of God is seeking to come through our lives as we are and as we reach out and as we respond and are responded to.

That's why Christians care about this world and not just about the church. It's why we spend only a few hours here and all the rest of our time there. It is why Christians care and care deeply when they see human society trying to build peace by preparing for war. It is why Christians care and care deeply when they see their fellow human beings living on the streets and eating out of garbage cans or living on a dole from a grudging government. It is why Christians care when they see pain and illness and suffering. It is why Christians call on all the rest of the world to join us in reaching out to and changing this world. Why? Because God calls you and me into the life of the Trinity, that life of sharing, of mutual exchange, of love and peace and joy, that life of which we have a foretaste as we gather here.

And so Jesus says, come into the love of God. Come and go, in the life of Father, Son, and Holy Spirit. Go out and bring all my people into this total life of exchange, of sharing, of coherence, of love, of peace and of joy. For we are called to be the manifestation and the active agents of God the Holy Trinity here and now, and forever.

Michael W. Merriman

R BODY AND BLOOD OF CHRIST

R *Ex 24:3–8; Heb 9:11–15; Mk 14:12–16, 22–26*

Several years ago I watched a television documentary that has impressed an image on my memory that I will never forget: the image of tiny, starving children whose eyes looked longingly for someone who would relieve their hunger. Some were mere babes in arms whose distended stomachs spoke of famine in a way no words could express adequately. Others were a little older, walking around half-naked, crying and reaching out for a bowl of some pasty substance which, to my eyes, looked less than appetizing—but then, I never have been really hungry.

It is most appropriate on this feast in which the symbols of bread and wine are so prominent, that we ask those who are hungry to help us understand the meaning of the eucharist, so central to us as a people. Catherine Doherty used to pray, "Lord, give bread to the hungry and hunger for you to those who have bread." In the context of today's liturgy, it would not be an overstatement to say that feeding the hungry and hungering for the bread of life are necessary prerequisites for participation in the eucharist for those of us "who have bread."

Created at a time in the church's history when faith in and devotion to the sacrament had waned, this feast of the Body and Blood of Christ was designed to assist Christian believers to enter more fully into the mystery of eucharist. By emphasizing its connection with the Passover event of Jesus, the church tries to instruct us about the dynamic nature of this sacrament which is both enacted and received.

Of significance in the Marcan account of the Last Supper in today's gospel is the choice of words which connects this event to two other events of miraculous feeding of the crowds in the gospel of Mark. Jesus *took* bread, *blessed* it, *broke* it and *gave* it to his followers. Jesus' sacrificial action of the gift of himself on the cross, remembered at every celebration of eucharist, is thus closely connected to Jesus' act of feeding the hungry multitudes. Far from being a ritual to observe, the eucharist is an act of God's love in Christ freely bestowed on a hungry people who look longingly for someone to feed them.

This eucharistic meal is intended as a bonding action as well, one that bespeaks the interdependence of all, the hungry and the fed alike. Through the shedding and sharing of his blood, Jesus binds all of humankind to God and to one another in a unique way. The church purposely evokes the memory of the sprinkling of the people by Moses in the Exodus account to remind us that our God desires to be bound to us, and wants us to understand the need to bind ourselves to God and with one another. Through the blood of the Lamb "poured out for many," we are one.

Through the repeated use of this account of Jesus' Passover in its community of worship, Mark's believers remembered the action of Jesus and celebrated the effects of that event in their own present reality. We, too, are invited by this feast and at every eucharist to celebrate with Christ our own present reality of dying and rising. We would be remiss if we came to celebrate eucharist merely as observers who look at an event that has happened in the past. Rather, called to be participants, we come ready to offer ourselves with Jesus, the Christ, by integrating our daily lives with what we proclaim together in our worship assemblies. The body of Christ which is broken and shared among us, the blood of Christ poured out for all, is what we are called to be for one another. We are the body and blood of Christ! We are expected to break and share the bread of life and to pour out our life's blood for those who look longingly to us for nourishment.

In the spirit of Catherine's prayer, we "who have bread" are asked to recognize our own great need to be fed. The eucharist is a gift freely offered to those who hunger along the way. Eucharist, a continuous sign of the graciousness of our God, challenges us to believe that no food on earth will satisfy our hunger completely. Only those who continue to acknowledge their hunger and thirst for the true bread and wine that nourishes for everlasting life can celebrate eucharist. Eucharist feeds us, yet eucharist makes us hunger and thirst even more.

The television documentary which I spoke about earlier tried to focus on those who were most affected by the famine, in order to urge first world countries to take responsibility for feeding the many who are hungry in the world. I hope that I never forget the image of those starving children, a constant reminder that I am called through eucharist to feed them and others like them; a reminder, too, that I need to experience hunger before I can truly celebrate eucharist.

Patricia A. Parachini, S.N.J.M.

R *Deut 5:12–15; 2 Cor 4:6–11; Mk 2:23–28*
E *Deut 5:6–21; 2 Cor 4:5–12; Mk 2:23–28*
L *Deut 5:12–15; 2 Cor 4:5–12; Mk 2:23–28*

In Monty Python's satire *The Life of Brian*, there is a scene resembling the Sermon on the Mount. After Brian says, "Blessed are the peacemakers," a small foolish-looking man far back in the crowd turns and asks, "Wha'd 'ee say?" "He said, 'Blessed are the *cheesemakers!*"[31] What a wonderful, though ridiculous, example of how we can twist things around so badly that their entire meaning is lost. Not only does the meaning of things get lost, but our priorities get changed as well.

You've probably heard the story about the Franciscan friar who said: "The Jesuits may be the greatest scholars, and the Dominicans may be the greatest preachers, but when it come to humility, we Franciscans have them all beat." Some people simply will not see the point. Jesus surely must have agonized over this as he spoke to the Pharisees, who had chided his disciples for breaking the Sabbath law.

It has been said that before we were Christians, we were Jews. Our heritage stems from those ancient roots. At the seder meal during the Passover, the words say that once *I* was a slave in Egypt, and God brought *me* out of bondage. The words are spoken in the first person even though the exodus of Israel occurred so long ago. Here we see a personal claim on heritage of salvation and an acknowledgement of God's interaction in each life.

The observance of the Sabbath had been for Israel a remembering, a bringing into the present the exodus story. It was not a nostalgic ritual, but a command to remember that God had loved Israel enough to bring the people into freedom. In a way, the Pharisees had forgotten to remember. They had forgotten the point and the priority of the Sabbath. Israel's memory had faded into laws and rules. Jesus reminded them that God is concerned for all our needs, not our rules. Even David ate the Bread of the Presence when hungry and in need. David's eating of the consecrated bread did not disturb or change its holiness. Rather, its holiness fed him both physically and spiritually.

Frederick Buechner writes, "Man does not live by bread alone, but he also does not live long without it. To eat is to acknowledge our dependence — both on food and on each other."[32] It is God who feeds us, not only manna in the wilderness of Egypt, but the real bread of heaven which is Christ. Do not be confused: God knows our need and our hunger. But do we? For as Simon Weil reminded us the danger is not that we doubt that there is bread, but that, by a lie, we convince ourselves that we are not hungry.

Our priorities must not be idols which we worship or laws which we contrive and control: we must know our need of God. Yet we celebrate that God always feeds us. In the wilderness of perplexity or affliction it is God who rescues us. In the midst of perplexity we do not despair. We carry the death of Jesus so that the life of Jesus may be made manifest. That is the greater truth; that in the midst of darkness, in the midst of this earthly Egypt, we are assured of God's faithfulness. Laws can never be ends within themselves, but only means to a greater truth.

What is our priority? It is God. God's is the final word in law and judgment. Incredible though it may seem, God's priority is love for us. That is not found in rules. It was found in Israel's exodus journey to Canaan and most importantly in Christ's journey to Calvary. In Jesus we have been set free from ultimate slavery. The resurrection on Easter morn was the fulfillment of the Sabbath. God has brought us not only out of Egypt but out of our bondage to sin and death.

We are bearers of that truth and that history. We have been touched by that history: that God has stooped down to enter our very humanity. We draw together in the breaking of bread because we are hungry: not only in body but in soul. And God feeds both, and that is a good and holy thing.

Because of the resurrection we can all respond to the seder meal's proclamation by saying, "Once *I* was a slave and God brought *me* out of bondage." Re-remembering that exodus is part of our journey towards God. It is almost as though God has given us transparencies through which to see a greater truth. The Sabbath, the exodus, and the resurrection all point to a greater truth, a greater priority. As the hymn so beautifully puts it,

> O Food to pilgrims given,
> O Bread of life from heaven,
> O Manna from on high!
> We hunger; Lord, supply us,
> Nor thy delights deny us,
> Whose hearts to thee draw nigh.
>
> O stream of love past telling,
> O purest fountain, welling
> From out the Savior's side!
> We faint with thirst; revive us,
> Of thine abundance give us,
> And all we need provide.[33]

Virginia L. Bennett

[31]Monty Python, *The Life of Brian* (Warner Broathers, 1979).
[32]Frederick Buechner, *Wishful Thinking, A Theological ABC* (New York: Harper & Row, 1973), p. 12.
[33]John A.L. Riley, tr., "O Food To Pilgrims Given," *The Hymnal 1982* (New York: The Church Hymnal Corporation, 1985), #308.

R   *Gen 3:9–15; 2 Cor 4:13–5:1; Mk 3:20–35*
E   *Gen 3:8–21; 2 Cor 4:13–18; Mk 3:20–35*
L   *Gen 3:9–15; 2 Cor 4:13–18; Mk 3:20–35*

The images of the Blessed Virgin come easily. Mary the Mother is a familiar figure for us. We do not doubt that she is the model mother. Caring for Jesus, that is her role. On Christmas Eve, the church bulletins show her in stately blue cradling the Christ child in her arms. "Mother and child," reads the caption. And at the end, Jesus is once more cradled by Mary. He is down from the cross and draped across Mary's lap. A model mother, Mary. But now look at her. Here she is in Nazareth convinced Jesus is crazy and trying to have him put away.

"He is crazy," says the mother. "Put him away." "Must be insane," chime in his brothers, "make him come home with us." The whole family is convinced that Jesus is mad. Not surprising, really. A boy from a small town goes off and returns different. The conventions of behavior are violated, the town's pecking order is disrupted. Jesus has returned to their midst but clearly without sanity. He is "in but not of" Nazareth. Remember *To Kill A Mockingbird*, the story of a black man unjustly charged and convicted of a crime in the South in the 1930's. The lawyer for the defense was Atticus Finch, a man of great integrity who went to Montgomery to read law and returned to practice it. All sorts of conventions were defied, the trial revealed. But most centrally breaking these unwritten laws was Atticus himself. He portrayed a relentless passion for justice in the midst of lies and deceit. Such a return to Maycomb County by Atticus was disruptive, unsettling. He never should have come back. And as for Jesus, he too should not have returned home. An embarrassment for his family. So they try to put him away.

"He is possessed," say the scribes. These things he does must be from Satan. To heal people of their illness must mean he is in league with the devil. It is through the ruler of demons that he casts demons out, they say. A delegation is sent down from Jerusalem to check into this. Such a situation threatens the whole community. Action is clearly needed. It is like when a denomination hardens its heart and turns inward. Soon there is a search for those who are "possessed," who do not subscribe to the official way of thinking. A delegation is sent from synod headquarters to investigate certain members of a seminary faculty. They arrive at the airport wearing power suits and carrying the same kind of attache cases. "We have come to resolve this problem," they tell a reporter. Then they get into a car driven by a local supporter and are whisked away to their motel. It's like that with these scribes. They are in town to deal with "this problem." The problem is Jesus. He is clearly possessed, and that can infect a whole community. So they come down from Jerusalem to control this infection.

Banish him, or put him away: that is what we must do. If he will not conform to us, he should be excluded from our world. If he acts to disrupt the world we have created, then declare him insane and restrain his activities. Either suppress Jesus within our conventions, or banish him from our living room. Otherwise, Jesus will disrupt our world with his healing and shatter it with his words. Look at this logic in action. A dissident speaks out on human rights in Moscow: an especially grave mistake since the Western press was in evidence. Such disruption is clearly symptomatic of insanity, so he is confined within a psychiatric hospital. But he will not recant and is consigned to the Gulag, that string of camps whose lights twinkle in the darkness of the Siberian night. Odd, what light shines in what darkness. Finally, with such madness persisting even under restraint, he is forced to emigrate, banished from the homeland. Cast out of the family. Possessed by demons or simply mad, he is restrained or exiled, on behalf of the world and its normalcy. So Jesus must be retrained, restrained or banished. For he threatens our world with his words and his actions. He must be suppressed or expelled, on behalf of our world and its ways.

Still, the crowd gathers around him. People hungering for acceptance jam into the house with him. There is good news here, and the crowd hears it gladly. They wait on Jesus' teaching and offer him their sick and their outcasts. But this crowd is a diverse people. Except for Jesus they would not be together in any other circumstance. They are all too different from each other. There is no natural bonding, only that Christ is the center of their new world. You see something like this when the Pope comes to visit, that diverse collection of humanity crowded into the stadium for mass. The devout from proper parishes in the suburbs mix with both charismatic folk and Trentine conservatives. Even the Protestant dignitaries are present, dressed in their odd assortment of vestments. A Hispanic choir sings *coritos* in honor of the occasion, a choir no doubt containing some undocumented aliens. All crowd into one place to hear the good news and to break bread with the Lord. The crowd gathers, diverse as they are, and Jesus is in their midst.

These, says Jesus, are the new family of God. "Who are my mother and my brothers?" he asks. Pointing around him, he answers, "Here are my mother and my brothers." Here is the family of God's new reign. Here are those who receive the good news gladly. Here are the ones who have come in faith to be healed. Here is the place where the world has been shattered and reformed. Who is part of this new family? Those who believe the gospel and do not oppose God's dominion. Welcome, brothers and sisters, mothers and fathers. Welcome to the family of God. Welcome home.

Richard Eslinger

R ELEVENTH SUNDAY IN ORDINARY TIME
E PROPER 6
L FOURTH SUNDAY AFTER PENTECOST

R *Ez 17:22–24; 2 Cor 5:6–10; Mk 4:26–34*
E *Ez 31:1–6,10–14; 2 Cor 5:1–10; Mk 4:26–34*
L *Ez 17:22–24; 2 Cor 5:1–10; Mk 4:26–34*

"While we are at home in the body," says the apostle, "we are
away from the Lord, for we walk by faith, not by sight." If so,
we nonetheless wish that we could see. Or rather, we would like
to know what sort of sight faith itself is, that it should be of help
in walking through this world. What do we "look at" with our
faith while we live in the only place we know, the body? What
do we walk toward?

By means of the gospel of this day, Jesus Christ stands in our
midst again to open to us the mystery of God's dominion. He
gives us parables, seemingly to help our faith see. But when we
hear him, at first things grow more dim. We learn what we had
already known, that what we trust with faith cannot be seen.
The very reign of God is a secret, both its method and its final
content, as hidden as is the harvest to the sower. Both the sower
and the believer are blind. "But privately to his own disciples
Jesus explained everything," says the text, seeming to shut us
out of the explanation. We could be forgiven if we wished that
this privacy might open to include us. Could we please know
the explanation?

But the second parable seems clearer. We see the great tree
which ancient religions, and the Hebrew Scriptures themselves,
proposed as the principal image for a king and his kingdom.
Now that image is used for the universal order, for the place
where all the nations, all the birds of the air, might find refuge
and creative rest. In the plan of God Israel would be such a tree,
the prophet had promised. It was a lie that the imperial pretensions of the kings of the earth would ever offer such refuge.

So, we have our answer. Walk toward the dominion-tree of God.
In faith, look there. But what does that mean? And where shall

we look? In this text, Jesus does not say "tree" at all. He says, "bush." The mustard bush, which starts as a tiny seed, may grow pretty big, sometimes even shoulder-high, but it is no tree. Indeed, it is only a annual bush, every year dying away. "Here is God's dominion, God's world-ordering Tree," says Jesus. "All the nations of the earth, all the needy birds, may take refuge in an annual bush!" But then we cannot see at all. How can that be so?

Dear sisters and brothers in the faith, this assembly is in on the secret. When we gather here, we gather in the house with Jesus and with all the disciples of the ages, to hear and trust the explanation. Jesus Christ, who was no king, who was cut down like an annual bush, who is still a little thing in the earth, is the center of refuge. God has raised him up, so that the branches of his tree offer shade that you may rest and fruit that you may live. God has made the little bush of the cross, one of the backwater cruelties from the imperial pretensions of one of the kings of the earth, to be the true center of world order. Here is no mighty competition with the empires. Here, in Christ and in the word at the center of this assembly, is service and love and thanksgiving to God. Here is the low tree made high, the dry tree made to flourish.

Come to the table. The explanation of the parables will be the bread and cup in your hands. Look there. Have the eyes of your faith trained again, looking at these little, hidden things. See the giving of Christ. See a refuge for yourself, for all that you are, together with all the others of the world. See the tree which is the very order of the world, bringing all things to stand before God. See the harvest already come.

In looking at the gifts on this table and walking toward this tree, let yourself learn how to look toward mercy and praise as you walk through the days of your life.

Gordon W. Lathrop

R *Jb 38:1,8–11; 2 Cor 5:14–17; Mk 4:35–41*
E *Jb 38:1–11,16–18; 2 Cor 5:14–21; Mk 4:35–41*
L *Jb 38:1–11; 2 Cor 5:14–21; Mk 4:35–41*

Have you ever been frightened? I mean really frightened. I bet that every one of us has at least once been scared out of our wits. Let me tell you about one experience of mine.

A couple of years ago a group of us was driving on a freeway in Los Angeles, which can be a frightening experience in itself. Our driver didn't see the bumper that had been knocked off a car and was lying in the middle of our lane, or he thought it was something else. We hit the bumper, and it became lodged under our car, grinding us to a halt. We were in the next-to-last left lane of a five lane highway with traffic going by at around sixty-five miles per hour. Traffic was zipping past us, with the faster traffic in our lane. Our driver had no alternative but to get out and remove the bumper and cast it to the side of the road. But in those thirty seconds, which seemed like hours, all I could do was look out the back window at the cars and trucks zooming toward us. As one truck swerved and missed us by what seemed to me less than a foot, I was absolutely terrified. They say that your life passes before you in moments like that. I don't know. I don't remember that happening. All I can remember is looking out that back window and thinking, "In the next ten seconds I'm either going to be alive or dead." Absolute terror controlled me. I can also remember that it took about an hour for my palms to stop sweating and my heart to stop pounding.

Perhaps I've succeeded in stirring up memories of similar experiences. If not, a rainy dark night with a good Stephen King novel can get your imagination back into shape. Yes, we know that the world can be a scary place. And there are moments when our fear can immobilize us.

Where is God in these moments? These are the times when it seems that God has abandoned us, doesn't really care, or is asleep at the back of the boat or the car or whatever. The burden of Scripture that we've heard today is that God never abandons us, no matter how much we feel God's absence. It's like that story I'm sure you've heard, "Footsteps." It seems to us as if we're walking with God, but when we are most afraid, most in pain, most confused, there is only one set of tracks in the sand. Those are the times, so goes the story, when the tracks are God's, and we are being carried.

We are like the disciples in Mark's gospel. Mark portrays them as notoriously slow learners. They seem to keep missing the point, the point of who Jesus is. They keep having to learn the same lesson over and over again. Perhaps that's why essentially this same story is repeated only two chapters later in the gospel. We too keep asking, "Teacher, do you not care if we perish?"

We are a lot like Job. In the body of the book of Job, the main character doesn't get rewarded in the end. The original version of the story ends with Job's acknowledging the magnificence of God in the midst of his own misery. Job hears the awe-inspiring speech of God, part of which we've just heard. God says: " I am God. So shut up: that should be enough for you." Of course, usually it is not enough for us, and we keep on questioning. I don't think that's bad. What is bad is if we can't hear the voice of God after our fear or our indignation has died down.

I'm not suggesting that we shouldn't be afraid, that it's wrong to be seized with terror in times of danger. It is at precisely those times that we must hold to our conviction that God is with us, that God is for us. Our ultimate confidence is that God has made us into a new creation, to use the words of Paul in 2 Corinthians, that God has entrusted us with a mission as ambassadors of reconciliation, the human and divine harmony that we celebrate week by week around this holy table. The love of Christ impels us to put our fears and terrors into perspective and to hear that same voice that the disciples hear in today's gospel: "Why are you afraid?"

John F. Baldovin, S.J.

R THIRTEENTH SUNDAY IN ORDINARY TIME
E PROPER 8
L SIXTH SUNDAY AFTER PENTECOST

R   *Wis 1:13–15,2:23–24; 2 Cor 8:7,9,13–15; Mk 5:21–24,35b-43*
E   *Deut 15:7–11; 2 Cor 8:1–9,13–15; Mk 5:22–24,35b-43*
L   *Lam 3:22–33; 2 Cor 8:1–9,13–14; Mk 5:21–24a,35–43*

Today's readings bring special light and warmth to this Sunday in what is called "ordinary time," a time for quiet, everyday deepening of the wonder of our Christian faith. The gospel is especially rich and touching, one of a series of healings related in Mark 1:14–8:26, a section which gradually reveals the mystery of Jesus and of his mission.

A synagogue official, Jairus, pleaded with Jesus to heal his daughter, and Jesus simply "went with him" (and on the way had time graciously to acknowledge the cure of a woman whose faith had worked a saving wonder). While they were on the way, Jairus is told with brutal directness that his daughter is dead, so he need not trouble the teacher any longer. How ordinary, how like us in their reaction: we know the limits of God, we know exactly what to expect. Healing, yes; "raising up," impossible! Certain small adjustments, some change, yes; but real change? A real turning-around from hatred to tolerance to love? Impossible! A real conversion from one kind of life to another? Impossible! We cannot believe that the fame or infamy already marking a person can be turned around. Jesus ignores their message and turns to Jairus: "Do not fear, only believe." Do not close the doors and windows to new possibilities; believe that there are new possibilities, new horizons, new ways of seeing and doing.

Those who cared about the girl and those who were sincere followers of Jesus were open to new facts, open to experience the reality of new life, open to imagine the unimaginable, the resurrection. Jesus did not command nor cry out in a loud voice, but simply took the child by the hand and said, "Arise," and she did.

What does this tell us about Jesus, about the mystery of Jesus? That he cared about people, that he went out of his way to give his help to those who asked for it. That he stood up to ridicule and went on about the business of caring for others. That, being human, he had an eminently human touch. Jesus was, and is, no distant cool character. He touched, he lifted up, he arranged to feed a hungry child. These miracle stories may cause problems in our scientific world; we may, in fact, interpret many of these cures as psycho-somatic illnesses and cures. No matter. What matters is the insight we gain into the mystery of Jesus and of his mission, and so into the reality of our lives as his followers. He was a healer, a giver of hope and new life. He was open to the needs and pain of others and he cared about them, cared enough to do something. And in the gospels we learn that his was not a pious do-goodism, but a caring and a curing intended to open people's eyes to the reality of God, to unheard-of possibilities made possible of realization through faith in Jesus.

The second reading shows us that Jesus' disciples shared his openness and his caring. Paul wrote to the Corinthians, exhorting them to give graciously in the collection for the needy church in Jerusalem. Paul sees this giving as an expression of genuine Christian love and as an expression of the unity of the churches, a unity transcending ethnic barriers: the Gentile Christians of Corinth coming to the aid of the Jewish Christians in Jerusalem. We can learn from this apparently mundane passage that Jesus' concern for the sick, the poor, the needy, was extended through the early Christian churches in sharing, and in the striving for equality within the Christian community.

The Christians of Corinth, living in a busy, bustling commercial city, were urged by Paul to express their care and concern for others, and to do so sincerely, graciously, because they had been graced, favored by God and were now being given the grace, the opportunity, to give. Grace, *charis*, is favor received from God, and the Christian response is to live in an attitude of self-giving, looking graciously, sincerely, favorably on others. Why? Because God does not look with favor on gross inequality, and Paul quotes Exodus to prove his point: "One who gathered much had nothing over, and one who gathered little had no lack." What we are hearing here is not about "charity" in the weakened, diluted sense of almsgiving by well-to-do to ne'er-do-wells. We are hearing, if we are open, that in a Christian community, inequality which is notable, which separates one group from another, is not compatible with a life of grace, with a life in which all are united in Christ as sisters and brothers.

And in the first readings we are given God's clear command to favor justice. The Book of Wisdom begins: "Love justice, you rulers of the earth, think of the Lord with uprightness and seek the Lord with sincerity of heart." And in an alternate reading from Deuteronomy: "You shall not harden your heart nor shut your hand against your poor neighbor." With the author of Lamentations, we can sing: "The mercies of the Lord never come to an end; they are new every morning."

In the Christian communities there is concern for sharing, for are not all one body of Christ? In the gospel today we have seen Jesus giving freely of his time and of his caring concern for anyone in need. Very soon we shall share in one bread and one cup, united in one act of thanksgiving, one eucharist: note again that root word, *charis*! We gather together as those graced, favored by God: we rejoice and give thanks for that grace, we join in eucharist. And we renew our will to express our care and concern, to look with favor on our sisters and brothers, never suffering any to be in need when we can help. Even when we think it is impossible to help, as did the mourners in the gospel, if we stay close to the Minister of the impossible, we may well discover unheard-of ways to extend our horizons of community. We may discover untried ways of effecting change in the direction of peace and justice that others, the mourners among us, deem impossible.

Marian Bohen, O.S.U.

R FOURTEENTH SUNDAY IN ORDINARY TIME
E PROPER 9
L SEVENTH SUNDAY AFTER PENTECOST

R *Ez 2:2–5; 2 Cor 12:7–10; Mk 6:1–6*
E *Ez 2:1–7; 2 Cor 12:2–10; Mk 6:1–6*
L *Ez 2:1–5; 2 Cor 12:7–10; Mk 6:1–6*

Many of us, when hearing the word "prophet," think of the Old Testament characters—Isaiah, Jeremiah, Amos, Ezra, or Nehemiah. We imagine them as wizened old men, thundering out God's judgment upon an unrepentant and unreceptive people. Prophecy, in that picture, is God's message showing how current actions are against God's will and predicting dire consequences. Sometimes the warning is accompanied by a promise of peace, prosperity and blessing if people will repent and return to God's will.

People in today's world are not usually identified as prophets. Our churches have not institutionalized the prophet in the same way in which they have the priest or the deacon. We think of prophets as distant and unfamiliar people.

Let me define what I mean by the prophetic word. Prophecy is naming the truth in a given situation and explaining the logical consequences of a course of action. God's word is the truth. And the prophet speaks God's word, often in a situation where people have been unable or unwilling to face the truth. Naming the truth, especially when people have denied reality, challenges people to accept the truth, to acknowledge their denial and to change their behavior. However, people can reject the truth, usually by rejecting the bearer of the word.

When we don't want to face the truth, we invent an amazing number of ways to deny reality. We perform the "happy family act" to deny that our marital relationship is dead. We stay very busy to deny the emptiness in our lives. We market the good features of a product to convince our customers that the benefits outweigh the costs. We call "disinformation" the lies our government tells. We become so dependent on our lifestyle that we no longer see it destroying the environment and impoverishing others. We have constructed reasonable explanations for what we do. Many of those reasons are lies we tell to avoid facing the truth.

The prophet comes into our world and names the truth. When the prophet is low key, we might protest mildly. But when the prophet is a whistle-blower in industry, a reformer in politics or a preacher who proclaims a God of love and justice, then the response can be much stronger. People don't like to hear the truth when it requires them to change who they are or how they live. So the whistle-blower gets fired, the politician doesn't get re-elected. And the preacher is scorned, avoided or "fired." Sometimes, even today, the prophet gets killed.

Probably all of us, at some time in our lives, are called to bring the prophetic word into a situation. All of us are called, at various points in our lives, to listen to the prophet's voice, even when we don't want to hear it. The word of God which the prophet brings is often rejected by the people. That is because God's word is the truth, and people often reject the truth. The prophetic vocation is a dialogical vocation: The prophet is called to speak the truth, and people's task is to listen.

We are called to listen to those people who identify the truth in a situation. We won't always like what they have to say; we may not agree with them. And not everyone who speaks up is right. But our first task is to listen, to set aside our objections, for the moment, to try to see things from that person's perspective. Then try to identify what is feeling threatened; see if just perhaps the person may be speaking the truth. What would happen to you if that really were the truth? The task of being a prophet is not easy, but neither is the task of hearing the prophetic word. Yet it is important to learn the discipline of both speaking and hearing the truth. For many of us, the discipline of hearing the truth will precede the courage needed to speak the truth.

God's truth cuts through the layers and reveals the true motives underlying our actions. God's truth shines a light on the connection between military spending and poverty, between the politician's power and an increasing drug market, between industry's profits and a child's death. God's truth uncovers the uncomfortable reality about ourselves, our concepts and our institutions that we've been unwilling to face.

Revelation of the truth is often experienced as judgment. And it is judgment, but not in the sense of condemnation. Rather, it is judgment in that there is a moment of decision. When we are faced with the truth, we have a choice. We can choose to accept the truth and then change the way we live, or we can reject the truth. It is not that God is inflicting punishment on us. Rather, in rejecting the truth, we will suffer the inevitable consequences. If we continue to make military spending a priority, people will die. They will die from lack of food and shelter. And they will die in industrial accidents while producing weapons, on the battlefields, in the refugee camps, in the fallout from bombs or missiles. That judgment is the logical consequence of rejecting God's truth and refusing to live God's will.

The other side of judgment is promise. God's promise is that walking in God's ways and living in accordance with God's commandments will bring us blessings untold. Again, that is a logical consequence of our actions. God created and redeemed a world in which we can live in love and harmony with each other and with all of creation. When we choose to live in community, as the people of God, the promises of God will be fulfilled. Christ has inaugurated the reign of God in our time; in and through Christ we can live in peace and harmony. But doing so requires us to name the truth, to hear the truth and respond to it. Jesus said, "I am the way, the truth and the life." It is in and through Christ that we can hear and be prophets, bearers of God's truth in and for our time.

Linda L. Grenz

R   *Am 7:12–15; Eph 1:3–10; Mk 6:7–13*
E   *Am 7:7–15; Eph 1:1–14; Mk 6:7–13*
L   *Am 7:10–15; Eph 1:3–14; Mk 6:7–13*

Jesus Christ had high hopes for his disciples. He hoped for apostleship now!

Jesus Christ has high hopes for us as well. From us too he has hopes for apostleship now!

Were those hopes, are those hopes, high-apple-pie-in-the-sky hopes?

Everything planned from before the foundation of the world by the Three-in-One was now being turned over to these two-by-twos. The lesson for us is not so much that we, too, are *supposed* to, but that we *can*. We can because God makes us able. The positive evidence that we can is that they could, and did.

What is remarkable here is that the Lord was ready to turn over his work on earth to these amateurs. They certainly were not ready. It is not until some time later that Peter is able to stutter out the amazing realization, "You are the Christ!" And even then Jesus "charged them to tell no one about him." But here, even less prepared, they are sent out to heal and to preach. He "began to send them out two by two," instructing them to go without even commonsense provisions, "no bread, no bag, no money in their belts, only one tunic." But "he gave them authority"! His purpose is to show them that they can, because God is able.

Jesus was not dealing with the disciples as we might with a child who wants to help paint the fence. We give a little brush and a pail of paint to our sons and daughters and set them to work on a part of the fence where their artistry won't show, intending to cover over their inadequacy later with our big brush. Yet this was no practice session for witness. Jesus' purpose was to teach them, and us, early on that we can do what God wants us to do because along with the command God gives the capacity. God wants us to spread the word. We are to understand that God will not have to follow us with a big divine paint brush, for the power is in that word. Jesus is convincing the disciples, and us, not that we are able but that God's word is able.

We often hear these expectations of apostleship now as commands to *do*, and we feel guilty because we don't. Our real guilt is that we so blatantly assume that we could if we only decided to. Our pride shows in our guilty feeling. We are as unlikely candidates for doing what God was trying to get done through Jesus Christ as were these disciples. Amos, in the first lesson, was a herdsman and a dresser of sycamores when God called him to prophesy in Israel. That word evidently got through to Amaziah the priest and Jeroboam the king, because they told Amos to leave the country and do his prophesying in Judah. But that word clearly had done its work also on Amos, because he insisted God had told him to prophesy in Israel, and in Israel he would prophesy.

God's word has always worked, because God is in it. When Moses tried to excuse himself from demanding freedom from Pharaoh, explaining "I can't, Lord, I stutter," God said, "You can, because I AM!" When Israel said, "We can't be sure if we will have extra manna for tomorrow," God said, "You can, because I AM!" That is what God is saying to us: Apostleship now! You can, because I AM!

Since the great I AM makes us what we are, how ought we to think of ourselves? The Scripture tells us not to think more highly of ourselves than we ought to think. Certainly we ought not think less highly of ourselves either. The second reading meets any hesitancy we might feel by reminding us of all that has gone into our preparation to be apostles.

Follow the list: God has blessed us with every spiritual blessing in Christ Jesus and chose us before the foundation of the world to be holy and blameless. Because God wanted it so and loves us in the beloved Son, God destined us to be children of God, we are made God's own by God's glorious grace. We have redemption through the blood of Jesus through God's grace. God gave to us wisdom and insight into the mystery of the divine will to bring all things in heaven and on earth into union in Christ. God appointed us to live for the praise of the Almighty, made sure we would hear the truth of the gospel and would believe and be saved, and guaranteed to us our inheritance of eternal life. The promise is sealed by the gift of the Holy Spirit, until God brings us into full possession of it.

If those first disciples had reason and confidence to do as they were told, we surely have more. If they were ready through the word, we also are ready, for apostleship now.

There are two more reasons for our confidence. Those disciples went out two by two. Another disciple is company, but if your companion is only as able as you, with the same mixture of faith and unfaith, of questioning and hesitancy, is there more than misery in company? But we are sent out with greater company. Remember our Lord's promise, "I am with you always." We go out two by two, but our companion is Jesus Christ himself.

The other source of our confidence is that we are well-fed. Those disciples were told to take a walking staff, but not bread, the staff of life. For our Lord gives us an invitation to gather around his table. He gives food for the journey, strength for the task, the bread of life, the cup of salvation. "Take and eat. Take and drink," he says, and gives us with his body and his blood the very life he gained for us.

Apostleship now is possible.

George W. Hoyer

R *Jer 23:1–6; Eph 2:13–18; Mk 6:30–34*
E *Is 57:14b-21; Eph 2:11–22; Mk 6:30–44*
L *Jer 23:1–6; Eph 2:13–22; Mk 6:30–34*

I've talked with enough parents of young children to know that one fond wish is a quiet place, a place of peace, and that for many, not even the bathtub is safe haven! And I've known parents who desire peace from worry about their adolescent children, and couples who long for peace between each other. I've met a Salvadoran refugee who seeks peace away from her village where her husband was murdered and where she was threatened with death. I've visited an older woman who prays for peace, a final respite from the pain of the cancer which is overcoming her. I've talked with an alienated son who wants to make peace with his father, and doesn't know how. I know a man in a psychiatric ward who aches for peace from his obsessive thoughts.

You know them too. So many people, crying out for peace. Quite possibly you yourselves and people you love: longing for peace in mind and heart and body, in relationships, in the workplace, city, nation, and world. In comparison to the size of some of these peoples' wants, the disciples' desire for a time of rest and quiet seems quite trivial. Yet, however small, this yearning and pining we all have, like that expressed in a poem-lament by Gerard Manley Hopkins:

> When, when, Peace, will you Peace? I'll not play hypocrite
> To own my heart: I yield you do come sometimes: but
> That piecemeal peace is poor peace . . . [34]

Piecemeal peace. That's about the best it seems we humans can do. Here and there by some miracle of good-heartedness, we see reconciliation, healing, harmony. But so often we use the word "peace" to mean lack of visible conflict, where hatred or mistrust simmers beneath the surface. All we can know is the "Pax Romana" type peace, peace enforced by threats of destruction, cold war, detente. We keep peace by exiting scenes of potential conflict, ignoring issues to be dealt with, glossing over strained relations with perfunctory pleasantries and saccharine smiles. Piecemeal peace. Pretender peace.

But God's peace is of a different sort. It is that peace which Paul says surpasses all understanding. It is, first off, pure gift, that for which we long from the marrow of our bones, that fundamental rightness with ourselves, each other, God, that we keep discovering, the world cannot give. It is a strange peace, a disruptive peace, a peace that often demands suffering, conflict, the pouring-out of self, all in the likeness of Jesus, who won our peace by his blood, who gave himself on a cross, uniting us "who were far off," who was killed to kill our hostility, who was broken for our wholeness.

This eucharist is celebration of the peace won by Jesus' cross, our place of rest. Here we, like the disciples, come apart for awhile; here we are taught by Jesus and fed by him, given refreshment, guidance, comfort. But as the disciples learned, the respite is all too short. For we are also challenged. Our God who is rest is also restless. There is work to be done in a world where so many people cry for peace. As the sign of our Christian call to unity, we share the sign of peace, sacrament of the shalom that Jesus established through his cross, an extension down through the ages of the peace he offered his disciples after the resurrection, that wonderful blessing of communion with God, world, neighbor, and self continually wrought by the Spirit who dwells among us. As sign of God's gift of unity, we share the living bread and the saving cup. Jesus' gift, this eucharist, banquet of peace, both fills us and makes us hungry: hungry enough to keep praying for the gift, hungry enough to keep striving for peace among our brothers and sisters. Let us go forth, to bring in word and deed the voice and embrace of our peacemaker God.

Janet Schlichting, O.P.

---

[34]"Peace," *Poems of Gerard Manley Hopkins*, 3rd ed., ed. W.H. Gardner (New York: Oxford University Press, 1948), p.85.

R SEVENTEENTH SUNDAY IN ORDINARY TIME
L TENTH SUNDAY AFTER PENTECOST

R *2 Kg 4:42–44; Eph 4:1–6; Jn 6:1–5*
L *Ex 24:3–11; Eph 4:1–7,11–16; Jn 6:1–5*

The crowd that gathered that day by the Sea of Galilee was hungry. They were hungry for food. The day had been long as they followed and listened to Jesus' teaching. They were hungry for leadership. The wait for a king, a messiah, had been long as the word of the prophets were passed on from one generation to another. And so when Jesus fed them, 5000 of them, plus women and children, from so little, five barley loaves and two fish, they thought they had found their king. They thought they had found the ruler who would take care of all their physical wants and needs. They thought they had found the long-promised one who would make everything all right again: no more hunger, no more sickness, no more oppression. Perhaps the story of the prophet Elisha, who fed one hundred men from a few barley loaves, was in their minds and on their lips as they ate the meal which Jesus hosted for them.

Scripture says that in their excitement the people were about to come and take Jesus by force to make him king. The experience of sharing that bountiful meal was quickly put behind them as they rushed to take care of their own desires and agendas. The crowd did not see that they were hungry for more than food and political leadership. The crowd did not see that they had been fed and filled by more than bread and fish.

The group that gathers in the award-winning Danish film *Babette's Feast* is also hungry. They are aged disciples of a sectarian religious leader long since deceased, their community dwindled, their inspiration diminished, and their unity disrupted by grudges and quarrels of long ago. They are called together to a meal, a feast of a meal, prepared as a gift by the French housekeeper Babette. The frugal Scandinavians are completely at a loss at a ten course French extravaganza. They don't know which fork to use or glass to sip from as one sumptuous course follows another. In spite of their stated intentions not to let the meal affect them, a miracle begins to unfold. Old grudges and grievances are put to rest and laughed about. Relationships—between husbands and wives, brothers and sisters, friend and friend—are restored and renewed. Joy is rediscovered in place of bitterness. Decisions of the past, for better or worse, are accepted with a sense of peace. "All is mercy—All is mercy," one man states. As the group disperses to return to their homes, the phrase repeated on everyone's lips is *tak*, thank you. Joining together under the stars in the town square, they form a circle with united hands and uplifted voices in a song of praise. Hungry in ways they had never imagined, they had now experienced a feast.

We are hungry people who gather in this place. In all likelihood, our stomachs are full, too full! We remember, pray for, and act to alleviate the physical hunger of others. Our hunger, though, goes beyond food, like those who gathered by the Sea of Galilee, like those who gathered in a remote Danish village.

We hunger for forgiveness. We hunger for reconciliation and restoration in our relationships. We hunger for joy in place of bitterness and cynicism. We hunger for peace over choices we have made. We hunger for a sense that "all is mercy." We hunger for unity, to be the one body, in the one Spirit, that the writer of Ephesians claims we are. We hunger for God.

For what is hunger, but an emptiness, a yearning that longs to be filled? What is hunger, but a reminder of our dependency upon the gifts of a Creator and the gifts of others?

And like those gathered by the Sea of Galilee, like those gathered in a remote Danish village, we too are fed. We share a feast called Holy Communion, the eucharist. From so little, a sip of wine and a nibble of bread, God provides so much. With this meal, we receive forgiveness of sins, life and salvation, says Martin Luther's Small Catechism.

Often, we too get caught up in our own desires and agendas. We rush from this meal to take care of our own business: the noon meal to get on the table, the plans for the rest of the day, the errands to be run. We don't stop to acknowledge our hunger. We go on with business as usual. We forget that we have been fed! A miracle has happened. We have shared a meal together. We have been made bread-sharers, literally com-panions, by our host Jesus Christ who has fed us himself.

As we leave this gathering, may the phrase repeated on all of our lips be *tak*, thank you. For, like the Israelites in ancient days, we beheld God, and ate and drank.

Kendra Nolde

E   PROPER 12

E   2 Kg 2:1–15; Eph 4:1–7,11–16; Mk 6:45–52

In some respects, the entire Bible is a commentary on the exodus. In that passage through the water and the wilderness, from slavery to freedom, Israel met God and forged its identity as God's people. All of Genesis is built on the experience of God that Israel had at Sinai and on the stories of the ancestors who formed the tribes that went down to Egypt. The forging of the kingdom under Saul, David and Solomon led to a re-examination of the promise of a land to settle—a more militant reinterpretation of history. But the exile in Babylon crushed all of that and forced the people to look once more at their understanding of God and themselves.

Key figures in the people's history are associated with the passage through the water because they seem to offer a new hope for liberation or a new understanding of God. Three of those people appear in today's readings: Elijah, Elisha, and Jesus.

Elijah is the one most associated with Moses and the exodus. He crosses the Jordan dry-shod with his partner, Elisha, and he goes up to heaven in the same area where Moses was buried. Ancient legend links him to Moses as the two people for whom God cared personally: that is why no one knows "to this day" where their graves are.

Elisha receives Elijah's mantle of prophecy and leadership. He returns across the Jordan as Elijah did, as the tribes of Israel did long before. And Elisha went on to do greater things than Elijah.

Jesus walked on the water. Whether a resurrection experience or an event from his ministry, the story links Jesus to the exodus and the God of the exodus. His control of the wind and the waves on the lake alludes to God's control of the waters of the sea. In fact, the two events seem to blend and overlap in the lyrics of Psalm 77:

> When the waters saw you, O God,
> when the waters saw you, they were afraid,
> yes, the deep trembled.
> Your path was through the sea,
> your path through the great waters;
> yet your footprints were unseen.

Jesus' followers didn't understand, as they didn't understand about the bread. Their hearts were hardened, as were the hearts of the people in their desert wanderings, as were the hearts of those who refused the ministry of Elijah and Elisha.

How about us? Do we understand what God has done for us and is doing in our lives now? We are children of the exodus; we have gone through the waters of liberation. We have crossed the Jordan to share in the bread that is God's gift. We are the heirs of Elijah, draped in the mantle of the prophets. As Elisha did in Elijah, we recognize in Jesus a presence more important than all of Israel's horses and chariots, more important than all the world's weapons and armies.

We profess with the author of Ephesians that there is "one body and one Spirit, just as you were called to the one hope that belongs to your call, one Lord, one faith, one baptism, one God and Father of us all, who is over all and through all and in all." We profess, but do we understand? Do we understand that we should be changed by the water and the bread, the faith we profess and the heritage we share? Our faith should issue in action; it should change us. Ephesians suggests what I'm talking about: Life "with all lowliness and meekness, with patience, forbearing one another in love, eager to maintain the unity of the Spirit in the bond of peace."

I'm not talking about lists of do's and don'ts, about regulations that try to apply the ten commandments to every aspect of our lives. I'm talking about a stance in the world, an attitude that Moses looked for in the desert, that Elijah and Elisha looked for in the people of the kingdom, and that Jesus looked for in his disciples. It is the stance of a community under God, in which the concerns of others come first for us, the poor and oppressed first of all. It is a stance that shows our faith in ourselves, our belief that God has chosen us, for whatever strange reason God may have had, and our hope that there is something we can offer to God and the world. We have heard about God's great works in the exodus, the prophets, and Jesus. We have seen God's great works in creation and redemption. We know God's great works in our time, in movements of liberation, justice, and peace. And we have found God in ourselves, bound together as the church. Greater works than these shall you do.

Gordon E. Truitt

R EIGHTEENTH SUNDAY IN ORDINARY TIME
E PROPER 13
L ELEVENTH SUNDAY AFTER PENTECOST

R *Ex 16:2–4,12–15; Eph 4:17,20–24; Jn 6:24–35*
E *Ex 16:2–4,9–15; Eph 4:17–25; Jn 6:24–35*
L *Ex 16:2–15; Eph 4:17–24; Jn 6:24–35*

In an age when many people experience abundance with plenty of bread, fresh meat, canned goods and fast foods, it can be difficult to imagine people wandering hungrily in a wilderness. When our bounty is compounded with a plethora of books and magazines featuring quick-and-easy diet methods, a generally overweight contemporary society takes manna-from-heaven for granted. The Exodus story of the provision of manna by God to a wilderness people could be taken merely as another television episode, suitable even for children.

A conflicting picture is provided through the news media. There are people experiencing serious poverty, hunger, and starvation. No book, regardless of how carefully written, can be a quick-and-easy remedy for abject poverty and starvation. In fact, many of the people in contemporary wildernesses are unable to read due to the perpetual lack of food and water. The Exodus story could in this instance be given a different reading and hearing. The luxurious television interpretation might be instead the agonized question, "Are we not God's people?"

People of faith live in constant tension between the meaning and message of biblical stories for today and the reality of life today. Since the good news has been made available through Jesus the Christ to all the world, persons will hear through the ears of their existential situations. Clearly, the message in today's pericopes highlights the faith of God's people rather than physical food. How can anyone who is hungry, without visible evidence of food that will satisfy and nourish one's physical body, hear the message initially? On the other hand, there is a message about feeding the hungry which is bound up in faith.

On one level we could stick to the story. Israel's faith was being tested. God had made promises to these people, and surely God had not left them at a time when divine guidance was needed. Here they were, out in the wilderness, but with nothing to eat. Utilizing their most powerful human defense, the people attacked their visible leaders, Moses and Aaron. They could not attack God, whom they had not seen. Furthermore, God had given signs of divine presence previously, so it was not as if they did not have any faith at all. Israel lacked the courage to confront God with what surely looked like divine betrayal.

God's faithful generosity bursts forth in spite of Israel's complaining. The testing involved waiting, something humans have difficulty doing. We are an impatient people. Saturated with doubt, the people of God had made a golden calf in the days of Moses.

Saturated with fear and pride, people throughout the ages have relied upon weapons which continue to destroy God's creation.

God's promise is fulfilled, and the people are instructed to follow God's directions: Gather only as much as you can eat; don't leave any 'til the morning; bake and boil what you need and lay by that which is left to keep; tomorrow is a day of solemn rest; the food will not become foul: trust me! Contrary to the instructions, some of the people made pigs of themselves. They took more than they needed.

The story is familiar. Unfortunately it is most familiar among contemporary people of faith, or those who claim to be of faith. We know we are to love one another, to share, to trust, and to wait, and yet we gather more than our share. We know this story quite well. We can quote many of the familiar passages. We close the book and then continue to live like those who have not heard. We can carefully dry off the waters of our baptism and move ourselves toward the concrete wilderness which we helped to build. A golden calf? Surely not.

God came into our midst in human form and found evidence of people still seeking bread for life, bread which would satisfy their stomachs. The gospel lesson picks up the theme of bread in the wilderness where the Exodus story ends. The people had just experienced the feeding of the five thousand, and they were anxiously seeking the prophetic rabbi to see additional miracles and to eat. These people knew the wilderness story and immediately related it to Jesus. What they received instead was the meaning of the story: that God gives the true bread from heaven and that Jesus is that bread. Bread is used here as a metaphor for Christ's teaching, as well as for the Torah. Even then, the people heard little beyond the words.

We cannot manipulate manna from heaven in our own lives nor in the lives of those whose lands are barren, whose cupboards are empty, who for political reasons are unable to work. If we come merely to eat the bread in "human" memory and not as remembrance of Christ's teaching, we misunderstand the meaning of the Living Bread as a source of spiritual nourishment. So nourished, we can hear the story as if we were hungry or unemployed. Where we have been provided enough or more than our share, we can share with others. We can give what we have to those in our community, the city, suburbia, and wherever next door might be. We can live out our baptism even when we are not facing the font. How easily we forget the promises of God, the instructions that we are given, and the meaning of baptism and the table.

Melva Wilson Costen, Ph.D.

R   NINETEENTH SUNDAY IN ORDINARY TIME
E   PROPER 14
L   TWELFTH SUNDAY AFTER PENTECOST

R   *1 Kg 19:4–8; Eph 4:30–5:2; Jn 6:41–51*
E   *Deut 8:1–10; Eph 4:30–5:2; Jn 6:37–51*
L   *1 Kg 19:4–8; Eph 4:30–5:2; Jn 6:41–51*

It is comforting to know that the God who has sent Jesus also "draws" us to Jesus. We have time and freedom to explore the wonders of this world, one another, and the process by which God our Father does this "drawing." We don't always appreciate the route designed for our drawing—or "dragging" as the case may be, since the word can mean that as well. It sometimes takes effort to recognize God as the one who is pulling on our lives.

Consider Elijah. To be such a prophet was no small matter. When Jezebel threatened his life, he headed for the wilderness, seeking some respite under a broom tree, there wishing to die. "It is enough," he said, "I might as well be six feet under." This is the drawing of God? Elijah was hungry for some safety, a share of security. Instead he found himself in the wilderness. What is this? he likely said.

Consider the people of Israel. Delivered from Egypt only after disgrace and the discomforts of the plagues, they were drawn (dragged at times) by God via a circuitous route through the wilderness. Theirs was a long trip, often without water and food. The divine itinerary led these chosen ones, these hungry and homeless people here and there and nowhere for forty years. What is this?

Consider the crowds following Jesus. At last the people of Israel got to see the age-old promises of God enfleshed in a human. Here was one who said words that made sense, words that softened the hours and paths to come. Here was one who healed diseases. Yet, God's route still led to the unknown and the harsh, for the crowds followed Jesus to the hills where there was no food. Hungry again were those who were drawn and dragged. What is this?

Consider ourselves. Under the vision and plan of God we are drawn to this place and time. If we are hungry, there isn't much to eat. After all, we don't really expect to be satisfied by the food received here, do we? What's worse, the wilderness we know as the liturgy provides hungers we've never named or never wanted: it asks us to be hungry for kindness, tenderheartedness, and a spirit of forgiveness. It assumes that we will look for every opportunity to offer ourselves up in the name of God. What is this? We don't need it, do we?

Perhaps it's not so comforting to know that God draws us to Jesus. Murmurs come easily and their swelling is no surprise. Elijah complained too; the people of Israel murmured, so did the five thousand, and if you listen in the halls of your hearts you will hear murmurs as well. What is this?

Certainly it's not a macho exercise in building character. There must be a better way—as Calvin and Hobbes reasoned in the face of a camp-out in the rain: "Why can't we ever build character at a Miami condo or casino somewhere?"

There are plenty of religious condos and casinos. But it is in the wilderness that we know and feel the fullness of God's love. Our murmurs don't go unnoticed. Face to face with our own utter dependence upon God's nurturing love, we are surprised by being fed for the rigors of the way.

Consider Elijah. In the midst of a sleep that he wished would turn into death, an angel touched him and left behind a strange cake under a broom tree. Nourishment for the hungry one.

Consider the people of Israel. Wandering here and there and everywhere in the wilderness, food and drink eluding them, murmurs were answered by strange morning bread. "Manna," they said, which means "What is this?" But "What is this?" was not murmur, for their hunger was satisfied. Nourishment was provided.

Consider the five thousand hungry in the hills. Murmurs were transformed by a strange measure of provisions which multiplied unbelievably.

What kind of God is this who leads us to helplessness and hunger and thirst, there to be fed with the most unlikely morsels of nourishment? Oh, what a God, Jesus would say. And that is the point, especially for our wanderings. For the question about food in this wilderness of ours is not so much a question of "what is it?" but rather of "who is it?" Cakes and manna and fishes and loaves are mere tokens of God's full love for wilderness wanderers. But in this wilderness God is nourishment. I, I am the Bread of Life, Jesus says. I am the nourishment for the hungers you have, hungers you've never named, hungers you didn't know you had.

Who is this, this bread and this wine? It is Jesus who turns our cold hearts into warm centers of tenderheartedness and forgiveness, hearts which transform us to be fragrant offerings, eager to seek life which is eternal, eager to be life which is eternal.

Who is this, this bread and this wine? It is Jesus who transforms all our murmurs into sweet melodies, lives which together are the new Song of Jesus Christ, for he satisfies hungry hearts.

No wonder that St. Ignatius said: "I take no delight in corruptible food or in the dainties of this life. What I want is God's bread."[35]

What I want is God's bread.

Mark P. Bangert

[35]Ignatius, Romans 7:3, *Early Christian Fathers*, The Library of Christian Classics I, ed. Cyril C. Richardson (Philadelphia: Westminster, 1953), p. 105.

R TWENTIETH SUNDAY IN ORDINARY TIME
E PROPER 15
L THIRTEENTH SUNDAY AFTER PENTECOST

R *Prov 9:1–6; Eph 5:15–20; Jn 6:51–58*
E *Prov 9:1–6; Eph 5:15–20; Jn 6:53–59*
L *Prov 9:1–6; Eph 5:15–20; Jn 6:51–58*

Here we are again this morning. For most of us this is a familiar scene indeed: coming to church to worship God, praying and singing with other Christians, sitting where we usually sit, settling in to hear the word of the Lord and to share in the supper.

Here we are again this morning. Once again the lesson is from the sixth chapter of the gospel of John. How many weeks can this go on? We wonder whether there has been some mistake, whether perhaps the same lessons have been assigned for two weeks in a row. "I am the bread of life . . . ." Yes, but haven't we heard that before? Haven't we already gotten the message?

But the author of the fourth gospel thinks that we haven't. The method of this gospel is to take fewer themes than we find in the other three, but to explore them in great depth. Rather than pushing on to a new story of Jesus, a new miracle or new parable, John prefers that we linger, savoring the complex meaning of a few key events.

And Jesus as we meet him in this gospel is rather demanding, almost a little aggressive. He takes on the crowds, and through them attacks our ignorance, our listlessness, our too comfortable sense that we have been here before. This is done by challenging us to consider the connections among four things that we might not necessarily bring together: Jesus, bread, life, and God.

"I am the bread of life," Jesus tells us again this morning. It sounds lovely, hopeful, reassuring. But consider it for a moment. What a strange thing for our Lord to say! He seems to want to make the point almost literally: My flesh is food indeed. This bread I will give for the life of the world.

Those long ago or today who have been drawn to Jesus only by his wisdom or his kindness or his fame are certain to be troubled at this point. It is almost as it our Lord is shocking us into thinking on a warm Sunday morning, about who he is, about who we are, and about how we receive him in this meal today. He calls us to an intimacy of relationship with him that goes beyond even what many Christians are seeking. Unless you eat his flesh, you have no life in you.

But just when we begin to get somewhere with connecting Jesus and bread, John throws another term in for our consideration: life. Ordinary bread will not sustain us forever. Even those who ate manna in the wilderness, which was also bread from heaven, finally died. But Jesus promises that those who eat his flesh and drink his blood have eternal life and will be raised up at the last day. Jesus is the bread of life.

I had a dear aunt who used to panic from time to time and want to be taken off to receive communion in case she would die during the next week. Most of us can make some connections between Jesus and bread and life on that level. We might long to hear these words, and even to eat this bread, on our deathbeds.

But in this great text Jesus invites us to think not only of life after death (although his promise seems a great hope for that too) but how even now we receive life from him. Jesus invites us to consider that we are now on our deathbeds, unless we have found the life that sustains us in the One who is our way, our truth and our life. He is the head, ready to love us, to teach the path of wisdom to us, even to feed us. In such a moment our present and our future blend together in one joyous eternity with God, the Father of our Lord Jesus Christ.

And that brings us to God, the final term of the four. All of this talk about Jesus and bread and life that never ends would be poetic dreaming except for the claim of faith that Jesus was indeed the one who came in the name of the Lord, the One that the living Father sent. He is the heavenly bread because he comes from God.

So God in great love for this perishing world sends Jesus to us. God not only speaks to our minds, but touches our bodies with the bread that we receive this morning. Here we are again, but as always, so much more is going on here than we had dreamed when we walked into the church.

So much is going on here, and yet in the end this deep and complex gospel is rather a simple matter. It all comes down to the naming of God. In this place we are in God's presence, touched by God's love in Jesus, fed by the bread of life, renewed for our life this day and into all of eternity. And if that is our situation, we cannot sit here without response; we do not get credit for mere attendance. If in this hour Jesus, and bread, and life and God all come together, then we must rouse ourselves, wake up, and live as the epistle to the Ephesians invites us to live:

"Be filled with the Spirit, addressing one another in psalms and hymns and spiritual songs, singing and making melody to the Lord with all your heart, always and for everything giving thanks in the name of our Lord Jesus Christ to God, the Father."

So here we are again. But consider what a joy and a privilege it is to be here in light of the mystery of what is offered here. And then join in the celebration to receive the strength that you need for whatever lies ahead for you until here we are again.

Timothy F. Lull

R   *Josh 24:1–2a,15–17,18b; Eph 5:21–32; Jn 6:60–69*
E   *Josh 24:1–2a,14–25; Eph 5:21–33; Jn 6:60–69*
L   *Josh 24:1–2a,14–18; Eph 5:21–31; Jn 6:60–69*

Today we are presented with two questions—one calling for reflection, the other for decision. "Whom *do* you serve?" and "Whom *will* you serve?" We will give some attention to both this morning, but perhaps you should return to them again in the course of this day or this week. I ask you again, "Whom do you serve?"

Very often we find ourselves at Sunday worship feeling fragmented and frenzied. For a week we have been tied in knots over problems at the office, difficulties with the children, frustrations with those who seem to put too many demands on us. Perhaps you have come here to seek refuge this morning, to take time out from your frenetic life.

Gathered here together, very much the way the tribes might have been gathered together by Joshua, we find ourselves caught off-guard and strangely confronted by the question, "Whom do you serve?" The answer should be obvious from the very fact that we are here, but this isn't always the case for us, any more than it was for the tribes Joshua gathered together. Rather, it is a question we ought to ask ourselves periodically, especially when we are feeling depleted.

"Am I serving God or am I serving myself?" is how I phrased the question for myself when I began to consider these readings. When I serve myself, once my energy is gone, it's gone. I work myself to the point of exhaustion on some self-ordained project, usually accompanied by totally unreasonable expectations. When I try to serve God, however, and allow God to set the agenda, God provides me with all the energy I need, often in the most surprising ways. Similar to the appearance of manna in the desert, God provides resources needed for the day, not the warehouse of reserves I would like to have provided.

Serving God doesn't necessitate leaving our jobs or present responsibilities and going off to impoverished corners of the world. Ironically, for some individuals such a radical shift might be serving self rather than serving God. Serving God means having a right order in our lives, remembering that we are human beings created in the image and likeness of God, not machines designed to operate around the clock, in season and out. It means recognizing that God is at the center of our lives and that all our actions flow from that realization.

Paul's letter to the community of Ephesus speaks about right order within the household of the social order of his day. Although the terms which Paul uses might seem jarring and even contradictory to us in the twentieth century, their key concept ought to be harmonious with what we understand Christianity to require: loyalty. Right order requires us to be loyal to ourselves and to our relationships with others. We are loyal to ourselves when we refuse to abuse our minds or bodies, gifts or talents. We are loyal to our relationships when we nurture them with care and attention. We are loyal to our families when we try to be agents of reconciliation. We are loyal to God when we listen for God's word with open hands and open heart. Loyalty, for the Christian, necessitates fidelity to the gospel of Jesus Christ and to the community gathered in his name.

This brings us to the decision required by the second question, "Whom will you serve?" The choice is ours to make, not only today, but daily in life. Each time we gather for eucharist, our action rededicates us to the terms of the covenant with God and the community we originally made at baptism. It is the actions of our everyday life, however, that manifest our true intentions.

Whom will you serve? God? Self? Money? Country? Culture? The choices seem endless, and some persons have broken away from the community of believers before us, but I would hope that we could each make Peter's words our own this day. "Lord, to whom shall we go? You have the words of eternal life."

"Choose this day whom you will serve." Will you serve God or will you serve the culture?

Julia Upton, R.S.M.

R   TWENTY-SECOND SUNDAY IN ORDINARY TIME
E   PROPER 17
L   FIFTEENTH SUNDAY AFTER PENTECOST

R   *Deut 4:1–2,6–8; Jam 1:17–18,21b-22,27; Mk 7:1–8,14–15,21–23*
E   *Deut 4:1–9; Eph 6:10–20; Mk 7:1–8,14–15,21–23*
L   *Deut 4:1–2,6–8; Eph 6:10–20; Mk 7:1–8,14–15,21–23*

The Olympic figure skater seems so free. Gliding over the ice she twirls and flies, and it looks so easy. The professional singer opens his mouth and those wonderfully rich sounds flow out true and clear. The major league hitter swings and the ball lands perfectly in the space between the second baseman and the right fielder for a single.

We who sit and watch envy their freedom sometimes. We think fleetingly, "I could do that," before our "too, too solid flesh" reminds us of ineptitude. But why are the singer, the skater, the athlete so free? Is it only talent that separates them from the rest of us? Talent there certainly is. But there is one other essential ingredient in their achievement of success: discipline. Only the daily, repetitious practice which builds habit makes possible the full freedom of human artistry. The gift without discipline is a gift buried in clay.

Israel knew that life, fullness of life, was a gift from God. Israel knew also that the gift of life could be stunted, distorted, even lost without the corresponding gift of the law. For Israel the law was the practice manual for forming the habits which would make possible their freedom to live. Only daily practice would clear the eye and tone the muscles, fill the lungs and secure the balance so that one could leap freely into the joy of living. In this is wisdom, the understanding from experience of how to live well.

In the last centuries before the Christian era a sect of Judaism called the Pharisees developed a set of regulations or practices intended to be a "fence around the law." This oral tradition set out an added discipline to refine the skills for living. But in some cases the technique became more important than the art, the exercises became more important than the freedom to live. Jesus' disciples meet just such a situation in today's gospel: the washing of hands becomes more important than the inner cleanliness it signifies. In response to the criticism of the Pharisees, Jesus does not deny the importance of the law; rather he points out the true purpose of the law, to liberate people so that they become capable of genuine living.

It is this genuine living that is the true gift from the Father. The law is the corresponding gift which both supports the freedom to live and protects against the bad habits which would destroy that freedom.

A parent who gives a child a piano also gives that child the opportunity of taking lessons, buys the child practice books and books of recital pieces, and insists that the child practice every day—even with tears. The lessons, the exercise, the daily drudgery may seem a burden for a very long time. But they are truly part of the gift. The child who perseveres in the discipline until the habits of fine piano playing are second nature will gradually become free to play the piano. Free not to practice but to play. Free not just to make sounds but to speak what is in the heart.

God who gives us life also gives us the law, with teachers and examples and exercises, and insists that we practice every day— even with tears. But the law is indeed part of the gift of life. St. Benedict in his rule says that eventually those things which the monk once practiced out of fear he will begin out of habit to do with love. He will become free to run the way of God's commands. So too with all Christians. As we practice the discipline of the law, we will become free to play, we will become free to live.

Irene Nowell, O.S.B.

R   *Is 35:4–7a; Jam 2:1–5; Mk 7:31–37*
E   *Is 35:4–7a; Jam 1:17–27; Mk 7:31–37*
L   *Is 35:4–7a; Jam 1:17–22,26–27; Mk 7:31–37*

The car would go neither forward or back. I sat in the marshy gully as cars slithered past on the ice-coated highway. Darkness fell and the snow continued to fall. A figure blocked out the tail-lights of a car that had pulled over. Two more figures appeared, then three. Directions were yelled through the windshield, and four pairs of hands literally lifted my car up and back onto the highway. "Happy New Year!" floated into the falling snow and all four were gone. They never learned my name and I have no idea who they were, but those four people made my day. They *were* my Happy New Year.

We welcome the word into our hearts every time we read it or hear it proclaimed. What we often miss is that we ourselves *are* a word before we speak or do anything. The medium is indeed the message.

What kind of word are we? There are people whose very presence is peace. When they walk into a room, we breathe a sigh of relief. There are others who lift our spirits when we merely set eyes on them. And there are those whose presence sends a chill up our spine or floods us with pity.

Like fine-tuned sonar instruments we receive and transmit who we are. But the fine-tuned humanness that is the basic resource of each of us is tenuous at best. We have a sneaking suspicion that we can easily lapse into wording nothing but our egotistic self-interest. Faith will not settle for us being but a voice in the void. We are called to be words for a far greater word. We are to be voices for the fullness of the word that waits to be revealed in us.

There is a Presence waiting to be tended behind the gaunt eyes of the have-nots of our neighborhoods. There is Someone who longs to serve behind the arrogant eyes of those among us who think they have everything.

What prevents us from being a good word for the word of God? Today's gospel makes it quite clear. We may be pitifully deaf and thus unable to sound who we are to those we live with or meet. We may be so plugged up with self-importance or self-interest that the sound of who we really are cannot get through. Like a stopped-up flute we cannot sound a true tone. What does emerge is the whine of self-centeredness. We need to be opened up. We need to be healed. Isaiah announces that we needn't be afraid. Our God is here and will do it. This God has spoken a divine word indeed, and it stands before us in our history clothed in human flesh. We the human words will be vindicated. The divine word will be sounded and through our crippled humanness a wonderful exchange will take place. God's word will take on our crippledness. In exchange this word comes with human fingers that can be placed in human ears, and blockage melts away at his touch. This word comes with a tongue, and its saliva can snap our tongue-tiedness to speak our own trueness and integrity. We are the deaf ones and the voiceless ones who prefer not to hear the cries of our brothers and sisters, and who prefer not to speak up for those who have no voice. But when this Word touches us, he indeed does all things well. We hear and we speak and we do, and the Word is no longer bound up tight in our locked-up lives.

It is dangerous for us to be here today in this place. To gather here in his name is to risk being touched by him. When this happens we can no longer remain deliberately deaf and safely silent. But we are here. So let us take the risk of that touch. Let us present ourselves for that sweet contact that works conversion in the heart, and let us then move out from this assembly opened and ready.

Someone is waiting for a good word today. Someone is waiting for us. Go then, and be a good word in the marketplace.

Carla Mae Streeter, O.P.

R   *Is 50:5–9a; Jam 2:14–18; Mk 8:27–35*
E   *Is 50:4–9; Jam 2:1–5,8–10,14–18; Mk 8:27–38*
L   *Is 50:4–10; Jam 2:1–5,8–10,14–18; Mk 8:27–35*

Were I to tell you the truth, I would have to say, "I am afraid." I am afraid that this gospel cannot be spoken. It is an unspeakable gospel. But there is more, much more. It is not only that there exists no spoken word for this gospel. I am also afraid of what this gospel would do if it were done in a way other than words.

How can one talk about the will of God in connection with the Messiah's rejection, suffering, and death? How can one even think of God's will for the Messiah in these terms? Never mind speaking about it. How can one even think about the necessary death of the promised Christ?

Will theories of atonement fill the void that such a truth creates? Will exquisite soteriologies conceal the ugliness implicit in this unspeakable gospel? Will complicated Christologies diminish the pain such a silent word evokes? I wonder. Can all our theological words be an authentic expression of the Christ who must die? Or are they not rather like my many preachings?—parodies of truth, shadows of objects too fearsome to behold, caricatures of a Christ we dare not hear or see, for fear of the danger to which he must expose himself and us.

No, our many words betray us. Rather than keep proper silence before this unspeakable word, we have committed ourselves to a sort of verbal masturbation, a frivolity with which we amuse and sedate ourselves in a shadow dance with death. All our words are a kind of prophylaxis designed not to tell the truth, but rather to avoid its awful pain: if Christ must suffer and die, then so must we.

The Christ commands silence. And the silence hangs like a casket suspended above an open grave waiting to be let go, waiting to be covered over and forgotten, waiting to be marked with some slight arithmetic inscription, as though statistical precision might prevent the pain. We compose epitaphs: The man from Nazareth. Great Teacher. Friend of Sinners. Carpenter's Son. Son of Mary. Does any of this really matter? He must be rejected, suffer, die, and be raised on the third day. Anything else is like a eulogy spoken by a stranger over a stranger's grave: a pretense, a pointless drama enacted for the sake of form.

One suspects, and the Christ confirms, that the silence leads to the very place the unspeakable word declares: the cross. "Those who would come after me, let them deny themselves and take up their cross and follow me." These are not human thoughts. These are God's thoughts, of a piece with Christ's own identity and destiny. They point to Easter, but only by means of death. And not a grand, self-fulfilling sort of death, not a death my way, but rather a self-denying sort of death, a death God's way. The way of the Christ in this world is the way of suffering and death; it is the unspeakable way of self-denial for the sake of the gospel. It is the way through death to Easter life. The cross is a taking hold of death and life, bound together in a sacred equation: Cross death equals cross life.

In an age of too many words about the gospel, of too many preachers telling about the Christ, of too many well-dressed lecturers talking about the liberation of the poor, the unspeakable gospel becomes the litmus test of truth.

There is nothing new here. Nor is there anything particularly exciting. In fact, what this unspeakable word proposes is likely unexciting and terribly old: human suffering shared. We are to enter into another's pain, to be vulnerable to those who would take us for all we've got. This is a word which when talked about loses any claim to authenticity, which is perhaps why Jesus instructs those who would follow him, not to talk about a cross, but rather to take one up.

James is an apostle of the unspeakable gospel. On the subject of authentic faith, a faith conveyed by more than words, what Luther called the "Epistle of Straw" shines pure gold: "If a brother or sister is ill-clad and in lack of daily food, and one of you says to them, 'Go in peace, be warmed and filled,' without giving them the things needed for the body, what does it profit? So faith by itself, if it has no works, is dead. But some one will say, 'You have faith and I have works.' Show me your faith apart from works, and I by my works will show you my faith."

There can be no denying that taking up the cross is work, and that this work involves self-denial. Christ speaks the truth when he makes a connection between the work of the cross and the denial of self. Peter speaks for all of us when he expresses his horror of the cross. We flee from the unspeakable gospel, we hide from the cross, and we escape to our many words about it, to our preachings of concern, liberation, and inclusivity. We run to the enhancement of ourselves in the weary world of verbal religion, upon which the Christ invokes an injunction of silence.

The unspeakable word flows out of silence. It was hinted at by Isaiah, "The Lord GOD has given me the tongue of those who are taught, that I may know how to sustain with a word those who are weary." The tongue of those who are taught is silent. And it is out of silence that the unspeakable gospel flows. It is silence as at the dawn of creation, when the Spirit brooded over the face of the deep. We have been sealed by the Holy Spirit and marked with the cross of Christ forever. The silent cross-word is anchored in our baptism. In baptism it is etched into us as God leads us through death to life, following Christ toward Easter. The silent word bears Easter life.

But for now the weary ones wait for the baptized to do the silent word, to take up the cross for the sake of Christ in demonstration of Easter life. The silent word sustains the weary. It leads them and us to the sacrifice of thanksgiving, to Christ the victim, to Christ the feast. It leads us in silence to loud songs of Easter joy. Alleluia!

Franklin A. Wilson

R *Wis 2:12,17–20; Jam 3:16–4:3; Mk 9:30–37*
E *Wis 1:16–2:1,12–22; Jam 3:16–4:6; Mk 9:30–37*
L *Jer 11:18–20; Jam 3:16–4:6; Mk 9:30–37*

There is an image of my daughter's childhood indelibly etched in my mind's eye. She is playing in our backyard with soap bubbles. One bubble in particular fascinates her. It is huge and hangs just out of her reach, tantalizingly near. Mesmerized by this bubble, Katherine drops her plastic bubble maker. She stretches our her arms; her hands reach up for the bubble just beyond her reach. Her smile is so full as to nearly crack her face wide open with delight. But it is especially her eyes that I remember. They are shining with fascinated delight. In the depths of her bright eyes the bubble itself is reflected. And when I look at the bubble, it too catches and reflects her eyes. Both bubble and Katherine's eyes hold such wonder and delight, such fascination and celebration.

Nikos Kazantzakis wrote about the eyes of a child as being most like God's eyes:

> Truly, nothing more resembles God's eyes than the eyes of a child; they see the world for the first time, and create it. Before this, the world is chaos. All creatures—animals, trees, men, stones; everything: forms, colors, voices, smells, lightning flashes—flow unexplained in front of the child's eyes (no, not in front of them, inside them) . . . Chaos must have passed in front of God's eyes in just this way before the Creation.[36]

Could not these eyes of a child inform our understanding of today's gospel?

The ninth chapter of Mark's gospel is alive with visionary wonders. It begins with the narrative of the transfiguration in which Peter, James and John behold the Christ with new eyes. Yet Jesus orders them not to tell anyone what they have seen until he has risen from the dead. Jesus is teaching his disciples about the coming passion, but they are fearful and fail to see what he means. At Capernaum, the disciples are arguing about who among them will be the greatest. Into their midst Jesus takes a child and says: "Whoever receives one such child in my name receives me; and whoever receives me, receives not me but the one who sent me."

Who was this child? From where had she come? The text moves swiftly from passion prediction through teachings about servanthood to receiving a child in Jesus' name. It is a movement from death through confronted ambition to a new insight into what it means to be a follower of Christ. And it is the child in Jesus' arms who incarnates this revelation of discipleship.

Jesus speaks to the disciples, and in a very real sense, through them to us. He speaks of his passion. The disciples may not see, but we with our post-resurrection eyes see clearly, that he refers to the cross, to a sacrificial death. Jesus speaks of servanthood, of becoming last and servant to all. The disciples may be blind with guilt, but we observe the teaching clearly, reinforced by our memory of Jesus' basin and towel on the night before his death. But then Jesus takes the child in his arms and speaks. And even we are uncertain as to what he signifies.

In taking the child, Jesus incarnates his teaching. Jesus lays aside his own status in reaching out to a child, a symbol of the marginalized within any community. In his reception of the child Jesus models the openness, vulnerability and humility to which we are invited. Jesus invites us to receive Christ in the same way that we receive a child-like one.

The so-called "church growth" experts advocate the absence of children in corporate worship. Send them away; provide nurseries. Make Sunday School concurrent with worship: give parents an hour free from child care. But such an attitude contributes to the marginalization of children. Where else than in the liturgy will children see the gathering of God's family? Where else than in the liturgy will children perceive God's people eating at the table of the Lord?

We are thus called to stand with the child-like ones, for they may help us to see. We are bid to stand among the marginalized, to invite them in Christ's name within the community that bears Christ's name. We are drawn to receive the ones whom Kazantzakis envisioned as having the eyes of new creation. And in so doing, of course, we shall find that we are among them. We shall see anew and discover that we, too, are marginalized and in need of God's gracious reception. We are called to see the passion with child-like newly created vision, to see beyond the cross, torture and execution, to see in the cross a path to new life, to see in servanthood not a demeaning of personhood but an enhancement of life.

We bring this narrative of reception with us this day to Christ's table. We discover here forgiveness for our own disciple-like arrogance and ambition. We encounter here ministry to pattern our own feeble attempts at servanthood. In our welcome here we experience hospitality which in turn will shape our own ministries of hospitality.

Come to the feast of Christ. Come with hands outstretched in need. Come, perhaps to kneel in image of loyalty or devotion. Come, perhaps to stand in image of readiness for service and ministry. Above all, come with the eyes of a child to see in this meal Christ present. Witness for yourself the wonder and celebration, the delight and fascination of God who comes to us incarnate in Jesus of Nazareth. Behold with your own eyes of new creation the meal of the dominion of God.

Stephen M. Larson

[36]Nikos Kazantzakis, *Report to Greco* (New York: Simon and Schuster, 1965), p. 40.

R   *Num 11:25–29; Jam 5:1–6; Mk 9:38–43,45,47–48*
E   *Num 11:4–6,10–16,24–29; Jam 4:7–12; Mk 9:38–43,45,47–48*
L   *Num 11:4–6,10–16,24–29; Jam 4:7–12; Mk 9:38–50*

The story is told among Zen Buddhists that an earnest student sought out a Zen master for instruction in the true meaning of Zen. The student had spent many years studying sacred texts of Buddhism. But his mind was filled with many questions. Which teacher of Buddhism was the most trustworthy? Which sacred writing was the most reliable? Which monastery should he join?

He took all these questions to the Master. Upon hearing his questions, the Master immediately threw all of the student's books into the fire, refused to answer any questions and dragged the student into the marketplace where he confronted him with a poor, crippled beggar. "Learn righteousness," he admonished the student.

They came to Jesus, perhaps as we have come to him today, to learn more about how to be a more faithful disciple. Who is the true disciple? The teacher must distinguish between true and false faith, right and wrong belief. And that's what we often expect of a homily. In the sermon, the preacher elucidates the faith, helping believers to distinguish between the true and the false.

"Teacher, we saw a man casting out demons in your name," said John, "whom we forbade, because he was not following us."

Now let us not demean the disciples' questions about this questionable man. Proper, careful distinctions make a difference. Sometimes, in the American church, people try to short-cut the need for careful thinking and theological clarification with slogans like, "It doesn't really matter what you believe as long as you are sincere." Too often, such talk is an excuse for not taking the effort to think things through. Beliefs do make a difference. All sorts of terrible things have been done by people who sincerely believed that what they did was right. Wrong thinking can lead to confused, chaotic, miserable lives.

So, when the disciples ask about the place of this man who was busy exorcising in Jesus' name without being part of Jesus' community, Jesus does not reply, "Don't worry about it. It doesn't really matter."

Rather, Jesus instructs them by noting that good works done in his name are to be celebrated and acts of kindness toward Jesus' disciples are to be gratefully acknowledged by disciples. Even if the agent's words are not right or his or her membership credentials are not in order, disciples can rejoice that good work is being done.

During the scandals surrounding the escapades of television evangelists a few years ago, I thought of all the good, sincere people who lost money and even faith because of the actions of some of these TV preachers. I also recalled all the people who, every time some impropriety had been charged, said, "Well, I don't agree with everything those people believe, but they do a lot of good." The mere fact that these evangelists attracted millions who gave millions was proof enough that they were about the Lord's work. Was it not more accurate to say that anyone who invoked the name of Jesus on TV was immune from accountability?

In today's gospel, Jesus does not say that anyone who works under the guise of religion is immune from accountability. There is a means of measurement: the gospel. The gospel does have something theological to say about the identity of Jesus. But the gospel is also a matter of mighty works of compassion as well as even relatively small works of love, such as the cup of cold water in Jesus' name. It is not a matter of believing and doing anything we want with nothing more to commend us than a muddle-headed warm glow of religion. It is a matter of being faithful to the peculiar shape of the gospel which, unlike some religions, puts high value on concrete, visible, practical love in action.

No doubt the early church had to struggle with Christian identity. It had to answer questions about discipleship and to make
proper distinctions between those who actually follow Jesus and
those who are terribly confused about Jesus. "Not being one of
us" is not an adequate criterion for determining who is or who is
not a Christian. More segments of the church would be at peace
with one another today if we all remembered this.

So we can rejoice when good work is done, whoever the agent.
As Christians, we believe that every instance of the advancement
of justice, of compassion and love, is an indication of the
inbreaking dominion of God. Knowing that God's kingdom is
bigger than our particular church's definitions of it, we can expect to be pleasantly surprised by the rich array of response
which the presence of Christ evokes. We can be reminded, as
we come to the Lord's Table, that our faith is a matter of correct
doctrine, orthodox belief, clear thinking, but it is also a matter of
the cup of water, as well as the cup of eucharistic wine, given in
the name of the one who so richly offered himself to us that we
might offer ourselves to others.

William H. Willimon

R   TWENTY-SEVENTH SUNDAY IN ORDINARY TIME
E   PROPER 22
L   TWENTIETH SUNDAY AFTER PENTECOST

R   *Gen 2:18–24; Heb 2:9–11; Mk 10:2–12*
E   *Gen 2:18–24; Heb 2:9–18; Mk 10:2–9*
L   *Gen 2:18–24; Heb 2:9–11; Mk 10:2–16*

No one wants to talk about divorce, least of all pastors. It's not
the kind of topic that makes for good stories and stimulates
church growth. Meanwhile our divorce rate has escalated over
the last twenty years, with more and more clergy themselves
divorcing.

It is precisely because divorce is so painful that the church must have something to say. It is not enough for the church to avoid the topic, trying to escape the guilt. Precisely because the divorced are guilty, the church must have something to say which takes account of them and their history. We cannot assume that the mercy of Jesus is so small that it cannot speak to the guilt of divorced people. The truth in fact is that the word of Christ is so boundless that it calls us all to account and then gathers us all in.

The Pharisees want to know if it is lawful for a husband to divorce his wife. Is there an acceptable time and an appropriate way to put away another person? What is the acceptable time, the appropriate way, for people to be free of their duties and promises to each other? Is there a divine rite for divorce?

Jesus answers with a question: What does Moses say? Jesus says that Moses' law, which allows the man to divorce the woman, reveals the ways of humankind, the hardness of the human heart. The words in the text literally mean, "a heart dried up." Jesus underscores that although divorce proceeds from the ways of humankind, from the beginning God made them male and female.

Suddenly there is much more at stake than the Pharisees had imagined. They asked a question about the acceptable conditions for a man responsibly to put way his wife. Now Jesus confronts them with the primal reality of human createdness and with the intended partnership of male and female as mutual and equal creatures. Jesus illustrates the unity of human flesh, the bondedness of humankind, with the metaphor of marriage. Human beings are made to cleave to each other. God joins male and female as mutually dependent partners in humanity. What therefore God joins, humans and their ways are not to put asunder.

It is not for men to figure out acceptable ways to put away women as if they were property to be ritually disposed of. Further, Jesus speaks beyond this Hebrew custom to the Roman one, where also the woman could put away the man. All these are signs of parched hearts. The dissolution of marriages and the will to shed off responsibility become, in Jesus' hands, a metaphor for the human condition. The basic unity of human flesh and the intended mutuality between men and women is disrupted. And one of the ways we see this is marital divorce.

But all of us, single or married, widow or widower, male or female, gay or straight, all of us stand under the experience of divorce. That experience is the limits of our human flesh, the gnawing sorrow that we are not able to be what we hoped or to create what we promised. We stand together under the experience of brokenness and need. We all fail one another, we all are faithless, we are all much less than we had desired. We are a company of hearts dried up.

So, for the morally conscious, all divorce, particularly divorce in a marriage, is an experience of one's weakness and finitude and death. Particularly when people have striven so hard to find life and strength in their promises, divorce becomes so intensely a painful death, for divorce is the failure of the future. The adulteration of the future is an adulteration against both partners. Both partners are cut through; the victims are the whole people involved.

The Pharisees were tested in their testing. Faithfulness is suddenly much more than a matter of acceptable times and appropriate rituals. Faithfulness and adulterated partnership intertwine at the creation of one humankind, male and female. Even the morally conscious Pharisees are a company of parched hearts, dried up, unable to pump the life-blood of grace and hope.

We are unworthy to bring ourselves to Jesus that his healing hands might touch and bless us. But turning aside from the Pharisees, Jesus blesses the children. As the powerless, as the least, as those without means to pay or secure their own passage, the children are welcomed into Jesus' arms. The powerless, the least, those without means to secure passage, the ones whose lives are sundered from the society, those who stand under the experience of their own brokenness, all these hearts dried up, Jesus takes into and under the waters of death and blesses them. For Christ does not put away humankind. Rather,

Christ joins us, cleaving to us in suffering and death so that we might be brought into God's dominion in glory and honor.

No one wants to talk about divorce. What we have to say is only this: God quickens the most parched hearts with the balm of mercy. For this balm, come now to the table.

Jann Esther Boyd Fullenwieder

R TWENTY-EIGHTH SUNDAY IN ORDINARY TIME
E PROPER 23
L TWENTY-FIRST SUNDAY AFTER PENTECOST

R *Wis 7:7–11; Heb 4:12–13; Mk 10:17–27*
E *Am 5:6–7,10–15; Heb 3:1–6; Mk 10:17–27*
L *Am 5:6–7,10–15; Heb 3:1–6; Mk 10:17–27*

In *You're a Good Man, Charlie Brown,* Lucy spins a fantasy for herself: "When I grow up, I'm gonna be the biggest queen there ever was. I will live in a big palace with a big front lawn. And when I go out in my coach, all the people will wave at me. . . . And in the summertime, I will go to my summer palace—and I will wear my crown in swimming, and everything."[37] Linus interrupts her with a little reality-testing, explaining that the only way to become a ruling queen is to be born into a royal family. After protesting that this is undemocratic, Lucy recovers her fantasy, now transformed into an authentically American dream: "Then I will work very hard, and get very, very rich, and I will buy myself a queendom! I'll buy myself a queendom, and I'll throw out the old queen—I will be head queen. And when I go out in my coach . . . ."

The young man who comes to Jesus with his anxious question is also seeking a royal inheritance; he wishes to inherit eternal life. He thinks the way to qualify for this inheritance is to keep all the rules, to do all that is required. Yes, he says, he has kept all the rules he's aware of. And Jesus' heart goes out to him. Why is Jesus not angry at him, as Jesus was often angry at those who claimed to have met the law's demands? Perhaps because he saw in this young man not a proud hypocrisy, but an anxious perfectionism, making him worry that there might be other rules he hasn't heard of. If only this good rabbi would lay out for him the definitive requirements!

Jesus' response seems to be just what a perfectionist would dread: a new, unheard-of requirement, stricter than the old rules, a yoke too heavy to bear. Sell all you have, give it to the poor, follow me: the young man hears an unmeetable demand, and goes away sad. But perhaps if he had not come expecting a demand, he might have heard something different in Jesus' reply: an offer of an entirely different way of living. He might have heard Jesus coaxing him to unclench his hands, to spread them open to give and to receive. With his hands grasping his possessions he will not be able to catch the life God is tossing him. Giving to the poor is not so much a good deed he must do to qualify for life, as it is the inseparable flip side of living in grace. Our hearts cannot be open to God without also being open to those in need.

Like the rich young man, the disciples hear Jesus making an impossible demand. If it's harder than a camel squeezing through a needle's eye, then who can be saved? Yet the disciples had heard, as we did last week, to whom God's dominion belongs: to little children. Is it because of their perfect obedience, their ability to meet the strictest demands? (What child you know is perfectly obedient?) Or is it because of their trust, their open hands ready to receive what is offered?

If we must become as little children, though, that also seems humanly impossible. As another rich man, Nicodemus, pointed out, it's not possible for a grown-up to be born again; the birth passage is too narrow, it might as well be a needle's eye. But God has a womb large enough for all humanity to be reborn in, and even the dinkiest font is big enough for us to enter again and again and again. At last, if we are born anew each day, we may grow up into full childhood and learn how to open our hands in trust, in generosity, in praise. We cannot buy ourselves a queendom, not by working very hard, not even by acts of charity. But we can be born into a royal family; in baptism, that has already happened. So come to the royal banquet table; you have only to open your hands to receive the inheritance of eternal life. Pray that they stay open this week, to receive what you need, to give to others in need. If by your hands the hungry are fed, then you will know that the queendom of God is within you. And look in the font as you pass by; there's grace there deep enough for you to dive in. You can wear your crown in swimming, and everything.

Elaine J. Ramshaw

[37]Clark Gesner, *You're a Good Man, Charlie Brown,* based on the comic strip by C.M. Schulz (New York: Random House, 1967).

R   TWENTY-NINTH SUNDAY IN ORDINARY TIME
E   PROPER 24
L   TWENTY-SECOND SUNDAY AFTER PENTECOST

R   *Is 53:10–11; Heb 4:14–16; Mk 10:42–45*
E   *Is 53:4–12; Heb 4:12–16; Mk 10:35–45*
L   *Is 53:10–12; Heb 4:9–16; Mk 10:35–45*

"This man for others" is the phrase Dietrich Bonhoeffer used to describe Jesus. It is apt description of the Jesus we meet in the gospel reading for today and an apt description of the suffering servant of whom Isaiah speaks in the first reading, though we might add "this man who *suffers* for others." Jesus suggests in the gospel reading that it would also be an apt description of the followers of Jesus, those who would bear his name and who intend that their lives reflect the life of Jesus.

The gospel reading comes from a section of the gospel of Mark called "the way of the cross." It is so named because the journey of Jesus described in chapters 8–10 is a journey toward Jerusalem and the cross that awaits him there. Jesus knew that his foot was set firmly on the path that would lead him to Calvary, but the minds and hearts of his disciples were elsewhere. On three different occasions Jesus spoke in clear and direct terms about the suffering that lay ahead of him. In each case his disciples turned a deaf ear, and Jesus then attempted to instruct them that the kingdom of God comes not through power but through suffering love. The gospel reading relates the story of one of those occasions.

Immediately before the gospel reading, Jesus had said to his disciples: "Behold, we are going up to Jerusalem; and the Man of Heaven will be delivered to the chief priests and the scribes, and they will condemn him to death, and deliver him to the Gentiles; and they will mock him, and spit upon him, and scourge him, and kill him; and after three days he will rise." Instead of responding to what Jesus said, James and John asked Jesus if they could be in positions of authority when he came into power. Jesus answered their question with a question: "Can you endure the suffering that I am about to endure?" That is the question of the hour, and it is obvious from the behavior of the disciples throughout Christ's hour of trial that they were woefully unprepared to face it.

Measured by time and miles, we are far distant from Calvary and the one who suffers there for us. And yet that distance evaporates in the invitation extended to us to taste the body of Christ which was broken for us and to sip the blood of Christ poured out as a ransom for our sins. The full meaning of "this man for others, this man for us" gets embodied in this meal and embedded in us who are privileged to be the body of Christ in the world today. What a gracious gift—this forgiveness-food which so richly nourishes our spiritual lives! What an awesome responsibility—that we are now the body of Christ to be broken for others!

To receive the gift without accepting the responsibility is cheap grace and likens us to the disciples who wanted the crown without the cross, and Easter without a Good Friday. However, I must quickly add that they were on the other side of Calvary, and we are on this side. They had not yet received the full gift of Christ's ransom. We have. And after they had made their passage through Good Friday to Easter, they were prepared to drink the cup of suffering for others and did so.

Brothers and sisters in Christ, come to the feast which is prepared for you. Receive the gift of Christ's body and blood freely and gladly. There are no conditions. It was for you that Jesus suffered. And then go from this assembly as this man, this woman for others, holding fast to your confession. You do not go alone. The Lord Christ, "who in every respect has been tempted as we are," accompanies you, strengthens you, suffers with you, and will not let you go.

Thomas Droege

R THIRTIETH SUNDAY IN ORDINARY TIME
E PROPER 25
L TWENTY-THIRD SUNDAY AFTER PENTECOST

R *Jer 31:7–9; Heb 5:1–6; Mk 10:46–52*
E *Is 59:9–19; Heb 5:12–6:1,9–12; Mk 10:46–52*
L *Jer 31:7–9; Heb 5:1–10; Mk 10:46–52*

As you listen attentively for a word from God, I invite you to close your eyes. Real tight. Try to imagine absolute darkness. A country road on a moonless night. Your home in a storm when the fuse blows, and you haven't got a candle, and you can't find a match, and the batteries in the flashlight in the drawer are dead. Even if you have 20/20 vision, you still can't see in the dark. Imagine what it would be like to be permanently blind. Try to feel for a moment, from the inside out, the agonized cry of the blind beggar, Bartimaeus: "Jesus of Nazareth, I want to see!"

Now open your eyes. What do you see? People, pews, pulpit, preacher, snatches of color, a hundred and one bits of sensory data assault your sight on every side. But what do you really see? What sense do you make of that level of reality lying just below the surface of things, that world of meaning and purpose where religion is at home, where sight is really insight or wisdom, where vision is not something in the eye of the beholder but a conviction in the heart of the believer? What do you see of this inner world of sensitivities beyond the senses? So many of us walk through life with our eyes wide open, yet we comprehend little of its meaning, because we are inwardly blind. The physically blind are well aware of their handicap. The spiritually blind usually are not.

The times we live in demand of us a clear inner vision. Without such a vision to enlighten and sustain us, we are in danger of succumbing to the dark, terrifying forces of fear within and around us, fear of failure, fear of cosmic annihilation, fear of a loss of faith as moral principles and religious practices, one after another, fall out of fashion and disappear. In the prophetic words of Isaiah, we are like those without eyes groping for light in our existential darkness, searching blindly for meaning and for justice and for truth amid falsehood all around. The blind Bartimaeus cried out from the dark night of his own soul and spirit: "Jesus, have mercy on me!" And Jesus turned to him and said, "What do you want me to do for you?" "Let me receive my sight. I want to be able to see."

When was the last time you asked Jesus for sight or for insight? It would mean having to admit that we don't really see things all that clearly. We would have to admit that we don't know all there is to know about God, about religion, about ourselves and one another. It would mean that we would have to be open to dealing with the possibility that God might answer our prayer. If we should really look into our behavior and our beliefs, we might see that some rules need rewriting, some roles need rearranging, some rites and rituals need reworking, some attitudes need reforming, some convictions need renewing. That's a tall order, wanting to see things as they really are or as God intends them to be, not as we would have them.

There is no doubt that God can handle such a request for genuine spiritual insight; but can we? We may want to see with the eyes of faith, but we are afraid of the consequences. "Take courage," said the friends of Bartimaeus as the blind man stood on the threshold of no return. "Don't lose heart. Jesus is calling you." Don't lose heart, dearly beloved in Christ. Jesus is inviting us to tell him what we would have him do for us. Say to him, "I want to see!"

Jesus performed two miracles for Bartimaeus. He restored sight to eyes long physically blind and gave insight to a heart that longed to see. A newly liberated Bartimaeus perceived as in a mirror darkly that there was even more to be seen, so he followed after Jesus, intrigued by the startling words, "It is your faith that has made you whole." As the faith of Bartimaeus gave rise to miracles, so too our own faith will work wonders for us. Faith means believing that God will lead the blind back to clarity from the far corners of confusion, as the prophet Jeremiah foretold, that God will bring the outcasts back from the margins of credibility into the mainstream of religious life, that God will form a great company from the prophetic remnant of the faithful, calling all into one common covenant of intimate relationship with God.

Faith means believing that Jesus as the Christ intercedes before God on our behalf as our one-only high priest, as flesh of our flesh, as one of us and yet One beyond us, as child of God, as God of God. "Jesus, I want to see!" Indeed, we do want to see what all this means for us and what this requires of us. Our intuition tells us it may mean at times being less priestly and more prophetic, living justly, loving tenderly, walking humbly before God. It may mean that we who ought to be teachers have still much to be taught, that we who are called to proclaim the good news have yet to learn the basic principles of applying God's liberating word. It may mean that we who have been fed on the solid food of faith must admit to a spiritual immaturity and turn again, like a child, to a nurturing God as we grow spiritually strong.

Today's gospel is about the spiritually handicapped, not the visually impaired. It speaks a hard word. It calls for a faith strong enough to make miracles happen, and for courage and determination to live with the miracle once it has occurred. Bartimaeus received his physical sight and followed after Jesus. His friends surely thought he was crazy. There was so much he could finally do, now that he could see. Why was he running after that Nazarene, throwing his life away, wasting the miracle? But Baritmaeus followed Jesus precisely because he could see at last with the eyes of faith far more than the eye could see. He was now a person of vision amid the blindness of his friends. How ironic. The blind in a flash see clearly that which the supposedly enlightened somehow fail to see. Christianity is accustomed to paradox. Those who are blind see, those who are lame walk, those who relinquish their lives find life, while those who cling to what they cherish most will feel it slip-sliding away. Amazing grace. How can this be? "I once was lost, but now am found, was blind, but now I see."

Miriam Therese Winter, S.C.M.M.

R   THIRTY-FIRST SUNDAY IN ORDINARY TIME
E   PROPER 26
L   TWENTY-FOURTH SUNDAY AFTER PENTECOST

R   *Deut 6:2–6; Heb 7:23–28; Mk 12:28b-34*
E   *Deut 6:1–9; Heb 7:23–28; Mk 12:28–34*
L   *Deut 6:1–9; Heb 7:23–28; Mk 12:29–34*

In a sense we could call our liturgy today a celebration of "down to basics," since it celebrates love of God and neighbor, covenant and kingdom, priesthood and sacrifice. Furthermore, we are invited to enter into the mystery of Christ, the Word of God. Again, Old and New Testament illumine our faith and move our hearts to respond.

First, let us savor the fare served us in the selection from Deuteronomy. This passage is part of a liturgy of covenant renewal, and it is an urgent appeal to covenant fidelity. An appeal to keep the law is always part of covenant renewal, for the law is there to protect the bonding between God and the people. The land flowing with milk and honey belongs to the Israelites by reason of God's promise, not because they have appeased the Baals, the fertility deities.

In that promised land they lived among the Canaanites and were in constant danger of adopting some of the cult of the Baals, the deities of fertility. The Israelities needed to hear the serious injunction introduced by the solemn formula, "Hear, O Israel: The LORD our God is one LORD; and you shall love the LORD, your God. . . . " This reveals the kind of response in keeping with the dignity of the people of God. It does not call primarily for any specific exterior behavior, but it reveals the need for deep interior motivation in the words: "with all your heart, and with all your soul, and with all your might." We must be in touch with our own deep desires and know that no matter what our external work may be, we can take to heart these words which are enjoined on us today, as we are assembled here to celebrate the new and everlasting covenant.

At first glance it may seem that the gospel is little more than a repeat of much of the text of Deuteronomy. However, close inspection will reveal significant additions. In the first place, the text from Mark 12 is probably the single example of open dialogue between Jesus and one of the scribes. Lawyers of that time often engaged in argumentation over which commandment was the first or the foundation upon which the numerous commandments of the Torah rested. When the lawyer put forth the question, Jesus replied without any hesitation: "This is the first." He proceeded to quote the Deuteronomic text along with its solemn introduction: "Hear, O Israel: The LORD our God, the LORD is one."

As usual, these words contain power. Jesus is himself present when the word is proclaimed in the assembly. Jesus is the only one with power to call us away from the temptation to think we are able to save ourselves. We live amid the manifold advances in technology. Many are lured to think that our scientific advances will save us, and that military might alone will give us victory. We are tempted to consider ourselves gods who can determine the lives of other peoples, even the fate of other nations. We are in danger of overlooking the fact that God is the Lord of human history.

Jesus also adds the same emotive depth to the commandment of love of God and adds "with all your mind." What is completely original with Jesus is his uniting the love of neighbor inseparably to the love of God. Leviticus 19:18 exhorts the Israelites to love others as themselves, but it does not join this to love of God. The lawyer recognizes this, adding that such a combination is better than burnt offerings or sacrifice. Jesus, in his turn, gives the scribe the assurance that he is not far from the reign of God. The lawyer is close to allowing inner motivation, where alone God can reign as the guiding force in the human heart.

You are not far from the kingdom of God! These words have a special flavor now that we are approaching the close of the church year. At this season we are celebrating, not just the end of the year with its gospel of the end of the world and the Feast of Christ the King, but we are also celebrating the assurance that deep within our hearts the kingdom is very near.

When we look at the kingdom of God in the light of the second reading, we find that Jesus' reign is an entirely interpersonal reality. Jesus has a priesthood that will not pass away. He stands forever between God and us who wish to approach God. He personally intercedes for us. He did not offer sacrifices: he offered himself once and for all. We are still the beneficiaries of that love.

We have said that the readings give moral instruction; they also give the power to carry out what they enjoin. Hence we can enter into the eucharistic liturgy with love. We can be challenged to respond to Christ's own love. Love is undoubtedly the strongest power on earth to evoke love in return. When we share the consecrated food and drink, we know again that we are sharing both the power to love God and to love our neighbor as ourselves.

Mary Pierre Ellebracht, C.Pp.S.

R THIRTY-SECOND SUNDAY IN ORDINARY TIME
E PROPER 27
L TWENTY-FIFTH SUNDAY AFTER PENTECOST

R 1 Kg 17:10–16; Heb 9:24–28; Mk 12:41–44
E 1 Kg 17:8–16; Heb 9:24–28; Mk 12:38–44
L 1 Kg 17:8–16; Heb 9:24–28; Mk 12:41–44

Archeologists have learned new things about the Christian centers in Rome in the first two "downstairs" centuries of the church's life, before we moved "upstairs" into basilicas. They have learned that Christians sometimes met in the homes of widows. They may have been widows of Christian martyrs, or of men who had fallen out of favor with the successive tyrannies of the empire, or women who had been child brides to men much older than themselves, who had now died. The law provided civil penalties if they did not soon remarry. But remarriage meant that their dowries and inheritances would soon enrich some other, usually pagan, gentleman. Slick televangelists have a similar scam with lonely survivors in our own time. Mark's gospel warns, "Beware of those who devour widows' houses."

As Christian missionaries like Peter and Paul arrived in Rome on their visits, they sometimes stayed in the homes of Christian widows. These houses thus became meeting places for Christian worship. They were the safe houses for the illegal Christian revolutionary movement.

Every revolutionary movement has widows. One of the striking things about Central America is the number of widows, thousands of women whose husbands and sons have been "disappeared" by military governments and death squads. Violent oppression there creates a whole class of widows. The murder of their families has always politicized women, to the point that they become willing, if they were not so earlier, to commit themselves, their lives and property, in witness to the rule of justice to the kingdom of God in their own time and place. Jesus urged our attention to one such poor widow in an alien land, and proclaimed God's special attention to her, in his first sermon at

Nazareth. He outraged his neighbors by preaching that although there were many widows in Israel at the time of the famine, Elijah was sent to none of them, but to an alien woman of a despised race. You may remember that his neighbors tried to "disappear" Jesus off a cliff after that homily.

It was during an ideological war that Elijah made his pilgrimage to the alien town on the Philistine coast. The wealthy people there worshiped prosperity: Baal was their god. Today, a fertile brand of Baalist televangelism offers such instant prosperity to its devotees. In those days, it was rain, always on tap for the crops of the true believer. But Elijah asked the true God of Heaven to turn off the tap and show that such manipulation wouldn't work. Three and a half years, no rain! Even Elijah got thirsty, even Elijah got hungry! God then sent him to the alien widow, the Palestinian woman, to be cared for: in solidarity with each other, each would now survive the famine. Her last shared tortilla never disappears, her last cup of cooking oil keeps filling itself up. There is food enough so that "she and he and her household ate for many days." Can it be that in Central America, in Ethiopia, in Azania, on many strange coastlands today, God is visiting the widows with special favor? That the humble gifts of the poor, of peasants and of the persecuted, are being used by God to preserve their lives and witness in the world?

Jesus pointed to another widow closer to home: the one he noticed in the court of the women at the Jerusalem Temple. (Was it because his disciples included women that they sat there, instead of in the all-male court of Israel?) Thirteen trumpet-shaped boxes there received the gifts of the people, and Jesus noticed that rich people came and gave large gifts. Suddenly, along comes a woman with two little copper coins, the *lepton*, only about a quarter inch in diameter. Since this Greek coin was not used everywhere, Mark explains for his readers that they were worth a *quadran*: together the coins amounted to half a *denarius*, a day's wages for a laborer. Jesus said that she gave all that she had to live on—100%! Not a tithe, not the 50% standard of Luke's gospel, but the 100% standard that Mark always holds up.

Jesus then puts her gift in perspective, along with the gifts of the rich. The value of the gift cannot be set by its inherent cash value, he teaches us, but by what it represents for the giver. What do our gifts cost us, in terms of commitment? A drop in the bucket? Or a full bucket? The Palestinian widow gave a bucketful to Elijah. She gave her last meal to share with the God-sent visitor, her life in a measure of meal, a cruet of oil, just as the woman with the copper coins gave her all. Elijah asked for solidarity and sharing, even of the poor. Jesus praised it. God expects it.

No one gets off the hook by claiming, "There are people who have more than I do who should be doing their share, in witness and in giving." The fact is they will rarely carry the load. Christianity got on the move in the Roman empire with the help of the poor. There are still wealthy patrons of the kingdom, but God goes especially to seek the help of the poor, that the poor themselves may be helped. Jesus says the widow of Zarephath was favored by the prophet's need, by his demand for commitment. She got to invest in the future, to share in the meals of many days, to pour from her cup until the famine ceased.

Our own sacrificial giving—not stingy parting with privilege, but commitment to and solidarity with the coming age—will bring us at last to a banquet of endless blessing, of which we have fore-taste today in the sharing of the loaf and cup of the eucharistic meal.

Grant M. Gallup

L TWENTY-SIXTH SUNDAY AFTER PENTECOST

L *Dan 12:1–3; Heb 10:11–18; Mk 13:1–13*

Have you ever met a hypochondriac? Have you ever acted like one? These are people who do not have organic illness or disease, but who do suffer in thinking they are ill. Many of us are part-time hypochondriacs; when reading a list of physical symptoms we immediately conclude, "That's me! I've got that," whatever the condition may be. We draw our conclusions from the signs, and certainly symptoms are a very real help in diagnosis. Awareness of the meaning behind the signs can often prevent tragedy.

We live our lives surrounded by all sorts of signs. In traveling there are directional signs, speed limits, and hazard warnings. Sometimes they are indirect, like the ominous rattle under the hood. Smelling gas alerts us to a household danger; smoke is not to be ignored. Parents can be especially perceptive to signs of changed behavior in their children; parents even become uneasy when things are "too quiet." Our bodily attitudes and gestures are as clear as speech to those who are trained or sensitive. The list of signals which affect our lives is endless.

One universal group are the weather signs. We listen to forecasts and we study winds, temperatures, fronts, trends, whatever. Every fall we hold discussions on the woolly-bear caterpillars, the activity of squirrels, the flight of birds, or some other natural factor that helps to predict the winter. We plan outings according to weather phenomena, we climb mountains or stay home, we launch our boats or put up our storm windows, all according to the signs around us. And humans try to predict an event more significant than the coming of winter: the arrival of the last days, the end time, the final judgment of the world.

From the Scriptures we know that the disciples of Jesus and the members of the early Christian communities shared this concern. They realized a period of great distress was to come, and many believed it was just around the corner. Disturbing weather phenomena, upheavals, tribulations of all kinds: these were to precede the triumphant return of Christ. Although his followers yearned for the completion of his mission and the final redemption of all creation, they were still anxious. They wanted to be ready. They wanted what we all want: a sign that everything will be all right.

In the passage from Mark read in today's liturgy and in those passages immediately following, Jesus emphasizes the need to be prepared and tells the disciples to be on guard. He calls for fidelity to the end, with all the harsh consequences which those who follow him can expect. Faithfulness is never easy. Like those early believers, we, too, hear the warnings and become anxious when we consider the coming of the great judgment. We, too, keep studying signs and looking for some kind of direction.

Among all the possibilities we might ever imagine, there is only one which will truly help. It is the great and holy sign of the cross—the sign of contradiction which proclaims the fullness of our sanctification. We now exist in a double dimension of time. On the one hand, we are those in the process of being sanctified, and, on the other, those who are finished, completed, and perfected, because of the sacrifice of Christ. Today's reading from Hebrews, when we look to the original Greek tenses, makes this clear: "For by one offering he *has perfected* in perpetuity those *being sanctified*. Christ has, indeed, made our peace, our reconciliation with God, through the blood of the cross.

That cross speaks both a fact and a promise. Through accepting death on a cross, Jesus has already won our victory. We are still struggling on the way, and that cross is promise that we will share in that triumph. As the first reading from Daniel indicated, someday we shall shine like stars, but only if we make the contradiction of the cross ours. The incident preceding today's gospel is that of the widow's mite. It, too, is a sign: will we be able to give all that we have? Will our loyalty and our generosity persevere to the end? By accepting and sharing in the sign of the cross, we will be able to answer "Yes."

Katherine A. Lewis, O.P.

R *Dan 12:1–3; Heb 10:11–14, 18; Mk 13:24–32*
L *Dan 7:9–10; Heb 13:20–21; Mk 13:24–31*

In the first pages of John Bunyan's remarkable book *The Pilgrim's Progress*, the Pilgrim begins a long and arduous journey towards eternal life, and he's met by a man named Evangelist. "Then said Evangelist, pointing with his finger over a very wide field, Do you see yonder wicket gate? The man said, No. Then said the other, Do you see yonder shining light? He said, I think I do. Then said Evangelist, Keep that light in your eye, and go up directly thereto; so shalt thou see the gate."[38]

You're aware that the date of Easter is movable. Thus the season "after Pentecost," this season of "ordinary time," is long in duration of weeks, or short, depending on whether Easter is early or late. So it's not very often that we get this deep into the shadows of this season at the end of the church's year.

And it's rather spooky here, isn't it? The selections of Scripture chosen for these last Sundays of the church's year are not for the faint-hearted: they're full of unsettling, apocalyptic images, hell-fire-and-damnation, "next-time-no-more-Mister-Nice-Guy," that kind of talk. I have a difficult time with passages like the ones the church puts before us in these last weeks: some of them are, well, just plain spooky.

But another part of me is glad they're there. I need to be reminded, you need to be reminded, the world needs to be reminded, of at least two things these texts hold up.

First, I hear a reminder in these selections from our Scriptures that time has meaning.

That's worth recalling, in a cynical age like ours, when meaning of any kind is often the last thing anyone worries about. How you live your life, how you spend your time, how you invest your time, has significance. It's curious, isn't it, and insightful, that our language about time should borrow from the world of business and finance: your time, rightfully so, is something you "spend," something you "invest."

These passages from Scripture call me to remember that investment. My time is precious, my "three score years and ten," or whatever my gift of days or moments: these are mine to squander—or to invest, in intentional decisions of humility and gratitude. And when I hear in these awesome, rolling, majestic phrases about the Man of Heaven coming in clouds with power and glory; or when I hear of the Ancient of Days whose throne is fiery flames; when I hear all that, I am reminded that there is One who will come to judge how I spent my time, how I invested my moments and my years.

That is a sobering thought, and ought to be. Your gift of days, your gift of hours and moments, is precious, sometimes precious beyond counting. It's good to remember that, and resolve to make time matter. Among other good reasons, we come together this morning as a community of Christ's people who know and celebrate the gift of time.

There is a second good reason for recalling these texts: if time in this life has meaning, if time is one of God's good gifts to be cherished and honored and respected, so also then are the people, and the things, and the events of this life. If we are to remember that our days and our moments are precious and pregnant with possibility, we are also to remember that everything else we have comes from the hand of a gracious God.

These texts call us to look at all of life from the perspective of the Last Judgment, when God who is the righteous Judge will speak the final word over this world. The first word God spoke over the world was *tov*, in the Hebrew of the first book in our Bible: the word means "good." God saw everything that God had made, and "behold, it was very good."

We have the promise in Christ that God's final word will also be good. God will speak an affirmation, a "yes," not only over against our moments and our days and our decisions, but over against— yes! —the world itself and its peoples and its stuff. "The world was created as the 'matter,' the material of one all-embracing Eucharist," wrote Alexander Schmemann, and you were created as "priest of this cosmic sacrament."[39]

"Priest of a cosmic sacrament": that is how we are to view our work in the world. In the words of the second lesson, we are to be ready to do God's will in any kind of good action in the world God loves and has called good. We are born to be priests of a cosmic sacrament, nothing less. The world itself is the matter, the material, the sacramental "stuff" for you to consecrate. There is incredible power and promise in that reminder. It is one of the things that keeps me going, when the sky is dark.

Keep that light in your eye: so shall you see the gate.

Paul F. Bosch

[38]John Bunyan, *The Pilgrim's Progress* (Boston: Houghton Mifflin, 1969), p. 94.
[39]Alexander Schmemann, *For the Life of the World* (New York: St. Vladimir's Seminary Press, 1973), p. 15.

E PROPER 28

E   *Dan 12:1–4a; Heb 10:31–39; Mk 13:14–23*

It was the third time he had entered Jerusalem. Three strikes and you're out. It would be the last time he would depart from that city as he had entered.

Jesus came to the city of Jerusalem, or more specifically to the temple, with a warning. The message was clear to all who had eyes to see. In many ways Jesus told of the truth that was soon to be revealed to all.

First there was the fig tree, a barren fig tree. The day before, Jesus had pronounced judgment upon this seemingly alive tree that did not bear fruit. Now, the next morning, as they passed by it again they saw the tree dead to its very roots. A warning: it was a picture of what was to come.

Next was the teaching, Jesus' teaching in the temple. Here is the word of God, the very being of God present in the midst of God's house. Yet here he was challenged. Here this Jesus was questioned by the religious authorities who were to speak for God. The temple could not, would not, accept the very word of hope it was called to house. A warning: it was a picture of impending doom.

There are also parables, stories that challenge and open the world to a different reality. On this journey to the temple Jesus tells the difficult parables of the Wicked Tenants and the Fig Tree. And a living parable is seen by Jesus, as he points to the widow who from her poverty shares her whole living. Jesus gives pictures of warning and of new reality that will soon break in upon this world.

Jesus also condemns the temple. It is no longer a cleansing that is proclaimed. It is condemnation. The temple is disqualified as the house of God. A new temple is soon to raised from the rubble.

In the midst of this hectic journey to the temple, this journey that seals Jesus' fate, a strange discourse is shared. The language is outside of time. The images are not part of the story. The pictures are abstract. The message is in code, deciphered only by those who have seen the truth. Those who can see God's word in a fig tree, a parable, or a widow's penny, can catch this message.

The image is clear. Tribulation and sacrilege will mark the day. The world will be a tragic place to live. People will flee. Stability and security will be lost. Families will be fractured and left empty of life. Creation will be experienced as chaos, and order will be lost. False prophets will seek to provide answers, but their hope, spoken of in grand and beautiful words, will be as vacant of life as is the temple.

These are but images, descriptive of what will be, not prescriptive. They are pictures full of color and movement, but without clear definition. It is the image of a world that has lost its center and thus its meaning. The words are a warning that soon the faithful will be called to undertake a journey, to travel light, and to be on the way. The temple and all that it stands for will not be the place to see God clearly.

So we come to a temple, to this church. We come sometimes full of wonderful theological debates. Our offices and libraries are full of weighty thought. Parables, some still to be lived out in our very midst, are overlooked because of our sophistication. We are often like the fig tree, full of wonderful foliage, but bearing no fruit.

The words and images of Jesus are words to us. Finally, in the midst of the terror of those words, we might ask, "Where can we look for hope? Where is God present for us? If not the temple, if not the church, where?"

The simple truth is that Jesus is the new temple. Jesus is the hope for the journey. Jesus, the crucified one, is the house of God in this world. Jesus is our security and our stability.

He is here. Not in the shape of a building, not in the clarity of our theology, not in our pride of beauty and glory. Jesus is here. He is here in bread and wine, body and blood. He is here to nourish you for the journey. He is here to feed you for the struggle. He is here to be carried in your heart as you face the tribulations and sacrilege of this world.

Come, the table is set. Jesus, the crucified one, is present. Hope and courage will be fed to you on your journey of faithfulness in a dangerous world.

Mark A. Olson

R LAST SUNDAY IN ORDINARY TIME, CHRIST THE
  KING
E PROPER 29
L CHRIST THE KING, LAST SUNDAY AFTER
  PENTECOST

R *Dan 7:13–14; Rev 1:5–8; Jn 18:33b-37*
E *Dan 7:9–14; Rev 1:1–8; Jn 18:33–37*
L *Dan 7:13–14; Rev 1:4b-8; Jn 18:33–37*

The Bible readings portray Jesus Christ as King, the King of all
kings, the Ruler of all rulers, the Power of all powers. The reading from the Book of Daniel portrays Christ being crowned as
King. The reading from the Book of Revelation portrays Christ
already enthroned as King. Jesus Christ portrayed as King: What
might this mean for our faith?

To portray Christ as King certainly does not mean that we think
of Christ as up in the sky controlling the world by invisible
strings or undetectable ray guns. This would distort a matter of
faith by trying to turn it into a matter of fact. To speak of Christ
as King is a matter of faith. Through the eyes of faith we picture
our world as ruled over by Christ. With the psalmist, we can
picture earth as Christ's footstool and heaven as his throne. We
can picture the whole world as a kingdom ruled over by Christ
the King.

But often the hard facts about our world seem to deny our
faith's picture of Christ as King, do they not? For example, the
world seems to be ruled by evil and destructive forces, does it
not? Hate seems stronger than love. Conflict is more prevalent
than peace. Lies win out over truth. Pain often overshadows
happiness.

What hope is there then for the future? Can we hope for a victory of love and peace and truth over hate and conflict and lies?
Can we hope that goodness and happiness will win out? It is
easy to lose hope. Life sometimes seems to be a tragedy, ruled
over by a malevolent fate, doomed to an unhappy end no matter

what we do. And when we lose hope, when we give up, that's when life really becomes hopeless, for hopelessness is a self-fulfilling prophecy.

Where can we find a sure and certain hope for the future? The Bible readings point us beyond the world as it is to the world of faith. Not a hopeless faith in fate or in the powers of evil and destruction. Not a hopeless faith that hate and conflict and lies and pain rule the world. No! The faith which the Bible readings proclaim is faith in Christ the King. Christ is portrayed as ruling over all other powers.

Christ our King reigns. The whole world is under the kingship of Christ. This is the faith assertion for today. The powers of evil and destruction have not got out of hand. They are still subject to Christ our King. Hate and conflict and lies and pain do not rule the world. Christ our King rules the world.

Why Christ our King permits or decrees malevolent powers to operate can be a perplexing puzzle. Why can't there be more good and less evil? More love and less hate? Why can't there be more peace and less conflict? More truth and fewer lies? Why isn't there less pain and more happiness in a world over which Christ reigns as King?

These puzzling questions are often without answers. But even so, we have the faith assurance that Christ is King and, further-more, that Christ is a good and benevolent King. Christ our King has made himself one of us. Christ is not only King. Christ is our Friend, our Brother, our Lover. Whatever suffering our King permits or decrees for us, he suffers with us. Christ suffers hate and conflict and lies and pain along with us. Although we cannot solve the puzzle as to why our King permits or decrees the evil and destruction which rack our world, we still have the assurance that Christ our King is a good and benevolent King—a King we can trust. We can trust Christ to be with us and to be for us.

This faith picture of Christ as King makes us feel more confi-dent. In faith we can see beyond hate and conflict and lies and pain to Christ the King—the King who is our Friend and Brother and Lover. As it was when we were children, when we had a strong big brother to back us up, we felt confident even when the neighborhood bully was walking by.

And doesn't this faith picture of Christ as King give you a more sure and certain hope for the future? Christ the King holds the future in his hands. Sometime, in some way, our King will work things out for good. In some way, at some time, we can hope that evil and destruction will be completely subdued. Then life will be truth, not lies. Life will be peace, not conflict. Life will be love, not hate. Life will be happiness, not pain. Christ promises us that such a life will come. Because Christ is King, he has the power to pull it off. Christ the King is our confidence. Christ the King is our sure and certain hope.

Kathe Wilcox and Milton Crum

R   *Jer 33:14–16; 1 Th 3:12–4:2; Lk 21:25–28,34–36*
E   *Zech 14:4–9; 1 Th 3:9–13; Lk 21:25–31*
L   *Jer 33:14–16; 1 Th 3:9–13; Lk 21:25–36*

We gather on this first Sunday of Advent, at the beginning of this new year of grace, in order to recount in word and meal and song the ancient story of our salvation. We gather as frail children of the Light who, as T.S. Eliot once wrote, hold the little lights of our lives toward the great mystery of God's light. We mark in sacred Scripture the truth of our frailty and the still greater truth of God's light revealed in human flesh and blood. We join our voices in hymn and acclamation to sing of that Light whose presence we experience in shadow and glimmer and dappled flame.

There is, burning before us, one small light: not enough to warm our bodies, certainly inadequate to illuminate this place in which we gather, a frail sign itself at the beginning of our Advent vigil. Next to the vision of the last day proclaimed in the gospel, this flame, our song, our word and meal appear insignificant. "There will be signs in sun and moon and stars," says Jesus. The sea will roar and the heavens will be shaken and the people of the earth will be overtaken by fear and anguish of what is to come.

For some today, such visions of the end of history appear harmless if not silly, a vision drawn from an out-moded cosmology based upon the rather remarkable belief that the Creator of heaven and earth desires the destruction of all living things. For others, however, these images of the last day evoke a thirst to discover the precise moment when the Man of Heaven will appear in glory to judge the living and the dead, the righteous and the sinner.

And yet neither will do for us. To conjure out of our ancient book the calamitous moment of judgment is simply one more way of diverting us from what Paul says is our fundamental hope and project in life: that we may overflow with the love of Christ for one another and for all. But at the same time we must recognize this anxious truth of the modern age: that if the Creator does not desire our destruction and the obliteration of all that lives, we now have the power within our hands to ignite the nuclear flame, the final holocaust. Before the eyes of the human race there now appears this apocalyptic image of a world engulfed by searing light, a world laid waste by human recklessness.

To dwell at length on this vision can only lead to despair, for it seems that human freedom cannot readily save us from human folly. And perhaps then it is here, within us and within the struggles of the world, at the juncture of our freedom to create life and our propensity to do violence to the same life, that we must take to heart the ancient word of the prophet, we must let it be that word of grace which directs our freedom toward the dawning Light: "I shall cause a righteous Branch to spring forth, who shall execute justice and righteousness in the land."

Brothers and sisters, we gather as one in an anxious age. We gather to hear the words of the prophet who names our hope in this nuclear age as "The Lord our justice." We gather in the name of the one who is our Security, our Strength, our Holiness, our Ransom. We hold before him our frail lights, our fears for the present day and our hope for the world to come. We sing and proclaim and pray the story of his life, his cross, his resurrection so that we ourselves might become his story, his word of grace, his body broken for the life of the world, that we might stand secure and strive to ensure the progress of justice and peace for the children of the earth.

And at last, we come to his table. We eat a bit of bread and sip from the cup of blessing. We feast on the death of the Just One and proclaim, in our eating and drinking, that he who is coming on a cloud with great power and glory, is already with us, embracing the darkness of our human folly and thus transforming it into our prayer, our cry for salvation: a glimmering light of hope.

Dear friends of the Light, in this word and meal God is giving us the power to live and do the divine will, which is nothing less than God's intention to ransom the world from its own folly, its violence, its darkness. We sing and pray and eat this story, this power, this will, so that with patience, with strength, and yes, with suffering we might serve the dominion of God wherever we may find ourselves in the days ahead. May our witness to Christ, like dappled flames, enliven with hope the circles of life in which we move. May our prayer for the full revelation of that light who is Christ now shape and suffuse our work for peace in a world now living in the shadow of nuclear death. And at last may the gift of faith enable us to stand with those who curse the darkness: the lowly, the hungry and the weak who have no bread and cup, no hope and peace. May our work with them become our cry of expectation: Lord Jesus, quickly come, and night shall be no more.

Samuel Torvend, O.P.

R E L SECOND SUNDAY OF ADVENT

R *Bar 5:1–9; Phil 1:4–6,8–11; Lk 3:1–6*
E *Bar 5:19; Phil 1:1–11; Lk 3:1–6*
L *Mal 3:1–4; Phil 1:3–11; Lk 3:1–6*

Each year during Advent we turn our attention back to John the Baptizer. Part folk hero to be sure, he remains for people of all ages a model of trust and confidence. Oddly dressed, and coming from the wilderness, John caught people off balance. Proclaiming a baptism of repentance for the forgiveness of sins, his message brought to mind the words of Isaiah, "Prepare a way of the LORD; make straight the paths of the LORD."

Deutero-Isaiah was describing the return from the Babylonian exile in terms of a new exodus, of leading the people across another Sinai to a new and glorious land. John heralds yet another exodus, one which will lead all people to salvation. Surely it must have been his enthusiasm for the message that attracted people to John, for everything else we read of him paints him as a person from whom people would turn their faces.

The personality and conviction of the messenger is of great importance, as Madison Avenue has taught us. Bill Cosby could probably convince the American public to buy anything these days. Perhaps John did not have Bill Cosby's gift for comedy, but he certainly must have had a personality that was appealing to people and a sense of conviction and dedication that led others to follow in his way.

Down through these long corridors of time, the message proclaimed in this season is unchanged: repent, change your ways, make straight your paths, for the Righteous One is coming. The message urges us to be enthusiastic in preparing for his coming, not lethargic.

The reading from Baruch puts the message a different way, beginning with a very direct command: "Take off the garment of your sorrow, and put on the beauty of the glory from God." Written by an anonymous author, and hesitantly dated around the fourth century before the coming of Christ, the words sound to the modern ear either like a scolding for people who are wallowing in self-pity or an enthusiastic recommendation from the best-seller *Dress for Success*. A similarly rousing message is found in the text from Malachi today, "Who can stand when he appears?"

Paul's commendation of those who have shared in spreading the gospel is made to people who have accepted the challenge with enthusiasm. The fact that our mission is to spread the good news of Jesus Christ does not for a second deny that there is intense suffering all over the face of the earth, nor does it deny that this suffering is most often caused by injustice. Wearing a mantle of joy does not necessitate cloaking ourselves in denial, but taking joy in the mission.

Discouragement weighs heaviest on us when we think that we are working alone. What brings us around this table today, what binds us in community, is the realization that we are not solitary workers, but a family of believers. In baptism we first received our mantle of joy, and even though we might travel through alien territory at times, it is important to remember that God will never cease to be a source of strength for us.

Look down at your own robes. What are you wearing this morning? Do you see yourself wrapped in misery, or cloaked in joy?

Perhaps you see yourself wearing that garment of misery. It is natural for us to feel discouraged when we take a close look at the world around us. Endless wars and unspeakable violence characterize daily life in many corners of the world. Children are raised, marry, and give birth to the next generation knowing only a world of terrorism. Millions of people, but mostly children, live on the brink of starvation, on a planet with plentiful resources, sufficient to satisfy everyone's need. Thousands of people live and die on the streets of our major cities, without ever a nutritious meal or a warm bed to welcome them.

Yet the faces of the poor are juxtaposed every day with images that subtly urge us to ignore their need to satisfy our greed. Billboards, magazines, radio and television blare out the message, "Clothe yourselves in riches, for the feast is now!"

Overwhelmed by so much suffering, it seems quite natural for one to be clothed in misery. To be dressed otherwise might even seem to be a denial of the plight of the poor. To be clothed in riches would seem to align us more with the raucous huxters than with the just stewards of the gospel. For this reason the command from the prophecy attributed to Baruch catches us by surprise. "Take off the garment of your sorrow and put on for ever the beauty of the glory from God." It might leave you questioning, "How can I rejoice in the midst of so much suffering?"

We might find ourselves looking at John the Baptizer as an historical oddity today, as one whose message was applicable only to Jesus' first coming. The "way" might appear to be so scrambled to us that there is no way in which we might conceivably make it straight in our own day.

These can be discouraging times, but we must keep in mind that God is the ultimate source of our confidence and our rejoicing. For a thousand generations God has proved worthy of that trust. The marvels recounted over and over again in the Scriptures in those centuries before the incarnation have been outdone repeatedly in our own day, as we stand in ever-widening circles of wonder. Even though we might seem to be working against much greater odds than our ancestors did, God has never failed to provide us with sources of strength and models of courage.

Now, take off that cloak of misery, put on your mantle of joy, and come to be nourished by the One who is our joy.

Julia Upton, R.S.M.

R E L THIRD SUNDAY OF ADVENT

R   *Zeph 3:14–18a; Phil 4:4–7; Lk 3:10–18*
E   *Zeph 3:14–20; Phil 4:4–7; Lk 3:7–18*
L   *Zeph 3:14–18a; Phil 4:4–7; Lk 3:7–18*

The days continue to shorten, the nights grow longer, the temperature continues to drop and we enter winter. "Love winter," wrote Thomas Merton, "when the plant says nothing."[40] For most of us that is a major challenge. Nature's decay, mute signs of winter dormancy, the long darknesses are hard to love because they speak of silence, of death, of the end of things.

Yet it was precisely at this time of year that the ancient, Western church set the celebration of the appearance of the Lord in the flesh. The feast invites us now to confront the surrounding darkness, to put aside our despair and to look for a new birth of life through the power and warmth of the Son of Justice.

I like to view the darkness which surrounds us in this season not so much as the darkness of death and sin which one strongly senses, for example, at the celebration of the Easter Vigil, but rather as the darkness of a womb, a place not of sin and death, but rather of new life and rapid, albeit silent, growth.

The church describes this as a joyful season of expectation, not one of penance. So we might ask ourselves: What do I expect? Some of us may find it difficult to expect anything better than "more of the same." Does your worldly wisdom instruct you to be cynical about any attacks of hope? It seems that society, at this time of year, gets more than usually disturbed by the evil around and within us, the violence people bring against one another: neighbor against neighbor, nation against nation. This heightened awareness could be, in itself, a positive sign. We recognize that we are terribly disordered, that we need the Messiah. Some of us turn to look at the creche scene, the child. It might be only a desperate exercise of nostalgia. But it need not be.

New life. What needs to be born in you, in us this Christmas? What new gift does the Prince of Peace need to bring us? Have you given up on some relationship which should be looked at again? Have we, as a community, given up on a noble mission because our courage or stamina failed? Has the fervor of our hope in the kingdom already arrived and still coming cooled? "The Lord is at hand," we heard in the second reading. "In everything by prayer and supplication with thanksgiving let your requests be made known to God. And the peace of God, which passes all understanding, will keep your hearts and your minds in Christ Jesus." There is no person frozen in destructive patterns that the Lord cannot free. Zephaniah's prophesy commands us to hope: "The LORD, your God, is in your midst, a mighty one who gives victory; the LORD rejoices over you with gladness, and will renew you in love."

Have confidence. Look into the darkness for the light. It may not resemble the Easter sun leaping over the horizon announcing a new day, but it might be the fragile, yet stable light of a star in the night sky. Many new beginnings are fragile, but nonetheless truly new. Look into the darkness and see if some unused or underused capacity of yours might not be ripe for growth.

Christ is our hope even in the face of intimidating, paralyzing odds. He came to us in the strange power of poverty and weakness and died for us in the wisdom of God that was folly to the world. He has baptized us in fire as John prophesied in Luke. It is a precious time to stir up the gifts given us; we, the holy people of God, can dream of new birth because his Spirit dwells in us, powering us to always try anew.

We are about to undertake a holy remembrance of the dying and rising of Jesus. As we commune in the Lord all the power of his Spirit is made available to us; the Spirit transforms our poverty into richness and our dying into new life.

Lawrence J. Madden, S.J.

[40]Thomas Merton, "Love Winter When the Plant Says Nothing," *The Collected Poems of Thomas Merton* (New York: New Directions), 1977 p. 353.

R E L   FOURTH SUNDAY OF ADVENT

R   *Mic 5:1–4a; Heb 10:5–10; Lk 1:39–45*
E   *Mic 5:2–4; Heb 10:5–10; Lk 1:39–49*
L   *Mic 5:2–4; Heb 10:5–10; Lk 1:39–45*

If you're anything like me, you dislike meetings intensely. Meetings are when you have to go and listen to people taking up lots of time. Most meetings take up all the time allotted to them, even if the business is finished long before the scheduled amount of time is up. Sometimes it seems as if we do nothing but spend time in meetings, time when we could be getting something done, or even better, enjoying ourselves.

Of course I'm aware that what we're involved in right now can be called a meeting. In fact "meeting" was one of the earliest names given to Sunday worship in the church. Maybe all meetings aren't the same. After all, even I go away from some meetings with the feeling that something has been accomplished, that the time has been worthwhile, perhaps even that I've enjoyed myself.

Today we have a model of a meeting. This one is a simple encounter between two women. Perhaps it can help us in figuring out what our meetings can look like. The setting is familiar to you. The scene takes place in Luke's gospel just after the annunciation of Jesus' birth by the angel Gabriel, and in a wonderful way links up the two great births that Luke is describing in his infancy narrative. One of the items on Luke's agenda is to show the superiority of the birth of Jesus to that of John the Baptist.

Mary has just heard that her relative Elizabeth is pregnant— because of Elizabeth's age a miraculous event. Elizabeth will confirm the angel's message of Mary's own pregnancy. So Mary undertakes a journey from Galilee to Judea (no trains or automobiles, mind you), a journey to support someone in need. And what does she get when she arrives at this holy meeting? She hears the same greeting she received from the angel, from God's messenger: "Blessed are you," truly happy are you; you're what a human being is supposed to be, you trust in God. And Mary's response is to praise God the more in the beautiful and powerful poetic song we call the Magnificat.

What Mary has done is similar to what the letter to the Hebrews tells us that Jesus himself has done. He has come into the world to do God's will, a more important activity than anything specifically religious, more important than prayers or sacrifices. The true prayer offered by the Christian is the constant striving to respond to God's will. This is what makes Mary blessed, what a human being is supposed to be.

"I come to do your will." That's not a bad motto for any meeting, especially the holy meeting of these two women or the holy meeting that we're involved in today, in which we respond to the invitation to meet around the Lord's own table. This meeting is a constant reminder that the Lord has come to meet us and to make us a people, despite all of our difference, and in all our uniqueness. That is what we celebrate in this season of the Lord's coming, this season of Advent, and what we look forward to celebrating with special joy in the upcoming feasts of Christmas and Epiphany. Just as Mary's visit fills Elizabeth to the brim with joy, so the Lord's own encounter with us does the same thing. Why? Because he is our way of doing God's will by self-sacrificing love. Even here as we ponder his incarnation, we know that it leads to the cross, as he offers his life to the One he called Abba.

It is that offering, the fact that it is life-giving, that we celebrate every time we meet around this holy table. And our joy is only as real as we make our self-offering to God in our daily lives, for it is our response to the will of God for us to be blessed, to be true human beings, that makes sense of the holy meeting we partake in today.

Let us pray that we can bring the peace, the respect, the reverence and the joy of this meeting into our lives, and especially into the lives of all we encounter in this holiday season. Let us pray that we can bring the joy of doing God's will back here every time we meet.

I guess that all meetings aren't bad. Some of them, like the meeting of Mary and Elizabeth, or the meeting the Lord Jesus with all of us, or even our meetings here, can fill us with joy and purpose. Let us then continue to celebrate.

John F. Baldovin, S.J.

R   CHRISTMAS MASS AT MIDNIGHT
E   CHRISTMAS DAY I
L   THE NATIVITY OF OUR LORD, 1

R   *Is 9:2–7; Tit 2:11–12; Lk 2:1–14*
E   *Is 9:2–4,6–7; Tit 2:11–12; Lk 2:1–14*
L   *Is 9:2–7; Tit 2:11–12; Lk 2:1–20*

Tonight, God's first-born, the sun of righteousness, rises from the winter darkness to restore the splendor of God's creation. But Christmas is not Saturnalia, as though our revels were needed to keep the light from dying, or a coronation, as though third-century Christians had created a ritual for the annual enthronement of their king. Rather, the lectionary for the Christmas liturgy at midnight points beyond these rites to their fulfillment in a new harmony. It focuses on the Messiah's appearance, the story of Jesus' birth, and on the church that continues as his poor body for the world's sake.

Mysteriously and with unsurpassable simplicity, the tale of Mary's child gathers up and transforms the ancient Roman and Canaanite figures, beloved as they are in the world's history and echoing still in the deep longings of the human heart. The baby constrained in swaddling clothes is infinite God hidden in the opaqueness of conditioned, created, bodily existence. Uncreated love, power and wisdom—the one in whose image humankind was made—is here, tonight, reversing forever the dying of the light and the precariousness of government. God comes, though we see only ourselves—safe for a moment in each other's care and united in loving this child, our child, whatever problems our relationships may have had, whatever troubles are still to come.

We are not mistaken: love and parenting and birth are natural signs of peace and new life, and, as such, they are nature's gift to the meaning of Christmas. But the metaphor of the family is offered here not as the reason for our festival or as an escape from the world's complexities. To celebrate Christmas as though it were only a warm and intimate family holiday trivializes its meaning. Luke's portrait of a nearly perfect holy family is not the whole story. By itself seeing the nuclear family as a symbol of wholeness is even dangerous. After all, Joseph and Mary were en route when the baby was born, their thoughts distracted by dreams and political events, their hearts disturbed by circumstances.

Christmas is the far deeper story of who, where and why we are. It tells us that God is father and mother to us though we must consent over and over again to having been born; and it tells us that we must accept, along with the gift of existence, the sheer madness of dependency. Wrapped in swaddling clothes and warmed by the sweet breath of animals—that's us, at the beginning of our lives and again before we die. How fortuitous and fragile our lives are. We are strangers to ourselves, as Jesus was. In becoming human, Jesus put aside divinity, left the self that was equal to God and became God's firstborn through the body, not in spite of blood and bone, but incarnate, available to others, and embodied. Christmas involves us in the mystery of ourselves; we cannot love the Lord and hate this bodily life that expresses God to us.

The Christmas story presents us to ourselves. Incarnate life is where we are, where we stand, what we are made of. We are in a world of distinct manners, forms and purposes. We are surrounded by structures: governments requiring that we be counted; economies requiring that we work; nature and family requiring that we deliver them from chaos, that we care for what we have named. In some of these purposes we see ourselves, from others we are alienated. But the Christmas story speaks to us as embodied ones; it tells us that the truth of our existence is in the person next to us; we taste and touch life in the other; we feel connectedness and come to life.

The Christmas story gathers up the old poetry and the earliest revelation and gives us ourselves in covenant, consent, contract. The body it praises is the church, the body of Christ. It is not for ourselves or for our family that we labor to make the world holy, but for everyone. The surprises we give one another this Christmas, the beauty of the poinsettia that decorates this church, and all the other joys of this season I wish you in abundance. But only if our desire for tidiness and order is balanced by a willingness to go humbly into the dark places of human need will we inherit the peace and joy that these gifts portend.

This is why we hear the echo of time in all the readings appointed for Christmas: Isaiah looks for the fulfillment of Israel's hope, but the vision is not yet, and while it is delayed the people suffer. We feed the hungry, comfort the dying, overcome loneliness, and so live, until the one comes whose dominion is vast and forever peaceful. In time, the zeal of the Lord will do this. Only hold on, only wait. It is just around the corner.

And in the meantime, we stay behind, as Titus stayed in Crete, knowing that God's grace has indeed appeared and taught us to live just lives, temperate and devout lives, while we look for the appearance in glory of our God and Savior, Jesus Christ. The peace is won by sacrifice, by the waiting, the sobriety and the kindness, now, as it was in the beginning. Only this time it is clear that the final redemption and our blessed hope is Jesus, the sun of righteousness, the Messiah whose birth is now.

In the gospel, Joseph and Mary fulfilled their time and the requirements of their history. They were included in the census. They accepted the inchoate signs, longing that the good they did would come out right in the end. Jesus' birth is a storybook's happy ending to their time and God's beginning of a new time. For us, who live in that new time, the angels sing joyfully of grace and peace on earth. Let no one disregard their song.

Rachel Reeder

R CHRISTMAS MASS DURING THE DAY
E CHRISTMAS DAY III
L THE NATIVITY OF OUR LORD, 2

R   *Is 52:7–10; Heb 1:1–6; Jn 1:1–18*
E   *Is 52:7–10; Heb 1:1–12; Jn 1:1–14*
L   *Is 52:7–10; Heb 1:1–9; Jn 1:1–14*

The fourteenth verse of the first chapter of John is a marvelous summary of what Christmas is all about: "And the Word became flesh and dwelt among us, full of grace and truth."

Almost two thousand years ago in a smelly stable in a small, insignificant town called Bethlehem, in a country smaller than many of our states, the Word became flesh, the divine became human, the deity took on humanity, God became a man, the infinite became finite, the high became low, the creator became the first born of creation. This is what happened in that wooden cradle in that smelly stable. But for many this is difficult to accept in a time that makes God seem so very far away.

For many people today the idea that God became a human male with our own flesh is offensive. Many of us still think of human flesh in such low terms. But we must get over this and realize that God has affirmed our human flesh by assuming it in the incarnation. And in the person of Jesus Christ we see most fully what God is like.

There is a story about a man who went to Africa and during his first night heard an animal that he could not identify. The next day he described to a native of the country the sound the animal made, and the native said what he heard was a tree-bear. But since the man had never seen a tree-bear before, the word "tree-bear" was just a vague impression; it was just a word to him. Several days later the native brought the man a tree-bear. Now he could see it, touch it and handle it. The words had become flesh, full of meaning. And this is what God has done in Jesus Christ. Here we see what God is really like.

Try to define truth. It is very difficult to do. We know truth best when someone utters a truthful statement. Try to define love. It is very difficult to do. We know love best when we see Jesus touching a leper and making him clean. Try to define obedience. It is very difficult to do. We know obedience best when we see Jesus setting his face toward Jerusalem to do his Father's will. Try to define forgiveness. It is very difficult to do. We know what forgiveness is when we see Jesus say to the woman taken in adultery, "Go, and from now on sin no more." Try to define goodness. It is very difficult to do. We know what goodness is when we see Jesus eat with the outcasts of his day.

When someone comes to see you, whom you are not expecting but would love to see, one of your children may call out, "So-and-so is here in the flesh!" This is what happened on that "Silent Night, Holy Night": God came in the flesh.

Our text not only states that the Word became flesh, but also that he "dwelt among us." There is no question that Jesus lived in Palestine and that he died there. He dwelt with his own people and his own people received him not. He ate with them. He fed the hungry; restored sight to the blind; and helped the crippled to walk. He worshipped in their synagogue, and he went to Jerusalem for the Passover. There he was arrested and beaten. He was crucified on a cross outside of the city on a garbage heap and was buried in a borrowed grave. And on the third day God raised him up. There is no question that he "dwelt among us."

But even more exciting is the reality that he continues to dwell among us in his word and sacraments. This is how he dwells with us now. The very same Word that became flesh comes to us in these words and in the sacraments of baptism and the Lord's Supper. The sermon is not just reciting the mighty acts of God in the past; it is not just a description of how we should live; it is not a lecture about God. It is the means God uses to be present among us. Through it we are reconciled to God. The Word become flesh, who forgave the woman taken in adultery, comes to us in the sermon and forgives us. The same is true of baptism. Baptism is not just a symbolic gesture, but in baptism the same Word become flesh comes to us and claims us as his own. The Lord's Supper is more than mere bread and wine. Here the same Word become flesh, who was broken on the cross, comes to us in the broken bread. Here the same Word become flesh, who drank the cup of suffering, comes to us in the cup of wine with his forgiving message.

As the Word of God became flesh in Jesus Christ, so the words of the gospel should become flesh in our lives. As Jesus revealed God to us, so we tell the world about this Jesus. As he healed the leper, so we touch the wounds of the world. As he loved the lawyers who tried to trap him with their questions, so we love those out to get us. As he wore that crown of thorns, so we are willing to be pricked by the thorns of the world. This is what it means to be the church, to be the body of Christ.

As the body of Christ we are to love, serve, and tend the world. As the body of Christ, as the church, we do not merely draw people into the contemplation of its navel and the decoration of its nave, but by word and sacraments we equip people to continue the reconciling ministry of Jesus Christ. The church, the body of Christ, exists for the world. As William Temple, the Archbishop of Canterbury, once said: "The church is the only institution which exists for the benefit of those who do not belong to it."

God has become flesh, and dwells among us in word and sacraments, so that we might be the body of Christ in the world.

Donald S. Armentrout

R HOLY FAMILY
L FIRST SUNDAY AFTER CHRISTMAS

R *1 Sam 1:20–22,24–28; 1 Jn 3:1–2,21–24; Lk 2:41–52*
L *Jer 31:10–13; Heb 2:10–18; Lk 2:41–51*

Have you seen the bumper sticker that says "There's no free
lunch"? I like that kind of sassy irreverence; and it came to mind
as I looked at the texts for this first Sunday after Christmas.
There is truth worth looking at in that bumper sticker; it says a
lot about human frailty and the pain and frustration of human
limitation.

In any case, I see this winsome account of Jesus at twelve in
the temple as a glowing example of family life for us today, and
not incidentally as a charming commentary on the fourth commandment.

First, I see this remarkable family keeping the fourth commandment by keeping the first: "I am LORD your God; you shall have
no other gods before me." The very first words of Luke's account show this family putting first things first: "Now the parents of Jesus went to Jerusalem every year at the feast of the
Passover. And when Jesus was twelve years old, they went up
according to custom."

This reminds us that we cannot truly keep the fourth commandment, or the fifth or sixth or any of them, without first keeping
the first commandment. God alone is Lord of life, Jesus himself
reminds us: "Seek first the dominion and the righteousness of
God." "You shall love the Lord your God with all your heart,
and with all your soul, and with all your strength, and with all
your mind; and your neighbor as yourself." That's important to
remember. It keeps your priorities straight.

Secondly: This year, Jesus is given a measure of independence, a
measure of freedom: "And when the feast was ended, as they
were returning, the boy Jesus stayed behind in Jerusalem." His
parents supposed him to be somewhere in the company. Jesus'

parents apparently felt he could be trusted with a measure of freedom and independence this year.

Scholars have suggested that perhaps at age twelve Jesus was this year making a kind of Bar-Mitzvah, entering the world of responsible Jewish adults, leaving behind his childhood. In any case, this is the kind of mutual respect and trust between parent and child that is my model of what our families ought to be like. Jesus' parents recognize that their son possesses his own center of freedom and responsibility. And such recognition begins, not when the child reaches twelve, but the day of birth, and it continues life-long. Respect and honor are like love: you learn them by experience. You learn to love by being loved; you learn to respect and honor others by being respected and honored yourself.

The actual text of the fourth commandment reads, "Honor your father and mother." Following the example of Mary and Joseph, I would be willing to emend that to read: "And honor also your children." It should work both ways. A mutual trust, a mutual affection, a mutual respect gives honor in both directions, from child to parent, and from parent to child.

Thirdly: Both parents and child are acting responsibly, although in Luke's account we puzzle over this. Usually we search for blame in a given situation. We're tempted to ask here, as elsewhere in human life: Who's to blame here? Who is at fault, Jesus, or his parents? Three days of anxious searching, his parents perhaps haggard with looking, perhaps beside themselves with fear over what might have happened to their son: surely here is indication that Jesus was wrong, worrying his parents so. Or perhaps these parents were wrong: worrying about him, or letting him slip away in the first place. So we attempt to fix the blame.

In the face of these contradictory events and emotions, let me suggest this possibility: that both were right, Jesus acting as a model of responsible behavior, obedient to the will of God, and Mary and Joseph, acting as they knew and cherished God's will for them in the moment.

This kind of thing often happens in human life: Mary and Joseph not really understanding their son, but trying to act out their love for him; and Jesus, not really understanding his parents any better, but trying to act out his love. In life there is often a conflict of misunderstandings, a conflict in values. You simply can't say with any certainty who in a given situation is right or who is wrong.

"There's no free lunch," says the bumper sticker. We simply don't have the security of making ultimate judgments in much of life. Usually life isn't a case of true or false, good or bad, right or wrong. It is most often muddy and unclear, full of moral compromise and ethical ambiguity. Probably what hurts the most about being human is that there is almost always a price to pay. The price is paid not so much in being wrong, as in being uncertain, in simply not knowing.

It is unsettling for me that we read this charming and unsettling story in Luke's gospel during the Christmas season. Christmas is the reminder that God has not abandoned us to a world of uncertainties and ambiguities, but enters that world with us, alongside us. The message of Christmas is supremely that: God's own hands in the muck and mud of life, God's own hands bloody with the wounds of our own moral compromises and our own ethical uncertainties, God's own feet bloody with the wounds of our own not knowing where to walk, of our own simply not knowing.

The God we meet in bread and cup today is the God who has honored and respected us that much: to join us at Christmas as Emmanuel, "God-with-us"—even here, even in this, even in the full limitation and moral anguish of our humanness. For me, no other kind of God would be worth my worship.

Paul F. Bosch

R *Sir 24:1–2,8–12; Eph 1:3–6,15–18; Jn 1:1–18*
E *Is 61:10–62:3; Gal 3:23–25;4:4–7; Jn 1:1–18*
L *Is 61:10–62:3; Eph 1:3–6,15–18; Jn 1:1–18*

How do you pronounce a word? Your mouth seeks the proper shape to enable the word to emerge; your brain must contemplate the image you are about to speak; your vocal cords must vibrate at just the proper speed; and then the word finally tumbles forth to crack open the space in front of you with sound, to emerge as coherent speech in order that a new reality might stand where previously there was only the image. The word brings truth to bear upon reality; the word outlines in sound what was previously only seen with the eye. Now the picture can be transmitted because there is a word to create it for another person's mind.

The hearer, too, must be prepared for the word; when you hear you must be able to decode this set of sounds to make sense of them. When you hear, you are surrounded by sound; words are inescapable. On the other hand, when you see, you embrace only the silent vision, and that right in front of you. You cannot share your vision with another person unless you speak it forth again as you have recorded it, and then discuss what you have said about what you have seen.

Many words pummel us and fall at our feet, but they have no power to change our lives in any significant way. At this time of the year we celebrate a counterpoint of truth, that it is not impossible for words to promise and to give life. For we have heard this peculiar word in which we claim that we gain life and that most abundantly. Jesus is the Word in the telling of which God comes among us. In the telling, God. . . . But how are we to tell?

We tell by our lives, but only if we have heard with our hearts. The consequence of hearing the Word is that the light of our faith shines in all that we do to embrace the other. Christ has broken down the dividing wall of hostility and offered a way of unity, says the writer to the Ephesians. By hearing the promise which comes in Christ, we are turned from introspection and egocentricity and brought into life together with others in love. Or so the word says.

How difficult it is to affirm this word, to hold it fast in practice. We are tempted at every turn to run from the promise of life given in the birth of Christ, because we would prefer to invent our own answers to the problem of life. We turn aside from steadfastly gazing upon Christ to focus on ourselves, and in the process we lose our way. In seeking to inspire ourselves, we lose sight of the one who breathes life into us. In Christ there is no east or west, as the old hymn puts it, in him no north or south, but trouble comes because we hear this not as wisdom but as an affront to our individualism. Even the call to common sharing with brothers and sisters at the eucharistic table can become a call that frightens us because it seems naive. The promise that we shall be and are, through baptism, incorporated into the body of Christ can make us run in the other direction.

I would rather live alone if I could manage it. Who of us would not, really? To live dependent on others is bothersome and wearisome and takes time and robs us of our personhood. So we think. The Word comes to relieve us of self-centeredness, but we will not be prepared to hear it until we learn that we cannot live all by ourselves. First of all, we live dependent on many others to feed and clothe and house and educate and sustain and nurture us. But even this is not yet the recognition that is called for, the word to be heard.

What is called for is nothing less than the willingness to give up our very image and idea of ourselves into the hands of God, to float free in the creative power of God, to be upheld only by God's sustenance. When Christ comes among us, this is the word he bears: what life we have is given only by God, and so we are called to give our lives back to God. Christ is the one who will preach and teach and heal and sing our way into the embrace of God, if we but follow. This is a promise, and like all promises it can only be fulfilled when those who hear it take up the offer it makes.

Faith indeed does come by hearing, but in order to hear we must stay close to the speaker. We see in the speaker the light and the life and the glory which is promised in the Word. Christ invites us to the highest in human development which is rooted in selflessness. It is not that we shall become Jesus Christ; we are given the promise that, in Christ, we shall become ourselves. When we focus on Christ's offering to us and forget ourselves, we are strangely given back ourselves. We receive ourselves back transformed so that we no longer cling to ourselves as prize but may receive ourselves as gift. This is a word of promise which, once we have heard it aright, we cannot ever forget. We may turn aside from the word of promise, but the word of promise will never turn aside from us. Grace and truth have indeed come through Jesus Christ. "No one has ever seen God: the only Son, who is in the bosom of the Father, has made God known." What cannot be seen can be heard. And in the speaking it is made real for us and among us.

Our fascination deepens as we know that we are ourselves words spoken into reality by God. Following Christ as disciples we learn how to pronounce ourselves. The body of Christ extends into the world through our actions and our demeanor and our words, so that, through us now, the grace and truth Christ spoke into the world may be multiplied. For this calling we need sustenance.

So we come to this bread and wine, broken and poured out for us. The Word speaks them into being as more than bread and wine. The Word calls them body and blood of Christ, given for the forgiveness of our sin. In this meal, then, we receive the promise of our own place as words of God. The word embraces the bread and the wine and kisses them into another zone of reality. The same word embraces us and kisses us so that we become really ourselves in God through Christ. This meal is given to us as a remembrance of the Word made flesh in Christ, a foretaste of the feast to come, and a sign of God's power to transform us through the word into our deepest selves, that we might be filled with the light of the Word so the light of our faith may shine in all that we do.

Jay C. Rochelle

E SECOND SUNDAY AFTER CHRISTMAS

E *Jer 31:7–14; Eph 1:3–6,15–19a; Mt 2:13–15,19–23*

The Coptic church of Abu Serghis stands in one of the poorest sections of Egypt's capital, Cairo, which is to say it is in one of the poorest places on earth. This little church claims two honors. It is the oldest Christian church in Cairo, and it claims to be the site of the refuge to which Joseph and his family fled from Herod. Their cave-home is beneath the church, an old and simple room with a square altar in the center and a dirt floor.

This church is only one of the places that claim the honor of being the holy family's home in Egypt. There are at least three others. One of them is at a place called Matariyah, just northeast of Cairo, near Heliopolis. There is a legend that Jesus got involved with some balsam or palm trees here: he planted them or blessed them. Raymond Brown describes what happened to these trees. The "balm from the balsam trees of Matariyah was used by both Christians and Muslims of the Middle Ages as a cure-all, healing anything from snake bite to running nose."[41]

Jesus is remembered among the poor in Cairo; his healing was shared by the people of Islam and the people called Christians. This memory and healing may be based on unsubstantiated legends, but they are consistent with the biblical understanding of Jesus as the one who stands with the poor and exiles, the one who takes them into himself and makes them a source of life and healing for the world.

That is the point, after all, of Matthew's story of the flight into Egypt. The children of Israel fled a famine in Canaan by going down to Egypt, only to be enslaved there. They fled Egypt, finally, and returned home, coming back changed, transformed by their experience. In a similar way, Jesus fled Herod's persecution in Judea, living in Egypt until his father dreamt of a return home. But that return brought the family back transformed. According to Matthew, they were no longer citizens of Bethlehem; they moved to Galilee, and Jesus was called a "Nazarene," which could mean a citizen of Nazareth, a branch of David's royal line or a holy person dedicated to God.

Jesus is identified with Israel, that small collection of tribes, poor and oppressed, that spoke God's presence to the world. The same point is made by the use of Jeremiah's poem today: Jesus is with the exiles, whose return transforms the land itself. The prophet sings about a procession of the blind and the lame, the broken and the weak, accompanied by the women who bear the promise of new life for land and nation. Hosea identified Israel in Egypt as God's child: "When Israel was a child, I loved him, and out of Egypt I called my son." With the same prophetic vision, Jeremiah saw the returning exiles as born of God: "I am as a father to Israel, and Ephraim is as my first-born."

Those identities remain today, won at great cost. The assembly of the poor and the broken, of the exiles and of those who hold the promise of new life is still the body of God's elect. Their healing and return still promise renewal for the earth. Sometimes it seems they are the earth's only hope of renewal. And Jesus stands with the broken, the oppressed, and the "woman with child and she who is in labor."

Does this special election of the oppressed leave us out in the cold? Not at all, and for two reasons. The letter to the Ephesians describes the first reason: God has chosen us in Christ "before the foundation of the world, that before God we should be holy and blameless." And the second reason is that because we are chosen in Christ, we can affirm our identity as God's elect. That is, we are among the broken, the exiles, and the life-givers.

By accepting our solidarity with the poor and the weak, we accept our unity in Christ and our identity as God's child: "this was God's good pleasure and will, to the praise of God's glorious grace freely bestowed on us in the Beloved." Our identity redounds to God's glory most completely when we accept it as a sacramental identity, that is, when we let God work through us to renew the world. The way to do that is to call on God's gifts, listed in Ephesians: the spiritual powers of wisdom and revelation, inner illumination, hope, and a glorious inheritance.

Our sacramental focus is on the rest of God's elect, God's chief sacrament of the outcasts, the poor, the marginalized. In them lies the world's hope. It is our task to make that hope a reality, in God's grace. God's elect must know the truth of the Lord's promise: "With consolations I will lead them back, I will make them walk by brooks of water, in a straight path in which they shall not stumble; for I am as a father to Israel, and Ephraim is as my first-born." Our work is to make that promise come true to bring a new dawn for the earth and its people, and, perhaps, to inaugurate justice and peace.

Gordon E. Truitt

⁴¹Raymond Brown, *The Birth of the Messiah* (Garden City, New York: Doubleday & Co., 1977), p.204.

R　E　L　THE EPIPHANY OF OUR LORD

R　*Is 60:1–6; Eph 3:2–3a,5–6; Mt 2:1–12*
E　*Is 60:1–6,9; Eph 3:1–12; Mt 2:1–12*
L　*Is 60:1–6; Eph 3:2–12; Mt 2:1–12*

A few weeks ago I sat entranced as I do each year with a presentation of Gian Carlo Menotti's one-act opera, *Amahl and the Night Visitors*. The story is about three magi who stop on their way to Bethlehem at the hovel of a poor crippled boy named Amahl. When Amahl hears of their mysterious search for a child, he secretly follows behind. He watches in awe as the magi present their gifts to the child. He is disturbed that he has no suitable gift for the child until it occurs to him to offer the only things he possesses, his crutches. As he presents his crutches, he is healed. The same theme is played in slightly more sentimental tones in our popular Christmas carol, "The Little Drummer Boy." Both works have drawn on Matthew's well-staged drama and focus on the contrast between the regal gifts of these impressive travelers and the unpretentious gift of a simple child. While such colorful recreations of the gospel story are irresistible as drama, they rather miss the point of Matthew.

In Matthew's spare and seemingly simple story, much more is said. In the first place, the evangelist tells the story of the magi and the star after he has already identified the child being sought as God-with-us, the Christ, a child conceived through the Holy Spirit, and therefore the son of God. That provides the background for today's reading.

Today's gospel selection is laden with concrete details: this child is born of Mary, in the days of Herod, in Bethlehem, named Jesus, in the line of David. These details are not intended as an eyewitness account of the birth of Jesus. Rather, they interpret the faith and serve to tell us something of who God is and what God's own deepest concerns are.

With the birth of this child, God comes into our history. God breaks into the particularity of the Jewish people and is manifest in person for all of us. In this act there stands open to us the reality of God, whose power is grasped not so much in terms of force as in terms of love. The mystery long hidden is now revealed. The birth of this man Jesus, and indeed his entire life, should make it possible for us to see that God's own deepest concern is our salvation. In this birth, God identifies with our cause and our concerns. In the humanity of Jesus, God is present in the struggle to overcome the movement of evil, both individual and social, that is the stuff of human life and human history. Our old human history takes on a new orientation. Its course is changed. God has stepped in and rescued human history so that it is now the agent, not the enemy, of human salvation. And we cannot hesitate to acknowledge that our salvation will be accomplished not in flight from this world, but within this wounded world of our fellow human beings.

The mystery of God's saving work in Jesus is further delineated by the characters playing roles in this drama: Herod, the chief priests, the scribes, and the magi. They make it clear that this new way of salvation is made known by revelation and not invented by human beings. No political philosophy that we may adhere to (Herod), no religious ideal that we may espouse (the chief priest and scribes), and no scientific knowledge that we may gain (the magi) can procure for us the promise of salvation. The kingdom comes unearned.

Moreover, the sphere of God's reign remains hidden to us. It is present to us, who must believe in it, hope for it, and love it without seeing it clearly. The magi, in seeing the star of the king of the Jews at its rising, see one whose kingship is not visible. Only by a series of signs (the star, Herod's fear, their quest for and adoration of the child) is Jesus manifested as the epiphany of God in the world.

Finally, Matthew's account is a dramatic presentation of the truth that is spoken in the reading from Ephesians: that the Gentiles "are heirs with us, members of the same body, and partakers of the promise in Christ Jesus." Traditionally, the Gentiles were excluded from the promise to Israel given through Abraham. Thus they were thought to be alienated from God. Matthew's magi represent the Gentiles—they come from the East and they receive a revelation from nature—and they are portrayed as the first to pay homage to the king of the Jews. The impenetrable wall between Jew and Gentile has been overcome. The revelation made to the Jews is made to the Gentiles, and now both have access to God. God's salvation is for all the world.

The prophet of the Book of Isaiah dramatizes for us too the universality of salvation. Jerusalem, pictured as a woman mourning in the dust, is bid to lift up her eyes to see all nations and rulers of the earth coming to her through the deserts and across the seas. Here Jerusalem is a symbol of the heavenly Jerusalem to come, where all differences that divide us pale into insignificance in the light of God who offers salvation to all.

The feast of Epiphany celebrated today is a celebration of gifts. But not gifts of gold, frankincense and myrrh; not gifts of crutches or drums. Epiphany is a celebration of the unfathomable gift of the birth of Jesus and of the new possibilities that exist for the human race because of this gift of God to us.

Kathleen Cannon, O.P.

R L   THE BAPTISM OF OUR LORD
E   FIRST SUNDAY AFTER EPIPHANY

R   *Is 42:1–4,6–7; Acts 10:34–38; Lk 3:15–16,21–22*
E   *Is 42:1–9; Acts 10:34–38; Lk 3:15–16,21–22*
L   *Is 42:1–7; Acts 10:34–38; Lk 3:15–17,21–22*

Imagine a world without mirrors. Eliminate as well from that imaginary world reflecting pools and polished silver, bright store windows and other places where we catch a glimpse of ourselves.

The loss of the looking glass might lessen the temptation to self-absorption. It might be that in such a world our focus would be less self-directed and increasingly other-directed. "Here's lookin' at 'you', kid!"

The crowds were beginning to look to John ("whether he was the Christ"). The Baptist saw beyond that. John points to Jesus. And our Lord, the baptized Son of the Father, sees beyond himself. This Jesus is beyond basking in the accolades of the Heavenly Voice. He is the very image of the Servant of whom Isaiah sings. This is the one for others. This is the One who shall bring forth justice to the nations, open the eyes that are blind, bring out the prisoners from the dungeon, from the prison those who sit in darkness.

The Baptism of our Lord might help us to shift our focus. His baptism and ours might help us to see beyond ourselves.

Discover the view from another pew. Shift your focus to our parish family. Comfort and console one another over coffee. Greet one another in peace, with genuine affection. Pray for one another.

> For our parish, our school, and opportunities to serve your people,
> We thank you.
> For making us dear one to another, for good times in happy union, and for all our many blessings,
> We thank you.

That you would lead us day by day in ways of love and
tenderness one to another,
We pray, Lord Jesus.
That each may stay close to all the rest, that we may be
mindful one of another with sympathy and understanding,
We pray, Lord Jesus.
That honest and cheerful, brave and true, we may be quick
and ready to help each other meet the day's work and
cares,
We pray, Lord Jesus.[42]

Catch a glimpse of genuine catholicity. Let's put a dent in our
denominationalism. Focus on Christian unity. Begin to make the
people-to-people connections with other parishes, other congregations. It is his death into which we have been baptized, and
not our denomination. Baptized Christians have a great deal in
common. One Lord. One faith. One baptism. One passion. One
death. One resurrection. Exploration and celebration of the "oneness" of the Christian faith expands our vision and broadens our
horizons. The gospel provides an appropriate prelude to the
Week of Prayer for Christian Unity. The week provides an annual occasion and opportunity which ought not be ignored.

Let us resolve to enlarge our worldview. Beyond the bounds of
the church there is a world of sin and strife, a world of unre-
lieved suffering. Let us resolve to include in our field of vision
those whom we too easily overlook. Those too far removed to be
easily seen. Afghan rebels and Sandinistas. Cambodians, Pales-
tinians, and Namibians. Political prisoners and victims of torture.
Those with diseases of which we are terrified: AIDS, Alzheimers,
alcoholism, mental retardation, addictions of various sorts and
descriptions.

Holy baptism, his and ours, is a mirror-shattering event. This is
rebirth on a grand scale. It is a familial event designed to improve our sight lines, increase our vision, and help us to look
beyond ourselves. In our adoption as daughters and sons we
experience a divine exponential explosion of those to whom we
are related. We are, by the power of the Spirit, by water and the

word, swept away on the tide of his grace to larger pools where we are comparatively smaller fish.

The Baptism of our Lord refreshes our recollection of our own and moves us beyond ourselves. This is the One who in the throes of death prays, "Father, forgive them." This is the One who in greatest need looks to the needs of others: "Woman, behold your son. Son, your mother." This is the One whose sandals we are not worthy to untie, who offers himself to us again: "My body, my blood, given for you."

See for yourself.

Look beyond yourself, for his sake.

Christopher Hoyer

[42]Adapted from *Prayers New and Old* (Cincinnati: Forward Movement Publications), pp. 101–102.

R SECOND SUNDAY IN ORDINARY TIME
E L SECOND SUNDAY AFTER EPIPHANY

R *Is 62:1–5; 1 Cor 12:4–11; Jn 2:1–11*
E *Is 62:1–5; 1 Cor 12:1–11; Jn 2:1–11*
L *Is 62:1–5; 1 Cor 12:1–11; Jn 2:1–11*

It is an abrupt transition. For weeks on end we have proclaimed those cherished stories of annunciation, chanting angels and foiled kings. Suddenly, however, with only a single week's notice under the guise of last Sunday's celebration for the Lord's baptism, we are catapulted out of infancy narratives into the adult life of Christ.

This unceremonious transition from the festive to the commonplace may seem even more arduous, given the somewhat enigmatic gospel proposed for today's worship. It is a curious story in which Jesus offers a brusque response to his mother's advocacy, needs to be coaxed into miracle working, and may even have contributed to the wine shortage by arriving with an uninvited band of fishermen in tow.

This rapid transition from Bethlehem to Cana, however, may not be as disjunct as it first appears: especially when recalling that, unlike the civil calendar, the church year did not begin on January first. Rather, our yearly pilgrimage through the Christian mysteries began back in frantic November. It was in that unlikely moment, between turkey leftovers and "The First Noel," that our watch for the eternal dawn began. The four week preparation for the liturgical solstice built to an enthusiastic climax on December 25th. Despite the season's focus on nativity, however, the church's revelatory cycle did not end on Christmas Day. Rather, the weeks that followed were filled with accounts of temple presentations, hasty departures, and a baptist's profession: further unfolding the incarnational mystery of God's self-speaking. Now, though the creche is packed away and "Silent Night" is just a faded memory, we realize that the revelation begun in Advent and momentarily resolved in the nativity continues on this ordinary Sunday of the year. Today is another epiphany, in Jesus' first miracle and public ministry.

Making connections between infancy stories and the wedding at Cana, therefore, is not an exercise in imaginative exegesis, but an acknowledgement of the fundamental unity in Jesus' life and the church year. The Johannine writer acknowledges such connections in today's gospel which anticipates cross and Calvary, with allusions to the final manifestation and the hour yet to come. More than literary flourishes, these references affirm that Jesus' entire life was an ongoing preparation for his final manifestation in death and resurrection. Thus birth, baptism, and first miracle were not isolated events to be eclipsed by Calvary, but were part of that continuum of praise and commitment which led to Calvary.

Given our sometimes disjunct approach to word and season, it is possible to miss this progression, and instead focus on a single gospel event each week. One challenge of the word, however, is to acknowledge the continuity in Jesus' mission as well as the integrity it calls forth in our own lives, a challenge reflected in that vocational choice which sets the context for much of today's word: marriage.

Weddings hold a special fascination for us: the bridal march, the dentine smiles, and all those rented clothes. Despite the allure of these externals, however, we know that the ritual is not magic, automatically turning strangers into committed spouses or agnostics into believers. Instead, weddings express and nourish an already existing love and faith. Consequently, it is not the marriage ritual as much as the faithful living as husband and wife which is truly sacramental.

In many respects, therefore, Christian marriage parallels the mission of Jesus and stands as a powerful symbol for our own baptismal journey. Just as the reality of marriage is not contained by an isolated ceremony but realized in a lifetime of vowed love, so was the mission of Jesus uncontainable by a single deed and only realized in the sweep of events which led to death and resurrection. Just as the exchange of vows finds its true significance in the daily struggle to live in covenant, so are the individual acts of birth or epiphany or first miracle significant only to the extent that they reveal the covenant consummated on the cross. And just as the challenge of marriage is not met merely by marching down the aisle, and Jesus' mission was not complete with one fanciful miracle late in the wedding reception, so is the essence of the Christian vocation not to be found in occasional donations and obligatory Sunday worship: for as isolated events, these are empty events. It is not such individual moments, but the ongoing commitment in faithful love which is the true manifestation of God among us. May this day be for us a true epiphany: a living response to God's self-speaking in our own lives.

Edward Foley, Capuchin

R   *Neh 8:2–4a,5–6,8–10; 1 Cor 12:12–30; Lk 1:1–4;4:14–21*
E   *Neh 8:2–10; 1 Cor 12:12–27; Lk 4:14–21*
L   *Is 61:1–6; 1 Cor 12:12–21,26–27; Lk 4:14–21*

Her name was Tiffany, said the nurse who called, Tiffany Nicole. A sixteen month old black child from Harlem was dying, and her mother wanted someone to come to the hospital and pray. Once again I was presented with a frustration we all face, the frustration of not having good news, freedom, or recovery to offer someone. Once again I was not able to look a sickness or disease in the eye and say: Be healed! If there were one more gift that I would ask of God in doing my ministry, that gift would be the power to restore the many Tiffanies, the many suffering people I see. "Lord, will you help?" you too may have asked. Or, "Lord, *can* you help?"

Someone has calculated that every human being, on average, has some medical complaint or problem every three days. An aspirin will usually do, or Bandaid, or a good night's sleep. But occasionally we need greater healing. In the next year, many of us will undergo batteries of tests and diagnostic procedures. We will endure CAT and NMR scans, myelograms or discograms. We will require therapies, treatments or surgeries; be bombarded by laser, sound or radiation; measured and fitted with heart valves, knuckle joints or pace makers; and mobilized once again with braces, crutches, a walker or wheelchair. The arsenal to overcome our tendency toward illness is impressive, the cost staggering. Yet, though treated, counseled, or operated on, all of us will eventually lose the battle.

You see, the bodies we inhabit for what we call a lifetime are imperfect vessels, jars of clay, as Paul said. Their resistance to attack has limits; their endurance under severe stress or trauma has a breaking point. Without food, as we know, these bodies last only weeks; without water, only days; without air, but a few minutes.

Has God, our almighty Creator, failed us somehow? Is the design so fraught with flaw and imperfection that God has had to depend on the medical establishment to undo these divine blunders?

I don't believe so. God has not failed in carrying out a better creative plan. Nor do I believe that we are flawed when we should have been perfect, or weak when God intended strength and invincibility. Weakness is not an absence of strength: it is rather the means to strength. The struggles that you and I must go through to survive, to deal with our pain and our suffering, to conquer our imperfection, occur not because God hasn't *succeeded* creating us, but because God hasn't *finished* creating us.

As I sit with a family who has lost a child, I know how difficult it can be to place that catastrophe into some kind of understanding of a loving and gracious God. It is a temptation to say that God planned it this way, that God sends us our trials and tribulations to test or teach us. In Jesus Christ, however, we are revealed a God who is loving and compassionate. He said, "In this world, you will have tribulation, but fear not, I have overcome the world." Our troubles are not sent to us by God; they are already here. The Scriptures reveal quite clearly that brokenness and fallenness are the basis of this world. From the opening verses of Genesis, the Hebrew people described it so well: "The earth was without form and void, darkness was on the face of the deep." Rather than sending us trials, God's Spirit is still at work calling us, bringing something out of nothing, light out of darkness, life from death.

A little girl, upon finding a butterfly cocoon, brought it home and planned to care for it until the butterfly came out. She waited with eager expectation until the day finally arrived. A tiny head appeared, munching its way through the gray, paper thin wall. She viewed the little creature with such love, but what she wasn't prepared for was how long it would take and how difficult a time the butterfly would have.

With a small stick, ever so carefully, she decided to give the butterfly a helping hand. And within moments instead of hours the butterfly was free. Then it tried to fly, but when it stretched its wings, it fell and died. "What happened?" she pleaded, teary eyed, to her father. "I even helped." "The caterpillar needed that struggle," her father answered. "Without it, it was never able to strengthen its wings to fly."

When we struggle, God wants us to become something through that struggle. The real miracles that occur in hospital rooms are not the ones where suffering has been canceled in a moment, at the end of a prayer, but where, through the suffering, someone has courageously lived. Even when a child dies at two, or twenty, what has been demonstrated is not failure, but a miracle of life being called out of chaos.

Jesus began his ministry with these words read from a scroll of the prophet Isaiah: "The Spirit of the Lord is upon me to proclaim the acceptable year of the Lord." The arrival of the dominion of God was, in those words, inextricably tied to helping the poor, releasing prisoners, healing the sick. And yet, the poor remain in our streets, our prisons are overcrowded as never before, and everyone of us will eventually succumb to ill health and physical death. Had Jesus failed? Was it a mistake to announce that Isaiah's prophecy had been fulfilled in this reading by Jesus?

Following in his steps from that early synagogue worship service, to the hills of Galilee, on the road to Jerusalem, and the way of the cross, we discover that suffering is not God's will. Rather, life in the face of suffering is God's will; courage in the face of fear; faith in the face of doubt and abandonment; love in the face of hatred and prejudice.

God's will is to call these things out of the hurt and brokenness that we are and that we find around us. Yes, you and I need good news, freedom and healing: that is, in Christ, healing of our minds and hearts, freedom from our attitudes and outlook, good news to speak as we get up in the morning, and new hope for what we are doing with our lives. With Christ, the prophecy is fulfilled, in you and in me.

Bruce J. Evenson

R   *Jer 1:4–5,17–19; 1 Cor 12:31–13:13; Lk 4:21–30*
E   *Jer 1:4–10; 1 Cor 14:12b–20; Lk 4:21–32*
L   *Jer 1:4–10; 1 Cor 12:27–13:13; Lk 4:21–32*

I suppose a hometown can be any size, but I always think small, perhaps because my own hometown is just over a thousand people. New York and Chicago, Paris and Moscow are also somebody's hometown, but the picture isn't quite the same. I know something of what it's like to go to such a town as Nazareth, to be back in a congregation where you grew up. It is a strange thing: only the children seem to have gotten older. The grownups are still the same age, for old people seem to remain the age you remembered when you left at eighteen.

There's something comfortable about going home to such a town and such a congregation. You can feel assured that some things never change. But you know you have, and that means you can also feel uncomfortable. No longer are you home in the same way as when you sat in those very pews years before. I can't pretend to know how Jesus felt going back to Nazareth. But it seems clear that the people were amazed at the child now grown. "Is not this Joseph's son?" they asked each other. And we can imagine them remembering the young boy who came to synagogue with his parents. So nice to have him back, isn't it? And so good to know he hasn't forgotten his religious training.

Religion can be like a hometown: familiar, traditional, unchanging, a constant in a chaotic, fast-moving world. We want religion to stay the same, to look as it looked when we were children. We want to sing hymns with tunes we know and be able to follow the service without looking. This is the faith of our ancestors, the faith of our childhood. We can wrap religion around us like a homemade quilt, assured that God is in heaven and all's right with the world.

It seemed right in Nazareth when they heard Jesus read. "And all spoke well of him, and wondered at the gracious words which proceeded out of his mouth." They had heard Jesus read from the scroll of Isaiah the prophet. It was familiar: some of them knew the words by heart. "Today this scripture is fulfilled in your hearing," Jesus said as he sat down. Perhaps it seemed to them a liturgical response, a bit like singing, "Thanks be to God!" It didn't sink in that Jesus was talking about himself. Did that even occur to them? After all, this was Joseph's son, their hometown boy.

But something happened that day in Jesus' hometown, something that moved those who knew him from delight to rage. In just seven verses, the story changes dramatically, from "all spoke well of him" to "all in the synagogue were filled with wrath." Of course we cannot read their minds, but we do see the picture: those who smiled with approval at the boy grown-up soon led him to the edge of the city to throw Jesus down headlong. You don't have to be a mind reader to know something has happened.

It is more than disappointment over not seeing a miracle. Oh, perhaps that started it. Jesus told them he knew what they were thinking, and few of us like to be second-guessed. Then he told them that "prophets are not acceptable in their own country." What right did he have to think of himself as a prophet? They might have simply gone home in a huff. Young upstart, who does he think he is, telling us he won't heal anybody here? Who knows if the stories from Capernaum are even true?

But the hometown folks didn't get into a huff: they were all filled with wrath. They didn't head for home at all, but tried instead to kill the one they thought they knew. Their "Hosannas" of praise had quickly turned to "Crucify him," though this time they did not succeed. If not anger for lack of a miracle, what then? What could have been so terrible, so life-threatening?

Jesus had stripped away their quilt. The ancient quilt, worn and familiar, had assured them of God's favor. "There were many widows in Israel," Jesus said, but Elijah the prophet was sent to a widow in the land of Sidon. "There were lepers in Israel," Jesus continued, but Elisha cleansed only Naaman the Syrian. They knew those stories; Jesus had learned them there—hearing them read again and again in this very synagogue. Yet, perhaps they hadn't heard them, any more than they had really heard the prophet Isaiah: good news for the poor and liberty for the oppressed. For such prophecy to come true, things would have to change. The boundaries around the chosen people would be broken down. The hometown would have to extend hospitality to sojourners and strangers, tax collectors and sinners.

"Today this word is fulfilled in your hearing." They didn't get it at first, but it was becoming clear. Jesus would not let them stay the same. Jesus would not allow God's love and mercy to be so small. Elijah had gone to Sidon; Elisha had cleansed a Syrian; and Jesus had healed in Capernaum. No one was going to tell them religion had to go that far! There had to be some clear boundaries; there had to be outsiders! You can spot the outsiders in your own hometown; you know who belongs.

Religion can be like that, familiar, comfortable, unchanging. But Jesus comes into our streets, into our sanctuary, saying that the prophet's words are now fulfilled. All sorts of people we'd never invite to dinner are being welcomed to the table, to break bread and drink wine. We can no longer hear the words "given for you" without also hearing the very same words said to someone we had condemned to hell. This is not what we had in mind! We feel the old quilt slipping off our shoulders. Frantically we grasp at the edges, desperate to know God loves us still, in the midst of these strangers. Then, if we stay, our odd thing happens. We feel the quilt grow larger. Still around us, it is also around the one we named outcast. The widow from Sidon, Naaman the Syrian, a child from Capernaum, and the person we can't stand. It's not quite the same hometown, but it's a lot more like the dominion of God.

Barbara Lundblad

R   *Is 6:1–2a,3–8; 1 Cor 15:1–11; Lk 5:1–11*
E   *Jud 6:11–24a; 1 Cor 15:1–11; Lk 5:1–11*
L   *Is 6:1–8; 1 Cor 14:12b-20; Lk 5:1–11*

What will it be? the Fish, the Sea, or Me? For some infants at baptism the choice must seem predetermined—someone wants to turn them into fish. Which they are not, but water everywhere seems that to be a fish is the only way to survive. Baptismal outbursts, perhaps, tell us of the struggle.

In it all there comes also some comfort. Mother's voice, possibly, or the smoothness of oil. Do not be afraid, little one, the water will not overtake you.

We know the event runs much deeper. For in the water, in my water, in my baptismal water there was at battle those primal powers of which the hymnist sings: "Death and life have contended In that combat stupendous."[43] And still the oil soothes: You are sealed by the Holy Spirit, and are Christ's forever. Do not be afraid. This is the Spirit of him who leads as a gentle Shepherd, not as a ruthless despot with holocaust on his mind. "Do not be afraid," Jesus said to Peter, who grasped at his knees, fearful of the power behind that draught of fish.

The question then, and the question now, is: What will it be? the Fish, the Sea, or Me? The answer, we have said, is the answer of Peter and John and James: they left everything and followed him.

What will it be? We follow, but often not with that same kind of abandon. The distractions aren't all that different, however. Think about the fish, for example. Don't you think that Peter, astonished by the nets bursting with fish, entertained the potential of such a catch? Fish were his business. Suddenly there are more than he ever imagined. Selling would be easier than ever. If Jesus could do it once, couldn't he do it again? Think of the profit.

The world's history is full of those who have tried to harness the power of God. Some of us pray for new bikes or for a win at the lottery. Others try for political clout powered by morality. How is profit on your agenda for life after baptism? What will it be? the Fish? the Sea? or Me?

We follow but often not with the same kind of abandon. Think about the sea, for example. It was their vocation, Peter's, James's and John's. How well Peter did at it we don't know. Whatever he set himself to, he did with determination and with that kind of single-mindedness which was bound to lift him to the top of the industry. His vocation was the sea, and through tough competion it held promise for achievement and for the sense of accomplishment.

Peter left the Sea behind. Others have not. The power of water in our own lives often leaves us hankering after profit or desiring new ways to compete or seeking opportunities to achieve status. That's in the church. And outside, while we are given by God to excel in whatever we do, too often we follow by using ourselves as the end of every pursuit. What will it be? the Fish, the Sea, or Me?

"Do not be afraid," Jesus said once to us as we were covered by the waters of life. Then the deep yielded more than a great shoal of fish. Flowing from the water was the power of him who died and rose again; from the waters came a surge of power which is eternal life unleashed within each of us by the breath of the Holy Spirit. "Do not be afraid," Jesus said.

Today the gospel calls us to follow him with greater abandon. Who knows where all we will be led? Through sickness? through hardship? through danger? through death. "Do not be afraid," Jesus says. For as the water yielded the great catch, so it is that the waters of rebirth have made you mine forever.

Today the call is back to that promise and that power. And we are following, even without his asking us to, because following we know we have found eternal life. As with Peter, he says to us: "Do you love me?" And we say, "Yes, Lord." So we follow him, follow him to the sheep out there who need to be fed, the sheep for whom Fish and Sea exist and make sense.

"Do not be afraid," Jesus says. What will it be? the Fish, the Sea, or Me? And they left everything and followed him.

Mark P. Bangert

[43]"Christians, to the Paschal Victim," *Lutheran Book of Worship*, #137.

R **SIXTH SUNDAY IN ORDINARY TIME**
E **SIXTH SUNDAY AFTER EPIPHANY, PROPER 1**
L **SIXTH SUNDAY AFTER EPIPHANY**

R *Jer 17:5–8; 1 Cor 15:12,16–20; Lk 6:17,20–26*
E *Jer 17:5–10; 1 Cor 15:12–20; Lk 6:17–26*
L *Jer 17:5–8; 1 Cor 15:12,16–20; Lk 6:17–26*

Blessed are we who this day hunger for the Lord, love with a spirit of sacrifice, and act for the kingdom's coming on earth as it is in heaven. Now is the day of blessing or of curse, of conversion of heart or of hardened heart, for now is the time to choose. This is one emphasis in Luke's Sermon on the Mount that Matthew does not have in a similar sermon. Following the Lord is done everyday, or it is not well done on any day. "Blessed are you poor . . . who hunger now . . . who weep now . . . who are hated now. . . . and woe to you who are rich now, who are full now, who laugh now. . . ." The gospel couldn't be clearer. Now is the time of salvation.

Jeremiah has another version of a similar message stated in the present tense of now. "Blessed is the one who trusts in the LORD . . . and cursed is the one whose heart turns away from the LORD." It is important to sense this direction of the heart, for the difference is one of blessing or of curse, of life or of death. Are our hearts restless because they already know and desire to seek the Lord more fully? Or are they restless because they wish more of that which is temporarily satisfying? Is the restlessness merely an impatience in being satisfied because we want more and better clothing, cars, houses, VCRs, acclaim, friends, careers, and so on?

Those who hunger for the Lord now, who recognize their need for the Lord now, have restless hearts in spite of the good and the bad in life. Today we hear about the poor in spirit, those who acknowledge this day that they know about poverty of the heart. This is the reason they seek and so need the blessing of God's dominion, the presence of Jesus Christ, now.

Luke contrasts two expressions of hearts. The hearts of the poor are set in opposition to the hearts of the rich. The poor, the hungry, the weeping, and the persecuted who look to the Lord are blessed. The popular, the rich, and the satisfied who need only themselves are cursed.

For the Jewish audience of Jesus Christ, the urgency of the woes and blessings for this day would be clear. The word of God addressed to the heart demanded action. Living the word in deed was a blessing, because this was a means of being united with the Lord of all. Refusing to hear God's word, which meant refusing to live in a manner of union with God, was a denial of the commandment. For Jewish hearers, blessing statements are commandments. For us, as for them, the blessings are set before the community and within the community. Action must follow if there is a hearing, a conversion of heart to the Lord.

Today, Jeremiah sets forth the two directions for this journey of the heart. Cursed be the heart that turns from the Lord. . . . Blessed be the heart that looks to the Lord in hope. Paul assures us that Jesus Christ is our hope, our blessing, our way to the kingdom. In Jesus Christ, the first fruits of the new creation continue to be revealed. Those who can hear his words to the heart, those who hunger now, who thirst now, who look to Christ now in their need, are the ones who shall be blessed.

This day of celebration of the new creation in Christ is the day to search our hearts and choose blessing or curse. We come around the table of blessing, invited to share a blessing cup, not a cup of woe. Dare we eat this bread and drink this cup as sign of the restlessness that is turned to the Lord? We dare if we know in our hearts that we do desire to be among those poor, those who hunger now, those who thirst now, those whose hearts are willing to be converted now to love in spite of the costs.

What is the cost of loving until the Lord comes in glory? The cross reveals an answer. Our lives reveal an answer as well. C.S. Lewis states the challenge, the cost of blessing and curse this way.

> To love at all is to be vulnerable. Love anything and your heart will certainly be wrung and probably be broken. If you want to make sure of keeping it intact, you must give your heart to no one, not even an animal. Wrap it carefully around with hobbies and little luxuries; avoid all entanglements; lock it up safe in the casket or coffin of your selfishness. But in that casket—safe, dark, motionless, airless—it will change. It will not be broken; it will become unbreakable, impenetrable, irredeemable. . . . The only place outside heaven where you can be perfectly safe from all the dangers and perturbations of love is hell.[44]

Blessed are you who hunger, who thirst, who are poor now: yours is the dominion of heaven.

Shawn Madigan, C.S.J.

[44]C.S. Lewis, *The Four Loves* (N.Y.: Harcourt, Brace, Jovanovich, 1960), p. 168.

R   *1 Sam 26:2,7–9,12–13,22–23; 1 Cor 15:45–49; Lk 6:27–38*
E   *Gen 45:3–11,21–28; 1 Cor 15:35–38,42–50; Lk 6:27–38*
L   *Gen 45:3–8a,15; 1 Cor 15:35–38a,42–50; Lk 6:27–38*

"How are you dying?" In common parlance the familiar greeting would be, "How ya doin'?", certainly not "How are you dying?" The person posing the question would no doubt anticipate the answer "Fine, and how are you?" One assumes that the questioner is indeed concerned about the health and state of affairs of the other. An opportunity for dialogue is evoked; the respondent is to say something about herself or himself.

"How are you dying?" Like the first Adam, perhaps, merely as a living human being? Or is our living into hope exemplary of the last Adam, a life-giving spirit, Jesus the Christ? We are not conditioned to think of such spiritual matters as part of our day-to-day existence. At holy baptism and the Lord's supper we are reminded of our dying and rising with Christ, but somehow this matter is left inside the church. Away from the altar or holy water, it's back to business as usual. What matters is that we are living, we are doing whatever is necessary to survive.

It is easy to ask people if they are healthy, successful, rich, happy, staying busy. Too often greeters are anxious to get the conversation going merely in order to tell how well life is treating them. This is apparent when the response is, "I'm really not doing well at all. The last few years have been terrible for me." We cannot end such a conversation merely with expressions of sympathy. How many greeters are truly prepared to enter into dialogue when they have received such an honest answer? The question actually raised in this instance is "How are you dying?"

The Scriptures for today ask and answer the questions of "doing" and "dying." In the Old Testament passage, there is new life even in the midst of stories full of death. Paul's analogy of a seed underscores the Old Testament passage by demonstrating continuity when there has been dissolution, difference and death. The seed is dissolved before it can produce new life. As the outer shell of the seed dissolves, the seed remains essentially the same. When it bursts forth into a new form and a new life appears, it continues to be the same seed. There can be disintegration, difference, and yet continuity in the life and death of seeds as well as of humans. At the core of a destructible human facade is the possibility of new life, a spiritual dwelling that can experience divine metamorphosis only by the grace of God.

Another form of death underscored by the gospel pericope is set forth in the form of divine law: love unselfishly! One can grasp the essence of these words of Jesus when viewed in the context of the preceding section, Luke's version of the Beatitudes. Luke assumes that these words of Jesus are addressed to the disciples in the second person and that they emphasize the reversal of values that will take place in the age to come. The "law of love" follows and is made relevant to daily choices. To love unconditionally helps one avoid the kind of death which has stagnated the Dead Sea. Since the Dead Sea has no outlet, it takes everything into itself and gives nothing out. Thus it is motionless and stagnant, producing nothing.

How are you dying? Like the Dead Sea, humans can slowly strangle themselves to death with their own greed and selfishness. Jesus summarizes the great commandment by reminding us to love our neighbors as ourselves, thus indicating a healthy form of self-love. To love self is to want the best for self and to reach out to get it. In the process we should recognize that the real values of life are those which God would have us gain. As we reach for the ultimate enrichment which God alone can give, we will also love and recognize the worth of our neighbors, praying for the best in life that God can make available to them. This is the supreme ideal: we expect nothing in return when we give truly of ourselves.

We live in an age when the accumulation of wealth is viewed as a sign of success. Many of the wealthy among us profess to be people of faith. Unfortunately, many people are miserable in the midst of their possessions. Their pride drives them to maintain the facade of apparent sufficiency when their lives within are empty. The years of gathering material goods without lovingly sharing with others has created a Dead Sea: motionless stagnation, spiritual death.

Joseph the dreamer provides for us a model of one who had all the reasons to be typically human. As a favored child with an unusual talent, many options were placed before him. We assume that his time in the pit, his being a victim of slave trade, and his sojourn in a strange and alien land provided him an opportunity to hear and respond in a positive manner to God. He died into new life. From self-sufficiency he was plunged into helplessness and a desperate need for God. For this reason he surrendered to divine leadership. Rather than emerging as a cynical, rebellious and revengeful person he became an agent of God's love and forgiveness. His memory of his brothers and his father evoked tears rather than anger. He reached out in love rather than passing harsh judgment on those who had persecuted him.

Martin Luther King, Jr. often spoke of unmerited suffering and God's intervention. When his efforts were stymied, King could feel the great benign Power who is God transforming our "dark yesterdays into bright tomorrows."[45] Perhaps what appears to be dying moments and experiences of the pit are actually God's interventions causing us to die from worldly direction. Such moments remind us of our need to be concerned with others and the will of God rather than for ourselves alone.

We can die and shed the destructive elements of our being and live into the hope granted us in Jesus the Christ. "How are you dying?"

Melva Wilson Costen, Ph.D.

[45]Martin Luther King, Jr., *Strength to Love* (Philadelphia: Fortress, 1963), p. 114.

R   EIGHTH SUNDAY IN ORDINARY TIME
E   EIGHTH SUNDAY AFTER EPIPHANY, PROPER 3
L   EIGHTH SUNDAY AFTER EPIPHANY

R   *Sir 27:5–8; 1 Cor 15:54–58; Lk 6:39–45*
E   *Jer 7:1–7; 1 Cor 15:50–58; Lk 6:39–49*
L   *Jer 7:1–7; 1 Cor 15:51–58; Lk 6:39–49*

"Words are cheap." It's a common saying. Proverbial wisdom gives us many sayings to indicate that actions are the real test of a person, not simply words. "Easier said than done." "Beauty is as beauty does." "A lot of hot air." "Don't just sit there, do something." "A smooth talker." Obviously, it is common human experience that great dreams and wonderful promises do not always become reality. Words and actions do not always agree.

Today's Scripture readings present us with two views of the relationship between words and actions: a challenge and a fulfillment. The portion of the Sermon on the Plain read today is a whole chain of thought about words. A person's words reveal the truth about the person's nature just as the fruit reveals the tree. The sage Jesus ben Sira had proclaimed the same fact two centuries earlier. Besides the image of the fruit as proof of the tree, he used yet another image: words test a person as the kiln tests the pot. The first point is therefore that the words themselves are a test and a revelation of a person.

The gospel continues, "Why do you call me 'Lord, Lord,' and not do what I tell you?" Words without actions are nothing. The person of words alone is like one who builds on sand. The prophet Jeremiah tried to convince the Jerusalemites of his time that trust in the magic formula, "The temple of the LORD! The temple of the LORD," was not enough. Only righteous actions—justice toward one another, obedience to God's commands—would convince God to stay in their midst, would save them from exile.

The American political process is an ongoing witness to the difficulty or even impossibility of transforming grand speeches into practical action. Candidates give promises concerning farm subsidies, social security, national defense, peace. But voters consistently return to the candidate's previous record. "How did you vote on this issue? What was your role in this event? How have your constituents benefited by your actions?" A candidate whose previous record contradicts current promises will not gain many votes. A voter who is swayed simply by campaign rhetoric can be badly deceived.

The same principle holds in our lives as well. The challenge is twofold: Our words must be good, for they are the key to the truth of who we are. But our words must also be given flesh in action, for words alone are not enough. Trust in words alone is folly.

The reading from 1 Corinthians shows another side of the relationship between words and actions. The whole of chapter 15 is a treatise on the resurrection, the ultimate realization in action of a promise beyond our imaginations. We are put in a position which tests our trust in the words of God. Paul says earlier in chapter 15 that if Christ's resurrection, which he preaches, is not true, then we are indeed the most pitiable of people.

But the resurrection is true. The word of God has become flesh in order to turn the promise of life into the full-blown wonder of immortality. The word of God through whom all was created has become incarnate in order to bring to reality the new creation, free from sin, free from death. This is the ultimate unity between word and action. This is the final reality, the rock, the word of God, on which our faith is built.

Irene Nowell, O.S.B.

E   LAST SUNDAY AFTER EPIPHANY
L   THE TRANSFIGURATION OF OUR LORD

E   *Ex 34:29–35; 1 Cor 12:27–13:13; Lk 9:28–36*
L   *Deut 34:1–12; 2 Cor 4:3–6; Lk 9:28–36*

The gospel reading for today is the story of Jesus revealing his glory upon the holy mountain. Jesus and the "inner circle," Peter, James and John, went up on higher ground to pray. Mountains in Scripture have always symbolized a place of meeting between heaven and earth, a place where people felt it appropriate, with some fear and trembling, to hobnob with the Most High.

While they were on the mountain, Jesus prayed. We are told that "the appearance of his countenance was altered, and his raiment became dazzling white." Moses and Elijah appeared in glory and spoke with Jesus. Meanwhile Peter and the others fell into a deep snooze. When they finally woke up, they beheld his glory and the two others who stood with him. As they departed Peter suggested constructing three booths, one for Moses, one for Elijah, and one for Jesus. A cloud hovered over them, and they were scared. The voice said, "This is my Son, the chosen one; listen to him!"

Now what are we to make of all this? A trip to the montains, drowsy disciples, altered states, dazzling attire and a proposed construction plan? Deep within these curious goings on are spiritual truths, truths that speak to modern people in the modern church.

First we have the setting, a mountain top. Make no mistake: I am not advocating that we pack our bags and head for the hills to have a spiritual experience. The fact is that with all those U.F.O. hunters and people seeking a cosmic convergence in New Age fashion, there would scarcely be enough room on the mountains for us anyway. Rather, it is indeed a good and joyous thing, it is indeed right and salutary, that we should gather together on "higher ground" to pray. It is still worth the effort to gather together in a holy place to focus our prayer in the company of the baptized.

Once on higher ground, we have a lot in common with the disciples. While Jesus was before them in all his glory, Peter and the others fell fast asleep. All heaven was breaking loose, and all they could manage was a yawn! I can imagine it, because I see it on many each Sunday morning. Here we are in church, on higher ground, and Jesus is here among us in word and meal. All of heaven is breaking loose, and sometimes all we can muster is a yawn.

There are many people today who are seeking God, a lot them in bizarre ways. Your local "spiritual supply store" offers crystals, cards, boards, powders and various other gadgets for the expressed purpose of cosmic convergence of your coming in contact with God. The greatest search in our time and for all time is the search for God.

Christian people proclaim that God cannot be found, but has found us in Jesus the Christ. With this great knowledge, the knowledge of salvation, it is our task to go into the world and say that Jesus is Emmanuel, God with us.

The task of pointing others to God can scarcely be done if we ourselves are sleeping. Thus the summons from the gospel today is clear and simple: "Awake, awake!" This summons is for those of us who regularly go to higher ground, for us who are used to hobnobbing with the Most High. It is easy for us, as it was for the disciples, to fall asleep in the dazzling light of God's presence.

God tabernacles among us in people gathered in Christ's name, in wine poured and bread shared. All of heaven breaks loose for us in the weekly assembly, but we will miss it if we are sleeping. However, if we wake up, we will behold his glory, the glory of the only Son coming from the Father full of grace and truth.

Awake, O people of God! Let us not be found asleep in the light. As we awake to God's presence let us not lock it away in booths of our own security and salvation. Instead of snoozing, let us be dazzled, opening our hearts to God's presence. God's presence will be a source of courage, a source of power and might that will motivate us to go out into the world and point others to God's most brilliant light. This light shines on all who dwell in darkness. This light will guide us into the way of peace. Jesus is here, and all heaven is breaking loose; so awake, sleepers! Arise, rise from the dead, and Jesus will give you his light.

Karen M. Ward

R E L   ASH WEDNESDAY

R   *Joel 2:12–18; 2 Cor 5:20–6:2; Mt 6:1–6,16–18*
E   *Joel 2:1–2, 12–17; 2 Cor 5:20b-6:10; Mt 6:1–6,16–21*
L   *Joel 2:12–19; 2 Cor 5:20b-6:2; Mt 6:1–6,16–21*

God touches us today not only through word and bread, but also through one of the humblest of all signs: ashes. I invite you now to share the images I have of ashes, or to bring forth from your own memory and imagination a set of your own.

Ashes. The side of a hill leveled by a forest fire; hiking ankle-deep in soggy soot; discovering new growth under the layer of ashes.

Ashes. Cleaning an ash-tray for the last time, after my mother, hemorrhaging from the lungs, was taken to the hospital.

Ashes. The cremated remains of Dominican Sister and peace activist Margie Tuite, delivered at her request to the people she loved in Nicaragua to be buried in that bloodied, battered land as a sign of hope.

Ashes. The debris from a car bomb in Belfast, a community center in Soweto, and the homes of the poor in our own inner cities that burn because of faulty furnaces and unscrupulous landlords.

Ashes. Hundreds of thousands of pounds of garbage and trash burned daily as the refuse of an affluent and throw-away culture.

Ashes. Scenes from these same garbage dumps in Mexico City, Calcutta and Cairo where human scavengers survive by rooting through the ashes for their livelihood.

Ashes. A line from one of the most humanly appealing of all biblical stories. God's servant Job, after a profoundly humbling confrontation with his God: "Now my eye sees you; therefore I despise myself, and repent in dust and ashes."

We begin this Lenten season in dust and ashes. With Job, and in the spirit of the texts we have heard proclaimed, we too begin again the process of repentance, a conversion of life to which the church so wisely calls us as we prepare for its greatest mystery.

The Lenten Scriptures are consistent in their message. The prophet Joel calls us to return, to turn again: our hearts must be conformed to the Lord and to the justice that is expected of God's people. Paul instructs the citizens of Corinth that Jesus himself, though innocent, immersed himself in the ashes of our sinfulness so that he might liberate us for freedom and holiness. And Matthew reminds us that this endeavor can so easily be turned into hypocrisy. Even the ashes that we will wear today as our badge of membership in a community of sin can become an empty sign.

For some of us, this may be the first time we have seriously heard a call to conversion. A personal crisis may be the grace that has prepared others for a sincere effort at prayer and penance. For many, I suspect, this Ash Wednesday brings memories of annual attempts, failed resolutions, and eventual indifference. Most of us, I fear, if we could verbalize our ambivalence about this season, would choose words from T.S. Eliot's poetry. Like his "hollow men" we must admit that

> Between the idea
> And the reality
> Between the motion
> And the act
> Falls the Shadow.[46]

The Shadow is the debris of our own life's ashes, layer upon layer, until whatever life might survive is stifled.

Or like Eliot's weak-willed Prufrock, the Shadow is procrastination echoed in the lines:

> And indeed there will be time . . .
> Time yet for a hundred indecisions,
> And for a hundred visions and revisions[47]

before we will admit that this call to conversion is meant for us this year. We must pray for the grace to realize that this Lent is our acceptable time. It is "kairos," a time for decision and action.

The perspective of Lent is not navel-gazing but forward-looking. The debris of our wasted lives is not the final word, and the repentance and conversion of heart to which we are called should not invite us to discouragement and despair—the preoccupation of a soul obsessed with its guilt. (Eliot again: "Because I do not hope to turn again/ Because I do not hope/ Because I do not hope to turn . . ."[48]) There is a cause, rather, for profound optimism in this season that will see, even in nature, a springtime renewal. We do hope to turn again. What we anticipate is the greatest victory of life over death; what we foster is the growth that can occur only when the ashes that prevent new life have been cleared away.

So what shall we resolve as we move from these sacraments of word, of bread, and of ashes into the "acceptable time" of our salvation? Perhaps God desires us this year to address in humble peace the most persistent deposit of ashes in our own personal lives so that we can enjoy the liberating peace of reconciliation. Then, reconciled, we can better join in the task of building the City of God.

Ruth Caspar, O.P.

[46]T.S.Eliot, "The Hollow Men," *The Complete Poems and Plays 1909–1950* (N.Y. Harcourt, Brace and Company, 1952), p.58.
[47]Eliot, "The Love Song of J. Alfred Prufrock," *The Complete Poems and Plays 1909–1950*, p. 4.
[48]Eliot, "Ash Wednesday," *The Complete Poems and Plays 1909–1950*, p. 60.

R   *Deut 26:4–10; Rom 10:8–13; Lk 4:1–13*
E   *Deut 26:5–11; Rom 10:8b–13; Lk 4:1–13*
L   *Deut 26:5–10; Rom 10:8b–13; Lk 4:1–13*

"Lead us not into temptation." Let this be our prayer as we enter into Lent. It is the prayer that Jesus taught us to pray, a prayer that Jesus himself must have prayed when, filled with the Holy Spirit, he was led by the Spirit into the wilderness and into the midst of temptation.

We expect better things of the Spirit of God. We expect to be gifted, not tempted, to be drawn toward spiritual not physical concerns, to be delivered from the devil's domain. Yet we read in today's gospel that Jesus was led by the Spirit into the wilderness and into the thick of temptation. Why? To learn about the pitfalls of life. To teach us how to pray.

As he listed the essential elements of prayer in a much later sermon on a Galilean hillside, surely Jesus was remembering his struggle with evil and the temptations he had overcome. Temptations are often camouflaged as blessings which offer the unsuspecting an exit when there seems to be no way out. The most dangerous come in the guise of goodness when a person is down for the count. Such were the temptations Jesus encountered during his forty-day sojourn in the wilderness as he prepared for an intensive ministry among us. Such are the temptations we too encounter as we carry out our own ministries in the world.

If you are who you say you are—Satan sets Jesus up, then tosses him the challenge—turn these stones into bread! An irresistible temptation, a double-pronged temptation, the chance to alleviate an excruciating hunger and to show that it is God who is in charge. Yet Jesus resisted the temptation, for only God calls forth the power of God. The Israelites in their wilderness wandering were given manna to sustain them. We are given the bread of life. "I am the bread of life," says Jesus. I was once hungry, desperately hungry. Come to me, all you who hunger, and you will never be hungry again. Only one who has experienced real hunger understands what hunger is about. "Give us this day our daily bread." This prayer is for all who hunger for survival, who like Jesus are tempted to compromise their souls to satisfy the hunger within.

Jesus endured three temptations in the wilderness. The final two seem intertwined. One addresses political power and the human tendency to dominate and control other people; the other, religious power, as it puts to the test the extent to which religion seeks control over God. Power and prestige are promised to all who would worship other gods. The molten calf of the Israelites, the metallic missiles our technology has spawned, the dogmatic assumptions that proliferate when we are no longer in control: how prone we are to bow down before the gods of our own making, to proclaim ourselves invulnerable, to pronounce our systems impregnable when we preach from our holy places and parade from our pinnacles of power. Jesus resisted on our behalf, then taught us to pray to the one holy God, incarnate on earth, transcendent in heaven, "hallowed be your name." Like Jesus, in baptism, we too renounce Satan's seditious, seductive ways. We pray for the dominion of God to come on earth as it is in heaven, where justice prevails, where domination and oppression are no more.

The temptation to succumb to irresponsible sensuality, religious domination, and oppressive power will haunt us all our personal and political lives, distracting body and mind and spirit with issues of status and control. Jesus was besieged by these temptations when he was least able to resist them. How he handled the onslaught, what we might learn from his experience, are our lessons for today.

At the heart of temptation is the tiny word "if." If you really are of God, Satan said to Jesus. If there really is a God, we are prone to say in times of anguish, then what we want will surely be done. If we do not fail to worship, then God will see to our reward. That "if" is the evil among us.

"Deliver us from evil." Only a person who has been seriously threatened emphasizes liberation. Only one who has known the influence of evil and the relief of divine deliverance could promise us that we will encounter no temptation that is more than we can bear.

There is no escaping the wilderness. It guards every promise and surrounds all success. The wilderness is teeming with temptation. After the devil departed in defeat, Jesus returned to Galilee in the power of the Spirit, and all who heard him were amazed. Like Jesus, we are led by the Spirit into the wilderness, to and through temptation, on route to our promised lands. Like Jesus we emerge in the power of the Spirit to preach good news to the poor, to free those who are imprisoned, to liberate those who are oppressed, to proclaim the victory of God, and to pray:

> Forgive us our sins
> as we forgive those who sin against us.
> And lead us not into temptation
> but deliver us from evil,
> for yours is the sovereignty and the power
> and the glory forever. Amen.

Miriam Therese Winter, S.C.M.M.

R SECOND SUNDAY IN LENT

R *Gen 15:5–12,17–18; Phil 3:17–4:1; Lk 9:28b-36*

We have arrived at one of those high points in our liturgical calendar. Today Luke's gospel takes us up on the Mount of Transfiguration, along with Jesus, Moses, and Elijah, and Peter, James, and John. From atop this mountain we can look back to the peaks of Christmas, Epiphany, and the baptism of Jesus. Back there we also heard the word, "This is my Son." From atop the mountain today we can see also in the other direction, toward Jerusalem, and Mount Calvary, where another voice will say, "This was the Son of God." This time, though, it would be the Roman centurion who spoke, and Jesus would be dead. Today, however, we can see for a moment beyond even that mountain, to the peaks of the resurrection. Today's mountain is something of a midpoint in the journey we take each year with Jesus.

There was plenty of conversation on the Mount of Transfiguration it seems, but only Luke tells us what Jesus, Moses, and Elijah talked about. Most literally, Luke's summary says they spoke of the exodus which Jesus was to complete at Jerusalem. That is, they spoke of the work which Moses had never quite finished. Moses had been to the top of the mountain before. He had worked so hard, struggling with Pharaoh, with the murmuring wilderness generation, and mostly with God. And he had got through the wilderness, to the mountain from which he could see the promised land off in the distance. But he got no further. There God took him. It is difficult to imagine that was not a disappointment.

Elijah had been to the mountain before, too, just before God took him home in that sweet, low-swinging chariot. He had been on the mountain to pray, in great discouragement, thinking himself to be the last faithful person left on earth. He had worked and worked, this tireless prophet of God, and look where it had got him! Nowhere, he thought. And then God took him.

That could easily be a picture of most of our lives. We work and work, believing always that soon will come the day when things will fall into place. The struggle will finally be over . . . when I finish school, get a job, get married, recover from this divorce, when my children are grown, when the loans are paid off. Tomorrow. Next year. And sometimes we do make it to the mountain. Things do fall into place and make sense, but then we stumble into another valley beyond. Somehow we never seem to finish, and then God takes us. It is easy enough to know Moses's and Elijah's disappointment.

Luke would invite us, however, to think of ourselves, along with Moses and Elijah, as runners in a race, a long and difficult race, but a race we do not run alone and in which we can hand off to another runner. Moses handed off, finally, to Joshua, and Elijah passed the baton to Elisha. Today we see Moses and Elijah making the last handoff, as it were. They pass the baton to Jesus for the last lap, the anchor stretch. It would be a difficult lap, with the finish line just outside Jerusalem, at Golgotha. There would be no cheering crowds at the finish, but jeers and taunts, and a voice would say, "If you are the Son of God, come down from there!"

We are poised today to run that last lap with Jesus in the season of Lent. We hear the voices, too, some of them from others, the worst from inside ourselves. "You are wrong. You are a fool. You have lost your touch. I'm sorry, there is nothing more we can do for you."

But we hear also that voice which spoke to Jesus, and speaks to us in our baptism, "You are my son, my daughter, the delight of my soul. I give thanks for you every time I think of you." That is the truest truth about any one of us. That voice which drowns out the jeers and criticisms sustains us on this last lap. That voice gives us strength also to carry on for Jesus as his arms and legs and body in the world.

There is also the meal which sustains us on this long run. It is a mountain meal, a share in the banquet at which we will rejoice at the end of all the running on the last holy mountain, where God shall wipe away every tear. It was that meal which Jesus gave to the disciples as they remembered the exodus on the night of Passover, and it is the meal he gives us now for our wilderness journey, our run for Jerusalem, for Golgotha, and finally for the empty tomb. And also on to the holy mountain where we shall join with Moses and Elijah and Jesus, eating and drinking and rejoicing, washing our feet, and telling running stories.

Frederick A. Niedner, Jr.

E   *Gen 15:5–12,17–18; Phil 3:17–4:1; Lk 13:31–35*
L   *Jer 26:8–15; Phil 3:17–4:1; Lk 13:31–35*

The temple in Jerusalem and the palace in Jerusalem sat as two powerful symbols. They were the dwelling place of God and of the king. The Davidic dynasty was viewed as the human manifestation of God's reign. And this extended to the people dwelling in Jerusalem. The expectation was that the Davidic dynasty, the city and the people would receive an abundance of material and spiritual blessings forever.

Loyalty to the temple and to the city of Jerusalem did not fade, even during the exile. From the time of the prophets onward, Jerusalem became even more broadly identified with the people. "Jerusalem" was God's people in every time and place. Jerusalem became the symbol of divine protection. It also became the focus of God's judgment. The prophets ascribed the sins of the nation and its citizens to the city. They saw Jerusalem as an idolatrous city, an unfaithful harlot, the one who chooses political power over faithfulness to God. Jeremiah saw the city as oppressive; Micah saw its ethical and social sins as arising out of the people's religious sins. The prophets preached that only radical conversion could avert the judgment of God who would bring the city, and by extension all the people of God, to account. For their warning, the prophets usually suffered rejection, punishment and even death.

But the people believed that Jerusalem, God's holy city, would always survive. God's blessings would eventually flow from Jerusalem again. The hope was that God would create a new Jerusalem, an even more glorious city. To this glorified city the faithful remnant would return, and God would draw all nations to the new Jerusalem. The inhabitants of the new Jerusalem would live a secure and abundant life, enjoy prosperity and live in joy, giving God thanksgiving and praise. This new Jerusalem would be inaugurated by the king or messiah who would usher in an even more glorious reign of God.

When Jesus laments over Jerusalem, he evokes in his listeners a host of images and expectations: Jerusalem the center of political and religious power, the symbol of God's people, the sign of the people's rejections of God's word, the focus of God's judgment, the hope for peace and prosperity. To all this Jesus preaches judgment. The prophet is going to Jerusalem to pronounce God's word and to face a prophet's death. God's word will be rejected, and God's word incarnate will be killed.

In Lent we travel to Jerusalem with Jesus. We travel a spiritual journey to our own Jerusalem, to our center of power and our place of hope, to hear the word of God to us.

For many of us, our personal Jerusalem is still a combination of the real and symbolic, both palace and temple. For some of us, the primary source of power is political power in Washington. Government will save the world by transforming it. Patriotism becomes a significant part of our religion, and to challenge the government is to challenge God. The temple and the palace, still side by side, imply that the work of the palace is the work of God. For others, the primary source of power is religious power. They look to the church to save the world by transforming it. The church becomes our religion, and to challenge the church is to challenge God.

These places often become our centers of power and hope. We assume that God's power is resident in the places of power in our lives, the government and the church, or perhaps business, the courts or the schools. We assume that when those institutions prosper, their work is of God and is blessed by God.

And when things are going well, it does in fact seem as if that were true. When government regulations benefit me, I do prosper. When the church's ministry affirms me, I feel blessed. When my job pays well and my business makes a healthy profit, I am comfortable and confident. And so it is easy, when things are going well, to assume that the Jerusalem I have created for myself is, in fact, the place of God's dwelling, that I rightly receive God's blessing.

But when the institutions which served as my centers of power and hope judge me; when the government fails me and lowers my standard of living; when I lose my job or my business goes bankrupt; when the church challenges my comfortable lifestyle and says that my living at the cost of others is sinful; when all is not well, my Jerusalem, like the Jerusalem of old, becomes the place where I experience life's failings. Christ's entry into Jerusalem was a messiah's triumphant entry. But, although he spoke God's prophetic word, he did not only die a prophet's death. His resurrection ushered in a new Jerusalem. So we now live in a different world. It is still a world where we encounter injustice, rejection, deprivation and violence. And in this Lenten season we know ourselves a broken and sinful people, living in a broken and sinful world. And yet, we are simultaneously a redeemed people, living in a redeemed world. Christ's life, death and resurrection is salvation for all of us, and it marks the beginning of the new Jerusalem in our midst.

We are called to make the Christ of the new Jerusalem the center of our lives. Through the power of Christ we become partners in transforming the world. None of the institutions of our society, not the government, business, education, the judicial system, not even the church, can transform the world. When we put our faith in those, we discover they give only illusionary peace and prosperity. God may choose to work through those institutions. And we may, at many times in our lives, find God in and through those institutions. But ultimately God is not tied to any given Jerusalem; God in Christ will meet us at any time and in any place, often when and where we least expect it!

"Oh Jerusalem, Jerusalem! How often would I have gathered your children together as a hen gathers her brood under her wings, and you would not." Christ calls us into that eschatological community which is the new Jerusalem. Christ calls us into the protection and care of God, into the challenge and responsibility of being God's people. Christ calls us to face rejection when we proclaim God's word, to receive and bear God's life and love. Christ call us to be Jerusalem, the people of God.

Linda L. Grenz

R   *Ex 3:1–8a,13–15; 1 Cor 10:1–6,10–12; Lk 13:1–9*
E   *Ex 3:1–15; 1 Cor 10:1–13; Lk 13:1–9*
L   *Ex 3:1–8b,10–15; 1 Cor 10:1–13; Lk 13:1–9*

What is it in human nature that we feel the need to blame the victims for their circumstances? In response to the woman beaten or raped, the person with AIDS, the homeless person on the street, the family with a developmentally disabled child, we want to ask: what did they do to deserve this misfortune? What offense did they commit to bring such hardship onto themselves? Implicit in the question is a connection between sin and suffering.

Today's gospel lesson reminds us that such questions are not new to the twentieth century. People approach Jesus about two contemporary disasters. Innocent folk who apparently had come to the temple to offer their sacrifices had been caught in the crossfire of a riot and Pilate's military police. A tower had collapsed and killed eighteen people in Siloam. Telling Jesus the stories, the people wonder: "Were they worse sinners that such suffering befell them?"

What is it in human nature that we feel the need to blame the victims for their circumstances? Perhaps we feel threatened ourselves, and therefore desire to separate ourselves from "those people." We are not like them; "they" are different. What happened to them cannot happen to us. Separated, we will not be contaminated, "catch" whatever it is they have. Or perhaps we simply crave an answer, an explanation, a cause-and-effect equation with which our minds can ascribe sense to something which is senseless.

To those who approach him, Jesus does not answer in the form of an explanation. He answers in the form of a response. "Do you think that these Galileans were worse sinners than all the other Galileans, because they suffered thus? I tell you, no; but unless you repent you will all likewise perish."

With his response, Jesus shifts the focus from "them" and "those people" to "all of us." Jesus does not allow us any false distinctions with which to protect ourselves or think ourselves superior. He rejects the notion that calamities come to people in some kind of payment for their sins. The point is not that "those" people who died in the two disasters were more or less sinful, but that all are sinners and will perish if they do not repent.

All of us stand in need of repentance. A part of our Lenten journey with ashes on our foreheads is the reminder that each one of us carries within the weakness to sin, the vulnerability to suffering, pain, and death. We participate in a society that allows violence toward women in their homes and on the streets. We participate in a society where people are left without shelter or food, fallen in between society's cracks. Psychotherapist John Fortunato encourages us to see that we have participated in a culture that has defined homosexual persons totally by their sexual behavior, refusing to see them as whole persons. Thereby, all of us have fostered some of the promiscuity that is one factor in the spread of AIDS. Our culture's stress on instant self-gratification and our inability to provide a nuclear-free future have contributed to the current drug crisis, yet another factor in its spread.

Jesus' words seem to imply: in all of your concern for "those people," don't think that you are any better. Don't think that you are standing firm and secure. Life for my followers is lived moment by moment, by faith, without any easy guarantees. Placing one's faith in false security is an attempt to live beyond faith in Christ, who is our only security. False security can be the notion that "they" somehow deserve what happens to them. False security can also be the overconfidence in our participation in the sacraments that St. Paul condemns in the second lesson.

With Christ as our security, the question is changed from "where does tragedy and suffering come from?" to "where does it lead?" Does it lead to faith or to despair? Does it lead to compassion or to apathy? Does it lead to an affirmation of life and hope, or to rejection?

Dorothee Soelle, the German theologian, speaks of God's martyrs and the devil's martyrs. Martyrs are people who die in such a way as to bear witness to their faith. By remembering their faith, our own faith is strengthened. Soelle maintains that the forces of despair and disbelief have their own martyrs, people whose suffering and death weakens other people's faith in God and God's world. It is not, however, the circumstances of their death that make them witnesses for or against God. It is our response to their death. Illnesses, accidents, human tragedies kill people. But they do not necessarily kill life or faith. If the death and suffering of someone we love makes us bitter, jealous, against faith, and incapable of happiness, that person has become one of the "devil's martyrs." If suffering and death in someone close to us bring us to explore the limits of our capacity for strength and love and hope, if we are led to discover sources of consolation we never knew before, then with God's help that person has become a witness for the affirmation of life.

We don't need to blame the victims. We don't need to make devil's martyrs. The Lenten call to repent echoed in Jesus' words of this Sunday offers another possibility. There is still time. The parable of the fig tree says that the story is not over yet. The vinedresser says, wait, give more time. And as long as there is still bread and wine for us to share at this table today, as long as there is still water for us to remember our baptism, then there is still time and hope. Time to repent, time to receive forgiveness, and time to live with compassion.

Kendra Nolde

R   *Jos 5:9a,10–12; 2 Cor 5:17–21; Lk 15:1–3,11–32*
E   *Jos 5:9–12; 2 Cor 5:17–21; Lk 15:11–32*
L   *Is 12:1–6; 1 Cor 1:18–31; Lk 15:1–3,11–32*

Forgiveness is both one of the more consoling and one of the more challenging themes in the gospel. The consoling aspect consists in God's mercy and compassion. The challenge lies in our capacity to forgive others. Jesus taught us to pray, "Forgive us as we forgive others." Forgiveness is a major ingredient of salvation.

The Lucan parable raises two questions for us. How can I accept God as the one who forgives? And, how can I begin to be as forgiving and as compassionate as God?

Sometimes we prefer not to talk any longer about sin. How can sin be good news? I grant that much preaching about sin has led to a denial of an individual's self-worth. Yet we must be conscious of our sinfulness in order to hear the good news of God's love. This does not mean putting us down in order to try and pick us back up. But we still need to understand that we are all sinners.

Being a sinner does not mean that I am worthless. Indeed, we have all been created as images of God. The parable of the talents and the industrious servant encourages us to make good use of the gifts God has given us. Even as a sinner I am not devoid of self-worth. But I am *undeserving* of God's infinite, compassionate, generous, faithful love. Although I must accept and never dismiss my created worth, I still must acknowledge my undeservedness before God.

Without having this healthy sense of being a sinner, of being one who does not deserve God's continuing love, of being one who in fact hurts God and offends God's sense of justice, I cannot appreciate one of God's greatest gifts: God's forgiveness and love. Our experience of human relationships can be the same. I cannot identify my own personal worth with deserving another's love. Love is always experienced as grace, as receiving something that I don't deserve. The only proper response is one of gratitude. Gratitude is the capacity to accept my sinfulness and to focus upon God's loving forgiveness.

I have a friend with a philosophical bent. Often when one asks the simple question, "How are you?" his response is, "Better than I deserve." This is not self-rejection but religious insight. Happy is the person who knows God's love. Like the forgiving father in the parable, God is a forgiving mother or father to us.

But the deepened awareness of God's great forgiveness and mercy is not something to take for granted. Rather God challenges us to forgive as we have been forgiven. We may recall the Matthean parable of the debtor whose debts were forgiven but who then exacted strict payment from the servant who owed him. We are outraged at such a person. Yet are we not like that person, like the jealous or unforgiving brother in today's parable? We want justice when it comes to our neighbors but mercy when it comes to God. "An eye for an eye" more often guides our responses to those who have offended us, while at the same time we address God and say, "Forgive me." Such is hypocrisy. We know that God wants us to forgive and love each other just as God forgives and loves us.

In what does such forgiveness consist? Forgiveness does not mean liking someone, or agreeing with them, or setting myself up for repeated hurt. But forgiveness does mean not cutting someone off, not blocking the person from some presence in my life. Forgiveness remains open to reconciliation, healing, and a relationship, whatever form that may take. Forgiveness does not mean denying pain, dismissing hurt, or disregarding feelings. But forgiveness does imply a sense of hope that the future can be different from the past.

Forgiveness is not just a question of personal and interpersonal relationships. Sometimes the greater need may be to forgive myself, or my parents, or a group of people. There must be forgiveness among peoples and nations as well. We must always be the ones ready to forgive. Forgiveness means a willingness to let go of offenses as God does, not storing them up, not letting them harden like cement, not letting them become resentments and bitternesses. Forgiveness implies hearts of flesh rather than hearts of stone.

Who among us would want God to judge us with a heart of stone or in accord with strict justice? So, go and do likewise.

Donald J. Goergen, O.P.

R   FIFTH SUNDAY IN LENT

R   *Is 43:16–21; Phil 3:8–14; Jn 8:1–11*

"Remember not the former things, nor consider the things of old. Behold, I am doing a new thing." Thus God admonishes us as we enter the last week of Lent: Prepare yourselves, for something you have not imagined is about to happen. The day that is coming will not be like any former day. It will come fresh and dazzling as a bright sunrise after a lifetime of drizzle and gloom.

We all know how it stirs us when someone does something really unexpected. The child everyone thought was "slow" suddenly speaks wisdom; the boring teacher one day gives a riveting lecture; the politician manages to break away from posturing and to perform an act of real integrity. Such moments wake us up, put grins on our faces and a new gleam of hope in our hearts.

Yet in all such instances there will be those unwilling to believe any real change has taken place. They will insist that the appearance of "a new thing" is mere deception, or perhaps a fluke. Likewise, we who hear the Scriptures today may be inclined to mutter under our breath that there is nothing new under the sun. Nature will take its course, and what has happened before is what will happen next time. Indeed, most of us have experienced enough shattered expectations to salt us deeply with cynical despair. As we have failed in the past, so we will fail again. As others have failed us in the past, so they will fail us again.

But the Scriptures announce that a new thing is about to happen. The season that hangs heavy upon us now is already beginning to yield to the new growth pushing its way toward the light. Right here in our parish, we are all beginning to scurry about to get ready for the Easter celebration. There is a gathering intensity of singing and practicing and planning and baking. In the midst of all this busyness, which is only going to increase as we approach the great celebration, we will be well advised to take some serious time to ponder Paul's saying: "I count all things as refuse, in order that I may gain Christ."

The new thing that is almost upon us will relativize everything—even our best preparations. Christ, and the power flowing from his resurrection, will make us like people dreaming; on that night we will hardly believe the goodness that is flowing around us on every side.

I am painting this joyous picture for you because there is also another side to today's word: a hard side, a painful side. The joy comes first because it is the heart of the truth. The wealth of Christ is our heritage, and that is overflowing joy. But the pain cannot be ignored. It is the pain that Lent is all about, the purification that goes along with the "new things" of God.

When the wondrous light of Christ dawns in our hearts, the first thing it exposes is our own pettiness and hardheartedness. We, like the scribes and Pharisees of today's gospel text, have spent our life's energies angling to put ourselves up and others down. The scribes and Pharisees set the adulterous woman apart from themselves and accused her before the crowd. Jesus placed her back in their midst, an equal among equals. In doing so, he exposed their sin, equal to, if not greater than, hers.

It was undoubtedly a moment of anguish for them; the gospel depicts them slinking away, one by one. But surely among them were some who felt a dawning joy in this discovery of their membership in the fellowship of sinners, and, even more so, in the totally unexpected gift of Jesus' radical forgiveness of sinners.

This, above all, is the "new thing" God is doing: bringing us out of the isolation created by sin, into a communion of the forgiven. No matter how many times we experience it, no matter how many times we celebrate repentance, eucharist, and Easter, the forgiving embrace of God always comes upon us as brand new, totally unexpected, awesome in its revelation of ourselves and all others as beloved children of God. For over and over again we fall back into the same trap. Like the scribes and Pharisees, our fear causes us to divide the world into a prim circle of respectability (with ourselves inside) and a despised realm of "wild beasts" (where other folk live).

God is doing a new thing: God is breaking down the walls, taming the wild beasts, and bringing us all to a place where all fear and enmity have been cast out. Here in the eucharist, let us welcome one another joyfully as newfound sisters and brothers; and then let each of us go forth to proclaim this good news to whoever is, in our eyes, the least likely candidate for God's forgiving embrace. Only when we have the courage to do this will we know that we are fully ready to let God's new thing have its way with us.

Mary Frohlich

E L FIFTH SUNDAY IN LENT

E   *Is 43:16–21; Phil 3:8–14; Lk 20:9–19*
L   *Is 43:16–21; Phil 3:8–14; Lk 20:9–19*

Each year the readings for this last Sunday in Lent confront us with the Christian claim that the new life we have together is grounded in the suffering and death of Jesus. This is the last of the considerations about the Christian life with which Lent has to do. It opens before us the oldest of Christian convictions: that the suffering and death of Jesus are essential to the plan of salvation. It is with this in mind that we go forward to Holy Week and Easter.

The readings for this year are, frankly, not the easiest to deal with. The passage from the gospel of Luke is a case in point. It is a rather complicated and subtle retelling of the familiar parable of the vineyard which functions as an interpretation of the events which lie just ahead at Jerusalem. Like the other versions of this parable in the gospels, it relies on Isaiah's picturing of Israel as a vineyard about to be rooted up because it has not produced the fruit expected of it. Here, however, the vineyard, in its fourth season, is just about to produce the fruit the owner has been awaiting when the tenants conspire to kill the heir to the property and acquire it for themselves. The suffering and death of Jesus are foretold here as part of the struggle between God's interests and those of others. From the perspective of the author, seeing them in the light of the resurrection, they insure the success of God's plans rather than impeding them.

This point is made again when the words of the psalm are interpreted as foreshadowing what is about to happen: "The very stone which the builders rejected has become the head of the corner." The allusion is to the still-common practice, in that part of the world and elsewhere, of building dry-stone enclosures from the assortment of rocks lying on the hillside. The stability of the finished structure depends on the selection of the right boulder for the cornerstone. The rejection of that boulder—the suffering and death of Jesus—ensures the collapse of the structure and its rebuilding according to the right plan. Portrayed once again is a losing battle against the purposes of God.

The reading ends on an even subtler note. The telling of the parable is a self-fulfilling prophecy. It leads the religious leaders to try to lay hands on Jesus. It is itself part and parcel of the events which it interprets.

Thus far we have heard only that Jesus' suffering and death is an inextricable part of the struggle between God and the leadership over the purpose of Israel. The issues in that struggle, the acceptability of God's message of universal forgiveness and reconciliation, which might be thought to have been foreshadowed in Isaiah's prophecy about God's doing a new thing in contrast to the things of old, are only hinted at here.

The passage from the epistle to the Philippians does much more than that. Here the suffering and death of Jesus inaugurate a new way of life for humanity. The passage, in which Paul states his hope that his life will be conformed to the self-giving life of Christ, is part of the sequence of passages which flow from his account of Jesus as refusing to grasp equality with God, taking the form of a servant, suffering death on the cross, and for this reason being exalted. The name of Jesus, not that of Adam, gives humanity its true identity. Jesus is not merely an example of life lived in the service of God. In him that life is embodied. As Irenaeus would say later, it is made visible. It is rendered accessible for all who live. Paul says that he has given up everything in order to "gain Christ and be found in him," in order to "know Christ and the power of his resurrection," and to "share his sufferings, becoming like Christ in his death."

These words might be thought to flow from some special mysticism were it not that they struggle to say something about life as we all know it. Our lives are inevitably used up for something, even if that something is merely an inherited set of assumptions and conventions to which we conform. These assumptions and conventions may not be immediately or obviously self-serving. They may give meaning and purpose to daily existence. In the end, though, there is this curious contradiction about them: they have to do with a preservation of life which we secretly know is impossible.

In Jesus Christ we are confronted with something different. There we see human life used up and given away for God and others. In him there is missing the contradiction which besets our lives. For him, resurrection is not a reversal or a forestalling of the process of dying, but its conclusion. What is visible in him is life with God.

From this perspective, the suffering and death of Jesus are not merely incidental to the fulfillment of God's purposes. They are the inauguration of a new humanity into which we may hope, with Paul, that our lives are being taken up, freed from the self-serving assumptions and conventions which now inform the way we live them, placed already now at the service of God and others.

These readings, then, confront us once again with the Christian claim that the new life we have together is grounded in the suffering and death of Jesus Christ. In a different idiom but with no less persuasiveness, the eucharist we now celebrate confronts us with this same claim. To eat the broken bread and to drink from the cup, and to say Amen to the declaration that they are the body and blood of Christ, is to acknowledge that we have been given a share in the new human life of Jesus Christ. It is then for us to say in what other actions of ours that new life will be manifest.

Lloyd G. Patterson

R L SUNDAY OF THE PASSION
E   PALM SUNDAY

R   *Is 50:4–7; Phil 2:6–11; Lk 22:14–23:56*
E   *Is 45:21–25; Phil 2:5–11; Lk 23:1–49*
L   *Deut 32:36–39; Phil 2:5–11; Lk 22:1–23:56*

Jesus said to the thief, "Truly, I say to you, today you will be with me in Paradise." With what measure of confidence in that promise, do you suppose, did the thief live the rest of his life? With what measure of confidence in Jesus' promise do we live out our lives? Jesus said to his disciples and to us, "Lo, I am with you always, to the close of the age." The thief's life was only a matter of a few more hours. The test of his faith but brief. Our part of "the age" may last until three score or more.

The rest of the thief's life was spent hanging there in agony on his cross. After hearing that promise, it would be one thing to have some level of hope while there still was movement, even words, from that center cross. But what about after Jesus cried with a loud voice, "Father, into your hands I commit my spirit!"

What about the hours left to him after it was clear that Jesus "had breathed his last," that there was no evidence of any life or concern or possible help from that center cross? What could sustain confidence for the future when the promiser could not hold out in the present? And then, after hours of silence from a dead savior, soldiers came to break the legs of the crucified three, one more insult, one more demonstration of the domination by evil. They did not even bother to break the bones of Jesus, seeing he was already dead. No possibility for faith in the promise and the future: how could there be after that? We hear a sardonic testimony by the military on the impotence of deity.

Is our situation so very different? Hanging between earth and heaven, day by day, year by year: it is a description of human existence. For many of us suffering is as life-suffocating as Jesus' suffering. Some are tormented only with meaninglessness, guilty of sins not realized, under judgment for crimes too well remembered. Many of us are confused, ignorant of life's meaning and goal, certain only of doubt. What sustains faith when God is dead? Some circumstances would seem almost to justify a stance of doubt. How could a good God permit so much evil to fall upon creatures whom God proposes to love?

When with each Lent the image of the dying Jesus is impressed on the eyes of the world, even on those eyes which see only television, what are the reactions? There are the same unbelieving demands, "Are you not the Christ? Save yourself and us!" Some others acknowledge their own failures and admit responsibility, even rebuke the unbeliever, "Do you not fear God? We are receiving the due reward of our deeds." And some concede that he was a good man. "This man has done nothing wrong." There are some who cry for help, "Jesus, remember me if and when you come into your kingdom." But where are the throngs pressing into the kingdom to claim the promises of the Savior?

Is this only a description of lives in Lent, of lives that look to the future? What of our day-by-day lives when we think only of this time on earth? The promise made to us by God-in-Christ is, "Lo, I am with you always." That includes now, each now. And it extends to the end of the age, even to our old age. Like the first thief, do we call him the Christ but not really believe that he is God's Son, savior of the world? Some live through their days on earth as if God had neither made it nor redeemed it.

And yet, in the midst of all these passers-by, some wagging their heads, some looking the other way, some completely oblivious, God's only begotten Son was not spared, but God was delivering him up for us all. The Son had willingly given up godhead and taken on human nature, become subject to the law of God, submitted to the curse on others' sins, and offered his life in death on the cross. To despair of God in the face of what we know to be true—by faith, it is true—is but foolishness and inconsistency. God did not spare Jesus, the beloved Son: can we expect to be spared? But God did that all for us: can we expect anything less than that God will freely give us all things?

How could God prove trustworthiness, faithfulness? How could God keep promises? Think about the thieves again. What if the thieves had lingered on in their suffering, hanging between earth and heaven, for three days (or for the totality of three score years and ten, and even in spite of weakness, what would seem like four score years) as we do; and then, when the bone-breaking crunch came, the soldiers would say, "You know, that man who was crucified with you on the center cross, the one we took down on Friday late? Well, he was buried over in the garden, and some of the soldiers in our squadron were sent to guard the opening of the grave where they had rolled a great stone. You should hear their story! The stone was rolled away while they were shocked into some kind of trance. And when they came to and looked, the grave was empty! The word is that he is alive. He has risen from the grave, risen from the dead!"

What if the thieves had known of his resurrection even in their very moments of dying? Is not that the very way God has made good on the promise that whoever believes in Jesus Christ will not perish but have everlasting life? How differently the phrases "Today, paradise" and "with you always" sound when the "I lay down my life and on the third day I take it up again" is known to be true. How different all the promises sound when remembered with the resurrection.

The Lord is not content simply to repeat over and over, "It is I, myself. Behold, I live!" He says to us as he said to those first disciples, "Have you anything here to eat?" And when they gave him a piece of broiled fish, he took it and ate before them. To us he says, "Take and eat, take and drink." And so we eat with him and know he is risen, and we trust ever more surely that he is with us even to the end of the age.

Still the tendons tear, the bones are broken, the agony goes on. But the promise is made sure in the resurrection; the promise remains for every day. And look: the table is set, the cloth is spread. Come, for all things are now ready!

George W. Hoyer

R HOLY THURSDAY
E MAUNDY THURSDAY

R *Ex 12:1–8,11–14; 1 Cor 11:23–26; Jn 13:1–15*
E *Ex 12:1–14a; 1 Cor 11:23–26; Jn 13:1–15*

At any distance from childhood or poolside, there's a reluctance in our North American culture to go barefoot. "The soil is bare now, nor can foot feel, being shod,"[49] wrote Gerard Manley Hopkins, who saw there our distance from God and from nature. It was thought a personal idiosyncrasy of President Richard Nixon that he wore shoes even when out for a stroll on the beach, but perhaps it is more deeply characteristic of our paved-over civilization, our well-shod ways. C.S. Lewis thought that we all ought to be able to get outdoors some time every day and put our feet, not just our shoes, on the earth. Not just on blacktop or concrete, but the earth.

"Put off your shoes from your feet," God told Moses, "for the place on which you are standing is holy ground." Recently an illiterate but highly articulate campesino in El Salvador welcomed us North American visitors to the once bombed and now resurrected village near Agua Cayo. He stood unashamedly in his bare feet. "We have achieved coming here with thousands of sacrifices," he said. Helicopters scourged the noonday with noise above us. How beautiful are the feet of the one who brings good news, Isaiah sang. The campesinos had made their exodus from resettlement camps far away, across a wilderness, beyond the mountain. Their feet were bruised and blistered. But in exile at Patmos, John saw the feet of the heavenly Human One, and they were now beautiful, as burnished bronze.

There are many references to "feet" in any concordance of the Scriptures, but only a few entries for "shoes." With our shoes on, we have walked so far from this truth of Scripture that, until recently, the Lord's own service of footwashing was observed only in marginal communities of Christians, or at Rome once a year by the Pope. A liturgical fad a few years ago had the clergy shining shoes on Maundy Thursday, as an update of footwashing. But the New Testament connects footwashing to baptism, and to the church's preeminent style of ministry as hospitality to the shoeless poor, and it is hard to see how we could so easily have stomped through the centuries with our shiny shoes on. Jesus asks that our ministry partake of his own style of ministry. Jesus lays aside his garment, he divests and empties himself and pours out service to his own, as a sign and order to ministry, and Peter objects. Earlier in John's gospel, it is Judas who objects when Mary of Bethany kneels to splash the feet of Jesus with a costly ointment, and to dry them with her hair, which the apostle Paul calls a "glory." In the gospels, it is women and slaves who are associated with the ministry of footwashing, and it is a patriarchal, financially preoccupied church that objects. The church's managers, with pride and pretense, can easily turn away the Savior's style of ministry. But Jesus insists upon this ministry, and even identifies himself with the poor of history before whom the church is called to kneel in humble service. Footwashing requires divestment of privilege, the taking up of the towel of intimate service, the pouring out of self in renewed baptism, the use of what one is in fact wearing for the service of the poor. It is Jesus' style of ministry, and he ordains it, and names its sign.

The Velez-Paiz hospital in Managua is dedicated to children from all over the country who are burn and trauma patients. Some there are victims of Contra land mines, called in Spanish "quitadedos," because they "take off the toes." Children hobble about on crutches or lie legless, footless in their beds. How can we do Maundy Thursday with them? Liturgical forms cannot do all the truth. In John's gospel, the resurrected Christ will show a fearful young church his own wounded hands and side. Curiously, his wounded feet are not mentioned there. Where can we find them? Will we find a way to do the Maundy now, the new commandment of love? Can we trace the footsteps and kneel to clasp the feet of the Risen One? "Be swift my soul to answer him, be jubilant, my feet," sang Julia Ward Howe.[50] It may be that in the bruised bare feet of the world's poor, and in the burnished, wounded feet of the world's oppressed, God's truth is marching on. This may be the Maundy service Jesus spoke of when he said, "You also ought wash one another's feet."

Grant M. Gallup

[49]Gerard Manley Hopkins, "God's Grandeur, *The Poems of Gerard Manley Hopkins,* ed. W.H. Gardner and N.H. Mackenzie (London: Oxford, 1967), p. 66.
[50]Julia Ward Howe, "Mine Eyes have Seen the Glory," *Worship,* 3rd ed. (Chicago: GIA, 1986), #686.

L   MAUNDY THURSDAY

L   *Jer 31:31–34; Heb 10:15–39; Lk 22:7–20*

Looking back so that we can look forward is a common practice. We celebrated the bicentennial of the United States Constitution by first looking back. We remembered the struggle to overcome the injustice of a colonial power and the chaos following the victory at Yorktown. We rejoiced in awe that a debate among fine ideals and brutal interests could forge a new instrument of government.

From the distance of two hundred years of remarkable success under that instrument of government, we not only remembered, we rejoiced. We remembered and rejoiced for the gifts of the past to our present and, more importantly, for the gifts of the past to our future.

Whenever we look back as we did with the bicentennial of the Constitution, we take our bearings on this past and by means of these bearings mark out a path for our future. The fine ideals and brutal interests of the past have been replaced with new ones. However, the new ideals and interests also conflict. Precisely because chaos and injustice are at hand in the future, we create law to secure order and justice in our future. Through our ritual memory the past becomes present, and through this remembering and rejoicing we reaffirm the law and secure our future. We look back so that we can look forward.

Luke's account of the Passover meal of Jesus and his disciples has these same circumstances and motivations. The Passover is a ritual remembering, an anamnesis that is already many centuries old. Israel remembers as deliverance from bondage, the bloody sacrifices of lambs and Egyptians, its journey through the wilderness, the gift of the law from Sinai's smoking heights, the murmuring of the people as the journey lengthened, and the conquest of the promised land. Through this ritual remembering, the past is made present.

The law given at Sinai is made present. Children ask questions that lead to yet another generation's interpretation of that law. One more generation remembers, rejoices, and interprets the law. One more generation takes up the task of mapping out a secure future on the basis of the law.

Jesus' disciples, true to form, begin disputing among themselves their future. They disagree on which of them is to be regarded as the greatest. They are no fools; they know that what is taking place will be remembered and others will rejoice. They want to secure their futures. They know now is the time when they have a fresh beginning to establish their individual interests.

Jesus' reply is disconcerting. "The rulers of the Gentiles are domi-neering, and those in authority over them are called benefactors. But not so with you; rather let the greatest among you become as the youngest, and the leader as one who serves. For which is the greater, one who sits at table, or one who serves? But I am among you as one who serves."

His reply is disconcerting for many reasons. It imagines a great break with the normal way of securing our futures. It describes a world where the servants will be the greatest, not because they finally establish the dictatorship of the proletariat, but precisely because they serve. It points to Jesus' own serving as the trajec-tory of the future.

It disconcerts the disciples' neat pattern of looking back so that they can look forward. It imagines a new future so radically dif-ferent that it disrupts any easy continuities with the past. This future turns the law upside down and leaves the disciples with no security. They have no guarantees as to who will be on top. Jesus' reply disconcerts because it welcomes the chaos of the kingdom of God. It makes clear how radically different this do-minion is.

Jesus invites them to take this cup and bread. He identifies the bread as his body. He states that the chaos of this kingdom is so close that he will not drink of the fruit of the vine until the rule of God comes. He invites them to join him. This invitation changes the disciples' future. One will betray him. Others will flee in fear. The faithful will take on a new way of being in the world. Far from securing their futures, this meal is placing them in jeopardy.

What of us? What of our ritual remembering, our anamnesis? Are we not looking back so that we can look forward? Are we not busy securing our futures by making the past present?

We are. We are looking back. We remember this last supper. We remember how we too seek to secure our futures by acting domi-neering over others— spouse over spouse, marrieds over singles, parents over children, bosses over employees, clergy over laity,

Christians over Jews and every other religious force that threatens our image of the future.

We remember our Lord's disconcerting reply. It is at once both threat and promise, threat insofar as we act domineering, promise insofar as we are taken up into the rule of God. We remember his promise that through word, wine, and bread we are taken up, once again, into that rule of God. We are fed his body and made one with him in the will of his Father through the power of the Holy Spirit.

However, in this service, we do more than remember and rejoice. Over these next three days we enter the chaos that Jesus spoke of, the chaos of the passage from death to life. We step into our future; we are assured only by our baptism that we share Jesus' death and resurrection. Removed from any law that can secure our future, we enter the paschal mystery of the gospel. In this mystery we make no predictions. We secure no plans of government, family, or church. We simply are abandoned to the promise of life in Jesus Christ. We trust the promise and seek to be transformed by its power.

As you step forward this evening and receive our Lord's body and blood, you step forward into this promise. Beyond this meal there is only the certainty of God's rule in a future made present. Come. Our Lord earnestly desires to eat this meal with you. Come with your desire to secure your future by acting domineering and leave it at this altar. Come with all your memories, good and bad. Come into this future made present, in Jesus' name.

Patrick Keifert

R   *Is 52:13–53:12; Heb 4:14–15;5:7–9; Jn 18:1–19:42*
E   *Is 52:13–53:12; Heb 10:1–25; Jn 19:1–37*
L   *Is 52:13–53:12; Heb 4:14–16;5:7–9; Jn 18:1–19:42*

The silence and simplicity that surround us, gathered as a Christian community on Good Friday, are meant to focus our minds and hearts on the centrality of God's redemptive love poured out for us in the death and resurrection of Jesus Christ. In the early church, Good Friday, Holy Saturday and Easter Sunday comprised the Paschal Triduum. Each day honored one aspect of the single paschal mystery of Christ crucified, buried and risen. In the seventh century when Holy Thursday shifted from being a day for the reconciliation of public penitents to a time for commemorating the Lord's Supper, the old Paschal Triduum yielded to a new Triduum of Holy Thursday, Good Friday and Holy Saturday. The focused vision on the single mystery of Christ crucified, buried and risen was yielding to an attempt to recreate liturgically the historical sequence of Jesus' passion. The danger was that the celebration of the paschal mystery would be replaced by a liturgical passion play.

Although contemporary liturgical renewal has sought to restore the centrality of the paschal mystery during Holy Week, we must constantly refocus our vision on Christ crucified, buried and risen for our salvation. This is especially true with regard to Good Friday since its celebration represents the linking together of liturgical services from diverse traditions and different periods of history whose unity of focus is not always clear. Christians in this century observe Good Friday with a diversity of historical practices: the fourth century Roman tradition of readings and bidding prayers; the fourth century Jerusalem tradition of venerating the cross; and the early medieval tradition of receiving holy communion outside of the celebration of the eucharist itself. Besides these liturgical traditions from patristic and medieval times, there are also many devotional traditions from the Reformation on that have become associated with Good Friday.

In the midst of this collage of traditions and devotions that surround Good Friday, we must focus clearly on the readings of the day—the servant song from Isaiah, the passage from the letter to the Hebrews, and the passion according to St. John—to enter into the true meaning of this paschal celebration. The readings do not seek to evoke a sense of guilt in us because our sins have caused the sinless Jesus to suffer and die. Nor do the readings strive to create feelings of compassion to make us wish that we had been historically present at the crucifixion so that we could have consoled Jesus in his sufferings. The readings are not concerned with our personal feelings in relationship to Christ's passion. Rather they proclaim what God has done for us in Christ and bid us anew to receive the gift of God's redemptive love in our lives.

The opening words of the first reading from the prophet Isaiah proclaim the good news of God's paschal victory in Christ: "Behold, my servant shall prosper, shall be exalted and lifted up." Joined to that Isaian theme is the Johannine theme that permeates the passion narrative: "And I, when I am lifted up from the earth, will draw the whole world to myself." The Isaian text does not deny the terrible sufferings that the servant must undergo; but the emphasis is not upon the horror of these sufferings. Rather it seeks to proclaim their significance within God's plan of salvation: "But he was wounded for our transgressions, and was bruised for our iniquities; the chastisement that made us whole was upon him, by whose stripes we are healed." In identifying the Isaian servant with the Johannine Jesus, the liturgy of Good Friday sees the crucified one, lifted up, as drawing all humankind to himself, so that his wounds can be the source of healing unto new life.

On Good Friday we gather as a Christian community around the proclamation of the paschal mystery in Isaiah, Hebrews and John's passion narrative to receive God's gift of new life in Jesus Christ crucified and risen. We bring the truth of our wounded lives as individuals, as a community and as members of the human family. And in the very proclamation of the good news of God's redemptive love in Christ, we are embraced by the One lifted up in his crucifixion so that our wounded lives can be drawn anew into his life-giving wounds. The blood and water from his pierced side become a stream of new life racing as a torrent of healing and peace through all the ruins and desert places of our hearts. Here is the central message of the paschal mystery on Good Friday: by his wounds we are healed anew unto life and the compassionate service of others.

Let us in faith place the woundedness of our personal and corporate lives once more into the wounds of Christ so that we may receive the gift of new life and healing promised to us in the word of God. Let us allow God's gift of grace to make these gifts of life and healing a lived reality so that we witness in truth what we petition in the bidding prayers. Indeed let us lift high the life-giving cross as a sign of our faith in what God is ever doing for us in Jesus Christ crucified and risen. For in this celebration, the wounds of Jesus, the One lifted up on the cross, have become once more our reconciliation with God and with our sisters and brothers.

Thomas McGonigle, O.P.

R E L EASTER VIGIL

R   *Rom 6:3–11; Lk 24:1–12*
E   *Rom 6:3–11; Mt 28:1–10*
L   *1 Cor 15:1–11; Lk 24:1–11*

All over the Christian world adults are being initiated into Christ on this night. The saving waters of baptism are being poured on them, they are being sealed in the Spirit with chrism, and they are leading other believers toward the eucharistic table to partake of the bread and cup, Christ Jesus our Lord. These new Christians are not egregious sinners. Most of them are people of absolutely upright life whom the religious tradition of their childhood, if there was one, may have passed by. Their experience of life, their friendships, perhaps their marriage has led them to seek entry into a communion that keeps to the ancient ways. They are being initiated into Christ on Easter night with the full celebration of word and sacrament.

Whoever these candidates are and whatever action of grace brought them to font and altar, they are sinners. They are sinners because they are human beings. No one escapes the heritage of disobedience of our father Adam. Alienation from God is as much a part of us as breath and life as we come from the womb. That is why we say with St. Paul of our new Christians that they were baptized into the death to sin of Christ Jesus. United with him in a death like his, they hope certainly to be united with him in a resurrection like his. Their baptism anticipates it, of course. Resurrection has not happened yet to any of the baptized, only to him. But the one thing the persons washed with water and the Holy Spirit have put behind them is the hereditary sin which has death as its punishment.

St. Paul said of Christ that, having paid the penalty of sin, this sinless one was free of death's dominion. The baptized are like Christ in that they too have left something behind in the tomb of the waters that engulfed them. It is their old self, crucified with him. Their sinful selves have been sloughed off like a snake's skin. Slaves to sin went down into the baptismal bath. Free persons who need no longer be beholden to sin came forth.

Is it true? Are any of these things true that St. Paul believes and we, ever since, believe with him? Just ask one of these new believers, "new" in a public, sacramental sense. They will tell you that there is not a scrap of fiction about it. Figure, yes, but not fiction, for these great truths about new life are so great that ordinary language is not equal to them. Only metaphor can handle them.

Does it sound as if today's Easter celebration is mostly about risen Christians and only secondarily about the risen Christ? In fact, there can be no first or second importance here, for the two resurrections are totally correlative. "Christ died for our sins . . . he was buried . . . [and] was raised on the third day" only so that Cephas, the twelve and the more than five hundred at once, then James and all the apostles and Paul, and you and I, could hear the gospel and be raised up with him. The one is purposeless, or even impossible, without the other.

It is absolutely fitting to proclaim the account of Christ up from the tomb on a night such as this. To omit reading the gospel narrative would be like playing Hamlet without the prince of Denmark. The number of youths or messengers at the tomb is not important. Neither is the conduct of the women, aside from telling us of their fidelity and concern when all of Jesus' male companions were paralyzed with fear. St. Luke expresses well the central point of all the risen-life narratives: "Why do you seek the living among the dead?" Jesus is the living one. He is not merely a person resuscitated, like Lazarus and the daughter of Jairus and the son of the widow of Naim, but a person alive. Jesus' life is different. It is the life of the new age. It is the existence to which Israel felt called over many centuries and to which we look forward in virtue of our baptism.

We read a compendium of Bible readings tonight in the vigil service because we claim Israel's history as our history. From the story of creation to the writings of the prophets and the psalms, we experience ourselves to be a people called. Jesus' brief career is all of a piece with that of his people. In his death as a persecuted Jew, faithful to God to the end, he expects his friends to bring word of this reconciling act to a world dead in sin. The marvel has happened. The gospel has reached us. A question for us is, does it make any difference?

I do not put the question as it touches our individual lives of faith. Undoubtedly it does. We dare to hope that we shall live again. Our faith conviction is that if sin cannot master us, the grave cannot hold us. But that can be a private treasure, a product not for export. I ask another question. What difference does it make to world markets, to oppressed peoples, to the poorest of the poor, that we believe in resurrection from sin and death? Have *they* felt the difference that our faith has made? To whom, if to anyone, have we proclaimed, "He is not here. He is risen," in a way that made any real difference to them?

This is not an Easter question. It is the Easter question.

Gerard S. Sloyan

R E EASTER DAY
L THE RESURRECTION OF OUR LORD

R   *Acts 10:34a,37–43; Col 3:1–4; Jn 20:1–9*
E   *Acts 10:34–43; Col 3:1–4; Lk 24:1–10*
L   *Ex 15:1–11; 1 Cor 15:1–11; Lk 24:1–11*

The much disputed movie *The Last Temptation of Christ* had at least one triumphantly startling moment. That was the raising of Lazarus. In the chaos before the tomb, Jesus commands the stone to be removed. His uncertain cry, "Lazarus, come out," produces no effect. Jesus draws nearer the dark opening, and repeats the command. Then, in the eerie stillness, Jesus falls to his knees and prays.

The silence is overwhelming. The angle of the camera captures Jesus' struggle. Suddenly an alarming hand pierces onto the screen. Jesus, frightened, hesitates. Then he reaches into the darkness and takes the hand. For a moment, it seems like a battle, as the dead man seems able to pull Jesus into the darkness. But Jesus rallies and brings Lazarus, like a drowning man, forth from the tomb, ashen white and covered with dirt. Yet the momentary stark terror on Jesus' face as death dragged him into the darkness of the earth is what I remember.

This is what we have been doing this past week, following the steps of Jesus, going to the edge of the tomb, kneeling in trust at the very place of defeat, there to let the power of God show forth, however it will. We're not well rehearsed in this. We fear death with all its harbingers, old age and disease. Like those who fall down on their faces in terror at the tomb, we run from opportunities to witness the power of God over the power of death.

I see this battle worked out whenever we bury our dead. The liturgy for the burial of the dead is one of the most uplifting in the whole Christian liturgy. In it, questions about God's existence and the Christian life are decidedly sidelined by sure proclamation of the resurrection into life.

Meanwhile, the funeral director does his work. He and his impeccably dressed assistants have one goal. They don't want you to see the dirt. Unlike Lazarus, who comes from the tomb wearing the dust he had become, our dead are cosmetically reclaimed for final viewing. Thus, at grave side, morticians use a kind of green rug to cover the upper edges of the hole they've dug, with astroturf covering the mound of displaced earth. Nor do they want you to think about dirt. The big selling point in coffins is waterproof-ness: as long as they're greening up the dirt, they might as well sell you a rubber seal in the lid. When the assembly arrives at the grave, the funeral director always whispers to the pastor, "Do you use sand?" The funeral director is glad to assist, strewing on the casket his clean white sand.

Maybe they don't think people are strong enough to face the reality of "earth to earth, ashes to ashes, dust to dust." But if we are able this morning to come to the edge of this tomb, we are also able to sound a proclamation which all of Lent and Holy Week have been preparing us for. Whether we whisper it in prayer before the darkness, or dive in to grasp hold of it and pull it forth like a man drowning, we proclaim, Christ is risen!

The profound change we experience in Holy Week, beginning with Jesus' triumphal entry into Jerusalem but quickly transformed into cries of "crucify him," has hauled us through death. This story, central to the Christian Scriptures, teaches us closely to follow Jesus as he prepares for his transfiguration on the cross. Baptism itself, during the dark hours of the vigil, is another such foray. There is a death we die when we give ourselves wholly to God, and in the waters of baptism we are united to Jesus in death to be finally and irretrievably pulled from the tomb of mortal life into God's dominion. In our community we know both the reality of death and the unshakable promise of the empty tomb. Nor is it wise to stray too far from these profound truths, as each Sunday we evoke the empowering experiences of our hope in water, bread, and wine. The resurrection of Jesus has changed death. No longer can we look on death and see only death.

Moreover, we are called to go forth with the women from the empty tomb to all the places of struggle, all the greened-up tombs our culture makes, there to witness to the power of God. Our society has massively abandoned those defeated by AIDS, homelessness, and drugs. The thinly veiled mark of death terrifies people, and they run. But, given to forays into death, we know death has been defeated. Therefore we are called to wait for the power of God's promise to show itself in the lives of all the abandoned ones.

Jeffrey A. Merkel

R E L SECOND SUNDAY OF EASTER

R   *Acts 5:12–16; Rev 1:9–11a,12–13,17–19; Jn 20:19–31*
E   *Acts 5:12a,17–22,25–29; Rev 1:9–19; Jn 20:19–31*
L   *Acts 5:12,17–32; Rev 1:4–18; Jn 20:19–31*

Easter is a time of life triumphant over death, of light radiant beyond darkness. It is a festival of victory and triumph, of glad celebration and joyous festival. Yet, here we are one week after the feast, and the gospel confronts us with fear, doubt and uncertainty. The disciples are gathered in a room with the doors shut. They are afraid for themselves. After all, their teacher and Lord had just been executed; who among them would be next to die? They gather together in mutual support and solidarity as well as in shared terror.

Precisely in the midst of that fear, terror and isolation, Jesus came and stood among them. To their terror Jesus spoke words of peace. To their isolation Jesus spoke words of empowerment and forgiveness, words which strengthened and commissioned them for ministry.

There are parts of the church catholic today that know this very juxtaposition of fear with peace, isolation with empowerment. Consider Central America. In her poetry, Julia Esquivel voices the cry of fear and pain that Central Americans know too, too well. She articulates the cycle of death and despair that prevails, the fear that drives one indoors, the terror that isolates sister from brother as well as friend from foe. In poetic phrase and form she speaks of the magnitude with which death stalks the terrain:

> Now six of them have left us,
> and nine in Rabinal,
> and two, plus two, plus two,
> and ten, a hundred, a thousand,
> a whole army
> witness to our pain,
> our fear,
> our courage,
> our hope![51]

But look! As with John, Julia Esquivel couples pain with courage, fear with hope. She goes on to speak in this poem of being "threatened with resurrection":

> Because in this marathon of Hope,
> there are always others to relieve us
> in bearing the courage necessary
> to arrive at the goal
> which lies beyond death. . . .

In a similar way, Jesus threatens the disciples with resurrection. On the evening of his resurrection, Jesus calls the disciples forth from fear and gives them peace. Jesus breathes on the disciples and bestows on them the Holy Spirit. The scene evokes Genesis. In that creation account, God inspired the breath/spirit of life into the human one, and life began. In John's new creation account, Jesus breathes upon the disciples and a new creation is born: the disciples filled with the new life of the Spirit. Jesus further threatens the disciples with resurrection by commissioning them to a ministry of forgiveness of sins. They are called out of their isolation and fear into a ministry which re-presents Christ's own ministry of forgiveness and reconciliation.

Thomas, the Twin, eternally dubbed "The Doubter" by generations of Sunday School teachers, is also called away from isolation, fear and uncertainty into the community of peace, empowerment and ministry. With his own fingers in contact with the wounds of Christ, Thomas is threatened with resurrection and incorporated into the community of belief.

So it is for us. We who sometimes too easily call ourselves disciples, followers of Christ, Christians; we too are threatened with resurrection in our encounter with the wounded, yet risen Christ. Our encounters seem tame by comparison. We encounter this wounded, risen one in the word, in baptismal bathing, and in the shared meal. But such an encounter, far from being tame, confronts us to the core of our being and threatens us with resurrection.

In word and sacraments we are drawn away from isolation and fear, gifted with community, peace, forgiveness and power for ministry. We are threatened with resurrection in that we are dared to offer our lives to Christ and spend our lives for others. Our natural doubts are at once acknowledged, yet transformed within our liturgical encounter with the wounded, risen Christ.

In that encounter we are not abandoned and left alone. The same gifts that John describes as given to the disciples are also graciously, mercifully granted to us. In our baptism, by water and the Spirit we are washed into the community of believers. We encounter Christ's wounds and are marked with the cross of Christ. We are baptized into Christ's death that we might share Christ's resurrection. We are given peace, forgiveness, and community and are commissioned for ministry.

In the eucharist we feed upon Christ's broken body and shed blood. In so doing, we are intimately sustained and upheld by Christ's saving presence. We are fed and made companions of Christ. We are sent forth as ministers of Christ to share the peace which we have received, to proclaim the good news that we have heard, to announce the forgiveness of sins with which we have been blessed, to strive for the justice which we have experienced within the liturgical assembly.

> Accompany us then on this vigil
> and you will know what it is to dream!
> You will then know
> how marvelous it is
> to live threatened with Resurrection!

Stephen M. Larson

[51]Julia Esquivel, "They Have Threatened Us With Resurrection," *Threatened with Resurrection: Prayers amd Poems from an Exiled Guatemalan* (Elgin, Illinois: The Brethren Press, 1982), pp.59–63.

R E L THIRD SUNDAY OF EASTER

R *Acts 5:27b-32,40b-41; Rev 5:1–14; Jn 21:1–19*
E *Acts 9:1–19a; Rev 5:6–14; Jn 21:1–14*
L *Acts 9:1–20; Rev 5:11–14; Jn 21:1–14*

Have you ever found yourself in the pages of the Bible? You've been reading along, following some story, and then, suddenly, you discover events, situations, attitudes, and reactions which could be your own. You, and your problems, are no longer alone. You are there. You are somehow mirrored in Scripture. And others, you begin to realize, have been where you are. They seem to share your fears, your hopes, your doubts, your thoughts and passions, your quickly tiring resolutions, your sudden enthusiasms, and your own fragility of faith.

Perhaps you recognize something of yourself in the story of the apostle Peter. In many ways, he is just like us. He is so ordinary. So simple. And so complex! When life at home gets confusing, perplexing, too much for him, his strategy is quite direct and uncomplicated. No matter what is going on, he simply announces, "I am going fishing." And he is so impulsive. He had cut off someone's ear. And now, when he hears that someone important is nearby, someone he wishes to see, he rushes there. He takes off, jumping out of the boat, and leaving others behind to manage with the work. And he seems so insensitive. For when he does meet Jesus, meets Jesus after having denied him, Peter acts as if nothing really significant has happened. The momentous events—of betrayal, trial, crucifixion, and resurrection—are not even mentioned. Instead, there is an initial silence between them. Peter remains seemingly indifferent to his earlier denials and disloyalty; and all the excitement of the intervening events is unspoken. And then, as if nothing amazing has happened, as if nothing requires comment or repentance, Peter quietly eats his breakfast. He eats, as if nothing has happened. Peter, for once in his life, is quite speechless.

He has good reason to be. For he, after all, had denied Jesus. Not just once; but three times! And perhaps Peter is also thinking of that earlier moment when he had bravely wanted to follow Jesus, and had vowed passionate loyalty to Jesus. For then, Peter's hasty words were, "I will lay down my life for you." And perhaps now, next to a charcoal fire on which fish had been cooked, perhaps Peter was thinking of another fire. For Peter had warmed himself next to a charcoal fire, warmed himself during Jesus' trial, warmed himself while he denied Jesus. No wonder Peter was speechless. What could he say? What could make up for the past, his failures, his denials of his Lord? He can do nothing; and he is silent.

Jesus breaks the silence. He takes the initiative. He always does. He speaks to Peter. He calls him by name. He calls him by the name "Simon, son of John." The name itself is significant, for with it Jesus returns to an earlier name, to the name Peter had before he met Jesus. Peter is given a second chance. His life with Jesus begins over again. The miserable episodes of hasty vows and quick denial are now set aside. And Jesus' question is simply, "Simon, son of John, do you love me?" Three times he asks it. Three times, as if the three will somehow undo the fearful past, relieving Peter of the awful burden of guilt which has prompted his silence. Three times, as if, by the questions and answers, the three denials are overcome. And Peter's "Yes, Lord" marks the restoration of relationship. Peter, now, makes no bold claims, no rash promises. His faith is no longer in himself. It is in Jesus. "Lord, you know everything; you know that I love you." And so, "a chastened Peter rests his case on Jesus' knowledge of what is in his heart."[52]

It is a wonderful story, this story of Peter. There is, of course, much more to tell. More to tell as Peter follows Jesus with love, and faith, and courage. But for now, it is enough that in a curious way it is the story of our own lives. For us too, these days, just now, after Easter, these days are the right time for our own new beginnings. It is time to say "Yes, Lord. . . ."

John E. Burkhart

[52]R.E. Brown,*The Gospel According to John*,The Anchor Bible (Garden City, NY; Doubleday & Company, 1970), p. 1111.

R   E   L   **FOURTH SUNDAY OF EASTER**

R   *Acts 13:14,43–52; Rev 7:9,14b-17; Jn 10:27–30*
E   *Acts 13:15–16,26–33; Rev 7:9–17; Jn 10:22–30*
L   *Acts 13:15–16a,26–33; Rev 7:9–17; Jn 10:22–30*

I once asked a friend of mine, who knew a fair amount about farming, how much of a fence you need to keep cows in. He answered, "It depends on the farmer." What do you mean, the farmer? "Some farmers round the cattle up by herding them with a helicopter. They need 6-foot-tall, solid plywood fences. Some farmers go out in the pasture and call the cows by name. They need sticks and a strand of wire." I was assuming that the cows would want to get away and that the fence would have to forcibly prevent them from wandering off. My friend's response made me consider another possibility: that with the right kind of farmer, the cows wouldn't want to escape. It wouldn't be a question of the farmer's power over the cattle; the power at work would be a power between the farmer and the cows, a power of connection.

The people asking Jesus to tell them plainly if he is the Messiah may be making a mistake similar to mine. They expect him to do or say something that will establish his authority, to proclaim the power that resides within him. But Jesus responds by talking about a different sort of power. "My sheep hear my voice, and I know them, and they follow me; and I give them eternal life." Jesus' authority is found in the between, in the bond that gives life, an authority that is known only in relationship. "They hear, I know, they follow, I give." In that back-and-forth, call-and-response movement is the revelation of who Jesus really is.

We know the power of connection, of empathy, in our lives; it is so pervasive, undergirding all our living, that we often take it for granted. What does a baby need to live? If it is fed and warmed and cleaned but never held and smiled at and talked to, it will die. It is the living connection with the one who holds it that calls a baby into life. What greater power is there than that? Surely the power that calls into life is greater, more fundamental, more divine, than the power we work so hard to exert over each other and over nature, to coerce behavior, to force events.

Why then do we turn to coercion ourselves? Why do we expect it of God? Perhaps because the tragedy of human life is that where the necessary living connections have broken down, people build their selves around control. The baby in an orphanage beats her head against the wall because she can control the sensation. The teenager gets addicted because drugs are more dependable than people. The country loses faith in the democratic process and looks for a "strong man." And then, sometimes, it can be too late for empathy alone to call us back into life. The strong man's army may need to be fought. The addict may not be reachable; the neglected child may develop a personality whose very core is chaos. A 12-year-old murders a frail old lady and evinces no regret. Maybe if you took the child into your home and gave him the years of concentrated attention and empathy you'd give a baby, he might develop a self that could love. But who will do that for all the delinquents, all the self-abusing children and the child-abusing parents, all the torturers and death squads and genocidal dictators in the world? The power-between fails us; we look for the power-over to control our own vicious will to control.

Only Easter brings hope of a different ending, the ending hinted at in the poetry of Revelation. The lamb who was slain will be their shepherd. This shepherd's authority lies in his connection with the least powerful, those whose lives have been destroyed by torture and abuse. That connection is stronger than death itself, for the one who called Jesus to be our lamb raised him to be our shepherd. God entered into a new living connection with the slain Jesus, and created a new relationship between Jesus and his followers. This is the hope of Easter: that where evil has destroyed all possibility of relationship, God can create new bonds of life. It is not God's power over us that saves us; it is the power of the creative connection that God establishes with us where we are most powerless. Between God and your need are found the living waters.

Only within the relationship can we find out who Jesus really is. So come when the shepherd calls you, here to the place where he will feed you. It is only a foretaste of the feast to come. At that table God will kneel before you, like a mother before her crying child, and tenderly wipe your tears away.

Elaine J. Ramshaw

FIFTH SUNDAY OF EASTER

R   *Acts 14:21b–27; Rev 21:1–5a; Jn 13:31–33a,34–35*
E   *Acts 13:44–52; Rev 19:1,4–9; Jn 13:31–35*
L   *Acts 13:44–52; Rev 21:1–5; Jn 13:31–35*

In the Sundays of Easter, the first lesson is from Acts. Luke, the author of Acts, would undoubtedly approve of this ancient practice. On Easter we celebrate the resurrection of Christ. In the Sundays after, we explore the consequences of that great, wondrous event, the daily, continuing effects of what God did on Easter. The resurrection is not some isolated once-and-for-all event that happened to Jesus. It is a great cosmic reversal of everything that is usual and expected into things that are surprising, wonderful and unexpected.

Acts is filled with stories of how the power of God, unleashed so dramatically in the resurrection of Jesus on Easter, continues to be felt in the church as the gospel of Christ expands into the whole world, leaps over all boundaries, overcomes all obstacles.

Today's lesson is typical of this post-Easter emphasis of Acts. Paul and Barnabas preached and their preaching evokes spectacular results: they made many disciples. Acts loves to tell these tales of evangelical success. The great, cosmic wonder of Easter keeps on happening in the growth of the Church. Through these stories we learn that there is a power, a power let loose in the world, a power for you, a power for good. It is this Easter power which Paul and Barnabas preached.

Surely you have seen these "Christian Talk Shows" which specialize in this sort of testimonial. You know the show: Some celebrity appears on the show and tells of a particularly tragic time in life that he or she went through, some terrible tale of woe. "Then I found Jesus," the testifier says, "and now my life is wonderful." Jesus, we are told, can cure all our problems, meet all our needs, overcome all of our dilemmas, just like he did for that celebrity, just like he did for Paul, Barnabas, and the early church in Acts. Come to Jesus and plug into the power, the power of Easter, the power to set things right in your life.

Thus some have accused Luke, particularly in Acts, of "trium-phalism." After the tenth story in Acts of how hundreds were converted, sick people were miraculously healed, and all was set right by the power of the resurrected Christ, it does begin to sound like the "I-was-miserable-then-I found-Jesus" testimony is right. Being a Christian is the best deal in the world! You have a problem? Something not quite right in your life? Come to Jesus and plug into the Easter power. Get all that fixed.

But to accuse Luke in Acts of "triumphalism" is not to read the whole story. Yes, here is a story of great success. But here is also a story of happiness mixed with much pain, and success which comes through suffering. Luke says that only through many tribulations we enter the dominion of God. Through many tribu-lations, sometimes one trial after another. Read through the book of Acts: there you will find little of the superficial, naive triumphalism of the TV Christian talk-show panel. Placed next to every story of success, gain, victory, is a story of persecution, death, suffering, and defeat for the young church. The two go together for disciples.

Certainly, because of Easter, there is a power let loose in our world. That power, the power of the risen Christ, can be for you. But that doesn't mean that disciples are exempt from the same cares that afflict everybody else; in fact, your faith may at times, like in the tales of Acts, be the source of your suffering rather than the eliminator of all pain. There is for example the story of how Paul preached about Jesus and for his sermon got not success and new disciples, but a nasty beating that left him half dead.

The risen Christ at Easter still had nail prints in his hands. The food we enjoy at the holy feast is made in shed blood and bro-ken body. Disciples are still called to make difficult decisions, to face tough questions, yes, to suffer. Nothing about Easter changes any of that. What is changed is that we, like Paul and Barnabas, are able to testify that though we go through our share of many tribulations, we have caught a glimpse of God's new dominion prepared for us. Our times of difficulty are given new meaning because of the story that he has suffered and triumphed before us. As Augustine said, Christians differ from others in the way they respond to the evils they suffer.

We respond in faith born out of what we learned at Easter, that, in our suffering or set-backs, God is with us. Even in our tribulations, by the power of the risen Christ, we are entering God's kingdom.

William H. Willimon

R E L SIXTH SUNDAY OF EASTER

R *Acts 15:1–2,22–29; Rev 21:1–14,22–23; Jn 14:23–29*
E *Acts 14:8–18; Rev 21:22–22:5; Jn 14:23–29*
L *Acts 14:8–18; Rev 21:10–14,22–23; Jn 14:23–29*

Some editors of church school materials had gathered to discuss a proposed new curriculum. The guidelines had been prepared for every unit, for every age child. Each unit had a series of goals which were carefully reviewed. The editors progressed along until they got to the guidelines for the study of Jesus. The first goal of the study was "To learn to appreciate the life of Jesus." There was a studied silence in the meeting. Finally, one of the group blurted out, "Wait a minute. This 'appreciate' business is tricky. I thought we were to love Jesus."

Of course, loving Jesus is what we are to do. All life long we have been formed around this love. Whatever else we have been taught, the center is that Jesus is worthy of our love. Think back to your childhood in church. The Christmas pageants with the rustic manger and the baby doll playing the part of the holy child. Maybe we were shepherds in bathrobes or magi with gold-painted crowns, or maybe the virgin herself, draped appropriately with a blue veil. All of the attention, all of the love was focused toward baby Jesus. "Oh Come Let Us Adore Him," sang the angels with the cardboard wings and tinsel halos, and we joined in their song. It began back then and continues in the church, this love of Jesus. We have been taught well. There is everything in this love, for God is love, and we share in God's love for Jesus.

The problem is that our devotion can turn inward and become a very private thing. One version of this love for Jesus is syrupy sweet, sentimental love. At times we are tempted to turn our love for Jesus into an exclusive affair, me and Jesus in the garden alone. Most of us know it is rather adolescent to equate love with warm feelings alone; there must be more to love than glowing affect. Still the temptation is there, and this kind of private love is widespread these days. Some Sunday morning listen to the TV preachers talk about l-o-v-e, all of it offered to you through the television and in glowing warm feelings. There is not much emphasis on love for our sisters and brothers, especially for the poor and the outcasts. But look at the love we can have for Jesus there by ourselves alone. Oh, it's a private affair, utterly sentimental. When love turns inward, it can exclude almost everybody else in the world.

But our Lord speaks to us in a different way. Still insisting on our love, Jesus calls for our obedience. "Love me," he says, "then keep my words." There is a discipline to love in Christ, a discipline which reaches out to the world God loves. "Keep my words" is a way of saying "Do my love." If we are going to love like Jesus we need to heed his new commandment. Look at this Jesus whom we are to love; he's kneeling at our feet with a towel and basin, acting out his love for us. He asks, "Do you know what I have done to you?" And answering his own question, the Lord tells us, "I have given you an example that you should do as I have done to you." We copy Jesus. And maybe we wind up volunteering to help care for AIDS patients, mopping their brows and holding their hands. Kind of scary and strange, maybe. And whatever else, we are copying Jesus, loving Jesus. When Jesus invites us to respond in love, we have to leave the sentimental stuff behind. His words are hard words about tough love. He points us to a brutal world to do that love. Jesus tells us, that is how my love is; now copy my love.

But loving Jesus involves also another kind of hospitality. We are called to welcome his words; we are also called to welcome him. We are to receive Jesus with hospitality. He will dwell with us and make his home among us. In Jesus' farewell to the disciples, the church is urged to welcome into its midst the risen Christ. Look at all the preparations for welcoming Jesus. The altar cloths are all washed and carefully ironed, the choir prepares a new communion hymn. This week the youth group bakes the bread, along with loaves to be sent to the Food Bank. Then the people gather, with their minister, around the table. Bread and wine are offered. The choir sings "Draw us in the Spirit's tether." In welcoming Jesus, we bless the Father, and the bread is broken and shared. "Alleluia," sings the choir, "Touch we now your garment's hem." And Christ is welcomed and received. The promise is fulfilled. Christ arrives to make his home in us. We are fed, and in blessing we are blessed. Just as we are called to bid farewell to Jesus, there is Advent, and Christ dwells with us. Receive me with hospitality, Jesus says. Welcome me, and I will dwell with you.

There is a benediction, of course. The risen Christ blesses the faithful. Live in my peace, says Jesus. This shalom will be the sign of my presence among you. Not as the world gives does Christ give, and this peace abides within the body. Look at this peace where Christ is welcomed. See that those who are old are welcomed too. They sit in the church hall at places of honor, at tables heaping with good food. Among the tables, the children hurry to find their place as well, for no one is turned away. Then there is quiet, and God is blessed; for the meal, for this family of faith, and for Jesus Christ who brings us peace. Amen. Come, Lord Jesus.

Richard Eslinger

R   *Acts 1:1–11; Eph 1:17–23; Lk 24:46–53*
E   *Acts 1:1–11; Eph 1:15–23; Lk 24:49–53*
L   *Acts 1:1–11; Eph 1:16–23; Lk 24:44–53*

From the Bible reading from the Acts of the Apostles: "Jesus was lifted up, and a cloud took him out of their sight." Jesus ascended into a cloud. Jesus moved from earth where his presence was a matter of fact to a cloud where his presence with us is a matter of faith. Jesus moved from earth where what he said was a matter of fact to a cloud where what he says to us is a matter of faith.

Let's look at the ascension from this perspective. As Jesus of Nazareth, a man on earth, Jesus was an objective matter of fact. A few people saw him with their physical eyes. A few people heard him with their physical ears. There Jesus was—an objective matter of fact. But, as a factual person on earth, Jesus could be present only to those who could see him with their physical eyes or hear him with their physical ears or touch him with their physical bodies. So for most people in most parts of the world, Jesus as the factual person on earth was not present. Jesus could only be absent from most people.

Furthermore, when Jesus is experienced only as an objective matter of fact, he can be experienced only as part of a distant past in a distant place. As an objective matter of fact, Jesus could easily be only that—a distant fact, irrelevant to our lives today.

But the story of the ascension is the story of Jesus moving from being an objective matter of fact to being taken out of sight by a cloud. A cloud is a biblical symbol of the presence of God who can be seen only by faith. So the ascension is the story not about Jesus being taken away from us, but Jesus being given to us for all times and for all places as a matter of faith.

As a matter of fact, Jesus was present with a few people in the first century. But as a matter of faith, Jesus is present with each of us all the time and in every place. Can you feel this presence right now? Can you not feel Jesus sitting beside you? Feel him touching you. Feel him reach out and take your hand and hold it as would a friend, a brother, a lover. Can you feel his warmth, his care, his love for you? Even now he is closer to each of us than we are to each other. When we are separated from the people we love, when we are alone, Jesus is still present. As the ascended one, Jesus is always present. Through the eyes of faith, we can see Jesus. Through the ears of faith, we can hear Jesus. Right now, let's see Jesus; let's hear Jesus.

As a matter of fact, a few people saw and heard Jesus. A few people heard Jesus tell them that he did not condemn them but rather forgave them. As a matter of faith, all of us can at any time confess to Jesus our burden of guilt. We can do so right now. We can see Jesus listening to us with understanding love, and we can hear him say, "I do not condemn you. I forgive you. You are forgiven." We can hear Jesus say, "I will be with you to help you do better in the future. Don't give up. I will help you be a new person."

As a matter of fact, Jesus told a few people not to be afraid because he would be with them to guide them and to bring them into joy. As a matter of faith, all of us can hear Jesus speaking such words to us whenever we are afraid. When we are afraid of what might happen to us, when we are afraid of the future, Jesus speaks to us. Can't you hear him say, "I understand your fear. It's a scary world. But don't be afraid. You belong to me. I will never let you go. You do not know the way or what will happen. But I am the way. I will see you through whatever happens. I will take you into a new life of joy." Can't you hear Jesus say, "The world may be too much for you. But do not be afraid, for I have overcome the world. You can trust me. You can count on me. I will see you through."

The ascension, then, is not the story of Jesus going away. Quite the opposite! The ascension is the story of Jesus being present and seen and heard by each of us as a matter of faith at any time and in any place. When we become as a child, when we see and hear through the images of our minds, when we see through the eyes of faith and hear through the ears of faith, then we can penetrate the cloud to feel Jesus' presence with us, to see Jesus looking at us with understanding love, and to hear Jesus say, "I love you. I forgive you. Don't be afraid. I will see you through."

Kathe Wilcox and Milton Crum

R E L SEVENTH SUNDAY OF EASTER

R   *Acts 7:55–60; Rev 22:12–14,16–17,20; Jn 17:20–26*
E   *Acts 16:16–34; Rev 22:12–14,16–17,20; Jn 17:20–26*
L   *Acts 16:6–10; Rev 22:12–17,20; Jn 17:20–26*

An essential aspect of relationships is thinking, hoping, dreaming, wishing, praying for and about the future. We all know that even the beginning of pregnancy can set the parents' heads reeling with thoughts of baseball gloves, bicycles, prom gowns and tuxedos, music lessons and swimming lessons, kindergarten and college. Their minds are rushing ahead into the future. Not long ago a friend of mine spoke with great intensity about his hopes and dreams for his two children. In addition to expressing pleasure and optimism about their accomplishments and potential, he talked about the values he wanted them to learn. Especially important to him was to teach the kids to care about others and to serve their community. He hoped that they would be able to give something back to the world, to make a difference. Brian was deeply concerned about what he had managed to impart to his children, about his impact on their future life. This conversation was a poignant one, because my friend, the devoted dad of these children, was dying.

Today's gospel reading is the final section of a prayer. It comes at the very end of the part of John's gospel containing Jesus' farewell discourse to his disciples. These are the final words of Jesus to his followers before the crucifixion. These are words meant to be remembered by the disciples when Jesus is gone from among them. In these discourses, Jesus says many significant things to the disciples. Here, in the final section, the author of the gospel carefully frames the concluding words into a prayer, addressed to the one Jesus calls Father. Although the prayer is addressed to the Father, it is obviously meant to be heard by the disciples.

The portion of the prayer we hear today turns its attention to the future. Here Jesus, knowing he will die, expresses his deepest desires and hopes for the future of his followers. This is the natural result of his continuing love for the disciples. "Having loved his own who were in the world, he loved them to the end" is the opening image for the entire last discourse. In this prayer, Jesus reflects that love for his own. His concern now is for the future life and ministry of those gathered around him. As Jesus was sent by God, so now the disciples are sent, and through their words others will come to believe. In the complex and beautiful language of the prayer, we hear that the future for the disciples is possible because they are connected through Jesus to the Father. His desire is for the continuation of the relationship: "As you, Father, are in me and I in you," so also may they be in us; "that you have loved them even as you loved me;" "so that the love with which you loved me may be in them, and I in them." It is this love, this indwelling, this name made known, this glory, now given to the disciples, which the world will see and believe. Through the ongoing words and work of the disciples, people will come to put their faith in Jesus. So Jesus facing his death and resurrection prays for his followers, that being made with him and the Father, their words and lives will make a difference.

This prayer is an especially appropriate one for us to hear this day. As for the disciples, these words are meant for us to notice and to remember. This seventh Sunday of Easter finds us waiting between the feasts of Ascension and Pentecost. It is a peculiar time. We have marked the event of the risen Jesus' leave-taking from the disciples. We have not yet celebrated the coming of the Spirit. In our yearly retelling of the story, it is indeed a time to wonder about the future. We realize that we are not simply to stand looking into the sky after the ascension. There is life and mission ahead for us. And yet, as surely as the disciples were, we are left wondering how.

The crucial reminder for us is the reminder of God's love, of Jesus' hope and desire for our future. The words of Jesus' prayer are also words for us. We must recognize that we too are connected to God, that we are among those who come to believe. We are bound in that relationship of faith into oneness with the Father. We are touched by the love the Father had for Jesus, which was in the disciples and is now in us. We are sent forth because of that love, as the disciples were sent. Through us the world may come to see and to know that love. That is the desire and the confidence Jesus had for the future of his first followers. It is the hope held out for our future. It is our yearning to be united and connected to God that gathers us together here around this table to celebrate this eucharist.

The eucharist helps to satisfy our wondering about now. In this sacrament we are united with God through Jesus. In the traditional liturgy of the Episcopal Church, the eucharistic prayer asks that we be made one body with him, that he may dwell in us and we in him as we receive the body and blood of Christ. These words echo the prayer of Jesus in John's gospel. It is here that we come to experience the presence of God. It is here that we come to remember Christ's death, resurrection, and ascension. It is here that we come to be filled with indwelling love of Jesus Christ. It is here that we are fed and strengthened to be sent with that love into the world and to face the future of our ministry and mission.

In any relationship, it is natural to have hopes and dreams for the future of those we love. My friend gave a great legacy of serving and caring to his growing children. They will remember his words and be moved by his example long after his death. Jesus too cared deeply about the future of those he loved, and he hoped confidently for the impact his followers would make after he was gone. What he left to them, and to us, is more than a legacy or an example: it is an ongoing relationship, a continuing connectedness, a way of nurturing and sustaining. Because even though Jesus vanished from the sight of his disciples, the love of the risen Lord did not disappear. It is among us and with us each time we come together to break the bread and to share the cup. We are assured that Jesus dwells in us, and that if we dwell in him, others will come to know and to have faith in that love. The hopes, dreams, and final prayer of the Lord who loves us and dwells in us will be fulfilled. And it will make a difference.

Leslie G. Reimer

R PENTECOST SUNDAY
E DAY OF PENTECOST

R *Acts 2:1–11; 1 Cor 12:3b-7,12–13; Jn 20:19–23*
E *Acts 2:1–11; 1 Cor 12:4–13; Jn 20:19–23*

If there is one word which sums up the story of Pentecost, that word is unity.

All barriers of nation and language were broken down by the fusing power of the Holy Spirit. This was a noteworthy accomplishment, for the writer states that on this day there were in Jerusalem people "from every nation under heaven." There is a partial list of these nations in today's first lesson, and even this is rather impressive. So is the number of those who came to faith: three thousand in one day! And the most remarkable thing is how they immediately became one body. "They devoted themselves to the apostles' teaching and common life, to the breaking of bread and the prayers." Soon it was said of them that "all who believed were together and had all things in common," that is, they practiced a community of goods, a thing which would have been impossible if they had not been filled with the Spirit of faith and love. Pentecost was truly a miracle. It made one body out of many diverse people.

The second lesson underscores this fact. "There are varieties of gifts, but the same Spirit," it begins. What was said of the Corinthian congregation could be said of any authentic Christian community in any century. And whenever this sort of thing happens in history, you may be sure that God is at work, and whenever the opposite occurs, the devil is certain to be behind it. For Satan's constant purpose is to divide and separate human beings from one another and from God. In the Garden of Eden the devil succeeded in driving a wedge between our first parents and their Creator, and in the next generation caused such hatred to spring up between two brothers that one killed the other. So it always has been. Whenever there is trouble between husband and wife, whenever one class wars with another class, or one nation with another, you may be sure that the fomenter of the strife is the evil one. On the other hand, where people live in peace with one another, where justice prevails, and even love, there the Spirit of God has won a notable victory. It is no small task to overcome the petty jealousies, resentments, self-seeking, avarice, and lusts which so easily flare up into open hostility and loveless action. This requires the transforming power of God, precisely the kind of power which the Holy Spirit brings to bear upon the hearts and souls of human beings.

What is puzzling and disturbing, however, is the spottiness of results in the lives of the baptized. There are those who apparently are Christians; they say the creed, they make diligent use of the means of grace, they say their prayers. But they seem to have certain blind spots in their characters. It may be that they have a violent antipathy to other denominations so much so that it amounts to bigotry, which on the face of it is always a transgression of the law of love. It may be that they have strange prejudices toward liturgical practices or in manners and morals or that their politics are a bit on the wild side. It may be that they harbor certain weird ideas about other races, which ideas constitute a very effective block to their knowing these people personally and dealing with them in justice and love. Thus we have the strange and incongruous spectacle of church officers, Sunday School teachers, and otherwise active church members regarding other human beings with antipathies, suspicions, and feelings of hostility which are anything but Christian.

Obviously, if we are God's people, we are bound to function as divine agents to break down these walls, since God is consistently on the side of unity. God labors, and so must we, in the interest of understanding, justice, and love. Where there are feelings of hostility which are based on ignorance, these may be removed by education. Fear of another group or race may be dispelled by the Christian gospel, even when it happens as it did with the Nazis, that hatred of one kind of people grows to unbelievable barbarism. Now however, in most parts of the world, we have opportunity to batter away at divisive walls not with guns and bombs, but with words, or rather, with the word, through which the Spirit of power works. It's a word which must be spoken by us, into whom the Spirit has already come.

Today the wind of God is again blowing on our world. This is evident in two areas particularly. The one is the ecumenical movement. The change of climate among Christian denominations is evident to everyone. We have resumed speaking to one another as brothers and sisters in the Lord! The other area in which notable progress has been made is that of race relations. At the moment the outstanding illustration of this is the almost unanimous position of Christian churches to the apartheid of South Africa. In our own country we have a long way to go, of course, but we also have come a long way in the last century.

The key to all this lies in that God to whom we pray on this day: "Make us messengers of the good news that, through the power of your Spirit, everyone everywhere may unite in one song of praise, through your Son, Jesus Christ our Lord, who lives and reigns with you in the unity of the Holy Spirit, one God, now and forever."[53]

Herbert F. Lindemann

[53]*Lutheran Book of Worship*, p. 23.

L DAY OF PENTECOST

L *Gen 11:1–9; Acts 2:1–21; Jn 15:26–27; 16:4b–11*

The readings for this festival of Pentecost contain two contrasting stories about language and its power to create and destroy community. The story in the first reading is about the building of the tower of Babel. We are told that "The whole world had one language and few words." And people said to each other: "Come, let us build ourselves a city, and a tower with its top in the heavens, and let us make a name for ourselves." But God, displeased with the project, said, "Come, let us go down, and there confuse their language, that they may not understand one another's speech."

The second reading records the story of Pentecost. The apostles were assembled in Jerusalem. The city was filled with people from all over the empire. The apostles "were all filled with the Holy Spirit and began to speak in other tongues, as the Spirit gave them utterance."

The contrast between the two stories is obvious. At Babel people suddenly spoke in many tongues, and the result was confusion and loss of community. On Pentecost the apostles spoke in many tongues, and the result was increased understanding and the formation of community. At Babel people had to give up their plans because they could no longer understand each other. On Pentecost many people from different lands heard the gospel call to community because of an increased facility to communicate.

Language has the power to divide and the power to unite, depending upon the spirit of those who use it. Pentecost would remind us that the difference between the word that destroys community and the word that creates it is the Spirit of God.

What prompts the confusion of tongues at Babel and the resulting loss of community is apparent in the words of the tower builders: "Let us make a name for ourselves." The sin was not in the building of a tower any more than it is now in the exploration of outer space. The folly of the Babel project was the intention of the builders to make a name for themselves. The folly was not the project, but the pride. Building only for oneself is inevitably done at the expense of neighbor and even in competition with God, and this is sin. The result is always the same: people no longer speak the same language. Communication breaks down. Pride always means me rather than my neighbor, my way rather than her way: and so I no longer hear her, and soon she no longer hears me. There is confusion of tongues, no longer one language and one people.

Pentecost is God's answer to Babel. Hear the ancient prayer of the church for this day: "Come, Holy Spirit, fill the hearts of the faithful: and kindle in them the fire of Thy love." The Spirit's life-giving word is the answer to our death-dealing words. To pray for the Spirit is to pray for the Word that creates community. "In the beginning was the Word, and the Word was with God, and the Word was God." That Word took on human form in the person of Jesus Christ and was filled with the power of the Spirit of God. You could hear the power of the Spirit in the words that he spoke. You could see it and feel it in the life that he lived and the death that he died. And in his rising the Spirit of God burst the bonds of death and became the source and power of the new community born on Pentecost.

There is in all of us the spirit of Babel and the Spirit of Christ. If we are out to make a name for ourselves—as individuals, as a parish, as a nation—that will be obvious in what we say and do. The result will be a breakdown of community and a loss of communication. If we are filled with the Spirit of Christ, it will also be obvious in what we say and do. And the result will be the building of community and the increase of communication.

Holy Spirit, fill our hearts and kindle in us the fire of your love, so that what we say to each other and to all those with whom we come into contact may build community, until there is but one language and one people in the kingdom of God.

Thomas Droege

R *Prov 8:22–31; Rom 5:1–5; Jn 16:12–15*
E *Is 6:1–8; Rev 4:1–11; Jn 16:12–15*
L *Prov 8:22–31; Rom 5:1–5; Jn 16:12–15*

Have you been to any dances lately? Almost everyone enjoys some form of this activity, from pre-schoolers swinging to "Here We Go Looby-Loo" to senior citizens active at square dance clubs and polka parties. Dancing is a universal human pastime, and a great metaphor for life. Those who enjoyed the exuberance of the movie *Zorba the Greek* can readily testify to the power of dance, as can the many generations of fans who watch *Dance Party*. In earlier times, dance was also one of the verbal images used for the Holy Trinity; our culture is poorer because we no longer use it, and our appreciation of this great Christian mystery suffers without the richness of the dance.

God knows, and, truly, *only* God knows, how hard it is to speak about this doctrine. The reality which we acknowledge and celebrate today defies our understanding and our language. Perhaps we can rattle off definitions or quote famous writers on the meaning of the Trinity. If we are more sophisticated theologically, we may refer to the divine processions of the persons within the Trinity, or discuss the missions proper to each of these persons. Historians may concentrate on the controversies which have arisen about the Trinity, while those who are formulating contemporary feminist theologies find this dogma difficult, since our traditional ways of describing the Trinity rely heavily on masculine imagery and Father-Son terminology.

It's hard to envision a dance if we use such scholarly approaches. Our Western world seems to have chosen "procession" for the relationship among the triune persons. A procession is characterized by order and dignity, formality, and logical progression. A dance, on the other hand, is joyous, spontaneous, and vital. The God of the Trinity imaged as dance is lively. Life erupts in a celebration for which the Pentecost symbols of rushing wind and flaming tongues are totally appropriate.

The core to the meaning of the Trinity is life generating life. One person called Father, Mother, Yahweh, Great Spirit,—the terms may change in differing cultures and time periods—is so filled with the energy of Being-at-its-fullest, that this Being eternally generates the "Living One," a contemporary and beautiful title for the Risen Jesus. The Life which leaps and sparks between these two is itself so dynamic, so joyous, and so fertile, that another Living Person, powerful and generative, springs out into the eternal, never-ending Dance. As the life energy advances and retreats in the intricate pattern of full giving and full receiving, it overflows into the entire universe, creating and renewing the face of the earth. All created beings mirror and echo the richness that is there, and humans especially become the reflection of the Trinity-Family and its gift of life.

The celebration is repeated in microcosm each time husband and wife enter their own joyous dance of procreation and generation. Two become one, so enamored of each other's goodness and life that their intimacy calls forth another being. Each of us, every person, every new child witnesses to the reality of Trinity, and to the miracle of love diffusing itself. The author of the book of Deuteronomy reverenced this truth when he summarized the obligations of God's people in a simple phrase, "Choose Life." What is life-giving is of God; what creates, shares, and enriches life is of the Trinity. Imitating the Trinity means entering more and more fully into the life of God, a life which is never static or selfish.

Today, as every year, our liturgy celebrates this amazing gift of life in a special way by recalling the dance of life. God sends Jesus that we may have life to the full. Raised from the dead, this Living One destroys the power of un-life, and seals the promise of eternal life by the gift of the Spirit. The Spirit "inspires"— literally breathes into our being—and we, "in-spirited," produce a multitude of lovely fruits, such as love, joy, and peace.

And this is our challenge today: to bring forth these realities in our lives and in our world. We are asked to respect and to protect all life. We are asked to give up personal habits which harm us or those around us, either physically or emotionally. We are confronted with the obligation to abandon social and political habits not in keeping with life, if we are to resemble our God in heaven. Today, as every day, our God invites us to choose life, to join the dance, and live!

Katherine A. Lewis, O.P.

R   BODY AND BLOOD OF CHRIST

R   *Gen 14:18–20; 1 Cor 11:23–26; Lk 9:11b-17*

The taste of bread and wine is a good taste. The taste of body and blood is sweet, the milk of a mother. It is hard to think that something good and sweet is a symbol of death. Unless that death gives life. It certainly did in the case of Jesus. He was an innocent man who preached the love of God. He could not be tormented out of the truth. He blessed creation at the end, he did not curse it. And we can live off everything he said and did. We can feel the life-giving nature of him. We know it is the life of God, the life of God in someone's body and blood, translated into bread and wine, so everyone can eat.

We don't know Jesus dead, we know him living. He has absorbed death. Death is written all over him when he appears to his disciples. He has to remove from their minds the classical conviction that once dead, never alive again. Except perhaps as a memory. But Jesus is so physical to his disciples in apparitions to them! That is why they were so physical when they remembered him. They took the same bread he did, the same wine he did, they meant what he meant. We can live off his innocence, we can live off his love, we can live off his blessing of the earth and all creatures in it. Such living may cost us our lives, as it cost him his. But due to him, death does not have the final say.

There is no doubt that people the world over want death to be a birth. We find shells in ancient graves, we find figurines of fertile women, we find symbols of the moon. It is as if people were asking womanhood for one more, for one greater procreation, to take in death and give out life. And to come out of that experience rich with nourishment. It may be hard for us to think of Jesus as womanly, but that is what he is in eucharist. A modern parable may illustrate this.

There was a man who loved people's stories. He was a food salesman to institutions, hospitals, nursing homes, and the like. He felt obliged to eat in the places where the food he sold was served, the breakfasts, the lunches, the dinners, and he would sit with people, staff and patients, and just pretend to be there for a vague reason. But he would get listening to a story and forget to ask how they liked the food. The nursing homes were the most poignant. One in particular. A woman there thought he was her son John. As soon as he entered the lobby where everyone was sitting she would shout, "O, there he is, there is John, my son," and she would come alive with joy. As he got close to her, however, she saw he wasn't, and she would get very sad and retreat back inside herself. But he would crouch by her wheelchair and bring her back out enough so she could tell him John was to come soon. Then there'd be some hope and expectancy in her. One day over lunch with the staff, a lunch steamed to death he thought, he asked about the woman. She had a son, it was true, but he had been killed in World War II, a hero, but a crazy man from what the staff could tell. He got a super medal from leading a suicide charge to gain the top of a hill and the battle. He had succeeded but he also died. She had been in and out of institutions since that time, but now that she was old she was peaceful, so she could live easily with the others. "Not much to live on," the man thought, "a dream of a son." One day he tried saying to her, "John was a hero, wasn't he?" She seemed for a moment to reflect on something, then she said, as if not to him, "He loved to kill things. I have to teach him not to. That is why he doesn't come to see me." Then the man tried something further, "John died in action, didn't he?" "O, yes," she said, "but he still wants to kill things. I have to teach him not to. I must soon or no one will." "Why?" the man asked. "Why soon?" She lifted her head at him, almost fiercely, and whispered, "Well look at me!" Then she closed down on herself and drifted into sleep. And he did look at her. And he felt the power of womanhood as he had never felt it in his life. This woman would chase death to make it change its ways. "Crazy," he thought. "I just chase bad cooks. So they don't steam the red out of carrots." He stood up and touched the woman on the forehead and said, "I hope you find him." Then he left.

The story of the man changes into the story of the woman, then back into the story of the man. And that is the way the eucharist moves, from Jesus, to us, then back to Jesus. And the great purpose of his, to chase death down and make it yield life, becomes our purpose. There was an ancient way of praying to Jesus, my brother, my sister, my mother, my father, my all. There was so much love in him it called on every love.

Francis P. Sullivan, S.J.

R NINTH SUNDAY IN ORDINARY TIME
E PROPER 4
L SECOND SUNDAY AFTER PENTECOST

R *1 Kg 8:41–43; Gal 1:1–2,6–10; Lk 7:1–10*
E *1 Kg 8:22–23,27–30,41–43; Gal 1:1–10; Lk 7:1–10*
L *1 Kg 8:41–43; Gal 1:1–10; Lk 7:1–10*

Groucho Marx, so the story goes, once rejected an offer to join an exclusive country club, quipping, "I would never be a part of a club that would have someone like me as a member." That piece of reverse logic may strike us as funny, but it also touches a deep human nerve. We are, all of us, concerned about being accepted. We want people to like us, welcome us, gather us into the group, invite us to join the club. At the same time, though, we are worried that we are not good enough, that if the truth were known about us we would be rejected as unworthy.

In a recent study, researchers asked eminently successful business executives about their greatest fears. These were people of considerable power and influence, people who had climbed above, and sometimes over, the pack to get to their places of prominence. They seemed in many ways to be tough and fearless, even ruthless, but the research team found that the majority of them were haunted by one, secret terror: They were terrified that they would be found out, their hidden incompetence discovered. They were convinced that they had made it into the "club," but under false pretenses, and that one day the truth would be known that they really lacked the credentials.

In the deepest recesses of our lives, many people also feel as though they lack the credentials necessary to approach God with confidence and joy. William Muehl of Yale Divinity School once called upon the clergy to remember that many of the men and women sitting in the pews nearly did not come to worship this day, and "that in all probability most of them feel that they are there under false pretenses, that everyone around them feels more confidently Christian . . . than they do.[54]" J. Randall Nichols tells of a woman in his church who once explained to him why she so seldom came to worship. She said that she stayed away because she was afraid she would cry and that she knew you weren't supposed to do that. Nichols goes on to state that nothing he could say would persuade her that what she had learned was not true, "that personal vulnerability and 'coming to church' do not mix."[55] This woman felt that her vulnerability disqualified her from the "club." She lacked the credentials of strength and composure she was convinced were necessary to come before God.

What are the credentials necessary to come before God? Can we draw near to God with hope and in trust, or are we always in danger of being found out to be the spiritual weaklings and the impostors that we know we are? These are the questions which lie at the heart of the story in Luke's gospel about Jesus and the centurion.

The way the story unfolds, there was a centurion (we would call him a "company commander" in the army) whose servant was ill. The centurion had heard of the powerful and healing ministry of Jesus, so he sent some religious leaders to inquire if Jesus might come and cure his servant. Now these leaders were, as most people are, concerned about credentials, so they made the best case they could to Jesus. What they told Jesus was that the centurion was "worthy" to have this blessing because he was a racially open-minded man and a philanthropist. "He loves our people," they said, "and he built us our synagogue."

What the religious leaders were implying, of course, is that God's blessings come to those who are worthy, that there is some way to establish enough credit in the divine account to persuade God to be kind. Now, this centurion was not a member of the synagogue, to be sure. He was a Roman army officer, not the sort of person one would normally consider "in the church club," but he was not completely devoid of credentials. He was a good man, they said, and therefore worthy.

The centurion himself knew better, though. When Jesus came near to his house, what impressed the centurion most was not his own solid credentials as a good man, but rather his deep unworthiness in the face of this man Jesus. Thus he sent friends to Jesus with his honest cry: "I am not worthy to have you come under my roof." It is the cry made by every honest person before God. We hear its echo in the woman's voice, "I cannot come to church. I am afraid I will cry," and in the prayer of many others, "I am not strong enough in my trust. Help my unbelief."

And Jesus turned around and left. That is the way many people fear the story will end. No credentials, no blessing. Or, perhaps in some blazing moment of hope, we can imagine that the story will end, "Despite the centurion's unworthiness, Jesus healed the servant anyway." Nothing in our experience, however, prepares us for the true ending of this story: Jesus marveled at the centurion, *marveled* at him, and said, "I tell you, not even in Israel have I found such faith." Back at the centurion's house, the slave was a new, and whole, man. No doubt, the centurion was, too.

It was precisely the centurion's sense of unworthiness before Christ, his vulnerability in the face of Jesus' power, his openness to what he needed but knew he did not deserve, his reaching out to what can only be called grace, that Jesus calls "faith." It was and is the one and only credential necessary to draw near to God with joy and hope.

Thomas G. Long

[54]William Muehl, *Why Preach? Why Listen?* (Philadelphia: Fortress 1986), p. 11.
[55]J. Randall Nichols, *The Restoring Word* (New York: Harper & Row, 1987), p. 1.

R TENTH SUNDAY IN ORDINARY TIME
E PROPER 5
L THIRD SUNDAY AFTER PENTECOST

R *1 Kg 17:17–24; Gal 1:11–19; Lk 7:11–17*
E *1 Kg 17:17–24; Gal 1:11–24; Lk 7:11–17*
L *1 Kg 17:17–24; Gal 1:11–24; Lk 7:11–17*

In the Sundays after Pentecost, we see Jesus victorious. Luke proclaims the Christ who heals the sick, raises the dead, and forgives sins. Christ is the fulfillment of the promise which, according to Mary's song, God made to Abraham and to his posterity forever.

The readings this day hearken back to Easter, the power of God to bring life out of death. By means of Elijah, God restored life to a widow's dead son. Her son restored, the widow responds, "Now I know that you are a man of God, and that the word of the Lord in your mouth is truth." Jesus raises the only son of the widow at Nain, and the people respond, "A great prophet has arisen among us," and "God has visited the chosen people!" The apostle Paul, once an angel of death amid the church of God, preaches the gospel he once tried to destroy. On account of this astonishing news, the churches of Christ in Judea glorify God.

All three readings bear witness to the miraculous power of God to bring life out of death. Yet in a world littered with corpses the sign of the resurrection remains an alien sign. Authentic miracle remains but a flash in the pan, an all too brief beacon on death's otherwise dark horizon. How long, after all, does the power of miracle endure? Are widows' sons yet alive? Is the apostle to the Gentiles still preaching the faith? Even those who once stood in awe at the astonishing power of God have now gone to their graves and await with us the consummation of their hope and ours. Death will lay claim to us soon enough, and then what will become of our hope?

It is in this context that the gospel is spoken. The gospel of Jesus Christ is announced in the midst of death. But it is in the context of death that the gospel exercises its greatest power.

There is no mistaking a funeral procession. Few processions evoke as much awe as that which wends its way to the cemetery. It is so as on a crisp autumn afternoon the hearse drives through the streets of our town, followed by an automotive train of mourners. Headlights declare: "This is the march of death. Stand back! Do not enter." Cars stop at intersections, as drivers avert their eyes. Children, on the way home from school, mass at crosswalks, wide-eyed, mouths agape. Some adults stare as well. But most turn their heads, unwilling to witness yet another sign of the inevitable.

Entering the cemetery it is as though life had been left outside. This is not a living place, not part of the living world. Though we did not see it, the river Styx has been crossed, and we are in the land of the dead. We pass another service in progress. But that little assembly is made up of strangers, unknown to us. They are unreal, like plaster statues depicting the nativity of death. We pass unnoticed, each bound by our individual grief, denying the catholicity of the common event that binds us.

Outside the line of parked cars the air hangs heavy with impending finality. We stand in small groups remarking on the weather:

mourners are reluctant to get too near the grave. We are like tourists on the south rim of the Grand Canyon, afraid to get too near the edge, afraid we too might be swept over the side, down into the black hole hidden by the too-green outdoor carpet. Death's dark hole may be out of sight, but it is not out of mind. We must be coaxed toward the casket. "Come. Gather round so you can hear." Are you kidding? Nothing doing! We remain far back, looking down at grave markers, reading unknown names. Anonymous subtraction occupies the mind: Born, 1910; Died, 1982. 72 years. An average lifespan. It gives the illusion of statistical comfort: "We have time left. We have lots of time. There may yet be a way we can avoid this."

Only the widow has no illusion. She can hardly get near enough. This is the burial of her last hope. Her only child lies atop the sterile machinery of cosmetic death, ready to be lowered to his final rest. She is as present now as she was the day of his birth, mother now as she was mother then. If illusion would allow she would gather this son to herself and nurse life into his veins. But not even the awesome strength of mother love can bring back his life. She grieves as one who would change places with the deceased, as one who would willingly enter death in order to restore life. So powerful is her pain that not even her closest friends can comfort her. They are pushed away, held back as by some repelling force. Surrounded by friends, she is yet alone. This is the singular power of death.

"Do not weep. Young man, I say to you, arise." In this context the gospel bears Easter power. It comes to people who have no hope, to people terribly alone in their grief. It is announced as an alien word, as a shocking word, as a word that runs against the grain: "Do not weep. Young man, I say to you, arise." These ludicrous words fly in the face of all we see, know, and understand. And yet, they are pregnant with Easter promise.

Shall even we know the unbridled joy of a mother who again holds her once dead, now living son? Shall even we be visited by God in this way? Will there come a day when we are stunned by the peculiar fear that moves humankind to glorify God as on

Easter morning? Can it be that one day in a world strewn with corpses the promise of the gospel will be realized by all flesh?

"This is my body given for you. This cup is the new covenant in my blood, shed for you." Even now, even here, we may taste a bit of Easter! Here God feeds us on Christ the way a mother nurtures her child: Christ in, with, and under the forms of bread and wine. "Earth to earth, ashes to ashes, dust to dust, in sure and certain hope of the resurrection unto eternal life through our Lord Jesus Christ." Earth. Ashes. Dust. These are elements common with the stuff of bread and wine. These are elements common to us, redeemed by the crucified and risen Christ.

I say to you, "Arise and eat! Come and drink!" Here God visits us and beckons towards the great and promised feast. In this feast, we, like the widow's son, are restored to the one out of whose pain we were born. In this God is glorified!

Franklin A. Wilson

R ELEVENTH SUNDAY IN ORDINARY TIME
E PROPER 6
L FOURTH SUNDAY AFTER PENTECOST

R *2 Sam 12:7–10,13; Gal 2:16,19–21; Lk 7:36–8:3*
E *2 Sam 11:26–12:10,13–15; Gal 2:11–21; Lk 7:36–50*
L *2 Sam 11:26–12:10,13–15; Gal 2:11–21; Lk 7:36–50*

Before all of the children were settled in their desks, Henry went up to Mrs. Bender's desk in their fourth grade classroom and handed her a small potted plant which had but one tiny bud ready to open up any minute. As his eyes met hers, she smiled at him. Embarrassed, he quickly pushed the plant into her hands and rushed back to his desk. The other children looked on in amazement. None of them had brought her anything. Mrs. Bender smiled to herself as she looked back at the attendance sheet which she was marking. But her mind was elsewhere.

Thoughts of yesterday rushed through her mind. She couldn't believe this was the same Henry that had chosen to "take her on" in front of the whole class the day before. After getting back a math test with a low grade written at the top of the paper, he had stood up in front of the class and told her what a poor teacher she was. Some of the other children began making similar comments, as well. Fortunately, the recess bell had rung shortly after Henry's outburst. Mrs. Bender returned from her reverie and noticed that the bud on her plant had begun to open up, barely showing its delicate shade of pink. Henry looked at it, smiling.

Who among us is not able to relate to this or similar stories? For me it evoked different memories of my own experience. Perhaps after hearing a story such as this one, we would be inclined to approach future similar incidents with a different outlook. We might even choose to change our behavior in such situations.

Not unlike this type of story, biblical stories have had a strong, transforming effect on the Christian community throughout its history. In his book, *Stories of Faith*, John Shea gives us a clue about why the stories from the Bible have such an impact on their listeners. "The stories of scripture were remembered and today remain memorable because they are similar enough to our own lives for us to see ourselves, yet different enough from our lives for us to see new possibilities. . . . They come close to home and yet are an invitation to a journey."[56]

Today's gospel story from Luke can do just that for us. A deeply moving story, this account of the woman who anoints Jesus, displays his profound sensitivity to the longings of the human heart for God's love and forgiveness. In this story, Jesus directly confronts the leaders of the people, and us as well. He presents them with the example of a woman, a sinner, whose authentic faith and love moved her to anoint him, an act which the host had neglected. She acknowledged her sinfulness; the leaders' closed minds and hearts prevented them from admitting theirs. Aware of the way Jesus accepted her without condition, future generations remember this unknown woman by her act of anointing rather than by her sin. Because this description of God's relationship to sinners is deeply rooted in the Christian tradition and is closely aligned to other similar gospel stories, it challenges us to believe in God's merciful love with the same unquestioning attitude as the unnamed "woman of the city."

But the Lucan twist—the insertion of a parable within the story that seemingly contradicts the point of the story— stretches us to move beyond our own experience to examine new possibilities for our relationship to God. What is the key to forgiveness? Is it our great love which impels God to forgive us, or is it the magnitude of God's love which leads us to seek forgiveness in the first place?

I don't think today's lectionary asks us to choose betwen these two alternatives with an either/or response, although at first glance the first two readings seem to take a contradictory view. In the reading from 2 Samuel the emphasis is on the need for repentance and the seeking of forgiveness by the sinner. The focus of Galatians, on the other hand, is on the offer of God's forgiveness in Christ.

In its specific context in the Scriptures, each passage has its own role to play in forming the faith of the Christian community. By placing them together, however, and joining them with Luke's gospel today, the church forces us to grapple with the paradox involved in the process of being reconciled with God. As sinners, we are expected to repent and seek forgiveness in a spirit of faith and love; yet, it is only on God's initiative that we are able to believe and love at all.

Jesus said to the woman, "Your faith has saved you; go in peace." And for Henry the fourth grader, "As his eyes met hers, she smiled at him." We, too, are invited to believe in the possibility of the tranforming effects of God's love offered to us each day. May the bread and wine which we offer in Christ at this eucharist be symbols of the hope we have for that possibility, just as the budding of the small potted plant with its delicate shade of pink was for Henry.

Patricia A. Parachini, S.N.J.M.

[56]John Shea, *Stories of Faith* (Chicago: Thomas More Press, 1978), p. 89.

R   *Zech 12:10–11;13:1; Gal 3:26–29; Lk 9:18–24*
E   *Zech 12:8–10;13:1; Gal 3:26–29; Lk 9:18–24*
L   *Zech 12:7–10; Gal 3:23–29; Lk 9:18–24*

Perhaps you've seen those optical illusions which seem at first to be one thing but then suddenly become something else. The outline of a chalice turns into two faces, or an old haggard woman becomes a lovely young girl. It depends largely on what you expect to see, and sometimes, once you have seen one of the figures, it becomes difficult to find the other. What we believe to be there is what we tend to see. Once we think we understand something, it's difficult for us to go beyond that understanding.

In the realm of faith, too, there are things we think we understand. Certainly that was so for the disciples. When Jesus questioned them as to who people believed he was, Peter seemed to understand a good deal. Others may have thought that Jesus was John the Baptist or Elijah or one of the prophets, but Peter knew and declared him to be the Christ. After all, Peter had been with Jesus for some time. He had heard him teach, had seen him heal the sick, raise the dead, feed the hungry. It is not really surprising to hear Peter's confession: "You are the Christ of God." He had good reason to know and understand who Jesus was.

And yet, as Jesus then went on to talk about what it meant to be chosen by God, to follow God's anointed, it is likely that Peter and the others were surprised. Suddenly, like an optical illusion that seems to change before our eyes, their perspectives were reversed. Jesus spoke not of the power and majesty and dominion that they might have expected from the Messiah, but of suffering and rejection and death. These must have been hard and confusing words for them, because the words flew in the face of what they thought they understood. This was a view of discipleship that was new and difficult to take in.

For us, of course, it is no longer new. We have heard these words of Jesus before, so that they no longer shock us. We have the advantage of knowing what lay ahead for Jesus and those who followed him. Two thousand years of history and tradition have taught us that those who name the name of Christ pay a high price. Peter may have been amazed at Jesus' saying that he must take up his cross, but we know that he was indeed called to do just that, dying a martyr's death, nailed, head down, to a cross. All of that fits our understanding of what it means to be a Christian, and so it is not likely to shock us as it did those first disciples.

There is, however, another reason these words are less likely to trouble us. The reality is that most of us will never see a cross. Martyrdom is not likely to be required of us, and so the call to take up our cross is less frightening. But what if our perspective were suddenly to change, and a different understanding came to light? Might this call then take on a new meaning for us?

Jesus spoke of taking up the cross before his crucifixion linked that symbol with Christian martyrdom. Speaking to the twelve about a cross would not necessarily have made them think of death. Rather, it might have brought to mind the cross-shaped mark branded on cattle as a mark of ownership. That cross was, in effect, a mark of slavery, and that is a very different matter from martyrdom.

In a way, it is easy for us to talk about taking up the cross, if it means dying a martyr's death. We know that most of us will not be asked to make that sacrifice. But it is harder to talk of slavery, because that means giving up control of our lives, and we want to be in control. Acknowledging that we cannot provide for ourselves, that our every breath is dependent upon God, that all we have comes, not of our own doing, but as a gift from the Creator—this is the slavery we are called to accept, the cross we are summoned to take up. Following Christ then means offering whatever service we can, in gratitude for all that we have received. That service may not be grand or noble or earthshaking; it may mean visiting a nursing home, rather than becoming a missionary in South America. Nevertheless, the God who provides in love, who spreads the table before us, calls us to respond in humility. It is God who leads, not we ourselves. Take up your cross and follow.

Catherine A. Ziel

R THIRTEENTH SUNDAY IN ORDINARY TIME
E PROPER 8
L SIXTH SUNDAY AFTER PENTECOST

R   *1 Kg 19:16b,19–21; Gal 5:1,13–18; Lk 9:51–62*
E   *1 Kg 19:15–16,19–21; Gal 5:1,13–25; Lk 9:51–62*
L   *1 Kg 19:14–21; Gal 5:1,13–25; Lk 9:51–62*

Dostoevsky's Grand Inquisitor lets Christ be killed a second time in order to preserve peace, a peace that comes when all are satisfied with bread, when all accept their reward for unquestioning obedience to his authority. Freedom, he reasons, is not worth the suffering it causes. Better that people live like well-fed slaves than suffer the disorder that freedom brings. The Grand Inquisitor has understood that freedom is at the center of the Christian message. As indicated in today's readings the living Christ is indeed identical with the call to freedom. As Paul writes in Galatians 5:1, "For freedom Christ set us free." Let us examine how each reading presents apostolic freedom.

The first reading presents the call of Elisha by Elijah. A simple but prosperous farmer, Elisha experiences the call to prophecy as so immediate and unconditional that he needs to ask if he cannot return to say good-bye to his parents. He is scolded by Elijah for even thinking this would not be allowed. "What have I done to you?" Though the call to the prophetic life demands a break with previous attachments, symbolized by Elisha's burning his plow and sacrificing his oxen, family bonds are respected. Elisha is presented as one with the freedom to leave what he is doing and to follow the prophet. Yet the freedom to leave is determined by the call of the prophet. If Elisha had had no call, there would have been no reason for him to leave, and therefore no freedom to leave his family and the responsibilities he had there. The freedom which he has to leave the oxen and his family is complemented by the new responsibility which he undertakes by following Elijah.

Luke stresses the unconditional nature of Christian apostleship by contrasting the words of Jesus to the words of Elijah. The man Jesus calls says, "Let me first go and bury my father." Surely this obligation would be more pressing than that of leave-taking, yet Jesus is more demanding than Elijah. His admonition "Leave the dead to bury their own dead" is at once the command to follow Jesus immediately and the admonition to forget all the past. Conversion means a turning from death to life.

The disciples we see in Luke have already done what Elisha has done. They have left the security of their fishing nets and have assumed both the hardships and the freedom of traveling about the countryside. In another reference to 1 Kings, Luke contrasts the idea of discipleship in the old covenant with the new. In the question, "Lord, do you want us to bid fire come down from heaven and consume" the inhospitable Samaritans, the disciples are recalling Elijah who called down fire from heaven to consume the king's soldiers sent to capture him. Jesus' response, that the disciples should move on to another village, demonstrates that consent rather than force are the signs of his kingdom.

Are these two readings to be seen as counter-arguments to the charge of the Grand Inquisitor, that humanity prefers slavery and security to freedom and the risk and hardship it may require? These two stories do show that the call to freedom can be sounded and will be taken up.

In Galatians 5 Paul is writing to Christians who already have taken the first step toward following Christ by becoming members of his community. Paul is adamant in his insistence of the gift of freedom made to Christians through Jesus the Lord in the Spirit. Yet the freedom which has been won for us by Christ's saving death is not an effective gift without our exercising it daily. "For freedom Christ has set us free; stand fast therefore, and do not submit again to a yoke of slavery." The Christian is freed from the strictures of Mosaic law: yet the Christian lives constantly in the freedom to choose the way of the Spirit, or the way of the flesh. The challenge which this freedom presents is met in the tedium of daily encounters. Both freedom and love are essential for the stability of the community. They are in fact inseparable. Freedom allows us to serve freely from love rather than from obligation. The Spirit that calls us beyond the law, calls us to "love, joy, peace, patience, kindness, goodness, faithfulness, gentleness, and self-control."

Pamela Kirk

R FOURTEENTH SUNDAY IN ORDINARY TIME
E PROPER 9
L SEVENTH SUNDAY AFTER PENTECOST

R   *Is 66:10–14c; Gal 6:14–18; Lk 10:1–12,17–20*
E   *Is 66:10–16; Gal 6:14–18; Lk 10:1–12,16–20*
L   *Is 66:10–14; Gal 6:1–10,14–16; Lk 10:1–12,16*

Children know the wolf in grandmother's clothes that greets Red Riding Hood. Children know the wolf in whose woods Hansel and Gretel are lost, the place *Where the Wild Things Are.*

And children know just as well the welcoming mother who serves a portion of last night's sweet dessert with a glass of cold milk. They know her enfolding arms and her comforting kiss that make everything all right.

Children do not know the abstractions, but the experience; not violence and evil, brokenness and alienation, but "big and bad" like the wolf, "dark and deep" like the woods, and "wild and scary" like the monsters who live there. Neither is it consolation and security in mother's care which they know, but sucking the abundant milk from her breasts, riding on her hip, and playing horsy on her knee.

Even though children grow and their experience is widened, we are lambs still. The abstractions which the child could not express become for us the deepened reality of the world where the wolf will meet the lamb. Violence and evil are fierce, brokenness and alienation are real; consolation and security are the fondest hope.

Isaiah envisions a kingdom restored. Jerusalem, the city of the king, has been violently overthrown; the people have been transported into an evil exile, broken from their historic foundations, and alienated from their religious heritage. The wolf has been at work. But a homecoming is on the horizon. Like a nursing baby returned to the breast it knows, the nation will be return to its mothering land and capital city. Those who had been led off as lambs will be consoled in Jerusalem by the Lord who comforts like a mother. Security is sure for people of God's pasture, the sheep of the Lord's hand. There shall be prosperity, with peace and healing extended like a river. Hopefully, Isaiah sees this comfort for the lambs whose hearts shall rejoice and whose bones shall flourish like the grass.

Into the midst of wolves, as lambs without purse, bag, or sandals, Jesus sends seventy missionaries. Their only provision is a proclamation. It is Jesus' proclamation and those who hear it from the missionaries hear Jesus, who has said from the beginning of his ministry, "The dominion of God has come near to you."

Jesus' invitation into the kingdom has been accompanied by the signs of peace and healing. These the lambs bring with them, too. Their mission is Jesus' mission, and the gospel would be incomplete without them. "Peace be to this house!" they say. "The dominion of God has come near." In the towns they heal the sick and say, "The kingdom of God has come near."

Near, says Isaiah, as near as a mother who comforts her child on her lap. The kingdom of God is near, soon to be restored with peace and healing flowing like a river. Our hearts, Isaiah promises, shall rejoice.

And the lambs return to Jesus who sent them, astonished with joy. "Lord, even the demons are subject to us in your name!" they say. "The kingdom you gave us to proclaim is more powerful than ever we knew!" Yes, and Jesus has seen it, too: "I saw Satan fall like lightning from heaven."

But these are not the occasion for rejoicing. We shall not joy in the success of the mission, or the power God lends to wield over the wolves. It is finally only this, that we lambs are counted among those who belong to God's kingdom, a dominion of peace and healing and astonishing joy.

Isaiah knows, too, that God's is a peaceable kingdom in which the lambs will lie down with the wolves. And that kingdom is *near*, though not fully come.

And so the wolves gather. The woods are cut down for a gallows. The wild things prowl around a cross. Above them is a Lamb sacrificed.

And in this Lamb is the restored kingdom. In this Lamb and this cross the very presence of the peaceable kingdom is come. The glory we thought we saw in God's power over the demons, or even in the fall of Satan, was only the beginning. In this Lamb is the final confrontation with violence and evil, brokenness and alienation. In this Lamb is the glory and promise of a new creation. "Far be it from me to glory," writes Paul, "except in the cross of our Lord Jesus Christ."

The kingdom's ours forever. Our names are written in heaven where our mothering God comforts us. Our Lord sets before us not the dessert and cold milk we once craved as children, but the kingdom of God baked into this bread and poured out in this wine. It is for us lambs to share until the wolves shed grandmother's clothes and join us at the table prepared before us in the presence of our enemies. This new creation, this nearing kingdom, this promise of peace, this place of healing, is this table and this food, and our astonishing joy.

Mikkel Thompson

R *Deut 30:10–14; Col 1:15–20; Lk 10:25–37*
E *Deut 30:9–14; Col 1:1–14; Lk 10:25–37*
L *Deut 30:9–14; Col 1:1–14; Lk 10:25–37*

It has always somewhat amused me that Jesus answered the lawyer's question, "And who is my neighbor?" with this story about the good Samaritan. Jesus didn't respond in a way we might have expected: but then he rarely did. After describing the incident in which the man who had been victimized was ignored by both the priest and the Levites and then helped by the Samaritan, Jesus asked: "Which of these three, do you think, proved neighbor to the man who fell among the robbers?" Which of the three responses—that of the priest, the Levite, or the Samaritan—was truly neighborly? The lawyer had not asked how one is to be a loving neighbor; he had asked how one is to recognize the neighbors we are called to love. He asked who; he was told how. Maybe I have been making a bit too much of the distinction, but I think not.

The parable of the good Samaritan is undoubtedly one of the best known and loved of all the parables of Jesus. It follows Jesus' response to the lawyer's principal concern, namely, what are we to do to inherit eternal life? Each of the synoptics present a version of that question—although each does so somewhat differently. The basic message is the same: we are to love God with all our heart, soul, and mind; and we are to love our neighbor as ourselves.

In Mark a scribe asks Jesus which commandment is "the first of all." Jesus answers that there is no other commandment greater than these two. The scribe recognized the truth of Jesus' response and commented that such love for God and others is much more important than burnt offerings and sacrifices. Jesus was impressed and told the scribe in turn that he was not far from the dominion of God. Matthew says that the question comes from a Pharisee. His version of the incident emphasizes the fact that the command to love one's neighbor as oneself "is like" the command to love God with one's whole being. But it is only Luke who gives us the parable about the good Samaritan in response to the lawyer's further inquiry about the identity of our neighbor.

We are very familiar with the story. And we get the point. We recognize instinctively that the Samaritan expressed the kind of love that the gospel sets before us as the ideal. We know as well as the lawyer did that we are to "go and do likewise." But why didn't Jesus focus on the victim as neighbor rather than on the neighborly response of the Samaritan? Why didn't Jesus tell the lawyer whom we are to love? Why did he concentrate instead on how we are to love?

It often seems to me that it would be so much easier if I only knew who it is I have been called to love. It often seems to me that it would be better if I could identify those persons. If only I knew the names of those for whom I bear such awesome responsibility . . . but I don't. You don't. We are called by Jesus to an expansive love, to a love without limit that is potentially there for all. We are not provided with a category of persons or a list of individuals. No one is eliminated in advance. Jesus' description of how we are to love tells us that the who is open-ended.

That is not to say, however, that Jesus has not given us any guidelines about those for whom we bear special responsibility. Luke's account of this incident implies that we are to love the disenfranchised and alienated, the marginalized and oppressed; we are to care for those who have fallen among the robbers. Yes.

We are to love, however, not only those needy strangers whom we read about on the front page or pass by in the subway stations, but our friends, our relatives, and all those at the center of our political, social, and economic power structures. If we love like the Samaritan loved, we will be compassionate and generous to each person upon whom we stumble. We will be attentive and affectionate toward all. Neighborly love knows no limit.

Barbara Finan

R   SIXTEENTH SUNDAY IN ORDINARY TIME
E   PROPER 11
L   NINTH SUNDAY AFTER PENTECOST

R   *Gen 18:1–10a; Col 1:24–28; Lk 10:38–42*
E   *Gen 18:1–10a; Col 1:21–29; Lk 10:38–42*
L   *Gen 18:1–10a; Col 1:21–28; Lk 10:38–42*

My eyes were on Marsha's face. She was checking her watch. I repeated again what I had said. She blinked, not having heard it the first time. She was not really "with" me, and I knew it. Instead she was far off, already tending to business in the place where her mind had gone.

Each of us has known a Marsha in our experience; perhaps we have been one all too often in our encounters with others. We have not really been "all there." We really have not been present. The personal human mysteries of a *you* and a *me* have not really entered into an interpersonal bond. I go away distracted and you depart disappointed, or the other way around. The human sacrament of real presence has not been given or received.

When the mystery hidden for ages became manifest in the person of Christ Jesus, it forever changed the human mystery. The human face became the icon of God and continues to be such for those who know through faith. The Word is first of all a person, and from that personal presence we speak our humanness as a word to one another.

Mary in today's gospel entertains Real Presence with a real presence. She is all there for him, and he recognizes this as being top priority for her. No one with a sound mind would rate the meal preparation as unimportant. But Martha is upset while doing that preparation. Could it be that in her woman's heart she sensed that he was already being served by Mary's real presence in a way that far exceeded the spread of her table? Has Mary's attentiveness already nourished his humanness in a way that physical food could never do?

Abraham receives three guests in his vision. His focus in on *them*. His one request: "Do not pass by." His washing and waiting on them embellish this main focus. It is a practical manifestation of his real presence to them, not a substitution for it. Abraham is not upset. He is delighted.

The mystery hidden for ages and revealed personally in the face of the man-God Christ Jesus longs for our company. Our baptismal grafting has joined us to that vine, and the eucharist nourishes the bonding of that mystery with us in the tent of our own personal turmoils and tensions. Our communing brings us sooner or later to the table of the cross, for it is his mind to give of himself. As we gradually put on his mind, we find ourselves gradually released from the nausea of our own self-centered preoccupation.

In Abraham's vision, the guests reward Abraham's attentiveness with the promise of a son. Perhaps the reward of our attentiveness to the mystery we bear in our own bodies and that hidden in the hearts of loved ones, colleagues, and strangers, is the re-emergence of our own innocence and integrity. Perhaps we shall know ourselves as we really are for the first time, and be really present to our own authentic mystery. When others come to call, perhaps they will indeed find us "at home." We are then able to offer them the gift of our own real presence. Who knows: we may even entertain angels unawares.

Carla Mae Streeter, O.P.

R SEVENTEENTH SUNDAY IN ORDINARY TIME
E PROPER 12
L TENTH SUNDAY AFTER PENTECOST

R *Gen 18:20–32; Col 2:12–14; Lk 11:1–13*
E *Gen 18:20–33; Col 2:6–15; Lk 11:1–13*
L *Gen 18:20–32; Col 2:6–15; Lk 11:1–13*

We often hear the question, perhaps even ask the question ourselves: what is God really like? How can we know God? We
cannot fully know and understand God, but if we pay attention
to what God has empowered the writers of Scripture to say, we
may come a little closer to knowing the one who is source and
end of our human existence.

Today's Scripture readings, forming a thematic unity as they do,
can help us to know God better. In the first reading, we hear the
familiar story of Abraham's pleading for mercy for the people of
Sodom and Gomorrah. But this story also portrays certain characteristic of the God who is *hesed* and *emet*, loving-kindness and
faithfulness. Our passage begins: "Because the outcry against
Sodom and Gomorrah is great and their sin is very grave, I will
go down to see whether they have done altogether according to
the outcry which has come to me." Here we see one who does
not immediately accept as fact what has become the subject of an
outcry, but first investigates the validity of the outcry. This an-
thropomorphism, speaking of God in human terms, intends to
tell us something about the God we worship. Unlike us, God is
slow to believe in outcries, name-calling and condemnations.
God, the rightful judge of all humanity, is slow to pass judgment without proof, without verifying the facts. As Paul would
later say, how much better to be judged by God than by our
fellow human beings, even though God knows better than anyone the depths of our weakness, compromising and mixed-up
motivations? What do human judgments on our words and actions matter, in comparison with the judgment of one who
means to find out the truth before passing judgment?

In the Genesis reading Abraham persists in bargaining with God about how many or how few innocent people it would take to spare the city. Abraham is like a clever, well-loved child, whee-dling, playfully bargaining to spare the city, almost as if he wanted to see how far he could go. And God? God is shown to us clearly as one who is patient, one who leans toward mercy. The Lord is the judge of all the world, yet for the sake of only ten just people in the city will withhold destruction. God is Judge, God is just, yet the judgments of God lean toward mercy.

The reading from Colossians prepares us for the gospel message. The Lord of Abraham, the judge leaning toward mercy, is at once Father and friend. In Jesus Christ we have been brought to life, having had our transgressions forgiven, because Jesus Christ has obliterated the bond against us: "This, God set aside, nailing it to the cross." Because we have been regenerated, born again, the restricting bond of accusations, the legal claims, and the out-cry against us is removed. We dare stand up in Christ and say, as he teaches us in the gospel, "Father."

The gospel today speaks of prayer. Above all, it helps to answer our question, "What is God like?" God is as father and sustainer; God is friend to whom we may go, even in the middle of the night, and ask without shame or embarrassment; God is giver of all good things.

Luke's version of the prayer we call the "Our Father" is shorter than Matthew's, and probably closer to the original words of Je-sus. "Father," a form of address for God found in Jewish tradi-tions as well as in traditions of other faiths, is here used in the Christian prayer of choice. "Hallowed be your name": that God make holy the divine name by manifesting glory and power. "Your dominion come" is a call for the completion of Christ's work on earth. "Give us *each day* our daily bread" reminds us that God is sustainer now, tomorrow, each day. "And forgive us our sins." Why? "For (because) we ourselves forgive everyone who is indebted to us." This is the only place where this prayer refers to the action of Christians, and this forgiving is to be mod-eled on God's forgiving. "Lead us not into temptation" refers to a single, great future trial, the final onslaught of the evil one.

Here in Luke's gospel, Jesus tells a parable to show that petition for daily bread is always heard. In the original Greek text, the opening words are in the form of rhetorical question, demanding an answer of an emphatic No! Can you imagine that if a friend came at midnight asking for bread for unexpected guests, the friend would be refused? No, I can't imagine it!

Friendship, especially in Eastern cultures, within which Jesus was speaking, allowed such bold requests. One cannot say no, because of the bond of friendship. Again we return to our question: What is God like? God is a friend who will arise even at midnight to help a friend. God, who allowed Abraham to ask six times about reducing the number of just people required to spare the city, who removed restricting bonds and legal claims from us because of Jesus Christ, will surely not remain indifferent to us.

This gospel ends with a repetition of the theme: that we never ask, seek, knock in vain. What is God like? God is like a father who cares for, listens to, opens to those who approach. Jesus is teaching us how to pray, not what to pray for. We can expect always to be heard, to be attended to; we may not expect certain things, positions, promotions through prayer. God is the one who is not irritated by repeated pleadings on a behalf of others, by insistent questioning about the way the innocent must suffer along with the guilty. God, who is both father and mother, is one who does not stand on ceremony when friends are in need, one who accepts the shameless, unembarrassed importunities of a friend.

We will receive once more today the bread of life from God, our Father, our Mother, our Friend. In sharing together the bread of community in Jesus Christ, in becoming more and more his bread for the world, we may hope that God may enable us to be sparks of the God who is slow to judge and merciful toward others, who breaks constricting fetters, and who is willing to be disturbed and to give good things.

Marian Bohen, O.S.U.

R EIGHTEENTH SUNDAY IN ORDINARY TIME
E PROPER 13
L ELEVENTH SUNDAY AFTER PENTECOST

R *Ecc 1:2;2:21–23; Col 3:1–5,9–11; Lk 12:13–21*
E *Ecc 1:12–14;2:18–23; Col 3:12–17; Lk 12:13–21*
L *Ecc 1:2;2:18–26; Col 3:1–11; Lk 12:13–21*

The gastroenterologist made a big claim: the gastric bubble will make you lose 50% of your excess weight. Your body will be reshaped. (Like the story of Little Red Riding Hood, the wolf in bed will be reshaped, and supposedly, we too will live happily for some days after.) Vanity of vanities, living in a world of pretense. Our Scriptures name our sickness. Ours is a self-possessedness that worships the created rather than the Creator. We think substitutes will make us secure and strong.

Steroids seems to be one American answer for reshaping. But the athletes on *Sixty Minutes* were calling for the outlawing of drugs that set unretractable results—blocking of arteries, primitive facial features, heart attacks. Out of their own experiences of drug use which distorted them and blocked their health they identified idolatrous desires that left them sicker than they were before. When asked why they became addicted, they said, "The Russians." They believed that if we were going to win by lifting heavier weights and by playing tougher, they had to use steroids.

Our lessons show the personal and social vices resulting from being possessed. We are diminished when things we possess end up possessing us. Being self-possessed is a condition which results from being seduced by self-centered, self-gratifying, self-serving patterns of society.

Slander is labeled by the second lesson as an enemy. What soap will wash it away but kind, pure and true words. "Is it true?" Words are not to be obscene or insulting. Alteration of tone of voice, even a wink of the eye, or silence itself may mislead. Temper tantrums or angry outbursts are not the only evidence of this misshaping.

Sex can be idolatrous. Sex is to be respected. Sexuality relates us to one another in healthful and helpful ways. If wrongly possessed it manipulates even a king, like David, so that someone gets badly hurt, like Bathsheba's husband.

Stock can be named as a misshaping enemy. The Greek word for covetousness, *pleonexia*, means "more" and "to have." It is the desire to have more, the insatiate desire can ruin us and make us sick. The passion of acquisitiveness is a desire that leads us to want more than we need, and inevitably for that which belongs to someone else. It gets us things which we have no right to have. This getting sets us up to put things in the place of God. To worship things and not God is idolatry. We may even try to use God to obtain money, rather than to use money to serve God. Jesus' farmer is called foolish not because of his gift of entrepreneurship. He is not called unjust because his economic decision to replace old barns with larger ones. He's just foolish because he lives completely in and for himself. He congratulates himself, plans for himself. The poor fellow will soon die and he's failed to make the distinction between what one has and what one is. He's unable to know what is enough until he reaches the point of too much. His inordinate craving to hoard disregards those in need and places goods in the place of God. What does it profit him?

Starwars is yet another illustration of our attempt to be secure. Vanity of vanities! The cartoonist shows the Pentagon painting "In God We Trust" on a missile nose cone. The caption reads, "Isn't that a wee bit hypocritical, General?" Those who advocate "a vote for me is a vote for God" and then advocate our trusting in Star Wars illustrate a society that is reshaped by militaristic and materialistic ways.

Scrabble is not named in the Scripture and would not illustrate our sickness unless it too would so preoccupy us as to make us proud, or on the other hand, to make us reject ourselves because we can't spell as well as the Smiths. Whatever possesses us, whenever there is a possession by possessions, it needs to be put down.

Re-suit. Be God-possessed, urges Paul. That will give you a true intellectual propriety. Having received Jesus as Lord, live in him, since you have indeed been raised with Christ. You will have with this Christ-possessedness a true emotional propriety: your passions will be transformed. There will be a volitional propriety as you secure your confidence and trust in God with whom all things are possible. The metaphor is: Let the garment fit. Sit and rise with comfort. Christ tailor-makes us.

LeRoy E. Kennel

R NINETEENTH SUNDAY IN ORDINARY TIME
E PROPER 14
L TWELFTH SUNDAY AFTER PENTECOST

R *Wis 18:6–9; Heb 11:1–2,8–19; Lk 12:32–48*
E *Gen 15:1–6; Heb 11:1–3,8–16; Lk 12:32–40*
L *Gen 15:1–6; Heb 11:1–3,8–16; Lk 12:32–40*

Faith shines out from each of the three readings today. The selection from Hebrews serves well to bond them. In other words, we can say that by its position in the center of the table of God's word, this selection sheds light on both the first and the third readings. As members of the church through faith and baptism, we admire the faith of Abraham and Sarah, we hope to imbibe some of it, and we look forward to sitting down at the eucharistic banquet.

The readings tell us something important, too, about how the word of God is planted deep within the human heart. God does not lay commands nor promises on us as it were from the outside. Abraham and Sarah knew, in a beginning sort of way, that they were to have descendants as "many as the stars of heaven and as the innumerable grains of sand by the seashore." Our forebears in Egypt were trusting in the oath God made to Abraham and Sarah, Isaac and Rebecca, and Jacob and Leah, when they carried out what they knew they had to in Egypt. The servant in the gospel would have violated his very person by not staying alert until the return of the master.

All were in the dark, however, as to how and when the promise would be fulfilled. Abraham and Sarah, for example, tried several cultural solutions offered to childless couples of their day. They tried adopting as heir the first most trusted slave of the household, and they tried having offspring by Sarah's maidservant. But God made it clear to them that such was not the route they were to take. They grew in the confident assurance concerning what they hoped for, as they waited and waited for God to reveal the how and when. Consider that Abraham and Sarah never gave up responding to God in faith. When their confident assurance was stretched to the limit of its endurance, God fulfilled the promise planted in their hearts so many years earlier. Only when Sarah was long past the age and Abraham was as good as dead, did the answer come. They still trusted. Sarah received the power to conceive because she judged that God's promise would be kept. Again God's word became creative in a unique way. The act of intercourse in which Isaac was conceived proceeded from the faith of the couple, "the visible from the invisible," as Hebrews puts it. Those who were barren and dead became creative because Sarah and Abraham, judging God to be trustworthy, said "yes."

Since the desire to carry out God's plan is planted deep within the human heart, we collaborate with God in carrying out what is best for us. It is important, then, that we be in touch with our own deepest motives. We may have to struggle, to let go some cherished goods when the call to growth comes. We may have to be strangers and foreigners as we grapple with cultural solutions like abortion, surrogate motherhood, or countless others, to find in our day a city with foundations whose builder and maker is God.

Our confident assurance of hope is intensified in the gospel revelation, a precious little jewel within which the entire gamut of God's dealings with humankind is compressed. The injunction "Be dressed and ready" calls us to be prepared to move at once as the Israelites were on the night of the Passover in Egypt. Our lamps are to be burning, the light of faith as our guide. Jesus can reveal to us God's tremendous love only when we are willing to make the changes called for in the light of faith.

Again the imagery is vivid and appropriate. We are the servants awaiting the return of Christ, not only at the end of time when he will come again to judge the living and the dead, but also whenever he comes in the events of our daily life. Whenever the risen Lord comes upon servants who are alert, he exchanges roles with them: he invites them to sit at the banquet table, first of the word, then of the sacrament. He takes us into the mystery of his having emptied himself, taking the form of a slave. He draws us into his unique act of love whenever we discover him in the least of his children or in our act of worship.

The Lord is coming at an unexpected hour. This sounds like a final warning to remain alert. In order not to be caught off guard, we need to be in touch, as we said earlier, with our inner motives. We need to be aware of where God is luring our hearts to expand in love of God or love of neighbor. We need, therefore, to listen for that word which is meant to call us to growth at any given time. Something new, by way of insight, attitude, or behavior, does spring into life at the juncture where the word of God encounters deep within us the urge to grow.

Each such encounter with Christ in the liturgy of the word is a new wonderful deed of God accomplished through Christ. No wonder that when we are called to give thanks, we respond that it is right to give God thanks and praise. We who have all met Christ in our own way now join together to celebrate at the table where we are served. Together we learn anew Christ's own meaning of the meal he serves us. Our food is his body broken out of love for us, and our drink is his blood shed for the remission of sins. This becomes for us a moment of truth, a challenge to be alert; for when we least expect him, he will come again into our day-to-day living.

Mary Pierre Ellebracht, C.Pp.S.

R TWENTIETH SUNDAY IN ORDINARY TIME
E PROPER 15
L THIRTEENTH SUNDAY AFTER PENTECOST

R *Jer 38:4–6,8–10; Heb 12:1–4; Lk 12:49–53*
E *Jer 23:23–29; Heb 12:1–7,11–14; Lk 12:49–56*
L *Jer 23:23–29; Heb 12:1–13; Lk 12:49–53*

"Do you think that I have come to give peace on earth? No, I tell you, but rather division." These are deeply disturbing words for Christians to hear. We tend to pride ourselves on our efforts for unity, peace and harmony, whether in our personal relations or in the larger arenas of civil and ecclesiastical affairs. And so we should; the gospels, taken as a whole, are abundantly clear on the centrality of our call to the work of peacemaking.

But today's gospel presents another face—a hard face—of that call. The peace we are called to make is not always sweet, for ourselves or for others. Sometimes it shatters our best-laid plans and burns up our fondest hopes. Sometimes its fruit is defeat and humiliation. This peace does not necessarily feel peaceful; it feels more like death by fire.

The peace Jesus came to bring was the peace of God, not peace as humans define it. The difference is that human peace is basically a matter of trade-offs: "I'll scratch your back if you'll scratch mine, and as long as this arrangement is mutually satisfying we'll avoid hostilities." The peace of God, on the other hand, is basically a matter of truth, integrity, and love: "I'll do this because it is the right and true and loving thing to do, not because of what I'll get out of it."

The reason this causes division is that there is nothing more annoying to human beings than for someone to refuse to participate in the normal and customary trade-offs. Trade-offs seem to us to be the very stuff of human relations; our very identities are built on the trade-off of playing a role in exchange for approval and status. For people suddenly to claim that they can build their identity on another foundation—namely, God's love—shakes the whole system of human relationships to its roots.

Prophets are people who make that claim. Jeremiah, for example, refused to participate in the patriotic project of bolstering the faltering confidence of the soldiers when Jerusalem lay under siege. He spoke the truth as he heard it from God; and the political leaders knew that he had to be gotten rid of. His life was saved in the end, but not before he was physically abused and profoundly humiliated.

The supreme prophet, of course, is Jesus Christ, the pioneer and perfecter of our faith. His word of truth is cast upon us like fire, burning up every false foundation upon which we try to base our individual and communal identities. For casting this fire upon us, he was crucified. Neither then nor now can the powers that be permit the status quo to be confronted by the truth.

At our eucharistic table today we celebrate unity and reconciliation. Yet let us not imagine that these come lightly. The unity celebrated in the eucharist requires that we relinquish every false unity, every merely human trade-off, every false identity, and take up the cross of love.

Mary Frohlich

R TWENTY-FIRST SUNDAY IN ORDINARY TIME
E PROPER 16
L FOURTEENTH SUNDAY AFTER PENTECOST

R *Is 66:18–21; Heb 12:5–7,11–13; Lk 13:22–30*
E *Is 28:14–22; Heb 12:18–19,22–29; Lk 13:22–30*
L *Is 66:18–23; Heb 12:18–24; Lk 13:22–30*

People love to tell this story on themselves, no matter what their denominational affiliation. Hans dies and is welcomed at the pearly gates. He is given a tour of the mansions of heaven by the angel in charge. As they pass various chambers, the angel identifies the inhabitants: "This is where the Roman Catholics reside, and here are the Methodists, and over there the Anglicans." Then, as they pass another room, the angel whispers: "Sh! This is where the Lutherans are. They think they're the only ones here."

The story is a humorous way of acknowledging our limited vision of the kingdom of God. We can laugh at the thought of our being in heaven without being aware of the presence of fellow Christians whom we confess to be part of the "one, holy, catholic church." But the story loses its humor for most people if it becomes as broadly inclusive as Jesus suggests in the gospel reading, when he says that people "will come from east and west, and from north and south, and sit at table in the dominion of God." This is not something new that Jesus made up. His words reflect the imagery in the Old Testament reading which speaks of bringing people from all the nations to the holy mountain of Jerusalem. If there are going to be people from Iran and Libya there, then maybe we wouldn't want to know who is in the next room of the heavenly mansion.

Jesus had been asked the question, "Lord, will those who are saved be few?" There are two surprising things about his answer. First, he implies that there will be people there that we would never have expected, people who are very different from us. That is both sobering and liberating: sobering, because it challenges the provincial way we envision the kingdom of God; and liberating, because it encourages us to think of all humanity not only as neighbors but as family. And if that will be so then, "at table in the dominion of God," why not now?

A second surprising and somewhat disturbing element in Jesus' answer to the question about who will be saved is that it prompts us to question whether we will be seated at the heavenly banquet. The story about a group thinking they are the only ones in heaven at least assumes that the group is there and can laugh about its provincialism. But Jesus suggests that many who think that they have assured seating at that wondrous feast are in for a rude surprise. Narrow is the door and stern the householder in passing judgment on who will enter and who will be thrust out.

This is a hard saying of Jesus and seemingly no word of gospel at all. What can it mean? Is Jesus laying down conditions that must be met for entrance into the kingdom? Will our souls in fact be weighed on the scales of justice on the day of judgment? Will we be facing an angry God when we approach the narrow door?

The key to understanding the warning of Jesus that "some are last who will be first" is to be found in the meaning of the metaphor "door," the narrow door by which we gain entrance to the kingdom of God. On another occasion Jesus said: "I am the door; any one who enters by me will be saved," or, as the writer to the Hebrews puts it in the second reading, Jesus is the "mediator of a new covenant." The door that serves as the entrance to the dominion of God is Jesus, the very Jesus who mediated the new covenant through the blood he shed for us, the very Jesus whose broken body and shed blood we receive in the banquet prepared for us today. There is no other door, no other way.

If that is so, then what makes the saying of Jesus hard? Because it exposes what Dietrich Bonhoeffer called "cheap grace." Because it is possible, as St. Paul warned the Corinthians, that when we meet together, it is not the Lord's Supper we eat. Because it will not be sufficient in that day to say, "Lord, open to us. . . . We ate and drank in your presence." Because it's possible for us to eat and drink judgment upon ourselves. To enter the narrow door that is Jesus is to enter the narrow way that is called the way of the cross. As the writer to the Hebrews reminds us, that narrow way calls for spiritual discipline, a discipline that often seems more painful than pleasant, and only later yields the peaceful fruit of righteousness to those who have been trained by it.

Let there be no doubts in your mind about the invitation of Jesus to share in the banquet he lays before us today and also in the heavenly banquet he is preparing for us. The invitation is extended to you freely without any conditions attached. But at the same time do not be falsely reassured that this gracious offer of forgiveness and fellowship is all there is to the Christian life. The reason that our Lord will say to some who expect to be at the feast, "I do not know where you come from," is because Jesus did not become "the way" for them. May the food and the fellowship we share here keep our feet firmly on the narrow way of the cross until we join together at the heavenly feast with people from all over the world who know the same Lord and have followed the same path.

Thomas Droege

R TWENTY-SECOND SUNDAY IN ORDINARY TIME
E PROPER 17
L FIFTEENTH SUNDAY AFTER PENTECOST

R *Eccs 3:19–21,30–31; Heb 12:18–19,22–24a; Lk 4:1,7–14*
E *Eccs 10:12–18; Heb 13:1–8; Lk 4:1,7–14*
L *Prov 25:6–7; Heb 13:1–8; Lk 4:1,7–14*

When I was in seminary, the pastor of my home congregation invited me to assist with the bread during the distribution at the eucharist. This was in the early seventies, and the people of that congregation still held to their old pietistic habits concerning holy communion. They would come to the table looking very somber and, upon reaching the altar rail, would fall to their knees, clasp their hands together, and bow their heads so low that they turned almost completely in on themselves. Since they received the bread in their mouths, it was quite a difficult operation to find their mouths! I began the distribution being slightly scornful of their piety (sophisticated seminarian that I was!). But as I went along from person to person, I realized something important: I knew all these people by their hands. I could not see their faces, but each pair of folded hands brought a name and a face to me. I knew in that moment the wonderful humility of being part of God's people, of what it meant to be one in Christ. These hands had nurtured and cared for me as I grew in the faith, and now I had the privilege of meeting those hands in the grace of the eucharist. This was a feast of the caring, embracing, loving reality of the community of faith.

Jesus tells of just such a banquet in the gospel for this day. He dismisses the honors and status of the world and calls everyone into the same meal, into the same place of caring and embracing hands. If you sit up higher than another, you cannot be cared for by the hands of love and mercy. But if you are brought into the feast to join the others, it is those hands of love and mercy which reach out to draw you in. It becomes the banquet which Jesus describes at the end of the gospel lesson, where all the people around the table reach out their hands to those who cannot provide a feast themselves but who need to share the feast. This is the feast of the poor, whose hands reach out in need. It is the feast of the maimed, who may not have hands to share the work. It is the feast of the lame, whose hands are crippled by disease. It is the feast of the blind, whose hands grope to feel life's realities.

The writer to the Hebrews reflects on the feast of the community of faith. We are told that on our Mount Zion love between sisters and brothers must continue, a love which knows no boundaries or distinctions or physical limitations. It is the love of God at work within us. The community is to be always hospitable; as God has invited us to the feast, so we share that invitation with all people. The feast is of the freedom of the children of God, and it speaks a word of hope to those imprisoned. It is a feast for the abused, for we are called to feel their bruises, since we are all one body. This is the banquet for all the children of God. We are called to the same table. There are no distinctions: all share the same food, and that food is the best meal we can ever have on this earth.

When we gather at the table now, we no longer bow our heads, fold our hands and turn in on ourselves. We have learned, as communities of faith, that the table is a place of joy and healing. And in that joy and health, we come in confidence to the feast of life. Our hands stretch out to receive the bread and the wine of life. Our confidence in receiving that gift is not human pride in our worthiness. It is, rather, the confident humility of the faithful. In our confidence in God's gift, we can also be gifts for one another. We gather as the friends of God, and friends always look to see that everyone is included. We gather at the same table and stretch our hands to receive the same gift. We are the household of God, gathered at the table for the family meal. We are the body of Christ, a body whose hands are strengthened in the meal to reach out in deeds of love and mercy. We stand at the table humbled by the presence of God and of each other. And our confident humility draws us into God's promise that we will know God and each other through our loving hands, and that the world will know God through us.

Nancy L. Winder

R TWENTY-THIRD SUNDAY IN ORDINARY TIME
E PROPER 18
L SIXTEENTH SUNDAY AFTER PENTECOST

R *Wis 9:13–19; Philem 9b-10,12–17; Lk 14:25–33*
E *Deut 30:15–20; Philem 1–20; Lk 14:25–33*
L *Prov 9:8–12; Philem 1, 10–21; Lk 14:25–33*

During the decade of the 1960's there was a great deal of talk in our society about commitment. The commitment often led to action that sought to effect immediate change. It was a time of high passion. It was not a time for compromise. *The Sophie Horowitz Story* by Sarah Schulman is a mystery novel set in that time. Near the beginning of the novel, Lillian is reflecting on her life as a revolutionary in the 1960's. "We had to give everything to the struggle," she says. "We had to smash monogamy, we had to break with our parents, we had to give up our white skin, and we had to fight the pigs."[57] Lillian felt powerful taking on the world, but eventually she gave up the struggle because it was too heavy. Most of all, she didn't like people telling her how to live.

Smashing monogamy may not be the best way to effect social change. And giving up our racial identity is probably impossible. But the intent behind the mandate for a revolutionary is clear: to be part of the movement requires total commitment. That's what it means to be a principled person, says Lillian later on. Personal feelings and personal relationships and personal possessions are set aside for a larger vision.

No one, says Jesus to the great crowd that followed him, no one who does not carry a cross and come with me can be a disciple of mine. The mandate for discipleship is clear. Nothing can be more important than following Jesus. Not family, not possessions, not even one's own life. The demands of Jesus are not violent but they are uncompromising. To be a disciple requires total commitment.

Just before these hard sayings about discipleship, Luke records the parable of the big dinner party. The invited guests have asked to be excused for a variety of spurious reasons. As Luke gives an account of the homily on the hillside, it is almost as if Jesus had those absenting guests in mind when he reminds the eager throng to count the cost of discipleship from the beginning.

Whenever it seemed to my mother that I was embarking on an adventure without considering all the consequences or at least all the consequences she had considered, she would ask me something like, "Do you know what you are getting yourself into?" Because my mother was a timid soul who was fearful about many things, it was easy for me to discount the question as one more effort at control. However, there was wisdom in my mother's question similar to the warning from Jesus. Before deciding to be a follower of Jesus, know what you are getting yourself into. It may require of you your life. Very likely it will limit what you possess. And most certainly it will change every significant relationship you have.

The message from Jesus is clear. And it sounds more like a warning than an invitation. It is costly to be a disciple. And one had better count the cost before making the commitment. That is not the kind of message that we usually give to people on an evangelism visit. Or when we are talking to an unchurched friend about what it means for us to follow Jesus. We are more inclined to say something about meaning or fullness in life. We are inclined to tell people that their lives will be easier or better or at least richer and deeper in the spiritual sense. An abundant life is always part of the gospel promise, but it is only part. For the other part, we are reminded by this harsh word from Jesus that everything we value is qualified by the demands of discipleship.

There is wisdom in the church's practice of the catechumenate. A six-week inquiry class is not long enough to consider the weightiness of the call to discipleship. It takes more time. People need time in order to know clearly what they are getting themselves into.

If we take seriously this word of Jesus, it is no wonder that we want to domesticate discipleship. Most of us are like Lillian. We don't want life to be too heavy. Nor do we like being told how to live. Nor do we like carrying crosses. We would like to have it all. Discipleship and the "good life." Not possible, says Jesus. And it is better you know that from the start.

Why then would anyone count the cost from the beginning and still choose to follow Jesus? Because, in a curiously paradoxical way, it is to choose for life rather than for death. The command given to Israel remains. To love and obey God, that is life rather than death. To keep God's commandments, that is life and not death. To participate in the death of Jesus in his holy meal, that is life. There really is no alternative.

Herbert Anderson

[57]Sarah Schulman, *The Sophie Horowitz Story* (Tallahasse, FL: Naiad Press, 1984), p. 3.

TWENTY-FOURTH SUNDAY IN ORDINARY TIME
PROPER 19
SEVENTEENTH SUNDAY AFTER PENTECOST

R   *Ex 32:7–11,13–14; 1 Tim 1:12–17; Lk 15:1–32*
E   *Ex 32:1,7–14; 1 Tim 1:12–17; Lk 15:1–10*
L   *Ex 32:7–14; 1 Tim 1:12–17; Lk 15:1–10*

"Now the tax collectors and sinners were all drawing near to hear Jesus. And the Pharisees and the scribes murmured, saying, 'This man receives sinners and eats with them.' "

I love it! Sometimes I think this Jesus thrived on creative tension. He seemed always to be pulling someone's chain, challenging the pious and powerful. The opening verses in today's gospel are a case in point.

It is extremely significant in Semitic circles with whom one eats. The very act of eating with someone creates a oneness and solidarity, a communion, if you please, with that person. John Navonne writes:

> The banquet is a most common motif describing the People of God. It is both a source and sign of communion among men, and also between men and God. Its participants share the same source of life, which creates among them an identity of life. Eating together establishes a covenant community on a purely human level. The shared meal commits one to a bond of loyalty.[58]

Thus it is not difficult to understand why Jesus was crucified; simply check out his list of dinner companions. They were not the people who make the guest list at White House state banquets or appear on the pages of our newspapers' "living" sections. Jesus' iconoclastic eating habits were forever getting him into trouble. Norman Perrin points out: "Jesus welcomed these outcasts into table fellowship with himself in the name of the Kingdom of God, in the name of the Jews' ultimate hope, and so both prostituted that hope and also shattered the closed ranks of the community against their enemy. It is hard to imagine anything more offensive to Jewish sensibilities."[59]

That offensiveness is at work in our text. Eating with rich Pharisees is one thing, but eating with folk like Zacchaeus, tax collectors for Rome, drove the Jerusalem establishment "up a tree." For this they inevitably "treed" Jesus.

Fifteen years ago Luther Place in Washington, D.C., opened its doors to the de-institutionalized homeless. They came into the church in droves out of the bitter cold January nights, filling the church to wall-to-wall capacity. The following December, when the congregation's parent body sent out its annual parochial-report forms to be filled out by the pastor, I entered "15,000" in the block slotted for "new members." It must have blown the computer at church headquarters. Forms were fired back with an accompanying letter: "Dear Pastor Steinbruck . . . you have not followed the criteria . . . this info does not compute." I responded: "My criteria for membership is Matthew, Mark, Luke and John. What's yours?" As a matter of gospel fact, by Jesus' criteria these are his sisters and brothers. Strangers or not, friend or foe, they are welcome to his banquet.

In fact Jesus goes *looking* for strays, along the by-ways of life. Talk about what the cat dragged in, Jesus instructs his host, "But when you give a feast, invite those who are poor, who are maimed, who are lame, who are blind, and you will be blessed, because they cannot repay you. You will be repaid at the resurrection of the just." I would love to see a modern day Leonardo DaVinci do justice to Jesus' supper community and fill the other side of the table, giving priority to those normally excluded from life's feasts. What a collage of humanity that would make! As Groucho Marx declared, "I wouldn't join any club that would have me as a member!" But God did, and does.

Biblical hospitality is not entertaining. It is not a performance at which we cast peripheral glances to gauge how our acts are received and applauded by guests. Rather, it is a selfless act, done out of poverty of spirit without regard for reward, even to the degree of being demonized and labeled a glutton and drunkard. Supper with the Lord, who may well come among us as a homeless stranger, results in a mutuality of giving and receiving, host and guest. All together become one and inseparable.

Biblical hospitality is evangelism. To welcome the stranger and sojourner into our midst and to our tables is to continue here on earth the messianic banquet. It is a foretaste of the marriage feast of the Lamb, to expand our communion circles to embrace into our community the least of these of whom Jesus was least of all. Biblical hospitality is to share the bread of life broken for us, to extend the cup of living water to all who thirst, to offer life in the hidden places where "lost coins" and "sheep" tend to hide, to invite each and all to the celebration that has no end.

Our calling is to exemplify the acceptance that is in Jesus, even and especially to sinners and outcasts. So we bear witness amidst the idolatries of this world to the difference that faith makes, in offering hospitality with the whole of one's being to the well-being of others, even unto martyrdom. That our fellowship is extended even to our enemies will make clear the difference that faith makes in the moral life of the covenant people. And so we know what is meant by "a light unto the nations."

Jesus the evangel; Yeshua, the one who will save. Evangelism is to live in the way that manifests and exemplifies the life and grace of Christ, the gentle, self-giving love that empties itself, being a servant and host to the other.

John Steinbruck

[58]John Navonne, "The Lucan Banquet Community," *The Bible Today*, December 1970, p. 155.
[59]Norman Perrin, *Rediscovering the Teachings of Jesus* (New York: Harper & Row, 1967), pp. 102–3.

R TWENTY-FIFTH SUNDAY IN ORDINARY TIME
E PROPER 20
L EIGHTEENTH SUNDAY AFTER PENTECOST

R *Am 8:4–7; 1 Tim 2:1–8; Lk 16:1–13*
E *Am 8:4–7; 1 Tim 2:1–8; Lk 16:1–13*
L *Am 8:4–7; 1 Tim 2:1–8; Lk 16:1–13*

It is a strange account just read in our midst, this parable of Jesus about the dishonest steward. The steward insures his own future by ingratiating himself to others; but this he does by cheating his master. And Jesus commends him. But for what?

For his dishonesty? Can it be that Jesus suggests a shady ethical stance, all too well known to us in the worlds of politics and commerce today? Surely not! No. Jesus commends the steward for taking an interest in the future. The steward is able to look ahead and see that after he is fired for incompetence, he will have little prospect of getting another job. So before the ax falls, he takes precautions to guarantee his own future. He puts others in his debt, so they will be obligated to him when he is unemployed. He foresees his future, and provides for it.

Concern for the future often gets bad press in religious circles these days. As we look back, it seems that for many Christians the chief concern has been to get to heaven after death. Too often a preoccupation for that aspect of the future created an indifference to human values while on earth. It was not without reason that critics could call religion "the opium of the people"— an escape from current unpleasantness into a dream-like trance.

That kind of concern for the future at the expense of the present we rightly reject. But care must be taken, lest in fleeing from a lion we encounter a bear instead. We cannot dismiss all thought of the future; rightly understood, concern for the future is a necessary consideration for Christians. And that is Jesus' point in the parable of the dishonest steward.

The future about which we are to think does not begin at some distant time after the resurrection of the dead. It begins now.

Always the future is simply a split-second ahead of us. What we do now has an effect immediately, not merely at some far-off time. Our problem has been that we defined the future too distantly, not that we were concerned about it.

The prophet Amos looked at the future of his people and cried out in protest. Greed and dishonesty abounded in the land. The wealthy exploited the poor, and justice was in shreds. Amos knew that no society could survive long under such conditions. The people were sealing their doom in the not-so-distant future by their shortsighted view in the present. Unlike the steward in the parable of Jesus, the people of the land did not look ahead and foresee what was about to happen unless they took drastic action. And so Amos rose up and argued against the values of his generation.

It is the task of the church in every age to look at present practices and policies and to ask, "How will these affect tomorrow and the next day? What are the unrecognized consequences of our actions today?" If the consequences are grim, then it is the task of the church to call for reassessment and reversal—or, to use the biblical word, repentance.

Such a mission rarely makes the church popular. When the church questions current problems of poverty or nuclear armament or the rights of women and minorities, for example, always someone says, "Why don't you people just worry about saving souls and leave society alone?" Which is exactly what the people said to Amos! But Jesus insists that the future which ends in heaven begins a split-second from now, not at some date remote from us.

It is not that we have no concern for the distant future. Instead it is that we believe the distant future should shape today and tomorrow.

Consider well the phrase we glide over without much thought every time we gather for worship: "Your will be done on earth as it is in heaven." This means that whatever we believe heaven to be like, we work to achieve even now. Is heaven a place of unity and peace for God's people? Then unity and peace are goals for which we strive here. Is heaven a place where righteousness reigns and all who seek admission are welcome? Then here and now we seek to set right all injustices, and we strive to insure that none are strangers to us. It is this kind of concern for the future that Jesus presses upon us with his parable.

So also the church impresses us with this concern. When we are baptized, we are baptized into the future. The water of the font is already the water of the river that flows through the eternal city of God, the river of the water of life. When we receive the eucharist, the future comes into our midst; for here on earth we are already enjoying the great banquet of heaven, when God's people gather from east and west, from north and south, and sit at table together.

For us the future is now; we are summoned to care about it earnestly, to protect it fervently. Therefore now we are called to live as we expect to live in the eternal habitations, that God's will may be done on earth as it is in heaven.

Laurence Hull Stookey

R TWENTY-SIXTH SUNDAY IN ORDINARY TIME
E PROPER 21
L NINETEENTH SUNDAY AFTER PENTECOST

R *Am 6:1a,4–7; 1 Tim 6:11–16; Lk 16:19–31*
E *Am 6:1–7; 1 Tim 6:11–19; Lk 16:19–31*
L *Am 6:1–7; 1 Tim 6:6–16; Lk 16:19–31*

An art professor once said to us, "You may delight in having a painting by Van Gogh on your living room wall, but you wouldn't want the real Van Gogh in your living room." I might make a similar claim in light of today's readings. We may have the Bible in our homes, even give the word of God a place of honor. But we'd be uncomfortable with the living Word, Jesus, there especially if he brought his friends.

What we hear in the first reading today, the psalm, and the gospel, all point to one thing: God is on the side of the poor, the outcasts, the prostitutes and tax collectors, widows, orphans, lepers, those whose bodies are twisted, and those who cannot see. God is for them. God cares about them and wants to gather them in to ease their pain and sorrow. And Jesus embodied that caring: consorting with all manner of folk, urging them to have faith, restoring their dignity. "Blessed are you poor," he said. "Blessed are you that hunger now, blessed are you that weep now." And he promised them the joys of the dominion of God.

And the rulers, the rich, the comfortable? "Woe to you," said Jesus, echoing the prophets, like Amos whom we hear today. But why? Because you are rulers or rich or comfortable? No: Jesus had no quarrel with the accidents of a person's birth. No; it is because you do not see. You do not notice that you are part of a system of oppression, you do not care. You do not share God's holy dissatisfaction with the way the world is, the world which is divided into haves and have-nots, powerful and powerless, oppressors and oppressed. You who so readily sing "Alleluia!" do not heed that for many people in this world, every day is Good Friday. Calvary happens over and over again and the weeping has not yet been stilled. For many, it is not yet Easter. It is with these that Jesus casts his lot, calling the better off to account. The sayings and parables are battering-rams against the fortresses of complacency. But we know the story: ears were closed and hardened hearts grew harder, and Jesus died, an outcast, poorest of the poor, naked on a cross, crying out as has many an anguished, despairing voice before him and since: "My God, my God, why have you forsaken me?"

But God had not forsaken Jesus. God stood by this Jesus, this suffering one, and raised him from death. He who bore the grief of the downtrodden rose, triumphant over the forces of sin and evil, bearing God's promise that there is a future of hope for those who despair, a day of laughter for those who mourn.

In today's Scriptures we are confronted with a question, and it is not "Are you rich or are you poor?" as if one or the other would make us morally better. It is not "How much do you have?" but

"How much do you care?" And this eucharist for which we
gather puts to us another question: "Will you come to the banquet?" We are here today as guests of the risen Jesus, at a banquet for which he is host. This banquet draws together Jesus'
friends in a soup kitchen in Chicago, a cardboard hut in a Calcutta slum, a refugee camp for the starving in Ethiopia, a barrio
in El Salvador, a black township in South Africa. This banquet is
spread not at the sumptuous table of a rich man, but outside his
gate, on a mat where a poor beggar lies. Will we come to table
with Jesus' friends? Will we sit beside bag ladies and boat people, AIDS victims and ADC mothers? Will we share bread and
cup with them? Will we share our faith? Will we share whatever
it is that is our wealth? Will we give them cause for hope? Then
we can claim, not, "God is on our side," but "We are on the side
of God."

Janet Schlichting, O.P.

R   TWENTY-SEVENTH SUNDAY IN ORDINARY TIME
E   PROPER 22
L   TWENTIETH SUNDAY AFTER PENTECOST

R   *Hab 1:2–3;2:2–4; 2 Tim 1:6–8,13–14; Lk 17:5–10*
E   *Hab 1:1–6,12–13;2:2–4; 2 Tim 1:6–14; Lk 17:5–10*
L   *Hab 1:1–3;2:1–4; 2 Tim 1:3–14; Lk 17:1–10*

Spenser Johnson, M. D., is known for his recent best seller *The
One Minute Manager*, a simple story that has helped many people
to reorganize and better manage their lives. What many of us
probably don't know about Dr. Johnson is that he reflects that,
having enjoyed a happy childhood, having achieved many academic accomplishments and having a lovely family and home,
he was basically unhappy and knew something was missing. He
searched for what was missing, and he has now brought us the
parable of the Precious Present.

This parable is a story of an old man who tries to share with a young man both the secret of how to be happy and the greater secret of how to remain in that happiness. The young man desires to be happy, yet fails to comprehend how that can happen, and it's not until he himself is an older man that he finally discovers what the Precious Present is. He says it this way:

> The Present is what is. It is valuable. Even if I do not know why. It is already just the way it is supposed to be. When I see the present, accept the present, and experience the present, I am well, and I am happy.

> Pain is simply the difference between what is and what I want it to be. When I feel guilty over my imperfect past, or I am anxious over my unknown future, I do not live in the present. I experience pain. I make myself ill. And I am unhappy.

> My past was the present. And my future will be the present. The present moment is the only reality I ever experience. As long as I continue to stay in the present, I am happy forever: because forever is always the present.[60]

This modern day parable is much the same story as is in today's gospel. The apostles ask for an increase in faith, and Jesus responds with the example of a mustard seed. He tells his followers that what is important in life is not the quantity but rather the quality of our faith. Dr. Johnson learned this when all the quantity of his life did not offer him the happiness that he longed for. What he had to search for, what the apostles had to discern, and what we have to discover is the quality of our faith, whether it be the size of a mustard seed or that of a sycamore tree.

It is interesting to note that nowhere in the teachings of Jesus does he ever give us a simple definition of faith. But the totality of Jesus' teaching makes it clear to us that faith is our unconditional acceptance of Jesus. It is our total "yes" to follow Jesus and like him to fulfill the will of our heavenly Father. St. Paul knew this well when he wrote his second letter to Timothy, reminding him "to rekindle the gift of God that is within you."

Paul is challenging Timothy never to be ashamed of witnessing for the Lord. He is reminding him that the rich deposit of faith found within himself is to be lived and shared with others. Paul's words are given to us, then, in the same spirit as they were given to Timothy, in the same spirit as they have been given to others that we have known in our witness for Christ. We too must be concerned with the quality of how we live our lives and not the quantity that the modern world wants us to consider. For us, too, our focus is not to look back to the past or to dream into the future, but rather to live the precious present.

Timothy O'Connor

[60]Spencer Johnson, *The Precious Present* (New York: Doubleday, 1984), pp. 64–68.

R TWENTY-EIGHTH SUNDAY IN ORDINARY TIME
E PROPER 23
L TWENTY-FIRST SUNDAY AFTER PENTECOST

R   *2 Kg 5:14–17; 2 Tim 2:8–13; Lk 17:11–19*
E   *Ruth 1:8–19a; 2 Tim 2:8–15; Lk 17:11–19*
L   *Ruth 1:1–19a; 2 Tim 2:8–13; Lk 17:11–19*

"Get your hot roasted peanuts here!" The hot, lazy days of summer foster our penchant for nostalgia. Open windows allow us to hear the freight train penetrating the quiet of the night. Holiday drivers pack up and set out for vacations in the mountains or in our national parks. The baseball season helps us remember the hysteria of fans cheering the home team and eating hot roasted peanuts in the midst of a seemingly happier, more halcyon era.

When Robert Redford played Roy Hobbs in the film *The Natural*, he played out the dream that is rooted in North American stories. The underdog can win out even in the face of evil, even against all odds, even when opportunity and skill seem worn out. The dream, mixed with steam from train engines and the fog of early morning, still tempts us summer after summer.

Somehow one gets a sense that the nostalgia and the dream get wrapped up together to say we are more comfortable with the positive side of life than the negative. We Christians are more comfortable with praising God than with lamenting before God. It is said that whole societies are built on the capacity to forget. We forget the victims of war and laud the returning soldier. We forget the rape of the land as we drive our superhighways. We forget the stories of the neglected nobodies in the lionized biographies of the rich and famous.

The stories we cherish as Christians bring us face to face with the lament of our ancestors. There is lament in the experience of Naomi and her daughters-in-law, Orpah and Ruth. All three wind up as widows. All three become marginalized. All three find cause for lament. Yet the Jewess Naomi and the Moabitess Ruth do not abandon or forsake one another. What does God work? They go up to Bethlehem at the beginning of the barley harvest. Out of lament comes blessing. Ruth's plight eventually gives us David.

Naaman, an outsider Syrian, has cause for lament. He is marginalized as a leper. At the word of Elisha, the man of God, he goes down to the Jordan and is plunged seven times into those life-giving waters. His flesh became like that of a little child, and he enters into allegiance with the God of Elisha. Out of lament comes blessing. Naaman not only finds wholeness and inclusion in society; he also finds faith.

The people with leprosy meet Jesus as Jesus journeys to Jerusalem and passes along the borderlands of Samaria and Galilee. All call out to him in a way we are accustomed to: Jesus, Master, have pity on us, have mercy on us. All are cured of their lamentable disease which cuts them off from society. But only one returns to praise Jesus. And that one belongs to an outcast group. He was a Samaritan, a foreigner. Out of lament comes blessing. Jesus tells the unnamed, cured leper: your faith has been your salvation.

Amid our desire for the nostalgia of passed, more wondrous days, we discover a wholesome word. We cannot forget. We cannot deny lament. What all these people have in common is their lament, their outsider status, their experience of human suffering and pain. In fact, one of the signs of cure from leprosy is the newfound ability to feel pain. Too often we take comfort in praise! We forget that there is something redemptive in pain and in suffering. Paul tells Timothy: "Remember Jesus Christ, risen from the dead, descended from David, as preached in my gospel, the gospel for which I am suffering and wearing fetters like a criminal." It is not that pain is to be dwelt in out of masochistic motives. Pain and suffering are real and are evils to be dealt with. They are not goods in themselves. But out of lament comes blessing. Pain and suffering disturb our desire for nostalgia. They become worthwhile when they enable us to turn to God, the source of blessing, the one who creates out of chaos.

There is something subtle here that we could easily overlook. Luke's gospel portrays Jesus as someone lamentable. He is the innocent martyr who goes up to Jerusalem. His message, a brutal cross-death and an innocent suffering Master, is not the stuff of nostalgic dreams. But out of the lamentable brutal paschal deed comes blessing. Blessing for the leper, a foreigner. Blessing for the Gentiles. Blessing for the man who is promised paradise. Blessing for the lost sheep, for the woman with the lost coin, and for the son seemingly lost in his irresponsible, dissolute living. The saving power of the Lord is for all the nations, all the peoples who lament, all the nobodies who yearn to be somebodies, all the unnamed who are graced with the name "God-lovers."

For us who gather to give praise at the table, we can depend on this: "If we have died with Christ, we shall also live with Christ; if we endure, we shall also reign with Christ."

John J. O'Brien, C.P.

R TWENTY-NINTH SUNDAY IN ORDINARY TIME
E PROPER 24
L TWENTY-SECOND SUNDAY AFTER PENTECOST

R *Ex 17:8–13; 2 Tim 3:14–4:2; Lk 18:1–8*
E *Gen 32:3–8,22–30; 2 Tim 3:14–4:5; Lk 18:1–8a*
L *Gen 32:22–30; 2 Tim 3:14–4:5; Lk 18:1–8a*

How long must the widow still knock at the door? Is the judge not yet worn down by the continual pleading? And what of the others? Along with this wretched Palestinian widow who has lost all her rights and protection we may see many, many other petitioners coming: the hungry, the tortured, the homeless, the saints of the ages, and all those whose only prayer is their own existence in need. They come to this self-centered judge, to all human judges, and beyond all judges they come to God who, we confess, judges justly. Then how long must they ask?

Or, to say it with other images, how long must Moses hold up his weary arms until the people of God may at last prevail? How long must terrified Jacob wrestle with the angel, begging for blessing? When will God vindicate the elect? The texts for this Sunday are filled with the ancient longing for the day of God, that day understood as the time when tears will be wiped away and justice done. The images are powerful because they mean to gather us in also: our own sense of the unconsoled suffering around us cries out with the widow.

But the texts are also full of promise. God does answer, more surely than does this sovereign and self-assured judge. Victory does come to Israel, the elect. God does give the blessing. When? Speedily, says Jesus in the gospel. Soon. That promise was given long, long ago. Does it still hold? Can we still believe it?

In fact, the gospel seems to have meant a very surprising thing. The promise that God will act to vindicate the elect was understood by ancient Christians to be fulfilled in the events at the conclusion of the gospel itself. The response of God was coming as soon as the end of the story of Jesus. Sharing the lot of pleading humanity, Jesus was crucified, and in his resurrection God acts to vindicate not just him but all the unconsoled ones. The resurrection is God's final judgment, spoken already now. And our assembly on Sunday always gathers to remember that final merciful judgment, to hear it spoken in all its strength again, and to encourage each other to live on the grounds of that judgment even when it doesn't appear to be effective in the world.

Or to say it in other images: The blessing of God in the midst of fear is the resurrection, spoken in Christ to our death. And the resurrection is the victory of Israel. For Christ's arms on the cross are the outstretched arms of Moses for us all.

But is that hope really for us, for our world? The suffering seems to go on and on. The doors of this earth's courtrooms seem hardly even to open. The judges have not heard our cries. And have we heard from God?

Listen to the letter to Timothy. Continue, abide, dwell in what you have heard in this assembly and in the Scriptures. When you eat and drink the gift of Christ here, eat and drink the signs of God's grace-filled judgment. Here is the answered cause, the redistributed wealth, the victory, the blessing. Trust it, in season and out. Live with your neighbor, not out of the fear based on yet more closed doors from the judges, but out of the mercy God has revealed as the final word in this world. Hear that mercy in this world. Eat and drink it at this table. Know it in the little signs of loving response to the needy ones with which the world is overflowing.

Still, there is one other thing. The mercy of God still remains so largely hidden, revealed only in this word and in little signs. Yet we can help one another heed the counsel of the text: Hold up the arms. Wrestle with God. And keep beating at the heavenly doors for the sake of your neighbor in this city and in the world. The grounds for our boldness is this: we already know what the answer is.

Gordon W. Lathrop

R   *Sir 35:12b-14,16–18a; 2 Tim 4:6–8,16–18; Lk 18:9–14*
E   *Jer 14:7–10, 19–22; 2 Tim 4:6–8,16–18; Lk 18:9–14*
L   *Deut 10:12–22; 2 Tim 4:6–8,16–18; Lk 18:9–14*

For some years, I served as chaplain to a medical center. I preferred working the night shift, for in the stillness of those late hours it was easier to talk with people about life, and faith, and God, without having to adjust to the busy, day-time hospital routines. My presence seemed more welcome during those late hours when friends, relatives, and physicians had departed, leaving the people alone with fear and weakness and pain.

On one night I heard a voice call out, "Hello! Chaplain!" Peering into the darkness of a nearby room, I noticed a very dignified older woman sitting up in bed as if ready to hold court. The proper simplicity of her appearance suggested hard work and country life. "I'm always glad to see a man of God," she said, graciously extending her hand. "So you're a person of faith, then," I ventured. "Yes, indeed!" she replied. "I'm against all this wickedness that goes on in our society today. I'm against all this sex before marriage, and changing husbands whenever you feel like it. I'm against all this abortion and pornography and drugs and drinking. I'm against all these men acting like women and the other way 'round. I tell you, I'm against all of it."

It struck me that were I sitting up alone in a hospital bed in the middle of the night, there would be other things on my mind besides society's immorality. So I suggested, "With all of those things that you're against, I'll bet there are some things that you're in favor of, too. Am I right?" For a moment she looked at me with puzzled expression, and then began again, "Well, it's like I said before. I'm against all this lawlessness and immorality, all this vice and depravity. It's not right. It's not God's will. I don't believe in it." Once again, I tried to find a way to share thoughts about what God does want for us frail and fragile human beings, created in the divine image and yet so pitifully prone to weakness, helplessness, sickness, pain and death. I tried to find a way for us to share what we did believe as people of faith. And once again I got a litany of sins that God and my patient were unanimously against.

Many people come to believe that being a Christian means being against other people, or, to use the words of St. Luke in today's gospel, trusting in our own righteousness and despising others. It seems to me that it used to be easier to be that kind of church-goer. The church used to offer us more encouragement in self-righteous contempt for those who failed to live up to our hypo-critical moral standards. Where are those people now who taught us that smugness was a Christian virtue, that sharing your faith meant making other people feel guilty?

Nowadays it seems hardly safe to despise anyone. On our con-gregational mailing list are singles who have the same address. Just last week was a "second marriage" at this altar. We used to be able to turn up our pious noses at those who hit the bottle, but now Alcoholics Anonymous meets right here in the church basement; and some of those people have joined our congrega-tion. Even a few short years ago, we could still take self-righteous comfort in the knowledge that drug addicts and homo-sexuals were surely beyond the reach of God's love and mercy, but today in our congregation there are self-avowed gay people urging us in God's name to minister to those who are suffering from the AIDS epidemic.

Why is today's church becoming so uncomfortable for the self-righteous and so comfortable for those miserable individuals who have nothing going for them besides faith and trust in Jesus Christ? It may be that God's Holy Spirit, promised by the risen Christ to this community of baptized people, is breathing down the neck of the church these days, convincing all of us of our solidarity in human sin, convincing all of us of our common need for God's forgiveness in Jesus Christ.

In our gospel for today, the Pharisee sounds rather like the woman I spoke with in the hospital and rather like people many of us have known. He may even sound a little like you and me when we're at our self-righteous worst. His idea of prayer is to offer God a list of all the things he's against: extortion, injustice and adultery. The tax collector, on the other hand, has nothing going for him except his faith in God's mercy. And if we were at our truthful best, we would certainly all describe ourselves in the same way. Not daring even to raise his eyes to heaven, the tax collector offers to God a prayer so very simple and yet so very perfect, "God, be merciful to me, a sinner."

According to our Lord it was the tax-collector, not the Pharisee, who went home right with God. And why should this be so surprising? Throughout the long and sordid history of God's people, divine mercy was always reserved for those who were ready to admit their true situation in the sight of God. Throughout the pages of the Hebrew Scriptures, God promises to hear the prayers of those who are honest enough to acknowledge their unworthiness, their insignificance in God's sight.

Indeed, the whole message of the Christian faith is that in Jesus Christ God has visited the humble. In Jesus Christ God has descended in person to those who dare not even raise their eyes to heaven, who recognize the hopelessness of human sin, who can do no more than cry to God for mercy from the depths of their hearts. In Jesus Christ God has descended to us, to share with us our failures and our griefs and our regrets, to identify with us even to the point of sharing our death, so that we might share in his resurrection. This is the faith we made our own at the beginning of our worship on this Lord's Day, when we gathered around the baptismal font to reflect together on who we really are in the sight of God, to confess together that each of us bears an equal share of the guilt for the sin of this world, and to hear again God's promise that our baptismal faith has made us right with God. And this is the savior that we will make our own when he descends to us today in this place, to share with us our lives and to make us part of his risen life. This is the savior whose body is given for us and whose blood is shed for us. This sacramental presence of the risen Christ among us is the sign and guarantee that God is eternally and unconditionally for us.

Martin Hauser

R THIRTY-FIRST SUNDAY IN ORDINARY TIME
E PROPER 26
L TWENTY-FOURTH SUNDAY AFTER PENTECOST

R *Wis 11:22–12:2; 2 Th 1:11–2:2; Lk 19:1–10*
E *Is 1:10–20; 2 Th 1:1–5,11–12; Lk 19:1–10*
L *Ex 34:5–9; 2 Th 1:1–5,11–12; Lk 19:1–10*

New Year's Eve is a curious and peculiar day of the year. Probably the first image that comes to mind when thinking about the Eve is the festive celebration where relatives and friends ring in the new year while ringing out the old. However, there is a second image about the Eve also present. It occurs at that moment prior to the festivities. The table is set and the food and drink have been prepared. The host stands in readiness and then there is a pregnant moment of silence. In the quiet of that moment, one remembers. It is a moment of memory when the rhythms and events of the previous year come to mind and we are invited to stand before the significance of the days and months that have passed: the successes, the failures, the joys, the missed opportunities.

In these next weeks, the Christian community is preparing for the end of this present church year and the beginning of another. Like a host family, we stand before our table and are enticed into that pregnant moment of remembrance. The people of God are called to reflect soberly upon our own successes and failures, our own joys and missed opportunities. Through the enlightenment of the Spirit, we are being called to a new understanding of the quality of our life in Christ as it has been lived these past days and months. It is in this light that we can come to appreciate today's gospel reading.

This familiar story contains four characters or groups that are extremely important. We have Zaccheus. He is a small person not only physically but also in the eyes of the society of his time. Zaccheus is a tax collector; he is unclean in the eyes of the law, for he is a collaborator with the hated Romans in the oppression of a poor and disenfranchised nation. The pious Jew could not even share the intimacy of a meal with him lest one risk cultic impurity. On the other hand, as a second set of characters, we have the "murmurers." These are those pious ones who viewed Zaccheus as an outcast and were horrendously shocked at Jesus' invitation to eat and be intimate with Zaccheus that day. Of course, the third, and central, character is Jesus himself. The Lord does not gather in those who are the self-righteous. Rather, this Jesus searches out and saves the lost even at the risk of reproach by those who are the self-styled guardians of religious truth. Finally, if you will, there is a last "character," more precisely a type of stage prop, whose presence is quite significant. Our "prop-character" is the sycamore tree, a short-trunked tree with wide lateral branches that made it easy for Zaccheus to climb and see this Jesus despite Zaccheus' lack of physical height.

Today, our story and our characters serve as a mirror of sorts. We are standing at the brink of the end of this church year and are poised to begin again. These next weeks are a time of reflection, a time to test the quality of our Christian life over the last months. To do so, we gaze into the mirror of the story of Zaccheus, and we ask ourselves which of the characters best fits our own characterization of our life in Jesus. We might have to admit to being all four. We are Zaccheus. Each of us is short. We have been outcasts even if only by merit of our lack of love of the persons that God has made us. It is possible that we might also have defrauded the poor in our midst; yet, there is always room for repentance. We also might very well be one of the murmurers. It is easy in a culture that discriminates to disenfranchise the unlovely in our midst simply because they do not look the proper part. But we, hopefully, have been the Lord as well. For it is our very vocation as church to go beyond the strictures of human logic and to welcome as equal members those in our community who seem the most lost and the most in need of salvation. Lastly, we might very well have been the good sycamore tree: short by our very nature, but with arms wide enough to gather in all those who by faith wish to see the Lord as he seeks out the lost and wayward.

The story of Zaccheus is our story as church and gives us much to reflect upon in these final weeks of this liturgical year. It is not a story of despair. We need not look into its mirror and engage in self-centered guilt for our weaknesses. Rather, the story is a tale of hope. Like Zaccheus we are challenged to go beyond the limits of the present and to permit the Spirit of God to bring us to a new identity in Christ, a new sense of mission for all the world, a new life together wherein the peace and justice of God are heralded. The story of Zaccheus is a story of salvation. Salvation: a word whose roots mean "health." Today, in the spirit of God, we bear one another up as so many sycamore trees that we might see the Lord of salvation. We lift today the cup of salvation that we might be steeped into the health that is the life of the Christ who is forever in our midst seeking the lost.

Edward Francis Gabriele, O. Praem.

R   THIRTY-SECOND SUNDAY IN ORDINARY TIME
E   PROPER 27
L   TWENTY-FIFTH SUNDAY AFTER PENTECOST

R   *2 Mac 7:1–2,9–14; 2 Th 2:16–3:5; Lk 20:27–38*
E   *Job 19:23–27a; 2 Th 2:13–3:5; Lk 20:27, 34–38*
L   *1 Chr 29:10–13; 2 Th 2:13–3:5; Lk 20:27–38*

What strange words the Lord has for us during these final weeks of the liturgical year, before the great cycle begins again with Advent! Luke's gospel places us in the midst of an eschatological debate. As is so often the case, even in our own times, an apparently academic issue is used as facade for a political agenda. We too in our days have divisions among us of liberals and conservatives, and our own attempts to nail our opponents are frequently every bit as transparent as the contrived account used by the Sadducees to embarrass Jesus. One wonders if they realized how effectively he avoided their trap.

The absurdity of the story of the poor woman who was given in marriage successively (but not successfully!) to seven brothers is typical of the type of moral casuistry that is so obsessed with hypothetical possibilities that it loses sight of the human dimension of the problem. A contemporary example might be that of a child born through one of the new reproductive technologies—or some combination of them. We might even be able to manage the same symbolic number of seven: let donor parent #1 contribute sperm to fertilize donor parent #2's egg; let these be cultivated "in vitro," until fertilization and initial cell division occurs. When this embryo is ready, let it be given to parent #3, a surrogate mother who will carry it to term, and then, by contract of course, surrenders it to adoptive parents #4 and #5, who attempt to raise it and do so lovingly until one day both are killed in an automobile accident. The child, now a toddler, is adopted by another couple who become parents #6 and #7. At the resurrection, whose child is this?

Our own culture must debate the ethical, legal, psychological, and sociological ramifications of these questions because there are persons involved in these arrangements, and real lives are at stake. The Sadducees had no real interest in what Jesus would say about the status of their hypothetical woman in life after death: they expected to expose what they took to be the absurdity of belief in resurrection. Jesus, however, had another agenda for them, and the church in selecting this text for our reflection directs our attention to an article of faith.

As followers of Christ we profess belief in the resurrection. The faith that we profess draws its confidence from the fact that God has raised Jesus from the dead, and Jesus has promised that we too shall share eternal life, a life described for us also as resurrection. The foundational belief of Christian anthropology is not the immortality of the soul but resurrection of the dead. It is our embodied human person that will be the continuation of our existence in eternal life, and not a disembodied soul or spirit. Mysterious as this must seem, and even Paul despaired of making sense of it to those who could conceive only of immortality, it has profound implications regarding the holiness of our bodies and of the created universe. No Christian can despise the human body, and surely none should abuse it.

It is sometimes instructive simply to review some of the central tenets of our faith to see what is said in them about the body. Three of the greatest mysteries of Christianity directly address human embodiment: the incarnation proclaims that the eternal Son of God took on human flesh, entering and transforming forever the created universe. The eucharist, the central mystery celebrated at this altar, is the legacy of Jesus for all subsequent ages of the gift of his body and his blood. The resurrection attests to Christ's victory over the forces of evil and of death. Through the glorification of his embodied human nature all who, in the words of today's gospel, are judged worthy of a place in the age to come are invited to share in the ultimate freedom of the body: resurrection.

These mysteries that recapitulate the liturgical cycle—life, death, and resurrection—all have profound moral significance for these bodies of ours which are the foundations of our personalities. It is because we ourselves are holy, as are our brothers and sisters, that we must refrain from overindulgence in food and drink, from drug abuse, from sexual exploitation. We are God's work of art, temples of God's spirit. All that we do to promote our own health and that of others, through good nutrition and fitness, all the legitimate pleasures that our bodies offer, all the labors that we do with our hands—all are part of the created order that will be transformed in the resurrection. We live even now in a "divine milieu," as Teilhard de Chardin so beautifully described it.

Paul in his letter to the Thessalonians speaks of the eternal consolation that the Father has given us out of mercy, and Jesus in his response to the Sadducees in today's gospel has named that consolation. God is not the God of the dead but of the living. All are alive in God. The living, breathing, loving, caring body that is my own temple already anticipates its own resurrection. Having been fed by God's word, we now profess our faith in the resurrection, and then celebrate the meal that is the promise of that eternal life.

Ruth Caspar, O.P.

R THIRTY-THIRD SUNDAY IN ORDINARY TIME
E PROPER 28
L TWENTY-SIXTH SUNDAY AFTER PENTECOST

R   *Mal 3:19–20a; 2 Th 3:7–12; Lk 21:5–19*
E   *Mal 3:13–4:2a,5–6; 2 Th 3:6–13; Lk 21:5–19*
L   *Mal 4:1–2a; 2 Th 3:6–13; Lk 21:5–19*

Jesus saw rich people putting their offerings into the temple treasury, and then he noticed a poor widow making an even more
lavish contribution to the temple worship. Next he realized that
his own companions were remarking with wonder at the very
sight of the building. Jesus himself seems to be more of an ob-
server than a participant in that place of worship.

What he sees is waste. Not that a waste of money would bother
him—unless some of it might have gone to the now penniless
widow to relieve her need. But it was a waste of spirit, a waste
of hope and confidence, wonder and awe being poured out on
the sacred architecture and all its sacred loot. "All these things
you're staring at . . . everything will be destroyed." While he
grieved at these people's misspent faith he may have remembered his own early boyish wonder in the face of God's holy
temple. Now he takes for granted its destruction, distressed by
the hollowness of the place and by his people's trust in its magnificence. He feels for the woman who invested in the temple
out of her own livelihood, and for his own gullible, awe-struck
companions. He would not question or damage the faith of these
little ones as they poured out their offerings on this sacred
precinct, but he could already grieve because of the suffering
and disillusionment that would surely come with its destruction.
(He would not stop an admirer who poured an expensive offering over his own feet, but he might well fear what would happen to her should he himself be brought to execution.) What
grieved him at the temple was the abuse of people's faith and
confidence.

Perhaps a warning would prevent their destruction. Words
spoken in time might prepare them, save them from bitterness.

What was it that had saved him, had tided him over that terrible realization that all that he had once thought to be the Holy of Holies would one day be destroyed? It might have been some words from the prophets, those people who had only words to offer, but words invested with hope, words that could sustain faith through terrible times and losses. Perhaps Malachi was on his mind: The Day, when it comes, will set evil-doers ablaze, like stubble . . . but you who fear God's name will only feel the healing rays of the sun of righteousness, you will come out leaping like calves from the stall. From what must have sounded like dark pessimism Jesus would make an offering of caution and hope, for the sake of his companions' simple, untried faith.

Their faith is not yet in him. Jesus still has to be tried and tested, and so "they put to him this question." (These children from Galilee sound like the delegations of the learned who put their questions to see if Jesus could stand up against their own wisdom and cleverness.) "When will this be, and what will be the sign when this is about to take place?" As though wisdom is proven in its details.

We might wonder whether the evangelist filled out with considerable detail Jesus' response to his examiners. Certainly he did, drawing from old prophecies and from the subsequent experiences of Jesus' followers: we have a prediction of would-be messiahs, rumors of war and social upheaval, national hostilities and nature itself joining in the strife, "terrors and great signs from heaven." Any statement about the future needs to be graphic. If you ever have anything to predict, remember that the more detailed you can be, the more certainly you will be believed. In the face of that recurrent apocalyptic instinct Jesus warns his companions: "Take heed that you are not led astray. . . ." Don't be swept away by fear, and do not think for a moment that you can calculate your own survival and triumph. "Settle it therefore in your minds not to meditate beforehand how to answer. . . ."

It seems a strange way to prepare such innocent faith for all the drastic trials these people would certainly suffer: go before your enemies, and accept all the grief and shocks, without defense, without even thinking beforehand of pleas for justice and mercy.

Just go into the uncertain future as defenseless as you are right now. Your defense will be an irresistible eloquence and wisdom—it will come to you at the right moment. Such an assurance is denied to those who march forward confident of their own resources, impressed by their own foreknowledge and tactical awareness. But it is promised to the little ones, for the safety and preservation of that naive faith that would, through trust and perseverance, come to maturity on "that Day." Could these disciples believe they would come through times of hellish testing "like calves released from their stalls"? Of course they could. Could they imagine themselves basking in the sun of righteousness once the storms and clouds had cleared? Of course they could. They were not wise enough to imagine otherwise. Prophecy and promises, and the faith to live by them, are God's gifts for those who don't know any better.

John Gerlach, O.P.

L TWENTY-SEVENTH SUNDAY AFTER PENTECOST

L *Is 52:1–6; 1 Cor 15:54–58; Lk 19:11–27*

The theme of Jesus' teaching in today's gospel lesson is surely not new or unique. The timid investor in Jesus' parable who hid his talent in a napkin lest he lose it learned a simple, capitalist principle: nothing ventured, nothing gained. No guts, no glory. There is seldom growth or profit without pain and risk. Jesus was not talking about money or a contest, however, but about risking faith and life itself.

Luke sets this parable between the story of Jesus' visit to the home of Zacchaeus, the tax collector, an incident which had set the pious folk to murmuring over Jesus' friendship with sinners, and Jesus' entry into Jerusalem, an event that also started some talk and accusations which eventually led to the crucifixion. The lesson for the pious people of Jesus' day was the suggestion that they had buried their faith or hid it away so as to keep it safe.

As a result, they could not think of sinners and tax collectors as part of the reign of God without their whole understanding of themselves and the world and God falling apart. Their ancestors had given their lives and the pious folk had suffered so much to preserve the Torah and be faithful to it, only to have this happen? They could not take such a risk.

We, too, are called by this parable to risk our faith and our very lives, and it is no easier for us than for the pious folk who first heard Jesus or read Luke. We are tempted to shun risk and to treat our faith like something fragile and precious to be hidden in a napkin. It was handed down to us and we must pass it along to the next generation like an heirloom, in perfect condition, safe and unscratched. We would not want to risk losing our faith by letting go for a moment, looking at ourselves or the world from another perspective, venturing to think differently of the reign of God.

The pious folk of Jesus' day simply could not see the dominion of God as big enough for tax collectors, sinners, and Gentiles. Today, however, in the largely Gentile Christian community, perhaps the tables are turned. Can we see the reign of God as big enough to include those different from us, both Christians of other kinds and perhaps also those who worship the same God we do but are not Christians, like pious Jews? Surely there is much we could learn of God and God's reign if only we could risk sitting at table with them. To be sure, we would have to change much of our thinking about ourselves, the world, and God to see the household of God as being great enough to hold all those who are different from us. But if God is so much a risking shepherd and friend of sinners, could it not be that God's reign is much broader than we have sometimes imagined? And if it is, would there not be much to be gained from understanding that and living accordingly?

There are other risks of faith and life to which Jesus' parable calls us. We always risk when we make ourselves vulnerable to another whose poverty or pain cries out to us. When we respond compassionately, for a moment we see the world from another's eyes, and we can never see the world, or ourselves, or

God the same again. We are changed, but we have not become smaller or lost our talent through risking compassion. We are richer. We have grown.

That is the truth of what Jesus taught as cross-bearing discipleship. Whoever would save life will lose it, and whoever will risk losing it for his sake will find it. It's like falling in love. You lose yourself in utter vulnerability to another, only to find yourself anew, grown infinitely richer for the losing. That is the way of Jesus, who after telling this parable went to Jerusalem and to the cross, risked everything so that Zacchaeus could be a part of God's reign, and healed the ear of one who came to arrest him, looked at the world through the eyes of those who crucified him, and prayed for their forgiveness; laying his life, finally, not in a napkin somewhere, but in God's hands. In those hands his life was found, resurrected, made new.

There, too, in those hands, are our own lives hid with Christ in God, by virtue of our baptism. Our lives cannot be ultimately lost. That is God's promise. No matter how incautiously we invest ourselves, no matter what risks we take, God will no more let go of us or let us be lost than God let the napkin of the grave clothes hide God's son, Jesus, forever.

Of that one's body and blood we now eat and drink. Still he invests himself in us through this supper, that his life might be in us, and that through us he might risk his life and God's very own life for the sake of the world so precious to God.

Frederick A. Niedner, Jr.

R   *2 Sam 5:1–3; Col 1:12–20; Lk 23:35–43*
E   *Jer 23:1–6; Col 1:11–20; Lk 23:35–43*
L   *Jer 23:2–6; Col 1:13–20; Lk 23:35–43*

Luke the evangelist is a great artist in the way that he has constructed his gospel. He says at the beginning that he made careful investigation of all that had happened, but it is clear in almost every section of the gospel that we heard this year that he has also left his own mark.

We see this morning that themes we have heard all year long now come before us for a last time. This is not the last scene in the gospel, of course, for that belongs to Easter and what happened between Jesus and his followers in the days after Easter. But on this last Sunday of the church year we visit again Luke's particular version of the story of the crucifixion of Jesus. And it is there, and only there in the New Testament, that we find this story of the different behaviors of the two thieves crucified with Jesus.

It isn't surprising to find this at the end, for all along Luke has reminded us of life's two ways: the way of fearing God and the way of taking care of self. The people of Bethlehem turned their back on Mary and Joseph, but the shepherds rejoiced and believed. Ten lepers were healed of their terrible disease, but only one returned to Jesus to give thanks. Two persons went to the temple to pray: one paraded his achievements before God, while another could only beg for mercy.

All the way through Luke many ignore God and court disaster, but a few heed God and find mercy and blessing. Even at the cross this human pattern of basic choices, of alternative paths, continues. The rulers scoff, the soldiers mock, the crowd stands by silently watching. At first it seems that only the way of death is represented. Even one of those who is dying with Jesus joins in the clamor.

But then another voice is heard, eloquent and surprising. There is no reason to glamorize the thief who repented; while he may possibly also have been an innocent victim of rough Roman justice, he says about himself that he is getting what he deserves. But he attacks the other criminal for joining in the assault on Jesus. Can he not see that this man is dying a death he did not deserve?

Before we rush on to even more remarkable things, we should remember how hard it is to make such an intervention when the crowd is running in a particular direction, full of emotion, not pausing to think. The courageous words of this dying man make him worth remembering at times when we have an obligation to put a stop to the terrible, hateful clamor that sometimes fills our world.

But there is more. Jesus in Luke's gospel is especially concerned to bring the gospel to the outcast, to the marginal, to the places where it is not expected. Thus it is appropriate that Jesus' last human contact be with such a person. Even on the cross he is still preaching release to the captive, as he proclaimed in his first sermon in Nazareth.

When the criminal turns to him, Jesus receives the request to remember him with words of gracious promise. Not a word here about it being too late. Not a word exploring whether his confession is sincere. Another prodigal has come home, and the dying Jesus welcomes him and promises him eternity, even as the waiting father rushed out to welcome his erring son.

In the course of this exchange, the repentant thief becomes the only person in the whole crowd to comprehend and to confess that Jesus, though he seems to be a dying and rejected failure, is in fact the true and righteous king. "Jesus," he cries out, "remember me when you come into your kingdom."

This Jesus who died for outcasts and executioners, for men and for women, for Jews and for Gentiles, for the righteous and for the prodigal, will welcome you today as well. If you look only to the surface, you must cast your lot with Herod and Pilate and the religious leaders or watch silently with the crowd. But the gospel of Luke has taught us the true marks of the king who comes in the name of the Lord. He is the child of peace, at whose birth the angels sing. He is the friend of sinners and outcasts. He is the radical who overcomes conventions to welcome Zacchaeus back to a righteous life and to call Martha from the kitchen to join Mary in the joy of learning.

He is our king, but nothing like the kings that you have read about in books and seen in movies. He is David's descendant but also David's Lord, for he is the promised heir of David who will deal wisely and execute justice and righteousness in the land.

He is our king, but we have to accept him as a king who rules from a cross, and who calls us not to sit upon thrones, but to paths of caring for the hungry, and sorrowful, and the persecuted. He redefines kingship, because he is the one who comes in the name of the Lord.

And we will see him this morning, in our great feast in this place, when we will welcome him with these words: Hosanna to the son of David! Blessed is Jesus our King who comes in the name of the Lord! And at that moment we will join those of every time and every place, like the thief on the cross, who knew what to look for in a king and where to find hope for eternity.

Timothy F. Lull

JANUARY 1
R MARY, MOTHER OF GOD
E HOLY NAME
L NAME OF JESUS

R *Num 6:22–27; Gal 4:4–7; Lk 2:16–21*
E *Ex 34:1–8; Rom 1:1–7; Lk 2:15–21*
L *Num 6:22–27; Rom 1:1–7; Lk 2:21*

The baby is sleeping, at least for the moment. She doesn't waken even at the sound of her own name spoken at the font. Gently, her sponsor rocks her while the pastor dries her off. She squirms a little, but doesn't waken for the prayer. Then, the sign marked on her forehead, just above her sleeping eyes: "Lisa Ann, child of God, you have been sealed by the Holy Spirit and marked with the cross of Christ forever."[2]

She might have been crying; the sign would have been the same. The parents were relieved for they remembered baptisms when it was impossible to hear the pastor over the screaming baby. (And even though they told themselves that God didn't mind, they knew that people often did and then were relieved.) But the sign was still the same: the cross on her forehead. By the time of the closing hymn, the cross was invisible. No mark was left above the child's eyes, waking or sleeping. No sign as clear as ashes for others to see when tomorrow she is in her stroller. No one who sees her in the park or at the pediatrician's office will remark, "Oh, she has been baptized."

The water dries quickly and the sign of the cross is invisible. Who will know that Jesus' name has been written on her forehead? Did I say "the name of Jesus"? Yes. The name of Jesus. One way to spell the name is by marking the sign of the cross. Jesus: the one who saves.[61]

For that is what the name means. Just as my name, Barbara, means foreign or strange, like the word "barbarian," Jesus and its Hebrew twin Joshua means "the one who saves." It is not a magic name reserved for God: it is a human name, blessed by

God and spoken by angels. At the end of eight days, on the day of circumcision, the name was given. The child's parents followed the ancient rite which tied this child to human ancestors, back beyond the Roman occupation, back to a people moving from place to place, living in tents, back to the burning bush when God's mysterious name was spoken to Moses: "I AM WHO I AM." Tell the people that is my name. But it was not the only name, that holy name which could never even be spoken aloud by the people of Israel. There was another name, a name with human names attached: I am the God of Abraham, Isaac and Jacob. It was as though God also had a last name, that God's full name always has human names attached. Sarah, Rebekah, Leah, Rachel. God's name would be made known with these human names attached. This, word, too, was given to Moses: "So shall they put my name upon the people of Israel, and I will bless them."

But God's name dried on their foreheads. The people forgot how they were named; the covenant was broken and they tried to make a name for themselves. A mighty nation was soon reduced to ashes, a holy people scattered in the winds of war. Then, to a remnant of the people, God made a new promise: A child will be born as a sign. I will put my word upon the earth.

And it came to pass, in the fulness of time, that the child was born to Mary, a descendant from the ancient line, circumcised as Joshua had been centuries before. But the child was named according to the word of the angel: "You shall call his name Jesus." It is a human name with God's name attached. Jesus is his name: Jesus, the suffering servant whose name brought hope to the outcasts; the name which redefined family as those who do the will of God; the name which was hanged between heaven and earth to reconcile all people to God. This name put God's name again upon the people, and wrote God's covenant within human hearts.

That name is written on our foreheads. Long after the waters of baptism dry, the name is still there. It is spelled with the sign of the cross and marks us forever, sleeping or waking. And people will come to know the name of Jesus with our very human names attached. Oh, the name can't be seen, and it is not so simple as wearing a button that says, "Smile, Jesus loves you," especially if you are glaring at someone in hate.

I heard such hatred not long ago in a story shared by a friend. She had participated in Gay Pride Day in Grand Rapids, Michigan. Some gay and lesbian people gathered in an auditorium; a minister from the Metropolitan Community Church was trying to speak over a group of jeering religious protesters. "Sinners!" the group at the back shouted. "Repent and be saved of your sick and evil ways!" The protesters got louder and angrier, waving Bibles as they shouted. The young minister invited the gay and lesbian folks to move forward, close to the front of the room. Then the group turned to face the protesters, chanting "Jesus loves me and Jesus loves you." Over and over, the gay group said to the protesters, "Jesus loves me and Jesus loves you."

The protesters went into a rage and jumped up on tables at the back of the room. In one voice they began to scream: "Jesus hates you! Jesus hates you! Jesus hates you!" My friend didn't tell me how long this went on, which side was loudest. But she said that some of the people who had come to the city for Gay Pride Day were terrified. They had never seen such hatred; some feared for their lives. My friend too was afraid, and more than that, filled with sorrow that the name of Jesus be so violently taken in vain. How many in that room heard the name of Jesus, attached to human anger and condemnation? How many will remember Jesus' name with hatred attached?

The sign of the cross is invisible on our foreheads. No one can read the name of Jesus there above our eyes. But the baptismal words remain true: "You have been sealed by the Holy Spirit and marked with the cross of Christ forever." The name of Jesus. How will people hear and see that name in my life and in yours?

Barbara Lundblad

[61]*Lutheran Book of Worship*, p. 124.

FEBRUARY 2
R   E   L   PRESENTATION OF OUR LORD

R   *Mal 3:1–4; Heb 2:14–18; Lk 2:22–40*
E   *Mal 3:1–4; Heb 2:14–18; Lk 2:22–40*
L   *1 Sam 1:21–28; Heb 2:14–18; Lk 2:22–40*

During the Advent–Christmas season we have gathered around the word and the sacrament to celebrate the dawning of the light of Christ amidst the darkness of sin and hopelessness. Today's celebration of the Presentation of the Lord marks a transition point between the Advent-Christmas cycle and the Lent-Easter cycle. For the readings remind us that Christ the light comes to bring salvation to the people of God through his death.

Like many celebrations of the liturgical year, today's feast has a complex history which we need to consider briefly as a background for the readings. Originating in the fourth century Jerusalem cycle of feasts, which sought to maintain a chronological remembrance of the events of Christ's life, this feast was celebrated on February 14th, forty days after the Jerusalem celebration of Christmas-Epiphany on January 6th. Called *hypapante* in Greek, "the feast of the Meeting," this celebration commemorated the meeting between Christ and the people of the Covenant, symbolized by Simeon and Anna, as narrated in Luke 2:22–39.

The Roman celebration of this feast, which followed the pattern of replacing pagan Roman festivals with Christian feasts, seems to have begun in the early fifth century. Its celebration on February 2, forty days after the Roman celebration of Christmas on December 25th, sought to replace a pagan procession of expiation around the city walls by a light procession which emphasized Christ as the true light and savior of the Roman people. The names for this celebration have varied considerably in the West: the Presentation of the Lord, the Purification of Mary, and Candelmas, depending upon which aspect of the feast was being emphasized at a particular point in history. Contemporary liturgical renewal in calling today's feast the Presentation of our Lord makes clear that we are celebrating the mystery of God's saving work in Christ as that begins to unfold even from the earliest days of Jesus' life.

In today's celebration the second reading from the letter to the Hebrews seeks to link the Lucan account of Mary and Joseph's observance of the ritual purification rites prescribed in Leviticus 12:1–8 to the Paschal Mystery. Jesus, the one presented to God in the temple by the hands of the priest in fulfillment of the Covenant, is himself the true priest who will offer himself to God on the cross to fulfill God's promise of life offered in the Covenant. In the view of the author of Hebrews, Jesus, the child of God, has become totally one with the human family so that he could be the merciful priest of our deliverance from death by his own death on the cross.

The final verse of today's second reading offers the connecting link between Jesus as merciful high priest and the Lucan account of Simeon and Anna as symbols of the people of God awaiting God's saving presence: "For because Jesus himself has suffered and been tempted, he is able to help those who are tempted." The readings of the Advent-Christmas season are filled with the wonderful promises of God about light, hope and peace through Jesus Christ. Yet in the winter days of January and February after the Christmas lights and decorations have been taken down and the festal atmosphere has died away, we are tempted to think that promises of God proclaimed anew at Christmas for a light greater than darkness, for peace stronger than war, and for a hope that dispels despair remain largely unfulfilled in our individual and corporate lives.

So in the feast of the Presentation we have a new winter encounter between God and the people of God in Jesus. But this meeting is between a helpless God-child and two old people who have spent a life-time waiting for the promises of salvation to be fulfilled. How often Simeon and Anna must have been tempted to think that things would never change and to despair that the promises would never be fulfilled.

Suddenly in the midst of darkness, war, and despair, the light of God appears as a helpless child come to be one with us in our weakness. There are no facile answers here but an invitation to embrace our lives and our world anew because we have been embraced by the helplessness of God in Jesus, the merciful one.

Simeon sings the song of redemption as the completion of a lifetime of waiting which has known the constant need of receiving the mercy of God to rekindle the light of faith. Anna gives thanks because the years of watching have yielded to a new life more than she could have ever dreamed of, the life of a fragile child that needs to be nurtured through the dead winter to the flowering spring tree of life.

Amidst the winter experiences of our own lives we are invited this day to bring our own temptations to despair that God's promises will never be fulfilled to the burning light of Jesus' Paschal Mystery. For he has chosen to be helpless so that he can embrace all our helplessness. We are asked by God's gift of grace to be guests at the table of new mercy and to believe anew in light, peace and hope. For God in Jesus Christ our high priest has chosen to meet us and to be one with us in our darkness, our wars, and our despair. Let us come anew this day to the temple of our lives to receive Jesus the merciful one whose helplessness embraces our helplessness and whose love gives us the courage to keep watching and waiting as we yearn for the fulfillment of the promises. Like Simeon and Anna may we too sing of new light and salvation, because the promises of the tree of life already shine forth in the helplessness of Jesus crucified whose arms are outstretched to receive us in mercy.

Thomas McGonigle, O.P.

MARCH 25

R   E   L   THE ANNUNCIATION OF OUR LORD

R   *Is 7:10–14; Heb 10:4–10; Lk 1:26–38*
E   *Is 7:10–14; Heb 10:5–10; Lk 1:26–38*
L   *Is 7:10–14; 1 Tim 3:16; Lk 1:26–38*

Who among us has spoken or heard these words, "I just don't know what to do! I just wish God would come right out and tell me what I'm supposed to do." Few have avoided the anxiety of trying to extract truth from a morass of choices. Most of us occasionally wish that God would make clear direct announcements and so release us from our confusion. The world chafes and whines for a solid indisputable word from God.

But examine our yearning for clarity. In truth, we are terrified of any direct announcement from God. We would have to choose for or against God. If God is true God, then what God announces, God does. What God says, God accomplishes, according to the logic of God.

Mary's encounter with the word of God is the image of what we simultaneously desire and dread with all our hearts. Overhearing Mary's reaction to the greeting, "Hail, O favored one, the Lord is with you," we smile faintly and nervously grin. One of the tenderest and most humorous lines of Scripture is the report of Mary's reaction: "But she was greatly troubled at the saying, and considered in her mind what sort of greeting this might be."

Well should Mary be troubled. This indeed was wisdom. A faithful Jew, Mary knew that the "favored ones" of God were a tried and tested company of stragglers and sufferers, wanderers and misfits. The central saints of her Hebrew tradition were the exiled Jacob, leprous Miriam, runaway Jonah, beguiled Eve, beleaguered Moses, abandoned Hagar, devastated Job, waiting Sarah, suicidally-depressed Elijah, and enslaved Esther. The favored ones of God, as Mary knew, were set on a fulcrum between life and death, blessing and curse, wisdom and folly, joy and despair.

A humble Jew, Mary knew likewise that rarely is God's logic ours. Rightly, Mary is greatly troubled. Unnameable and strange power greets her. The threat of her death salutes her. The cost of an irrefutable announcement from God cannot be calculated in advance. Maybe on second thought we do not envy Mary this direct address. Perhaps like ancient Ahaz we too would rather beg not to see a sign.

But we are too late to beg for God's silence. We have heard the greeting we desire and dread. We are here, set down between life and death, wisdom and folly, curse and blessing, joy and despair. The ever-living God has already spoken in the body of the only begotten one, Emmanuel. "The Lord with us." The one born of Mary is the one who said to God, "Lo, I have come to do your will."

In these last days we are hailed as favored ones. Or did we forget the meaning of the water on that day when, like Gabriel, the church said to us, "Hail, O favored one, the Lord is with you," baptizing you in the name of the Father and of the Son and of the Holy Spirit?

In cities and hill countries the Trinity greets us in a word alive in the womb waters of baptism. There God salutes our bodily selves saying, "Behold, you will receive and bear the life of God's Holy Spirit, and you shall call this life within you Christ."

This strange trinitarian announcement troubles us. Morning after morning, we rise to consider what sort of word this might be. Yet the living waters say again, "Do not be afraid." Their healing wash breaks the fever of our fear. As with Mary, God calls us out of fear into shamelessness as those beloved of God.

"How can this be?" How in ourselves can God conceive the life of God? The will of God comes pouring out upon us in the name of Christ who accomplishes God's will. Our small understandings are overshadowed by the Holy Spirit. Our logic dissolves in the flood of grace and mercy. The freedom of the Risen One summons us to fecundity in the image of God.

That we are virgin territory, unproven as capable of bearing life, is no matter. That we grieve, calling ourselves useless and barren, is no matter. No sorrow, no sterility, no death inhibits God's travail to bring forth the rebirth of the good creation.

The growth of God within Mary's womb was a unique mystery and sign. So too the life of Christ within us is a deeper mystery and sign. We are fed on bread and wine and dependent on the living waters as the life of Christ gestates in us. We fill out and change, according to the demands of the life within us. Like Mary, we wonder what the face of this life is, and what it will be at full term. Like Mary, we wonder if we are strong enough to labor for God's life in the world. We are not exactly sure.

What we do know is that the image of Christ in us is radiantly beautiful. That God creates and sees the good; that the baptismal words are chromosomes of the Holy One which form us in forgiveness and welcome; and that the Spirit of God in us bears the birthmarks of suffering: these things are sure.

Like all pregnancy, this life within demands our surrender to growth. This life within changes our habits, perhaps sickens, frightens or disturbs us. Yet it is the life God announces to us. We, like Mary, are favored. Aware of the mystery and possible scandal may we too offer our whole selves in whole worship, saying, "Let it be with us according to your will."

Jann Esther Boyd Fullenwieder

MAY 31
R E L THE VISITATION

R *Zeph 3:14–18a; Rom 12:9–16b; Lk 1:39–56*
E *Zeph 3:14–18a; Col 3:12–17; Lk 1:39–49*
L *Is 11:1–5; Rom 12:9–16; Lk 1:39–47*

The event of today's celebration is simple enough: Mary visits with her cousin Elizabeth. This is a very human, a very simple event, an experience similar to our own. We know the human experience of visiting those we love. Often something happens even before we see them; there is an expectancy that the meeting will enrich us. Then there is the mystery of what occurs when friends awaken each other to new life, to the goodness of life.

All this happens when the pregnant Mary and Elizabeth meet, but here there is more. Each woman recognizes what God has done for the other. Elizabeth blesses Mary: "Blessed is she who believed that there would be a fulfillment of what was spoken to her from the Lord"; and Mary praises God: "My soul magnifies the Lord." The faith of one aids the faith of the other. This is a story of faith. Two women opened themselves to salvation; they did not close off or neutralize God's love offered in abundance. The event is told simply, with no artificial adornment. Yet the element of mystery is uppermost.

This gospel dramatizes the beginnings of God's mysterious dealing with Mary of Nazareth. God's love and longing for Israel and for us—which is what we mean by salvation—is concentrated in Mary, and she accepts that love totally. Mary's "yes" is a consent not merely to motherhood, but to the whole redemptive event. Her assent to redemption ushers in the age of salvation, and she participates in its joy. She praises God, singing of the great things that God has done for her and in her: "My soul magnifies the Lord, and my spirit rejoices in God my Savior."

Mary knows God's power and understands it not as force but as love. Her welcoming God allows that love and mercy to extend to the whole world. What God has accomplished in her is a sign of mercy and love, not for her alone but for all, particularly for the poor and oppressed. In taking flesh in her, God has overturned proud expectations and raised up those who count for little in this world. God's action in Mary is a dramatic sign of what salvation is: concern with those who are lowly.

Mary received the love that God has for us, and she assented to that love in the name of everyone who would someday be numbered among those in the church of God. She played the role of the whole human race consenting to its salvation.

Mary's song of praise puts her in proper perspective as first and foremost a woman of faith, one who opens herself to the saving initiative of God in Christ. Mary of Nazareth was a flesh-and-blood woman of history, the very real history of God's dealing with humanity. During the incomprehensible events of her life she experienced the same difficulties with which we are so familiar. To make of Mary some sort of china doll is to deprive her of faith which is her real greatness. Blessed is she who believed the Lord's word! Her trust in God's word did not mean that she fully comprehended God's actions in her life or that she could foresee all that her "fiat" would entail. In her effort to trace the thread of salvation in the events of her own and her son's lives, she had to turn again and again to her initial response: "How can this be?"

We sometimes forget that Mary shares with us the ordeals of faith, the risks of our decisions, the price of committing ourselves to God's will. Her cooperation with the Holy Spirit persisted through the darkness. Her faith became real in the thousand decisions and risks of daily life. Mary is the exemplar or pattern of all those for whom belief is not mere lip service but surrender to the real and mysterious demands of God's work. "Blessed is she who believed that there would be a fulfillment of what was spoken to her from the Lord."

Kathleen Cannon, O.P.

AUGUST 6
R   E   TRANSFIGURATION

R   *Dan 7:9–10,13–14; 2 Pet 1:16–19; Mk 9:2–10*
E   *Ex 34:29–35; 2 Pet 1:13–21; Lk 9:28–36*

A little girl in Sunday School was asked by her teacher what she was drawing. She replied, "This is a picture of God." "But," said the teacher, "you know no one knows what God looks like." "Well," she said, "now they will."

Perhaps the reason we are so interested in what God looks like is that we hunger to experience God's presence. Yet, we are often frustrated by what seems to be God's absence. This can be a life-long struggle, a struggle to break free of square-cornered spaces and neatly pigeon-holed definitions of everything we experience as real. Archbishop Anthony Bloom writes:

> God is never really absent. It is important to remember that prayer is an encounter and a relationship, a relationship which is deep, and cannot be forced on us or God . . . We complain that he does not make himself present to us and for the few minutes we reserve for him, but what about the twenty-three and a half hours during which God may be knocking at our door and we answer 'I am busy,' . . . We have no right to complain of the absence of God, because we are a great deal more absent than he ever is.[62]

Many scholars tell us that the transfiguration is a post-resurrection occurrence, nestled in the middle of the gospels. This unsettles me: I prefer things neat and organized, coming one after another, logistically and chronologically. I am too contained by *chronos*, earthly time, which is a one-dimensional plane. Yet God's time, *kyros*, is not bound to limits or dimensions.

A while ago there was an article in the paper about our galaxy. It said that our galaxy and its thousands of neighbors stream across space at speeds of more than 400 miles a second. The implication is that galaxies are pulled by a huge gravitational force beyond the astronomers' vision. This fascinated me, for it pointed out that the world which I so much like to compartmentalize refuses to do so.

I remember walking into York Minster one fall afternoon. Evensong had started, and the minster was nearly empty. As I sat listening to the voices and felt the presence which occupies that holy place, I did not want to leave. I did not want it to end. There was something magnetic and timeless in that moment.

Moses entered the presence of God, and his face shone. When Peter, James, and John finally stirred themselves from sleep on the mountaintop, they found Jesus praying. As he prayed he was seen speaking with Moses and Elijah. Dear old Peter was so overwhelmed by the presence that he wanted to nail it down and stay. Who can blame him?

It would be easy to dismiss the transfiguration as a myth, or as illustrational material, but we are reminded that the disciples were eyewitnesses. We have run smack into history. Could it be that we are too one-dimensional? Frederick Buechner writes:

> If you spin time fast enough, the time-past, time-present, and time-to-come all blend into a single timelessness or eternity, which is the essence of all times combined. God, as Isaiah says (57:15), 'inhabiteth eternity' but stands with one foot in time. The part of time where he stands most particularly is Christ, and thus in Christ we catch a glimpse of what eternity is all about, what God is all about, and what we are all about.[63]

Jesus is finally found alone. God's voice in that mountain focuses on him only. Is it any wonder that the presence of God is so often spoken of as light, a light that is difference, a light that changes not only Moses, but Paul, and that settled on the face of Jesus and shone so brightly that his whole appearance is altered? To enter God's presence means to risk being changed.

The Greek actually says that they went "into" the mountain to pray. To me that says something about my one-dimensional nature. It breaks open the confines of my thinking. I am left to think that we must be speaking of God's time, of God's dimension entering into our own.

We can choose to sleep like Peter and the others and to moan about God's absence, or we can choose to enter into God's presence. God's presence is not something beyond the horizon of eternity or always in the future. We come to the eucharist because we too can go 'into' the mountain. We too can experience God's presence. We can be changed so that our whole being shines forth God's love.

No, we cannot stay in the mountain, for we are sojourners toward God's dominion. Yet in this holy moment and all holy moments we enter God's presence and experience God's love, mercy and long-suffering. That is a dimension far beyond our imaginings. Then we will be found with Peter to say, "Master, it is good to be here."

Virginia L. Bennett

[62]Anthony Bloom, *Beginning to Pray* (New York: Paulist Press, 1970), pp. 23,27.
[63]Frederick Buechner, *Wishful Thinking, A Theological ABC* (New York: Harper & Row, 1973), p. 23.

AUGUST 15
R ASSUMPTION OF THE BLESSED VIRGIN MARY
E ST. MARY THE VIRGIN
L MARY, THE MOTHER OF OUR LORD

R *Rev 11:19;12:1–6,10ab; 1 Cor 15: 20–26; Lk 1:39–56*
E *Is 61:10–11; Gal 4:4–7; Lk 1:46–55*
L *Is 61:7–11; Gal 4:4–7; Lk 1:46–55*

Other than the word love, there is probably no word that resounds so sweetly to our ears as the word victory! Whether it be the World Series, the Olympics, or even the lottery, the moment of winning seems to make all the hard work, stress and strain, tiredness, training and tension fall into oblivion in light of the prize.

Today, the church celebrates not just a fleeting victory, not just a passing trophy. Because of the victory of Jesus over sin and death, Mary enters into heaven, possessing now the eternal crown and everlasting love.

Our God has been faithful to the covenant. Mary, as a young Jewish woman, trusted in that God, believed in that God's word and promise, and acted accordingly. Not only once did she give a "yes" to life and to love, but over and over. Now, Mary's "yes" to God resonates with God's eternal "yes" to Mary.

A few years ago, a priest who was suffering from cancer said in a homily: "Death is not something that happens to us, but something that we do." He said that we are faced daily with opportunities to let go and let God be God. Again and again we are offered the challenge to surrender in trust to God's ways, to God's timing, to God's mystery and love. When God asks for the ultimate surrender of the core of our being, then our practiced "yes" can flow more easily from our trained lips and heart.

Mary is one who modeled this practiced "yes" for us. Too frequently, Mary has been placed on a pedestal as someone who was so gifted as to somehow be other than human. To do this is to remove any possibility of finding in her a model for our own human strivings and struggles. It is to diminish her real greatness, and it can be a cop-out for us who are likewise called to a life of faith and trust in the Lord Jesus. There is no question that, in the scheme of things, Mary was specially graced; but what is significant is that she was open to grace. She freely and actively gave her "yes" in faith and in trust in God's word and promise.

Mary was not a simple, naive, passive young girl that God used. Scriptures reveal an articulate, sensitive, intelligent young woman. She does not even get thrown by a visit from a heavenly messenger. She asks questions, discerns, and makes certain that she understands what is being asked. Assurance that the conception and birth of her child was of God was enough for her to give a "yes," but the messenger's response was certainly not enough to remove all questions, all mystery.

Mary's life was filled with questions and mystery. She was asked over and over to give a "yes" in faith and trust: yes to the circumstances of her child's birth, to flight as a refugee to a foreign land, to the three day distress of a mother's search for missing son. Mary had taught her son to say yes to God; then she let go, and she let him live out his yes in a ministry of preaching, teaching, and healing that she did not always understand, at least according to Mark's gospel.

Often Mary was asked to say yes, but she needed to give only one assent at a time, as is true for each of our lives. My mother tried to teach me this important lesson one October morning in a hospital. The doctor had just informed the family that surgery had discovered the much feared brain tumor in my young sister. They could not remove it. There were hard times ahead. "She may have to be institutionalized," said the doctor. "She may become violent." I could handle much, but at this news, I fell apart. My mother sat me down. "Now, you look, girl," my mother said, "you're all upset about something that hasn't happened and may never happen. You can't live tomorrow's crosses on today's graces. We have the help we need to get through today. If God is going to allow more to happen in the future, we'll get the help we need at the time. 'Sufficient for the day is the evil thereof.' " So true!

It was true as well for Mary. Each "yes" of Mary strengthened her faith for the capital Yes she was asked to give at the foot of the cross. Here, confronted by the mystery of evil and the horrible death of her innocent son, Mary kept faith and trust in a loving God. We are not looking at a weak, timid, passive woman who fell apart after all of this, but at a widow, a mother whose son was murdered. What is it that she does? She gathers with those who had deserted her son; she prays with the eleven; and she awaits the gift of the Spirit in faith.

Our celebration around this table today reminds us that our God in Christ Jesus has won the victory over sin and death. God who is mighty has done great things for Mary; in God, she too can claim the victory. God has promised to be with us as well. Truly, we are a people whom the Lord has blessed. We can trust God with our daily "yes" so that when the moment comes for us to do our death, with Mary we too will know the ultimate prize of eternal life and the sweet sound of victory.

Joan Delaplane, O.P.

R   MICHAEL, GABRIEL, RAPHAEL

E   L   ST. MICHAEL AND ALL ANGELS

R   *Dan 7:9–10,13–14; Jn 1:47–51*

E   *Gen 28:10–17; Rev 12:7–12; Jn 1:47–51*

L   *Dan 10:10–14;12:1–3; Rev 12:7–12; Lk 10:17–20*

Angels. Guardian angels. A distant echo from the past. Don't sit too close, leave room for your guardian angel. Don't be afraid. Your angel will protect you, guard you, support you, "lest you dash your foot against a stone." All night. All day. Angels watching over me. Over you. Over all the weary world.

Angels. Messenger angels. Bearers of the big news. Glory to God in the highest. Peace on earth to all of good will. God's efficient emissaries. The angel Gabriel. Bringing glad tidings of fertility to the barren womb of Israel and of all humankind. Fear not, Zechariah. Your wife, Elizabeth, will bear a child. Fear not, Mary. The child already alive in you is of the Holy Spirit. Fear not, all you people of faith and good will. Nothing is impossible with God.

Angels. Warrior angels. Michael, the principal principality, celestial troubleshooter, victorious, triumphant, defiant, one who defeats the dragon in defending good over evil. Fighting angels. Fallen angels. Lucifer, full of light, a/k/a Satan the deceiver, thrown out of heaven, thrown down to earth in contempt of the heavenly court to tempt the unsuspecting, spitting venom like a snake in the grass. War broke out in heaven, we read in the book of Revelation, and ex-angel Satan and legions of angels all fell like lightning, conquered by the blood of the Lamb. Angels and former angels. Principalities and powers. A hierarchy of angels, archangels, cherubim, and seraphim.

Angels. Ascending and descending the mystical ladder linking heaven and earth. Ten thousand times ten thousand angels serving the One whose everlasting dominion will never pass away. And every now and then, on a midnight clear, listen: you may hear once again a glorious song, of angels bending near the earth to touch their harps of gold.

We have grown so accustomed to the rumor of angels that we confuse rumor with reality here. Our written records suggest that all the really important angels are male. Michael. Gabriel. Raphael. Is this fact or is this fiction? Oral tradition adds its own whimsical touch. Harps. Halos. Wings. Angelic choirs. In the absence of physical evidence, our fantasy fills in the facts. We have never seen an angel, yet we picture fiery figures with flaming swords, or fat little cherubs, according to the circumstance of the liturgical year. And our assumption is that one day, we too will be angels, claiming our halo, earning our wings and a place in the heavenly choir. We have theologized and rationalized and romanticized through the centuries about the subject of angels, perhaps saying too much about something we know far too little about. Today is a feast of angels, but what are we to celebrate? What are angels for you and for me?

In the gospel according to John, Jesus makes a promise to Nathaniel the Israelite. Believe in me, says Jesus, and you will see even greater things than what I have revealed to you. You will see what Jacob and Daniel saw, and what the saints of God have envisioned. You will see the integral connection between God and humankind, between the mysteries of heaven and the realities of earth. You will experience the power of God and the energy of grace flowing with a fierce force between the heavenly and earthly realms. You will discern blessings ascending and descending through the Incarnate One who bridges the human and the divine. At times, you may even see angels, for angels signal God's presence and mediate God's providential care. Angels inhabit that realm of the spirit where we must learn more and more to dwell. And at decisive turning points in the history of faith, angels have been known to communicate to us and interpret for us the intricacies of grace.

Angels remind us that there is more to life than what is immediately apparent. As often as seeing is believing, even more often, really believing is seeing far more than meets the eye. Such spiritual insight born of faith bestows an inner authority that demons cannot withstand. Yet Luke reminds us not to rejoice in authority or power, but rather that our names are written in the heavens to shine forever like the stars.

We will understand the meaning of angels only if we learn to transcend the language telling us what angels are about. Forget the vain pursuit of halo and harp and eternal rest on a cloud. Enough of those larger than life, militant seraphim who support our propensity for war. Put aside the hierarchical, patriarchal imagery. Angels have something important to teach us about ourselves and God. Angels remind us that our material world is influenced by the world of the spirit, and that we are intrinsically capable of inhabiting both worlds with equal ease. Humanity may rank a little lower than the angels because we are flesh as well as spirit, yet through Jesus who is God's own Word made flesh, we can rise above the angels to share in the very life of God. Look close and you will see that angels reveal God's secrets, guard and protect the vulnerable, are witness to miracles, are called to unending praise. Today we celebrate not only their achievements, but also that potential in ourselves to be and do the same. So come on—be an angel. And may the grace of God flow in you and through you to all our weary world.

Miriam Therese Winter, S.C.M.M.

NOVEMBER 1
R   E   L   ALL SAINTS

R   *Rev 7:2–4,9–14; 1 Jn 3:1–3; Mt 5:1–12a*
E   *Sir 44:1–10,13–14; Rev 7:2–4,9–17; Mt 5:1–12*
L   *Is 26:1–4,8–9,12–13,19–21; Rev 21:9–11,22–27; Mt 5:1–12*

Have you ever tried to stop a fight? It is not easy. Whether among children on a playground, or among adults in an apartment building, it is a hazardous undertaking. If you don't believe it, ask some police officer who has tried. Perhaps it was late at night, following payday. And an unhappily married couple was engaged in a drunken quarrel. They were disturbing the peace. They were shouting angry threats. They were throwing things, dishes, pots and pans, and even knives. Perhaps they were armed. And nobody knew what they might do next. You could get killed, trying to make peace.

Many people, you soon discover, simply do not want peace. Peace scares them. It threatens their pride. So, despite the consequences, they cherish their anger, harbor their grudges, and hold on, ever so ferociously, to their hostilities. They would, it seems, rather fight than love. And no matter who gets hurt!

It is a sad, sad story. And, pathetically, it is not simply the story of playgrounds and apartments. It is also the story of classes and cultures, labor and management, men and women, nations and races, It is what happens when any person or group wants something at the expense of another. And it is the story of humankind, humankind at war with God. War is sin. And sin is war, war against a God who bothers us, bothers us by being generous and demanding. And we don't like that. We want to live our own lives, without any interference. We like our little wars, and our big ones, too. They make us feel important, powerful, godlike.

As proud sinners, we are troubled by the poor in spirit, those who mourn, the meek, those who hunger and thirst after righteousness, the merciful, and the pure in heart. And we resent the peacemakers. The saints, after all, are bothersome. They threaten our complacency. So we persecute them. We stifle them with derision. We think them unreal, claiming that they do not understand the "real" world. Or we get rid of them. Get rid of them through martyrdom. Or crucifixion! As sinners, we continue to conduct covert operations against sainthood. And, perhaps, most subtly of all, we honor the saints as somehow so unlike us that their lives have nothing to say to us here and now.

Nevertheless, God will not let us alone. God sent the prophets to Israel, seeking to make peace, to create shalom. And God sent Jesus, as a peacemaker, to bring peace. So Jesus was crucified by those who wanted the hostilities to continue. Making peace is hazardous. Yet God refuses to give up on us warring humans. God remains restless and active, running the risk of our rejection. God seeks to make peace. Making peace is what God is all about. Despite our hostilities, God seeks peace.

And, through the centuries, the saints are those who have shared in God's task of peacemaking. For some, it has led to martyrdom. Indeed, the Feast of All Saints was first created because the martyrs, the witnesses to God's peace, overflowed the calendar. There were simply too many of them to name. And yet they are, as the readings would remind us, called "the children of God." Through God's love and their faithfulness, they have become truly like God. They share a family resemblance, share it as they share in making peace. "Blessed are the peacemakers, for they shall be called the children of God."

And God still seeks peacemakers. God's family always has room for more sons and daughters, more saints who make peace. It may be difficult and hazardous, challenging the pride of nations and empires. Or it may be as simple and reassuring as reaching out a friendly hand to your neighbor. There is a creativity, even poetry, at work in peacemaking. And once peace begins, begins to work among us, who knows what may happen? Or what we may become? "Beloved, we are God's children now; it does not yet appear what we shall be."

John E. Burkhart

R FOR THE UNITY OF ALL CHRISTIANS
E FOR THE UNITY OF THE CHURCH
L UNITY

R   *Ez 36:24–28; Eph 4:1–6; Jn 17:20–26*
E   *Is 35:1–10; Eph 4:1–6; Jn 17:6a,15–23*
L   *Is 2:2–4; Eph 4:1–6; Jn 17:15–23*

"They are strangers in the world . . . ." There are aliens in our midst. There are people who appear to be ordinary human beings but who, in fact, are different. They hold down jobs, they marry and have children, they watch television and go to ball games, they worry about the state of the world or find ways to avoid worrying about the state of the world: but they are different. They are strangers.

But oddly, many of them don't know that they are strangers. I vaguely remember a science fiction story in which an alien came to love life on this planet so much that he forgot he was an alien. That has happened to many of us Christians, and it happens to all of us some of the time. We forget who we are and whose we are. We accustom ourselves to the ordinary ways of living and to the conventions of our culture so thoroughly that we are indistinguishable from those who do not believe.

The same is true for the church. It has so completely adapted itself to life in the world and to the structures of our society that it acts like merely one of the many social institutions competing for people's loyalty and commitment.

One of the ways this adaptation is manifested is our becoming a group of divided churches. If you drive through this country you will often see when entering small towns signs welcoming you to the town. There will be signs from the Lion's Club, Rotary, Optimists, Elks Lodge; and signs from the Methodists, Baptists, Catholics, Episcopalians, Lutherans, and Presbyterians. They are joined with advertisements from various businesses as well. The church, the body of Christ, is replaced by a number of social institutions offering a variety of services among which we can pick and choose: "Worship God this Sunday in the church of your choice," we are told. In other words, the church has so adapted itself to the world's patterns that it has become a number of religious service clubs offering a variety of activities and the chance to associate spiritually with the sorts of people we like.

Jesus described a different sort of church. What he describes is something strange to the world's conventions: a people who are united with each other in the way that Jesus is united with God, a people who share in the divine life, who are the glory of the world, and who reveal God's own perfection in the unity which they share.

In this eucharist today we are praying for that unity to be restored, or rediscovered, or once again made clear. This is not a comfortable subject for American Christians. It goes against the idea that every person should have the opportunity to chose freely from any number of competing groups those particular benefits and activities which are most attractive. Why shouldn't we have a large variety of church groups just as we have a wide variety of fast-food chains, service stations, television channels, or political parties?

Paul tells us that we should spare no effort to build up the bonds of peace and unity given us by the Spirit. Yet we would rather find comfortable ecclesiastical niches in which to worship God. It is bad enough that, as a result, those outside the churches find a profoundly confusing number of versions of the Christian gospel. But even worse is the fact that far too often each of those separated groups enshrines only one social and economic class and all too often only one ethnic or racial group.

There is a different picture in the Scriptures. The prophets look forward to a gloriously joyful time when all the creation will burst forth with gladness because all of humanity is streaming into its home as one people. Jesus prays for a united humanity which will reveal God to the world. Paul exhorts us to share in a oneness like that of God. What a strange thing it would be to see the divisions and estrangements of this world overcome: to see people of every sort united; to find Catholics and Protestants, capitalists and communists, first world and third world, black, white, brown, all joined together in peace with one another.

We are strangers in this world, strangers above all because we are united in one God, one faith, one baptism. No longer are any of the categories of the world able to keep one person apart from another. There is no longer an approach to God which excludes some people. There is no longer any national or political affiliation which keeps people apart. There is no longer Jew or Gentile, slave or free, male or female. All are one in God.

Here around this table we find ourselves more fully human than at any other place because we find that our citizenship is in heaven. We find that to be human is to be alive in God. We find that there is nothing more real and valid than joining with all people in sharing food and drink in the presence of God. Here we find that our baptismal bath has given us a new identity which is bound up in the lives of one another.

We are indeed strangers in this world, and the world is being led by us to find its true home. Pray, brothers and sisters, that we all may be one even as Christ and the Father are one. Amen.

Michael W. Merriman